GREAT CHRISTIAN JURISTS IN THE LOW COUNTRIES

What impact has Christianity had on law and policy-making in the Lowlands from the eleventh century through the end of the twentieth century? Taking the gradual "secularization" of European legal culture as a framework, this volume explores the lives and times of twenty legal scholars and professionals to study the historical impact of the Christian faith on legal and political life in the Low Countries. The process whereby Christian belief systems gradually lost their impact on the regulation of secular affairs passed through several stages, not in the least the Protestant Reformation, which led to the separation of the Low Countries in a Protestant North and a Catholic South in the first place. The contributions take up general issues such as the relationship between justice and mercy, Christianity and politics as well as more technical topics of state-church law, criminal law and social policy.

Wim Decock holds the chair of Roman Law and Legal History at the University of Louvain (UCLouvain). He is the author of the prize-winning books *Theologians and Contract Law* (2013) and *Le marché du mérite* (2019). In 2014, he was awarded the H.M. Leibnitz-Prize by the German Research Foundation.

Janwillem Oosterhuis is Assistant Professor in the Department of Methods and Foundations of Law at Maastricht University. He is the author of *Specific Performance in German, French and Dutch Law in the Nineteenth Century* (2011).

LAW AND CHRISTIANITY

Series Editor

John Witte, Jr., Emory University

Editorial Board

Nigel Biggar, University of Oxford
Marta Cartabia, Italian Constitutional Court / University of Milano-Bicocca
Sarah Coakley, University of Cambridge
Norman Doe, Cardiff University
Rafael Domingo, Emory University / University of Navarra
Brian Ferme, Marcianum, Venice
Richard W. Garnett, University of Notre Dame
Robert P. George, Princeton University
Mary Ann Glendon, Harvard University
Kent Greenawalt, Columbia University
Robin Griffith-Jones, Temple Church, London / King's College London
Gary S. Hauk, Emory University
R. H. Helmholz, University of Chicago
Mark Hill QC, Inner Temple, London / Cardiff University
Wolfgang Huber, Bishop Emeritus, United Protestant Church of Germany /
Universities of Heidelberg, Berlin, and Stellenbosch
Michael W. McConnell, Stanford University
John McGuckin, Union Theological Seminary
Mark A. Noll, University of Notre Dame
Jeremy Waldron, New York University
Michael Welker, University of Heidelberg

The Law and Christianity series publishes cutting-edge work on Catholic, Protestant, and Orthodox Christian contributions to public, private, penal, and procedural law and legal theory. The series aims to promote deep Christian reflection by leading scholars on the fundamentals of law and politics, to build further ecumenical legal understanding across Christian denominations, and to link and amplify the diverse and sometimes isolated Christian legal voices and visions at work in the academy. Works collected by the series include groundbreaking monographs, historical and thematic anthologies, and translations by leading scholars around the globe.

Books in the Series

Christianity and International Law: An Introduction edited by Pamela Slotte and John D. Haskell

Christianity and Market Regulation: An Introduction edited by Daniel A. Crane and Samuel J. Gregg

Christianity and the Laws of Conscience Jeffrey B. Hammond and Helen M. Alvare

Infidels and Empires in a New World Order: Early Modern Spanish Contributions to International Legal Thought David M. Lantigua

The Possibility of Religious Freedom: Early Natural Law and the Abrahamic Faiths Karen Taliaferro

Catholic Social Teaching: A Volume of Scholarly Essays edited by Gerard V. Bradley and E. Christian Brugger

The Immortal Commonwealth: Covenant, Community, and Political Resistance in Early Reformed Thought David P. Henreckson

Great Christian Jurists in American History edited by Daniel L. Dreisbach and Mark David Hall

Great Christian Jurists and Legal Collections in the First Millennium edited by Philip L. Reynolds

The Profession of English Ecclesiastical Lawyers: An Historical Introduction R. H. Helmholz

Law, Love and Freedom: From the Sacred to the Secular Joshua Neoh

Great Christian Jurists in French History edited by Olivier Descamps and Rafael Domingo

Church Law in Modernity: Toward a Theory of Canon Law Between Nature and Culture Judith Hahn

Common Law and Natural Law in America: From the Puritans to the Legal Realists Andrew Forsyth

Care for the World: Laudato Si' and Catholic Social Thought in an Era of Climate Crisis edited by Frank Pasquale

Church, State, and Family: Reconciling Traditional Teachings and Modern Liberties John Witte, Jr

Great Christian Jurists in Spanish History Rafael Domingo and Javier Martínez-Torrón

Under Caesar's Sword: How Christians Respond to Persecution edited by Daniel Philpott and Timothy Samuel Shah

God and the Illegal Alien: United States Immigration Law and a Theology of Politics Robert W. Heimburger

Christianity and Family Law: An Introduction edited by John Witte, Jr and Gary S. Hauk

Christianity and Natural Law: An Introduction Norman Doe

Great Christian Jurists in English History edited by Mark Hill, QC and R. H. Helmholz

Agape, Justice, and Law: How Might Christian Love Shape Law? edited by Robert F. Cochran, Jr and Zachary R. Calo

Calvin's Political Theology and the Public Engagement of the Church: Christ's Two Kingdoms Matthew J. Tuininga

God and the Secular Legal System Rafael Domingo

How Marriage Became One of the Sacraments: The Sacramental Theology of Marriage from Its Medieval Origins to the Council of Trent Philip L. Reynolds

Christianity and Freedom (Volume I: Historical Perspectives, Volume II: Contemporary Perspectives) edited by Timothy Samuel Shah and Allen D. Hertzke

The Western Case for Monogamy Over Polygamy John Witte, Jr

The Distinctiveness of Religion in American Law: Rethinking Religion Clause Jurisprudence Kathleen A. Brady

Pope Benedict XVI's Legal Thought: A Dialogue on the Foundation of Law edited by Marta Cartabia and Andrea Simoncini

Great Christian Jurists in the Low Countries

Edited by

WIM DECOCK

University of Louvain

JANWILLEM OOSTERHUIS

Maastricht University

CAMBRIDGE
UNIVERSITY PRESS

University Printing House, Cambridge CB2 8BS, United Kingdom

One Liberty Plaza, 20th Floor, New York, NY 10006, USA

477 Williamstown Road, Port Melbourne, VIC 3207, Australia

314–321, 3rd Floor, Plot 3, Splendor Forum, Jasola District Centre, New Delhi – 110025, India

103 Penang Road, #05–06/07, Visioncrest Commercial, Singapore 238467

Cambridge University Press is part of the University of Cambridge.

It furthers the University's mission by disseminating knowledge in the pursuit of education, learning, and research at the highest international levels of excellence.

www.cambridge.org
Information on this title: www.cambridge.org/9781108429849
DOI: 10.1017/9781108555388

© Cambridge University Press 2021

This publication is in copyright. Subject to statutory exception and to the provisions of relevant collective licensing agreements, no reproduction of any part may take place without the written permission of Cambridge University Press.

First published 2021

A catalogue record for this publication is available from the British Library.

Library of Congress Cataloging-in-Publication Data
NAMES: Decock, Wim, 1983– editor. | Oosterhuis, Janwillem editor.
TITLE: Great Christian jurists in the low countries / edited by Wim Decock, Catholic University Leuven; Janwillem Oosterhuis, Maastricht University.
DESCRIPTION: Cambridge, United Kingdom ; New York, NY : Cambridge University Press, 2021. | Series: Law and Christianity | Includes bibliographical references and index.
IDENTIFIERS: LCCN 2021009544 (print) | LCCN 2021009545 (ebook) | ISBN 9781108429849 (hardback) | ISBN 9781108555388 (ebook)
SUBJECTS: LCSH: Christian lawyers – Benelux countries – Biography. | Judges – Benelux countries – Biography. | Law teachers – Benelux countries – Biography. | Law – Benelux countries – Christian influences – History. | Law and Christianity – History.
CLASSIFICATION: LCC KJ122 .G74 2021 (print) | LCC KJ122 (ebook) | DDC 340.092/ 87492–dc23
LC record available at https://lccn.loc.gov/2021009544
LC ebook record available at https://lccn.loc.gov/2021009545

ISBN 978-1-108-42984-9 Hardback

Cambridge University Press has no responsibility for the persistence or accuracy of URLs for external or third-party internet websites referred to in this publication and does not guarantee that any content on such websites is, or will remain, accurate or appropriate.

Contents

List of Contributors — page ix

Introduction. Law, Christianity, and Secularization in the Low Countries
Wim Decock and Janwillem Oosterhuis — 1

1. Alger of Liège
   Emmanuël Falzone — 19

2. Arnoldus Gheyloven
   Bram van Hofstraeten — 38

3. Boëtius Epo
   Hylkje de Jong — 52

4. Leonardus Lessius
   Toon Van Houdt — 64

5. Franciscus Zypaeus
   Wouter Druwé — 80

6. Hugo Grotius
   Janwillem Oosterhuis — 97

7. Paulus Voet
   Johannes van Kralingen — 123

8. Ulrik Huber
   Atsuko Fukuoka   139

9. Zeger-Bernard van Espen
   Jan Hallebeek   159

10. Dionysius van der Keessel
    Egbert Koops   177

11. Pieter Paulus
    Matthijs de Blois   201

12. Guillaume Groen van Prinsterer
    Jan Willem Sap   219

13. Edouard Ducpétiaux
    Frank Judo   236

14. Charles Périn
    Fred Stevens   249

15. Léon de Lantsheere
    Peter Heyrman   266

16. Paul Scholten
    Timo Slootweg   284

17. Willem Duynstee
    Corjo Jansen   301

18. Jules Storme
    Dirk Heirbaut   320

19. Herman Dooyeweerd
    Bas Hengstmengel   338

20. Josse Mertens de Wilmars
    Laurent Waelkens   359

Index   375

Contributors

Atsuko Fukuoka is associate professor at the Department of Advanced Social and International Studies, University of Tokyo. She received her PhD degree from the Johan-Wolfgang-Goethe University in Frankfurt. Her English-language publications include *The Sovereign and the Prophets: Spinoza on Grotian and Hobbesian Biblical Argumentation* (Brill, 2018).

Bas D. Hengstmengel studied psychology, law, and philosophy at the Universities of Leiden and Rotterdam, the Netherlands. He works as an advocate and publishes on topics of jurisprudence, philosophy, and politics. He has written a dissertation on Herman Dooyeweerd and natural law.

Bram van Hofstraeten is professor of Limburgish legal history at Maastricht University (Netherlands). He has published on a variety of topics (church history, economic history, palaeography, and legal history) and is currently leading a VIDI-research project on the history of early modern company law. Van Hofstraeten is chief editor of the Belgian–Dutch journal *Pro Memorie*.

C. J. H. (Corjo) Jansen is professor of legal history and civil law at the Radboud University of Nijmegen. He is the chair of the Radboud Business Law Institute and a member of the Scientific Advisory Board of the Max Planck Institute for Comparative and International Private Law in Hamburg.

Dirk Heirbaut is Francqui research professor at Ghent University and member of the Royal Flemish Academy of Belgium for Science and the Arts. His research focuses on medieval feudal and customary law, the comparative history of private law codifications, private law in Belgium since Napoleon, and the methodology of legal history.

Egbert Koops is chair of the Legal History department and professor of legal history at Leiden University, the Netherlands.

EMMANUËL FALZONE is lecturer in history at the Haute Ecole (University College) Albert Jacquard of Namur, teaching assistant and researcher in legal history at the UCLouvain. Currently, he is completing his PhD dissertation at the Université Saint-Louis – Bruxelles. His research interests include the implementation of medieval canon law in practice, the ecclesiastical courts, and the administration of justice within the Medieval Southern Low Countries.

FRANK JUDO studied history, philosophy, law, and canon law at KU Leuven. He has been a lawyer in Brussels since 1998. He is co-editor-in-chief of the journal *Recht, Religie en Samenleving* and member of the board of directors of the Information and Advice Centre on Harmful Sectarian Organisations (IACSSO).

FRED STEVENS studied law and history. He is an emeritus full professor at the Faculty of Law of KU Leuven. His main areas of research are university history, the history of the notarial profession, and the influence of the Enlightenment and the French Revolution on law and institutions.

HYLKJE DE JONG studied classics, linguistics, law, and philosophy. She is the chair of legal history at the Vrije Universiteit Amsterdam. Her investigation is primarily focused on Byzantine law.

JAN HALLEBEEK is emeritus professor of legal history at the Vrije Universiteit Amsterdam. From 1986 until 2016 he taught canon law at the Old Catholic Seminary, affiliated to the Department of Philosophy and Religious Studies of Utrecht University.

JAN WILLEM SAP is professor of European law at the Open University in the Netherlands in Heerlen and associate professor of European law at VU University Amsterdam. He studied law at Leiden University. In 2006 he was a member of the National Convention on constitutional reforms in the Netherlands.

JANWILLEM OOSTERHUIS is assistant professor of foundations and methods of law at Maastricht University. His research focuses on the comparative history of commercial (contract) law and early modern Roman–Dutch criminal law.

JOHANNES VAN KRALINGEN studied classics (BA) and civil law (LLM) at Leiden University. In 2020 he obtained his doctorate at the Leiden Law School with a dissertation on the history of the indivisibility of security rights. He is currently working at the law firm Houthoff and specializes in (Supreme Court) litigation.

LAURENT WAELKENS (1953–2020) is the late emeritus professor of Roman law at the Faculty of Law at KU Leuven. He is the author of *Amne Adverso, Roman Legal Heritage in European Culture* (Leuven UP: 2015).

MATTHIJS DE BLOIS studied law at Utrecht University. He has worked at Leiden University, where he received his PhD. Since 1990 he has been an assistant professor at Utrecht University. Research interests include philosophical, religious, and historical aspects of law. Since retirement he has been active as a senior fellow of thinc. (the Hague Initiative for International Co-operation).

PETER HEYRMAN is an historian and Head of Research at KADOC-KU Leuven. His bibliography includes publications on various aspects of Belgium's socio-political history in the nineteenth and twentieth centuries, focusing on the history of small and medium-sized business and related organizations, and the relationship between religion and entrepreneurship.

TIMO SLOOTWEG studied philosophy and history. His dissertation dealt with the ethics of history and historical consciousness in the philosophies of Hegel, Heidegger, and Derrida. Since 2006 he has been teaching philosophy of law and ethics at the University of Leiden, Netherlands. He is especially interested in the subject of the aesthetics of law.

TOON VAN HOUDT received his PhD for his doctoral dissertation on the economic and ethical thought of the Flemish Jesuit Leonardus Lessius (1995). In 1999 he was appointed professor of Latin and cultural history at KU Leuven. He has published extensively on the history of late scholastic and humanist political, ethical, and economic thought.

WIM DECOCK is professor of legal history at the Universities of Louvain (UC Louvain) and Liège. He is the author of the prize-winning books *Theologians and Contract Law: The Moral Transformation of the Ius Commune (c. 1500–1650)* (Brill/Nijhoff: 2013), and *Le marché du mérite. Penser le droit et l'économie avec Léonard Lessius* (Zones Sensibles: 2019).

WOUTER DRUWÉ is assistant professor of Roman law and legal history at KU Leuven. Recent publications include *Loans and Credit in Consilia and Decisiones in the Low Countries (c. 1500–1680)* (Brill, 2020) and *candalum in the Early Bolognese Decretistic and in Papal Decretals (c. 1140–1234)* (Peeters, 2018).

Introduction

Law, Christianity, and Secularization in the Low Countries

Wim Decock and Janwillem Oosterhuis

The present volume aims to reveal the impact of Christianity on the development of law and societal policies in the Low Countries over a period of ten centuries. It starts with the seminal contribution to the medieval *ius commune* by the canonist Alger de Liège (c. 1060–1132) at the end of the eleventh century and ends with Josse Mertens de Wilmars's (1912–2002) protagonist role as a judge in the creation of a European *ius commune* in the second half of the twentieth century. The impact of Christianity on thinking and making the law is shown through essays on twenty Christian legal scholars and legal practitioners from the Low Countries. Historically speaking, the Low Countries cover a region which, today, corresponds more or less to Belgium, the Netherlands, Luxembourg, and parts of Northern France. Through these biographies from jurists from the Southern and Northern Netherlands, developments that are more general in nature can be recognized and established, about the changing roles of Christianity and law in Western societies more generally. As a matter of fact, the gradual 'secularization' of legal culture in the Low Countries is used as a framework to describe the general evolution of the impact of Christianity on the lives and writings of the twenty selected jurists.

CHRISTIANITY, SECULARIZATION, AND LAW IN THE LOW COUNTRIES

The impact of the Christian faith on law critically depends on the more general role of Christianity in society as a whole, so much so that an assessment of the impact of Christianity on legal thinking in Europe before the French Revolution may seem almost nonsensical.[1] Until the end of the old

---

[1] F. Audren and P. Rolland, 'Juristes catholiques', *Revue Française d'Histoire des Idées Politiques* 28 (2008): 227–231.

regime, European societies were imbued with Christian thinking. However, the concrete role of Christianity in Western societies – including the Low Countries – took on different forms throughout the centuries, even before the period of the French Revolution. The process whereby Christian belief systems gradually lost their impact on the regulation of secular affairs – often labelled a process of 'secularization' – passed through several stages, not least in the Protestant Reformation. It led to the separation of the Low Countries in the first place, with the Northern provinces chiefly embracing the teachings of Martin Luther and John Calvin, and eventually adopting the Reformed religion as public religion, and the Southern Netherlands remaining predominantly Catholic, first under Spanish and later under Austrian rule. This gradual process of secularization, then, provides an adequate framework against which the twenty jurists from the Low Countries dealt with in this volume can be discussed.

Different, often conflicting, views on the meaning of 'secularization' circulate.[2] In his influential work *A Secular Age*, the Canadian philosopher Charles Taylor famously distinguished between three types of secularization: the secularization of public life, including a strict separation between church and state; the decline of belief and practice; and the questioning of the conditions of belief and the practice thereof – today, belief has become a human possibility, one among many others.[3] Clearly, the widespread decline of belief itself is a rather recent phenomenon in the Low Countries. The latter two types of secularization were clearly not accepted by large parts of the population until the end of the eighteenth century. Only during the last five decades did indifference toward the Christian faith accelerate dramatically in countries such as Belgium and the Netherlands. But when it comes to the first aspect of secularization as singled out by Taylor, the realities of the institutional relationship between ecclesiastical and civil authorities have been subject to change and variation from the very period that this volume opens with: the eleventh century. The tension between church(es) and state has marked the destiny and identity of the Low Countries as it has marked Western political culture in general from at least that period onwards, as political scientists such as Francis Fukuyama have not failed to note following the work of Harold Berman.[4]

[2] K. Dobbelaere, 'The Meaning and Scope of Secularization' in *The Oxford Handbook of the Sociology of Religion*, ed. Peter B. Clarke (Oxford: Oxford University Press, 2009), 599–615.
[3] C. Taylor, *A Secular Age* (Cambridge, MA and London: The Belknap Press of Harvard University Press, 2007), 14–22.
[4] F. Fukuyama, *The Origins of Political Order: From Prehuman Times to the French Revolution* (New York: Farrar, Straus and Giroux, 2011), 245–289.

From a legal historical perspective, Berman's use of the term 'secularization' is particularly helpful.[5] Rather than concentrating on the loss of religious belief as such, Berman employed 'secularization' as a concept that designates the transfer of jurisdictional power from the church to worldly authorities in the age of Reformations in the sixteenth and seventeenth centuries. This transfer of power did not imply a loss of faith on the part of the majority of the population or its leaders, but did have major effects on the organization of law and society: the church lost its dominant role in the administration of justice, the regulation of the market, and the organization of charity. Martin Luther and John Calvin, who became very popular in the Netherlands, played a paramount role in this process. They undermined the jurisdictional power wielded by the church and denounced the clergy's involvement in legal and economic affairs. 'Luther emphasized that formal legal authority lay with the state, not with the church, with the magistrate, not with the cleric', as John Witte Jr aptly summarized this shift.[6] At the same time, the decline in the worldly power of clerics was accompanied by a process of 'spiritualization' of civil authority. Therefore, it would be misleading to think of 'secularization' in the early modern period in any of the senses that Taylor distinguished. As the example of many Dutch Reformed jurists in this volume will show, they did not ban religion from the public sphere, but rather conferred responsibilities in religious affairs to civil authorities. After all, civil authorities in the young Dutch republic were pictured after the model of leaders from the Old Testament like Moses, and they liked to think of themselves as governors of the new Israel.[7] Protestants urged the magistrate to lay down laws that were based on the Bible. Toward the mid-seventeenth century, the Dutch Calvinist jurist Anthonius Matthaeus II (1601–1645) based his treatise on criminal law decisively on the Decalogue.[8] Law and religion, then, continued to 'intertwine' in the Protestant territories that rejected the jurisdictional authority of

---

[5] H. Berman, *Law and Revolution: The Formation of the Western Legal Tradition* (Cambridge, MA: Harvard University Press, 1983), 29.

[6] John Witte Jr., *Law and Protestantism: The Legal Teachings of the Lutheran Reformation* (Cambridge: Cambridge University Press, 2002), 8.

[7] Gordon Schochet, Fania Oz-Salzberger, and Meirav Jones, eds., *Political Hebraism: Judaic Sources in Early Modern Political Thought* (Jerusalem; New York: Shalem Press, 2008), M. Totzeck, *Die politischen Gesetze des Mose. Entstehung und Einflüsse der politia-judaica-Literatur in der Frühen Neuzeit* (Göttingen: V&R, 2019). See also e.g. Todd M. Rester and Andrew M. McGinnis, 'Introduction' in Franciscus Junius, *The Mosaic Polity*. Translated by Todd M. Rester; edited by Andrew M. McGinnis (Grand Rapids, MI: CLP Academic, 2015), xli–xlvii.

[8] Janwillem Oosterhuis, 'Roman–Dutch Criminal Law and Calvinism: Calvinist Morality in De criminibus (1644) of Antonius Matthaeus II' in *Criminal Law and Morality in the Age of Consent. Interdisciplinary Perspectives*, ed. Aniceto Masferrer (Cham: Springer, 2020), 67–95.

Rome.⁹ In the Catholic Southern Netherlands, too, secular authorities drew inspiration from Christian sources, especially canon law and moral theology, while reducing the institutional power of clerics and ecclesiastical courts.¹⁰ In any event, religion was certainly not banned from the public sphere until much later, with the advent of the modern Belgian and Dutch states in the first half of the nineteenth century.

Even in the modern period, the radicalization of the secularization process in Berman's sense – which led to the constitutionally guaranteed separation of church and state – did not necessarily go along with the demise of belief in the Christian faith. In Belgium, where liberal-secularists and Catholics fought for power in the nineteenth century, secularists were anti-clerical, but not automatically anti-religious.¹¹ A good case in point is François Laurent (1810–1887), arguably the most famous anti-clerical jurist in the second half of the nineteenth century in Belgium. Although he opposed the Roman Catholic Church as an institution – proposing a new Code of Civil Law that would take away legal capacity from religious associations – he was a profoundly religious man, rejecting atheism and believing that 'mankind would not survive for a long time without believing, since religion is life'.¹² It was not until the twentieth century, as Berman has pointed out, that 'secularism itself became secularized', that 'God was no longer thought to be hidden in the secular world', and that secularization started to refer not only to the emancipation of secular rule from ecclesiastical hegemony, but also to the loss of faith itself.¹³

MEDIEVAL REFORM OF CHURCH AND MORALITY: GREGORIAN REFORMS AND MODERN DEVOTION

The individual, intimate, and almost hidden character of the impact of Christian faith on legal developments in the Low Countries in the twentieth century stands in marked contrast, of course, to the public and self-evident nature of Christianity as a belief system in the Middle Ages. The

---

9   Lisbet Christoffersen, 'Intertwinement: A new concept for understanding religion-law relations', *Nordic Journal of Religion and Society* 19 (2006): 107–126.
10 Laurent Waelkens, *Amne adverso: Roman Legal Heritage in European Culture* (Leuven: University Press, 2015), 113.
11 Dobbelaere, 'The Meaning and Scope of Secularization', 602.
12 E. Bruyère, *Principes, esprit et controverses. L'Avant-Projet de Code civil de François Laurent ou l'œuvre séditieuse d'un libre penseur* (Ghent, 2019 (unpublished PhD thesis)), 3.
13 Harold J. Berman, *The Interaction of Spiritual and Secular Law: The Sixteenth-Century and Today*. Fulton Lectures, 1997, https://chicagounbound.uchicago.edu/cgi/viewcontent.cgi?article=1008&context=fulton_lectures, 9. Also cited in W. Decock, 'Salamanca meets secularism. Clerics' role in the administration of justice and charity' (in press).

Low Countries harboured one of the great centres of religious life and learning in Europe, the prince-bishopric of Liège, which was integrated into the Holy Roman Empire by Emperor Otto III in 985. It was composed of territories that are now part of eastern Belgium and the southeast of the Netherlands. Alger de Liège was a major canon lawyer in the prince-bishopric at the turn of the twelfth century, and an advisor to prince-bishop Otbert. In his treatise *On Mercy and Justice* (*De misericordia et iustitia*), he captured the spirit of the Gregorian Reform and prefigured some of the ideas on ecclesiastical governance and criminal law in Gratian's *Decretum*.[14] The work of Alger de Liège underscores the common religious roots of the Low Countries, shared with large parts of Europe, and the struggle for 'ecclesiastical liberty' – that is the church's increasingly successful striving for independence from interference by worldly rulers in the eleventh and twelfth centuries. Ironically, Otbert, whom Alger counselled, was himself accused of simony.

Although the institutional church remained at the centre of jurisdictional power and organized life during the later Middle Ages, church and society witnessed already-important Reform movements that advocated a more spiritual, interiorized form of Christianity. A case in point is the Modern Devotion, a lay movement advocating the renewal of spiritual life, which took off in the Lowlands with reformers like Geert Groote (1340–1384) in the second half of the fourteenth century. It focused on the morality and holiness of individual Christian believers rather than the protection of jurisdictional interests of clerics and the church as an institution. Arnold Gheyloven van Rotterdam (c. 1375–1442), a canon lawyer and theologian, was influenced by the Modern Devotion. He came from the Northern Netherlands but settled in Groenendaal, near Brussels, in the Duchy of Brabant, where he prepared an influential manual for confessors and penitents (*Gnotosolitus parvus*) – featuring a synthesis of Roman law, canon law, and evangelical principles – for the advancement of the spiritual life of students at the newly founded University of Louvain (1425).[15] Gheyloven, as part of the Modern Devotion, made an important contribution to the emergence of a northern humanist culture. Also as a consequence of earlier medieval reform movements in the Low Countries, like the Modern Devotion, the Reformed religion would find many adherents in this region.

---

[14] See Chapter 1: Emmanuël Falzone, 'Alger of Liège', in this volume.
[15] See Chapter 2: Bram van Hofstraeten, 'Arnoldus Gheyloven', in this volume.

AFTER THE REFORMATION: RETHINKING THE RELATION BETWEEN LAW, RELIGION, AND SOCIETY

As a result of the Reformation, the unity of faith and church in the Low Countries was lost. The ensuing religious and confessional controversies also lay at the basis of the Dutch Revolt, which resulted in a painful separation of the Low Countries into the northern Dutch Republic and the southern Spanish Habsburg Netherlands. Boëtius Epo (1529–1599) embodies this painful and radical religious and political separation of North and South. Born in Friesland, he made a career in the Southern Netherlands. Initially charmed by the Reformed religion, later in life he opposed the Protestant movement that came to dominate the Northern Netherlands, profiling himself clearly as a Catholic. Epo even chose to teach at Douai instead of Louvain when the Catholic University of Louvain was accused of Protestant tendencies. His career illustrates how legal teaching was affected by religious tensions in the early-modern Low Countries. Epo's writings are mainly on canon law, emphasizing the benevolent and necessary influence of the canon law for society.[16] He consciously chose to become a Roman Catholic and reject the Protestant view of the Christian faith despite his initial enthusiasm for the Reform movement. Importantly, then, with the Reformation, religion became more a matter of choice.

Louvain, meanwhile, became one of the leading centres for Catholic scholarship in Europe. It was the domicile of one of the greatest legal–theological scholars of the early-modern period, Leonardus Lessius (1554–1623). Lessius was a Catholic moral theologian from Antwerp in the Southern Netherlands. He taught at the Jesuit College in Louvain and played a major role in the moral transformation of the *ius commune*, as exemplified through his treatise *On Justice and Law* (*De iustitia et iure*). At the same time, he was a bridge figure between the School of Salamanca and the northern natural law school.[17] Although less well known outside the Low Countries, Franciscus Zypaeus (1580–1650) was one of the most eminent jurists in the Southern Netherlands after the factual separation with the North. After graduating in both laws from Louvain, he made a career in the church and published widely on the theory and practice of customary law, Roman law, and canon law in the Habsburg Low Countries. Importantly, Zypaeus reflected on the relation between ecclesiastical and secular authorities. He wanted to limit the influence of the Roman curia as well as the Habsburg rulers on the Netherlandish Catholic Church. Moreover,

---

[16] See Chapter 3: Hylkje de Jong, 'Boëtius Epo', in this volume.
[17] See Chapter 4: Toon Van Houdt, 'Leonardus Lessius', in this volume.

he wrote an important work on the ethics of public law (*Iudex, magistratus, senator*), containing deontological guidelines for Christian judges and administrators.[18]

In the Dutch Republic, jurists also pondered the relation between secular and ecclesiastical authorities, and, more generally, what role religion should have in public life. One of the first professors at the University of Leiden – founded in 1575, formally by Phillip II as sovereign, but, importantly, instituted by William of Orange as a Calvinist alternative to the Catholic Universities of Louvain and Douai – was Justus Lipsius (1547–1606), a jurist by training who promoted humanist learning and religious tolerance. According to Hugo Grotius (1583–1645), an alumnus of Leiden University, religious tolerance could be guaranteed by acknowledging that the civil magistrate held the highest authority in religious matters. Grotius belonged to the moderate current within the Reformed religion in Holland. In his view, the public religion should be limited to a kind of natural religion, that is, a few necessary, fundamental dogmas that could be rationally understood. These elements can be retrieved in *On the Right of War and Peace* (*De iure belli ac pacis*), in which he unfolds an all-encompassing description of law and society. Although Protestant, Grotius clearly stands in the main European Scholastic tradition, like Lessius in the Southern Netherlands – Lessius actually being one of Grotius's major sources.[19] This changes with Paulus Voet (1619–1667), a major jurist in the Northern Netherlands who stands in the Calvinist tradition of learning and who ostentatiously rejected the corrupt learning of the Roman Catholic theologians.

Paulus Voet was the son of the theologian Gijsbert Voet, also known as Gisbertus Voetius (1589–1676), who was a staunch Calvinist and a professor of theology. Gijsbert Voet delivered the inaugural speech on the occasion of the foundation of the University of Utrecht in 1636. Gijsbert Voet belonged to the movement of the Further Reformation (*Nadere Reformatie*, comparable with English Puritanism and German Pietism), which emphasized practising Christian ethics in everyday life, against a worldly life. Paulus followed his father's convictions, firmly opposing René Descartes's new philosophy of religion and knowledge. Although Paulus Voet is most well known for his works on international private law (e.g. *De statutis eorumque concursu liber singularis*, Amsterdam 1661), he has also written on the relation between law and religion (e.g. *Theologia naturalis reformata*, Utrecht 1656).[20] Moreover,

---

[18] See Chapter 5: Wouter Druwé, 'Franciscus Zypaeus', in this volume.
[19] See Chapter 6: Janwillem Oosterhuis, 'Hugo Grotius', in this volume.
[20] See Chapter 7: Johannes van Kralingen, 'Paulus Voet', in this volume.

his son Johannes Voet (1647–1713), author of a commentary on Justinian's *Pandects*, became one of the most influential jurists of the Roman–Dutch Elegant School – the influence of which is still palpable in the legal culture of countries such as South Africa. It has become increasingly clear that the Voet family played a major role in bringing a strict form of Calvinism to bear on societal and legal issues. It succeeded in convincing practising lawyers such as Johannes Andreas van der Meulen (1635–1702), a judge at the Court of Brabant in Den Haag, of the necessity to transform daily activities on the basis of lived Christian values. Van der Meulen even went as far as publishing a legal–theological treatise (*Forum conscientiae seu jus poli, hoc est tractatus theologico-juridicus*), which contemplated the differences between judging a case from the point of view of the law of God and the law of the land.

Another legal scholar whose life course was profoundly influenced by the Further Reformation was Ulrik Huber (1636–1694), an alumnus of the University of Franeker (the University had been founded in 1585 to promote a Calvinist approach to learning and science in the region of Frisia). Huber resolutely denounced Hobbes's pro-state standpoints, but also rejected the clerical struggles, observable on both Catholic and Protestant sides, for supremacy over the secular authority. Central to Huber's middle-of-the-road standpoint is a distinction between *necessaria* and other matters. God's explicit command and prohibition, comprising the revealed and natural laws of God, bind human conscience with necessity, allowing no deviation. In contrast, the matters about which no such will of God has been expressed can and do vary depending on time, place, and other circumstances. This distinction serves in turn as the boundary that limits the otherwise absolute power of the sovereign. Only God may rule and judge the *necessaria*, which pertain to questions of conscience, while the sovereign may exercise their legislative, executive, and judicial powers over other affairs. In this context, Huber defends *jus internum conscientiae*, a series of entitlements that are similar to liberty of conscience and free exercise of religion. Each individual may exercise this *jus*, even against the will of human authority, primarily secular, but also ecclesiastical. Although Huber was thus critical about theocratic Calvinist ministers, he decidedly defended the inviolability of the human conscience and the Divinity of Scripture. Building upon, but also nuancing the ideas of Reformers such as Theodore Beza (1519–1605) or his own grandfather-in-law, Johannes Althusius (1557–1638),[21] Huber

---

[21] See e.g. John Witte Jr, *The Reformation of Rights: Law, Religion and Human Rights in Early Modern Calvinism* (Cambridge: Cambridge University Press, 2008).

emphasized the individual's freedom to defend against tyranny, that is, the sovereignty of a Christian people.[22]

In the Southern Netherlands, one of the most famous jurists to contemplate the relationship between church and state was Zeger-Bernard van Espen (1646–1728), a professor at the University of Louvain. Like other Louvain jurists at the time, such as Pieter Stockmans (1608–1671), he sympathized with Jansenism, a current in Catholicism that promoted a less lax understanding of Christian morality and that took its name from Cornelius Jansenius (1585–1638), a professor of theology at the University of Louvain who had expounded St Augustine's doctrine of divine grace and was fiercely contested by the Jesuits. Van Espen's principal work on ecclesiastical law (*Jus ecclesiasticum universum*) was put on the index of forbidden books but remained a reference work for canon lawyers for centuries, both in the Southern and Northern Netherlands, and beyond. It offered a way of thinking of church–state relationships in an increasingly secular context, that is, where the state wields the highest jurisdictional power. As a staunch defender of royal power, he notably advocated the *ius placiti* of the sovereign and the so-called *recursus ad principem*.[23] Van Espen also emphasized the rights of the local church against excessive interference by Rome and sought to restrict the jurisdictional primacy of the Pope within the church. As a result, he became a major authority among the secular clerics of the Church of Utrecht, who refused to accept the papal Bull *Unigenitus*.

LAW, RELIGION, AND ENLIGHTENMENT

By the end of the seventeenth century, but particularly during the eighteenth century, the universe and society came to be increasingly regarded as a purely rational order in Western societies, devoid of references to an actively interfering divine being: the world became 'disenchanted'. For example, Balthasar Bekker (1634–1698), a Calvinist theologian from the University of Franeker and a preacher in Amsterdam, wrote *The Enchanted World* (*De betoverde Weereld*). In this book he made fun of Christians who believed in witches and evil spirits, and he even doubted that the devil truly existed. He adhered to Descartes's rationalist philosophy and combatted what he considered to be superstitious readings of the Christian faith. He anticipated Enlightenment philosophers and the rise of Deism, emphasizing the rationality of the Creation. Important parts of society, such as the economy and law, became

---

[22] See Chapter 8: Atsuko Fukuoka, 'Ulrik Huber', in this volume.
[23] See Chapter 9: Jan Hallebeek, 'Zeger-Bernard van Espen', in this volume.

more or less objectified and emptied of higher meaning, even in the work of theologians such as Bekker. This changing spirituality inevitably had consequences for the relation between religion and law in the Low Countries. However, despite a gradual and partial change in spirituality, no serious decline in belief and worship can be established in this period.[24]

The slowly changing role and character of religion in the legal realm can be witnessed in the lives and works of two jurists from the Dutch Republic. Dionysius Godefridus van der Keessel (1738–1816), who had been a professor of law in Groningen and Leiden, is mostly known for his update of Grotius's *Introduction to the Laws of Holland*, which has been particularly influential for Roman–Dutch law in South Africa. However, van der Keessel was also convinced that Christian beliefs had certain consequences for practising law, which he discussed in his *Oratio de advocato christiano* (1792), a work about the deontology of a Christian lawyer.[25] In van der Keessel's view, positive law was conceived of in a rational way, and devoid of religious notions. Where Lessius and Grotius produced all-encompassing theories, wherein divine and natural law, Christian morality, state and church were brought together in one coherent system, aimed at the advancement of a Christian society and eventually the eternal salvation of the individual, van der Keessel devoted his life and work to the study of Roman Law and the positive, customary Roman–Dutch law. But within a well-ordered society, professionally trained lawyers played an important role – and for van der Keessel this still obviously meant professionally trained *Christian* lawyers. That explains why he wanted those lawyers to follow ethical guidelines based on Christian principles. For van der Keessel, Christian faith was still embedded in law and society as a whole, as had been the case for the fifteenth-century moral admonitions of Gheyloven[26] or the seventeenth-century deontology of Zypaeus for those working in public functions.[27] This stands in marked contrast to the work – one generation later – of one of van der Keessel's pupils, Joannes van der Linden (1756–1835). His deontology for legal advisers and barristers, *De Ware Pleiter* (*The True Counsel*, 1827) was almost completely devoid of any reference to Christian notions.

Near the end of the eighteenth century, the Christian religion was still considered relevant for the ordering of Dutch society. Although, since the Enlightenment, orthodox Christianity and Biblical Revelation came to be

---

[24] Compare Taylor, *Secular*, 176–196, 221–295.
[25] See Chapter 10: Egbert Koops, 'Dionysius van Der Keessel', in this volume.
[26] See Chapter 2: Bram van Hofstraeten, 'Arnoldus Gheyloven', in this volume.
[27] See Chapter 5: Wouter Druwé, 'Franciscus Zypaeus', in this volume.

questioned as the ultimate foundation of law, they could function well as – important – sources of morality justifying certain legal principles. Christian jurists also came to think and act along those lines. A case in point is the life and work of Pieter Paulus (1753–1796). He was a patriot and a firm believer in a republic, at a moment when European societies were shifting from the old to the new regime. In his writings on a constitution for a Dutch Republic, Paulus stressed the equality between all individuals, which he based on the equality advocated by Jesus in the Gospels. Paulus went to great lengths to demonstrate the biblical foundation of such equality, but hardly discussed the role of religion as such in society.[28] Although in this period, the conditions of belief had been under question for quite a while, Christian belief itself and the practice thereof in the Dutch Republic were apparently still so strong that Paulus thought his appeal to a biblical foundation of equality sufficient to convince many of his fellow citizens, admittedly, not as the ultimate foundation of the legal principle of equality in a new constitution, but as one of its possible justifications – in this case, Christian morality.

BELIEF AND REVOLUTION

After spells of dominance by French rulers, especially Napoleon, the Low Countries were reunited in 1815 under King William I in the United Kingdom of the Netherlands. North and South, however, appeared to have grown too far apart politically, culturally, and religiously to form a unity once more. In the wake of the French July Revolution of 1830, the Belgian Revolution took place and resulted in an independent Kingdom of Belgium. This revolution deeply shocked Guillaume Groen van Prinsterer (1801–1876), secretary of King William I at the time. Groen van Prinsterer belonged to the so-called Réveil movement, a pietistic movement, and he linked revolution and unbelief. According to him, the atheist French Revolution had led to a spiritual vacuum in Europe as a whole, including in the Netherlands. Instead, he defended the Gospel as the religious foundation for Dutch society, with separate responsibilities spread out over various levels and instances, accompanied by independence in one's own sphere, as a citizen, municipality, societal organization, etc. Groen van Prinsterer was, moreover, deeply concerned with poverty and set up several initiatives to combat it. Van Prinsterer was an antagonist of the liberal Lutheran Johan Thorbecke (1798–1872), who revised the Dutch constitution to increase the power of parliament.[29] But with the

---

[28] See Chapter 11: Matthijs de Blois, 'Pieter Paulus', in this volume.
[29] See Chapter 12: Jan Willem Sap, 'Guillaume Groen van Prinsterer', in this volume.

further democratization of Dutch politics, van Prinsterer saw the need to engage in politics and defend the rights of Protestants in the Dutch parliament, just like Abraham Kuyper (1837–1920), the famous founder of the Free University of Amsterdam (now VU University Amsterdam) and leader of the neo-Calvinist movement. Thus, Groen van Prinsterer illustrates well the initial uneasy and ambiguous attitude of orthodox Protestants to the upcoming liberal democracy in the Netherlands. Groen van Prinsterer regretted the decline of Christian belief and its waning influence on Dutch society, but also came to recognize that he had to use liberal democracy, that is, the secular public sphere, to realize Christian ideals for Dutch society.

In the Southern Netherlands, contrasting reactions among Christian jurists to Enlightenment and revolution can be identified as well. Edouard Ducpétiaux (1804–1868) studied law in Liège, Leiden, and Ghent before becoming a journalist. He was concerned about high poverty rates in Belgium in the first half of the nineteenth century and is remembered for his seminal contribution to more humane treatment of prisoners and reform of the Belgian prison system. In 1827, just a few years before the Belgian Revolution, he wrote a famous pamphlet against capital punishment. Arguments deduced from belief or philosophy are strikingly absent in this controversial work. Although Ducpétiaux did not hesitate to call himself a Christian, the only references to religion in his book seem to concern the condemnation of religious fanaticism that were a *topos* in contemporary post-Enlightenment literature. Indeed, Ducpétiaux firmly supported the Belgian Revolution and the ensuing liberal democracy in the new Kingdom of Belgium. But the liberal values of liberty and transparency also meant for him 'a free church in a free state'. Later in life, Ducpétiaux, as one of the initiators of the General Assemblies of Catholics in Belgium, mobilized his fellow Christians, propagating Catholic principles for the wellbeing of society.[30] For Ducpétiaux, the state was a secular public space and in the public debate he chose no longer to rely on religious arguments, unlike for instance Pieter Paulus earlier in the Northern Netherlands, who had given his defence of the principle of equality a biblical foundation. But within this secular order of society, for a liberal Catholic like Ducpétiaux, Catholics and Catholic principles were still an important force for the wellbeing of society.

This liberal Catholic attitude is in sharp contrast to the conservative attitude of Charles Périn (1815–1905) toward revolution and liberal democracy. Périn was an eminent jurist from Mons teaching public law, international law, and political economy at the University of Louvain. Himself a student of the

---

[30] See Chapter 13: Frank Judo, 'Edouard Ducpétiaux', in this volume.

conservative French Catholic lawyer Charles de Coux (1787–1864), Périn became the master of the well-known neo-scholastic jurist and political economist Victor Brants (1856–1917). From supporter of liberal Catholicism, Périn evolved toward the secular leader of the ultramontanes, opponents of constitutional freedoms. A first condition of progress of social life was the acceptance of the teachings and the discipline of the church. The church professed the principle of submission to God, from which followed, as a practical consequence, the duty of sacrifice and charity. The Revolution, however, professed man as master of himself. The idea of obedience was the guiding principle for the ideas of Périn. For Périn, in contrast to individualism, source of many evils, the church stood for charity. In all his work on political economy, the principle of 'Christian renunciation' constituted his guideline. As a political economist, he was intensely involved in the contemporary debate about the relationship between workers and their bosses, and more generally, the attitude of Catholicism toward the rise of socialism.[31] Like Groen van Prinsterer for the Northern Netherlands, Périn regretted the waning influence of Christian faith on society and principally rejected liberal democracy. When developing and defending his economic theory, Périn relied unconditionally on Christian principles and the authority of church and Pope.

ANSWERS TO MODERNITY IN THE LOW COUNTRIES: NEO-SCHOLASTICISM, PERSONALISM, NEO-CALVINISM, AND CHRISTIAN DEMOCRACY

According to Taylor, the 'secular age' has existed since the late nineteenth century. This has several consequences: (1) public space has now been entirely emptied of religious meaning – unlike in the early modern period, where the separation between state and church was initially accompanied by a 'spiritualization' of the civil authorities; (2) Christian belief and worship are in decline, particularly over about the last five decades; and, importantly, (3) the conditions of belief have changed fundamentally. While even during the Enlightenment, unbelief was still unthinkable for the majority of the people, in the current secular age, many find not believing in a transcendent God almost inescapable. This, now widely available, 'default' option of absence of belief in God has been coined by Taylor as 'exclusive or self-sufficient humanism': 'a humanism accepting no

---

[31] See Chapter 14: Fred Stevens, 'Charles Périn', in this volume.

final goals beyond human flourishing, nor any allegiance to anything else beyond this flourishing'.[32]

The exclusive humanism in Taylor's sense stands in marked contrast to the – often Christian – humanism of the fourteenth to sixteenth centuries – a humanist movement that sought to reconcile Christian values and ancient philosophical traditions, as can be witnessed in the work of Desiderius Erasmus (c. 1466–1536) or Justus Lipsius. Their humanist writings contributed to the Protestant tradition, in which flourishing on earth and striving for a transcendent goal came to be distinguished and paradoxically related. The disenchantment of the world included the religious life: for Protestants, even more so than for Catholics, God is sanctifying us everywhere, including in ordinary life, work, marriage, and so on. Salvation is in faith, and faith alone. Serving God in ordinary life, guided by his spirit, also means that things can be reordered freely. This confidence in our capacity to achieve a well-ordered society, a disciplined personal life and the right spiritual stance, enabled the move toward the current, exclusive form of humanism, as Taylor argues. Only the reference to God had to disappear. The goal of order had to become only a matter of human flourishing, and the power to pursue such order was to become a purely human capacity.[33] This exclusive and self-sufficient humanism of our current age has resulted in the predominance of a so-called 'immanent' worldview: human flourishing, the fullness of life, and the ordering of society must come from within humanity, without any reference to a transcendent world. This immanent worldview also came to dominate the way of thinking about law and society, as legal positivism illustrates. Legal positivism envisions legal rules as the product of pure human will – human will which is no longer embedded in a divine framework as was the case when medieval canon lawyers started to articulate the nature of 'positive law' as opposed to natural law. For the Low Countries, Taylor's observations about a secular age appear acutely correct as well. In confrontation with modernity, but unavoidably also influenced by it, Christian jurists in the Low Countries have formulated strikingly different answers to modernity.

Léon de Lantsheere (1862–1912) is a major representative of the Catholic neo-Scholastic revival movement in Belgium. Although reaching back to the first half of the nineteenth century, the renaissance of the Thomistic tradition in Belgium received a major impetus from the publication of Pope Leo XIII's Encyclical *Rerum Novarum* (1891) – which was partly based on Leo XIII's previous experience, as a papal nuntius in Belgium, of the destabilizing effects

---

[32] Taylor, *Secular*, 18.
[33] Compare Taylor, *Secular*, 18, 77–145, here in particular 77–84.

of social class struggles in the major birthplaces of modern industrialization such as Ghent, Charleroi, and Liège. De Lantsheere was less involved in the revival of the socio-economic doctrines of early modern scholastics such as Lessius than was Auguste Castelein (1840–1922), a Jesuit theologian and from 1892 to 1894 counsellor of the *Association des Patrons Catholiques de Belgique*, or Abbé Pottier (1849–1923), advocate of the interests of the working class.[34] But he wrote an influential article on the problem of poor people stealing bread (*Le pain volé*) and saw the need to defend the Thomistic, essentially teleological, view of human existence as a continuing, destined movement toward God against the dangers of secularism. His neo-Scholastic training would also determine de Lantsheere's legal work. As professor of criminal law, de Lantsheere joined numerous Louvain colleagues in their fight against legal positivism and especially against what they called 'the relativism of modern sociology'. With the Catholic jurist Théodore Fontaine (1858–1898), de Lantsheere was one of the founding members of the *Société philosophique de Louvain*, which promoted neo-Thomism among university students, including those enrolled at the law school. Besides his academic career at Louvain's law faculty, de Lantsheere was also a politician for the Catholic party, eventually becoming Minister of Justice.[35]

The answer of Paul Scholten (1875–1946) to rationality and scientism in law was more personalist. Scholten was a professor in Amsterdam and has profoundly influenced generations of Dutch lawyers with his ideas about how judges should eventually reach their decisions ('rechtsvinding'). Scholten became a convicted Christian only later in life, when he also joined the Dutch Reformed Church. His faith and Christian convictions increasingly guided his thoughts and activities in the field of law. Whenever, according to Scholten, fairness or custom were at stake, the final say was not left to legal doctrine, but a solution needed to be sought that was acceptable both practically and theoretically. The law itself is not of decisive importance, as there will always be a need for a conscientious interpretation of laws and facts. Scholten believed the principles of law to be embedded in the personal relationship of man and God, a relationship that translated into the 'encounter' of man and his neighbour ('I and Thou'). All his theoretical publications bear witness to this Christian existentialist or personalist principle. Scholten countered the rationality and scientism in law with his attention to concrete existence: to the

---

[34] Peter Heyrman, 'A conservative Reading of *Rerum novarum* through a Neo-Scholastic Lens. The Jesuit Auguste Castelein (1840–1922) and the Belgian *Patrons Catholiques*' in *Neo-Thomism in Action. Law and Society Reshaped by Neo-Scholastic Philosophy, 1880–1960*, eds. Wim Decock, Bart Raymaekers, and Peter Heyrman (Leuven: UPL (in press)).

[35] See Chapter 15: Peter Heyrman, 'Léon de Lantsheere', in this volume.

paradox, the person, and the personal decision. The infinite, qualitative differences, paradoxes or antitheses between time and eternity and between world and word, between the realm of God and the realm of Caesar, implicate a (similar) abysmal distance between law and justice, is and ought, will and knowledge. A decision is not a scientific judgement. Judicial adjudication always requires an act of will and a conscientious 'leap'. Justice and fairness (equity) are decisive for law. As such, they can never be codified and found in written human law. Scholten is generally acknowledged to be one of the greatest jurists in the Low Countries in the twentieth century, even among jurists who are not Christian.[36]

Willem Duynstee (1886–1986) is exemplary for the advent of neo-Scholastic thinking in the Netherlands and the emancipation of the Catholic part of Dutch society. He was a priest, but became professor of law at the Catholic University of Nijmegen later in his life. During the interwar period in the Netherlands, he blossomed into a Catholic figurehead, albeit on the sidelines of the law. After the Second World War, he published a neo-Scholastic treatise on *Recht en rechtvaardigheid* (*Law and Justice*), reminiscent of Lessius's and other early modern scholastics' treatises *De iustitia et iure*. Duynstee's legal principles lay firmly in the nature of people, which God had created, and in the natural order that He had also created. They were subject to the *lex aeterna* (eternal law). This eternal law was absolute – that is, immutable and valid as a general matter. Its content was natural law proper. Natural law proper formed the basis of natural–rational law. Natural reason had derived natural–rational law from the natural law proper. Duynstee's view was closely bound up with his Catholic faith. Although an orthodox Catholic and loyal to the church, he was also interested in and open to findings of the modern humanities, such as psychology. This brought him into conflict with ecclesiastical authorities in the Netherlands, although he was rehabilitated by Rome near the end of his life.[37]

Jules Storme (1887–1955) was one of the most eminent Catholic lawyers and politicians in twentieth-century Belgium. He is the father of Marcel Storme and grandfather of Matthias Storme, two jurists who have continued to play important roles as Catholic intellectuals in Belgium. Jules Storme became the dean of Ghent University's Law Faculty just after the Second World War. Although he was a jurist, in his opinion, law was not the best means for ordering society. In a text on the 'sociological' foundations of law, he stated that *boni mores* trump *bonae leges*. In this context, he not only referred to

---

[36] See Chapter 16: Timo Slootweg, 'Paul Scholten', in this volume.
[37] See Chapter 17: Corjo Jansen, 'Willem Duynstee', in this volume.

morals, but also to religion, which he deemed more important than law. For ordering society, Storme's fundamental axiom was: 'Love your neighbour as yourself' (Mark 12:31). Unsurprisingly, Storme acted as a political representative for the Catholic workers and the middle estate respectively, crucially shaping the Christian Democracy in Belgium. At the end of his life, he was awarded the *Pro Ecclesia et Pontifice* sign for his lifelong service to the Roman Catholic Church.[38]

Probably the most fundamental answer of the Low Countries to modernity came from Herman Dooyeweerd (1894–1977). Dooyeweerd was professor at the Free University of Amsterdam, founded by Abraham Kuyper, but lectured quite extensively abroad, for instance in the USA (see e.g. Alvin Plantinga). He developed a complete neo-Calvinist philosophy (*A New Critique of Theoretical Thought*), in answer also to neo-Kantianism: for example, reality was divided in certain law-spheres or modalities (*wetskringen*), which had their own internal sovereignty. A noteworthy element in Dooyeweerd's philosophy of law is the relationship between law and morality. Principles of law are not moral principles. They belong to the 'jural' aspect of reality, not the moral. Just like legal positivists, Dooyeweerd sharply distinguished between law and morality. Morality is not the foundation of law. That does not make Dooyeweerd a legal positivist: the jural aspect has its own normativity. Law cannot violate fundamental legal principles; otherwise, it cannot be law. The principles, however, are not understood as moral principles. The concept of law is what makes a phenomenon a jural phenomenon. There is, however, a moral analogy within the jural aspect. Law has a normative direction. It must be 'opened up'. Legal–moral principles, however, are regulating principles, not constitutive ones. Law is a normative phenomenon, not only because it proclaims a norm, but because it is rooted in the jural modal aspect, which is governed by normative legal principles. As one commentator rightly observes, Dooyeweerd developed 'a normative theory of law that is both part of the natural law tradition and highly critical of many natural law conceptions'. Although Dooyeweerd has been lauded – slightly exaggeratedly – as 'the most original philosopher Holland has ever produced, not even Spinoza excepted' and has been regarded – more realistically – as 'undoubtedly the most formidable Dutch philosopher of the twentieth century', his work is perhaps better-known outside the Netherlands than it is inside.[39]

Finally, Josse Mertens de Wilmars (1912–2002) exemplifies the important influence of Christian Democratic political philosophy on the foundation and

---

[38] See Chapter 18: Dirk Heirbaut, 'Jules Storme', in this volume.
[39] See Chapter 19: Bas Hengstmengel, 'Herman Dooyeweerd', in this volume.

development of the European Union.[40] Mertens de Wilmars was a jurist from a Catholic family and a politician trained at the Catholic University of Louvain. He devoted his life and work to the Christian People's Party (CVP) and became one of the first judges in the European Court of Justice, of which he became the President in the early 1980s.[41] For lack of clear, public statements about his intimate religious beliefs, Mertens de Wilmars's Christian faith remains difficult to gauge. In this regard, Mertens de Wilmars's life and career illustrate a larger phenomenon whereby Christianity's structural power to guide policy-making and legal thinking steadily waned over the last century in the Low Countries. Mertens de Wilmars lived in the age that saw 'secularism itself being secularized', to recall Harold Berman's words. As a result, secularization no longer merely implied a transfer of institutional power from ecclesiastical structures to secular authorities but also the loss of faith itself. Except for indirect influence, for example through Christian Democratic parties, the structural and public presence of the Christian belief system almost disappeared in the Low Countries. But that did not prevent Christianity from continuing to inspire major jurists such as Josse Mertens de Wilmars, or, for that matter, Paul Scholten, in their personal and professional life.

---

[40] Compare R. Domingo, 'Robert Schuman', in *Great Christian Jurists in French History*, eds. Olivier Descamps and Rafael Domingo (Cambridge: Cambridge University Press, 2019), 404–420.

[41] See Chapter 20: Laurent Waelkens, 'Josse Mertens de Wilmars', in this volume.

1

Alger of Liège

Emmanuël Falzone

BIOGRAPHICAL INTRODUCTION

Alger (*Algerus canonicus Leodiensis*) lived between the second half of the eleventh century and the first half of the twelfth century,[1] in the age of the Investiture Controversy.[2] His biography is mainly known through the *Elogium* written during his lifetime by the canon Nicholas of Liège, as an introduction to his 'redaction' of Alger's two treaties.[3] Neither the date nor place of his birth are known and the nickname 'of Liège' is more a reference to the city where he made his career as a member of the secular clergy, before entering the monastery of Cluny at a later stage in his life.

---

[1] Besides the concise and useful biography provided by Robert Kretzschmar (n. 10 below), 1–8, the main study on Alger was published by Maria Ludovica Arduini, 'Tra *Christianitas* e *contemplatio*: Algero di Liegi. Per una interpretazione storiografica', in *Chiesa, diritto e ordinamento della 'Societas christiana' nei secoli XI e XII. Atti della nona Settimana internazionale di studio, Mendola, 28 agosto-2 settembre 1983*, Pubblicazioni dell'Università cattolica del Sacro Cuore. Miscellanea del Centro di studi medioevali, 11 (Milano: Vita e pensiero, 1986), 340–400, who offers a critical (and inspiring) reading of Nicholas's *Elogium* and the other sources of Alger's biography; see also the recent account of Carlo Dezzuto, 'Una vicenda biografica esemplare del XII secolo: Algero di Liegi. Da canonico di successo a monaco di Cluny', *Benedictina* 57 (2010): 103–128.

[2] See Ortwin Huysmans, 'The Investiture Controversy in the Diocese of Liège reconsidered. An Inquiry into the Positions of the Abbeys of Saint-Hubert and Saint-Laurent and the Canonist Alger of Liège (1091–1106)', in Steven Vanderputten, Tjamke Snijders, and Jay Diehl, eds., *Medieval Liège at the Crossroads of Europe. Monastic Society and Culture, 1000–1300*, Medieval Church Studies, 37 (Turnhout: Brepols, 2017), 183–217.

[3] Nicolaus canonicus Leodiensis, *Algeri scholastici elogium*, was first published by Jean Mabillon osb, *Veterum analectorum* (Paris: apud Ludovicum Billaine, 1675), vol. 1, 303–307 and then by Edmond Martène osb and Ursin Durand osb, *Thesaurus novus anecdotorum* (Paris: sumptibus Florentini Delaulne – 1717), vol. 5, 1021–1022 (reprint Migne, *Patrologia latina*, 180.737A–738D).

Educated at a time when the masters of Liège were famous for the teaching provided in the schools of both the episcopal city and the entire diocese,[4] Alger was trained in the liberal arts and divinity. At the time, theology, canon law, and ecclesiastical history had not yet developed into fully distinct fields of knowledge.[5]

Although he remained a deacon, Alger became — maybe in 1072, following the hypothesis that he was born in 1052 — a canon and the *scholasticus* of the collegiate church of St Bartholomew in Liège. This chapter had been established only forty years before. It consisted mainly of canons of non-noble lineage, which could be an indication about Alger's own, relatively modest origins. In the early years of the twelfth century (*c.* 1101), he was called to the cathedral chapter of Our Lady and St Lambert. For a period of twenty years, under prince-bishop Otbert (1091–1119) and his successor Frederic of Namur (1119–1121), he was chancellor of the diocese of Liège.

Alger left the cathedral chapter in 1121/22, just after prince-bishop Frederic passed away.[6] According to some scholars, the suspicious circumstances of Frederic's death could explain why Alger left the episcopal city and moved to Cluny. Nevertheless, he was not the first canon of the cathedral chapter of Liège who became a monk in Cluny toward the end of his life. Moreover, connections between Alger and Cluny are attested before his move. For instance, between 1114 and 1116, when he was still a canon of the cathedral chapter, Alger sold an allodial land located near the priory of *Vilar* – Münchenwiler (*Villars-les-Moines*), today in the Swiss canton of Bern – to the prior John who committed to pay annually one silver mark to the Cluny abbey for the salvation of Alger's soul.[7] Therefore, the hypothesis that he left the world for mere spiritual reasons cannot be excluded.

---

[4] See Christine Renardy, 'Les écoles liègeoises du IXe au XIIe siècle: grandes lignes de leur évolution', *Revue belge de philologie et d'histoire*, 57/2 (1979): 309–328 and Jean-Louis Kupper, *Liège et l'Église impériale, XIe-XIIe siècles*, Bibliothèque de la Faculté de Philosophie et Lettres de l'Université de Liège, 228 (Paris: Les Belles Lettres, 1981), 375ff., esp. 382–383 where he discusses briefly the conclusions of Charles Defreine, 'L'école canonique liègeoise et la Réforme grégorienne', in Jean Cassart, ed., *Miscellanea Tornacensia. Mélanges d'archéologie et d'histoire (Congrès de Tournai 1949)* (Brussels: Labor, 1951), 79ff.

[5] Alain Boureau, 'Droit et théologie au XIIIe siècle', *Annales. Économie, Sociétés, Civilisations*, 47/6 (1992): 1113–1125.

[6] Jean-Louis Kupper, 'La double mort de l'évêque de Liège Frédéric de Namur (†1121)', in Natalie Fryde and Dirk Reitz, eds., *Bischofsmord im Mittelalter. Murder of Bishops*, Veröffentlichungen des Max-Planck-Instituts für Geschichte, 191 (Göttingen: Vandenhoeck & Ruprecht, 2003), 159–170.

[7] Alexande Bruel, ed., *Recueil des chartes de l'abbaye de Cluny* (Paris: Imprimerie nationale, 1895), vol. 5, 330, nr. 3973. The identification of the toponym *Vilar* with the priory of

We know very little about his life in Cluny. Peter the Venerable praised Alger's humility and his biographer, the canon Nicholas of Liège, wrote that he was famous for his knowledge. While he remained a deacon during the largest part of his life, in Cluny he underwent ordination to the priesthood. There is no certainty about when Alger died, although there are indications that he passed away in the second quarter of the twelfth century, and definitely before 1145 (*terminus ad quem*).

MAJOR THEMES AND CONTRIBUTIONS

Alger's Oeuvres[8]

Alger's two treatises are by far his main contribution to the history of both theology and canon law: on the one hand, the canonistic treatise *De misericordia et iustitia* (*On mercy and justice*) and, on the other, the eucharistic treatise *De sacramento corporis et sanguinis Domini* (*On the sacrament of the body and the blood of the Lord*). However, as has been pointed out before, neither theology nor canon law was a distinct field of knowledge in the late eleventh or early twelfth century. To understand Alger's thought in the framework of his time, we have to take into consideration that both treatises deal with what Alain Boureau has named 'liturgy' before the turning point of

---

Münchenwiler (*Villars-les-Moines*), suggested by Berlière, 'Alger de Liège', in *Dictionnaire d'histoire et de géographie ecclésiastiques* (Paris: Letouzey et Ané, 1914), vol. 2, 423, was contested by Dezzuto, 'Una vicenda', 105ff. The charter edited by Bruel is the confirmation (*rem renouaui et confirmaui*) by Alger, *ecclesie Cluniensis monachus*, in the presence of the abbot Peter the Venerable, the priors and some monks of Cluny, and the prior John of *Vilar*, that the priory of *Vilar* has to pay, every year on All Saints' Day, an annual *census* estimated at one silver mark, to the Cluny abbey, according to the convention of sale between Alger, *peccator cum adhuc essem in seculo ecclesie Leodiensis sancte Marie sanctique Lamberti indignus canonicus*, and the same prior John, representing the priory of *Vilar*, of an allodial land *juxta ecclesiam de Vilar*, concluded in the presence of the abbot Pons of Melgeuil, the prior Ivo, and monks of Cluny. The priory of Münchenwiler was a recent foundation of Cluny, which explains the presence of the abbot of Cluny alongside the prior of *Vilar* in both the confirmation (*c.* 1124) and the convention of sale (*c.* 1114–1116). On the priory of Münchenwiler, see Kathrin Utz Tremp, 'Münchenwiler', in Hans-Jörg Gilomen, coll. Elsanne Gilomen-Schenkel, eds., *Die Cluniazenser in der Schweiz*, Helvetia sacra. III. Die Orden mit Benediktinerregel, 2 (Basel–Frankfurt/Main: Helbing & Lichtenhahn, 1991), 364ff, esp. 379.

[8] On Alger's oeuvres, the most recent account is Lotte Kéry, *Canonical Collections of the Early Middle Ages (ca. 400–1140). A Bibliographical Guide to the Manuscripts and Literature*, History of Medieval Canon Law, 1 (Washington, DC: The Catholic University of America Press, 1999), 272–273; Michael McCormick, XIIe siècle. *Œuvres non hagiographiques*, Index scriptorum operumque Latino-Belgicorum Medii Ævi, III.2 (Brussels: Académie royale de Belgique, 1979), 20–28 remains useful.

the thirteenth century.[9] This 'liturgical field' included sacramental theology and was related to procedural law.

The *De misericordia et iustitia* was drafted in the framework of the Investiture Controversy within the diocese of Liège.[10] The dating remains uncertain. At the present state of research, scholars situate it between 1095 (*terminus a quo*), on the ground that Alger uses the *Prologue* of Ivo of Chartres, and 1121 (*terminus ad quem*), when he retired to Cluny. While other suggestions to refine the dating have been made, none of them is really convincing. The *De misericordia et iustitia* circulated anonymously before it was gathered in the so-called 'Nicholas' redaction'.[11]

Alger's *De misericordia et iustitia* opens with a 'preface' in the form of a letter addressed to all the Christians,[12] which is 'a programmatic-explicative personal comment' on his work.[13] The treatise is divided into three books. The first two books deal with the topic of mercy and justice regarding those who are within the church, while the third focuses on those who are 'without' or even outside the church, such as heretics, which in Alger's mind included simoniacs, and schismatics. Each chapter is introduced by a rubric (heading) that highlights and announces the issue that will be discussed. It is formed by one or more canons, which are identified by an inscription indicating the author and the

---

[9] Alain Boureau, *La Loi du royaume. Les moines, le droit et la construction de la nation anglaise* (XIe-XIIe siècles) (Paris: Les Belles Lettres, 2001), 75: 'Par "liturgie", on entend ici l'ensemble des règles qui gouvernent les gestes, paroles et attitudes et visent à discipliner une communauté religieuse et l'installer comme médiateur entre Dieu et le monde terrestre'.

[10] The major study is the introduction to the critical edition provided by Robert Kretzschmar, *Alger von Lüttichs Traktat 'De misericordia et iustitia:' ein kanonistischer Konkordanzversuch aus der Zeit des Investiturstreits. Untersuchungen und Edition*, Quellen und Forschungen zum Recht im Mittelalter, 2 (Sigmaringen: J. Thorbecke, 1985). See lastly a comparative study of Lotte Kéry, 'Kanonessammlungen aus dem lotharingischen Raum', in Klaus Herbers and Harald Müller, eds., *Lotharingien und das Papsttum im Früh- und Hochmittelalter: Wechselwirkungen im Grenzraum zwischen Germania und Gallia*, Abhandlungen der Akademie der Wissenschaften zu Göttingen. N. S., 45 (Berlin: De Gruyter, 2017), 189–212, esp. 203ff and Carlo Dezzuto, *Il 'Liber de misericordia et iustitia' di Algero di Liegi: contributo alla storia della scienca del diritto canonico*, iur. can. diss. (Rome: Pontificia Università Lateranense, 2005).

[11] Although Nicholas of Liège explained the anonymous character of the publication in terms of Alger's humility, Maria Lodovica Arduini argues that, like Rupert of Deutz, he was trying to proceed as prudently and reservedly as possible, considering the delicate political context of the diocese of Liège under the episcopate of prince-bishop Otbert. See Arduini, 'Tra Christianitas e contemplatio', 372.

[12] A translation of the 'preface' is included in Robert Somerville and Bruce C. Brasington, *Prefaces to Canon Law Books in Latin Christianity. Selected Translations, 500–1245* (New Haven, CT; London: Yale University Press, 1998), 165ff.

[13] As well as Rupert of Deutz, see Maria Lodovica Arduini, *Neue Studien über Rupert von Deutz*, Siegburger Studien, 17 (Siegburg: Respublica-Verlag, 1985), 107.

passus quoted. Alger's sources are Fathers of the Church, mainly Augustine and Gregory the Great, decretals, including Pseudo-Isidorian decretals, and a few canons from Carolingian councils. Alger is eager to cite ancient texts, since they had greater authority by virtue of their long age, and non-polemical texts, acceptable to supporters of the papacy as well as to supporters of the emperor, given the context of the Investiture Controversy. Sources are mainly borrowed from the Dionysio-Hadriana and the Collection in 74-Titles, without excluding the use of intermediate collections. Although direct use of Ivo's collections is excluded, Alger was obviously inspired by his *Prologue*.[14]

The *De Misericordia et iustitia* is a work of interpretation. Alger reworked passages borrowed from other authors. He uses dialectic, which structures the succession of the quoted passus, introducing and concluding as well as managing transitions with a personal intervention: the *dicta Algeri*. Peter von Moos has compared this type of narrative construction, which combines *auctoritates* and *dicta*, to a half-timbered house: the author's interventions are the mortar that holds the whole building together. In addition, the combination of *facta* and *dicta* appears as a double-entry mode of expression of both an idea and a methodological contribution.[15]

In his *Elogium*, Nicholas de Liège used the word *tractatus* for both the *De misericordia et iustitia* and the *De sacramento corporis et sanguinis Domini*. However, scholars argue that, strictly speaking, neither is a treatise nor a canonical collection. According to Kretzschmar, the *De misericordia et iustitia* is an oeuvre *sui generis*.[16]

The redaction of the treatise *De sacramento corporis et sanguinis Domini*[17] has to be situated in the debate, within the eucharistic controversy, between Alger and Rupert, a monk of the Benedictine abbey of St Lawrence in Liège

---

[14] On the tradition of Ivo's *Prologue*, see Bruce C. Brasington, *Ways of Mercy. The Prologue of Ivo of Chartres*, Vita regularis, 2 (Munster: Lit, 2004), 106ff.

[15] Peter von Moos, 'Die Kunst der Antwort. *Exempla* und *dicta* im lateinischen Mittelalter', in Walter Haug and Burghart Wachinger, eds., *Exempel und Exempelsammlungen*, Fortuna vitrea, 2 (Tübingen: Niemeyer, 1991), 23–57, reprint Peter von Moos, *Gesammelte Studien zum Mittelalter*, vol. 2, *Rhetorik, Kommunikation und Medialität*, ed. Gert Melville, Geschichte: Forshung und Wissenschaft, 15 (Berlin: Lit, 2006), 69–106, esp. 73.

[16] Kretzschmar, *Alger*, 58ff.

[17] There is neither a comprehensive study of Alger's eucharistic treatise nor a critical edition. See PL 180.739C-854C based on Malou's edition of Louvain 1847; Kretzschmar, *Alger*, 15–20 and also Guntram G. Bischoff, *The eucharistic controversy between Rupert of Deutz and his anonymous adversary: studies in the theology and chronology of Rupert of Deutz (c. 1076–1129) and his earlier literary work*, unpublished Theol. Diss. (Princeton University, 1965); Nicholas M. Haring, 'A study in the Sacramentology of Alger of Liège', *Medieval Studies* 20 (1958): 41–78; Louis Brigué, *Alger de Liège. Un théologien de l'Eucharistie au début du* XIIe *siècle*, Theol. Diss. (Paris: J. Gabalda, 1936).

and later abbot of Deutz. The debate first took place in a series of theological disputes (c. 1113),[18] which is indicative of Alger's fame rather than of rivalry between the pre-scholastic and the monastic cultures.[19] In September 1116, Rupert was on trial for heresy. John van Engen argues that Alger was one of the two *cognitores* designated to advise the archdeacon and suggests that the first book of the *De sacramento corporis et sanguinis Domini* was completed 'sometime after the trial'.[20] However, Maria Lodovica Arduini contests the suggestion that Alger was one of the two *cognitores* of Rupert's trial.[21] According to her, the *De sacramento corporis et sanguinis Domini* is Alger's answer to Rupert's *De diuinis officiis*,[22] and the first two books were drafted *c.* 1117–1118; the third book was drafted *c.* 1119–1122.[23] Kretzschmar argues that the *De misericordia et iustitia* and the *De sacramento corporis et sanguinis Domini* mutually influenced each other, suggesting that Alger drafted his eucharistic treatise first (c. 1113–1114).[24] The treatise *De sacramento corporis et sanguinis Domini* is divided into three books: Book I is dedicated to the truth of the eucharist and a refutation of Rupert's arguments, Book II to ten questions on eucharistic theology, and Book III to sacramental validity.[25]

The two treatises were included in the so-called 'Nicholas' redaction', when Alger was retired in Cluny. Alger's *De misericordia et iustitia* had limited circulation. At the present state of research, three manuscripts give the full version, including two manuscripts of the 'Nicholas' redaction' and two manuscripts give an excerpt.[26] According to medieval book lists, we also

---

[18] John van Engen, *Rupert of Deutz* (Berkley; Los Angeles; London: University of California Press, 1983), 135ff. Jay Diehl, 'Masters and schools at St Laurent: Rupert of Deutz and the scholastic culture of a Liégeois monastery', 167, recent dating suggests 'probably closer to 1113 than 1115'.

[19] See the recent account of Diehl, 'Masters and Schools', 151–182, esp. 166ff, which updates on that issue van Engen, *Rupert*, 137–138, 145, 154–155 and also Monique Close-Dehin, n. 82 below.

[20] Van Engen, *Rupert*, 158ff, esp. 162–164 and 169–173.

[21] Arduini, *Neue Studien*, 61–63 and Ead., 'Tra *Christianitas* e *contemplatio*', 372ff.

[22] Maria Lodovica Arduini, *Rupert von Deutz (1076–1129) und der Status Christianitatis seiner Zeit: Symbolisch-prophetische Deutung der Geschichte*, Beihefte zum Archiv für Kulturgeschichte, 25 (Köln: Böhlau, 1987), 101ff.

[23] Arduini, 'Tra *Christianitas* e *contemplatio*', 191ff, and Ead., 'Considerazioni sul Liber III del *De Misericordia et iustitia* e del *De sacramentis* di Algero di Liegi: ipotesi interpretative', in Peter Linehan, ed.,*Proceedings of the Seventh International Congress of Medieval Canon Law (Cambridge, 23–27 July 1984)*, Monumenta iuris canonici, series C, vol. 8 (Rome [Vatican City]: Biblioteca Apostolica Vaticana, 1988), 176–184.

[24] Kretzschmar, *Alger*, 19–20.

[25] See van Engen, *Rupert*, 171ff.

[26] A critical survey of the manuscripts is included in Kretzschmar, *Alger*, 157ff. Since his research, a new copy of the excerpt was discovered in Vienna by Bruce C. Brasington, 'Zur

know that three manuscripts of the 'Nicholas' redaction' are lost. It must be stressed that five manuscripts, out of a total of eight, are connected with Cistercian libraries, respectively four of the 'Nicholas' redaction' and one excerpt.[27] The circulation is not only limited, it is also local. All the manuscripts but two are located in Belgium and northern France, including the lost ones. Moreover, except for Alger's reception in Gratian, there is no evidence that he was known beyond medieval learned literature.[28] In contrast to the *De misericordia and iustitia*, Alger's *De sacramento corporis et sanguinis Domini* had better circulation during the medieval and early modern periods, since it deals with some issues of fundamental theology.[29]

Alger's oeuvres also include two remaining *epistolae*[30] and a statement written for the chapter of the cathedral church of Liège.[31] Scholars disagree on the attribution of the *Liber sententiarium magistri A*.[32] as well as the opuscule *De sacrificio missae* to Alger,[33] while the question remains unsolved regarding the *De gratia et libero arbitrio*.[34]

At the dawn of the twentieth century, Demeester identified two *epistolae* within the collected letters of the *Codex Udalrici* that could be attributed to Alger.[35] The first was addressed to the collegiate chapter of Aachen[36] and the

Rezeption des Prologs Ivos von Chartres in Süddeutschland', *Deutsches Archiv für Erforschung des Mittelalters* 47 (1991): 167ff, esp. 171–173.

[27] Compare with Ivo's anticipation of the challenges of new religious orders; Brasington, *Ways of Mercy*, 103.

[28] See a survey of canons and *dicta* borrowed by Gratian in Kretzschmar, *Alger*, 141ff.

[29] Kretzschmar, *Alger*, 15ff.

[30] Kretzschmar, *Alger*, 11–14. According to John van Engen, on the ground of Nicholas' *Elogium*, Alger 'produced an extensive correspondence now lost, probably something like Ivo of Chartres' in its penchant for canonistic advice'. See John van Engen, 'Letters, Schools and Written Culture in the Eleventh and Twelfth Centuries', in *Dialektik und Rhetorik im früheren und hohen Mittelalter. Rezeption, Überlieferung und gesellschaftliche Wirkung antiker Gelehrsamkeit vornehmlich im 9. und 12. Jahrhundert*, ed. Johannes Fried, Schriften des Historischen Kollegs, Kolloquien, 27 (Munich: R. Oldenbourg Verlag, 1997), 97–132, esp. 119.

[31] Kretzschmar, *Alger*, 14.

[32] Kretzschmar, *Alger*, 21. The attribution of the *Liber sententiarium magistri A.* to Alger by nineteenth-century German scholars was dismissed since Fournier. See lastly Paule H. J. Th. Maas, *The 'Liber sententiarum magistri A': Its place amidst the sentences collections of the first half of the 12th century*, diss., Middeleeuwse studies, 11 (Nijmegen: KU Nijmegen. Centrum voor Middeleeuwse Studies, 1995).

[33] Kretzschmar, *Alger*, 20–21.

[34] Kretzschmar, *Alger*, 9–10.

[35] Alphonse Demeester, 'Notice sur le canoniste Alger de Liège (xiie siècle)', in *Congrès archéologique et historique tenu à Bruges, du 10 au 14 août 1902*, Annales de la Fédération archéologique et historique de Belgique, 16 (Bruges: Louis de Plancke, 1903), 450–460.

[36] Philipp Jaffé, *Bibliotheca rerum Germanicarum* (Berlin: Weidemann, 1869), 5.262–267, nr. 146.

other one to the cathedral chapter of Utrecht.[37] Although both letters, dealing with canonical issues, were written in the name of the canons of the cathedral chapter of Liège, Demeester argues in favour of an attribution to Alger, mainly because he was the prominent expert in canon law within the cathedral chapter when it had to deal with those issues. He suggests indeed that those letters were written when Alger was a canon of the cathedral chapter, viz. between the years 1101 and 1121. Nevertheless, Demeester's attribution to Alger needs further investigation. Maria Ludovica Arduini has done part of the work regarding the letter addressed to the cathedral chapter of Utrecht. She compared it to the treatise *De misericordia and iustitia* and suggests it was written c. 1111.[38]

According to Nicholas's *Elogium*, Alger wrote a statement about the historical dignity of the cathedral church of Our Lady and Saint Lambert. For a long time, the work designated by the scholarly literature as the *De dignitate Ecclesie Leodiensis* (*On the honour of the Church of Liège*) was considered lost, until Monchamp[39] demonstrated the attribution to Alger of the appendix to the *Liber officiorum Ecclesiae Leodiensis*.[40] The statement was written during the twenty years when Alger was a canon of the cathedral chapter, viz. between the years 1101 and 1121, on the occasion of litigation between the cathedral chapter of Liège and the canons of the collegiate church of St Peter, which turned into a conflict of jurisdiction. Furthermore, Clemens M. M. Meyer suggests that one of the *tituli* of the cathedral's baptismal font – today in the church of St Bartholomew – echoes the resolution of the dispute and Alger's statement.[41]

Peace and Unity from Harmony Within the Canons:
Mercy and Justice in Alger's Thought

In his preface to the *De misericordia et iustitia*, Alger sketched a picture of a church in crisis, between the lines of which he hints at the Investiture Controversy within the diocese of Liège:

---

[37] Ibid., 373–379, nr. 206; Samuel Muller and Arie Cornelis Bouman, *Oorkondenboek van het sticht Utrecht tot 1301* (Utrecht: A. Oosthoek, 1920), 1.243–247, nr. 265.
[38] Arduini, 'Tra *Christianitas* e *contemplatio*', 367–369 and Appendix II, 397–400; Ead., 'Considerazioni', 176–184.
[39] Georges Monchamp, 'L'écrit d'Algerus sur la dignité de l'Église liègeoise identifié avec l'appendice du *Liber officiorum Ecclesiæ Leodiensis*', *Bulletin de la Société d'art et d'histoire du diocèse de Liège*, 12 (1900): 207–229.
[40] Stanislas Bormans and M. E. Schoolmeester, 'Le *Liber officiorum Ecclesiæ Leodiensis*', *Bulletin de la Commission royale d'histoire*, s. 2, 6 (1896): 445–520, esp. 505ff.
[41] Clemens M. M. Meyer, 'Les fonts baptismaux de Liège: qui les bœufs soutenant la cuve figurent-ils?', in Geneviève Xhayet and Robert Halleux, eds., *Études sur les fonts baptismaux de Saint-Barthélemy à Liège*, Ly myreur des histors, 2 (Liège: CEFAL, 2006), 43ff.

Pondering the fact that the state of the holy Church is shaken by various errors and schisms—since the precepts of the canons are either unknown to or neglected by the corrupt, while the simple grasp them neither in their meaning nor in their discretion [corr. discernment]—to the extent that omnipotent grace answered my prayers, I thus brought the matter of prominence for everyone, so that the devotion of good men might be aided by discernment of truth, and the contention of the corrupt might be overcome by the evidence of canonical authority.[42]

According to him, the misreading and even neglect of the canons by the 'corrupt', alongside the misunderstanding and lack of discernment by the 'simple', are the causes of that crisis and its remedy stands in the 'discernment of truth' and 'the evidence of canonical authority'. In other words, the causes as well as the remedy of the crisis experienced by the church are located at two levels: (1) the question of how to establish evidence of canonical authority and (2) the question of how to apply the canons with discernment. As far as Alger was concerned, his *De misericordia et iustitia* aimed to address both questions, framing them in the context of the Investiture Controversy against the backdrop of the Gregorian Reform.

Regarding the first issue, Alger states that 'some canonical precepts are for mercy, others are for justice, differentiated by diverse circumstances, persons, and times, so that now mercy may totally remit justice, now justice may totally disguise mercy'.[43] Therefore, at a first level, he uses 'mercy' and 'justice' as hermeneutical principles. Both compete in a technique of harmonization, since within diversity, there is 'a unity of intention, utility, and truth that might shine forth in the canons'. Alger concluded that 'any diversity in them would not yield a cacophony of contradiction'.[44] In other words, diversity within the

---

[42] Algerus canonicus Leodiensis, *De misericordia et iustitia* [hereafter: *DMI*], praef., dict. a, ed. Kretzschmar, *Alger*, 187: 'Perpendens sancte ecclesie statum uariis erroribus variisque scismatibus concuti pro eo, quod precepta canonum a prauis uel nesciuntur uel negliguntur, a simplicibus uero uel non suo intellectu uel non sua discretione capiuntur, prout uotis meis omnipotens aspirauit gratia, ita omnibus rem deduxi ad medium, ut discretione ueritatis bonorum adiuuaretur deuotio et canonice auctoritatis euidentia perversorum uinceretur contentio;' trans. Somerville and Brasington, *Prefaces*, 166: however, *discretio* must be translated by 'discernment' rather than 'discretion'.

[43] *DMI*, praef., dict. a, ed. Kretzschmar, *Alger*, 187: 'Quia enim precepta canonica alia misericordie, alia sunt iustitie, adeo discreta uariis ordinibus, personis et temporibus, ut nunc misericordia omnino remittat iustitiam, nunc iustitia omnino dissimulet misericordiam;' trans. Somerville and Brasington, *Prefaces*, 166.

[44] *DMI*, praef., dict. a, ed. Kretzschmar, *Alger*, 187–188: 'ut in canonibus adeo intentionis, utilitatis, ueritatis eluceret unitas, ut nullam contrarietatis discordiam pararet aliqua eorum diuersitas;' trans. Somerville and Brasington, *Prefaces*, 166–167.

canons does not mean either cacophony or contradiction. In that respect, Alger is obviously indebted to Ivo's *Prologue*.[45] First, he borrowed from him the distinction between 'precept' (*preceptum*), indulgence (*indulgentia*) and advice (*consilium*).[46] Then, seeking for harmony within the *prima facie* diversity of canons, Alger borrowed from Ivo a technique of harmonization based on the distinction between 'dispensation', which is 'mercy', and 'strict law', which is 'justice',[47] to face the issues his time had to deal with.[48]

In Alger's mind, harmony within the diversity of the canons was not an end in itself and the first issue is closely related to the second, which concerned the question of how to apply the canons with discernment. Just after expressing the distinction between 'mercy' and 'justice' within the canonical precepts, Alger goes on:

> Those who do not know how to apply such diverse things through discernment think them to clash in contradiction, not considering that the method of ecclesiastical guidance [corr. government] is this: whether by indulging or by punishing, to preserve the same intention of charity [corr. love], the same operation of salvation. Hence those using canonical rules noncanonically so impugn and assail precepts with precepts that at times they remove justice from its place through unwarranted grace, at times they remove grace from its place through untempered justice.[49]

The issue of harmony within the canons is a first level that aims to preserve the 'intention' and 'operation' of 'the method of ecclesiastical government'; these are respectively 'love' and 'salvation'. In other words, when applying 'mercy' and 'justice' through discernment (*descretio*), both of them contribute to the ecclesiastical government (*regimen ecclesiasticum*), which sometimes uses indulgence, sometimes punishment, both inspired by love (*caritas*) in the way of salvation. Therefore, at a second level, Alger uses the topic of 'mercy'

---

[45] Kretzschmar, *Alger*, 33, 59ff.
[46] DMI, I.2–4, ed. Kretzschmar, *Alger*, 194–196.
[47] Kretzschmar, *Alger*, 31ff.
[48] Kretzschmar, *Alger*, 63.
[49] DMI, præf., dict. a, ed. Kretzschmar, *Alger*, 187: 'qui per discretionem nesciunt tam diversa temperare, putant ea sibi per contrarietatem discorditer obuiare non attendentes nunc esse modum ecclesiastici regiminis seu indulgendo seu puniendo eamdem intentionem caritatis, eamdem operationem seruare salutis, ideoque canonicis regulis non canonice utentes sic precepta preceptis diuerberant et impugnant, ut aliquando per indebitam gratiam suum iustitie, aliquando per intemperatam iustitiam suum gratiae locum auferant;' trans. Somerville and Brasington, *Prefaces*, 166: however, *ecclesiastici regiminis* must be translated as 'ecclesiastical government' rather than 'ecclesiastical guidance' and *caritas* by 'love' rather than 'charity'.

and 'justice' in the framework of the government of men and souls within the church.[50]

Referring to the *Liber Regulae Pastoralis* (*Book of Pastoral Rule*) of Gregory the Great, according to which 'the government of souls is the art of arts (*ars est artium regimen animarum*)',[51] Alger states that the *cura animarum* is the *ars artium*,[52] which implies that canonical precepts are applied through discernment (*discretio*), considering both people and circumstances.[53] Michel Foucault demonstrates with accuracy that the definition of 'the government of souls' as 'the art of arts' is the ground on which the pastoral power of the Catholic Church was built. It treats each case as an individual matter.[54] Alger's thought is deep-rooted in the patristic tradition and the *De misericordia et iustitia* is not an exception when calling on the topics of the shepherd or the physician,[55] like Ivo of Chartres did.[56]

According to Alger, the 'Church is ruled by mercy and justice through discernment'[57] and that is why canonical precepts express both:[58] diversity is not contradiction, but takes into consideration variability, regarding people and circumstances.[59] This sometimes leads to tolerating those who are not corrected[60] and sometimes even tolerating the 'evil', through love, in order not

---

[50] See a recent (and inspiring) historiographical account by Corinne Leveleux-Texeira and Annick Peters-Custot, 'Gouverner les hommes, gouverner les âmes. Quelques considérations en guise d'introduction', in *Gouverner les hommes, gouverner les âmes: XLVIe Congrès de la SHMESP (Montpellier, 28–31 mai 2015)*, Histoire ancienne et médiévale, 144 (Paris: Publications de la Sorbonne, 2016), 11–35.

[51] Grégoire le Grand, *Règle pastorale*, I.1, introduction, notes and index by Bruno Judic, ed., Floribert Romme, trans. Charles Morel, Sources chrétiennes, 381 (Paris: Cerf, 1992), 128–129. Gregory the Great borrowed it from Gregory of Nazianzen, according to which the 'guiding of man' is the 'art of arts and the science of the sciences (τέχνη τις εἶναι τεχνῶν καὶ ἐπιστήμη ἐπιστημῶν)'; Grégoire de Nazianze, *Discours 1–3*, ed. and trans. by Jean Bernardi, Sources chrétiennes, 247 (Paris: Cerf, 1978), 110–111.

[52] *DMI*, I.23 dict., ed. Kretzschmar, *Alger*, 204.

[53] *DMI*, I.23, ed. Kretzschmar, *Alger*, 204–205.

[54] Michel Foucault, *Sécurité, territoire, population. Cours au Collège de France (1977–1978)*, ed. Michel Senellard, dir. François Ewald and Alessandro Fontana (Paris: Gallimard/Seuil, 2004), 128ff, esp. 154; trans. Graham Burchell, *Security, Territory, Population: Lectures at the Collège de France, 1977–1978* (New York/Basingstoke: Palgrave Macmillan, 2007), 150ff. See Ben Golder, 'Foucault and the Genealogy of Pastoral Power', *Radical Philosophy Review* 10.2 (2007): 157–176.

[55] Valentina Toneatto, 'Les lexiques du gouvernement ecclésiastique au haut Moyen Âge', in *Gouverner les hommes, gouverner les âmes*, 39ff.

[56] Brasington, *Ways of Mercy*, 27–28.

[57] *DMI*, I.26 dict. a, ed. Kretzschmar, *Alger*, 207: 'Quia ergo cum discretione misericordie et iustitie regenda est ecclesia'.

[58] *DMI*, I.82, ed. Kretzschmar, *Alger*, 248–250.

[59] *DMI*, I.26 dict. b, ed. Kretzschmar, *Alger*, 207.

[60] *DMI*, I.27, ed. Kretzschmar, *Alger*, 207–208.

to disturb peace and unity within the church: 'indeed, the evil sometimes should be tolerated so as not to disturb the unity of the Church and the peace, sometimes only by love and piety'.[61]

'Mercy', when it has come to be seen as *tolerantia* in applying the canonical precepts through discernment, should help to maintain the peace and unity of the church, preventing the scandal of schism and oppression, tolerating the 'evil' so long as they do not harm the church.[62] However, even if Alger is advocating tolerance, he is not lenient,[63] since 'mercy' is directed toward correction and those who are not corrected by 'mercy' should be punished.[64] Notwithstanding, 'mercy' stands alongside 'justice' in applying ecclesiastical discipline. Alger quotes Augustine (*Contra epistolam Permeniani*), according to whom 'the bounds of moderation (*modus*) and circumstances (*tempora*) must be observed within the discipline of the Church', which means that correction is aimed at the restoration of the sinner, not at killing him out of feelings of revenge (*studio sanandi, non odio perimendi*), in order to preserve the peace within the church: unity needs severe discipline, just as social ties need moderate sanction.[65] Ecclesiastical discipline should be applied with good intentions and great discernment.[66] Within ecclesiastical discipline, 'mercy' must take precedence over severity,[67] not, however, in favour of those remaining impenitent because they do not want to be corrected: correcting the bad is also the true 'mercy'.

Neither 'mercy' nor 'justice' are virtues in Alger's *De misericordia et iustitia*.[68] Nevertheless, application of those guiding principles of interpretation must be tempered by the Christian virtue of *caritas*.[69] Alger brings up the issue right from the opening of the first book. On the one hand, quoting Psalm 100:1, he makes a distinction between sins that could be absolved *in hac uita* to the penitent by

---

[61] DMI, I.43, dict. a, ed. Kretzschmar, *Alger*, 218: 'Sic aliquando tolerandi sunt mali, ne unitas ecclesie uel pax turbetur, aliquando solo caritatis et pietatis intuitu'.
[62] Kretzschmar, *Alger*, 40ff.
[63] DMI, I.28–30, ed. Kretzschmar, *Alger*, 208–209.
[64] DMI, I.25, ed. Kretzschmar, *Alger*, 205–206.
[65] DMI, II.1, ed. Kretzschmar, *Alger*, 257: 'in disciplina ecclesie modus temporaque seruanda sunt'.
[66] DMI, II.2, ed. Kretzschmar, *Alger*, 257.
[67] DMI, II.3, ed. Kretzschmar, *Alger*, 258.
[68] On 'justice' as a virtue, see István P. Bejczy, *The Cardinal Virtues in the Middle Ages. A Study in Moral Thought from the Fourth to the Fourteenth Century*, Brill's Studies in Intellectual History, 202 (Leiden; Boston: Brill, 2011) and ID., 'Law and ethics: twelfth-century jurists on the virtue of justice', *Viator* 36 (2005): 197–216.
[69] *Caritas* rather than *equitas*. See Peter Landau, 'Aequitas in the *Corpus iuris canonici*', *Syracuse Journal of International Law and Commerce* 20 (1994): 95–104. Comp. Brasington, *Ways of Mercy*, 26: 'the resolution of tension between rigor and mercy stands in love (*caritas*)'.

'mercy', and judgement *in hac uita et in alia*, both belonging to government of the church. On the other, he states, on the basis of the Scripture, that 'mercy' drawn from 'love' has to take precedence over 'justice'.[70]

'The theme of *iustitia et misericordia* emerges as an obvious area of study within the Latin Church as various currents of reform jostle with one another and move through the final decades of the eleventh century', according to Robert Somerville.[71] Words are not neutral and, in this context, one can eventually raise the question how 'mercy' and 'justice' had to be comprehended in Alger's thought. First and foremost, they refer to hermeneutical principles of harmonization within the canons based on the distinction between dispensation and strict law (first level), which Alger borrowed from the *Prologue* of Ivo of Chartres. Then, harmonization within the canons needs to serve the pastoral government of the church (second level), in which, according to Alger, 'mercy' (*misericordia, tolerantia*) and 'justice' (*iustitia, disciplina*) contribute to applying the canons, through 'discernment' (*discretio*), in the way of Salvation. 'Mercy' applies to those who have to (and can) be corrected and cured, 'justice' to those who have to be punished and condemned. However, both have to be moved by 'love' (*caritas*) rather than 'force' (*potestas*). Alger's *De misericordia et iustitia* is deep-rooted in the patristic tradition. The canons that he borrowed from Gregory the Great, Ambrose, and Augustine, in particular, play a decisive part in shaping the relation between 'mercy' and 'justice' in his thought. However, Alger deals with practice rather than theory.[72] When he discusses the topic of 'mercy' and 'justice', he uses guiding principles, seeking conflict resolution in the framework of the Investiture Controversy.[73] His legal background and historical background are indivisible, and they nurtured one another.[74] One hundred years later, the bond between 'mercy' and 'justice' was disrupted by the 'legal revolution' of the twelfth century.[75]

---

[70] DMI, d.a.c. I.1, ed. Kretzschmar, *Alger*, 194.
[71] Robert Somerville, 'Mercy and justice in the early months of Urban II's Pontificate', in *Chiesa, diritto e ordinamento della 'Societas christiana' nei secoli XI e XII*, 153.
[72] Kretzschmar, *Alger*, 59, 61.
[73] Kretzschmar, *Alger*, 31ff.
[74] Paul Fournier and Gabriel Le Bras, *Histoire des collections canoniques en Occident, depuis les Fausses décrétales jusqu'au Décret de Gratien*, vol. 2 (Paris: Sirey, 1932), 340ff. See in general Stephan Kuttner, *Harmony from Dissonance. An interpretation of medieval canon law*, Wimmer Lecture, 10 (Latrobe, Pa: Archabbey Press, 1960), esp. 7–8; reprint in *The History of Ideas and Doctrines of Canon Law in the Middle Ages* (London: Variorum reprints, 1980), I.
[75] Anders Winroth, 'The legal revolution of the twelfth century', in Thomas F. X. Noble and John van Engen, eds., *European Transformations: The Long Twelfth Century*, Notre Dame Conferences in Medieval Studies (Notre Dame: Univ. Press, 2012), 338–353, esp. 339–340.

Sacramental Validity in the Age of the Investiture Controversy: The Case of Baptism

The Investiture Controversy raises a number of questions regarding the validity of sacraments administrated by unworthy priests.[76] Among them, the case of baptism is very interesting, since Alger's statement, expressed in both *De misericordia et iustitia* and *De sacramento corporis et sanguinis Domini*, seems to be the key interpretation of one of the early twelfth-century masterpieces of Liège.

The third book of the *De misericordia et iustitia* is dedicated to those who stand 'without' the church, such as schismatics and heretics. Alger focuses particularly on the validity of the sacrament administrated by unworthy priests, and for how long the minister's merits or demerits affect the sacramental validity.[77] His thought on the issue is closely related to the doctrine of Peter Damian (d. 1072), the only one among his contemporaries who is quoted in the *De misericordia et iustitia*. While Alger agrees with him on the validity of the sacraments administered by simoniacs in the name of the Holy Trinity, extending his statement on baptism to all sacraments, he refutes the opinion of Peter Damian that in these circumstances the sacraments confer spiritual benefits.[78] Since Alger borrowed from Augustine the distinction between *sacramentum* and *effectus sacramenti*, he states that the sacrament administered by schismatics and heretics in the name of the Holy Trinity[79] is *uerum*, that is, valid, but *non ratum* (or *irritum*), that is without spiritual benefits regarding Salvation.[80] In Alger's thought, therefore, the minister's merits or demerits do not affect the sacramental validity, but rather the spiritual benefits. The question was of imminent concern under the episcopate of princebishop Otbert, since he was accused of simony and Alger assimilated simony with heresy.[81]

Monique Close-Dehin argues that the iconography of the early twelfth-century baptismal font of the former baptistery of the cathedral church of

---

[76] Kretzschmar, *Alger*, 48ff. See also Haring, 'A Study' and Brigué, *Alger de Liège*, 153ff.
[77] DMI, III.1–2, ed. Kretzschmar, *Alger*, 314–315.
[78] DMI, III.39–45, ed. Kretzschmar, *Alger*, 343–350. On sacramental grace, comp. Alger's arguments with those of Rupert of St Lawrence in van Engen, *Rupert*, 118ff, esp. 124.
[79] DMI, III.13, ed. Kretzschmar, *Alger*, 324; *De sacramento corporis et sanguinis Domini*, III.13–14, ed. Malou, reprint Migne, PL, 180.847D-854C.
[80] DMI, III.2, ed. Kretzschmar, *Alger*, 315.
[81] DMI, III.32, ed. Kretzschmar, *Alger*, 337–338. On the *symoniaca haeresis* within Rupert of St Lawrence and Alger's thought, see Maria Lodovica Arduini, *Non fabula sed res: politische Dichtung und dramatische Gestalt in den Carmina Ruperts von Deutz*, Temi e testi, 33 (Rome: Storia e letteratura, 1985), 101ff; Ead., 'Considerazioni', 171–195.

Our Lady and St Lambert (hosted by the former collegiate church of St Bartholomew since 1803) is closely related to Alger's thought on the sacramental validity of baptism in the age of the Investiture Controversy.[82] In the early twelfth century, Liège had two baptisteries: on the one hand, the baptistery of the city, depending on the cathedral, and on the other, the baptistery of the island, depending on the collegiate church of St John the Evangelist. According to Monique Close-Dehin, the scene depicting the baptism of the Roman centurion Cornelius emphasizes that the bishop is the ordinary minister of baptism. The scene echoes the issue of the sacramental validity of baptism administered in the early twelfth century. Since prince-bishop Otbert, who supported the excommunicated emperor Henri IV, was a reputed simoniac, it raises the question of the sacramental validity of baptism administrated under his episcopate. However, according to Alger, for baptism administered in the name of the Holy Trinity, which is depicted in the scene, the minister's demerits do not affect the sacramental validity, although such baptism does not confer spiritual benefits.

GENERAL APPRAISAL AND INFLUENCE

Since the second quarter of the nineteenth century, Alger's *De misericordia et iustitia* has been regarded as of significant interest in the history of canon law. Although his eucharistic treatise *De sacramento corporis et sanguinis Domini* had a broader diffusion during the Middle Ages and even in the early modern period, the legacy of Alger appears eventually through the use that Gratian made of the *De misericordia et iustitia*.

Richter was the first to suggest that Gratian borrowed some of his materials from Alger's *De misericordia et iustitia*.[83] Less than thirty years later, Hüffer went further, suggesting that Gratian also used the *Sententiae magistri A.*, which he attributed to Alger.[84] Both conclusions were admitted, even if they were discussed by scholars, such as Maassen[85]

---

[82] Monique Close-Dehin, 'Du signifiant au signifié: un autre regard sur les fonts baptismaux dits de Saint-Barthélemy à Liège', in *Études sur les fonts baptismaux de Saint-Barthélemy à Liège* 117–167, esp. 151–160.

[83] Æmilius L. Richter, 'Ueber Algerus von Lüttich und sein Verhältniss zu Gratian', in *Beiträge zur Kenntniss der Quellen des canonischen Rechts* (Leipzig: Kayser, 1834), 7–17.

[84] H. Hüffer, 'Ueber Algerus von Lüttich und einen noch ungedruckten *Liber sententiarum*, der wahrscheinlich von ihm versagt und van Gratian benusst worden ist', in *Beiträge zur Geschichte der Quellen der Kirchenrechts und des romischen Rechts im Mittelalter* (Münster: Aschendorff, 1862), 1–66.

[85] Friedrich Maassen, 'Z'ur Geschichte der Quellen des Kirchenrechts und des rom. Rechts im Mittelalter', *Kritische Vierteljahresschrift für Gesetzgebung und Rechtswissenschaft* 5 (1863): 186ff.

and also Friedberg.[86] Although scholars henceforth dismissed the attribution of the *Sententiæ magistri* A. to Alger, what about Gratian's use of Alger's *De misericordia et iustitia*?

Grabmann stresses the importance of Ivo and Alger on determining the principles of concordance adopted by Gratian and, in particular, regarding the influence of Alger's *dicta*.[87] In 1921, Le Bras published an enthusiastic contribution on Alger's *De misericordia et iustitia*, concluding that, although it is related to local issues in the age of the Investiture Controversy within the diocese of Liège, it had a decisive influence on Gratian.[88] Ten years later, the same Le Bras is more nuanced, considering that Alger's *De misericordia et iustitia* prefigured 'in a miniature without grace' Gratian's *Concordia*.[89] And after all, he underlines that, although Alger's *De misericordia et iustitia*, which related to local issues, is not a revolutionary work in the history of canon law, it had a decisive influence on Gratian's method, besides the canons and *dicta* borrowed by him.[90] In the second half of the twentieth century, Friedrich Merzbacher[91] and Kretzschmar[92] share the same conclusions, with a few qualifications.

However, reservations started to grow at the end of the twentieth century. Christoph H. F. Meyer states that, although Ivo and Alger both seek harmony among the diversity of the canons, the *dicta Algeri* are much more a moral, anthropological justification than are the *dicta Gratiani*. In addition, Alger knows only a single harmonization technique, based on the distinction between mercy and justice, and his intention, in the framework of the Investitures Controversy, is more limited than that of Gratian.[93] Without

---

[86] Emil Friedberg, ed., *Decretum Magistri Gratiani* (Leipzig: Bernhard Tauchnitz, 1879; reprint 1928).

[87] Martin Grabmann, *Die Geschichte der Scholastischen Methode*, vol. 2 (Freiburg/Breisgau: Herdersche Verlagshandlung, 1909–1911), 216–217.

[88] Gabriel Le Bras, 'Le Liber de misericordia et justicia d'Alger de Liège', *Nouvelle revue historique de droit français et étranger* 45 (1921): 80–118.

[89] Gabriel Le Bras, 'Alger de Liège et Gratien', *Revue des sciences philosophiques et théologiques* 20 (1931): 5–26.

[90] Fournier and Le Bras, *Histoire*, vol. 2, *passim*, esp. 336ff. See, in general, Christof Rolker, 'Fournier's Model and Its Merits', in Christof Rolker, ed., *New Discourses in Medieval Canon Law Research. Challenging the Master Narrative*, Medieval Law and Its Practice, 28 (Leiden: Brill, 2019), 4ff, esp. 13, 20, 29.

[91] Friedrich Merzbacher, 'Alger von Lüttich und das Kanonische Recht', ZRG, KA 66 (1980): 230–260 (reprint *Recht – Staat – Kirche. Ausgewählte Aufsätze* [Vienna – Cologne – Graz: 1989], 588–618).

[92] Kretzschmar, *Alger*, *passim*.

[93] Christoph H. F. Meyer, *Die Distinktionstechnik in der Kanonistik des 12. Jahrhunderts. Ein Beitrag zur Wissenschaftsgeschichte des Hochmittelalters*, Mediævalia Lovaniensia, s. 1, Studia, 29 (Leuven: Univ. Press, 2000), 141–143

minimizing the contribution of Ivo and Alger to Gratian, Anders Winroth states that they influenced Gratian's method, without constituting a model.[94] Atria A. Larson is very critical about Alger's influence on Gratian: 'While not connecting Gratian to any particular school, Le Bras's article nevertheless established a connection between Gratian and a rather obscure, north-western European, early twelfth-century text that has no extant manuscripts in Italy and that no other contemporary of Gratian quoted'.[95] She emphasizes the influence of the School of Laon on Gratian, suggesting that the author of the *Concordia* went to the north of France to study divinity. However, in denying that Alger had any influence on Gratian, how can it be explained that about one hundred canons and sixty *dicta* were borrowed from Alger's *De misericordia et iustitia* by Gratian? Martina Hartmann suggests that the connection between Bologna and Liège must be due to the political and even marital ties between Northern Italy and Lower Lotharingia, both being part of the Holy Roman Empire in the late eleventh and early twelfth centuries.[96]

Whatever Alger's influence on Gratian, his use of dialectic, giving a hermeneutical structure to his treaty, introducing every issue and making transitions through the technique of *dicta*, is an anticipation of Gratian's method and a contribution to the autonomy of canon law in the field of divinity.[97] His view of canon law remains inspiring,[98] and might find an echo in recent constitutions by pope Francis,[99] under the proviso of respect for both its historical and legal backgrounds.[100] Alger's *De misericordia et iustitia* does not embrace the whole canon law, because this was not his ambition. The treatise had an application limited to the hermeneutical principles set forth by Ivo of Chartres. Dealing with issues related to the

[94] Anders Winroth, *The Making of Gratian's 'Decretum'*, Cambridge Studies in Medieval Life and Thought, Fourth Series, 49 (Cambridge: Cambridge University Press), 17.3.
[95] Atria A. Larson, *Master of Penance: Gratian and the Development of Penitential Thought and Law in the Twelfth Century*, Studies in Medieval and Early Modern Canon Law, 11 (Washington, DC: The Catholic University of America Press, 2014), cap. 7, 271ff, esp. 275 for citation.
[96] Martina Hartmann, 'The letter collection of Abbot Wibald of Stablo and Corvey and the *Decretum Gratiani*', *Bulletin of Medieval Canon Law*, N. S., 29 (2011–2012), 35ff, esp. 48–49.
[97] Bruce C. Brasington, *Order in Court. Medieval Procedural Treatises in Translation* (Leiden: Brill, 2016), 33, n. 35. Comp. John C. Wei, 'Of Scholasticism and Canon Law: Narratives Old and New', in *New Discourses in Medieval Canon Law Research*, 105ff, esp. 116.
[98] Thomas G. Doran, *Canon Law in the Twelfth century: The Views of Bernold of Constance, Ivo of Chartres and Alger of Liège*, excerptum ex iur. can. diss. (Rome: Pontificia Universitas Gregoriana, 1979).
[99] Ruggero Maceratini, 'Misericordia e diritto in Algero di Liegi e Graziano', *Vergentis* 5 (2017): 61–79.
[100] Wim Decock, 'Light of the World: Reclaiming the Historic(al) Role of Canon Law', *Concilium: International Review of Theology* (2016): 15–23, esp. 16–18.

consequences of the Investiture Controversy in the daily life of the Christian community in Liège, Alger is seeking peace and unity within the church and that is what the *De misericordia et iustitia* aims to do: 'I composed this little work for the sake of brotherly utility'.[101]

RECOMMENDED READINGS

Arduini, Maria Lodovica. 'Tra *Christianitas* e *contemplatio*: Algero di Liegi. Per una interpretazione storiografica'. In *Chiesa, diritto e ordinamento della 'Societas christiana' nei secoli XI e XII. Atti della nona Settimana internazionale di studio, Mendola, 28 agosto-2 settembre 1983*, Pubblicazioni dell'Università cattolica del Sacro Cuore. Miscellanea del Centro di studi medioevali, 11, 340–400. Milano: Vita e pensiero, 1986.

Arduini, Maria Lodovica. 'Considerazioni sul Liber III del *De Misericordia et iustitia* e del *De sacramentis* di Algero di Liegi: ipotesi interpretative'. In *Proceedings of the Seventh International Congress of Medieval Canon Law (Cambridge, 23–27 July 1984)*, ed. Peter Linehan, Monumenta iuris canonici, series C, vol. 8, 171–195. Rome (Vatican City): Biblioteca Apostolica Vaticana, 1988.

Close-Dehin, Monique. 'Du signifiant au signifié: un autre regard sur les fonts baptismaux dits de Saint-Barthélemy à Liège'. In *Études sur les fonts baptismaux de Saint-Barthélemy à Liège, Ly myreur des histors*, 2, eds. Geneviève Xhayet and Robert Halleux, 117–167. Liège: CEFAL, 2006.

Dezzuto, Carlo. *Il 'Liber de misericordia et iustitia' di Algero di Liegi: contributo alla storia della scienca del diritto canonico*, iur. can. diss. Rome: Pontificia Università Lateranense, 2005.

Dezzuto, Carlo. 'Una vicenda biografica esemplare del XII secolo: Algero di Liegi. Da canonico di successo a monaco di Cluny', *Benedictina* 57 (2010): 103–128.

Doran, Thomas G. *Canon law in the twelfth century: the views of Bernold of Constance, Ivo of Chartres and Alger of Liège*, excerptum ex iur. can. diss. (Rome: Pontificia Universitas Gregoriana, 1979).

Haring, Nicholas M. 'A Study in the Sacramentology of Alger of Liège', *Medieval Studies* 20 (1958): 41–78.

Huysmans, Ortwin. 'The Investiture Controversy in the Diocese of Liège reconsidered. An Inquiry into the Positions of the Abbeys of Saint-Hubert and Saint-Laurent and the Canonist Alger of Liège (1091–1106)'. In *Medieval Liège at the Crossroads of Europe. Monastic Society and Culture, 1000–1300*, Medieval Church Studies, 37, eds. Steven Vanderputten, Tjamke Snijders, and Jay Diehl, 183–217. Turnhout: Brepols, 2017.

Kéry, Lotte. 'Kanonessammlungen aus dem lotharingischen Raum'. In *Lotharingien und das Papsttum im Früh- und Hochmittelalter: Wechselwirkungen im Grenzraum zwischen Germania und Gallia*, Abhandlungen der Akademie der Wissenschaften

---

[101] DMI, præf., dict. a, ed. Kretzschmar, *Alger*, 188: 'quia fraterne utilitatis causa hoc opusculum composui'; trans. Somerville and Brasington, *Prefaces*, 168.

zu Göttingen. Neue Folge, 45, eds. Klaus Herbers and Harald Müller, 189–212. Berlin: De Gruyter, 2017.

Kretzschmar, Robert. *Alger von Lüttichs Traktat 'De misericordia et iustitia:' ein kanonistischer Konkordanzversuch aus der Zeit des Investiturstreits. Untersuchungen und Edition*, Quellen und Forschungen zum Recht im Mittelalter, 2. Sigmaringen: J. Thorbecke, 1985.

Le Bras, Gabriel. 'Le *Liber de misericordia et justicia* d'Alger de Liège'. *Nouvelle revue historique de droit français et étranger* 45 (1921): 80–118.

Le Bras, Gabriel. 'Alger de Liège et Gratien'. *Revue des sciences philosophiques et théologiques* 20 (1931): 5–26.

Maceratini, Ruggero. 'Misericordia e diritto in Algero di Liegi e Graziano'. *Vergentis* 5 (2017): 61–79.

Merzbacher, Friedrich. 'Alger von Lüttich und das Kanonische Recht'. ZRG, KA 66 (1980), 230–260 (reprint in *Recht-Staat-Kirche, Ausgewählte Aufsätze*, eds. Friedrich Merzbacher et al., 588–618. Vienna; Cologne; Graz: Böhlau, 1989).

2

Arnoldus Gheyloven

Bram van Hofstraeten

BIOGRAPHICAL INTRODUCTION

Based on the manner in which Arnoldus Gheyloven refers to himself in his works, that is, Arnoldus Theoderici de Hollandia de Rotterdam, one may believe that Arnoldus was born in the city of Rotterdam, probably around 1375, but the exact date of birth remains unknown. Hardly anything is known about his younger years or the social environment in which he spent his childhood. After having studied in Vienna for a while, Gheyloven moved to Bologna around 1393 in order to study canon law under the supervision of Gaspar Calderini (†1399), a *subtilis canonista* according to Gheyloven, and son of the even more famous canonist, Giovanni Calderini (†1365). Arnoldus stayed for six years in the house of Calderini, where he was nourished by him as if he was his own son. But when Calderini died from the plague in 1399, Gheyloven moved to Padua, as a *baccalaureus decretum*, to continue his canon law studies, between 1401 and 1403, under the supervision and sponsorship of the great Italian canonist, Francesco Zabarella (†1417). Arnoldus said that Zabarella, who was known for his altruism toward poor students, took care of him as if he was his adoptive son and that he even paid for Arnoldus's doctorate in canon law, which he obtained in October 1403.[1] In his *laudatio*, Zabarella, one of the most famous canonists of his time, praises Gheyloven as a canonist but also for the manner in which he managed to overcome the obstacles in life, mainly referring to the poverty in which the young doctor had grown up.[2] After his doctorate, Arnoldus

---

[1] More details on Gheyloven's residence in the house of Zabarella can be found in M. Dyckmans, 'Les premiers rapports de Pétrarque avec les Pays-Bas', *Bulletin de l'Institut Historique Belge de Rome* 20 (1939): 111–116.

[2] The *laudatio* can be found in Ms. Vienna Österreichische Nationalbibliothek, *Vind. Pal.* 5513, ff. 180v–181r.

continued his studies elsewhere, but he remains silent about the exact locations where this formation took place.[3]

Before 1409, Arnoldus Gheyloven entered the monastery of Groenendaal (*Viridis vallis*) in Hoeilaart near Brussels as a canon regular of Saint-Augustine. The monastery was situated in the middle of the Sonian Forest and was still a young institution. Founded in 1343 as a private community of three canons (Frank van Coudenberg, Jan Hinckaert, and Jan van Ruusbroec) of the chapter of Saint-Michael and Saint-Gudule in Brussels who were looking for peace and calm outside the city, the community was soon formalized as a monastery of Augustinian canons regular in 1349. The great mystic, Jan van Ruusbroec (†1381), became the first prior of the Groenendaal Priory, and Jan Hinckaert, his uncle, was chosen as its first provost. The writings of Ruusbroec played a pivotal role in the growing importance and attractiveness of *Viridis vallis* during the fourteenth century, when Geert Groote (†1384), founder of the Brethren of the Common Life and key figure in the *Devotio Moderna* movement, also visited the priory. New priories were founded and by the beginning of the fifteenth century, Groenendaal led a congregation of five monasteries, eventually giving up its independent status on 7 May 1413 and being absorbed into the Windesheim Congregation of the *Devotio Moderna*.

Little is known about Gheyloven during his time as a canon regular of the Groenendaal monastery. Most likely, he lived a life devoted to books and piety. So, when he died at Groenendaal on 31 August 1442, he was praised as a jurist and for the number of books that he had brought with him.[4] In addition, he enriched the priory's library by means of his own writings. About thirty works have been attributed to Arnoldus Gheyloven, yet only eight have passed the test of time.[5] Unfortunately, the monastery burnt down entirely during Arnoldus's lifetime, in 1435, which might explain the

---

[3] Van Kuyck believes Gheyloven also visited the university of Heidelberg while making reference to the university's registers of enrolment where in 1414 a certain 'Arnoldus de Rotterdam' was registered. See J. van Kuyck, 'Gheyloven (Arnold)', in *Nieuw Nederlandsch Biografisch Woordenboek. II*, eds. P. J. Blok and P. C. Molhuysen (Leiden: Sijthoff, 1912), 1240–1241. The idea that this was indeed Arnoldus Gheyloven is implausible for two reasons. Firstly, the same Arnoldus de Rotterdam is mentioned in the respective registers of 1416 and 1418 as *baccalaureus artium* and *licentiatus artium*. Secondly, Arnoldus Gheyloven had already entered the monastery at Groenendaal before 1409.

[4] M. Dyckmans, *Obituaire du monastère de Groenendaal dans la forêt de Soignies* (Brussels: Palais des Académies, 1940), 238–240.

[5] A list of these thirty works can be found in N. Mann, 'Arnold Geilhoven: an early disciple of Petrarch in the Low Countries', *Journal of the Warburg and Courtauld Institutes* 32 (1969): 95–100. It is based on the *Catalogus scriptorium Windeshemensium* (ca. 1650) by Petrus Trudonensis (Ms. Vienna Österreichische Nationalbibliothek, *Vind. Pal. Series Nova 12694*). The other 22 works are known by their titles only. Moreover, several of them bear the same title

loss of various writings that had already been produced by him. Nevertheless, Gheyloven manifests, through his remaining oeuvre, first as a canon lawyer and a moralist. However, the diversity of his literary output gives proof of his broader interests, for example in history.

MAJOR THEMES AND CONTRIBUTIONS

Based on numbers of surviving manuscripts, Gheyloven's *Remissorium utriusque iuris* (fifteen manuscripts) and his *Gnotosolitos* (eleven manuscripts and one printed edition in 1476) can be considered his most important and influential works.[6] The other remaining works survive in no more than three, two or one manuscripts. Likewise, Arnoldus is to be qualified as a moral canonist in the first place. This is also attested by the titles of those writings that did not pass the test of time but which are also to be situated within the domains of canon law and moral theology.[7]

Arnoldus Gheyloven as a Canon Lawyer

Already as a canon law student in Bologna, and inspired by *repertoria* produced by Guillaume Durand (†1296) and, most importantly, Giovanni Calderini (†1365), Arnoldus started working on a 'reference book for both laws', his so-called *Remissorium utriusque iuris* (or *Concordantia juris*). It concerns an alphabetically arranged compendium of primarily legal and theological concepts, terms, and ideas, and also contains – albeit sporadically – concise rubrics on biblical figures as well as classical and medieval authors. Each entry in the repertory is first explained by means of a brief definition, followed by one or more (in some cases – for example, the word *excommunicatio* – up to five hundred) legal rules about the concept at hand and ends with references to the sources of law or scholarly works where these rules had been stated earlier.[8] Likewise, Gheyloven's *Remissorium*, the title of which refers to the Latin verb

---

as parts of Gheyloven's *Gnotosolitos*, which may suggest that they were merely extracts from it and not separate independent works.

[6] Mann, 'Arnold Geilhoven', 95–100; A. G. Weiler, *Het morele veld van de Moderne Devotie, weerspiegeld in de Gnotosolitos parvus van Arnold Gheyloven van Rotterdam, 1423. Een Summa van moraaltheologie, kerkelijk recht en spiritualiteit voor studenten in Leuven en Deventer* (Middeleeuwse Studies en Bronnen XCVI) (Hilversum: Verloren, 2006), 16–19.

[7] For a list of these lost works, see Mann, 'Arnold Geilhoven', 95–100.

[8] The entries for which Gheyloven reproduced more than two hundred references each are: *Privilegio* (222), *Prelatus* (227), *Clericus* (229), *Pena* (233), *Restitutio* (234), *Ordinatio* (237), *Abbas* (261), *Ecclesia* (263), *Procuratio* (263), *Monachus* (280), *Electio* (294), *Possessio* (296), *Papa* (338), *Iuramentum* (361), *Matrimonium* (368), *Appellatio* (401), *Sententia* (409), *Iudex*

remittere or 'to refer to', serves as a practical tool for (canon) lawyers in need of arguments about a specific legal concept.[9] Arnoldus finished a first version of the book before obtaining his doctoral degree in Padua in 1403, and reworked the compilation at least once in 1417, before producing a final version in 1429.[10]

After dedicating the final version of his opus to Johannes Bont (†1454), chancellor of the Duchy of Brabant between 1427 and 1429, Arnoldus described the mentors and sources on which he drew heavily in order to produce the compendium. These scholars mentioned in the preamble, as well as the assertions in the book itself, have been described – albeit rather briefly – by the nineteenth-century Brussels professor of international law, Alphonse Rivier (†1898).[11] Unfortunately, Rivier never had the intention of drawing major conclusions based on his gathering of legal sources used by Gheyloven. He merely aspired to call attention to Arnoldus Gheyloven, and his *Remissorium utriusque iuris* in particular, for he considered it a '*nicht ganz werthloses Werk*'.[12] And Rivier was right. As mentioned earlier, the significance of the repertory is attested by the fact that no less than fifteen manuscripts of the work survive today. Moreover, the *Remissorium utriusque iuris* found appraisal in the *Topica* (1516) of Nicolaes Everaerts (†1532).[13] Everaerts opens his preamble by saying that 'writings on the *loci* of the law are not only useful, but also most necessary, to candidate lawyers', after which the third president of the Great Council of Malines makes reference to Baldus de Ubaldis's commentary on C.1.3.15, an important *sedes materiae* with regard to the art of reasoning, Guillaume Durand's *Repertorium aureum*, the *Dictionarium iuris* of Albericus de Rosate and 'frater Arnoldus de Roterodam in suo remissorio'.[14] Subsequently, Cicero (*Topica*), Boëtius (presumably his *In Ciceronis Topica* and *De topicis differentiis*), Fabius Quintilianus (*De Institutione Oratoria*) and Rodolphus Agricola (*De Inventione Dialectica libri tres*) complete Everaerts's list of authorities.

---

(431), *Episcopus* (444), *Testes* (450), and *Excommunicatio* (514) (Ms. Karlsruhe, Badische Landesbibliothek St. Blasien 3–4).

[9] O. Weijers, *Dictionnaires et répertoires au moyen âge. Une étude du vocabulaire* (Civicima. Etudes sur le vocabulaire intellectuel du moyen âge IV) (Turnhout: Brepols, 1991), 137; H. Lange and M. Kriechbaum, *Römisches Recht im Mittelalter. Die Kommentatoren, II* (Munich: Beck, 2007), 420–429.

[10] Weiler, *Het morele veld*, 17; Mann, 'Arnold Geilhoven', 77.

[11] A. Rivier, 'Dr. Arnold Gheyloven, aus Rotterdam, Verfasser eines *Remissorium juris utriusque* und anderer juristischer Schriften', *Zeitschrift für Rechtsgeschichte* 11 (1873): 454–468.

[12] Rivier, 'Dr. Arnold Gheyloven', 468.

[13] Rivier, 'Dr. Arnold Gheyloven', 455.

[14] Nicolaus Everardi, *Topica iuris sive loci argumentorum legales* (Venice: Griffio, 1587), 2.

As mentioned by Gheyloven himself, the work of Giovanni Calderini was one of the main sources which he drew on while composing the *Remissorium*. One may even assume that Arnoldus started the *Remissorium* as a mere copy of Giovanni Calderini's *Repertorium utriusque iuris*, which he had access to during his stay in Bologna at the house of Gaspar Calderini. This assumption is confirmed by a (sample-based) comparison of the two repertories.[15] For example, when we compare the entries starting with the letter B in Calderini's *Repertorium* with those entries present in the final version of Gheyloven's *Remissorium*, it becomes clear that no less than 38 of the 43 entries in the work of Calderini were reproduced by Gheyloven in his own repertory.[16] Nonetheless, Arnoldus managed to turn his repertory into a truly original work, for the comparison also shows that Gheyloven altered various definitions and added numerous references to various sources of law which were absent from the work of Calderini. Moreover, Gheyloven integrated various new entries (49 starting with the letter B) in the *Remissorium*.[17]

Whereas the *Remissorium utriusque juris* could be considered Gheyloven's *chef-d'oeuvre* in the field of late medieval law, two other of his canonical treatises have been preserved. Both deal with subjects that were highly topical during the fifteenth century: the sale of indulgences and the nullity of usurious contracts.

Gheyloven's treatise on indulgences, entitled *Tractatus (compendiosus et utilis) de indulgentiis*, suits him, as a member of a priory inspired by the *Devotio Moderna*, perfectly. After all, the sale of indulgences by the Catholic Church was, in addition to processions, pilgrimages, and exuberant worshipping, one of the major criticisms of the movement. The exact date of the treatise's production is unknown and only one copy is currently preserved, in the Herzog August Library in Wolfenbüttel.[18] Here, the twenty-five-folio treatise is part of a fifteenth-century miscellany in which ten other treatises on indulgences have been collected, which belonged originally to the

---

[15] In order to compare both repertories, I made use of the digitized version of the Sankt Blasien manuscript of the *Remissorium utriusque iuris* (https://digital.blb-karlsruhe.de/blbhs/content/pageview/2787879) and the 1474 Basel print of Calderini's *Repertorium utriusque iuris* (http://daten.digitale-sammlungen.de/bsb00081728/image_1).

[16] Gheyloven did not reproduce the following entries: *Bacca, Balthasar, Bisancium, Boecius* and *Bucella*.

[17] For example, *Babilonis filia, Balista, Barba, Bastardus, Beatitudo, Belial, Benivolencia, Bicolitas, Bohemia, Bonafides, Breviatores, Bruchus, Bucolica, Burgenses*, etc. With regard to the letter D, Gheyloven's *Remissorium* counts 251 entries, whereas Calderini's *Repertorium* only has 167 entries. Arnoldus didn't reproduce 27 entries (starting with the letter D) that were being dealt with by Calderini.

[18] Ms. Wolfenbüttel, Herzog August Bibliothek, *Gudiani Latini* 4° 338 (4645), f. 95r–120r.

Onze-Vrouw-ter-Engelendale monastery (*Monasterium Beate Marie Virginis vallis anglorum*) in Leiderdorp near Leiden.[19] Like Gheyloven's Groenendaal monastery, the priory in Leiderdorp was a member of the Congregation of Windesheim.

With the ban on usury by church authorities in the early middle ages, the use of usurious contracts became a constantly debated topic, both by the canonists as well as the romanists, during the late middle ages. Gheyloven too produced an elaborate treatise on the topic, entitled *Tractatus de contractibus usurariis sive Foeneratorium* (*Confessionale foeneratorum*), in which he addresses usury in no less than 478 *quaestiones*.[20] In Part I, dealing with 252 *quaestiones*, Gheyloven discusses all kinds of usurious contracts and other illicit contracts. In Part II, addressing 226 *quaestiones*, Arnoldus focusses on the restitution of illicit profits. The treatise itself is dedicated to Walter, a cleric from Brussels, and Lufo de Monte, an Italian banker or money changer in the city of Malines, not far from Brussels. Only one manuscript survives, in Utrecht; it was completed in 1467.[21]

Arnoldus Gheyloven as a Moral Theologian

As a moral theologian, Arnoldus Gheyloven was and is best known for his *Gnotosolitos* or *Know yourself*, which he finished in the years 1423–1424. Anton Weiler describes the work as a '*summa* of moral theology, canon law and spirituality', emphasizing the scientific nature of the book, due to the numerous questions and answers which are being discussed, with this scientific nature rendering it beyond a mere *confessionale*.[22] Nonetheless, the work also served a moral and educational purpose. Arnoldus hoped that, through the study of his book, the reader would turn to introspection as reflection on one's own moral behaviour in light of the doctrine set out by Arnoldus in each specific chapter of the *Gnotosolitos*. Arnoldus advocates moral improvement through self-knowledge. Therefore, Arnoldus *summarized* the moral behaviour that can be expected from a proper Christian.

---

[19] O. von Heinemann, *Die Handschriften der Herzoglichen Bibliothek zu Wolfenbüttel. Abth. 4: Die Gudischen Handschriften: Die griechischen Handschriften bearbeitet von Franz Köhler; Die lateinischen Handschriften bearbeitet von Gustav Milchsack* (Wolfenbüttel: Zwissler, 1913), 255.

[20] A digitized version of the manuscript can be consulted at the website of the university library of Utrecht University: https://dspace.library.uu.nl/handle/1874/330804.

[21] Weiler, *Het morele veld*, 19.

[22] Weiler, *Het morele veld*, 72.

Despite Weiler's characterization of the *Gnotosolitos* as erudite, Arnoldus mostly refrained from giving his personal opinion on specific moral issues.[23] His goal consisted merely in providing an overview of those (relevant) opinions that existed already with regard to specific moral topics. Through erudition, Arnoldus hoped to serve the primary practical goal of the *Gnotosolitos*, that is, the moral improvement of the reader. This practical goal of the *Gnotosolitos* becomes even more apparent in the *Gnotosolitos parvus* or *Small know yourself*, an abridged version of the original *Gnotosolitos* – which is now designated the *Gnotosolitos magnus* or *Big know yourself* – with a clear and specific focus on the instruction of students (in Leuven and Deventer).[24] For those whom Gheyloven called 'the simple youngsters', he left out all the legal assertions and argumentation that were incorporated in the *Gnotosolitos magnus*. A complete version of the small *Gnotosolitos* is preserved in only one manuscript (Liège), while the entire text of the big *Gnotosolitos* still exists in two manuscripts (Berlin and Cambrai).[25]

Both the small and big *Gnotosolitos* are divided into two parts. The first part, finished on 26 July 1423, was based on the medieval doctrine on sins and virtues and organized in *rubricae*, *capitula*, and *quaestiones* that deal with topics like mortal sins, the Ten Commandments, the seven sacraments, the fourteen works of mercy, etc.[26] The second part, completed on 13 May 1424, addresses the so-called *casus reservati*, that is, those sins that can only be forgiven by the Pope, a bishop, a papal nuncio, or someone who had been authorized to do so.

Weiler, who studied, edited and translated (into Dutch) the *Gnotosolitos parvus*, identified a major source of quotes and references to canon law source material, more specifically the French canonist Henricus Boyc (†after 1350) and his *Distinctiones super V libros Decretalium* in the first place, but also Henricus de Segusio (Hostiensis) (†1271), and the famous Giovanni Andreae (†1348), who had written various commentaries on existing collections of canon law.[27] As far as theology is concerned, Arnoldus's major sources of

---

[23] Weiler, *Het morele veld*, 62–66.
[24] Weiler, *Het morele veld*, 26. The printed edition of the *Gnotosolitos* (1476) contains a slightly adjusted version of the *Gnotosolitos magnus* and is entitled *Gnotosolitos sive Speculum consientiae*. With regard to the diaspora of the remaining copies of the printed edition, see E. Cockx-Indestege, 'The Gnotosolitos of Arnold Geilhoven published by the Brothers of the Common Life in Brussels in 1476. Observations on the surviving copies as evidence for the distribution', in *Incunabula. Studies in Fifteenth-Century Printed Books presented to Lotte Hellinga*, ed. Martin Davies (London: British Library, 1999), 27–78.
[25] The other eight surviving manuscripts of the *Gnotosolitos* contain only parts of the whole text.
[26] Weiler, *Het morele veld*, 40.
[27] Weiler, *Het morele veld*, 51–62.

inspiration were Saint Augustine, the *Sententiae* of Petrus Lombardus (†1160), the *Compendium theologicae veritatis* of Hugo Ripelin of Strasbourg (†1268), and the writings of Thomas Aquinas (†1274).

Through the *Gnotosolitos* Gheyloven manifested himself as a moral theologian in the first place, while his educational concerns become apparent by means of the abridged *Gnotosolitos parvus*. These concerns kept Arnoldus busy not only during the day but also at night, as is shown by his *Sompnium doctrinale sive ymaginarium* or *Instructive Dream*, also known as *Tractatus de condicionibus scholarum*, which he probably wrote after 1425.[28] More than any other of Arnoldus's works, this text gives proof of his literary skills, since it concerns an educational treatise in the form of an allegorical dream.[29] Again, Gheyloven pursued a double goal. On the one hand, he aspires to demonstrate what it takes to be a good student, while at the same time he wants to show his reader that theology is still the most fundamental and sublime of all sciences.[30]

The latter is necessary, according to Gheyloven, because of the growing appeal of the new 'natural' sciences to contemporary students. Nonetheless, these sciences, which are challenging and attempting to supplant theological

---

[28] Weiler, *Het morele veld*, 18. Only two manuscripts survive, one in Cambrai and an autograph in Amsterdam. In 1836, a copy of the *Sompnium doctrinale* was offered for sale at Baynes & Son in London as part of the collection of manuscripts owned by the late Dr Adam Clarke (†1832), a British Methodist theologian and biblical scholar. In addition to Gheyloven's *Sompnium doctrinale*, the manuscript also contained a version of Suetonius's *De vita XII Caesarum* and Lucius Annaeus Florus's *Epitome rerum Romanorum*. (J. B. B. Clarke, *A historical and descriptive catalogue of the European and Asiatic manuscripts in the library of the late Dr. Adam Clarke* (London: John Murray, 1835), 34.) This copy of the *Sompnium doctrinale* cannot be identified with either of the two copies surviving today in Cambrai and Amsterdam. The Cambrai manuscript already belonged to the municipal library of Cambrai in 1833 and the Amsterdam autograph isn't a miscellany. (M. Le Glay, 'Catalogue descriptif et raisonné des manuscrits de la bibliothèque de Cambrai', *Mémoires de la société d'émulation de Cambrai. Séance publique du 18 aout 1831* (1833): 173; Bibliotheek der Universiteit van Amsterdam, *Catalogus der Handschriften II. De handschriften der Stedelijke Bibliotheek met de latere aanwinsten* (Amsterdam: De Bussy, 1902).) It remains unclear whether the 'London' manuscript of the *Sompnium doctrinale* has survived and, if so, where it is being preserved today.

[29] Again, the work of Gheyloven demonstrates the extent to which he was inspired by his former masters, for Arnoldus's stay in Padua at the house of Francisco Zabarella coincides with the time when the latter, in cooperation with Pier Paolo Vergerio the Elder (†1444/45), was working on his *De ingenuis moribus*, an educational treatise comparable to Gheyloven's *Sompnium doctrinale*. (Dyckmans, 'Les premiers rapports', 115.)

[30] The present analysis of the *Sompnium doctrinale* is based on: Mann, 'Arnold Geilhoven', 83–88; K. G. M. Pols, *De 'Sompnium Doctrinale' van Arnoldus Gheyloven in het handschrift IH5 (Universiteitsbibliotheek, Universiteit van Amsterdam). Verslag van een codicologisch onderzoek* (Unpublished master's thesis, University of Amsterdam, 2006), 10–13.

doctrines, should always be studied in a manner subordinate to the most fundamental and true science of all, theology. Arnoldus conveys this message to the reader after falling asleep somewhere in the Sonian Forest surrounded by the beauties of nature. A dream sets in and Arnoldus's journey commences. Phronesis, the *mater sophie* or 'mother of (practical) wisdom', and Mary, the Blessed Virgin, serve as his guides on his journey through the late medieval educational landscape. This brings Arnoldus to the great authors of all times and places; the eleven secular disciplines, or *studia secularia*, which young people can and should study, are presented to the reader: grammar, logic, rhetoric, music, arithmetic, geometry, astrology, poetry, medicine, philosophy, civil law, canon law, and theology. The structure used in the *Sompnium doctrinale* is consistent. For each discipline, Phronesis praises the subject at hand and enumerates its blessings, concluding with a reference to an *auctoritas*, often a classical one. Consequently, the other guide, Mary, the Blessed Virgin, warns of the dangers of each discipline and refutes Phronesis's arguments based on the writings of Saint Jerome before concluding with an *exemplum*. Likewise, Gheyloven demonstrates the superiority of theology within the world of science.

In addition to this goal, Arnoldus also wanted to show his reader what it takes to be a good student. As Arnoldus considered many fifteenth-century students to be too lazy, sloppy, or careless, too ambitious and cheeky, he sets out, in the second part of the instructive dream and after a concise elaboration on the places in Europe where one can study properly, the seventeen conditions for a successful education. These indispensable virtues of the good student are dealt with under headings like *magister ydoneus, constans et stabilis, paupertas mediocris, sociatus bonis sociis*, etc. Finally, in the third book of the *Sompnium doctrinale*, entitled *Pulchrito moralis silve* or 'a short sojourn in the forest', Arnoldus returns to the valley where he had fallen asleep earlier in the first book. Here, he awakens refreshed and inspired and praises the beauty of God's creation, more specifically the charm and beauty of the Sonian Forest, under headings like mountains, fish, flowers, beasts, etc.

At the end of the Amsterdam manuscript of the *Sompnium doctrinale*, one can find a one-folio fragment of a text entitled *Paupertatis et fortunae certamen*.[31] So far, scholars always considered this text to be an original writing by Gheyloven.[32] However, this is incorrect. In reality, the text is a copy of a fragment from the first chapter (*Paupertatis et fortunae certamen*) of the third

---

[31] Ms. *Special Collections*, University of Amsterdam, ms. I H 5, f. 128a–128b.
[32] Mann, 'Arnold Geilhoven', 95–100; Weiler, *Het morele veld*, 18; M. Haverals, 'Gheyloven (Arnold)', *Dictionnaire d'histoire et géographie ecclésiastiques* 20 (1980): 1166–1169.

book of the *De casibus virorum illustrium* (*On the fates of famous men*) by Giovanni Boccaccio (†1375).[33] In eight books, Boccaccio describes – in prose as well as in a moralizing manner – the unfortunate course of life of 56 famous persons, from Adam and Eve to King Arthur. As such, the work of Boccaccio perfectly fits Gheyloven's favourite themes and approaches.

Arnoldus Gheyloven and His Interest in History

Without a doubt Arnoldus Gheyloven's major accomplishments are to be situated in the fields of (canon) law as well as moral theology. Nonetheless, two of his other works provide proof that Arnoldus's interests were not limited to the aforementioned domains. Both the *Moralizatio currus triumphalis* as well as the *Vaticanus* are clear demonstrations of Gheyloven's interest in history. In the former text, Gheyloven operates as a moralist in the first place, yet at the same time demonstrating a strong curiosity about classical history. The latter work allows Arnoldus to present not only his skills as a compiler, but also his interest in European history and acknowledgement of earlier authors and their writings.

The *Vaticanus*, finished by Gheyloven in the years 1424 (part I) and 1425 (part II), has no connection whatsoever with the papal seat in Rome. On the contrary, its title refers to the word *vates* or 'poets', and offers an enumerative description of the persons and (literary) merits of poets.[34] As will soon become clear, these 'poets' are not merely poets, for Gheyloven defined the word *vates* in its broadest sense, thus including, in addition to poets 'proper', prose writers, theologians, and philosophers.

Gheyloven divided the *Vaticanus* into three parts of which the third part, the so-called *Tractatus de arte faciendi collationes*, on the art of preaching, is not an original work by Arnoldus Gheyloven, as he himself states, but is by the fourteenth-century Thomas de Tuderto (or Todi), who wrote it as *Ars sermocinandi ac etiam collationes faciendi*. Parts I and II, however, did originate from the mind of Arnoldus Gheyloven. The first part, 110 folios in total, is called *Speculum philosophorum et poetarum* and – giving proof of Gheyloven's historical interests – lists the seven ages of man, the popes, kingdoms, and wars that have taken place, followed by a catalogue of writers

---

[33] I would like to thank Klaas van der Hoek, custodian Special Collections (Manuscripts and Modern Literature) at the University of Amsterdam, for providing me with a scan of the folio at hand, which made a proper comparison with the work of Boccaccio possible.
[34] The *Vaticanus* survives in two manuscripts. One copy is being preserved in Vienna, while the autograph, which Gheyloven produced personally for Jean Bont, can be found partly in Paris (Part I) and partly in Brussels (Part II).

and brief histories of the religious orders. It is the catalogue of writers (*De viris illustribus omnium*) that constitutes the core of the first part. In almost eighty folios Gheyloven addresses numerous authors from the past, from Roman antiquity to the late middle ages: Aulus Gellius, Valerius Maximus, Saint Augustine, Gregorius Magnus, Saint Jerome, Boethius, Cassiodorus, Beda Venerabilis, Gratianus, Thomas Aquinas, Azo, Albertus Magnus, Petrus Comestor, Vincent de Beauvais, Johannes Scotus, Dante, Nicolaus de Lyra, Francesco Zabarella, Petrarca, etc.[35] Likewise, Gheyloven entered the world of late medieval bibliographies, somewhere between the *Catalogus de viris illustribus* of the twelfth-century Sigebert de Gembloux (†1112) and the *De scriptoribus ecclesiasticis* of Jean Trithemius (†1516), which was printed in 1494.[36]

The core of the *Vaticanus* as a whole, however, is to be found in the 337-folio second part, entitled *Vocabularium*. It constitutes an alphabetically arranged list of moral, legal, and theological subjects, starting with *Abstinentia* and ending with *Zizania*. Each entry is dealt with in a most systematic way: first, Arnoldus addresses biblical authorities with regard to the subject at hand followed by the canonists and the Church Fathers. Subsequently, he mentions those authors dealing with (civil) law, medicine, ethics, and philosophy, before finally leaving some room for the poets too.[37] Again, and to an even larger extent than in the *Sompnium doctrinale*, Arnoldus presents himself as an outstanding compiler. In the *Vocabularium* Gheyloven collected as much relevant material as possible regarding each topic out of the works of other authors or, as he qualifies them himself, '*auctoritates, flores sive dicta notabiliora et breviora tam sanctorum patrum, philosophorum quam poetarum*'.[38] In the explicit of the Paris manuscript of the *Vaticanus*, Arnoldus says that he wrote and completed this book personally on the basis of works produced by historians he had met and heard in Italy, both in Bologna and in Padua, while studying in those places.[39]

Written before July 1426, the – incomplete – *Moralizatio currus triumphalis* is a 10-folio historical and moralizing work, far from being concerned with canon law.[40] The text contains a description of a triumphal chariot, as also

---

[35] A more in-depth analysis of the catalogue can be found in P. Lehmann, 'Der Schriftstellerkatalog des Arnold Gheylhoven von Rotterdam', *Historisches Jahrbuch* 58 (1938): 34–54.

[36] Weijers, *Dictionnaires et répertoires*, 148–152.

[37] Pols, *De 'Sompnium Doctrinale'*, 22.

[38] Lehman, 'Der Schriftstellerkatalog', 38.

[39] Weiler, *Het morele veld*, 18.

[40] Only two manuscripts survive, one in Cambrai and the autograph in Brussels (Mann, 'Arnold Geilhoven', 97).

found in the *Gesta Romanorum*, and is divided into two parts. The first part is largely historical in nature and here Gheyloven discusses the actual constitution of a Roman 'triumph', with, first, the honours accorded to the winner explained, followed by a description of the *triplex molestia* which the winner must undergo in order not to lose themselves in arrogance. Gheyloven is primarily concerned with facts and illustrates the theme with quotations from historical sources (Valerius Maximus, Suetonius, Aulus Gellius, etc.).[41]

This approach alters in the second part where the theme of the triumphal chariot is set in the context of ecclesiastical governance. Gheyloven, now more a moralist than an historian, and thus primarily making use of theological sources (Bersuire, Hugo of Saint-Victor), explains how the chariot is to be driven by the prelates of the church (particularly high ecclesiastical dignitaries) in light of their powers and duties. In particular, because of the content of the second part, the *Moralizatio currus triumphalis* was most likely written as a prologue to the second part of the *Gnotosolitos*, where Gheyloven discusses the *casus reservati*.[42]

So, in addition to Gheyloven's primary interest in the fields of law and theology, his oeuvre also gives proof of his historical consciousness. But in these more 'historical' works, we encounter an author who is moralizing as well as compiling, and it is in these activities that we meet the true Arnoldus Gheyloven.

GENERAL APPRAISAL AND INFLUENCE

Arnoldus Gheyloven, presumably born in poverty, succeeded, thanks in part to the financial patronage of a number of prominent canonical teachers, in studying at various European universities and obtaining the degree of doctor of canon law. Afterwards, Gheyloven retreated as a canon regular to the Brussels Forest de Soignes and opted for a life dedicated to study and devotion, primarily within the domains of law and theology. For this, Arnoldus was explicitly praised in the community's obituary after his death in 1442, as was his leaving of his library to the priory. Whereas his personal works continued to circulate for a few decades after his passing, Arnoldus Gheyloven fell into oblivion from the mid-sixteenth century onwards. Nicolaes Everaerts praised him in his *Topica* (1516), but at the same time the latter's printed work rendered Arnoldus's *Remissorium utriusque juris*, still available exclusively in manuscript form, superfluous. Arnoldus's other main work, the *Gnotosolitos*,

---

[41] Mann, 'Arnold Geilhoven', 88–90.
[42] The text of the *Moralizatio currus triumphalis* has been edited by Nicholas Mann: Mann, 'Arnold Geilhoven', 100–108.

did become available in print from 1476 onwards, albeit in particular within the Congregation of Windesheim and the spiritual renewal movement of the Modern Devotion.

Only during the second half of the nineteenth century did Gheyloven reappear on the radar of a few historical and legal scholars. In 1873, the Brussels professor of international law, Alphonse Rivier, drew attention to the possible importance of a work such as Gheyloven's *Remissorium* by describing it as a '*nicht ganz werthloses Werk*', while the Amsterdam theologian and church historian Willem Moll described Gheyloven in his *Kerkgeschiedenis van Nederland voor de Hervorming* (1867) as a 'very learned humanist and great connoisseur of the classics'.[43] Just like Rivier, Moll called for renewed attention because of the oblivion into which Arnoldus had sunk. The modest renewed interest that resulted from these calls during the twentieth century soon led to the conclusion that for years the 'humanist label' had been wrongly attached to Gheyloven. Gheyloven was most likely the first author to introduce Petrarch's oeuvre to the Netherlands, and to name the three established Italian authors (Dante, Boccaccio, and Petrarch) together in one work. Nicolas Mann observes that, despite this and despite the numerous contacts within humanist circles in Padua that Gheyloven had during his formation in Italy, after a thorough analysis of Gheyloven's main works, 'it is more often his encyclopaedic side which dominates, and the conventional compiler overrides the man of culture'.[44] With regard to a work such as the *Moralizatio currus triumphalis*, whose design could undeniably be called humanistic in nature, Mann emphasizes the medieval stamp that typifies Gheyloven's undertaking.

From an overall perspective Arnoldus's main merit lies in his ability to compile. Within the domains of law, moral theology, and even history, he has mainly focused on collecting and systematically presenting the available relevant material. As such, he focused primarily on an inexperienced audience. His *Gnotosolitos parvus*, a short summary of standard morality, shows his concern for young theology students, while his *Sompnium doctrinale* served as a guide to every student-to-be. With his *Remissorium*, Gheyloven offered a helping hand to the lawyer starting out in his search for useful legal rules and arguments. So, Arnold was not a theorist, but first and foremost he was a practical guide, with a strong sense of responsibility that often broke into a moralizing tone. Likewise, his scholarly influence remained very limited.

---

[43] W. Moll, *Kerkgeschiedenis van Nederland vóór de Hervorming*, II.2 (Arnhem: Nijhoff, 1867), 269.
[44] Mann, 'Arnold Geilhoven', 95. However, the humanist label proves to be persistent in nature. In 1999, Cockx-Indestege still characterized Gheyloven as 'theologian, lawyer and humanist' (Cockx-Indestege, 'The Gnotosolitos', 28).

RECOMMENDED READINGS

Cockx-Indestege, E. 'The Gnotosolitos of Arnold Geilhoven published by the Brothers of the Common Life in Brussels in 1476. Observations on the surviving copies as evidence for the distribution'. In *Incunabula. Studies in Fifteenth-Century Printed Books presented to Lotte Hellinga*, edited by Martin Davies, 27–78. London: British Library, 1999.

Dyckmans, M. 'Les premiers rapports de Pétrarque avec les Pays-Bas'. *Bulletin de l'Institut Historique Belge de Rome* 20 (1939): 51–122.

Gheyloven, A. *Arnoldi Gheyloven Roterodami Gnotosolitos parvus: e codice Seminarii Leodiensis 6 F 18 editus* (Corpus Christianorum. Continuatio Mediaevalis 212). Edited by Anton G. Weiler. Turnhout: Brepols, 2008.

Haverals, M. 'Gheyloven (Arnold)'. *Dictionnaire d'histoire et géographie ecclésiastiques* 20 (1980): 1166–1169.

Lehmann, P. 'Der Schriftstellerkatalog des Arnold Gheylhoven von Rotterdam'. *Historisches Jahrbuch* 58 (1938): 34–54.

Mann, N. 'Arnold Geilhoven: an early disciple of Petrarch in the Low Countries'. *Journal of the Warburg and Courtauld Institutes* 32 (1969): 73–108.

Pols, K. G. M. *De 'Sompnium Doctrinale' van Arnoldus Gheyloven in het handschrift IH5 (Universiteitsbibliotheek, Universiteit van Amsterdam). Verslag van een codicologisch onderzoek*. Unpublished master's thesis, University of Amsterdam, 2006.

Rivier, A. 'Dr. Arnold Gheyloven, aus Rotterdam, Verfasser eines *Remissorium juris utriusque* und anderer juristischer Schriften'. *Zeitschrift für Rechtsgeschichte* 11 (1873): 454–468.

Weiler, A. G. *Het morele veld van de Moderne Devotie, weerspiegeld in de Gnotosolitos parvus van Arnold Gheyloven van Rotterdam, 1423. Een Summa van moraaltheologie, kerkelijk recht en spiritualiteit voor studenten in Leuven en Deventer* (Middeleeuwse Studies en Bronnen XCVI). Hilversum: Verloren, 2006.

3

Boëtius Epo

Hylkje de Jong[1]

BIOGRAPHICAL INTRODUCTION

Boëtius Epo is a jurist whose life reflects all areas of tension and all contrasts typical of the sixteenth century. Born in Friesland, in the Northern Netherlands, which were soon to struggle out of the grasp of the Spanish king, he was to find his ultimate destination in Douai, situated in the Southern Netherlands still under Spanish rule. In his young life attracted to the enticing approach of the awakening Reformation toward the primitive church, he nevertheless retraced his footsteps, recognizing the orthodox Catholicism in which he had been raised. More than that, he revealed himself as belonging to the considerably radical wing of the Counter-Reformation. In his scholarly attitude there was a certain ambiguity between, on the one hand, being inclined to adhere to a re-foundation (*ressourcement*) of the sources of canon law, especially the texts compiled in the *Decretum Gratiani*, and, on the other, still adhering to spurious texts, maybe because from an ideological viewpoint their content was dear to him.

Boëtius Epo was born in Roordahuizen in Friesland in the year 1529. The exact date of his birth is unknown. His original name was Bote Ypes. He must have been of rustic descent: A reference to the countryside as his homeland can be found at the end of one of his works. There, a trident or pitchfork is depicted, with the epigraph *Tridens laboriosus at beatus est* (the trident is laborious, but prosperous).[2] The sources display alternative readings of his name, sometimes with the addition '*Frisius*' (the Frisian). In addition to the prefaces of two of his works, Epo pronounced himself upon the correct way of spelling his name. He stated that Boëtius was derived from the Greek word for messenger or angel (βοηθός ἀπὸ τοῦ βοηθεῖν) and that it had to be written

---

[1] The author would like to thank Philippus Breuker and Jan Hallebeek for their help and Douglas Osler for further help and correcting the English.
[2] See *De iure sacro, vel principiorum iuris pontificii libri III* ([s.l.]: Bogard [s.a.]), 380.

without aspiration (*sine flatu*), that is, in accordance with the genuine sound of the name in his native language or in German. Moreover, the addition *Frisius* should be written without PH or Y, just as it was spelled by ancient Latin authors and many others.[3]

In 1543, at the age of 13 or 14, he commenced his studies in Latin, Greek, and Hebrew at the Laurentianum in Cologne, a grammar school which had originated from one of the minor colleges. On 11 July 1551 he matriculated as an arts student at the University of Cologne and graduated in December of the same year as Master of Arts.[4] From 1552 until 1554 he taught at the Latin school of the 'Brethren of the Common Life' in Zwolle. One of his students there was Jakob Middendorp (c. 1537–1611), who later became professor at various foreign academies and eventually in Cologne. In 1554, Epo went to Louvain, where he studied Homer, Hesiod, and other Greek authors. Subsequently he went to Nice at the invitation of Eustace Chapuys (1489–1556), a Savoyard diplomat who served Charles V (1500–1558) as Imperial ambassador. He soon left Nice and went to Paris to study law. In Paris he remained one year and then continued his studies in Toulouse, where in 1558 he took the doctoral degree in law under the auspices of Bérenger Fernand (†1567).[5]

In 1560, Epo returned to Louvain where he taught until 1562. He did not like that position very much. The Frisian scholar Suffridus Petrus (1527–1597), who taught Latin and Greek in Erfurt, suggested to him that both would move to settle in one and the same city. In a letter of 24 July 1560 Epo responded, saying that he would prefer Erfurt, where Suffridus was staying, and not Louvain, despite the fact that Suffridus might feel differently. Epo added that he would like the Frisian jurist Cyprianus Vomelius (c. 1515–1578), who held a number of influential positions in the various German territories, to advance his promotion to a Germanic Province. As a reason for his wish to leave Louvain

---

[3] See Epo's remarks after the *Praefationes dedicatorias* in his *Commentarii novem testamentarii* and his *Antiquitatum ecclesiasticarum syntagmata IV*.

[4] Hermann Keussen, *Die Matrikel der Universität Köln*, Zweiter Band (1476–1559) (Bonn: Hanstein, 1919), 1055 (nr. 650, 98). According to other sources, Epo would already have obtained the doctorate in Philosophy and become Master of Arts in 1549. De Wal, *Oratio de claris Frisiae jureconsultis*, 17–18 and 39–42, at 40. It is said that Boëtius also started studying medicine, but Feenstra could not find any proof of this. See Feenstra, 'Portretten van juristen uit de oude Nederlanden', 129–135, at 132.

[5] See Suffridus Petrus, De Scriptoribus Frisiae, fol. 42r in Hs 64/A. Compare Feenstra's remark in Bibliotheca Frisica Juridica, 130, note 37. See also Valerius Andreas, *Bibliotheca Belgica, de Belgis vita scriptisq. claris. Praemissa topographica Belgii totivs sev Germaniae inferioris descriptione* (Lovanii: typis Iacobi Zegers, 1643), 113 and De Wal, *Oratio de claris Frisiae jureconsultis*, 40.

he stated that 'all that can be expected there is vain'.[6] The desired promotion failed to occur, but Epo nevertheless left Louvain. In 1562 he was one of the first four jurists offered a chair at the University of Douai,[7] newly founded by King Philip II of Spain (1527–1598). Some friends had recommended Epo for that position to the King's advisors, cardinal Antonio Perrenotti (1517–1586), Viglius of Aytta (1507–1577),[8] and Joachim Hoppers (1523–1576).[9] The solemn inauguration of the university took place on 5 October 1562. The Jesuit College (Collège d'Anchin) that was connected to the university was only established in 1568. Epo became 'secondary' professor, holding the chair of *tiltres et reigles de droit* of both canon law and civil law. He requested to lecture not more than once a day, so that he would have time left for writing legal opinions.[10] In 1565, he became *lecteur ordinaire des Pandectes*. In 1569, Epo tried in vain to become a Royal Historiographer, as appears from Viglius's letters to Hoppers.[11] He did obtain, however, the title of Count Palatine (*comes palatinus*). From 1574 or 1575 onwards, he was *primarius* of canon law. Moreover, because of his moral authority, his character, and the quality of his writings, he became permanent administrator of the University next to the rector. This position Epo maintained until he died on 15 November 1599. He was buried in the Jesuit Church of Douai. Boëtius Epo was married to Maria Kabeljaau van Iperen. The couple had four daughters and five sons. Three other children died prematurely.[12] One of his sons, Epo Boëtius (1577–1642), continued his father's professorial position at the University of Douai.

---

[6] '*nam vana sunt omnia, quae hic possunt expectari*'. Simon Abbes Gabbema, *Epistolarum ab illustribus & claris viris scriptarum centuriæ três* (Harlingen: Hero Galama, 1663), Epistola 94, 227. In Epistola 95 (13 September 1561) (228–230) Boëtius noted that Suffridus was tired of Erfurt and wanted to go to Paris or to return to Louvain. In the event that the choice fell on Paris, Suffridus had requested Boëtius to take charge of his library. What the exact reason was for Suffridus's disgust (*taedere*) remains unclear. For Boëtius's efforts in helping Suffridus to acquire a new position, see 'Over het leven van Suffridus Petrus Leovardiensis: voorgelezen door J. C. Ottema', bij het Provinciaal Friesch Genootschap ter Beoefening der Friesche Geschied-, Oudheid- en Taalkunde, maart 1841, *Vrije Fries* II (1842): 413–459, especially 425–427 and also Epistola 96 (18 April 1562), 231–233.

[7] See Epistola 97 (24 May 1562), 233–234.

[8] In a letter to Boëtius Epo, Suffridus Petrus asked him to take care of Folcardus ab Acchelen, Viglius's nephew (Epistola 77 [22 March 1583], 416–417). See also Onno Hellinga and Paul N. Noomen, 'Genealogia Ayttana', *Genealogysk Jierboek* (2011): 125–306 (at 159).

[9] Suffridus Petrus, *De Scriptioribus Frisiae*, 260. Compare *Nieuwe Encyclopedie van Fryslân*. Boetius, Epo (Ype Boates) (Gorredijk: Bornmeer, 2016), 355; De Wal, *Oratio de claris Frisiae jureconsultis*, 40.

[10] Cardon, *La fondation de l'Université de Douai*, 382.

[11] Cornelis Paulus Hoynck van Papendrecht, *Analecta Belgica*, I (The Hague: Gerard Block, 1743), 501, 506, and 568.

[12] Suffridus Petrus, *De Scriptioribus Frisiae*, 261.

MAJOR THEMES AND CONTRIBUTIONS

Boëtius Epo wrote about diverse subjects, including antiquity, religious and ecclesiastical history, Roman law, and canon law.[13] Moreover, he wrote Latin poems for prominent Catholic individuals,[14] such as pope Sixtus V (1521–1590) and the cardinals Alessandro Farnese (1520–1589) and Antonio Perrenotim.[15] He did not forget the prominent Frisians either, and wrote epitaphs for Viglius of Aytta and Joachim Hopper. He wrote epigrams for, among others, Petrus Pappus von Tratzberg (1558, fl. 1605–1614), Richard White (Ricardus Vitus, 1539–1611), his student Petrus de Loubbéns, and his son Epo Boëtius.[16]

From his various writings, it appears that Boëtius Epo, although remaining a Catholic, in the days of his youth felt attracted to the teachings of the Reformation, especially its orientation toward the primitive church. In the fifties, he must have had a meeting with John Calvin (1509–1564) in Geneva. However, Epo returned to his old faith and frequently openly expressed his regrets for this youthful lapse. Eventually he became a fanatical adherent of the Counter-Reformation.[17] We will discuss first his editions of theological texts and subsequently his orations, works on canon law and Roman law, and other writings.

Editions of Theological Texts

Boëtius Epo edited various ancient, theological texts. In 1564 he edited the Προγνωστικῶν sive de futuro saeculo libri tres of archbishop Julian of Toledo (c. 642–690). This work was an early systematic discourse on Christian eschatology, originating from the year 688. It consisted of three books, which deal successively with death, the state of the souls before the Last Judgement, and the resurrection of the dead. The *praefatio* of the edition is dedicated to Philip II. Epo thanked the King for appointing him to the University of Douai. He

---

[13] Other works by Boëtius not discussed in this contribution are *Sententiae Homericae* (1555), *Dictata juris* (manuscript Royal Library Brussels 1620) and *De regalibus in beneficiis ecclesiasticis* (René Dekkers, *Bibliotheca belgica juridica: een bio–bibliographisch overzicht der rechtsgeleerdheid in de Nederlanden van de vroegste tijden af tot 1800* [Verhandelingen van de Koninklijke Vlaamse Academie voor wetenschappen, letteren en schone kunsten van België, Klasse der Letteren, Jaargang XIII, No. 14] (Brussel: Koninklijke Vlaamse Academie voor Wetenschappen, Letteren en Schone Kunsten van België, 1951), 21–22). The latter could be the sixth question of the *Heroicarum et ecclesiasticarum quaestionum libri VI*.

[14] Wumkes, *Paden fen Fryslan, Samle opstellen*, 104.

[15] See at the beginning of *Heroicarum et ecclesiasticarum quaestionum libri VI De iure sacro, vel principiorum iuris pontificii libri III*.

[16] See at the end of *Antiquitatum ecclesiasticarum syntagmata V*.

[17] Andreas, *Bibliotheca Belgica*, 113.

described the various religious communities, which, driven by pride and hate, were combatting the Catholic religion, thereby damaging the Christian Republic. According to Epo his text edition was aimed at bringing all religious controversies to an end.[18] In addition to the text of Julian, Boëtius also edited some fragments from the works *De vitae monasticae variis generibus et institutis* and *De percipienda Eucharistia* of Isidore of Seville (c. 560–636).

Two Early Orations

In 1564, two years after his appointment in Douai, Boëtius Epo published two orations. The first, dedicated to Valerandus Hangvart, chancellor of the University and almoner of the King, dealt with the various designations for scholars in the course of history (*De honorum academicorum titulis et insignibus eorumque origine, progressu et legitimo usu*). The second oration, dedicated to his host Balduinus Glendius (Baudoin de Glin?), dealt with the true fruits of the perfect Roman jurisprudence (*De Romanae perfectaeque jurisprudentiae fructibus genuinis*). In the dedication of the latter book, Epo thanked his host for allowing him to live in his house without any charge. The same year the orations appeared for the first time, and both were later reprinted as one volume.[19]

Works on Canon Law

In 1576, twelve years after the publication of the two orations, Boëtius Epo published a work under the title *Antiquitatum ecclesiasticarum syntagmata IV*.[20] The preface was addressed to the King and the States-General. It contained autobiographical elements. Boëtius explained that the work, consisting of four 'syntagms' or 'composed texts', was aimed at strengthening the Catholic religion. Moreover, he mentioned the subjects he was teaching in Douai. These appear to include pacts, transactions, the *condictio* (Roman law) and celibacy of clerics, property of monasteries, and monks called to the Episcopacy (canon law). The first syntagm discussed the issue of ecclesiastical

---

[18] *En passant*, Boëtius pointed out that the famous German Benedictine abbot and polymath Johannes Trithemius (1462–1516) had mistaken archbishop Julian for the priest Julian Pomerius (†c. 500). See also the *Dedicatio* in the oration *De Romanae perfectaeque jurisprudentiae fructibus genuinis oratio*.

[19] *Orationes duae, una de honorum academicorum titulis et insignibus eorumque origine, progressu et legitimo usu, altera de Romanae perfectaeque iurisprudentiae fructibus genuinis* (Douai, 1564, also printed Leipzig, 1727).

[20] *Antiquitatum ecclesiasticarum syntagmata IV, Ad sacrosanctos Patres Patriae Belgicos, Regem nempe Catholicum ac Ordines vel Status universos Belgii* (Douai, 1576).

revenues, described in their historical development (*De jure proventuum ecclesiasticarum*) and contained a commentary on some of the decretals contained in the title on last wills of the *Liber Extra* (X 3,26). The second dealt with the Decalogue as a source of all ecclesiastical laws (*De legum ecclesiasticarum, quinimo cunctarum fontibus vel Decalogo*), the third with the Lord's Prayer (*De rudimentis admirabilibus vel precatione dominica*). The fourth and last syntagm described the life of St. Yves, the patron saint of law students, especially those studying canon law (*De vita D. Ivonis*).

In 1578 the *Antiquitatum ecclesiasticarum syntagmata IV* was published for a second time, together with a sequel, entitled *Antiquitatum ecclesiasticarum syntagmata V*. This time both were provided with an index.[21] In the preface to the new collection of 'syntagms', dedicated to pope Gregory XIII (1502–1582), Epo started by taunting the Protestants. As an example of how one can be stained by false doctrine, he referred to his own meeting with Calvin and subsequently explained how he returned to the pure Catholic religion:

> (...) I give an explanation concerning myself, who, hunted by different tails of different foxes, smeared with the dregs of these and then again those doctrines, now even rejoicing and bragging about a salute by Calvin in the vicinity of Geneva itself as if by some God of many peoples, once as a youth on the road in very dangerous wanderings, and indoctrinated by the Calvinists in the Kingdom of France and by stinking rules, I apparently knew nothing about the vicious approach of the Reformation towards worshipping the pure and orthodox Christian faith of Antiquity, I lapsed through a huge misstep, then again I thought to remain unhappy by a far too idealistic and very definite mistake, until finally having become a well–formed man through the purest sources of ecclesiastical antiquity, led by the Spirit of God, who clearly took care of me in spite of my offence, and working according to the holy instructions of Catholic men, while all things were rejected and brought into line with the infallible judgement of the highest Catholic mother church (as is the correct thing for all faithful) and by seeing that these promises of new doctrines actually stood and stand away from the truth of ecclesiastical antiquities. For a long time I have been deeply ashamed of the most horrible errors and I regret those. And the most gracious mother church, embracing me in her womb, strengthened me with the proper ritual (...).

Again, he presented himself as an example in order to point out that many can return from their mistakes (*ut exemplo meo plurimi resipiscant ab erroribus*).

---

[21] *Antiquitatum ecclesiasticarum syntagmata V, Ad Dn. Gregorium XIII Pont. Max. ... Accesserunt Auctoris aliquot epigrammata* (Douai, 1578).

After this short personal excursion about the meeting with Calvin, Epo pointed out seven – no exhaustive enumeration – tempting promises of the *Secta*, which are illustrative of his attitude toward the Protestants. Time and again he introduced his statements with the words '*secta pollicetur*' (the sect promises). All these promises, which seem to make human life easier, he considered dangerous, deceptive, and apt to lead astray: (1) The sect promises that in the world no one is in conscience subordinated to a superior authority. (2) The sect promises that solely through a strong faith can sins be taken away and this without confession to a mortal person. (3) The sect promises that everyone will be granted salvation as long as he firmly believes himself to be saved. (4) The sect promises that the Kingdom of Heaven is accessible for snorers and drinkers. (5) The sect promises that we will be accepted in grace by our faith and that all types of penance and all the fruits of such penance are foolhardy, superstition, and hypocrisy. (6) The sect promises a life that is pleasant in all respects; if you can believe, all things suddenly become light-coloured, without the hard trials of the truly Christian life for the weak body and the shameless or unmanageable soul, without submission of the proud soul and without restraining the overconfident body. (7) The sect promises that Evangelical freedom is incompatible with all kinds of servitude and therefore no one is bound by duties, despite accepting these of one's own free will. Furthermore, Boëtius referred to the support of Catholicism by three famous academies: Cologne as the mother, Louvain as daughter, and Douai as granddaughter.

The five syntagms of ecclesiastical antiquities which are dealt with in the volume are the age of the term 'Mass' (*de antiquitate Missae*), a historical overview of idolatry (*de idololatria*), the Pope as visible head of the hierarchy (*de hiërarchia*), Conciliarism (*de provocatione*), and jubilee and ordinary indulgences (*de iure iubilei et indulentiarum*).

In a letter of 26 March 1578 Epo asked Elbert de Leeuw, alias Leoninus (1518–1598), who was a member of the Council of State, what the best way would be for offering his two–part work to the government: personally or by letter, publicly or privately, after a week or some months, in the presence of the King and the States-General or surrounded by other persons? He also pointed to the fact that he hoped to be an example (*exemplum meum*) for the people of the Northern Netherlands, showing that it is possible to serve again the Catholic Church after taking an erroneous interest in the Reformation.[22] De

---

[22] See Jan Roelink, *Een honderdtal brieven, uit de correspondentie van Elbertus Leoninus* (Nijkerk: G. F. Callenbach, 1946), 149–150.

Leeuw's answer remained unforthcoming for some time, as appears from a second letter, dated 19 May 1578. In this letter, Epo informed De Leeuw that he had decided to present his work to his friend Nicolas Du Lis, Pensionary of Douai. The latter was delegate of Douai in the States-General. In so doing, Epo intended 'not to split hairs and to avoid that it would lose all its effect through late delivery'.[23]

In 1588, Boëtius published his most extensive work, which in fact consists of various writings, all starting with new pagination, but bound in one volume. There are two main title pages. The first, which mentions Douai 1588, has the title *Heroicarum et ecclesiasticarum quaestionum libri VI De iure sacro, vel principiorum juris pontificii, libri III*, which is followed by the subsequent elements: a preface (*praefatio dedicatoria*), an oration entitled *De gente Frisica*, six books of questions, viz. (1) competences of the sovereign, (2) temporal jurisdiction of the church, (3) ecclesiastical immunity (X 3,49), (4) life of clerics (X 3,1), (5) prohibition against clerics interfering in secular affairs (X 3,50), and (6) exchange of prebends. The fifth question has an appendix: the oration *de aureola doctorali*. The second main title page, which does not display a place or the year of the edition, has the title *De iure sacro, vel principiorum iuris pontificii libri III*. The title page is followed by a short instruction for the reader and the three books, dealing with (1) the true purpose of ecclesiastical law (*De vero iuris pontificii fine*), (2) the history of ecclesiastical law (*Historia simul et ars iuris pontificii*) and (3) remarks on the *Liber Extra* (*Paratitla Decretalium Gregorii IX*). These *Paratitla* had already been published, in 1581 and 1582.

Boëtius Epo addressed the *praefatio dedicatoria* to his five sons, viz. Epo, Angelus, Johannes, Thomas, and Petrus. He expressed his wishes concerning the place where he should be buried and suggested a text for an epitaph. He recommended to his sons a distinct way of life, dedicated to Catholicism, in austerity and modesty, and avoiding games of dice or cards. He also recommended pursuing an academic career. The oration *De gente Frisica* had been delivered on 20 December 1587 in addition to a series of *quaestiones quodlibeticae*. Some twenty years earlier Epo was already involved in acquiring materials for this oration. In a letter of 1 March 1567, addressed to the Chancellery and Council of the Court of Gelre in Arnhem, he had asked

---

[23] See Amsterdam, UVA: UB: HSS-mag.: 31 As 2. Compare Roelink, *Een honderdtal brieven*, 153–154: 'ne vel nodus videatur quaesitus in scirpo vel oblatio tam sera prorsus omnem perdat gratiam'.

for sentences of the Court and a list of councillors, which he considered helpful for investigating the history of Friesland and the Frisians.[24] The oration *de aureola doctorali* had been delivered on 4 December 1582. In the instruction to *De iure sacro* Boëtius excused himself for not having composed an *Index rerum verborumque* of the works, edited in 1588. Finally, he referred to some writings he had composed but which were not yet ready for publication, such as the *Paratitla civilia* and *In utrumque ius commentarii*.[25] The second book of *De iure sacro*, which contains an external history of canon law, had already been written in 1580, that is, before the promulgation of the Roman edition of the *Corpus iuris canonici*. In the margin there are, however, some references to this new edition.

Works on Roman Law

Boëtius Epo wrote only one work dealing extensively with Roman law. This was his *Commentarii novem testamentarii*, published in 1581 and dedicated to King Philip II of Spain. As the title indicates, it is a commentary, composed of nine parts, of which five deal with texts of Roman law from the Digest and the Codex (D. 28,2,29, D. 35,2,91, D. 35,2,86, D. 35,2,22, and C. 3,36,24). Four other parts deal with canon law, that is, with decretals X 3,26,16 and X 3,26,18 and decretals from the title on last wills in the *Liber Extra* (X 3,26), which had not yet been dealt with in the *Antiquitatum ecclesiasticarum syntagmata IV*.

Other Works

Furthermore, Boëtius Epo wrote an elegy for Philip II, which was published in 1599.[26] The preface was addressed to the King's daughter, Isabella Clara Eugenia (1566–1633), heir to the Netherlands Provinces and married to Albert VII of Austria (1559–1621). Boëtius Epo pointed out that the death of a parent is a reason for grief, but that the life of the deceased can be a source of inspiration for further life.

---

[24] See J. S. van Veen, 'Een brief van Boëtius Epo', *Vrije Fries* 23 (1915): 219–221.

[25] These works could be those mentioned by Foppens (*Reliquit vero affectos Commentarios IX. selectiores*). See Jean François Foppens, *Bibliotheca belgica sive virorum in Belgio vitâ, scriptisque illustrium catalogus, librorumque nomenclatura* (Brussels: Per Petrum Foppens, 1739), 140–141.

[26] *Oratio funebris nomine totius Universitatis Duacenae piisimis Philippi Secundi Regis Catholici fundatoris eiusdem Universitatis optimi manibus habita tertio novembris 1598* (Douai, 1599).

GENERAL APPRAISAL AND INFLUENCE

We have already seen that Boëtius Epo took a clear and firm position against the ideas of the Reformation. However, his main occupation must have been teaching canon law and to some extent also Roman law, and scholarly research in this field. We also see that he participated in the scholarly discourse of his day. Sources reveal that his contemporaries took him seriously as an expert in canon law. In a didactic–lyric laudatory poem on purchase (*de emptione*) Jan Fongers (†1612), rector of the Latin School of Leeuwarden, called him a 'legal expert in the doctrines of canon and Roman law'.[27]

During his academic career, Epo ran into conflict with some of his contemporaries. We can mention two examples. In the most extensive part of his *Commentarii novem testamentarii* (1581), that is, his commentary on the *lex Gallus* (D. 28,2,29), he had uttered serious criticism of some statements of the Portuguese jurist António de Gouveia (1505–1566). The debate focused on the question whether a son, having been disinherited, would still remain *filius familias* and *suus heres*. This would have had consequences for the possibility of bringing a *querela inofficiosi testamenti* and thus for children to take a father's place in the hereditary succession. According to António de Gouveia disinheritance would render the son extraneous.[28] According to Epo it did not.[29] Epo was in his turn criticized, which made his student Petrus Gilkens (c. 1558–1606) defend his master with even stronger arguments.[30] Epo also took a position against the opinion of Johannes Molinaeus (†1575), who in 1561 had edited the *Decretum* of Yves of Chartres (c. 1040–1115), which he considered a better compilation than that of Gratian.[31] In *De iure sacro* Boëtius Epo rejected this view.[32]

The *Decretum Gratiani* was one of the main legal sources Epo focused on. He was in favour of a critical approach toward the texts adopted in this work

---

[27] '*iuris coryphaeus dogmata ... pontificum et legum*'. See Joannes Fungerus, *Sylva carminum, in qua varia epigrammata et epitaphia doctorum ac illustrium virorum patriae continentur* (Antwerp: Christophorus Plantinus, 1585), 142.

[28] Antonius Goveanus, *Opera* (Rotterdam, 1766), 149 (ad D. 18.6.35). Feenstra, 'Bibliotheca Frisica Juridica', 134, note 59.

[29] *Commentarii novem testamentarii*, fol. 57r.

[30] Petrus Gilkenius, *Commentarii in praecipuos universi codicis titulos*, Tom. II (Frankfurt, 1606), 736 (ad D. 28,2,29,10 n. 19–23).

[31] Johannes Molinaeus, *Decretum Ivonis Episcopi Carnutensis septem ac decem tomis sive partibus constans* (Louvain: Gravius, 1561).

[32] *De iure sacro, vel principiorum juris pontificii, libri III*, 175. See also Friedrich Maassen, *Geschichte der Quellen und Literatur des canonischen Rechts*, I (Gratz: Akademische Druck-U.Verlagsanstalt, 1870), xxxiv–xxxvi.

and regretted that the texts were taken out of context, while the original works were grossly neglected or were lost: 'Now we have a work which is sadly so perverted, that water from brooklets is given to the sources, while, on the contrary, the sources themselves continuously ought to supply water to the brooklets.'[33]

According to Boëtius Epo, Gratian should, like Isidore, have reproduced the texts according to their chronological order and in their original shape.[34] He proposed arranging the texts according to the original sources. This would also greatly contribute to new editions of the texts of the Councils. Based on the inscriptions in Gratian's *Decretum*, he produced alphabetical surveys of the various categories of sources: (1) Scripture, (2) Apostolic canons, (3) Papal decretals, (4) Councils, and (5) authors.[35] Furthermore, Epo showed where the canons can be found in the edition of Lorenz Sauer (Laurentius Surius, 1523–1578) or in the compilations of Burchard of Worms (965–1025) and Yves of Chartres (c. 1040–1115). He also noted which canons were not published elsewhere and which canons, adopted by Burchard, Yves, and Gratian, were lacking in Sauer's edition, and he provided a survey of authorities cited.

Despite his support for a critical approach toward the texts in Gratian's *Decretum*, Boëtius Epo rejected the idea that the Pseudo-Isidorian Decretals could be spurious, although from 1559 onwards this was already defended by the Centuriators of Magdeburg. Moreover, he considered that Isidorus (Mercator) had been the genuine compiler of the texts, which at a later stage could have been supplemented by others.[36] It is difficult to say what made him take this stand. As we saw, Boëtius Epo was a strong supporter of papal authority and showed an enormous respect and loyalty toward popes Gregory XIII and Sixtus V. This may explain why he was not inclined to consider the *Decretum* of Yves of Chartres, which tended to a more moderate stand in the Investiture Controversy than that of Gratian, to be preferable to Gratian's compilation. Similarly, this may have prevented him from admitting that the Pseudo-Isidorian Decretals, which greatly supported the central and powerful position of the Roman Pontiff, are spurious.

---

[33] *De iure sacro*, 206: 'Nunc opus habemus (quod ut triste sic praeposterum est), ut ex rivulis aqua suppeditetur fontibus; ubi contra fontes ipsi perenniter aquam debebant subministrare rivulis'.
[34] *De iure sacro*, 205.
[35] *De iure sacro*, 211–217.
[36] *De iure sacro*, 220–253.

RECOMMENDED READINGS

Cardon, Georges. *La fondation de l'Université de Douai*. Paris: Alcan, 1892.

Collinet, Paul. *L'ancienne faculté de droit de Douai (1562–1793)*, [Travaux et mémoires de l'Universitè de Lille, IX]. Lille: Au siège de l'Université, 1900.

Feenstra, Robert. 'Bibliotheca Frisica Juridica. Bio–bibliografische notities over enkele weinig bekende Friese juristen'. *Tijdschrift voor Rechtsgeschiedenis* 75 (2007): 125–137.

Feenstra, Robert. 'Portretten van juristen uit de oude Nederlanden'. *Tijdschrift voor Rechtsgeschiedenis* 79 (2011): 129–135.

Perrin, Bernard. *Hommes et choses des Facultés utriusque juris de l'Université de Douai*, [Université de Lille, IVe Centenaire 1560–1960, II]. Lille: Etablissements Douriez–Bataille, 1966.

Petrus, Suffridus. *De scriptoribus Frisiæ, decades XVI, et semis* ... Coloniae Agrippinae: apud Henricum Falckenburch, 1593.

Wal, Gabinus de. *Oratio de claris Frisiae jureconsultis, dicta Franequerae d. VII Octobris MDCCCXVIII, Accedunt Annotationes de vita, fatis ac scriptis jureconsultorum*. Leeuwarden: J. W. Brouwer, 1825.

Wumkes, Geert Aeilco Durks. *Paden fen Fryslan, Samle opstellen IV*. Boalsert: Osinga, 1943.

4

Leonardus Lessius

Toon Van Houdt[1]

BIOGRAPHICAL INTRODUCTION

In 1640, the Society of Jesus proudly, if somewhat defensively, celebrated the centennial anniversary of its official recognition by Pope Paul III. In order to make a lasting contribution to the anniversary, the Dutch-Flemish Province was asked to compose a commemorative volume, the copious, lavishly illustrated *Imago primi saeculi Societatis Iesu*, in which the many impressive achievements of the order and its more illustrious members were duly highlighted. One of them was the Flemish Jesuit Lenaert Leys or, to use the Latinate name under which he gained international fame during his lifetime, Leonardus Lessius (1554–1623). After his studies at Louvain, Douai, and Rome, Lessius was appointed professor of scholastic theology at the Jesuit college of Louvain in 1585. From 1600 onwards, he was released from most of his teaching and other obligations to focus as much as possible on writing and publishing learned treatises, beginning with the encompassing work *On Justice and Right and the Other Cardinal Virtues* (*De iustitia et iure ceterisque virtutibus cardinalibus*), which grew out of his previous lectures on the *Secunda Secundae* of Thomas Aquinas's *Summa Theologiae*. The work, dedicated to Archduke Albert, sovereign ruler of the Catholic Netherlands, was first issued in Louvain in 1605 and would be reissued time and again in the course of the seventeenth century (and even later).[2] As early as 1608, the Jesuit bibliographer Petrus Ribadeneira was able to announce a new, revised edition

---

[1] I should like to thank Dr Ingrid Sperber for having corrected my English.
[2] For a detailed printing history, see Toon van Houdt, *Leonardus Lessius over lening, intrest en woeker. De iustitia et iure, lib. 2, cap. 20. Editie, vertaling en commentaar* (Brussel: Koninklijke Academie voor Wetenschappen, Letteren en Schone Kunsten van België, 1998), xviii–xxv. On Lessius's life and work, see Toon van Houdt, with Wim Decock, *Leonardus Lessius: traditie en vernieuwing* (Antwerpen: Lessius Hogeschool, 2005), 11–39.

to be published by the prestigious Plantin Press in Antwerp and, with unconcealed pleasure and pride, noted that the volume had been favourably received and was eagerly consulted by many a reader.[3] Thanks to the publication of his learned legal–moral treatise, Lessius had joined the select club of internationally renowned theological authorities which the Society of Jesus had engendered. Carolus Scribani, one of his former students, did not fail to mention this in his eulogistic anti-Calvinist tract *Amphitheatrum honoris* of 1606, one of the many attempts made by early modern Jesuits to defend the honour of their order and extol its glory against the attacks of Protestant and Catholic adversaries alike.[4]

It was an attempt that culminated in the aforementioned *Imago primi saeculi*, in which Lessius was unambiguously elevated to the rank of intellectual, moral, and spiritual paragon worthy of imitation, emulation, and even devout veneration. A fairly long hagiographical account is contained in the sixth book, which is devoted to the marvellous deeds exhibited by the Dutch-Flemish Province. Due attention is given to the success of Lessius's treatise *On Justice and Right* and, as a corollary, to the reputation which the author enjoyed as being one of the most acute moral problem-solvers of his age. Prelates and princes alike consulted him about the doubts that burdened their conscience. Among his numerous 'clients' and readers were Archduke Albert and Pope Paul V, or so it is purported. The biographical account ends with a brief description of Lessius's death and ascension to heaven, where he is said 'to be dwelling in the abode of the Blessed, where, as the Holy Book has it, Teachers of Justice shine like stars'.[5]

The same biblical image appears in both the text and the emblematically devised frontispiece of the even more excessively hagiographical description of Lessius's life and morals, which the Jesuit Jacobus Wijns, one of his nephews and self-appointed executors, published in Brussels under the name of the Norbertine friar Leonardus Schoofs, another nephew of Lessius's, in the year 1640. The personal commemoration of the Flemish Jesuit neatly blended into the jubilant celebration of the Society as a whole.[6] In both the *Imago* and the *Vita*, Lessius is hailed as a learned theologian, a virtuous and pious man, who

---

[3] Petrus Ribadeneira, *Illustrium scriptorum religionis Societatis Iesu catalogus* (Antverpiae: apud Ioannem Moretum, 1608), 135.

[4] Carolus Scribani [Clarus Bonarscius], *Amphitheatrum honoris in quo Calvinistarum in Societatem Iesu criminationes iugulatae* (Palaeopoli Aduaticorum: apud Alexandrum Verheyden, 1606), lib. 2, cap. 13, 205.

[5] *Imago primi saeculi Societatis Iesu* (Antverpiae: ex officina Plantiniana Balthasaris Moreti, 1640), lib. 6, 877. Cp. Daniel 12, 3.

[6] Leonard Schoofs [Jacobus Wijns], *De vita et moribus R. P. Leonardi Lessii e Societate Iesu theologi liber ad utramque provinciam Societatis Iesu per Belgium iubilaeum anno seculari suo celebrantem* (Bruxellae: apud Godefredum Schovartium, 1640). The original, unpublished

deserves to be officially beatified. Small wonder that Wijns himself played an active role in promoting the popular cult that had established itself around his uncle's tomb soon after his death in 1623. Wijns's arduous efforts to have Lessius canonized proved vain, though.[7]

What do all these – truthful, embellished, or utterly fictitious – hagiographical pieces of information amount to? One simple but pertinent, albeit negative, conclusion can readily be drawn: Leonardus Lessius was no lawyer or jurisprudent in the proper, professional sense of the word, nor was he perceived or described as one. However, his biography from 1640 provides us with several interesting details which clearly indicate that the moral theologian and ethical expert was thoroughly acquainted with both civil and canon law and was familiar with the works of important medieval and early modern jurists.

As a matter of fact, the young Lenaert Leys only narrowly escaped being drawn into the intricacies of contemporary legal matters. After having finished primary school at his home village of Brecht near Antwerp, he was strongly encouraged by his tutor and uncle Huibrecht Leys to follow a practical commercial training which would undoubtedly have provided him with at least a rudimentary knowledge of contract law. Fortunately, a scholarship for bright but poor children allowed him to study the arts at the pedagogic residence 'Het Varken' (*Porcus*) at the university of Louvain, where, on 19 February 1572, he was proclaimed *primus* of all the philosophy students of the entire university. Immediately thereafter, heavy pressure was exerted on him to pursue higher education in either theology or law. However, Lessius decided to enter the Society of Jesus instead. In October, he arrived in Douai where he began to teach Aristotelian philosophy at the Jesuit college of Anchin. Meanwhile, he taught himself Greek and also became proficient in ancient literature, Bible studies, patristics, theology and, last but not least, Roman and canon law.[8]

In 1583, Lessius was sent to Rome to the famous Collegio Romano to complete his theological studies under the guidance of Augustinus Giustiniani, Robertus Bellarminus, and Franciscus Suárez, the latter appearing to have acted as his principal mentor. It was through Suárez in particular that Lessius was introduced to the new approach to scholastic theology which had

---

version of Lessius's life, probably composed sometime between 1623 and 1628, is preserved at the Royal Library of Belgium, Brussels, ms 4070.

[7] On the vicissitudes of Wijns's *Vita* and its close connection to the *Imago primi saeculi*, see Diana Stanciu, 'An Aristotelian, an Example of Virtue and/or a Mystic? Learned Conventions Disguising Polemic Goals in the Biography of Leonardus Lessius', *Ephemerides Theologicae Lovanienses* 88.4 (2012): 369–393.

[8] Schoofs [Wijns], *Vita*, cap. 3, par. 9, 10: '*Canonibus et iuribus (studuit)*'; cap. 3, par. 12, 17: '*Utriusque iuris et antiquorum Patrum cognitionem adjecit*'.

been developed by leading theologians of the university of Salamanca and which had been spreading to various other universities in Spain and elsewhere, including the Jesuit university at Rome. It was an approach characterized by, among other things, a notable shift toward resolving the practical moral problems that were deemed imminent and pressing at the time, as well as by an intimate combination, if not a complete fusion, of (Aristotelian) philosophy, (mainly but not exclusively Thomist) moral theology, and (Roman and canon) law. This is the intellectual profile which Lessius learnt to adopt with the help of his Roman professors, in particular his mentor Suárez, and which would subsequently pervade his entire future career. This career spanned numerous aspects. There was Lessius as professor of scholastic theology at the Jesuit college of Louvain. There was Lessius as director presiding over seminars during which diverse cases of conscience were discussed and resolved on the basis of the work of the well-known canon lawyer Martín de Azpilcueta or Dr Navarrus. There was Lessius as author of a monumental treatise on the cardinal virtues, which for the most part deals with matters of contract law and contractual justice, and which neatly combines general moral and legal considerations with the discussion of particular issues related to concrete circumstances and specific types of contract. Last but not least, there was Lessius as ethical expert eagerly solicited from far and near to shed light on intricate, vexing problems, which, being more often than not as much of a legal as of a moral nature, required a thorough command of both moral theology and jurisprudence for a satisfactory resolution to be achieved.[9]

In all these areas of professional activity, Roman law, as received and combined with canon law in the course of time (the so-called *ius commune*) provided the legal vocabulary, concepts, and framework that enabled Lessius – and his fellow-theologians of the Jesuit order – to tackle the multifarious legal–moral problems with which they were invariably confronted. Small wonder, then, that Lessius's Spanish colleague and correspondent Ludovicus Molina was praised for his exceptional command of 'the science of law' (*iuris scientiam*). His voluminous treatise *On Justice and Right*, the first part of which was issued in 1593, revealed itself to be thoroughly based on a crystal-clear legal disposition; Molina was as much a jurist as a theologian, so it appeared. The same could rightly have been said about Lessius. His biographer Wijns, for one, was eager to point out that his treatise *On Justice and Right*, much shorter

---

[9] Many but by far not all of his resolutions were later collected by Jacobus Wijns in the *Variorum casuum conscientiae resolutiones* attached to Lessius's *De beatitudine, de actibus humanis, de incarnatione verbi, de sacramentis et censuris praelectiones theologicae posthumae* (Lovanii: typis Cornelij Coenestenij, 1645).

but no less impressive than Molina's, was even used by judges in court eager to extract the appropriate rules of law from it.[10]

MAJOR THEMES AND CONTRIBUTIONS

Natural Law and Contractual Justice

Just like Molina and many other Spanish colleagues, Lessius pays much attention to economic–ethical problems, which are systematically recast as economic–legal problems. A simple comparison will suffice to highlight the preponderant place that contract law occupies in his treatise on justice and the other cardinal virtues. The treatise is formally a commentary on Thomas Aquinas's *Secunda Secundae*. The latter's discussion of economic–ethical problems was basically limited to analysis of purchase–sale (quaest. 77) and loans for consumption and usury (quaest. 78). Lessius's discussion, on the other hand, turns out to be much more extensive. Under the heading 'On contracts' (*De contractibus*) and after a lengthy analysis of contract and obligation in general (lib. 2, cap. 17: *De contractibus in genere*), the following types of contract are dealt with: promise and donation (cap. 18: *De promissione et donatione*); testaments and legacies (cap. 19: *De testamento et legatis*); loans for consumption and usury (cap. 20: *De mutuo et usura*); sale–purchase (cap. 21: *De emptione et venditione*); rents or annuities (cap. 22: *De censibus seu redditibus annuis*); money-exchange (cap. 23: *De cambiis*); lease–hire, emphyteusis and feudal contracts (cap. 24: *De locatione et conductione, emphyteusi et feudo*); partnerships and companies (cap. 25: *De contractu societatis*); games and gambling (cap. 26: *De ludo et sponsionibus*); deposit and loan for use (cap. 27: *De deposito et commodato*); suretyship, insurance, pawn, and mortgage (cap. 28: *De fideiussione, assecuratione, pignore et hyptheca*). The moral theologian Lessius appears indeed to have become something of a regular lawyer.[11]

---

[10] Ribadeneira, *Illustrium scriptorum catalogus*, 139 (Molina); Schoofs [Wijns], *Vita*, cap. 6, par. 35, 38. It can easily be inferred from Wijns's account that he had no intention whatsoever of presenting his uncle as being essentially an Aristotelian, as Stanciu claims in her contribution 'An Aristotelian, an Example of Virtue and/or a Mystic?'

[11] On Lessius's role in the early modern reconceptualization of contract law, see Wim Decock, *Theologians and Contract Law. The Moral Transformation of the Ius Commune (ca. 1500–1650)* (Leiden; Boston: Brill/Nijhoff, 2013) and Wim Decock, 'Law of Property and Obligations. Neoscholastic Thinking and Beyond', in *The Oxford Handbook of European Legal History*, eds. Heikki Pihlajamäki, Markus D. Dubber, and Mark Godfrey (Oxford: Oxford University Press, 2018), 623–629. A modern English translation of chapters 21 and 28 is to be found in Wim Decock, 'Leonardus Lessius, S. J., On Buying and Selling (1605).

Lessius's *De iustitia et iure* is a quintessentially legal or juridical treatise in yet another, perhaps more fundamental, sense of the word, in so far as it refers to, and is intimately linked to, confession and hence to the court of conscience (*forum conscientiae*). Confession was conceived of as a real tribunal, with the confessant and the confessor playing specific, typically juridical roles – those of plaintiff and defendant on the one hand, and on the other those of lawyer or judge.[12] The overall importance of regular confession in the reformed, post-Tridentine Catholic Church is sufficiently well known, as is its central place in the Jesuit order. Many Jesuits were active as confessors, and it was on this aspect of the care of souls that the moral–theological training its members received was substantially based. As future confessors, they were trained to subject the behaviour of the faithful to minute inspection and moral–legal judgement. In order to perform his task adequately, the confessor or aspirant confessor was, of course, required to know precisely what was licit and what was not. The treatises *On justice and right* published by Lessius and many other moral theologians were meant to guide him in this learning process by providing the criteria he needed in order to be able to judge the deeds of the faithful correctly.

It is no coincidence, then, that 'law' and 'obligation' were key concepts in the moral–theological discourse in which the (aspiring) confessor was instructed. This is manifest in Lessius's discussion of the various contracts mentioned above. In chapter 20 on moneylending and interest-taking, for instance, the author goes to great lengths to determine which loan contracts may or may not be concluded, which forms of interest are licit or, on the contrary, illicit. Now, as Thomas Aquinas had already emphasized in line with Aristotle's ethics, the licit or illicit character of a particular contract depends on contractual or commutative justice (*iustitia commutativa*), which is itself governed by the principle of objective equality – a principle that is unambiguously written into the law of nature (*ius naturae*), the body of principles and precepts which every man has to recognize as morally binding on the grounds of just reason (*recta ratio*) as they are firmly rooted in the 'nature of things'

Translation and Introduction', *Journal of Markets & Morality* 10.2 (2007): 433–516 and Wim Decock and Nicholas De Sutter, *On Sale, Securities, and Insurance. Leonardus Lessius* (Grand Rapids, MI: CLP Academic, 2016). A fairly extensive German summary of the main chapters dealing with contractual justice is offered by Toon van Houdt in Bertram Schefold, ed., *Leonardus Lessius' De iustitia et iure. Vademecum zu einem Klassiker der Spätscholastischen Wirtschaftsanalyse* (Düsseldorf: Handelsblatt, 1999), 103–142.

[12] Wim Decock, 'Jesuit freedom of contract', *Legal History Review* 77 (2009): 423–458 (esp. 432–433) and Wim Decock, 'From law to paradise: confessional Catholicism and legal scholarship', *Zeitschrift des Max-Planck-Instituts für europäische Rechtsgeschichte* 18 (2011): 12–34 (esp. 22).

(*natura rerum*) themselves.¹³ In the case of loans for consumption (*mutua*), the nature of things consists in the fact that they are an exchange of two sets of fungible goods which, as Roman law teaches, have a fixed value determined entirely by their measure (wine or grain), weight (raw precious metals), or number (coined money). It is therefore only natural and right that a fungible good is lent in return for a similar good of the same quality and quantity, no more and no less.¹⁴

The principle of *objective* equality also determines the *subjective* natural rights and obligations of the contracting parties. It bestows a subjective right (*ius*) on the lender, the faculty or power (*facultas, potestas*) to claim an equal amount in return, while imposing a concordant debt or obligation (*debitum, obligatio*) on the borrower, whom the principle of equality forces to make an equivalent recompense.¹⁵ A lender who claims interest violates contractual equality in the objective sense that he receives more in return than he has given. This violation of objective equality also implies a breach of natural law and its provisions, which obliges the interest-taker or usurer to right the unequal contractual relationship and forces him to make restitution. As a consequence, in the late scholastic moral and legal thinking to which Lessius fully adhered, licit is what is not unjust and what is not at variance with natural law. Or, to put it otherwise, justice and right in the objective sense of the words have their foundation in natural law, which determines the extent of what is licit and hence delineates the scope within which people can act freely.¹⁶

Moral Doubt, Probable Opinion, and Freedom of Action

Following the lead of his Spanish colleagues, Lessius adopted an ethics that was firmly based on 'law' and 'obligation'. However, this moral–legal system did not induce him to adopt an inflexible, intransigent attitude toward the faithful and the moral doubts and quandaries with which they were

---

[13] *De iustitia et iure*, 2, 2, 1, 1 (*ius* as *aequalitas*) and 2, 2, 2, 9 (*ius naturale* as stemming from the nature of things themselves).

[14] *De iustitia et iure*, 2, 20, 1, 4. Cp. Dig. 12, 1, 2, 1. In the scholastic doctrine on moneylending and interest-taking, the Roman legal concept of fungible goods was, not without difficulty and controversy, equated with the notion of *res usu consumptibiles* (goods which are consumed by their use), first introduced by Thomas Aquinas. See for instance Odd Langholm, *The Aristotelian Analysis of Usury* (Bergen: Universitetsförlaget, 1984), 82–90.

[15] *De iustitia et iure*, 2, 2, 1, 1 and 2, 2, 2, 8.

[16] See further Toon van Houdt, 'Tradition and renewal in late scholastic economic thought: the case of Leonardus Lessius (1554–1623)', *Journal of Medieval and Early Modern Studies* 28.1 (1998): 51–73 (esp. 56–58) and Decock, 'From law to paradise', 16–17.

confronted. Quite the contrary appears to have been the case. In his assessment of what was licit and what was not, Lessius more often than not showed himself to be quite lenient and accommodating. He consciously aimed to extend the scope of human freedom and, conversely, limit the field of obligations arising from natural law. In order to do so, he had recourse to a probabilistic line of reasoning.

As an ethical expert, Lessius was invariably asked to analyze and resolve moral problems, difficult cases (*dubia*) about which a man's conscience doubted in actual practice. Thus a businessman may wonder if the contract he intends to conclude is just. It was Lessius's task as an ethical expert to expel this practical doubt. For as long as the businessman's conscience is not satisfied that he can do so without sinning, he is not allowed to conclude the contract. Now, Lessius was well aware of the fact that absolute certainty can never be achieved in human affairs. At best, a moral theologian is able to formulate an opinion that is so probable that it can be regarded as 'certain' from a practical moral point of view. In many other cases, however, uncertainty remains. A theologian is able to formulate a solution that, at the very best, can be called only probable. He takes a theoretical standpoint, without having been able completely to exclude the opposite viewpoint; on the speculative level, then, doubt remains.

Anyone acting on the basis of such a probable opinion acts with a 'probable conscience'. But is the probable opinion declared by the theologian sufficient to dispel practical doubt? May one, in other words, act with a 'probable conscience'? Lessius answers this crucial question in the affirmative. According to him, it is not necessary that the licit nature of an action be totally certain on the speculative level in order for one to be able to act with a practically certain conscience. This is a probabilistic standpoint, pure and simple, which Lessius wholeheartedly endorsed and frequently applied in his analysis and assessment of complex moral–legal issues. In essence, probabilism states that one may perform an action, provided serious or probable reasons can be advanced that argue in favour of its licit nature, even if there are other, more probable grounds that argue against it. Even if the licit or illicit character of an action is still the subject of doubt and discussion on the speculative level, that action may nonetheless be performed with a certain conscience in daily life. Practical certainty threatens to be eroded by speculative uncertainty: so long as such uncertainty remains it will suggest arguments that will cause the practical conscience to doubt the licit nature of the action. In other words, it will be a constant source of scruples, of anguish of conscience. The aim of probabilism is precisely to hinder speculative doubt from being transformed into practical uncertainty. The doctrine ensures that, as soon as they are found probable, many actions can be performed without anguish of conscience. In this way, it serves to give the faithful greater peace of mind and, at least to a certain extent, a 'freer' conscience. Henceforth, in the court of conscience, the virtuous, scrupulous man, thoroughly backed up with the probable opinions provided by probabilistic theologians like Lessius, can play the role of 'plaintiff', 'defendant', *and* 'judge' himself.[17] In the end, the overzealous hagiographer Jacobus Wijns may well have hit the nail on the head when he wrote that his uncle, although extremely strict and severe to himself, nonetheless showed a remarkably mild disposition toward other people, not in the least toward devout but conscience-stricken persons who came to visit him in order to confess or listen to his moral advice.[18]

Defending the Montes Pietatis 1: Legal Rules and Juridical Arguments

To gain a more profound understanding of the way Lessius integrated law and legal thinking into his work as a moral theologian and ethical expert, it may be useful to focus our attention on a particular 'case of conscience'. There are various reasons why his lengthy discussion of the licit or illicit nature of the so-called Montes Pietatis, charitable pawn banks, or public microfinance institutions, constitutes an excellent starting point for such a detailed analysis. The author treats the subject in the very last chapter of the section devoted to moneylending and interest-taking in his *De iustitia et iure*. In 1621, he added a much longer discussion of the Montes Pietatis, as they were devised and established in the Catholic Netherlands by the Antwerp polymath architect Wenzel Cobergher on behalf of Archdukes Albert and Isabella. This discussion is contained in a separate appendix attached to the fifth, revised edition of his monumental treatise. In an unpublished document, which unfortunately cannot be dated with certainty, Lessius once more tackled the issue and repeated the favourable standpoint which he had previously taken: the Montes Pietatis are entirely licit.[19]

---

[17] For a more detailed account of Lessius's probabilism, see M. W. F. Stone and Toon van Houdt, 'Probabilism and its methods: Leonardus Lessius and his contribution to the development of Jesuit casuistry', *Ephemerides Theologicae Lovanienses* 75 (1999): 359–394. An interesting juridical perspective on both Lessius's probabilism and his insistence on human freedom is offered by Decock, 'Jesuit Freedom of Contract'. There is a vast literature on the history of probabilism; for the sake of brevity, I would like to refer the interested reader to Rudolf Schüssler, 'Probabilism and casuistry', in *A Companion to the Spanish Scholastics*, eds. Harald E. Braun and Paolo Astorri (Leiden; Boston: Brill, in press).

[18] Wijns, *Vita*, cap. 9, par. 40–45, 63–69.

[19] The document is preserved at the archiepiscopal archives in Mechelen (Malines), Belgium, under the number AA, Boonen, 20A/9. A transcription is to be found in Toon van Houdt,

All these texts eloquently testify to the practical nature of Lessius's moral theology: far from limiting himself to a consideration of general moral principles and an analysis of various types of contract in the abstract, he did not shun discussing and defending a very specific institution, which had been created in accordance with the express wish of the archdukes and with the explicit approval of the local episcopate but which nonetheless continued to stir fierce controversy among lawyers and theologians about its true, licit or illicit nature. Were the Montes usurious and consequently to be condemned as being at variance with ecclesiastical and, more importantly, natural law? Or were they, on the contrary, beneficial institutions perfectly in line with the natural law principles of equality in exchange and proportionality in distribution? That is the core of the question which Lessius set out to answer. In so doing, he showed himself to be a skilful moral and political counsellor at the same time: by defending the Montes Pietatis, he eased the conscience of the archdukes and actively supported their economic and social policy. In short, spiritual and political counselling, moral guidance and social commitment went hand in hand. In that respect, too, Lessius proved to be a loyal executor of the Jesuit order's ambitious corporate programme.[20]

Apart from considerations of 'public utility' or 'political expediency', legal texts and arguments play a crucial role in Lessius's defence of the Montes Pietatis. Pope Leo X had unequivocally approved of the institution in a papal bull promulgated during the fifth Lateran council in 1515: the Monti di pietà, he stated, could licitly demand a moderate interest from their clients in order to compensate for their operational costs; the contribution paid by the borrowers should by no means be considered usurious. However, even though this strong papal approval was confirmed during the council of Trent, it did not prevent prestigious theologians from continuing to cast doubt on the institution or even downright condemn it as being illicit and nefarious; according to the Dominican friar Dominicus Sotus and others, the papal bull was invalid. In the first part of chapter 23, Lessius goes to considerable lengths to counter their objections and affirm the validity of papal legislation. The second part of his discussion is much more interesting from a moral–legal point of view: here the author sets out to defend the controversial institution on

---

Leonardus Lessius over lening, intrest en woeker, volume 3 (unpublished PhD diss., University of Leuven, 1995), 171–172.

[20] For the close connection between spiritual and political counselling in the Jesuit order, see e.g. Nicole Reinhardt, *Voices of Conscience. Royal Confessors and Political Counsel in Seventeenth-Century Spain and France* (Oxford: Oxford University Press, 2016) and the special issue of the *Journal of Jesuit Studies* 4 (2017), admirably introduced by Harald E. Braun with his contribution 'Jesuits as Counsellors in the Early Modern World: Introduction', 175–185.

the basis of rational argumentation. The outspokenly legal nature of his line of reasoning immediately strikes the reader. Indeed, his exposition is mainly based on two simple legal rules which turn out to have far-reaching consequences. The first rule was widely accepted in the scholastic discussion of economic ethics, in particular that of moneylending and interest-taking; it formed part of what the intellectual historian Odd Langholm has labelled the 'double rule of just pricing': 'No equity demands that one should lend to one's own detriment.'[21] In order to lend out money to people in need, a 'Mount' inevitably has to incur certain expenses. To cover these it may licitly demand recompense. The second legal rule invoked specifies whom the Mount can ask for compensation: 'He who bears the burden has to enjoy the benefit and vice versa.'[22] The Mount incurs expenses only for the benefit of its borrowers. On the other hand, a Mount cannot possibly survive without incurring any expenses. Therefore, it is only just and fair that the borrowers help to cover the necessary costs and, by doing so, make sure the institution continues to exist.

Defending the Montes Pietatis 2: The Political Contract and the Benefit Principle

A simple conclusion can be drawn from this line of reasoning. Far from being a usurious profit, the surplus which a Mount receives is a just compensation which the borrowers are obliged to pay on grounds of commutative justice. The obligation arises, so to speak, from a second, additional contract: 'If someone wants to enjoy the benefits of a Mount, a pact can be concluded with him in order to make him contribute toward its expenses in accordance with his share.'[23] The Spanish theologian Joannes Medina had already suggested that the borrowers enter into a kind of hire or employment contract with the staff working at a Mount, a suggestion that was taken over but deftly

---

[21] 'Nulla aequitas postulat ut quis cum damno suo mutuet'. It formed the rationale behind the well-known and at the time generally accepted extrinsic title *damnum emergens* ('damage incurred'). See further Odd Langholm, *Economics in the Medieval Schools. Wealth, Exchange, Value, Money and Usury according to the Paris Theological Tradition, 1200–1350* (Leiden: Brill, 1992), 232–234 and *passim*.

[22] 'Qui sentit onus, sentire debet commodum, et e contra'. Liber Sextus Decretalium, lib. 5, tit. 12, reg. 55. Cp. Detlef Liebs, *Lateinische Rechtsregeln und Rechtssprichwörter* (Darmstadt: Wissenschaftliche Buchgesellschaft, 1991⁵), 173, nr. 46 and 177, nr. 78. The rule was invoked by Pope Leo X in his Bull *Inter multiplices* on the Montes Pietatis.

[23] *De iustitia et iure*, 2 20, 23, 193, Primo: 'Si quis cupiat frui commodis Montis, potest cum eo iniri pactum ut pro sua parte ad illas expensas contribuat'.

adapted by Lessius.[24] According to him, the persons who run a Mount do not relate to the borrowers as if they were their employees, entitled to receive a just wage from them, but rather they function as the borrowers' managers or caretakers (*negotiorum gestores*). Caretaking or managing someone else's affairs (*negotiorum gestio*) was already a well-known concept in Roman law, where it was defined as a quasi-contract: someone looks after another person's interests without having received an order or mandate (*mandatum*) from him to do so.[25] This quasi-contract creates a personal obligation compelling the beneficiary to indemnify the caretaker or manager for all the necessary expenses he has incurred in his favour. Crucially, the beneficiary is supposed to agree with the caretaking, unless he explicitly says he does not. In fact, the second rule of law mentioned above is activated here: he who enjoys the benefit should also bear the burden. The rule makes it perfectly clear that the Montes Pietatis are fully in accordance with the principle of equality, the cornerstone of commutative justice. At the same time, it proves that the institution is not at variance with the equally crucial concept of distributive justice, based on the principle of proportionality. The rule can, indeed, be easily rephrased as follows: those who, comparatively speaking, enjoy more benefits, are obliged to bear more burdens and vice versa.[26]

It is interesting to note that Lessius continues to emphasize the principle of indemnification in his Appendix of 1621 but now develops a new line of reasoning that puts the whole discussion about the Montes in a much wider political framework. The focus remains nonetheless thoroughly legal: the starting point for the argumentation in favour of the institutions created in the Catholic Netherlands is the political contract which Archduke Albert is said to have entered into with his subjects. While the monarch commits himself to serving the interests of his subjects to the best of his abilities, the latter in turn promise to provide him with the means he needs to execute his task properly. It is on grounds of this political contract that the subjects are assumed to agree with all the measures which the ruler takes in order to ensure the common good. The establishment of Montes Pietatis is unquestionably such a measure; their beneficial effects on the political community as a whole are obvious, their main advantage lying, of course, in the fact that people in dire need of ready money can be rescued from the jaws of unscrupulous

---

[24] *De iustitia et iure*, 2, 20, 23, 194. Cp. Joannes Medina, *De poenitentia, restitutione et contractibus* (Ingolstadii: ex officina typographica Davidis Sartorii, 1581), tom. 2, quaest. 10, par. *Ad secundum*, 320.

[25] Reinhard Zimmermann, *The Law of Obligations. Roman Foundations of the Civilian Tradition* (Cape Town; Wetton; Johannesburg: Juta & Co, 1990), 433–450.

[26] *De iustitia et iure*, 2, 20, 23, 194.

private moneylenders (the so-called lombards) demanding a usurious interest for their loans. As the Montes are so beneficial, the monarch can be said to have a duty to establish them. The only question is how. Where does he find the means necessary for creating and maintaining them? Instead of imposing unpopular taxes the ruler can demand a contribution based on the so-called benefit principle: a person pays a specific contribution for his particular use of a certain public service; a person who does not make use of it does not have to pay for it. As a matter of fact, the benefit principle is – implicitly, if not explicitly – contained in the second rule of law which we have met before. Indeed, the rule legitimizes the imposition of burdens which are not proportionally distributed among all members of the political community.

Lessius sees no harm whatsoever in applying the benefit principle to the Montes Pietatis established in the Catholic Netherlands. As the archduke has created a highly beneficial service, he is perfectly entitled to ask its users to help cover the expenses it necessarily incurs according to the benefit they receive from it. On the basis of the political contract they have concluded with the ruler, they are assumed tacitly to have agreed with the creation of the Montes. On the basis of the same contract they are assumed indirectly to agree with the contribution they are asked to pay. Lessius concludes that it is absolutely licit for a Mount to demand compensation from its clients, even if they have not explicitly agreed to pay such compensation by means of a mandate (*mandatum*). For, as the theologian somewhat patronizingly pronounces, in matters which are found to further the common good, the ruler acts as the tutor or curator of his subjects; as their tutor or curator he eminently incarnates the consensus of all his subjects.[27] The archdukes who had explicitly asked Cobergher to create Montes Pietatis in their country could rest assured, and those subjects who gratefully made use of them, either by borrowing from them or by depositing their savings in them, had no reason whatsoever to worry: in no way was their conscience in peril.[28] And Lessius? Well, the moral theologian and ethical expert could pride himself on having

---

[27] *De iustitia et iure*, Appendix, nr. 49. Elsewhere, Lessius presents the political contract between ruler and ruled as a kind of employment contract. See especially *De iustitia et iure*, 2, 1, 3, 13. An analysis of Lessius's essentially contractual political thought is to be found in Toon van Houdt, 'Leonardus Lessius (1554–1623): politiek en moraal, recht en religie', in *Een nieuwe wereld. Denkers uit de Nederlanden over politiek en maatschappij, 1500–1700*, ed. Erik De Bom (Antwerpen: Polis, 2015), 183–215. His views are less detailed but very similar to those developed by his former teacher and mentor Suárez. On political contract theory in the latter's work and the Jesuit order at large, see especially the standard work by Harro Höpfl, *Jesuit Political Thought. The Society of Jesus and the State, c. 1540–1630* (Cambridge: Cambridge University Press, 2004).

[28] *De iustitia et iure*, Appendix, nr. 91.

successfully battled the mortal sin of usury. A heroic feat, indeed, achieved by a truly saintly scholar, as the authors of the self-laudatory *Imago primi saeculi* did not fail to stress.[29] The lavish praise bestowed on Lessius was not entirely undeserved. Thanks to the formidable combination of Cobergher's skilful planning, the legal and jurisdictional power of the archdukes, the ecclesiastical pressure exerted by the local bishops, *and* Lessius's strong intellectual support, private moneylending at an exorbitant interest rate almost completely disappeared from the Catholic Netherlands in the course of just a few decades.[30]

GENERAL APPRAISAL AND INFLUENCE

In the preceding pages I have paid no attention at all to the instrumental role which Lessius's outspokenly juridical approach to moral problems played in expanding and even breaking down the late scholastic paradigm of economic ethics. This is revealed most clearly in his introduction of the so-called extrinsic title *carentia pecuniae* ('lack of money') into the discussion of moneylending and interest-taking and in his daring defence of commercial capitalism while analyzing partnerships and the so-called *contractus trinus*, on the one hand, and, on the other, the interactions of professional businessmen as exemplified in the famous case of 'The Merchant of Rhodos'.[31] Nor have I dwelt upon the profound impact which his legal–moral thought has had on Protestant natural law thinkers such as Hugo Grotius. Old and new scholarly work has convincingly shown that the Jesuit functioned as a transmitter of the Spanish scholastic strand in Catholic moral theology, providing Grotius with important ideas and concepts in the field of contract law and, more generally, legal thought.[32] No less conspicuous is Lessius's role in the later history

---

[29] *Imago primi saeculi*, cap. 6, 793. Interestingly and typically, Lessius's performance is presented as being part and parcel of a collective Jesuit enterprise aimed at reforming morals in general.

[30] See Paul Soetaert, *De Bergen van Barmhartigheid in de Spaanse, de Oostenrijkse en de Franse Nederlanden (1618–1795)* (Brussel: Gemeentekrediet, 1986), 111–117. Regrettably, Soetaert's standard work has been overlooked by Nicola Lorenzo Barile in her otherwise comprehensive article 'Renaissance Monti di Pietà in modern scholarship: themes, studies, and historiographic trends', *Renaissance and Reformation / Renaissance et Réforme* 35.3 (2012): 85–114.

[31] See Toon van Houdt, 'Lack of money. A reappraisal of Lessius' contribution to the scholastic analysis of money-lending and interest-taking', *European Journal of the History of Economic Thought* 5.1 (1998): 1–35; Wim Decock, 'In defense of commercial capitalism: Lessius, partnerships and the Contractus Trinus', *Max Planck Institute for European Legal History Research Paper Series*, no. 2012-04; Wim Decock, 'Lessius and the breakdown of the scholastic paradigm', *Journal of the History of Economic Thought* 31.1 (2009): 57–78.

[32] See the monumental work by Decock, *Theologians and Contract Law*.

of political–economic thought, as is revealed by, for instance, the Catholic German jurist Kaspar Klock, who wrote a lengthy cameralist treatise on taxation and state financing in which he lavishly drew on the Jesuit's *De iustitia et iure*, as well as by the historical linkage that connected Lessius and his Spanish predecessors through Hugo Grotius and Samuel von Pufendorf to Scottish Enlightenment philosophers and political economists such as Francis Hutcheson and Adam Smith.[33] To be sure, while Lessius's outspokenly 'Molinist' views on the delicate issue of divine grace and human free will had already met with serious criticism during his lifetime, his probabilistic approach to moral issues was viciously attacked by Blaise Pascal as a stunning example of reprehensible 'Jesuitism', and his star unquestionably began to fade somewhat after the rigorist turn in Catholic moral theology which began around the middle of the seventeenth century. However, his name never disappeared entirely, and theologians, probabilistic and anti-probabilistic alike, continued to refer to him as an authority to be reckoned with. From the late nineteenth century onwards, his theological, political, and economic thought was rediscovered and reinterpreted in light of the neo-Thomist trend that was rapidly spreading throughout Catholic academia. While enthusiastic admirers such as the Louvain professor of political economy Victor Brants (1856–1917) succeeded in putting Lessius's scholarship and ethical expertise back on the intellectual map, the unremitting efforts made by ardent devotees such as the Jesuit author Karel van Sull (1859–1952) nevertheless failed to turn him into an officially recognized saint.[34]

All these omissions notwithstanding, I hope to have shown that Lessius was, indeed, an important scholar who managed to resolve complex moral problems and to give sound political advice on issues and institutions of topical interest by fully integrating law and legal thinking into his moral theology. In his work, scholastic theology and juridical thought merged, resulting in an exceptionally fruitful cross-fertilization. Wielding his pen, Lessius arguably made moral theology more juridical than it had been ever before and, conversely, submitted law and legal thought to a profound moral reconfiguration.

---

[33] See Bertram Schefold, 'Cameralism as an intermediary between Mediterranean economic thought and classical economics', in *The Dissemination of Economic Ideas*, eds. Heinz D. Kurz, Tamotsu Nishizawa, and Keith Tribe (Cheltenham, Northampton, MA: Edward Elgar, 2011), 3–40 and Stephen J. Grabill, 'Leonard Lessius and the prehistory of economics', *Journal of Markets & Morality* 10.2 (2007): 257–259.

[34] Eleonora Rai, 'The "Odor of Sanctity". Veneration and politics in Leonard Lessius's Cause for Beatification (Seventeenth–Twentieth Centuries)', *Journal of Jesuit Studies* 3 (2016): 238–258.

RECOMMENDED READINGS

Decock, Wim. 'Lessius and the breakdown of the scholastic paradigm'. *Journal of the History of Economic Thought* 31.1 (2009): 57–78.
Decock, Wim. 'In defense of commercial capitalism: Lessius, partnerships and the Contractus Trinus'. *Max Planck Institute for European Legal History Research Paper Series*, nr. 4 (2012).
Decock, Wim. *Theologians and Contract Law. The Moral Transformation of the Ius Commune (ca. 1500–1650)*. Leiden; Boston: Brill/Nijhoff, 2013.
Decock, Wim. 'Law of Property and Obligations. Neoscholastic Thinking and Beyond'. In *The Oxford Handbook of European Legal History*, edited by Heikki Pihlajamäki, Markus D. Dubber, and Mark Godfrey. Oxford: Oxford University Press, 2018.
Decock, Wim and Nicholas De Sutter. *On Sale, Securities, and Insurance. Leonardus Lessius*. Grand Rapids, MI: CLP Academic, 2016.
Grabill, Stephen J. 'Leonard Lessius and the Prehistory of Economics'. *Journal of Markets & Morality* 10.2 (2007): 257–259.
Rai, Eleonora. 'The "Odor of Sanctity". Veneration and Politics in Leonard Lessius's Cause for Beatification (Seventeenth–Twentieth Centuries)'. *Journal of Jesuit Studies* 3 (2016): 238–258.
Schefold, Bertram, ed. *Leonardus Lessius' De iustitia et iure. Vademecum zu einem Klassiker der Spätscholastischen Wirtschaftsanalyse*. Düsseldorf: Handelsblatt, 1999.
Schefold, Bertram. 'Cameralism as an intermediary between Mediterranean economic thought and classical economics'. In *The Dissemination of Economic Ideas*, edited by Heinz D. Kurz, Tamotsu Nishizawa, and Keith Tribe. Cheltenham, MA: Edward Elgar, 2011.
Van Houdt, Toon. *Leonardus Lessius over lening, intrest en woeker. De iustitia et iure, lib. 2, cap. 20. Editie, vertaling en commentaar*. Brussels: Koninklijke Academie voor Wetenschappen, Letteren en Schone Kunsten van België, 1998.
Van Houdt, Toon. '"Lack of Money". A reappraisal of Lessius' contribution to the scholastic analysis of money-lending and interest-taking'. *European Journal of the History of Economic Thought* 5.1 (1998): 1–35.
Van Houdt, Toon. 'Tradition and renewal in late scholastic economic thought: The case of Leonardus Lessius (1554–1623)'. *Journal of Medieval and Early Modern Studies* 28.1 (1998): 51–73.
Van Houdt, Toon. 'Leonardus Lessius (1554–1623): politiek en moraal, recht en religie'. In *Een nieuwe wereld. Denkers uit de Nederlanden over politiek en maatschappij, 1500–1700*, edited by Erik De Bom. Antwerp: Polis, 2015.
Van Houdt, Toon, with Wim Decock. *Leonardus Lessius: traditie en vernieuwing*. Antwerp: Lessius Hogeschool, 2005.

5

Franciscus Zypaeus

Wouter Druwé

BIBLIOGRAPHICAL INTRODUCTION[1]

François vanden Zype (or in Latin: Franciscus Zypaeus) was born in Mechelen in 1580. A son of Henri vanden Zype and Claire du Carne, he grew up in a devout Catholic aristocratic family. His father was lord of Kauwendael (near Mechelen) and Audermeulen (near Berlaar). In the roaring times of the 1580s, when Catholic liturgical celebrations were prohibited in Mechelen, Henri and Claire had been forced to travel to Antwerp to get François baptized in the Catholic Church. François's parents succeeded in transferring their faith to their offspring. Out of eight children, no less than four chose an ecclesiastical career. Franciscus's brothers Henri and Philippe entered the Benedictine order. The latter was a religious in the abbey of Saint John in Ypres; the former even became abbot of the Saint Andrew monastery in Bruges and was known for his theological books.[2] Franciscus himself and his brother Rombaut opted for the secular clergy, and both were promoted to the canonicate. Another brother, Pierre, became bailiff of the margraveship of Lede. In 1585, when the 'Calvinist Republics' in the Southern Netherlands had been recaptured by Alexander Farnese on behalf of the Spanish king, the vanden Zype family moved back to Mechelen, where François received his elementary education.

On 29 December 1593, François was tonsured. He went to Louvain to study at the Faculty of Arts, where he obtained the degree of *magister artium* on

---

[1] This section is mainly based on the following biographical article: Léon Verbeek, 'François Zypaeus (1580–1650). Juriste belge', *Tijdschrift voor Rechtsgeschiedenis* 36.2 (1968): 267–311.

[2] For an overview of Henri's publications on Gregory the Great, on the rule of Saint Benedict, on the life of Saint Scholastica and on the utility of religious life, see Alphons van Dijk, W. M. Perquin, and Lucidius Verschueren eds., *Bibliotheca Catholica Neerlandica Impressa, 1500–1727* (The Hague: Martinus Nijhoff, 1954), nrs. 5759, 7460, 8426–8428.

1 December 1599. He continued his studies in Louvain at the law faculties, and received a baccalaureate in both laws on 28 April 1603. He subsequently joined the college of *baccalaurei* and had even been elected treasurer of that college on 1 March 1604 when Joannes Miraeus, the diocesan bishop of Antwerp, called him to his palace as diocesan secretary in April 1604. Meanwhile, François continued his law studies, and obtained his licence *utriusque iuris* on 10 January 1605. In 1607, Zypaeus was ordained a priest,[3] and immediately appointed as secular canon of the chapter of the Antwerp cathedral.[4] He remained a secretary to the diocesan bishop, before being named *officialis* (ecclesiastical judge) in 1614. Ten years later, Zypaeus received the honorary title of apostolic protonotary and was appointed archdeacon of Antwerp. His last will of 30 July 1633 suggests that Zypaeus was well-off; he bequeathed his goods in an Antwerp polder near Sas-van-Gent, in Berlaar, and in Schoten, as well as a wood in Putte, and his rights in Kauwendael and Audermeulen.[5] In 1638, he became vicar general of the Antwerp diocese. In 1642, he was additionally appointed *provisor* of Saint Jérôme in Antwerp. He remained in office until his death on 4 November 1650.

Zypaeus was a prolific author. Several of his writings have been published. His first publication from 1619 concerned the procedure at the ecclesiastical curia of the diocese of Antwerp; an extended version – valid for the province of Mechelen – was published in 1625 (and again in 1665, 1667, and 1759). In his *Jus pontificium novum*, first published in 1620 and again in 1624, 1641, and 1675, this Antwerp canonist gave an overview of canon law as adapted by the Council of Trent. A volume on the deontology of judges and on the administration of justice, entitled *Judex, Magistratus, Senator*, appeared in Antwerp in

---

[3] On 13 April 1607, Zypaeus had received all minor orders. A day later, he was ordained a subdeacon. On 8 June, he received the diaconal ordination, before being ordained a priest on 22 December 1607. Interestingly, in his *Jus pontificium novum* (lib. 1, tit. *De ordinandis*, nr. 25), Zypaeus explained that the Council of Trent had prohibited the simultaneous reception of several orders, but that a contrary custom in the Southern Low Countries admitted the reception of all minor orders in one single celebration.

[4] Despite his own position as a member of the cathedral chapter and contrary to some of his colleagues, Zypaeus had no problem accepting that the Council of Trent had granted the diocesan bishop certain jurisdictional competencies which had traditionally belonged to the Antwerp cathedral chapter. See *Jus pontificium novum*, lib. 1, tit. *De officio ordinarii*, nr. 19–20. On the other hand, he did explain why the Antwerp secular canons – contrary to the general rule that every cleric should have only one benefice – were allowed to combine several benefices: *Jus pontificium novum*, lib. 3, tit. *De clericis non residentibus*, nr. 4–5.

[5] See, for an edition of Zypaeus's last will: Henricus Joannes Feije, *De Francisci Zypaei vita et meritis oratio quam die XXVIII mensis Julii MDCCCLI habuit Henricus Joannes Feije* (Louvain: Fonteyn, 1852).

1633 (repr. 1673 and 1675).[6] An overview of the civil law of the Southern Low Countries was given in his *Notitia juris belgici*, first published in 1635 (repr. 1640, 1642, 1665, and 1675). In a reaction to the opinion by the French author Jacques Cassan, Zypaeus rejected the French claims to the Southern Netherlands in his *Hiatus Jacobi Cassani obstructus* (1639, repr. 1640 and 1675). His activities as a legal counsellor are reflected in his *Consultationes canonicae pleraeque ex jure novissimo concilii Tridentini recentiorumque pontificiarum constitutionum depromptae* (1640, repr. 1675), and in his *Responsa de jure canonico, praesertim novissimo* (1645, repr. 1675). Finally, in 1649, he published a treatise on the highly controversial issue of ecclesiastical and civil jurisdiction (*De jurisdictione ecclesiastica et civili libri IV*, repr. 1675).

MAJOR THEMES AND CONTRIBUTIONS

Diligent and Well-Regarded Legal Practitioner

Franciscus Zypaeus was first and foremost a legal practitioner: an ecclesiastical judge, archdeacon, and vicar general. He was well-respected for his acquaintance with legal procedure. In his capacity as *officialis*, the 1617 provincial synod of Mechelen entrusted him with the uniformization process of the statutes of all Southern Netherlandish ecclesiastical tribunals, a process which he brought to a successful conclusion.[7]

Moreover, the many *consilia* written by Zypaeus are an indication that he enjoyed a good reputation as a jurist too, both in civil and canonical matters. His independent stance must have struck his contemporaries. He was regularly asked for as an arbiter in disputes between bishops and their subjects. Verbeek suggests, however, that Zypaeus's willingness – if need be – to render judgements against the bishops' interests might have been an explanation for his not having been named a bishop himself.[8]

It seems that Zypaeus has also been a diligent worker. Thus, he was the first to keep consistent and coherent registers of judicial practice at the

---

[6] On this work, see Randall Lesaffer, 'Iudex, magistratus, senator (1633): Franciscus Zypaeus over het publiekrecht', in *Interactie tussen wetgever en rechter voor de Trias Politica*, eds. Erik-Jan Broers and Beatrix Jacobs (The Hague: Boom Juridische Uitgevers, 2004), 29–49.

[7] Franciscus Zypaeus, *Modus procedendi in curia ecclesiastica* (Antwerp: Verdussen, 1619), with a preface by bishop Joannes Malderus. In his *Jus pontificium novum* (lib. 2, tit. *De iudiciis*, nr. 5), Zypaeus explains that this procedure was implemented in all diocesan administrations of the province of Mechelen with some minor adaptations to the local situation. The augmented and revised version was later published as: Id., *Statuta omnium curiarum ecclesiasticarum provinciae Mechliniensis* (Mechelen: Jaye, 1625).

[8] See for this hypothesis: Verbeek, 'François Zypaeus (1580–1650)', 273–274.

ecclesiastical court of Antwerp. As archdeacon of Antwerp, Zypaeus was responsible for the examination of candidates to benefices or ordination,[9] for accompanying the diocesan bishop on his visitations,[10] but also for the economic and financial administration of the diocese. He was trusted by his contemporaries and regularly named executor of last wills, inter alia for the testaments of the Antwerp bishops Joannes Miraeus (1603–1611) and his successor Joannes Malderus (1611–1633).[11]

Scholar Serving Legal Practice

Next to his activities as a practitioner, Zypaeus was also a prominent scholar, clearly inspired by the late humanist movement in Louvain.[12] In his *Judex, Magistratus, Senator*, our Antwerp canonist showed off his erudition with frequent quotes from the classical authors and poets. Interestingly, his clearest interest seems to have lain in (legal) history, as he frequently derived legal historical arguments from the *Corpus iuris civilis*, the *Corpus iuris canonici*, or even the Bible. He also enjoyed dwelling on the history of Rome and of the Low Countries. References to classical authors like Livy and Tacitus are legion. Other references include contemporary historians like Petrus Divaeus (1535–1581) and Franciscus Haraeus (1555–1631) on the history of Brabant,[13] Carolus Scribani (1561–1629) on the origins of Antwerp,[14] and Jacobus Marchantius (1537–1609) on Flemish history.[15]

Zypaeus was well-versed in moral theology and the writings of the followers of the School of Salamanca. He regularly referred for instance to his contemporary, the Jesuit Leonardus Lessius (1554–1623), whom he praised for his knowledge of Antwerp legal practice and his many efforts to converse with

---

[9] In his *Jus pontificium novum* (lib. 1, tit. *De ordinandis*, nr. 24), Zypaeus emphasized that the decrees of the Council of Trent did not abrogate this competence of the archdeacon, although they had required additional examiners.
[10] *Jus pontificium novum*, lib. 3, tit. *De clericis non residentibus*, nr. 18.
[11] See, with further references: Verbeek, 'François Zypaeus (1580–1650)', 275–276.
[12] On that movement, see e.g.: Jan Papy, ed., *Het Leuvense Collegium Trilingue 1517–1797: Erasmus, humanistische onderwijspraktijk en het nieuwe taleninstituut Latijn-Grieks-Hebreeuws* (Louvain: Peeters, 2017); Toon van Houdt and Erik De Bom, 'The artistry of civil life. Deliberative rhetoric and political pedagogy in the work of Nicolaus Vernulaeus (1583–1649)', *Journal of the History of Rhetoric* 35 (2017): 259–284.
[13] E.g.: *Consultationes canonicae pleraeque*, lib. 1, tit. *De constitutionibus*, cons. 1.
[14] E.g.: *Jus pontificium novum*, lib. 3, tit. *De testamentis*, nr. 3.
[15] *Jus pontificium novum*, lib. 1, tit. *De constitutionibus*, nr. 11.

Antwerp merchants.[16] Nevertheless, in his legal works, Zypaeus emphasized that moral–theological theories were limited to the *forum internum* and should not be extended to the external forum of the secular and ecclesiastical tribunals. Thus, our Antwerp canonist argued that for reasons of procedural economy, limited punitive interests were acceptable in the *forum externum*, even if in the internal forum a case-specific evaluation was preferred.[17] Regarding the sale of perpetual annuities, Zypaeus required unconditional redeemability in the external forum in order to discourage usurious contracts, even if he knew that as to the *forum internum* the mere compensation of the disadvantages to the seller–debtor of a non-redeemable annuity sufficed.[18]

In his writings as a scholar, Zypaeus always maintained the link with legal practice. Some published writings directly result from his counselling activities. Thus, 215 *consilia* were published in 1640 (*Consultationes canonicae pleraeque*). A second collection of 124 consultations appeared in 1645 (*Responsa de iure canonico praesertim novissimo*). Also, in other works, for example, in his introduction to the canon law of the Southern Low Countries (*Jus pontificium novum*), our author frequently refers to his personal experiences as an ecclesiastical judge and counsellor. His treatise on the division of competences between ecclesiastical and civil tribunals (*De jurisdictione ecclesiastica et civili*) has to be situated in this judicial context too. In May 1645, he finished a thematically structured *compendium* of the decisions of the first and second synod of Mechelen (1570 and 1609), as well as of the first two Antwerp diocesan synods (1571 and 1576), presumably meant for Netherlandish canon law practitioners (but never actually published).[19]

---

[16] *Notitia juris belgici*, lib. 4, tit. *De emptione et venditione*, § *De cambiis*. On the influence of neoscholasticism on Zypaeus's views on public law: Lesaffer, 'Iudex, magistratus, senator (1633)', 36.

[17] *Consultationes canonicae pleraeque*, lib. 5, tit. *De usuris*, cons. 1.

[18] *Notitia iuris belgici*, lib. 4, tit. *De emptione et venditione*, § *De reditibus, et eorum luitione*.

[19] KBR, ms. 6261–62, 57 f.: *Summaria Compilatio synodorum Mechliniensium prime et secunde et diocesarum Antverpiensium prime itidem et secunde auctore clarissimo viro D. D. F. Zypaeus J. C. A. A.* A first title concerns the profession of faith. The following titles deal with the sacraments (in general, baptism, confirmation, penitence, indulgencies, Holy Eucharist, extreme unction, holy orders, marriage), with preaching and liturgy, with fasting, images and relics, and with superstition. The subsequent titles focus on the hierarchy and the administration of the Church (bishops and their seals, ministers of the Church, archpriests and pastors, the clerical lifestyle, the correction of clerics, ecclesiastical benefices and offices), on schools, Sunday classes and seminaries, on the unions of churches, on the conservation and administration of ecclesiastical goods, and on their recovery. Final – very short – titles concern the jurisdiction of the Church, regular clergy, usury, visitations, last wills, witnesses and the synodal procedure.

Jurist Utriusque Iuris *from and for the Habsburg Low Countries*

Zypaeus's complete ecclesiastical and juridical career has been at the service of the Church in the Habsburg Low Countries. This is reflected both in his choice of topics for his writings, and in the ideas presented therein. Thus, in his *Ius pontificium novum*, Zypaeus commented on the titles of the *Liber Extra*, but with a strong focus on the canon law as it was applied in the Southern Netherlands. The same focus on the Low Countries is present in his other works too, except for his more general approach in *Judex, Magistratus, Senator*.

Of course, Zypaeus often referred to the decrees of the Council of Trent and also to later papal constitutions. His writings attest to his high esteem for the Tridentine legislation as inspired by the Holy Spirit,[20] even if occasionally he admitted that an old customary practice continued to apply in the Low Countries, for example, with regard to the laws of patronage (*patronatus*).[21] As to the interpretative constitutions by the Congregation of the Council, however, Zypaeus was more on his guard. When decisions by the Congregation did not fit within his line of thought, he regularly pointed at the unrealistic nature of the decisions,[22] at the uncertainties related to their authenticity,[23] or at the clarity of the decrees of Trent, which did not need any interpretation. Many so-called 'interpretations' were, as far as Zypaeus was concerned, in fact subtleties to strengthen the central control of the Roman curia and were alien to the *ratio legis* of the conciliar decrees.[24] Moreover, as to the post-Tridentine papal decretals, Zypaeus emphasized that many of them

---

[20] *Jus pontificium novum*, lib. 1, tit. *De summa trinitate et fide catholica, pr.*; ibid., lib. 1, tit. *De constitutionibus*, nr. 6–9 (where Zypaeus refers inter alia to the fact that even King Philip II and Governor Margaret of Parma had ordered the publication of the Tridentine decrees); *De jurisdictione ecclesiastica et civili*, lib. 4, cap. 7, nr. 1–4.

[21] *Jus pontificium novum*, lib. 3, tit. *De jure patronatus*, nr. 3: '*receptio Concilii Tridentini in his partibus speciatim exclusit quamcumque innouationem in praeiudicium patronatuum Principis aut Vasallorum*'. See also: *Responsa de iure canonico novissimo*, lib. 3, tit. *De jure patronatus*, resp. 2, nr. 12. He explained that this practice did not aim at disrespect for the Tridentine decrees, but only at mitigation (*accommodatio*) of the enforcement of these decrees: *Jus pontificium novum*, lib. 1, tit. *De constitutionibus*, nr. 6.

[22] E.g. concerning a letter by the Congregation of the Council to the bishop of Antwerp in 1608, in which it was stated that the maximum rate of a benefice granted to a vicar should still not exceed the amounts set in a papal constitution by Pope Pius V (1566–1572), whereas major monetary fluctuations had taken place: *Jus pontificium novum*, lib. 3, tit. *Ut ecclesiastica beneficia sine diminutione conferantur*, nr. 8.

[23] *Consultationes canonicae pleraeque*, lib. 1, tit. *De electione*, cons. 1: '*Sed, ut omittamus huiusmodi declarationes non tantum non exhiberi authenticas, et omnes impressas declarationes iam saepius Romae esse damnatas, ut adulterinas; ego tantum provoco ad ipsum textum Concilii (...)*'.

[24] See Léon Verbeek, 'Franciscus Zypaeus en het kerkelijk gezag', *Bijdragen tot de geschiedenis* 52 (1969): 106–107.

had never been received in the Low Countries.²⁵ Admittedly, *de iure* Zypaeus stated that if the Pope explicitly decided that the publication of a particular ordinance in Rome sufficed, the Holy Father's decision had to be respected. If, however, it was doubtful whether the Pope himself had given the relevant order, the Supreme Pontiff should expressly be asked for his decision.²⁶ De facto, the application of papal legislation in Netherlandish judicial practice required the publication of the norms by the diocesan bishops of the Southern Low Countries; mere publication in Rome did not suffice.²⁷ Exception was made only for new legislation that abrogated an older prohibitive norm. Thus, the decree that limited the scope of the diriment impediment of cognacy was also applicable in areas where it had not (yet) been published.²⁸

In principle, bishops were obliged to publish and enforce papal decretals in their own dioceses.²⁹ Nonetheless, Zypaeus thought it wise to give the diocesan bishops some leeway as to enforcement, as they were best aware of the local situation and of contrary ecclesiastical customs in their diocese. Our archdeacon stated that the climate of the Low Countries had formed the people's character and even physical condition, with different legislation required from that applied in Rome.³⁰ He argued that – for reasons of peace

---

25 See for some examples: *Jus pontificium novum*, lib. 3, tit. *De clericis non residentibus*, nr. 27 (regarding the decretal *Ex proximo* by Pius V on financial sanctions in case of non-recitation of the liturgical hours); ibid., lib. 3, tit. *De regularibus*, nr. 40–41 (regarding the decretals *Circa* by Pius V and *Deo sacris* by Gregory XIII on the strict observation of the cloister by all female religious who had taken the vows of poverty, obedience, and chastity). The latter decretals endangered the functioning of many hospitals erected in the Low Countries by female congregations. It was not uncommon in the Low Countries to hold that certain papal bulls had not been received, even though opinions differed as to which papal decretals were concerned. See for instance: Leonardus Lessius, *De iustitia et iure* (Antwerp: ex officina Plantiniana, apud B. Moretum, 1621), lib. 2, cap. 25, dub. 3, nr. 33, where this Jesuit and moral theologian defends the non-reception of the 1586 bull *Detestabilis avaritia* by Pope Sixtus V on the triple contract, whereas Zypaeus positively referred to that bull: Zypaeus, *Responsa de iure canonico*, lib. 5, tit. *De usuris*, resp. 1, nr. 19.

26 *De jurisdictione ecclesiastica et civili*, lib. 1, cap. 63, nr. 15.

27 *Jus pontificium novum*, lib. 1, tit. *De constitutionibus*, nr. 1.

28 Zypaeus gave the example of Scotland. See *Consultationes canonicae pleraeque*, lib. 4, tit. *De cognatione spirituali*, cons. 1.

29 *De jurisdictione ecclesiastica et civili*, lib. 1, cap. 63, nr. 2–3. During the *ad limina*-visits, bishops could inform themselves on the novel papal legislation. See also: Bart Wauters, *Recht als religie. Canonieke onderbouw van de vroegmoderne staatsvorming in de Zuidelijke Nederlanden* (Louvain: Universitaire Pers Leuven, 2005), 166–167.

30 Verbeek, 'Franciscus Zypaeus en het kerkelijk gezag', 109–111. He even stated that the types of physical illnesses in the Low Countries were different from those in Italy and other warmer places. Therefore, the prohibition by Pius V (in his 1566 bull *Supra gregem*) for a medical doctor to attend an ill person for the third consecutive day if this patient had not yet confessed, should not be applied to the Low Countries. See *Jus pontificium novum*, lib. 5, tit. *De poenitentia et remissione*, nr. 18. More than elsewhere, Netherlandish inhabitants uttered

and order – it was better to tolerate those local customs which deviated from new papal constitutions, than to create scandal among the flock by a radical effort to enforce the novel pontifical legislation.[31] The multiplicity of papal constitutions created legal chaos: as far as Zypaeus was concerned, some popes had simply been too volatile in their application of the Tridentine decrees.[32]

Contrary to his Gallicanist colleagues, however, Zypaeus respected the primacy of the Pope, especially as to ecclesiastical discipline, and even with respect to conciliar decisions.[33] That is why he expressly emphasized that these local customs enjoyed at least the implicit consent of the Supreme Pontiff,[34] even if the papal constitution stipulated that publication in Rome sufficed.[35] Zypaeus therefore presumed – until convincing proof to the contrary was produced – that a diocesan bishop's decision not to publish a papal decretal had been made in accordance with the Pope and his curia. Bishops had received their jurisdiction directly from Christ, but the Pope could limit their competencies on the basis of his primacy.[36] Of course, irrational customs, which the Pope would never consent to and which gave rise to endless litigation, should definitely be disregarded.[37]

Interestingly, Zypaeus was not opposed to the broad application of the *ius de non evocando* to procedures involving the Roman curia. According to the Golden Bull of 1349, Brabantian citizens could not be cited by foreign tribunals. Our Antwerp canonist seemed to extend this rule to the 'foreign' tribunal of the Roman Rota. Southern Netherlandish first instance cases, even concerning the possession of reserved benefices, could perhaps be dealt with by an apostolic delegate in the Low Countries, but parties could never be

---

threats which they would never actually put in practice. Consequently, one should not too easily believe in the actual presence of fear that would allow fiancées to renounce their marriage. See *Consultationes canonicae pleraeque*, lib. 4, tit. *De sponsalibus et matrimonio*, cons. 1.

[31] Preface to the reader (*Benevole lector*) to *De jurisdictione ecclesiastica et civili*. Zypaeus's basic message is that 'better times will come', but that – for the time being – it would not be clever to insist on every detail: *Necessitas tempestatum, quod sereno coelo illicitum est, licitum facit.*

[32] Verbeek, 'Franciscus Zypaeus en het kerkelijk gezag', 105.

[33] *Jus pontificium novum*, lib. 2, tit. *De appellationibus*, nr. 16 (on the prohibition of appeal against papal decisions with a future council). See also: *Consultationes canonicae pleraeque*, lib. 1, tit. *De rescriptis*, cons. 3: *De evocatione*, where Zypaeus mentions that the Council could not bind the Pope as to the form which had to be used to evoke a case; the Council could only instruct him.

[34] *Responsa de iure canonico*, lib. 2, tit. *De feriis*, resp. 1, nr. 11: *Quid dicendum ubi publicatio non fit?*

[35] *Jus pontificium novum*, lib. 1, tit. *De constitutionibus*, nr. 1.

[36] *Jus pontificium novum*, lib. 1, tit. *De officio delegati*, nr. 1.

[37] *Judex, Magistratus, Senator*, lib. 2, cap. 6, nr. 22–23.

summoned to Rome.[38] Contrary to the Tridentine regulations and despite Zypaeus's theoretical remark that a privilege by the Pope should be asked for, Zypaeus accepted in practice that even appeal procedures in ecclesiastical cases should be decided in the Low Countries by apostolic delegates. The Pope should be asked to send a delegate in order to avoid forcing the parties to travel to Rome. This solution would also facilitate the enforcement of judgements with the help of the secular authorities.[39]

Zypaeus was interested not only in the canon law of the Low Countries, he also wrote an overview of 'Belgian' civil law. The early seventeenth century was marked by a growing interest by jurists in the *ius proprium*, the particular law of a region. Southern Netherlandish scholars, such as Zypaeus's master Petrus Gudelinus (1550–1619) and Paulus Busius (1570–1610), had made extensive use of the law particular to their region in their learned commentaries. In 1631, Hugo Grotius published his *Inleidinge tot de Hollantsche Rechtsgeleertheit*. Clearly inspired by that example, but in Latin, Zypaeus's *Notitia juris belgici* appeared in 1635. In that treatise Zypaeus tried to give a systematic overview of the law in the Low Countries. He largely followed the order of the Code of Justinian (albeit mixed with titles from the *Liber Extra*), but attributed precedence to the *ius proprium* over the learned law. Great value was given to custom, which could abrogate earlier princely constitutions. Customs could of course be abrogated by later princely constitutions too, but they did not need an express homologation.[40] In his consultations, local customary law was often invoked against the application of the written (i.e. Roman) law, and this on very diverse subjects. Thus, he argued that Southern Netherlandish courts no longer granted a privileged defence of non-payment of money lent (*exceptio non numeratae pecuniae*) to the lender, nor the Anastasian benefice.[41] Contrary to Roman law, married partners and priests were automatically emancipated.[42] Tutors were obliged to render accounts annually, rather than only at the end of the term as Roman law provided.[43]

In the *Notitia juris belgici*, regular references are also made to the case law of the Southern Low Countries. Other sources include the treatise on the

---

[38] *Jus pontificium novum*, lib. 2, tit. *De iudiciis*, nr. 1.
[39] *De jurisdictione ecclesiastica et civili*, lib. 2, cap. 26, nr. 1–2. See Verbeek, 'Franciscus Zypaeus en het kerkelijk gezag', 119–120.
[40] Verbeek, 'François Zypaeus (1580–1650)', 307–311.
[41] *Notitia iuris belgici*, lib. 2, tit. *De exceptionibus*; ibid., lib. 4, tit. *De hereditate vel actione vendita*.
[42] *Notitia iuris belgici*, lib. 4, tit. *Ad Macedonianum*.
[43] *Notitia iuris belgici*, lib. 5, tit. *De tutoribus*.

abrogated laws in France by Philibert Bugnyon (1530–1590), as well as writings on French customary law, although Zypaeus emphasized that authors who relied exclusively on French customs neglected the particularities of the Habsburg Low Countries.[44] In legal historical overviews, Zypaeus is often presented as the person who introduced customary law into the civil law of the Habsburg Low Countries. To a certain extent, as he explained, local customary law and princely ordinances were also applied in the ecclesiastical courts (just like civil courts sometimes relied on canon law principles).[45]

Zypaeus clearly was a proud citizen of the Habsburg Low Countries, and of Antwerp in particular. In his *Hiatus Iacobi Cassani obstructus*, our canonist defended the position of the Habsburg monarchs and reacted harshly against alleged French claims on the Southern Low Countries.[46] The French royal councillor Jacques Cassan and some French contemporaries had argued that the *dominium* of the complete territory of the Low Countries belonged to the French king.[47] In his *Mars gallicus*, the theologian Cornelius Jansenius (1585–1638) had already countered those claims. In line with Jansenius, Zypaeus used juridical arguments to consistently reject all of Cassan's arguments and accused the French Kings of having supported heretical movements.[48] His very critical stance toward the 'Calvinist heresy', and the oppression of the Catholic Church in the Dutch Republic, is also regularly brought to the fore.[49] Within the Habsburg Low Countries and within the Duchy of Brabant, he defended the rights of the margraveship of Antwerp as

---

[44] *Notitia juris belgici*, lib. 1, tit. *De legibus*, nr. 11.

[45] *Jus pontificium novum*, lib. 1, tit. *De constitutionibus*, nr. 12. Canon law principles applied by the civil courts include the canonical computation of degrees of consanguinity, the formal requirements for last wills, and the process of law. The concordates between Charles V and the bishops of Liège and Cambrai on the enforcement of last wills required ecclesiastical judges to take secular legislation into account.

[46] The full title explains that Zypaeus will argue that the Netherlandish provinces should belong to a Catholic king (including the provinces that had become part of the Dutch Republic) and that the French claims on the Low Countries were unfounded: *Hiatus Iacobi Cassani obstructus, ubi immensa illius totam Europam scriptione deuorantis ambitio nullo Iure niti demonstratur: ditiones Belgicae Iuri Regis Catholici asseruntur: foederum regiorum vis atque virtus comprobatur: hodierni denique belli Hispano-Gallo-Belgici iustitia ostenditur. Quibus illapsa est disceptatio de pace Pragensi MDCXXXV aduersus Deplorationem Iusti Asterii: accessitque caput Posthumum super Vindiciis Gallicis.*

[47] Zypaeus reacted to the following tract by Jacques Cassan : *La recherche des droits du Roy et de la Couronne de France, sur l'Empire, Duchez, Comtez, villes et païs occuppez par les Princes estrangers appartenans aux Roys tres-chrestiens par conquestes, successions, confiscations, et autres titres légitimes* (Paris, 1632).

[48] Verbeek, 'François Zypaeus (1580–1650)', 301–304.

[49] E.g.: *Hiatus Cassani obstructus*, lib. 3, cap. 3, where Zypaeus inter alia complains – with reference to the situation of the Catholic faith and Catholic ministers in Maastricht and Breda – that the Protestants did not respect the treaties they had entered into. Unsurprisingly,

a separate political entity. In a consultation on the enforceability of the Perpetual Edict of 1611 by Archdukes Albert and Isabella in the city of Antwerp before it had been published over there in 1617, Zypaeus stressed that for the Edict to be enforceable, publication in Antwerp itself was required. Mere publication in the Brabantian chancellery in Brussels did not suffice. The margraveship of Antwerp should be regarded as a separate province, and the city as a metropolis in the technical sense.[50]

Mild Defender of Ecclesiastical Privileges Against Princely Authority

In ecclesiastical affairs, Zypaeus can hardly be called an ultramontanist, as he often stressed the importance of local ecclesiastical customs and practices from the Low Countries as an argument against the application of papal legislation. Nevertheless, as far as internal relations between the ecclesiastical and the civil authorities in the Habsburg Netherlands were concerned, Zypaeus often minimized the role of secular legislation[51] and pleaded against royal interventions in ecclesiastical affairs. Certainly in matters of faith, such as the regulation of marriage, the Church was to be solely competent. Thus, Zypaeus countered Gallicanist pleas to grant the king the right to decide upon diriment impediments.[52] Moreover, bishops should be respected by the secular princes, and must not be regarded simply as 'inferior ministers of the altar'.[53]

Our Antwerp canonist was not convinced of the need of a royal *placet* for the application of papal ordinances and limited the *placet*-procedure to rescripts that granted benefices.[54] It has been suggested that this explained the foreign publication of his *Ius pontificium novum* in Cologne, outside of

---

Zypaeus also argued that the Catholic members of monasteries and holders of benefices who had been expelled from their premises in the Dutch Republic kept their privileges and benefices, even if Protestants factually occupied them. See e.g.: *Consultationes canonicae pleraeque*, lib. 5, tit. *De privilegiis*, cons. 5.

[50] *Consultationes canonicae pleraeque*, lib. 1, tit. *De constitutionibus*, cons. 1: 'Publicata constitutio in Aula Belgica ac Metropolian (sic) Antuerpiae liget?

[51] Thus, except if it had been confirmed by a concordate, imperial legislation was not binding in conscience (*in foro interiori*). See *Jus pontificium novum*, lib. 3, tit. *De successionibus quae ab intestato deferuntur*, nr. 2.

[52] *Jus pontificium novum*, lib. 4, tit. *De sponsalibus et matrimonio*, nr. 15 (where Zypaeus claimed that the Edict of Nantes by the French King Henry IV could not validly dispense from canonical form, nor from the diriment impediment of sacred orders); *De jurisdictione ecclesiastica et civili*, lib. 1, cap. 33, nr. 2.

[53] *Jus pontificium novum*, lib. 1, tit. *De maioritate et obedientia*, nr. 3.

[54] *Jus pontificium novum*, lib. 1, tit. *De constitutionibus*, nr. 2-4. See also: Wauters, *Recht als religie*, 196; Verbeek, 'Franciscus Zypaeus en het kerkelijk gezag', 100-103.

the Low Countries. Anyhow, Zypaeus's teachings on *placet* belong to the most quoted passages of his oeuvre. Given the regular quotes of that fragment in the Jansenist controversy in the early eighteenth century, van Espen thought it necessary to rebuke Zypaeus's arguments against the *placet* in his treatise *De promulgatione legum ecclesiasticarum*, which in its turn gave rise to responses in 1718–1719 by Léger Charles de Decker, dean of Mechelen, and Petrus Govarts, apostolic vicar of the diocese of 's-Hertogenbosch.[55]

Zypaeus emphasized the liberty of the Church vis-à-vis the secular legislator and defended the *privilegium fori* and the right of the Church to employ coactive force.[56] Of course, as was the common opinion of the early modern canonists, the Church relied on the secular authorities (*bracchium saeculare*) for the enforcement of canonical penalties.[57] For some civil pecuniary claims[58] and in extreme penal cases, such as treason and (a strict conception of) lèse-majesté, (some categories of) clerics could be directly subjected to princely jurisdiction.[59] Whether Zypaeus recognized in the Low Countries a competence of the Prince to render provisional judgements (to decide *in possessorio*), which existed in France on the basis of a papal privilege, is less clear.[60] If a cleric possessed feudal goods, disputes concerning them had to be brought within the feudal courts.[61] In the case of doubt regarding the division of competences, Zypaeus argued that the question had to be decided by the Pope: 'If today controversy exists as to what matters belong to God and what matters to the Emperor, the response of Christ has to be interpreted by the Vicar of Christ.'[62] With a reference to Christ's granting jurisdiction to the church, our Antwerp canonist heavily criticized an edict by Charles V of 4 October 1540 which stipulated that disputes on jurisdiction had to be

---

[55] See, with further references: Wauters, *Recht als religie*, 196–205; Verbeek, 'Franciscus Zypaeus en het kerkelijk gezag', 93–95.
[56] *Jus pontificium novum*, lib. 5, tit. *De poenis*, nr. 1.
[57] *De jurisdictione ecclesiastica et civili*, lib. 4, cap. 3, nr. 17–21.
[58] *Jus pontificium novum*, lib. 2, tit. *De foro competenti*, nr. 3–4 (on the responsibility of the duke of Brabant as protector of monasteries, and thus as competent judge for civil and pecuniary claims by and against abbots and abbesses).
[59] *Jus pontificium novum*, lib. 2, tit. *De foro competenti*, nr. 36 (on the secular prince's competence to conduct proceedings regarding atrocious crimes by some minor categories of clerics, namely *clerici simplicis tonsurae*).
[60] *Jus pontificium novum*, lib. 2, tit. *De causa possessionis et proprietatis*, nr. 1 (where the existence of such a competence is recognized).
[61] *De jurisdictione ecclesiastica et civili*, lib. 1, cap. 29, nr. 1–3. Of course, crimes by clerics – even if the punishment included confiscation of feudal goods – were to be punished by an ecclesiastical judge.
[62] *De jurisdictione ecclesiastica et civili*, lib. 4, cap. 15, nr. 10–11: '*Si ergo hodie controuersia occurrerit, quae sint Dei, et quae Caesaris; proponenda est Vicario Christi qui interpretetur Christi responsum* (...)'.

decided by the sovereign tribunals, and that ecclesiastical judges must not impose censures against their secular counterparts.[63]

As a defender of the ecclesiastical jurisdiction and in line with the Tridentine decrees, Zypaeus was clearly opposed to the *recursus ad principem*, a procedure of appeal to the secular prince against apostolic letters, ecclesiastical censures, and sentences by ecclesiastical tribunals, except maybe in cases of notorious invalidity.[64] Nevertheless, sometimes he considered the possibility of recourse to the secular authorities against a decision by an ecclesiastical tribunal, especially if the ecclesiastical court had exceeded its own jurisdiction or endangered the privileges of the land. Zypaeus called the possibility for secular magistrates of the Southern Netherlands to cassate sentences by ecclesiastical tribunals an *usurpata consuetudo* which had been applied since time immemorial and therefore had binding force, as long as it was used exceptionally and not as a replacement for the normal intra-ecclesial appeals procedure.[65] He rejected the Gallicanist view that recourse against sentences by ecclesiastical courts could always be had with the secular prince: the normal power of oversight resided with the Pope.[66]

His *consilia* and *responsa* reflect his protective stance vis-à-vis the Church and its privileges. He often defended the patrimonial rights of churches, abbeys, and other pious causes. A good example of Zypaeus's stance in this regard can be found in his opinions on the redeemability of ecclesiastical annuities. In an effort to avoid usurious contracts, by the mid-sixteenth century it had become the *communis opinio* of the jurists – and it was later also supported by imperial ordinances of Charles V and Philip II – that pecuniarily constituted annuities were redeemable out of their very nature. This rule did not apply to annuities that had been constituted through other means (e.g. a foundation, bequest, or donation). In principle, our Antwerp canonist was in favour of this principle of redeemability of pecuniarily constituted annuities. Many churches, abbeys, and pious foundations were, however, (at least partly) financially dependent on the payment of annuities. Allowing debtors of ecclesiastical annuities to redeem them would have been disastrous for the financial situation of churches. Zypaeus proposed a solution based on the law

---

[63] *Jus pontificium novum*, lib. 2, tit. *De foro competenti*, nr. 26–27. For the edict of 4 October 1540, see: *Édit de l'Empéreur ...*, in Jean Lameere and H. Simont, eds., *Recueil des anciennes ordonnances de la Belgique. Deuxième série – 1506–1700, volume 4* (Brussels: Goemaere, 1907), 235–236.

[64] *De jurisdictione ecclesiastica et civili*, lib. 1, cap. 5, § 9, nr. 3 (*nisi forte tam notoria sit invaliditas, ut ipse censuram passus possit se gerere pro libero*).

[65] *De jurisdictione ecclesiastica et civili*, lib. 4, cap. 9, nr. 4 (where the exceptional nature of this procedural means is emphasized); ibid., lib. 4, cap. 13, nr. 10–11.

[66] *Jus pontificium novum*, lib. 1, tit. *De rescriptis*, nr. 7–8.

of evidence. Whereas for private annuities he assumed pecuniary constitution until proof to the contrary,[67] as to ecclesiastical annuities our Antwerp canonist proposed the opposite solution. He emphasized that the early Christians had always donated their income to the Apostles without requiring anything in return. Similarly, ecclesiastical annuities had normally been constituted through a foundation, bequest, or donation. As long as the debtors did not prove the original pecuniary constitution of the ecclesiastical annuity (a burden of proof which was often impossible to meet for the ancient ones), the annuity had to be considered perpetual and irredeemable.[68]

Zypaeus also pleaded in favour of the principle of immunity of ecclesiastical goods from secular taxes.[69] Nevertheless, his position was nuanced. Despite his arguments in favour of immunity from secular taxes, he accepted that the papal bull *In Coena Domini* – which extended this immunity to all goods of clerics – was to be interpreted strictly. On the basis of ecclesiastical custom in the Low Countries, taxation of clerics could be tolerated, as long as the local ecclesiastical authority had given its assent.[70] Voluntary contributions by clerics were possible to fund the war against the Protestants.[71] He was not necessarily opposed to the limitations on the acquisition of ecclesiastical goods imposed by Charles V and his successors, even if he tried to limit the consequences thereof.[72]

Despite his strong opinions, Zypaeus was not a polemical figure. He usually struck a conciliatory tone, definitely as far as internal relations within the Church and within the Habsburg Low Countries were concerned. In his preface to the *Consultationes canonicae pleraeque*, which was dedicated to

---

[67] *Consultationes canonicae pleraeque*, lib. 3, De emptione et venditione, cons. 2.
[68] *Consultationes canonicae pleraeque*, lib. 3, De emptione et venditione, cons. 3; *Notitia iuris belgici*, lib. 4, tit. De emptione et venditione, § De reditibus, et eorum luitione. See, on this debate: Wouter Druwé, 'De aflosbaarheid van renten in Nederlandse *consilia* en *decisiones* (ca. 1500–1670)', Pro Memorie 19 (2017): 139–159.
[69] The secular princes could not impose taxes on e.g. abbeys, even if they enjoyed a right of patronage, unless they had been given a special privilege by the Pope. See *Jus pontificium novum*, lib. 3, tit. Ut ecclesiastica beneficia sine diminutione conferantur, controversia quinta.
[70] *De jurisdictione ecclesiastica et civili*, lib. 3, cap. 17. Although the *libertas ecclesiae* concerned both the person and the goods of clerics, the former freedom was more essential than the latter, especially as far as the personal goods of the clerics were concerned.
[71] *De jurisdictione ecclesiastica et civili*, lib. 3, cap. 8, nr. 13. In principle, clerics were not allowed to voluntarily contribute to secular taxes without the Pope's consent. The funding of the 'holy war' against the heretics was, however, admissible.
[72] See, for an evaluation: Verbeek, 'Franciscus Zypaeus en het kerkelijk gezag', 120–121. An example of such a limitation can be found in his effort to interpret all redeemable annuities – even those which had been constituted on a piece of land – as movables. Movables were not subject to the limitations of the mortmain. See *Jus pontificium novum*, lib. 2, tit. De foro competenti, nr. 14 and 19.

the margrave, the consuls, the senate, and the people of Antwerp, our canonist praised the good cooperation of the ecclesiastical and secular authorities in his home town. In the years when Zypaeus had been active at the ecclesiastical court, uncertainties regarding the division of competences with the secular tribunal had always been solved amicably (*amico sermone*). Zypaeus was also pragmatic. In principle, Zypaeus agreed with Cardinal Robertus Bellarminus – who had taught at the Louvain Jesuit college – that the Church was superior to the Prince and had an indirect power (*potestas indirecta*) over it. In practice, though, it was better not to use that power to excommunicate a prince, but instead to convince the prince of the (Catholic) truth.[73] Or, to give another example: if a secular prince obliged the Church to ask his prior consent before it organized a provincial or diocesan synod, it was sometimes better for it to do so in order to prevent the ecclesiastical jurisdiction being questioned.[74] In his *Ius pontificium novum*, Zypaeus even praised the Habsburg monarchs, who – contrary to some of their colleagues of neighbouring nations (not to mention France) – had always been very diligent when using their right of patronage, granted by a papal indult, to nominate candidates for vacant episcopal sees.[75]

GENERAL APPRAISAL AND INFLUENCE

In his own time, Zypaeus's works were widely read by colleagues such as Paulus Christinaeus and the great Louvain canonist Andreas Vallensis, as well as by Northern Netherlandish jurists such as Willem de Groot.[76] Outside the Low Countries he was less well known. Famous scholars like Agostinho Barbosa (1589–1649) and Antoninus Diana (1586–1663) do not quote him.[77] The greatest quality of Zypaeus was undoubtedly his ability to systematize, which made of his writings – definitely his *Jus pontificium novum* and *Notitia*

---

[73] *De jurisdictione ecclesiastica et civili*, lib. 1, cap. 2, nr. 16–17. See Verbeek, 'Franciscus Zypaeus en het kerkelijk gezag', 128–129.

[74] *De jurisdictione ecclesiastica et civili*, lib. 1, cap. 63, nr. 19–21 ('*ex duobus malis minimum esse eligendum*').

[75] *Jus pontificium novum*, lib. 1, tit. *De electione*, nr. 2. On papal indults and their use by Charles V for nation building in the Low Countries, see Paul van Peteghem, *De Nederlanden en het Vrijgraafschap Bourgondië tussen paus en keizer. De rol van het apostolische indult in de staatkundige centralisatie en desintegratie onder Karel V (1500-55-58)* (Deventer: Kluwer, 2015).

[76] His most-quoted work in the Dutch Republic is undoubtedly his *Notitia iuris belgici*. See e.g.: Margreet Ahsmann, 'Willem de Groot (1597–1662) en zijn studie te Leiden in het licht van brieven van zijn broer Hugo', *Tijdschrift voor Rechtsgeschiedenis* 50 (1982): 379.

[77] Verbeek, 'Franciscus Zypaeus en het kerkelijk gezag', 92.

juris belgici – useful works of reference for many generations of Netherlandish jurists and canonists. In the second half of the seventeenth century, Zypaeus's writings were still regularly quoted, especially by authors who were looking for information on the particular canon and civil law of the Low Countries, or for an authority to support ecclesiastical claims for jurisdiction. There is even evidence that his works were used for teaching purposes at the Louvain university in the 1670s. The great Louvain canon lawyer at the turn of the eighteenth century, Zeger Bernhard van Espen, also cited Zypaeus as one of his main authorities, although he often disagreed with him.[78]

Despite his rather nuanced views and positions, soon after his death Zypaeus was generally regarded as an ultramontanist. When the bishops of Mechelen and Ghent in the 1650s were accused of being Jansenists, the famous Brabantian lawyer Petrus Stockmans (1608–1671), later president of the sovereign Council of Brabant in Brussels, came to their aid. When censors then had to decide upon the catholicity of Stockmans's works on this issue, Zypaeus's views were apparently used as a reflection of the orthodox stance.[79] In the early eighteenth century, the famous church historian Jean-François Foppens (1689–1761) praised Zypaeus as an ultramontanist in his *Bibliotheca belgica*.[80] That passage was copied over and over again in later biographical pieces.[81] Léon Verbeek s.d.b. was the first to successfully question that reputation.[82] We have seen how Zypaeus, as archdeacon and vicar general of the Antwerp diocese, was first and foremost a pragmatic defender of the

---

[78] See, for instance: Carlotta Latini, 'Le droit d'asile dans la pensée de van Espen: profils juridiques de la formation du *ius publicum ecclesiasticum* dans les Pays-Bas catholiques', in *Zeger-Bernard van Espen at the Crossroads of Canon Law, History, Theology and Church-State Relations*, eds. Guido Cooman, Maurice van Stiphout, and Bart Wauters (Louvain: Peeters, 2003), 127–128.

[79] Lucien Ceyssens, 'Pierre Stockmans et ses opuscules jansénistes', *Archives et bibliothèques de Belgique* 36 (1965): 67, footnote 7.

[80] Joannes Franciscus Foppens, *Bibliotheca belgica* (Brussels: per Petrum Foppens, 1739), vol. 1, 317–318: 'Authoritatis Pontificiae et Jurisdictionis Ecclesiasticae assertor strenuus, ac Molinaei, Fevreti, Espeniique pseudo-principiis omnino oppositus'. On Foppens, see Bert Woestenborghs, *Jan Frans Foppens (1689–1761): kerkhistoricus* (Louvain, 1989); Frédéric baron de Reiffenberg, *Notice sur Jean-François Foppens* (Brussels, 1839), 4: '[Il] se piquait de la plus scrupuleuse orthodoxie'. In the earlier 1643 edition of the *Bibliotheca belgica* by Valerius Andreas, Zypaeus was mentioned but no reference was made to ultramontanism. See Valerius Andreas, *Bibliotheca belgica* (Louvain: Typis Iacobi Zegers, 1643), 247–248.

[81] For similar remarks, see Petrus Josephus Goetschalckx, *De geschiedenis der kanunniken van O.-L.-V.-kapittel te Antwerpen (1585–1700)* (Antwerp, 1929), 160–163; Johann Friedrich von Schulte, 'Zype, Franz van den (Zypaeus)', *Allgemeine deutsche Biographie* 45 (1900), 579 ('Sein kirchenrechtlicher Standpunkt ist der streng curiale (…). [Er] ist (…) durch seine Schriften besonders in Rom zu Ansehen gelangt und eine Stütze des Ultramontanismus geworden'); Feije, *De Francisci Zypaei vita* (Louvain, 1852).

[82] Verbeek, 'Franciscus Zypaeus en het kerkelijk gezag', 91–135.

rights of the Netherlandish Church against too much involvement by the Habsburg monarchs, but also against too great control by the Roman authorities.

RECOMMENDED READINGS

Feije, H. J. *De Francisci Zypaei vita et meritis oratio quam die XXVIII mensis Julii MDCCCLI habuit Henricus Joannes Feije*. Lovanii: typis C.-J. Fonteyn, 1852.

Lesaffer, R. 'Vernulaeus, Zypaeus en Tuldenus: het recht van de oorlog in de Spaanse Nederlanden tijdens de laatste fase van de Tachtigjarige Oorlog (1621–1648)'. *Ex officina* 8 (1991): 32–70.

Lesaffer, R. 'Iudex, magistratus, senator (1633): Franciscus Zypaeus over het publiekrecht'. In *Interactie tussen wetgever en rechter voor de Trias Politica*, edited by E. J. M. F. C. Broers and B. C. M. Jacobs. The Hague, 2004, 29–49.

Verbeek, L. 'Franciscus Zypaeus en het kerkelijk gezag'. *Bijdragen tot de geschiedenis* 52 (1969): 91–135.

Verbeek, L. 'François Zypaeus (1580–1650). Juriste belge'. *Tijdschrift voor Rechtsgeschiedenis* 36.2 (1968): 267–311.

Wauters, B. *Recht als religie. Canonieke onderbouw van de vroegmoderne staatsvorming in de Zuidelijke Nederlanden*. Louvain: Universitaire Pers Leuven, 2005.

6

Hugo Grotius

Janwillem Oosterhuis

BIOGRAPHICAL INTRODUCTION[1]

Hugo de Groot (alias Hugo Grotius, 1583–1645) lived his entire life during the Dutch Revolt (1568–1648) against Spain. This revolt was importantly about maintaining local privileges and autonomy against the Habsburg centralization politics but also about the profession of the new Reformed religion in the Low Countries.[2] Particularly in Grotius's native Holland, the Reformed religion traditionally had included 'strict' ('precise', *precieze*, later also called Calvinist) and 'moderate' ('pliable', *rekkelijke*, later also called Arminian) denominations.[3] The consolidation of the Dutch Republic as an independent power and the simultaneous controversies between the various Reformed denominations that were tearing his native Holland apart would crucially shape Grotius's life and work.

Grotius was born on 10 April 1583 in Delft, Holland, into a respected, wealthy, and learned patrician family, as Cornets de Groot, son of Jan (Cornets) de Groot (1554–1649) and Aeltje Borre van Overschie (1561–1643). His father adhered to the Reformed religion, whereby the family would be characterized as moderate.[4] Grotius had an important teacher and example in

---

[1] My thanks to the participants in this volume's symposium held at Maastricht University in March 2019 for their comments, particularly Jan Hallebeek and Matthijs de Blois.
[2] Jonathan Irvine Israel, *The Dutch Republic: Its Rise, Greatness, and Fall, 1477–1806* (Oxford: Clarendon Press, 1998), 129–196.
[3] See e.g. A. Th. van Deursen, *Bavianen en slijkgeuzen: kerk en kerkvolk ten tijde van Maurits en Oldebarnevelt* (Franeker: Van Wijnen, 1991), 1–5, 227; Israel, *Dutch Republic*, 392. On the ambiguity of the term Calvinism, see Todd Rester, 'Describing Calvinism', in *Cultures of Calvinism in Early Modern Europe*, eds. Crawford Gribben and Graeme Murdock (New York, NY: Oxford University Press, 2019), 15–36.
[4] See Henk Nellen, *Hugo Grotius: a lifelong struggle for peace in church and state, 1583–1645*, trans. J. C. Grayson (Leiden; Boston: Brill, 2015), 16–17. His mother was most likely still Roman Catholic when she married Jan de Groot in 1581 and his father would only become a member

his father, including in respect of his irenicism.[5] Between 1594 and 1598, at Leiden University, Grotius appeared to have mainly read philosophy, philology, classical languages – Latin, Greek, and Hebrew – and law. His teachers notably included Joseph Justus Scaliger (1540–1609) and Franciscus Junius (1545–1602).[6] During the last two years of his studies, he boarded with the Junius family. In these formative years, Grotius appears to have been crucially shaped by the strong irenic convictions and devout Christian lifestyle of his teacher Franciscus Junius, a strict but irenic Calvinist.[7] Near the end of his studies, in March 1598, Grotius accompanied a diplomatic mission to France, led by inter alia Johan van Oldenbarnevelt (1547–1619), the Grand Pensionary of the States of Holland. On this journey, Grotius received a doctorate in Law of the prestigious Orléans University. In 1599, he established himself as advocate in the legal and political centre of Holland, The Hague. In his first Hague years, he boarded at the house of Johannes Wtenbogaert (1557–1644), one of the leaders of the moderate denomination within the Reformed religion and chaplain of stadtholder Maurice of Nassau (1567–1625). These were formative years, too: Wtenbogaert had a deep impact on Grotius by way of his Christian admonitions and irreproachable conduct.[8] Unsurprisingly, in 1603, Grotius strongly supported the appointment of Wtenbogaert's friend Jacobus Arminius (1560–1609) – leader of the moderate denomination and the giver of

---

of the Dutch Reformed Church in 1614. Before officially joining the Reformed Church, many people were 'devotees' ('*liefhebbers*') of the Reformed religion: the difference, however, between member ('*lidmaat*') and devotee should not be exaggerated, see e.g. van Deursen, *Bavianen*, 128–129.

[5] See Nellen, *Grotius*, 16–24, 30–31. Jan de Groot had studied philosophy and law at Douai and subsequently Leiden University, where he had been a pupil of Justus Lipsius (1547–1606). See also G. H. M. Posthumus Meyjes, 'Hugo Grotius as an Irenicist', in *The world of Hugo Grotius (1583–1645): proceedings of the International Colloquium organized by the Grotius Committee of the Royal Netherlands Academy of Arts and Sciences, Rotterdam 6–9 April 1983* (Amsterdam [etc.]: APA-Holland University Press, 1984), 43–63, at 48; Edwin Rabbie, 'Het irenisme van Hugo de Groot', in *Jaarboek van de Maatschappij der Nederlandse Letterkunde te Leiden (1992–1993)* (Leiden: Maatschappij der Nederlandse Letterkunde, 1994), 56–72, at 56.

[6] See Nellen, *Grotius*, 36–40.

[7] See Nellen, *Grotius*, 35–36, 77. On Franciscus Junius, see B. A. Venemans, 'Franciscus Junius', in *Biografisch lexicon voor de geschiedenis van het Nederlandse protestantisme*, ed. D. Nauta (Kampen: Kok, 1983), 275–278; Todd M. Rester and Andrew M. McGinnis, 'Introduction', in Franciscus Junius, *The Mosaic Polity*. Translated by Todd M. Rester; edited by Andrew M. McGinnis (Grand Rapids, MI: CLP Academic, 2015), xix–xxvi. Todd Rester, *Theologia Viatorum: Institutional continuity and the reception of a theological framework from Franciscus Junius's De Theologia Vera to Bernhardinus De Moor's Commentarius Perpetuus* (PhD diss., Calvin Theological Seminary, 2016).

[8] See e.g. Nellen, *Grotius*, 74–77. See also H. J. M. Nellen, 'Een tweespan voor de arminiaanse wagen: Grotius en Wtenbogaert', in *De Hollandse jaren van Hugo de Groot (1583–1645)*, eds. H. J. M. Nellen and J. Trapman (Hilversum: Verloren, 1996), 161–177.

its name – as Divinity professor at Leiden, as successor to the deceased Junius.[9] During these years, Grotius must have formed most of his ideas and convictions about faith, religion, and society, convictions to which he would adhere for the rest of his life.[10] In 1607, at the age of 24, he became Advocate-Fiscal of Holland, Zeeland, and West-Frisia. The next year, he married Maria van Reigersberch (1589–1653), member of a prominent, rather 'precise', Zeeland family. In 1609, the Twelve Years' Truce was established between Spain and the new Dutch Republic: as many had feared, among them Grotius himself, the smouldering dispute between 'precise' and 'moderate' soon erupted, particularly in Holland, culminating in the feud between Arminius and Franciscus Gomarus (1563–1641), also a Divinity professor at Leiden. The religious controversy ultimately concerned the issue of predestination: was faith the result of predestination, that is, God's will, as Gomarus – in line with Calvin – learnt? Or was predestination the result of faith, that is, the free human will, as Arminius learnt?[11] Importantly this religious controversy soon concentrated on the States' authority in confessional and ecclesiastical matters.[12] During the Troubles of the Truce Years (*Bestandstwisten*, 1609–1621), Grotius strongly supported the policy of Oldenbarnevelt and the States of Holland to enforce confessional tolerance within the Reformed Church, in spite of a large group within the church wanting to uphold

---

[9] See Nellen, *Grotius*, 84.
[10] See Nellen, *Grotius*, 759–763.
[11] See A. Th.van Deursen, 'Maurits van Nassau, 1567–1625. De winnaar die faalde', in *De Gouden Eeuw compleet* (Amsterdam: Uitgeverij Bert Bakker, 2010), 839–1128 at 1035. See also e.g. van Deursen, *Bavianen*, 227–229; Edwin Rabbie, 'Introduction Ordinum', in *Hugo Grotius, Ordinum Hollandiae ac Westfrisiae pietas. Critical edition with English translation and commentary by E. Rabbie* (Leiden: Brill, 1995), 2–10; Edwin Rabbie, 'Grotius' denken over kerk en staat', in *De Hollandse jaren van Hugo de Groot (1583–1645)*, eds. H. J. M. Nellen and J. Trapman (Hilversum: Verloren, 1996), 193–205; Harm-Jan van Dam, 'Introduction', in *Hugo Grotius. De imperio summarum potestatum circa sacra (1617/1647). Critical edition with introduction, English translation, and commentary by Harm-Jan van Dam*, Volume I. (Leiden: Brill, 2001), 7–8; Nellen, *Grotius*, 124–127. Recently on Arminian theology, see Jordan J. Ballor, Matthew T. Gaetano, and David S. Sytsma, eds., *Beyond Dordt and 'de Auxiliis': The Dynamics of Protestant and Catholic Soteriology in the Sixteenth and Seventeenth Centuries* (Leiden: Brill, 2019).
[12] On the deep interrelation between church and state in this period, see van Deursen, *Bavianen*, 298–309; van Deursen, 'Maurits', 1035–1078. For Early Modern Calvinist ideas and theories on the relation between church and state, see e.g. John Witte Jr, *The Reformation of Rights: Law, Religion and Human Rights in Early Modern Calvinism* (Cambridge: Cambridge University Press, 2008), 62–76, 89–94, 122–134. Although since the beginning of the Dutch Revolt around 1568, the Reformed Church had developed relatively independently from the authorities, soon the various States started to take more and more control in Church matters. See Rabbie, 'Introduction Ordinum', 11–29; van Dam, 'Introduction', 10–13.

Calvinist orthodoxy.¹³ In 1613, Grotius became Pensionary of Rotterdam and Delegated Member of the States of Holland. In this capacity, he drafted and enforced the Resolution for Confessional Peace (1614) and, more controversially, the Strict Resolution (1617): in trying to get a grip on the escalating confessional troubles, Oldenbarnevelt and the States decisively strengthened Holland's independence from the rest of the Republic, thus weakening its fragile unity and threatening Maurice's position as Captain General. In response, Maurice together with the States-General seized control: in 1618 Oldenbarnevelt, Grotius, Rombout Hogerbeets (1561–1625) and Gilles van Leedenberch (1550–1618) were arrested on suspicion of treason.[14] A year later, Grotius was sentenced to lifelong imprisonment in Loevestein castle. In 1621, Grotius, with the help of his wife, famously managed to escape in a book chest. Until 1631, he stayed in exile in Paris, where he wrote two of his most influential works, *De iure belli ac pacis* (1625) and *De veritate religionis Christianae* (1627).[15] In 1631, he returned to Holland, in vain expecting amnesty from Maurice's successor, Frederick Henry (1584–1647). The following year, Grotius had to flee Holland again and this time for good.[16] After living for two years in Hamburg, he was appointed in 1635 as Swedish ambassador with the French king, which he remained for ten years, with varying success.[17] In this period, he finally finished his Bible Annotations.[18] Returning from a visit to Queen Christine in Stockholm, where his ambassadorship was not extended, Grotius was shipwrecked at the Baltic Sea and died in Rostock at 28 August 1645. He was buried in the New Church in Delft.[19]

---

[13] See Nellen, *Grotius*, 171–177. On the ecclesiastical side of the conflict, see fundamentally van Deursen, *Bavianen*, in particular 241–245.
[14] In general e.g. van Deursen, 'Maurits', 1035–1078. On Grotius's role, see Nellen, *Grotius*, 171–191, 224–232, 264–272; Rabbie, 'Grotius', 202–203; Harm-Jan van Dam, 'De imperio summarum potestatum circa sacra', in Henricus Johannes Maria Nellen and Edwin Rabbie, eds., *Hugo Grotius – Theologian. Essays in Honour of G. H. M. Posthumus Meyjes* (Leiden: Brill, 1994), 19–39, at 20–21; van Dam, 'Introduction', 13–30. See also e.g. van Deursen, *Bavianen*, 241–275.
[15] See Nellen, *Grotius*, 272–442.
[16] During this interlude, he also stayed at Rotterdam where he paid a visit to the statue of Erasmus that he as a Pensionary had helped to erect, showing his identification with his famous compatriot. See Nellen, *Grotius*, 443–462.
[17] See Nellen, *Grotius*, 486–719.
[18] On these annotations, see e.g. H. J. de Jonge, 'Hugo Grotius: exégète du Nouveau Testament', in *The world of Hugo Grotius (1583–1645): proceedings of the International Colloquium organized by the Grotius Committee of the Royal Netherlands Academy of Arts and Sciences, Rotterdam 6–9 April 1983* (Amsterdam [etc.]: APA-Holland University Press, 1984), 97–115.
[19] See Nellen, *Grotius*, 720–736.

MAJOR THEMES AND CONTRIBUTIONS

A Humanist Christian

Grotius was born and raised a Protestant in a fundamentally changing Europe: the unity of faith was lost in the Reformation and the many ensuing Christian denominations and religions became entangled in bitter controversies and wars: struggling for internal dominance within emerging separate states, while Christian states were also vehemently fighting each other.[20] For Grotius, as a humanist Christian, the glorification of God on earth through a pious, virtuous, and above all peaceful life, and the eventual unity with Him in the afterlife, appear to be fundamental for his thinking and writing: all existence had teleological significance.[21] The glorification of God as the ultimate purpose of human existence can already be found in a religious play of 1601, *Adamus exul*, written shortly after his studies and probably while boarding with Wtenbogaert:[22] Adam and Eve were meant to glorify

---

[20] See e.g. Brian Tierney, 'Grotius. From Medieval to Modern', in *The idea of natural rights: studies on natural rights, natural law and church law, 1150–1625* (Atlanta, GA: Scholars Press, 1997), 316–342, at 341–342; Charles Taylor, *A Secular Age* (Cambridge, MA; London: The Belknap Press of Harvard University Press, 2007), 159–160, 237.

[21] See Olivier O'Donovan and Joan Lockwood O'Donovan, 'Hugo Grotius (1583–1646)', in *From Irenaeus to Grotius: A Sourcebook in Christian Political Thought, 100–1625*, eds. Olivier O'Donovan and Joan Lockwood O'Donovan (Grand Rapids, MI: Eerdmans, 1999), 787–820, at 789, and more recently Janne E. Nijman, 'Grotius' Imago Dei Anthropology: Grounding Ius Naturae et Gentium', in *International Law and Religion: Historical and Contemporary Perspectives*, eds. Martti Koskenniemi, Mónica García-Salmones Rovia, and Paolo Amorosa (Oxford: Oxford University Press, 2017), 87–110, particularly 94. Compare also e.g. Posthumus Meyjes, 'Grotius', 39; Posthumus Meyjes, 'Introduction', in *Hugo Grotius, Meletius, sive de iis quae inter Christianos conveniunt epistola. Critical Edition with Translation, Commentary and Introduction by G. H. M. Posthumus Meyjes* (Leiden: Brill, 1988), 38; Henk Jan de Jonge, 'Grotius' view of the Gospels and the Evangelists', in *Hugo Grotius – Theologian. Essays in Honour of G. H. M. Posthumus Meyjes*, eds. Henricus Johannes Maria Nellen and Edwin Rabbie (Leiden: Brill, 1994), 65–74, at 65–66; Jan Paul Heering, 'De veritate religionis christianae', in *Hugo Grotius – Theologian. Essays in Honour of G. H. M. Posthumus Meyjes*, eds. Henricus Johannes Maria Nellen and Edwin Rabbie (Leiden: Brill, 1994), 41–52, at 44–49; Jan-Paul Heering, *Hugo Grotius as Apologist for the Christian Religion: A Study of His Work De veritate religionis Christianae (1640)*, transl. J. C. Grayson (Leiden: Brill, 2004), 64. For a detailed review of works on Grotius as a theologian, see Florian Mühlegger, *Hugo Grotius: ein christlicher Humanist in politischer Verantwortung* (Berlin: Walter de Gruyter, 2007), 6–82.

[22] Together with his more Calvinist student friend Daniel Heinsius (1580–1655), later to become professor and librarian at Leiden, and secretary to the Synod of Dort (1618–19), Grotius wanted to improve classical drama; both were to write several plays. Grotius, as a true irenic, had intended *Adamus exul* as a play for all Christians, as he wrote in rather high hopes to Lipsius, who had returned to Leuven and Catholicism. See Nellen, *Grotius*, 30, 57–63.

God.[23] Moreover, they were able to do so, as they were created after the image of God, with reason, free will, and sociability, and even after the fall, they retained their divine spark.[24] Grotius considered human beings after the fall thus not completely deprived of all virtues:[25] rather, because of his remaining rationality, a human being is master over his own actions, that is, he has free choice, meaning that he can control other things[26] – in line with Erasmus and Arminius, but also Spanish Scholastics.[27] Created in God's image as sociable beings, a virtuous, God-pleasing life implied living in harmony and peace with fellow human beings, before ultimately being united with Him.[28] God had created society and human relations within it and God's laws thus had universal competence for society.[29] Although Grotius was educated decisively as a jurist, these theological opinions about the purpose and essence of humans and God's universal competence would fundamentally influence his legal writings.[30] Concerning the implications of God's universal competence, Grotius, although Protestant, stood essentially more in the Scholastic than in the recent Reformed tradition.[31] In several controversial legal issues, particularly the relation between state and church and more fundamentally the competence of divine law, Grotius would come into conflict with precise Calvinists. In these legal issues his

---

[23] Hugo Grotius, 'Adamus exul', in *The Celestial Cycle*, ed. Watson Kirkconnell (Toronto: University of Toronto Press, 1952), 139: 'Adam: "Let us give worship to that Author of all good, Him love the first, and follow equally the laws His wisdom hath ordain'd to avoid the fatal taste Of the forbidden tree, and feast on all the rest."'
[24] E.g. Grotius, 'Adamus exul', 103, 117, 119, 123. See also Nijman, 'Grotius', 94–95.
[25] Grotius, 'Adamus exul', 109. Nijman, 'Grotius', 95.
[26] Grotius, 'Adamus exul', 103, 107, 117, 119, 139, and 148–149. Nijman, 'Grotius', 102.
[27] See e.g. Eef Dekker, 'Was Arminius a Molinist?' *Sixteenth Century Journal* 27.2 (1996): 337–352; Nijman, 'Grotius', 91–93; Richard A. Muller, 'Arminius's "Conference" with Junius and the Protestant Reception of Molina's Concordia', in Ballor, Gaetano, and Sytsma, *Beyond Dordt*, 103–126; Jordan J. Ballor, 'In the Footsteps of the Thomists': an Analysis of Thomism in the Junius-Arminius Correspondence', in Ballor, Gaetano, and Sytsma, *Beyond Dordt*, 127–147; Keith D. Stanglin, 'Scientia Media: the Protestant Reception of a Jesuit Idea', in Ballor, Gaetano, and Sytsma, *Beyond Dordt*, 148–168.
[28] See e.g. Posthumus Meyjes, 'Grotius', 45; Heering, 'Vertiate', 44; Heering, *Grotius*, 67–69; De Jonge, 'Grotius', 66.
[29] See e.g. O'Donovan, 'Grotius', 789; Nijman, 'Grotius', 97.
[30] See e.g. Erik Franz Wolf, 'Hugo Grotius', in *Grosse Rechtsdenker der deutschen Geistesgeschichte* (Tübingen: Mohr, 1951), 252–305, at 254–256; O'Donovan, 'Grotius', 787–790; Olivier O'Donovan, 'The justice of assignment and subjective rights in Grotius', in *Bonds of Imperfection: Christian politics, past and present*, eds. Oliver O'Donovan and Joan Lockwood O'Donovan (Grand Rapids, MI: Eerdmans, 2004), 167–203, at 172–174; Nijman, 'Grotius', 97–98.
[31] On the Reformed tradition, see e.g. John Witte, Jr., *Law and Protestantism: the Legal Teachings of the Lutheran Reformation* (Cambridge [etc.]: Cambridge University Press, 2002); Witte, *Reformation*.

undogmatic irenicism[32] and disagreement with Calvinist theology became more outspoken, notably when comparing *De Indis* (1604–1606) with *De iure belli ac pacis* (1625), written respectively before and after Grotius's period in political power. This contribution will highlight the development of Grotius's Christian humanism – importantly also in contrast with Calvinist orthodoxy – and its influence on his legal works, notably *De Indis* and *De iure belli ac pacis*.

God's Universal Competence Through His Divine Will

God's universal competence appears central to Grotius's first more-sizeable legal treatise. The specific occasion was the capture of a rich Portuguese carrack, resulting in the question whether and when Christian states were justified in attacking another Christian state. In 1603, the Amsterdam Admiralty asked him to write a justification of the right to take prizes. Between 1604 and 1606, Grotius wrote *De Indis* (*On the Indies*, later called *De iure praedae, On the law of prizes*, 1604–1606).[33] In line with the occasion – and with the classics – Grotius in his introduction observed that justice could be a mean: 'It is wrong to inflict injury, but it is also wrong to endure injury.'[34] Generally, the foreign policy and the position of the new Republic in relation to the new world were at stake: 'To ascertain how much is owed to others and how much to oneself?'[35] To convince his Catholic, but nonetheless Christian, adversaries, Grotius started from common ground: God's will was the ultimate foundation or source of law and primary law of nature: 'What God has shown to be His Will, that is law.'[36] Grotius nevertheless immediately stressed the

---

[32] See e.g. J. Trapman, 'Grotius and Erasmus', in *Hugo Grotius – Theologian. Essays in Honour of G. H. M. Posthumus Meyjes*, eds. Henricus Johannes Maria Nellen and Edwin Rabbie (Leiden: Brill, 1994), 77–98, at 94.

[33] Hugo Grotius, *Commentary on the Law of Prize and Booty (De iure praedae commentarius)*, edited and with an introduction by Martine Julia van Ittersum (Indianapolis, IN: Liberty Fund, 2006).

[34] Grotius, *De iure praedae*, 12. O'Donovan, 'Justice', 175. For Tuck, this is an important reason to consider Grotius as precursor of Hobbes, Richard Tuck, *The Rights of War and Peace: Political Thought and the International Order from Grotius to Kant* (Oxford [etc.]: Oxford University Press, 1999), 88–89, 109.

[35] Grotius, *De iure praedae*, 13–4. See e.g. Nijman, 'Grotius', 102.

[36] Grotius, *De iure praedae*, 19. Grotius therefore distinguished clearly between God's will – including divine law originating from this will, as revealed e.g. in Scripture – and natural law, laid down in nature – thus created by God as well. Reformed theologians such as Calvin, Beza, Althusius, or Knox generally did not make such clear distinction between divine law and natural law, see e.g. Witte, *Reformation*, 59, 127, 157–158 and Stumpf, *Grotian*, 75–78.

rationality of this law, knowable via the human ratio.[37] God created all living beings with self-love to preserve their existence, but also with love for others thanks to the natural properties of *ratio* and *appetitus societatis* imprinted in the human mind.[38] Shaped after the image of God, human beings – even after the fall – thus had free will, and were rational and social, and there was universal consensus about this ('*consensus gentium*'): this was the secondary law of nature or the primary law of nations.[39] The rules on self-defence, on the acquisition of property, and on the defence of ownership thus had a legal basis in the natural law principle of self-preservation and self-love.[40] Consequently, Grotius acknowledged a right of resistance of the Dutch against their sovereign prince, Philip, in defence of 'lives, property and lawful liberty'.[41] Self-love, however, needed to be kept within the limits of justice, and Grotius considered humans – created after God's image – by nature capable and obliged to 'care for the welfare of others'.[42] In this scheme of laws and rules, and also using Roman legal concepts,[43] human sociality – 'the welfare of his fellow beings', 'justice properly' or 'social virtue' – thus sets limits to the rules of self-love and self-preservation.[44] Mutual care generates laws of non-maleficence, respect for property, rectification of injuries, and repayment of benefits, leading to rules of commutative justice that prevail between private parties.[45] In the course of a revision of the manuscript, Grotius distinguished between 'distributive'[46] and 'compensatory' justice, the latter including justice in punishment:

---

[37] Grotius, *De iure praedae*, 53–54. See Tierney, 'Grotius', 327, who argues that a possible shift from a voluntarist position in *De Indis*, to a more rationalist approach in *De Iure Belli ac Pacis*, is primarily a matter of emphasis. In addition, Besselink argues that Grotius did not adhere to a strict voluntarist position in *De Indis*; rather, Grotius considered God, who is just, as the ultimate source of law, because God willed his creation. See Leonard Besselink, 'The impious hypothesis revisited', *Grotiana* 9 (1989): 3–63, at 47–54.

[38] Grotius, *De iure praedae*, 20–21, 24–25. Nijman, 'Grotius', 94–95, 98, 102. On a possible Stoic influence on Grotius in this respect, see Hans W. Blom and Laurens C. Winkel, eds., *Grotius and the Stoa* (Assen: Royal van Gorcum, 2004); Taylor, *Secular*, 156.

[39] Grotius, *De iure praedae*, 25: 'What the common consent of mankind has shown to be the will of all that is law'. Nijman, 'Grotius', 96, 99.

[40] Grotius, *De iure praedae*, 21. See O'Donovan, 'Justice', 175; Nijman, 'Grotius', 102.

[41] Grotius, *De iure praedae*, 400; compare also 140, 244–247, 399. See e.g. Arthur C. Eyffinger and Bernardus Petrus Vermeulen, *Hugo de Groot. Denken over oorlog en vrede* (Baarn: Ambo, 1991), 15.

[42] Grotius, *De iure praedae*, 24–28. Nijman, 'Grotius', 103.

[43] See Laurens Winkel, 'Problems of legal systematization from *De iure praedae* to *De iure belli ac pacis*', *Grotiana* 26–28 (2005–2007): 61–78.

[44] Grotius, *De iure praedae*, 24, 28. O'Donovan, 'Justice', 175.

[45] Grotius, *De iure praedae*, 27. According to Tuck, Grotius limits justice to commutative, i.e. distributive, justice. Tuck, *Rights*, 88–89. See also O'Donovan, 'Justice', 174–175.

[46] Or, probably more correctly, 'assignative' justice, see O'Donovan, 'Justice', 175–177.

Compensatory justice, on the other hand, is concerned not only with the preservation of equality among individuals, but also with the bestowal of appropriate honours and rewards upon deserving patriots, and with the punishment of persons who are injuring the community.[47]

Here, Grotius thus generally limited justice in punishment to compensatory justice; he would revisit the question of justice in punishment several times in later writings.

In *De Indis*, Grotius leaned heavily on the learned Roman law, biblical sources, and antiquity (Cicero, Seneca), but also derived arguments from Early and Late Scholastic scholars, particularly Thomas Aquinas, Suarez, Vittorio, and likely – although without explicitly mentioning him – Lessius.[48] Grotius would apply this typically legal technique – using an adversary's own arguments – throughout his apologetic works, whether legal, theological, or political.[49] The biblical passages, from both the Old and the New Testament, he often interpreted in his own way, in typical Protestant fashion.[50] *De Indis* remained unpublished during Grotius's lifetime.

A few years later, however, after he had become Advocate-Fiscal (1607–1614), he published a chapter of *De Indis* where he defended the principle that the seas are open to all states, as *Mare liberum* (*The open sea*, 1609). He changed very little of the content or ultimate justification, and hardly used new sources, although in the introduction he unambiguously rejected the opinion that justice and injustice do not essentially differ.[51] *Mare liberum* had been published primarily to justify Dutch maritime politics and colonial expansion in the new world. More specifically, the book was meant to support the position of the Dutch Republic as an independent state vis-à-vis Spain in the negotiations for a truce.[52] In 1609, the Twelve Years' Truce was indeed concluded.

---

[47] Grotius, *De iure praedae*, 29, 37.
[48] Fundamentally, see Peter Haggenmacher, *Grotius et la doctrine de la guerre juste* (Paris: PUF, 1983). See also e.g. R. Feenstra, 'Quelques remarques sur les sources utilisées par Grotius dans ses travaux de droit naturel', in *The world of Hugo Grotius (1583–1645): Proceedings of the International Colloquium organized by the Grotius Committee of the Royal Netherlands Academy of Arts and Sciences, Rotterdam 6–9 April 1983* (Amsterdam [etc.]: APA-Holland University Press, 1984), 65–81, at 73–81; Nijman, 'Grotius', 99, 103–105.
[49] See e.g. Tierney, 'Grotius', 316.
[50] Compare e.g. Mark Somos, 'Secularization in "De iure praedae": from Bible criticism to international law', *Grotiana* 26–28 (2005–2007): 147–191.
[51] Hugo de Groot, *Mare liberum, De vrije zee*, translation in Dutch and introduction by Arthur Eyffinger (Den Haag: Jongbloed, 2009), Ad Principes populosque liberos orbis Christiani § 1 ('iustum atque iniustum non suapte natura').
[52] See Eyffinger, 'Inleiding', in De Groot, *Mare liberum*, 11–87, at 14, 47, 67–68.

Natural Religion

During the Truce, the controversy between strict Calvinists and moderate Arminians flared up, in what came to be known as the Troubles of the Truce Years. Grotius did what was in his power to appease the opposing parties. In 1610, he published *De antiquitate reipublicae Batavicae* in which he created a common birth myth for Holland, arguing that since Roman times the Batavians had always had an independent, aristocratic form of government. His indirect plea to overcome religious diversity by looking at historical commonalities was ignored.[53] Importantly, Grotius considered taking a stance in and about the confessional controversy between Arminius and Gomarus itself. Earlier, in an unpublished juvenile tract *De republica emendanda* (c. 1600),[54] Grotius had already expressed his concern about religious controversies threatening a peaceful, virtuous life within the new Dutch Republic:

> The one and true religion is now publicly accepted; however, our sinfulness has effectively prevented God from reaching his aim, that is, the unanimous embracing of this religion by the whole nation. In this respect one must not underestimate the extent to which the furtherance of the true religion can be impeded by the overcharged fanaticism of one group and the indifference of others: the one has led people to set off in the wrong direction, the other to the right path being neglected altogether.[55]

With overcharged fanaticism, Grotius most likely had the dogmatism of precise Calvinists in mind: in his play *Adamus exul*, Satan's reference to predestination seems at least ambiguous.[56] This struggle between 'precise' and 'moderate' had been inherent to the Reformed religion ('the one and true religion') within the emerging Republic.[57] In 1611, Grotius wrote *Meletius*, named after an Eastern orthodox patriarch, Meletius Pegas (1549–1601).[58] In this apologetic but also irenic work, Grotius stressed the unity between Christians and their religions. He applied a similar method to

---

[53] See Nellen, *Grotius*, 110–112.
[54] Hugo de Groot, 'De Republica Emendanda: a juvenile tract by Hugo Grotius on the emendation of the Dutch polity (ed. by Arthur Eyffinger; in collab. with P. A. H. de Boer, J. Th. de Smidt, L. E. van Holk)', *Grotiana* 5 (1984): 3–135.
[55] Grotius, 'Republica', § 6, 70–71. See also e.g. Grotius, 'Republica', § 57, 114–115.
[56] Admittedly, Grotius appears to mock the Calvinistic dogma of predestination when he made Satan reply to Eve: 'Do not believe that through the loss of one small apple Thy certain death must straightway be the consequence. How can those perish whom to everlasting life God hath predestined?' Grotius, 'Adamus exul', 161.
[57] Van Deursen, *Bavianen*, 227ff; Israel, *Dutch Republic*, 129–196.
[58] Posthumus Meyjes, 'Introduction', 17–18. See also Mühlegger, *Grotius*, 83–137.

theology as he had applied to law in *De Indis*. Grotius concentrated on those elements of Christian faith that were necessary or fundamental to lead a God-pleasing life:[59] these elements had to be rationally developed, to create consensus among all people.[60] If unnecessary or not fundamental, dogmas had to be left open, particularly if they could not be rationally understood. Essential for Grotius's argument was again the principle that humans were rational, social beings with a free will – including after the fall in Paradise.[61] This view on humanity, already present in *Adamus exul*, Grotius stressed at various places in *Meletius*.[62] Because humans are rational, social, and with a free will – and thus responsible for their deeds – they can understand or recognize natural law and natural justice.[63] Moreover, humans have a social appetite, because as created after God's image, they have a natural inclination and duty to love other humans, who are equally bearers of God's image.[64] As a humanist Christian, the Early Church exemplified for Grotius the idea that religious diversity had been tolerated initially.[65]

Grotius sent a manuscript to several friends for critical comments, including to a more precise Calvinist theologian, Antonius Walaeus (1573–1639).[66] Walaeus lauded the purpose of the work, but was critical on three points, namely: that the community of Christians seemed to include even Roman Catholics; the question of why the trinity was not included as an essential element of true faith; and the emphasis on the free will of humankind. As regards the inclusion of the Catholics, Grotius referred to Junius, a teacher they had in common and whom both revered, while the dogma of the Holy Trinity Grotius still thought incomprehensible and thus necessary. And although Walaeus thought the third point on free will the lesser problem,

---

[59] Hugo Grotius, *Meletius, sive de iis quae inter Christianos conveniunt epistola. Critical Edition with Translation, Commentary and Introduction by G. H. M. Posthumus Meyjes* (Leiden: Brill, 1988), § 13.

[60] Grotius, *Meletius*, § 6. Posthumus Meyjes, 'Introduction', 31–2. See also e.g. Christoph A. Stumpf, *The Grotian Theology of International Law: Hugo Grotius and the Moral Foundations of International Relations* (Berlin: De Gruyter, 2006), 51–57. On a possible Stoic influence on Grotius in this respect, see Blom and Winkel, *Stoa*; Taylor, *Secular*, 156.

[61] Grotius, *Meletius*, § 18. Even Calvinists, such as Duplessis Mornay (1549–1623) and later also Paulus Voet (1619–1667), importantly founded their apologetic works on the fact that humans were not completely deprived of rationality. See e.g. Heering, 'Veritate', 44–45; Johannes van Kralingen, 'Paulus Voet', in this volume.

[62] Grotius, *Meletius*, §§ 27–30, 35–36.

[63] Grotius, *Meletius*, §§ 41, 44, 55.

[64] Grotius, *Meletius*, §§ 68, 35, 9. They thus also have a natural duty to keep their promises, to stick to their given word, Grotius, *Meletius*, §§ 22, 83–86.

[65] See e.g. Eyffinger and Vermeulen, *De Groot*, 15; O'Donovan, 'Grotius', 789.

[66] See Posthumus Meyjes, 'Introduction', 44–60.

this was for Grotius apparently reason not to publish the manuscript: the free will or rather his Arminian anthropology was fundamental to the whole enterprise.[67] In the debate between Arminians and Calvinists, he tried to be acceptable to both parties in creating a common ground, a minimum set of principles acceptable to all. In the creation of this common ground, however, he needed a rational, social human being with a free will – completely in line with Arminian theology, but alienating for Calvinists.

Sovereignty of State over Church

Meanwhile the confessional dispute had obtained strong political dimensions, concerning the States' authority in confessional and ecclesiastical matters.[68] The States of Holland supported the appointment of the highly controversial Conrad Vorstius (1569–1622) as successor to the deceased Arminius. Vorstius was considered a Socinian and this made him unacceptable, particularly for the Calvinists, including for his intended colleague at Leiden, Gomarus, but also for Sibrandus Lubbertus (1555–1625), Divinity professor at the Franeker University, Frisia. Lubbertus informed the Archbishop of Canterbury of the heresies of the designated professor and the role of the States of Holland, and he in turn notified King James I (1566–1625) of the matter. King James immediately demanded the States to cancel the appointment. In May 1613, Lubbertus published a massive book against the appointment of Vorstius, in which he discredited him and the Arminians as Socinians and criticized the confessional policy of the States of Holland. Primarily in reaction to Lubbertus's last attack, Grotius, having meanwhile acted as Pensionary of Rotterdam, fiercely defended the position of the States of Holland in *Ordinum Hollandiae ac Westfrisiae pietas* (1613).[69] Elegantly and with great erudition, he not only defended the States' course of action in appointing Vorstius[70] – although without defending Vorstius himself – but also emphasized the orthodoxy of Arminius and the traditional tolerance within the Dutch Reformed Church.[71] Finally, and at length, he stressed the supremacy of the States of Holland in religious matters and thus the right to enforce religious

---

[67] See Posthumus Meyjes, 'Introduction', 46–57. Also Nijman, 'Grotius', 94–96.
[68] See e.g. Rabbie, 'Introduction Ordinum', 11–16.
[69] See e.g. Rabbie, 'Introduction Ordinum', 1–35; van Dam, 'Introduction', 1–13; Mühlegger, *Grotius*, 139–143; Nellen, *Grotius*, 171–173.
[70] Hugo Grotius, *Ordinum Hollandiae ac Westfrisiae pietas. Critical edition with English translation and commentary by E. Rabbie* (Leiden: Brill, 1995), §§ 9–34. See Rabbie, 'Introduction Ordinum', 83–84.
[71] Grotius, *Ordinum*, §§ 35–96. See Rabbie, 'Introduction Ordinum', 85–87.

toleration,[72] precisely to facilitate people in living a virtuous and peaceful life – to the glory of God and with the aim of being ultimately united with Him.[73] This last topic, supremacy in religious matters, had been debated for years in the Republic and in Holland in particular.[74] In the States' policy of tolerance, 'moderate' ministers were allowed to be ordained, including in congregations with an opposing 'precise' Calvinist majority. Generally, Calvinists considered the state responsible for the defence of the true religion, which truth should be defended by and in the public Reformed Church. Importantly, many Arminians, including Grotius, considered sovereignty in religious matters as belonging to the States of Holland,[75] while most Calvinists considered the States-General sovereign in these matters.[76]

A few years before *Ordinum pietas*, in 1610, Wtenbogaert, on commission of the States of Holland, published a *Treatise concerning the Office and Authority of a High Christian Government in the Matters of Church*,[77] defending the supremacy of the States of Holland in religious matters. Grotius's own preference for supremacy of the state in religious matters can already be found in *De republica emendanda*, written around 1600, in his Hague years as an advocate, while boarding with Wtenbogaert. When discussing improvements to the young republic, comparing it to biblical Israel, Grotius appears to take the supremacy of the state in religious matters more or less for granted. Ultimately, rulers were deemed responsible for the worship of God in correspondence with the true religion.[78] Grotius favoured a strong central government preventing internal strife, neglect of the true religion, and, foremost, civil war.[79]

---

[72] Grotius, *Ordinum*, §§ 97–203. See Rabbie, 'Introduction Ordinum', 87–91.
[73] Grotius, *Ordinum*, § 135. See Rabbie, 'Introduction Ordinum', 83–84.
[74] Compare e.g. Junius, *Mosaic*.
[75] Grotius, *Ordinum*, §§ 97–199 (174–239).
[76] See Margaret Hewett and Jan Hallebeek, 'The Prelate, the Praetor and the Professor: Antonius Matthaeus II and the Crimen Laesae Majestatis, Utrecht 1639–1640', *Legal History Review* 66 (1998): 115–150, at 123–126; Rabbie, 'Introduction Ordinum', 13–16; van Deursen, *Bavianen*, 298–309; van Deursen, 'Maurits', 1035–1078.
[77] Johannes Wtenbogaert, *Tractaet van t'ampt ende authoriteyt eener hoogher Christelicker overheydt in kerckelicke saecken* (The Hague: Hillebrant Jlacobsz., 1610). In detail, see Atsuko Fukuoka, *The Sovereign and the Prophets: Spinoza on Grotian and Hobbesian Biblical Argumentation* (Leiden: Brill, 2018), 18–25. See also van Dam, 'Introduction', 13.
[78] Grotius, 'Republica', § 8, 72–73. On political Hebraism, see e.g. Arthur Eyffinger, 'How wondrously Moses goes along with the House of Orange!' Hugo Grotius's 'De Republica Emendanda' in the context of the Dutch revolt', in *Political Hebraism: Judaic sources in early modern political thought*, eds. Gordon Schochet, Fania Oz-Salzberger, and Meirav Jones (Jerusalem; New York: Shalem Press, 2008), 107–147; Todd M. Rester and Andrew M. McGinnis, 'Introduction', xli–xlvii.
[79] See Grotius, 'Republica', § 57, 114–115. During his political career, he came to favour the States of Holland as the more appropriate body sovereign in these matters, see Leonard

An important improvement would be an aristocracy or even monarchy, but at a minimum a more centralized state led by a Council that was also experienced in church administration was needed.[80]

The publication of *Ordinum pietas* in 1613 turned out to be disastrous. Grotius lost all his carefully maintained impartiality: from now on, he became entrenched in the Arminian faction and the States' policy of enforced tolerance.[81] Many of Grotius's books written between 1613 and his imprisonment in August 1618 related to the confessional disputes and form an attempt to justify himself, but also a sincere effort to find a – rational – way out of these disputes together.[82]

In 1617, Grotius wrote *De imperio summarum potestatum circa sacra* in which he defended the supremacy of state over church in religious matters in far more detail. *De imperio* was also a response to Wallaeus's *The Office of Church-ministers* (1615).[83] Herein Wallaeus defended the principle that ministers stood directly or immediately below God – a counterattack against Wtenbogaert's *Treatise* of 1610 and also against *Ordinum pietas*.[84] The first chapter of *De imperio* dealt with the question why states were supreme in religious matters. Grotius gave a range of arguments, but importantly, secular authorities were entrusted to create a peaceful society in which people could live a virtuous and pious life. Moreover, it was in accordance with *ratio* to have just one supreme authority. To cement the supremacy of the state in religious matters, Grotius referred to a huge number of biblical and historical examples where this had been the case.[85] Magistrates should thus not depend on ministers for the truth in religious matters, because then the magistracy would become effectively dependent on church ministers.[86] For Grotius this had become a fundamental matter: it had to do not only with who mediated God's will to His people, but rather about the certainty of the divine will's mediators. According to Grotius, contemporary mediators – magistrates as well as churchmen – could not have absolute certainty about God's will

---

F. M. Besselink, 'The place of De Republica Emendanda in Grotius' works', *Grotiana* 7 (1986): 93–98, at 97–98.

[80] Grotius, 'Republica', § 59, 116–117.

[81] See e.g. C. van der Woude, *Hugo Grotius en zijn 'Pietas Ordinum Hollandiae ac Westfrisiae Vindicata'* (Kampen: J. H. Kok, 1961), 27–31; Rabbie, 'Introduction Ordinum', 61–72; Nellen, *Grotius*, 171–186.

[82] See e.g. van Dam, 'Introduction', 13–30.

[83] Antonius Wallaeus, *Het ampt der kerckendienaren* (Middelburg: Adriaen vanden Vivere, 1615).

[84] In detail see Fukuoka, *Sovereign*, 25, 28–34. See also van Dam, 'Introduction', 17.

[85] Grotius, *Imperio*, 1.4–14, 163–183. See also Mühlegger, *Grotius*, 374–383.

[86] Grotius, *Imperio*, 1.3, 159–163.

apart from via another divine revelation or indubitable proof of the mediator's truthfulness. The capacity for truthfulness was not a given, for instance, by virtue of being a Reformed minister or the Catholic Church.[87] Ecclesiastical judgements as source of law or truth were thus made unavailable by Grotius as an argument in the debate about the church–state relationship. Calvinist Reformers, on the other hand, had explicitly built law and society on their knowledge and mediation of the divine will, of which the Decalogue was the ultimate expression of the moral and enduring laws in the Bible.[88] *De imperio* would appear only posthumously, in 1647.

Vindicating the Lawful Order of the Universe

Around the same time as writing *De imperio*, Grotius published *Defensio fidei catholicae de satisfactione Christi adversus Faustum Socinum senensem* (1617) against the accusation that Arminians adhered to the heresy of Socinianism. Grotius chose to refute Socinus's theory about satisfaction through Christ, a relatively safe battleground.[89] According to Grotius, satisfaction was necessary before unity with God could be reached.[90] In a clear, unambiguous, and thoroughly juridical defence of the Protestant doctrine of satisfaction through Christ, Grotius also came to expand his theory on justice in punishment, touched upon in *De Indis*, and central to the question as to the capacity in which God inflicted or remitted punishment.[91] Although Socinus stated that God acted as a ruler, he essentially thought of the relation between God and sinner as that of commercial creditor and debtor, whereby God could waive his right to punish. According to Grotius, however, only superior authorities could inflict punishment, not private parties. Moreover, although Grotius submitted that God could indeed be considered an injured party, God had the right to punish or grant impunity in his capacity as superior authority, not as injured party. Rather, by nature an offended party had no right in punishment: only restoration or damages might be due. Therefore, superior authorities might justly remit punishment although restitution by damages is imposed on the guilty: 'So we see kings and other

---

[87] Grotius, *Imperio*, 6.3–6, 293–301 in particular 6.4, 294. In detail, see Fukuoka, *Sovereign*, 26–27, 43–52.
[88] See e.g. Witte, *Reformation*, 127–129, 183; Witte, *Protestantism*, 113–115; Janwillem Oosterhuis, 'Roman-Dutch Criminal Law and Calvinism: Calvinist Morality in De criminibus (1644) of Antonius Matthaeus II', in *Criminal Law and Morality in the Age of Consent. Interdisciplinary Perspectives*, ed. Aniceto Masferrer (Cham: Springer, 2020), 67–95, at 69–70, 73–81, 89–92.
[89] See Rabbie, 'Introduction Satisfactione', 1–26, particularly 16; van Dam, 'Introduction', 23, 29.
[90] See De Jonge, 'Grotius', 66.
[91] See O'Donovan, 'Justice', 176–177.

sovereign rulers pardoning the guilty and demanding only compensation for the damage.'[92] Contrary to God, however, secular authorities were not always free to remit from punishment, because they were subject to superior or even divine laws:

> The fact that lower magistrates cannot remit corporal punishments has nothing to do with any supposed right of the victim in punishment, for they would still not be able to do so even if the victim agreed; it is simply that the law of the superior has not devolved this power upon them – has explicitly ruled it out, in fact. A parallel situation must be supposed in the relation of kings to God, in respect of those crimes which they are absolutely required by divine law to punish.[93]

In inflicting or remitting punishment, superior authorities thus acted as rulers, like God vindicating the lawful order of the universe.[94] Finally, the right of punishment in the ruler is not a right of ownership or credit, because such rights are for the benefit of their possessor. Rather, the right of punishment is for the sake of the community, for punishment aims at the common good, and particularly at the preservation of order and deterrence.[95] *De satisfactione* shows that Grotius was not anti-dogmatic, just undogmatic.[96] The dogma of satisfaction through Christ was necessary and fundamental for living a virtuous life on earth and for unification with God in the afterlife and, importantly, could be rationally defended. This treatise, however, fell on unfertile soil: Grotius had made himself suspected of Socinianism and there was very little that he could do himself to rectify his name. Still, his treatise became one of the clearest and most influential descriptions of the substitution theory.[97]

God's Universal Competence Through Natural Law

Almost immediately after his imprisonment in August 1618, Grotius started to work on rehabilitation, including via writing works for a greater audience,

---

[92] Hugo Grotius, *Defensio fidei catholicae de satisfactione Christi adversus Faustum Socinum senensem* (1617). Edited by Edwin Rabbie, translated by Hotze Mulder (Assen: van Gorcum, 1990), 2.13.

[93] Grotius, *De satisfactione*, 2.13.

[94] See Grotius, *De satisfactione*, 2.4–15. See Rabbie, 'Introduction Satisfactione', 66–67; O'Donovan, 'Justice', 184; O'Donovan, 'Grotius', 792.

[95] On this teleological dimension of punishment, e.g. Jeremy Seth Geddert, 'Too subtle to satisfy many: was Grotius's teleology of punishment predestined to fail?' *Grotiana* 38 (2017): 46–69.

[96] See O'Donovan, 'Justice', 173.

[97] See e.g. Rabbie, 'Introduction Satisfactione', 40–50; O'Donovan, 'Justice', 173; O'Donovan, 'Grotius', 791–792.

such as the *Inleiding tot de Hollandsche rechts-geleertheyd* (*Introduction to the jurisprudence of Holland*), written around 1621 and published in 1631, but also an apologetic poem, *Proof of the true faith* (*Bewijs van den waren godsdienst*, 1622), expounding the views taken in *Meletius*.

Although the *Inleiding* concerns the customary laws of Holland, cast in a Roman law framework, in the Prolegomena Grotius unfolded some more general ideas about law. In contrast to the introduction to *De Indis*, Grotius now took his starting point in reason and innate natural law.[98] First, he distinguished between Right widely and narrowly understood,[99] where he immediately emphasizes the rationality of Right: 'Right widely understood is the correspondence of the act of a reasonable being with reason, in so far as another person is interested in such act.'[100] Right in a wider sense had to be conducted according to sociability – similar to Suarez, who had also included the element of sociability in his description of *ius*[101] – which enabled Grotius to include a wider sense of justice in his description of the positive laws of Holland. Subsequently, reworking Aristotelian and Thomist Scholastic distinctions, Grotius tried to incorporate this sociality in right narrowly understood – corresponding with subjective right – which can relate to merit or property:[102]

> Of the justice which has regard to right narrowly understood the kind which takes account of merit is called distributive justice; the other kind which gives heed to property is called commutative justice: the first commonly employs the rule of proportion, the second the rule of simple equality.[103]

Also, in his definition of law, Grotius stressed both rationality and sociality:

> Law (which is also sometimes called Right because it determines what is right) is a product of reason ordaining for the common good what is honourable, established and published by one who has authority over a community of men.[104]

---

[98] Compare e.g. Benardus Petrus Vermeulen, 'God, wil en rede in Hugo de Groots natuurrecht', *Wijsgerig Perspectief* 23 (1982/83): 54–59; G. A. van der Wal and B. P. Vermeulen, 'Grotius, Aquinas and Hobbes. Grotian Natural Law between Lex Aeterna and Natural Rights', *Grotiana* 16 (1995): 55–83, at 72–74.

[99] Grotius, *Inleiding tot de Hollandsche rechts-geleertheyd* ('s Gravenhage: Weduwe Hillebrant Iacobsz. van Wou, 1631), 1.1.4.

[100] Grotius, *Inleiding*, 1.1.5.

[101] See O'Donovan, 'Justice', 198.

[102] Grotius, *Inleiding*, 1.1.6–8. See O'Donovan, 'Justice', 199–202.

[103] Grotius, *Inleiding*, 1.1.10.

[104] Grotius, *Inleiding*, 1.2.1.

Grotius distinguished law in innate or natural law, which is dictated by reason, and positive law, which can be either human or divine: 'As Divine Law we acknowledge, since the coming of Jesus Christ, no other than that which God the Father has revealed to us through our Lord Christ.'[105] A few years later, Grotius would elaborate these ideas in *De iure belli ac pacis* – there he would also clarify what should *not* be acknowledged as universal divine volitional law.

After his escape from Loevestein, Grotius and his family went to Paris and lived for ten years on an allowance of the French king. In these years, he wrote and published *De iure belli ac pacis* (1625) and also *De veritate* (1627).[106] *De iure belli ac pacis* stands in the tradition of just war literature and is a kind of mirror for princes, dedicated to the French king Louis XIII. As with *De Indis*, Grotius was heavily indebted to the Late Scholastics, he picked up many themes of the moral theologians and fitted those in his own exposition.[107] Using for instance contract law theories of the Late Scholastics as his model of choice, he could treat states and individuals in a similar way.[108] Grotius, however, wrote in a lucid, humanist style, not limited in the way that the style of his Scholastic contemporaries was. In *De iure belli ac pacis*, Grotius managed to develop a profoundly social natural law.

In the Prolegomena, Grotius again refuted that there is no such thing as justice or Right.[109] To a far greater extent than in *De Indis*, Grotius's systematization of Right in *De iure belli ac pacis* is, importantly, inspired by Thomist–Aristotelian theories, as in the *Inleiding*.[110] Right is grounded in human nature – innate, as in the *Inleiding* – and one of the distinct features of human behaviour is desire for society. This social instinct is the source of a right in the technical sense of the term (i.e. a subjective right): restoring or not touching the property of others; keeping promises; paying damages; deserving punishment. From this sense of Right there flows a second, wider sense, viz. the capacity to exercise judgement. To this belongs inter alia the prudent allocation of resources in adding to what individuals and collectives

---

[105] Grotius, *Inleiding*, 1.2.9.
[106] *De veritate* is not further discussed, as it expands ideas developed already in *Meletius*, and was moreover published after *De iure belli ac pacis*. In detail on *De veritate*, see Heering, 'Veritate'.
[107] See again Haggenmacher, *Grotius*; Feenstra, 'Droit naturel'.
[108] See e.g. Wim Decock, *Theologians and contract law: the moral transformation of the ius commune (ca. 1500–1650)* (Leiden: M. Nijhoff Publishers, 2013), 208–212.
[109] See Grotius, *De iure belli ac pacis*, Prolegomena, 4–5.
[110] See e.g. Grotius, *De iure belli ac pacis*, Prolegomena, 42. See O'Donovan, 'Justice', 178–185, 187, 191–195, 198–202; O'Donovan, 'Grotius', 790; Stumpf, *Grotian*, 47. Winkel, 'Systematization', 74–77; van der Wal and Vermeulen, 'Grotius', 72–74.

own, depending on what is being done in each case and what the business in hand requires.[111] Then follows probably the most famous passage of *De iure belli ac pacis*, here quoted with the surrounding text:

> [11] These observations [on the narrower and wider senses of right] would have a place even were we to accept the infamous premise that God did not exist or did not concern himself with human affairs. As it is, however, rational reflection and unbroken tradition combine to inculcate the opposite presumption, which is then confirmed by a range of arguments and by miracles attested in every period of history. From this there follows a further principle: that we must obey God without qualification, as our creator to whom we owe ourselves and all that we possess. Especially must we do so since he has shown himself by many means to be both Supreme Good and Supreme Power. To those who obey him he is able to give the highest rewards, eternal rewards, indeed, since he is himself eternal; that he is willing to, is something we should anyway believe, but all the more so if he has promised it explicitly. And that, as we Christians believe with an assurance based on proofs of unquestionable reliability, is precisely what he has done. [12] This consequently affords a second source of Right to complement natural Right, a Right which originates in the free will of God, to which our very reason itself categorically demands that we defer. But, of course the natural Right we have discussed, both the 'social' and its wider sense, though deriving from principles intrinsic to man, can also be appropriately attributed to God, by whose will these principles have come to be operative in human nature.[112]

Although Grotius thus started to ground Right in human nature – the solid rationality of which Right he asserts by invoking the Scholastic commonplace that such Right would even exist God being absent[113] – the mere existence of such natural law[114] invokes the principle that we have to glorify God.[115] Our own reason indicates thus that natural law is complemented by divine law. Rather, natural law, both narrow and wide, as intrinsic to human nature, can ultimately be attributed to God, who created human nature. However, unlike

---

[111] See Grotius, *De iure belli ac pacis*, Prolegomena, 6–10. See Stumpf, *Grotian*, 30–36, 48–49. Compare also e.g. van der Wal and Vermeulen, 'Grotius', 75–77.

[112] Grotius, *De iure belli ac pacis*, Prolegomena, 11–12 (translation O'Donovan, 'Grotius', 794).

[113] Fundamentally still Besselink, 'Impious'.

[114] O'Donovan uses natural Right in his translation. Despite the merits of doing so, for reasons of consistency the term natural law is used throughout the text instead of natural Right; both denote law in an objective sense.

[115] On this teleological dimension, see Nijman, 'Grotius', 100–101; Stumpf, *Grotian*, 51–58; Taylor, *Secular*, 183–184.

in *De Indis*, Grotius no longer started with the divine will.[116] For Right, the starting point is natural law, knowable via reason. Right originating from divine will, that is, divine law, is merely complementary to natural law. That also may not come as a surprise, after Grotius argued extensively in *De imperio* that the divine will cannot be known with absolute certainty by humans, otherwise than through direct divine revelation.[117] Grotius underlined this complementary nature of divine law when he made a methodological point about the use of Scripture. First, he indirectly dismissed the Calvinist doctrine of equalizing the Old Testament, and particularly the Decalogue and the Mosaic Law pertaining to it, to natural law:[118]

> There are some who urge that the Old Testament sets forth the law of nature. Without doubt they are in error, for many of its rules come from the free will of God. And yet this is never in conflict with the true law of nature; and up to this point the Old Testament can be used as a source of the law of nature, provided we carefully distinguish between the law of God, which God sometimes executes through men, and the law of men in their relations with one another.[119]

Although the Mosaic laws were given to the Jews and obliged only them,[120] Grotius regularly referred to the Old Testament, including the Decalogue and the Mosaic rules pertaining to it, as the Mosaic laws necessarily cannot be contrary to the law of nature.[121] Grotius for example justified his rejection of capital punishment of thieves with reference to the Law of Moses:

> Altogether worthy of approval is the opinion of Scotus, that it is not right to condemn any one to death except for the crimes which the law of Moses punished with death, or, in addition, for crimes which, judged by a fair standard, are equally heinous. For in this so serious matter it seems possible to obtain a knowledge of the divine will, which alone gives peace of mind from no other source than from that law, which does not with certainty appoint for the thief the penalty of death.[122]

---

[116] See e.g. Nijman, 'Grotius', 100. Compare also e.g. van der Wal and Vermeulen, 'Grotius', 72–74.

[117] See e.g. Grotius, *Imperio*, 6.4, 294.

[118] Reformed theologians such as Calvin, Beza, Althusius, or Knox generally did not make a clear distinction between divine law and natural law; see e.g. Witte, *Reformation*, 59, 127, 157–158 and Stumpf, *Grotian*, 75–78, and neither would a Calvinist legal scholar such as Antonius Matthaeus II, see Oosterhuis, 'Calvinism', 89–92.

[119] Grotius, *De iure belli ac pacis*, Prolegomena 48 (remaining translations Hugo Grotius, *The Law of War and Peace*, transl. F. W. Kelsey (Clarendon/Milford: Oxford, London, 1925)).

[120] See e.g. Grotius, *De iure belli ac pacis*, 1.1.16.

[121] See Grotius, *De iure belli ac pacis*, 1.1.17.

[122] Grotius, *De iure belli ac pacis*, 2.1.14. See also Janwillem Oosterhuis, 'A staunch Protestant on an irenic Remonstrant: Matthaeus's references to Grotius in *De criminibus*', in *De rebus divinis et humanis: essays in honour of Jan Hallebeek*, eds. Harry Dondorp,

Divine volitional law that obliged the human race as a whole was only given trice: after the creation of man, upon the restoration of humankind after the flood, and under the Gospel by Christ[123] – in the *Inleiding*, Grotius solely referred to the latter. Indeed, Grotius acknowledged that in the most holy law of the New Testament, which he, contrary to others, admittedly again orthodox Calvinists, clearly distinguished from natural law, 'a greater degree of moral perfection is enjoined upon from us than the law of nature, alone and by itself, would require'.[124]

Still, more than in *De Indis* and the *Inleiding*, Grotius succeeded in *De iure belli ac pacis* to have the common good – sociality – taken into account in Right. In book one, in describing how Right functions in the Right of War and Peace, he started with a threefold distinction of Right.[125] The first sense of Right is simply what is just, just being understood in a negative rather than a positive sense, to mean 'what is not unjust'. 'Unjust' in turn means what is inconsistent with the nature of a society of rational beings.[126] A second sense of right is a moral quality attaching to a subject enabling the subject to have something or do something justly. A moral quality can be perfect, in which case it is a 'faculty', or less than perfect, in which case it is called a 'fitness'. The faculty is a right in the strict sense; a fitness is that which is suitable. To a faculty corresponds expletive justice, what Aristotle called 'justice of transactions' – which was too restrictive according to Grotius, because returning something to an owner is not a transaction. To a fitness corresponds attributive or assignative justice (distributive justice according to Aristotle); this is associated with those virtues which serve the interest of other people, such as liberality, compassion, prudent government. Finally, the third sense of Right, which means the same as law, understands law in a broad sense as a rule of moral action obliging us to do what is correct.[127]

Martin Schermaier, and Boudewijn Sirks (Göttingen: V&R unipress, 2019), 225–240, at 234–235.

[123] See Grotius, *De iure belli ac pacis*, 1.1.15.

[124] Grotius, *De iure belli ac pacis*, Prolegomena 50. See also e.g. Stumpf, *Grotian*, 71–82.

[125] See on this threefold distinction also Tierney, 'Grotius', 324–329; Janne E. Nijman, 'Images of Grotius, or the international rule of law beyond historiographical oscillation', *Journal of the History of International Law* 17 (2015), 83–137, at 113–120; Jeremy Seth Geddert, *Hugo Grotius and the modern theology of freedom: transcending natural rights* (New York; London: Routledge, Taylor & Francis Group, 2017), 35–61.

[126] Grotius, *De iure belli ac pacis*, 1.1.3. According to O'Donovan a 'decisively Protestant' formulation of Right, in the sense that Right is the correction of the failure to be sociable, see O'Donovan, 'Justice', 200.

[127] Grotius, *De iure belli ac pacis*, 1.1.4–9. See in detail O'Donovan, 'Justice', 194–203.

The second sense of right in particular, more precisely the fitness, that which is suitable, enabled Grotius to include sociability in justice: the Right of War and Peace was not just governed by expletive justice, but was also governed by attributive justice, whether something is in accordance with sociality.[128] Two examples of the right of resistance and punishment serve to illustrate the centrality, but also the elusiveness, of the concept of the common good: it could easily be used to justify the existing societal order – and tacitly reject Calvinist doctrines.

A sovereign had to pursue the common good for his subjects, maintaining public peace and good order. Apparently, this justified Grotius in restricting – compared to *De Indis* – a right of resistance only to situations of extreme necessity. Lower magistrates were explicitly denied a right to resist injuries emanating from their sovereign.[129] Grotius thus distanced himself from the recent Calvinist tradition whereby a strict adherence to the Decalogue gave munition to a wider right of resistance for lower magistrates against – ungodly but also unjust – sovereigns.[130] In particular, ungodliness of a sovereign played a limited role for Grotius, as natural religion and the one true religion held only a limited number of rationally understandable dogmas, developed earlier for instance in *Meletius*.

The common good also appears central to Grotius's theory on punishment in *De iure belli ac pacis*. This theory, earlier developed in for instance *De satisfactione*, is based on the social relation between offender and society: the punishing authority has a right to punish, because this has been tacitly conferred upon it by the offender. The authority acts thus not in a capacity as creditor, who could waive his right of punishment, but as judge or rather ruler, vindicating the lawful order of the universe.[131] This teleological approach is also present when Grotius discusses pardoning crimes. According to positive laws and certainly divine law, certain crimes required capital punishment, a position that Grotius appeared to have himself defended earlier in *De satisfactione*.[132] In *De iure belli ac pacis*, however, Grotius nonetheless allowed to sovereigns discretion to remit punishment even for capital crimes, if the goals of criminal justice – special and general

---

[128] See O'Donovan, 'Justice', 201–203; Stumpf, *Grotian*, 47–49; van der Wal and Vermeulen, 'Grotius', 75–77.
[129] Grotius, *De iure belli ac pacis*, 1.4.2–7. Compare also e.g. van der Wal and Vermeulen, 'Grotius', 77–78; Tierney, 'Grotius', 333–338; Taylor, *Secular*, 159–160, 237; Geddert, *Grotius*, 87–106.
[130] See e.g. Witte, *Reformation*, 81–141.
[131] Grotius, *De iure belli ac pacis*, 2.20, particularly, 2.20.2–4; Grotius, *De satisfactione*, 2.4–15. See O'Donovan, 'Justice', 184. Compare e.g. Geddert, *Grotius*, 110–137.
[132] Grotius, *De satisfactione*, 2.13. See above.

prevention and deterrence – were no longer met: natural law requires, but does not determine, punishment.[133] At this point, Grotius again alienated himself from Calvinists, who considered the Decalogue and the Mosaic Laws pertaining to it as enduring moral principles, due to which capital punishment had to be exacted for certain crimes.[134]

Fundamental notions of Grotius's Christian humanism – the teleological significance of all existence and God's universal competence – remain unmistakably at the basis of both *De Indis* and *De iure belli ac pacis*.[135] But to a greater extent than in *De Indis*, Grotius managed in *De iure belli ac pacis* to include these notions on a rational basis in Right, creating a profoundly social natural law – importantly also as a result of his intermediate altercation with orthodox Calvinism.

GENERAL APPRAISAL AND INFLUENCE

In a world torn apart by confessional disputes and religious wars, living a pious, virtuous, and above all peaceful life for the glory of God, and being united with Him in the afterlife, was for Grotius the ultimate purpose of all human beings.[136] As an irenic, humanist Christian, Grotius emphasized ethics and defended a natural religion, containing only necessary, fundamental, and rationally defendable dogmas – uniting Christianity.[137] During his life, by taking human beings as rational, social, and of free will, created after the image of God, Grotius developed a profoundly social law of nature.[138] Grotius thus placed himself firmly in the tradition of the Scholastics, in the sense that the universal competence of the divine will was indirect, via *ratio* and human nature. As a Protestant, however, Grotius was much freer than his Scholastic moral theologian contemporaries, and in that way he could restate the relation between sociality, mutual care, the common good, and self-love and self-preservation – which were all part of God's law for society – as belonging to the law of nature. Although Grotius in this way incorporated the divine will on a general level in the laws for society, direct reference to divine law – particularly in the form of Scripture and

---

[133] Grotius, *De iure belli ac pacis*, 2.20.6–22. Maybe Grotius also had the capital punishment of Oldenbarnevelt in mind. See O'Donovan, 'Justice', 186.
[134] Such as Antonius Matthaeus II, *De criminibus*, 48.XIX.V.2. See Oosterhuis, 'Protestant', 238–240.
[135] See e.g. O'Donovan, 'Grotius', 789; Stumpf, *Grotian*, 30–36, 48–49.
[136] See e.g. O'Donovan, 'Grotius', 789; Nijman, 'Grotius', 97–101.
[137] See e.g. Posthumus Meyjes, 'Grotius', 49; Rabbie, 'Irenisme', 59.
[138] See e.g. O'Donovan, 'Justice', 187–203; Nijman, 'Grotius', 94–96; Taylor, *Secular*, 126–128.

Decalogue – was complementary and no longer decisive.[139] This is in sharp contrast to the Calvinists, who took the universal competence of the divine will and divine law far more literally and used the Decalogue and the Mosaic laws pertaining to it as a blueprint for society.[140] During his life, and particularly when in political power, Grotius came to distance himself further and further from the recent Calvinist tradition. Importantly also, in contrast and in opposition to Calvinist theology, Grotius thus developed his own humanist Christian ideas, which profoundly influenced his legal writings.[141]

Although this firm stance in the Scholastic tradition made him controversial for many Calvinists,[142] his original restatement of mainstream Scholastic legal scholarship in a Protestant fashion in *De iure belli ac pacis*, played a major role as a catalyst for new ideas, for instance in the early German Enlightenment. Despite critique of methodological shortcomings and accusations of scholasticism, *De iure belli ac pacis* was considered a divine instrument to overcome the internal corruption of Christianity, and simply impossible to bypass, until Pufendorf and Wolff took over.[143] In the eighteenth century, interest in Grotius's main legal work, *De iure belli ac pacis*, waned. Indeed, internationally Grotius had been initially most well known for his religious, apologetic works, such as *De satisfactione* and *De veritate*.[144] However, particularly since the beginning of the nineteenth century, *De iure belli ac pacis* definitively eclipsed the success of *De veritate*. Also, as a result of the atrocities of the First World War, van Vollenhoven heralded Grotius as a prince of peace, because of his consistent emphasis on living a peaceful life.[145] Some decades after the Second World War there was a reaction from scholars like Tuck, who read Grotius mainly through the lens of *De Indis*, emphasizing absolutistic or modernizing tendencies.[146] In similar fashion, scholars have branded Grotius an important secularizer of

---

[139] See Nijman, 'Grotius', 104. Compare also e.g. van der Wal and Vermeulen, 'Grotius', 70–77.
[140] See e.g. Witte, *Reformation*, 127–129, 183; Witte, *Protestantism*, 113–115; Oosterhuis, 'Calvinism', 89–92.
[141] See e.g. Posthumus Meyjes, 'Grotius', 55–56; Rabbie, 'Irenisme', 64–67.
[142] See e.g. H. J. Erasmus, 'Natural Law: Voet's Criticism of De Groot', *Fundamina* 22 (2016): 40–52; Kralingen, 'Voet'.
[143] See Frank Grunert, 'The Reception of Hugo Grotius's De iure belli ac pacis in the Early German Enlightenment', in *Early Modern Natural Law Theories*, eds. T. J. Hochstrasser and P. Schöder (Dordrecht, etc.: Kluwer, 2003), 89–105, at 94–97. See also Wolf, 'Grotius', 299–300.
[144] See Heering, 'Veritate', 41, 51–52.
[145] See e.g. Nijman, 'Images', 89–94. Compare e.g. Wolf, 'Grotius', 300.
[146] See Tuck, *Rights*. Compare e.g. Tierney, 'Grotius', 317–324; Nijman, 'Images', 94–98; van der Wal and Vermeulen, 'Grotius', 78–83.

natural law.[147] In the last decades, several scholars have tried to again read and understand Grotius in his own time and place:[148] as a humanist Christian, restating mainstream, Scholastic legal scholarship in a Protestant fashion – although importantly in opposition to Calvinist orthodoxy – promoting above all a peaceful society, where humans could live their lives to the glory of God.

RECOMMENDED READINGS

Besselink, Leonard F. M. 'The impious hypothesis revisited'. *Grotiana* 9 (1988): 3–63.
Fukuoka, Atsuko. *The sovereign and the prophets: Spinoza on Grotian and Hobbesian biblical argumentation*. Studies in Intellectual History, Volume 268. Leiden: Brill, 2018.
Mühlegger, Florian. *Hugo Grotius: ein christlicher Humanist in politischer Verantwortung*. Berlin: Walter de Gruyter, 2007.
Nellen, Henricus Johannes Maria and Edwin Rabbie, eds. *Hugo Grotius – Theologian. Essays in Honour of G. H. M. Posthumus Meyjes*. Studies in the History of Christian Traditions: 55. Leiden: Brill, 1994.
Nijman, Janne Elisabeth. 'Grotius' Imago Dei Anthropology: Grounding Ius Naturae et Gentium'. In *International Law and Religion: Historical and Contemporary Perspectives*, edited by Martti Koskenniemi, Mónica García-Salmones Rovia, and Paolo Amorosa, 87–110. Oxford: Oxford University Press, 2017.
O'Donovan, Oliver. 'The justice of assignment and subjective rights in Grotius'. In *Bonds of Imperfection: Christian politics, past and present*, edited by Oliver O'Donovan and Joan Lockwood O'Donovan, 167–203. Grand Rapids, MI: Eerdmans, 2004.
O'Donovan, Oliver and Joan Lockwood O'Donovan. 'Hugo Grotius (1583–1646)'. In *From Irenaeus to Grotius: a sourcebook in Christian political thought 100–1625*, edited by Oliver O'Donovan and Joan Lockwood O'Donovan, 787–820. Grand Rapids, MI: Eerdmans, 1999.
Oosterhuis, Janwillem. 'A staunch Protestant on an irenic Remonstrant: Matthaeus's references to Grotius in De criminibus'. In *De rebus divinis et humanis: essays in honour of Jan Hallebeek*, edited by Harry Dondorp, Martin Schermaier, and Boudewijn Sirks, 225–240. Göttingen: V&R unipress, 2019.
Posthumus Meyjes, Guillaume H. M. 'Hugo Grotius as an Irenicist'. In *The world of Hugo Grotius (1583–1645): proceedings of the International Colloquium organized by the Grotius Committee of the Royal Netherlands Academy of Arts and Sciences, Rotterdam 6–9 April 1983*, 43–63. Amsterdam: APA-Holland University Press, 1984.
Rabbie, Edwin. 'Introduction'. In *Hugo Grotius, Defensio fidei catholicae de satisfactione Christi adversus Faustum Socinum senensem (1617)*. Edited by Edwin Rabbie, translated by Hotze Mulder. Assen: Van Gorcum, 1990.

---

[147] For an overview, see Geddert, *Grotius*, 8–14.
[148] See e.g. van der Wal and Vermeulen, 'Grotius'; Tierney, 'Grotius'; O'Donovan, 'Grotius'; O'Donovan, 'Justice'; Stumpf, *Grotian*; Taylor, *Secular*; Nijman, 'Images'; Nijman, 'Grotius'; Geddert, *Grotius*.

Rabbie, Edwin. 'Introduction'. In *Hugo Grotius, Ordinum Hollandiae ac Westfrisiae pietas (1613). Critical Edition with English Translation and Commentary by Edwin Rabbie*. Studies in the History of Christian Traditions, Volume 66. Leiden: Brill, 1995.

Stumpf, Christoph A. *The Grotian Theology of International Law : Hugo Grotius and the Moral Foundations of International Relations*. Religion and Society. Berlin: De Gruyter, 2006.

Tierney, Brian. 'Grotius. From Medieval to Modern'. In *The idea of natural rights: studies on natural rights, natural law and church law, 1150–1625*, 316–342. Atlanta, GA: Scholars Press, 1997.

Van Dam, Harm-Jan. 'Introduction'. In *Hugo Grotius, De imperio summarum potestatum circa sacra (1617/1647). Critical edition with introduction, English translation, and commentary by Harm-Jan van Dam*. Studies in the History of Christian Traditions, Volume 102/I. Leiden: Brill, 2001.

Van der Wal, Goossen Albertus and Bernardus Petrus Vermeulen. 'Grotius, Aquinas and Hobbes. Grotian Natural Law between Lex Aeterna and Natural Rights'. *Grotiana* 16 (1995): 55–83.

7

Paulus Voet

Johannes van Kralingen

BIOGRAPHICAL INTRODUCTION

Paulus Voet (alias Paulus Voetius) is probably the least well known of three generations of the Voet family. His father was the famous reformed theologian Gijsbert Voet (alias Gisbertus Voetius, 1589–1676) and his son was Jan Voet (alias Johannes Voetius, 1647–1713), the famous exponent of Roman–Dutch law. Paulus Voet however was a formidable academic himself. This paper will throw light on the life and works of Paulus Voet from the perspective of his work as a Christian jurist during the seventeenth century in the Dutch Republic.

Paulus Voet was born on 7 June 1619 as the son of Gijsbert Voet and Deliana van Diest (also known as Deliana Jans), in Heusden, a small, fortified city in the county of Holland.[1] Paulus was born at a time of religious and political debate. His father took part in many of these debates and Paulus, as will be shown, inherited many of his father's ideas and feuds. Gijsbert Voet was minister of the Dutch Reformed church of Heusden when Paulus was born and went on to become a professor of theology, Hebrew and oriental languages in 1634 at the Illustrious School in Utrecht, which became the University of Utrecht in 1636. Gijsbert Voet was one of the leading figures of the so-called

---

[1] For biographical information see especially the extensive biography of Paulus's father by Arnoldus Cornelius Duker, *Gisbertus Voetius*, 4 vols. (Leiden: E. J. Brill, 1897–1915). Duker cites all the relevant contemporary sources and his work contains a lot of biographical information about Paulus Voet. See also A. J. van der Aa, et al., *Biographisch Woordenboek der Nederlanden, vol. 7* (Haarlem: Van Brederode, 1852–1878), 91; P. C. Molhuysen, J. van Kuyk, et al., *Nieuw Nederlandsch Biografisch Woordenboek. vol. 7* (Leiden: Sijthoff, 1911–1937), 1329–1330; K. R. G. Kuipers, 'Paulus Voet (1619–1667). Enkele opmerkingen over deze 17e eeuwse geleerde en zijn werken, in het bijzonder met betrekking tot het internationaal privaatrecht', in *Uit bibliotheektuin en informatieveld: Opstellen aangeboden aan Dr. D. Grosheide bij zijn afscheid als bibliothecaris van de Rijksuniversiteit te Utrecht* (Utrecht: Universiteitsbibliotheek, 1978), 51–63.

'Nadere Reformatie' ('Further Reformation' or 'Second Reformation'). This pietistic movement aimed to reform every aspect of private and public life according to Reformed principles. Gijsbert Voet opposed any social habit which in his opinion encouraged man's natural inclination to sin. He was for example opposed to dancing, gambling, and 'unnatural' hairstyles. As a staunch Calvinist Gijsbert Voet also used every opportunity to polemicize against the adherents of what he considered heresies. He polemicized against Arminians, Socinians, Jansenists, and Jesuits, like Bellarminus, Lessius, and Beccanus. Gijsbert was also a firm opponent of Descartes, which led to a famous and long-lasting dispute with Descartes. Paulus joined his father in his feud with Descartes and the latter's followers. Later in his life, for example, Paulus Voet tried – in vain – to prevent a colleague from Utrecht, professor De Bruyn, from giving 'Cartesian lectures'.

In his early years Paulus Voet was educated by his father. Gijsbert Voet in particular seems to have taught Paulus Greek and Hebrew. Paulus went on to study at the University of Utrecht and was awarded the title of 'master of arts' (*magister artium*) in 1640. In the following year he became a professor of metaphysics (*professor extraordinarius metaphysices*) at the same university. His father had used his influence to persuade the university to appoint his son a professor. Paulus was appointed on the condition that he would give at least one lecture on ancient Greek per week. From this period stem Paulus's works on the classical authors Herodianus, Callimachus, and Musaeus.[2] In 1644 Paulus was appointed *professor ordinarius* of philosophy.

During this period Paulus also managed to study law in his spare time.[3] In the year 1645 he was promoted to 'doctor in both laws' (*doctor utriusque iuris*), namely in civil law (Roman law) and canon law. By the age of 26 he was already a Master of Arts, Doctor of Laws, and professor of philosophy. In his private life Paulus Voet also thrived. In 1646 Paulus married a noble woman, Elisabeth van Winssen, with whom he had two sons, Jan (Johannes) and Paul. Paulus was a devout Christian and became a deacon in the Dutch Reformed church in Utrecht in 1645 and became an elder of the same church in 1666.

In 1648 the university ordered Paulus to teach logic as well. At the same time he was allowed to give private lectures on ancient Greek. Paulus however began more and more to shift his attention to the study and practice of the law.[4] He was appointed judge in the court of Vianen (*Souveraine camer van*

---

[2] See Margreet Ahsmann, *Bibliografie van hoogleraren in de rechten aan de Utrechtse universiteit tot 1811* (Amsterdam; Oxford; New York; Tokyo: North Holland, 1993), 143 and 148.
[3] Duker, *Gisbertus Voetius*, 3:183.
[4] There is a juridical opinion of Paulus Voet recorded in the *Utrechtse Consultatiën III*, nr. 162 (available online via Google Books).

Iustitie)⁵ and in 1652 he started to give private lectures on civil law. Between 1652 and 1653 he was rector of the University of Utrecht. In 1654 he was discharged from his task to teach philosophy and appointed a professor of law (*professor iuris ordinarius*).⁶ His specific task was to expound the *Institutiones* of Justinian. In order to be appointed professor of law Paulus was required to abandon his position as judge in the court of Vianen. He managed however to persuade the senators of the university to let him stay on the court.

Paulus Voet died at the age of 48 on the 1 August 1667. He was survived by his father, his wife Elisabeth Reuffert, whom he had married after his first wife had passed away, and his sons with his first wife, Jan (Johannes) and Paul. Paulus's father was very distressed by his passing. Gijsbert Voet regarded his son as the pillar of his house, the protector of his name, and the defender of his work.⁷ Paulus's son Johannes later continued the work of his father and developed his ideas in the *Commentarius ad Pandectas*.

MAJOR THEMES AND CONTRIBUTIONS

Paulus Voet's academic career was relatively short compared to that of his father Gijsbert and his son Johannes. This is probably one reason why Paulus is less famous than his family members. Another reason is that Paulus did not, unlike his father and his son, single-mindedly pursue just one academic discipline. The topics of his writings range from philosophy and theology to ancient Greek and civil law. His method usually consists of a systematic exposition of his arguments supported by allegations of authorities, of which the Holy Scriptures form an important part. Paulus Voet was very well read in other areas as well, as can be deduced from the wide range of authors he cites in his writings: they range from classical authors (Caesar, Cicero, Suetonius, Tacitus, Vergil, etc.) and church fathers (for example Augustine) to jurists (Azo, Baldus, Donellus, Faber, Rebuffus, etc.) and contemporary writers (Thomas Hobbes). Voet's first major works were published after his tenure as a professor of metaphysics and logic. The University of Utrecht did have

---

5   In honour of his 'lord protector' Paulus wrote a history in Dutch of count Brederode and his ancestors: *Oorspronck, voortganck en daeden der doorluchtige Heeren van Brederode, bij een gesteld door Paulus Voet der Rechten Professor in de Acad. tot Utrecht, en Raetspersoon in de Kaemer van Iustitie 's Lants Vianen* (Utrecht: Johannes van Waesberge, 1556 [=1656]).

6   Another son of Gijsbert Voet, Paulus's brother Daniël Voet (1629–1660), was Paulus's successor as professor of philosophy. Paulus edited and published the works of Daniël after Daniël's dead in 1660. See Ahsmann, *Bibliografie van hoogleraren*, 146.

7   Duker, *Gisbertus Voetius*, 3:185.

a chair of metaphysics, unlike most other universities in the Dutch Republic.[8] Aristotelian philosophy was seen by Gijsbert and Paulus Voet as a necessary tool for the study of theology.[9] The study of Aristotelian logic and metaphysics enabled students of theology to understand the orthodox authors and by studying the orthodox authors they would be able to refute heresies.[10] Paulus Voet's works *Theologia naturalis reformata* (1656) and *Prima philosophia reformata* (1657) fit this project of using philosophy as subordinate to theology.[11] The titles of these works are programmatic. Paulus Voet tried to reform the philosophical projects of the past. In the *Theologia naturalis reformata*, for example, Paulus expounds his theory of a natural theology. Natural theology was a branch of theology dealing with the knowledge of God based on the study of nature aided by reason, as opposed to the knowledge of God based on the revelation of the Holy Scriptures. For Paulus and Gijsbert Voet natural theology ought to be subordinated to theology based on revelation. The authority of the Holy Scriptures was paramount.

This project of reformation concerned not only philosophy, but also extended to other disciplines. His first legal writings show that Paulus Voet wanted to reform this academic discipline as well. In the same year as his *Prima philosophia reformata* Paulus Voet's treatise 'On the use of civil and canon law in united Belgium and on the custom to promote doctors in both laws' was published.[12] The first part of this treatise is a long indictment of canon law. According to Paulus Voet canon law did not have, nor had it ever had, formally or materially force of law in the Dutch Republic.[13] It in no way derogated from Roman law and none of the canon law rules were binding in court (*in foro*). Furthermore, canon law rules should not be accepted for their intrinsic value, because – a few exceptions aside – the papal laws are full of

---

[8] Theo Verbeek, 'Tradition and novelty: Descartes and some Cartesians', in *The Rise of Modern Philosophy: The Tension Between the New and Traditional Philosophies from Machiavelli to Leibniz*, ed. Tom Sorell (Oxford: Clarendon Press, 2000), 182.

[9] Gijsbert Voet's theological project has been described as the systematization of Protestant dogma in Aristotelian terms. See *Dictionary of Seventeenth- and Eighteenth-Century Dutch Philosophers*, vol. 2 (Bristol: Thoemmes Press, 2003), 1034.

[10] Verbeek, 'Tradition and novelty', 182.

[11] The complete titles of these works are Paulus Voet, *Theologia naturalis reformata cui subjecta brevis de anima separata disquisitio* (Utrecht: ex officina Johannis a Waesberge, 1656) and Paulus Voet, *Prima philosophia reformata* (Utrecht: ex officina Johannis a Waesberge, 1657). These works have not been reprinted.

[12] Paulus Voet, *De usu juris civilis et canonici in Belgio unito deque more promovendi doctores utriusque juris etc. liber singularis* (Utrecht: ex officina Johannis a Waesberge, 1657). This treatise has never been reprinted. It is freely available online via Google Books.

[13] Voet uses the term 'United Belgium' by which he meant the sovereign states of Holland, Zeeland, Groningen, Utrecht, Friesland, Gelderland, and Overijssel.

inextricable contradictions and are not in accordance with natural and divine law. The second part of the treatise is a logical and more practical follow-up to the first part. Paulus criticizes the custom observed at universities of the Dutch Republic to confer the degree of 'doctor in both laws' (*'doctor utriusque iuris'*). This title had been used since the 1590s at the universities, most probably to keep pace with degrees conferred by foreign universities.[14] The expression 'both laws' referred to Roman law and canon law, which, significantly, Paulus calls 'caesarian and papal law'. Although Paulus Voet is critical of this custom he admits that it is observed even at Protestant universities. He therefore handles the subject very carefully. Paulus concedes that a custom is almost always introduced with a reason and that a custom can still be law even when it lacks a rationale. The custom should nevertheless be discarded, concludes Paulus, for it was erroneously introduced in the Dutch universities (*'non ratione, sed errore introductum'*). Paulus Voet invokes several arguments to support his claim. One of his arguments is that the conferment of the title is not appropriate, because canon law is not taught at the faculties of law. Students are therefore not examined on the canon law and this makes the title of *doctor utriusque iuris* pointless.

Paulus Voet probably wrote his treatise as a reaction on the work of Cyprianus Regneri ab Oosterga (1614–1687). Regneri ab Oosterga was Paulus's colleague in Utrecht and had already in 1644 written a *dissertatio* about the same subject,[15] in which he claimed the opposite of what Paulus Voet claimed.[16] Voet does not refer to Regneri ab Oosterga, but he most probably knew this *dissertatio*.[17] The public debate about the conferment of the title *doctor utriusque iuris* seems to have ended with Paulus's treatise. Paulus Voet's ideas were not taken over by others. The custom to confer the title *doctor utriusque iuris* remained observed at the Dutch universities until 1815.[18] It remained a misleading and incorrect title as Paulus Voet was already keen to show in 1657, for most *doctores utriusque iuris* probably did not have any knowledge – or very little – of canon law. Joannes van der Linden

---

[14] Robert Feenstra, 'Canon law at Dutch universities from 1575 till 1811', in *Canon Law in Protestant Lands*, ed. Richard Helmholz (Berlin: Duncker & Humblot, 1992), 125.

[15] The complete title was *Dissertatio de jure canonico, quomodo et quando vim legis habeat in foris nostris, deque recepta consuetudine qua hodie in Academiis etiam Reformatorum I. U. Doctores renunciatur* (Utrecht, 1644). This *dissertatio* was also published in 1669 as an appendix to the sixth volume of *Censura Belgica* of Regneri ab Oosterga. Regneri does not mention Paulus Voet in this work.

[16] Regneri ab Oosterga claimed for example that *'juste et consulto adhuc in Academiis nostris J[uris] U[triusque] Doctores pronunciari'*. See Feenstra, 'Canon law', 129.

[17] See Feenstra, 'Canon law', 130.

[18] F. P. Th. Rohling, 'Canoniek Recht', in *Streven* 1 (1947–1948): 627.

(1756–1835) was aware of this as he urged law students to study canon law, because 'it is surely absurd to style oneself a *doctor juris utriusque,* and at the same time to know nothing of canon law'.[19] This raises the question of how students could study canon law. A faculty of canon law or a chair of canon law was inconceivable at the universities of the Dutch Republic.[20] This is not surprising since these universities were instituted during or after the revolt of the Protestant Dutch Republic against Catholic Spain. Canon law remained however an integral part of the law of the various states within the Dutch Republic, mainly in the field of civil law.[21] In particular, marital law and the law of inheritance were based on canon law. Civil law professors would therefore sometimes have to refer to canon law. A genre of treatises concerned with comparisons between civil law and canon law, '*differentiae*', seems to have been used for this purpose.[22] There were some more general books on canon law published, but they were few and probably not used for educational purposes. In 1669 Regneri ab Oosterga for example published the sixth volume of his *Censura Belgica,* a multivolume work on the differences between the law of inter alia the *Corpus Iuris Civilis* and the customs of the Dutch Republic (*mores Belgii*). In this sixth volume of *Censura Belgica* he discusses the differences between canon law and the *mores Belgii.* In more than 300 pages Regneri ab Oosterga discusses all the '*canones*'. A few other general books on canon law also appeared during this period. There was for example a 'manual' ('*manuductio*') on canon law by Antonius Matthaeus III (1635–1710), which was published in 1696 in Leiden. This was, however, despite its title, probably not written for educational purposes. It was a learned treatise about – among other things – the origins of canon law and was full of general and antiquarian knowledge. Another manual on canon law was written by Arnoldus Corvinus, who had been converted to the Roman Catholic faith around 1644.[23]

Although the study of canon law was in general thus quite marginalized and implicit at Dutch universities, it remained nevertheless an integral part of the

---

[19] J. van der Linden, *Regtsgeleerd, practicaal, en koopmans handboek* (Amsterdam: Johannes Allart, 1806), xl–xli. The English translation is taken from J. van der Linden, *Institutes of Holland, or Manual of Law, Practice, and Mercantile Law,* trans. H. Juta (Cape Town: Juta, 1884), xl–xli.

[20] Feenstra, 'Canon law', 124.

[21] See John Jr. Witte, 'The plight of canon law in the early Dutch Republic', in *Canon Law in Protestant Lands,* ed. Richard Helmholz (Berlin: Duncker & Humblot, 1992), 135–164.

[22] Feenstra, 'Canon law', 127.

[23] Antonius Matthaeus, *Manuductio ad Jus canonicum* (Leiden: Frederik Haaring, 1696); Arnoldus Corvinus, *Jus canonicum per aphorismos strictim explicatum* (Amsterdam: Ex Officina Elzeviriana, 1648).

law and of legal education. This was still not to the liking of strict Calvinists like Paulus's father Gijsbert Voet.[24] When Gijsbert was appointed professor of theology in Utrecht he gave a sermon in the Dom of Utrecht about the use of science and universities ('*Sermoen vande nutticheyt der Academiën ende scholen, mitsgaders der wetenschappen ende consten, die in deselve gheleert werden*').[25] It was a programmatic sermon. Gijsbert Voet explained the benefit of the university and how the different sciences were all in accordance with the Protestant Christian faith. He tried above all to show how the different sciences could be useful to theology, for theology formed the pinnacle of the university to which all other studies ought to be subordinated. Naturally, this also applied to the study of law. Gijsbert Voet first showed that the study of law is in accordance with the Holy Scriptures. Laws are necessary to regulate life within society, of which the church itself is a part. The main purpose of the study of law, according to Gijsbert Voet, is however the same as the purpose of the other sciences, namely as an aid to the study of theology and as a helper of the true church. The study of law could for example be helpful in explaining many passages of the Bible, like the Ten Commandments, dogmas like justification, and other legal terms in the Bible. The purpose of the study of law is clear, but what did the study of law according to Gijsbert Voet consist of? Gijsbert Voet does address this question. The object of the study of the law should be the 'Roman or Caesarian laws' ('*Roomsche of keyserlijcke rechten*').

This praise of pagan laws written for a wholly different society by a strict Dutch Calvinist in the seventeenth century seems odd. Gijsbert Voet even claimed that the source of the Caesarian laws is the Holy Scriptures ('*De Schriftuere is de suyvere ende onvervalschte Fonteyne van alle rechts-geleertheyt, en volgens dien van de Roomsche wetten of de Keyserlijcke rechten, die in de academien uyt-geleyt ende gheleert werden*').[26] There is however an explanation for this appraisal by Voetius. The reformers in the sixteenth century were strong opponents of canon law. It is well known that Luther burned a copy of the *Corpus Iuris Canonici* in Wittenberg. Other reformers like Melanchton were also opposed to canon law. They understood however that some other system of law had to be used if the papal laws were to be discarded. Luther was

---

[24] The following part is mainly based on the analysis of Fruin, see Jacobus Antonie Fruin, 'De strijd tusschen het Canonieke en het Romeinse recht in de middeleeuwen en het tijdvak van de Republiek der Vereenigde Nederlanden [oration 1879]', in *Jaarboek der Rijksuniversiteit te Utrecht 1878 – 1879* (Utrecht: J. L. Beijers, 1880), 31–71.

[25] This sermon was published in 1636 in Utrecht. The relevant parts of this sermon can be read in Duker, *Gisbertus Voetius*, 1:134 and Fruin, 'De strijd'.

[26] Duker, *Gisbertus Voetius*, 1:134.

very much in favour of using Roman law as an alternative to canon law, probably because he understood that the national laws of Germany were not yet suitable. The Reformation led therefore – in short – to a renaissance of Roman law. The disgust with canon law was mostly because it was *papal* law. The *source* of canon law and not the intrinsic quality of canon law rules was suspect. This can for example be seen from the fact that the prohibition of usury, which was a typical medieval canon law dogma and contrary to Roman law, was upheld by Luther and Melanchton. John Calvin was one of just a few reformers who seem to have drawn the obvious conclusions from the abandonment of canon law, for he was not principally against usury. This aversion of the early reformers to canon law ('papal law') and their fervour for Roman law seems to have been the inspiration of Gijsbert Voet in the seventeenth century. Paulus's treatise about canon law can be seen as an elaborate and more juridical exposition of the ideas of his father. Paulus does not refer to his father in the treatise, but it is telling that Paulus Voet refers to canon law as 'papal law' and contrasts it with 'Caesarian laws'. In view of this it is ironic that the same treatise of Paulus contains an '*appendix apologetica*' wherein Paulus Voet defends himself against claims of Samuel Maresius (1599–1673) that not Paulus, but his father Gijsbert, had written *Prima philosophia reformata* and *Theologia naturalis reformata*. The allegations of Maresius seem not to have been entirely unwarranted. Another joint project of father Gijsbert and son Paulus Voet was their contribution to a topical debate in the Dutch Republic about the relation between the state and the church.[27] The Arminians, among which Grotius was an important adherent, supported a firm grip by the state on the church, while the followers of Gomarus, like Gijsbert Voet, were in favour of a self-governing and independent church. One of the contested issues for example was the question whether magistrates could appoint and dismiss ministers. In 1662 Paulus Voet's 'Sacred jurisprudence' (*Jurisprudentia sacra*), in which he discusses several of these issues, was published. It was dedicated to his father and his brother Nicolaas. Paulus's father published his 'Church politics' (*Politica ecclesiastica*) about the same subject in several volumes from 1663 until 1676.[28] Both works deal with the governance of the church and the relation between the church and the state. The works can best be seen in contrast to the work of Grotius and others who were in favour of

---

[27] About this subject, see Witte 'The plight of canon law', 144–147, and Douglas Nobbs, *Theocracy and Toleration. A Study of the Disputes in Dutch Calvinism from 1600 to 1650* (Cambridge: Cambridge University Press, 1938).

[28] Compare Sijbrandus Johannes Fockema Andreae, 'Kerkrecht onder de Republiek', *Tijdschrift voor Rechtsgeschiedenis* 22.4 (1954): 435.

the authority of the state and its magistrates over church matters.[29] During the seventeenth century these ideas of Grotius resurged after the synod of Dordt (1618–1619) had failed to settle the matter.[30] Grotius's works were reprinted and in addition several new pamphlets were published. There appeared for example a pamphlet by Blondel against the authority of the congregation in ecclesiastical matters and a booklet about the competence of magistrates to remove ministers.[31] Paulus Voet opposed these views of Grotius and others in his *Jurisprudentia sacra*.[32] According to Voet, the prince, by which he means the secular authorities, does not have unlimited power. The prince is bound not only by natural law and divine law, but even by some civil laws. The prince can have no authority in religious matters and matters of conscience. The appointment of ministers is not in the power of the prince, nor can he remove ministers or other church officials. Another contested issue which Voet discusses is the ownership of goods legated for pious purposes (*pia causa*). Voet asserts that temporal goods can be owned by the church. These goods are not the property of the prince; the prince can only take care of these goods like a guardian takes care of the goods of a minor ('*ad instar bonorum minoris*'). Voet also discusses the governance of the church. The ministers ('*pastores*') and elders ('*episcopi*') should be chosen by the church itself. Paulus Voet then proceeds to explain what their task is. The elders for example should visit schools, including universities, because they must see to it that no false dogmas are taught at these institutions. The governance of the church should be regulated by the church itself. In the last part of the book Paulus discusses the jurisdiction of church officials. The censorship of the church is independent of the secular authorities, because the civil and ecclesiastical jurisdictions are separate. A lot of the ideas of Paulus Voet however – like the ownership of temporal goods by the church, the limitations of the authority of the secular state, and the validity of civil jurisdiction vis-à-vis ecclesiastical censorship – were at odds with what for a long time had been accepted at law.[33] It is therefore no surprise that *Jurisprudentia sacra* was not accepted in practice. Furthermore, there are hardly any references to this work in later legal and political writings.[34]

[29] See for example Hugo Grotius, *De imperio summarum potestatum circa sacra* (Paris: 1647); Compare Fockema Andreae, 'Kerkrecht', 435.
[30] Nobbs, *Theocracy and Toleration*, xiii.
[31] David Blondel, *De jure plebis in regimine ecclesiastico* ('s-Gravenhage: Adriaen Vlacq, 1661); A. C. E. M. G., *Officium Magistratus Christiani* ('s-Gravenhage: Adriaen Vlacq, 1662).
[32] Paulus Voet, *Jurisprudentia sacra, instituta juris Caesarei cum divino, consuetudinario, atque canonico, in multis, collatione* (Amsterdam: ex officina Johannis a Waesberge, 1662).
[33] Fockema Andreae, 'Kerkrecht', 436.
[34] Fockema Andreae, 'Kerkrecht', 436.

Paulus Voet's works on canon law and the relation between the state and the church were not very influential in his own time, nor were they ever after. Canon law continued to form an integral part of the law of the reformed states of the Republic, while Paulus's ideas about the relation between state and church were not in accordance with what had, for a long time, been accepted at law. Paulus Voet has however managed to establish his reputation as a jurist with a single work in the field of what is now called 'international private law' or the 'law of conflicts'. With his *Monograph about statutes and their concurrence* (*De statutis eorumque concursu liber singularis*) Paulus Voet showed himself able to develop the civil law in accordance with the needs of his time.[35] With the term *statutum* (statute) Paulus referred to the particular laws promulgated by sovereign states as contrasted with the 'common law', that is, Roman law and canon law.[36]

With regard to these local laws, conflicts of laws could arise. Already, from the thirteenth century, Italian and French jurists had written about the question of which law ought to be applied when a conflict of laws occurred. Several jurists from the Dutch Republic joined the debate. They were concerned with the division of statutes into personal, real, and mixed statutes, but they were above all concerned with the justification of the application of foreign laws. It is this last aspect which is typical of the so-called 'Dutch school' of statutists, which consisted of Christiaan Rodenburg (1618–1668), Ulrik Huber (1636–1694), Paulus Voet, and Johannes Voet.[37] These jurists all wrestled with the same problem. The Dutch revolt against Spain and the newly acquired independence made them adhere to theories of territorial

---

[35] On this subject see Basil Edwards, *The selective Paulus Voet: being a translation of those sections regarded as relevant to modern conflict of laws, of the De statutis eorumque concursu liber singularis (Amstelodami, 1661) by Paulus Voet (1619–1667) as a single book on statutes and their concurrence: an abridgement* (Pretoria: University of South Africa, 2007); Roeland Duco Kollewijn and Th. A. Fruin, *Geschiedenis van de Nederlandse wetenschap van het internationaal privaatrecht tot 1880/Geschiedenis van de wetenschap van het Nederlandsch Burgerlijk proces recht na 1811* (Amsterdam: Noord-Hollandsche Uitgeversmaatschappij, 1937); Niek Peters, *IPR, Proces & Arbitrage: over grondslagen en rechtspraktijk* (diss. Groningen) (Apeldoorn: Maklu Uitgevers, 2016); J. M. B. Scholten, *Het begrip comitas in het internationaal privaatrecht van de hollandse juristenschool der zeventiende eeuw* (Utrecht/Nijmegen: Dekker & van de Vegt, 1949); J.Ph. Suyling, *De statutentheorie in Nederland gedurende de XVIIe eeuw* (PhD diss., Utrecht) ('s-Hertogenbosch: Robijns, 1893).

[36] *De statutis*, sect. 4, cap. 1, nr. 1: '*Sequitur jus particulare, seu non commune, quod uno vocabulo usitatissimo, statutum, dicitur*'.

[37] According to Meijers, Arntzenius and van der Keessel should also be counted among the members of this school, Eduard Maurits Meijers, 'L'histoire des principes fondamentaux du droit international privé à partir du Moyen-Age spécialement dans l'Europe occidentale', *Recueil des Cours de l'Académie de droit international* 49 (Leiden; Boston: Brill/Nijhoff, 1934): 543–686.

sovereignty. According to them the laws of a sovereign state should apply not only to the subjects of that state, but to everyone in the territory of that sovereign state. Furthermore, there existed no obligation for a sovereign state to apply the law of another sovereign state. In practice however, the courts of sovereign states often deferred to the laws of other states. This posed a difficult question. How could statutes apply outside the territorial boundaries of the state that had created these statutes? Strict adherence to the principle of territorial sovereignty would preclude the application of any foreign law. The Dutch jurists however did not want to accept this consequence, because this would have meant a serious hindrance to trade between states within and outside the Dutch Republic. Christiaan Rodenburg was the first to acknowledge and address this problem.[38] He claimed that a legal obligation existed for states to apply foreign law *'ipsa rei natura ac neccesitate'*. This was not very convincing as it contradicted the territorial sovereignty premise from which all the abovementioned jurists reasoned, Rodenburg included.[39] In contrast, Paulus Voet denied that there was a legal obligation for a sovereign state to apply the laws of another sovereign state. In *De Statutis* Paulus Voet gave a justification for the fact that sovereign states applied the laws of other sovereign states. According to Voet this practice was based on the *comitas* between states. The term *comitas* can be described as 'courtesy', 'benevolence', or 'goodwill'. Voet does not define this concept, but he contrasts it with terms like *de iure, de juris rigore*, and *de necessitate iuris*.[40] *Comitas* meant therefore for Paulus Voet predominantly a negation of a legal obligation to defer to the statute of a foreign state. A sovereign state *could* apply the law of another sovereign state, namely *ex comitate*, on the basis of respect. On the other hand, the application of foreign laws was not entirely a matter of arbitrariness. In its positive effects *comitas* is sometimes described as a moral obligation of sovereign states to defer to the law of another sovereign state.[41] By way of this doctrine of *comitas gentium* Paulus Voet managed to salvage both the doctrine of territorial sovereignty and the useful practice of the extraterritorial effects of foreign laws.

---

[38] Christiaan Rodenburg, *Tractatus praeliminaris de jure, quod oritur ex statutorum vel consuetudinem discrepantium conflictu* (Utrecht, 1653). Rodenburg was *'le fondateur réel de la doctrine hollandaise'* according to Meijers; see Meijers, 'L'histoire des principes fondamentaux', 666. He first formulated the problem, but Paulus Voet was the first to come up with a convincing solution to the problem.

[39] Kollewijn and Fruin, *Geschiedenis van de Nederlandse wetenschap*, 82 and *passim*.

[40] Scholten, *Comitas*, 29; Meijers, 'L'histoire des principes fondamentaux', 664.

[41] Scholten, *Comitas*, 45.

The concept was not used in legal writings before Paulus Voet.[42] Paulus Voet probably took the term *comitas* from the works of moral theologians like Aquinas (1266–1273), Cajetanus (1519), Danaeus (1577), Lessius (1605), etc.[43] This ethical concept of *comitas*, which the moral theologians applied to relations between individuals, was taken over by Paulus and applied in a juridical context to the relation between sovereign states. Paulus Voet sometimes also uses other words like 'equity' (*aequitas*) and 'courtesy' (*humanitas*) in *De Statutis* to give a justification for the application of foreign law. It was the concept of *comitas* which was taken over by other jurists. It was first and foremost his son Johannes Voet who endorsed it in his *Commentarius ad Pandectas*. Johannes Voet systematized and perfected his father's theory of *comitas*.[44] Ulrik Huber also used the concept of *comitas* in his *De iure civitatis*. Huber's theory of *comitas* was however different from the theory of Paulus and Johannes Voet. He claimed – like Rodenburg – that there was a *legal obligation* of sovereign states to defer to the law of other sovereign states. The concept of *comitas* changed with Huber from a moral obligation to a legal obligation.[45] Huber based this obligation on the *ius gentium*. Huber's work is predominantly cited in Anglo-American law since the eighteenth century and in the work of Supreme Court judge Joseph Story.[46] Ironically, Huber was misunderstood by Joseph Story. According to Story 'comity' entails no legal obligation for states to apply the law of other states, but it means that states could voluntarily apply foreign laws.[47] This view is more in accordance with Paulus and Johannes Voet's understanding of *comitas* than with Huber's understanding of *comitas*. Traces of the *comitas* doctrine of both Paulus and Johannes Voet can also be recognized in the Supreme Court's 'classic statement' of comity per Justice Gray in *Hilton v. Guyot* (1895):

> Comity, in the legal sense is neither a matter of absolute obligation, on the one hand, nor of mere courtesy and good will, upon the other. But it is the recognition which one nation allows within its territory to the legislative, executive or judicial acts of another nation, having due regard both to

[42] Meijers, 'L'histoire des principes fondamentaux', 664; Scholten, *Comitas*, 29.
[43] Scholten, *Comitas*, 79–126.
[44] Kollewijn and Fruin, *Geschiedenis van de Nederlandse wetenschap*, 109; Scholten, *Comitas*, 54.
[45] Scholten, *Comitas*, 66.
[46] Th. M. de Boer, 'Living apart together: the relationship between public and private international law', *Netherlands International Law Review* 57.2 (2010): 6.
[47] Story: '[Huber's] doctrine owes its origin and authority to the voluntary adoption and consent of nations. It is therefore in the strictest sense a matter of the comity of nations, not of absolute paramount obligation, superseding all discretion on the subject'. As cited in De Boer, 'Living apart together', 6.

international duty and convenience, and to the rights of its own citizens or of other persons who are under the protection of its laws.[48]

Paulus Voet wrote another book in the field of international private law on the nature of mobile and immobile goods (*Mobilium et immobilium natura*).[49] This work is characterized as an appendix to his monograph about the conflict of statutes (*De statutis*), but is quite an extensive work in itself.[50] Paulus not only discusses the distinction between mobile and immobile goods, but he also reacts to critique by Abraham van Wesel (1635–1680) on his *comitas* theory. Abraham van Wesel was a colleague of Paulus in the Court of Vianen. According to van Wesel it was 'evidently law' ('*certissimi iuris est*') that the personal statute of a person follows this person wherever he goes and that a sovereign state should defer to the law of another sovereign state.[51] This shows that in the seventeenth century there was not yet a *communis opinio* on the application of foreign law and that Paulus Voet did not state a common theory about the application of foreign law. Paulus however stuck to his theory. *Mobilium et immobilium natura* contains a succinct summary of Paulus's theory: 'Statutes, of whatever kind, do not exceed their territory, unless on the basis of *comitas*.'[52]

Voet's last work was his commentary on the Institutes of Justinian, which was published posthumously in 1668.[53] There have been many commentaries on the Institutes of Justinian. Voet's commentary is not the most well known. Johannes Voet refers to it several times '*piae memoriae*' in his *Commentarius ad Pandectas*. Paulus Voet's commentary is an interesting work, because Paulus points out the differences between Roman law and Roman–Dutch law. Paulus Voet not only discusses Roman law and Dutch customary law, but also the law of the old testament (*mos Hebraeorum*) and even canon law. This is puzzling, because he had claimed in his treatise *On the use of canon law* that canon law had no force of law in the Dutch Republic. It could be that

---

[48] As cited in Joel R. Paul, 'The transformation of international comity', *Law and Contemporary Problems* 71 (Summer 2008): 19–38 (available via https://scholarship.law.duke.edu/lcp/vol71/iss3/2).
[49] The full title was *Mobilium et immobilium natura, modo academico et forensi ad evidentiorum juris statutarii intellectum strictim proposita* (Utrecht: ex officinaa Johannis Ribbii, 1666). It has been reprinted twice, see Ahsmann, *Bibliografie van hoogleraren*, 147.
[50] Edwards, *The Selective Paulus Voet*, 9.
[51] Kollewijn and Fruin, *Geschiedenis van de Nederlandse wetenschap*, 100.
[52] C. 12, nr. 2: '*Statuta, cujuscumque sint generis, territorium non egrediuntur, nisi ex comitate*'.
[53] Paulus Voet, *In quatuor libros institutionum imperialium commentarius, ubi juris civilis tum antiqui, tum novi cum divino, forensi, canonico et feudali in multis collatio instituitur* (Utrecht: Apud Johannem Ribbium, 1668). It was printed in the same year in Gorinchem as well and the second edition was published in 1691 in Leiden. See Ahsmann, *Bibliografie van hoogleraren*, 147–148.

Paulus Voet incorporated it in his commentary, because he 'must have been aware of the role which canon law played in mitigating much of the severity of the civil law, not to mention the indelible imprint which canon law left on the institution of marriage and testamentary dispositions generally'.[54] An interesting passage in Voet's commentary is his discussion of the ideas of Thomas Hobbes (1588–1679). It shows that Paulus Voet was aware of contemporary movements and ideas. In discussing the several meanings of natural law (*'ius naturale'*) Voet discusses a 'heterodox theory', namely Hobbes's fictitious 'state of nature'.[55] According to Hobbes this state of nature was the state of man before there was a society. This state of nature was a state of war in which everyone had to fight for his own survival. There were no laws, and nobody was bound to any rule or code of conduct. Paulus Voet deemed this theory dangerous (*'perniciosa dogmata'*) and in his typical way disputes the theory of Hobbes by referring to the apostle Paul. Paulus Voet based his view that after the fall of Adam people still had a sense of right and wrong inherent in them on the authority of the apostle.[56] Johannes Voet also refers in his *Commentarius ad Pandectas* to this point of view when he discusses natural law.[57] Johannes insists that there was a rudimentary knowledge of right and wrong, even in times when savage mortals fed on herbs and acorns, lived in the forests, and had woodland beds spread by their hill wives. Even after the Fall of Man there were 'some sparks of principles of right and wrong' (*'scintillae quaedam principiorum justi et honesti'*).[58]

GENERAL APPRAISAL AND INFLUENCE

At his funeral Paulus Voet was called an 'ornament of the university' by Antonius Matthaeus. A contemporary portrait of Paulus Voet can still be seen in the senate room of the University of Utrecht as testimony of this statement. Although Paulus Voet's works are very varied in subject there is a certain unity in them. His life and works were in support of the project of his father to reform the academic disciplines. Paulus's legal writings on canon law

---

[54] Edwards, *The Selective Paulus Voet*, 9.
[55] Voet, *In quatuor libros institutionum imperialium commentarius etc.* book I, tit. II, nr. 7.
[56] Voet, *In quatuor libros institutionum imperialium commentarius etc.* book I, tit. II, nr. 7: 'Non denique negari poterit, esse aliquam legem, aliquod Jus Naturale cordibus hominum insculptum, id est, menti et conscientiae cujusque inditum, adeoque omnem hominem venientem in mundum illuminari ab auctore universi, id est, ei quasi ingenerari semina scintillasque boni maliqe, justi et injusti'.
[57] See also H. J. Erasmus, 'Natural law: Voet's criticism of De Groot', *Fundamina* 22.1 (2016): 40–52.
[58] Johannes Voet, *Commentarius ad Pandectas*, book 1, tit. 1, nr. 1.

and the relation between state and church bear witness to this. These writings have not been very influential. His *Theologia naturalis reformata* and *Prima philosophia reformata* on the other hand are still mentioned in reference works. Both works are described as 'exemplary of Dutch reformed scholasticism' and 'examples of Calvinistic metaphysics in the 17th century'.[59] Among jurists Paulus Voet is remembered for just one single opus. His *De statutis* is called 'a classic of international private law'.[60] This work and selections from it have been reprinted several times. The most recent is a bilingual edition of the most important passages of the *De Statutis* with an introduction and commentary by Basil Edwards. Paulus Voet's *De statutis* continues to receive scholarly attention and has been discussed in several dissertations. In particular Paulus Voet's doctrine of *comitas* has been transplanted to other jurisdictions, such as the United States of America and South Africa. Joseph Story, Dane professor of law at Harvard, justice at the Supreme Court and the 'father of the American law of conflicts', refers several times to Paulus Voet in his famous treatise 'Commentaries on the conflict between Foreign and Domestic Laws' (1834). The doctrine of comity has entered Anglo-American and South African case law from the eighteenth century. Although Huber is often cited as an authority in these cases, it has been shown that it is not Huber's, but Paulus Voet's, doctrine of *comitas* that has been adopted. Paulus Voet's authority as an exponent of Roman–Dutch law has been surpassed by that of his son Johannes Voet. It has however been said that what Johannes wrote about international private law in his *Commentarius ad Pandectas* is essentially what Paulus had already stated in his *De statutis*.[61]

RECOMMENDED READINGS

Ahsmann, Margreet. *Bibliografie van hoogleraren in de rechten aan de Utrechtse universiteit tot 1811*. Amsterdam; Oxford; New York; Tokyo: North Holland, 1993.

Duker, Arnoldus Cornelius. *Gisbertus Voetius*. Leiden: E. J. Brill, 1897–1915 (4 volumes).

Edwards, A. Basil. *The selective Paulus Voet: being a translation of those sections regarded as relevant to modern conflict of laws, of the De statutis eorumque concursu liber singularis (Amstelodami, 1661) by Paulus Voet (1619–1667) as a single book on statutes and their concurrence: an abridgement*. Pretoria: University of South Africa, 2007.

---

[59] Ferdinand Sassen, *Geschiedenis der wijsbegeerte in Nederland tot het einde der negentiende eeuw* (Amsterdam; Brussel: Elsevier, 1959), 137; *Dictionary*, 2: 1029.

[60] Siehr, K., 463.

[61] Kollewijn and Fruin, *Geschiedenis van de Nederlandse wetenschap*, 109.

Fruin, Jacobus Antonie. 'De strijd tusschen het Canonieke en het Romeinse recht in de middeleeuwen en het tijdvak van de Republiek der Vereenigde Nederlanden [oration 1879]'. In *Jaarboek der Rijksuniversiteit te Utrecht 1878–1879*, 31–71. Utrecht: J. L. Beijers, 1880.

Helmholz, Richard H., ed. *Canon law in protestant lands*. Berlin: Duncker & Humblot, 1992.

Kollewijn, R. D. and Th. A. Fruin. *Geschiedenis van de Nederlandse wetenschap van het internationaal privaatrecht tot 1880/Geschiedenis van de wetenschap van het Nederlandsch burgerlijk proces recht na 1811*. Series: Geschiedenis der Nederlandsche rechtswetenschap, vol. 1. Amsterdam: Noord-Hollandsche Uitgeversmaatschappij, 1937.

Kuipers, K. R. G. 'Paulus Voet (1619–1667). Enkele opmerkingen over deze 17e eeuwse geleerde en zijn werken, in het bijzonder met betrekking tot het internationaal privaatrecht'. In *Uit bibliotheektuin en informatieveld: opstellen aangeboden aan Dr. D. Grosheide bij zijn afscheid als bibliothecaris van de Rijksuniversiteit te Utrecht*, 51–63. Utrecht: Universiteitsbibliotheek, 1978.

Meijers, Eduard Maurits. 'L'histoire des principes fondamentaux du droit international privé à partir du Moyen-Age spécialement dans l'Europe occidentale'. Recueil des Cours de l'Académie de droit international, vol. 49, 543–686. Leiden; Boston: Brill/Nijhoff, 1934.

Scholten, J. M. B. *Het begrip comitas in het internationaal privaatrecht van de hollandse juristenschool der zeventiende eeuw*. Utrecht; Nijmegen: Dekker & Van de Vegt, 1949.

Suyling, J. Ph. *De statutentheorie in Nederland gedurende de XVIIe eeuw* (PhD diss., Utrecht). 's-Hertogenbosch: Robijns, 1893.

8

Ulrik Huber

Atsuko Fukuoka

BIOGRAPHICAL INTRODUCTION

Ulrik Huber was born in 1636 at Dokkum in Friesland as the sixth child of Zacharias Huber (c. 1601–1678), who was then a local notary (*procureur*).[1] Zacharias's father, Heinrich (or Hendrik, c. 1557–1641), was born in Altikon, a small village at the northern periphery of the canton Zürich. He came to the Low Countries during the Eighty Years War as a mercenary—according to Ulrik's account, as 'one of the vanguards of Dutch liberty and the Reformed Religion against the Spanish tyranny'.[2] Heinrich's military honour[3] probably helped his resettlement in the Low Countries and his son Zacharias to marry a woman from the Frisian *eigenerfden* (proprietors) class, Sjoukje Jensma (c. 1603–1644), in 1626.[4] Ulrik was born of this marriage. The political and social structure of Friesland was more democratic than that of other provinces

---

[1] For Huber's biography, see especially Theo J. Veen, *Recht en nut: Studiën over en naar aanleiding van Ulrik Huber (1636–1694)* (Zwolle: Tjeenk Willink, 1976); Veen et al., eds., *Ulrici Huberi: Oratio [III]* (Zwolle: Tjeenk Willink, 1978); Margaret Hewett, ed., *Ulric Huber (1636–1694): De ratione juris docendi et discendi diatribe per modum dialogi nonnullis aucta παραλιπομένοις, with a Translation and Commentary* (Nijmegen: Gerard Noodt Instituut, 2010). An annotated bibliography of all works by Huber is included in Robert Feenstra et al., *Bibliografie van hoogleraren in de rechten aan de Franeker universiteit tot 1811* (Amsterdam: Koninklijke Nederlandse Akademie van Wetenschappen, 2003), 47–98 (hereafter *Bibliografie Franeker*).

[2] The translation is based on the quotation by Veen from a lawsuit document which Huber submitted to the Court of Friesland when he sued Jacobus Perizonius (1651–1715) in 1693 for defamation (Veen, *Recht en nut*, 2).

[3] See the lawsuit document mentioned in the previous note and Ulrik Huber, *Historia vitae meae vernacule scripta ob certam rationem*, in Veen, *Recht en nut*, 247–264 (249); Campegius Vitringa, *Oratio funebris recitata in exsequiis amplissimi et gravissimi viri Ulrici Huber* (Franeker: Leonardus Strickius, 1700; *Bibliografie Franeker*, nos. 283–284), 7.

[4] On *eigenerfden* and the political structure of Friesland, see Hosto Spanninga, *Gulden vrijheid? Politieke cultuur en staatsvorming in Friesland, 1600–1640* (Hilversum: Verloren, 2012), 46–51.

of the Netherlands and it offered the extraordinarily talented boy a place to flourish. Ulrik climbed the ladder of society higher than any of his ancestors, eventually becoming a judge of Friesland's highest court and one of the most renowned Dutch jurists of its Golden Age.

Franeker was the primary locus of Huber's study and career. On 4 July 1651, at the age of fifteen, Huber matriculated at the university of this town. His first year was devoted to the study of philosophy, history, and classical languages. And yet Huber was 'destined to the study of law by his father', and started to study jurisprudence the next year, combining its study with that of languages and history.[5] His multidisciplinary talent was soon recognized by Johannes Jacobus Wissenbach (1607–1665), a jurist belonging to the tradition of humanist textual criticism, and then *professor primarius* of the law faculty. Probably on Wissenbach's recommendation, Huber went on to study law at Utrecht in 1654 but, due to the sudden death of his supervisor Antonius Matthaeus II (1601–1654), Huber returned to Franeker the following May without receiving his doctoral degree.[6] His promotion to *doctor iuris utriusque* eventually took place at Heidelberg in April/May 1657 after a year-long search in Germany for the right place to obtain the degree. Almost simultaneously with his promotion, the Friesian Government (*Gedeputeerde Staten*) appointed him professor of *eloquentia, historia, et politica* at the Faculty of Arts of his home university, probably as a result of the manoeuvring of his father and Wissenbach. From his inauguration in November of the same year until his death in 1694, Huber taught at this university (from 1665 at its Law Faculty). He was only absent when he worked as judge at the *Hof van Friesland* at Leeuwarden (1679–1682).

Loyalty to Franeker and Friesland characterizes Huber's career. The University of Leiden offered Huber a professorial post at least twice (in 1670 and 1681), but each time Huber declined.[7] Following the 1681 invitation, which occurred during the concluding phase of Huber's career as judge (*senator*) at Leeuwarden, the Frisian Government gave him the honorary title *ex-senator*, placed him at the exceptionally privileged position within the university immediately under the *rector magnificus*, and furnished him with the extraordinary salary of 2000 guilders per year. In freeing him from the duty to give public lectures, the government expected Huber to produce works

---

[5] Vitringa, *Oratio funebris*, 10.
[6] Wissenbach probably recommended Huber to Matthaeus II. Wissenbach himself had studied at Groningen in the early 1630s under Antonius Matthaeus I (1564–1637), the father of the Utrecht professor.
[7] Veen, *Recht en nut*, 3 (at n. 14). Compare J. van Kuyk, 'Ulrik Huber', in *Nieuw Nederlandsch biografisch woordenboek*, 1: 1165–1168, 1166.

on Roman Law, Public Law, and Frisian Law.⁸ This was a duty which Huber most gladly fulfilled.

MAJOR THEMES AND CONTRIBUTIONS

Huber's Love for *humaniora* and *jus publicum universale*

Huber loved *studia humaniora* and made use of neighbouring disciplines for a deeper understanding of jurisprudence in his own way.⁹ His first reaction to being made professor of *eloquentia, historia, et politica* not only testifies to his initial upset about the unexpected appointment, but also his deep respect for these disciplines:

> I have always loved those studies of humanities [*humaniora illa studia*] and made efforts not to be entirely ignorant in these subjects. And yet everyone knows what is required to make a profession of them and what excellence in knowledge one must possess in order to execute that profession becomingly and honourably. I am certain that I would prefer death, or life as an obscure and unknown man, than to turn my mind to, or embark on anything which later people would judge me to have been mismatched or undeserving.¹⁰

When Huber moved to the law faculty, he recommended that young law students acquire basic knowledge in *litteras ac artes*, which for Huber refers to Latin and Greek literature, history, logic, ethics, rhetoric, and (with some reservation) politics.¹¹ Moreover, Huber explored the intersection of jurisprudence and humanities in his own *Digressiones Justinianeae quibus humaniora juris continentur* (Franeker, 1st edn 1670), while focusing on *mere juridica*, with modest references to *humaniora*, in *Praelectiones juris Romani et hodierni* (Franeker, 1st edn 1678).¹² Both works went through several editions and secured Huber a Europe-wide reputation.¹³

---

⁸ The original text of this decision is quoted in Hewett, *De ratione juris docendi et discendi*, 82 (n. 23).

⁹ On Huber's 'ambivalent' relationship with legal humanism, see Govaert C. J. J. van den Bergh, *Die holländische elegante Schule: Ein Beitrag zur Geschichte von Humanismus und Rechtswissenschaft in den Niederlanden 1500–1800* (Frankfurt am Main: Vittorio Klostermann, 2002), 184–187.

¹⁰ Huber's letter to his father, Heidelberg 21 April 1657, in Veen, *Rechts en nut*, 281–283.

¹¹ Hewett, ed., *Huber: De ratione juris docendi et discendi*, 51–53. On politics, 'I do not wish politics to be studied in advance but I wish it rather to accompany the study of law' (translation by Hewett).

¹² Ulrik Huber, *Digressiones Justinianeae* [...] *quibus varia et imprimis humaniora juris continentur* (Franeker: Johannes Gyselaar et al., 1688), praefatio, *3v; Huber, *Praelectiones juris civilis* (Franeker: Henricus Amama et al., 1687), praefatio, *2r; Vitringa, *Oratio funebris*, 15.

¹³ *Bibliografie Franeker*, nos. 140–144 (*Digressiones Justinianeae*); 180–181, 246–263 (*Praelectiones*).

As the overlap of subjects in *Digressiones Justinianeae* suggests,[14] Huber's learning in *humaniora*, especially his critical examination of politics in comparison to jurisprudence, paved the way for his landmark publication *De jure civitatis libri tres, novam juris publici universalis disciplinam continentes (Three Books on the Law of the State, Containing the New Discipline of Universal Public Law*, 1st edn 1672[15]).[16] Transferring the Grotian method of *De jure belli ac pacis* from international to domestic relations,[17] and transforming Hobbesian social contract theory from the platform of absolutism to that of constitutionalism,[18] Huber made a fundamental step in the history of public law and earned the fame of *juris publici universalis doctrinae pater*.[19] In the harsh religio-political constellation of his age, Huber sought to establish his position between the Hobbesian fear of 'unbound contumacy of citizens' and the Monarchomach suspicion of 'unbridled impetus to rule'.[20]

Huber's Religious Development in Pietism

Religion played a significant role in Huber's intellectual formation. In particular, his early life shows several traces of personal contact with the current of Dutch Reformed Pietism (*gereformeerd Piëtisme*).[21] After his matriculation at the University of Franeker, but before commencing his study there, Huber

---

[14] Veen, *Recht en nut*, 78. Huber remarks that the process of writing *Digressiones Justinianeae* was 'permixtas publici juris' (blended with public law). Huber, *Digressiones Justinianeae*, *3v.
[15] *Bibliografie Franeker*, nos. 145–157. The title is according to the third, definitive edition published in 1694 (no. 150). Succeeding references to this work are to this 1694 edition.
[16] Veen, *Recht en nut*, 77–80.
[17] Huber, *De jure civitatis*, praefatio, 4.
[18] Noel Malcolm, *Aspects of Hobbes* (Oxford: Clarendon Press, 2002), 526. Malcolm emphasizes Huber's affinity to Hobbes under the cover of overt criticism.
[19] Hartog Hyman Tels, *De meritis Ulrici Huberi in jus publicum universale* (Leiden: Hazenberg, 1838), 67. On the discipline of 'universal public law', see Michael Stolleis, *Geschichte des öffentlichen Rechts in Deutschland* (Munich: Beck, 2012), 1 (2nd edn): 291–297.
[20] Huber, *De jure civitatis*, 1.2.3, 33–34, §§ 3, 9. E. H. Kossmann, *Political Thought in the Dutch Republic: Three Studies* (Amsterdam: Koninklijke Nederlandse Akademie van Wetenschappen, 2000), 117–119; Gustaaf Nifterik, 'Ulrik Huber on Fundamental Laws: A European Perspective', *Comparative Legal History* 4.1 (2016), 2–18.
[21] In using the term 'Dutch Reformed Pietism ([*Nederlands*] *gereformeerd Piëtisme*)' and 'Further Reformation (*Nadere Reformatie*)' in the succeeding part of this article, I follow the terminology articulated by C. Graafland, W. J. op 't Hof, and F. A. Lieburg in 'Nadere Reformatie: Opnieuw een poging tot begripsbepaling', *Documentatieblad Nadere Reformatie* 19 (1995), 105–184. For a concise reformulation in English, see Willem J. op 't Hof, 'Willem Teellinck and Gisbertus Voetius', in *Protestants and Mysticism in Reformation Europe*, eds. Ronald K. Rittgers and Vincent Evener (Leiden: Brill, 2019), 389–408 (389–390). According to this current of research, pietism as religious orientation to personal conversion and devoutness is not exclusive to Lutheran tradition, but more widely applicable to other confessional groups

spent one semester private tutorship of Calvinist pastor Johannes Nisener
(?–1654), lodging at his home in Hallum, a small village situated between the
university town and Dokkum.[22] This pastor, known for his 1639 translation
of one of the pietistic works by the English puritan William Bradshaw
(1571–1618), *A Preparation to the Receiving of the Sacrament, of Christs Body
and Bloud* (London, 1st edn 1617),[23] taught Huber the basics of logics and
dialectics, Greek of the New Testament and Hesiod, as well as some Hebrew.
The name Bradshaw, as well as Nisener's affiliation with the University
of Franeker from 1627 to the early 1630s, suggest a link to William Ames
(1576–1633), who himself had translated Bradshaw's *English Puritanisme*
([London] 1st edn 1605) into Latin in 1610.[24] Ames, active, as professor of
theology at Franeker from 1622 to 1633, established one important, non-
scholastic branch of Dutch Pietism different from that of the Voetians,

including English Puritanism and Dutch Protestantism. Besides Mennonite, Remonstrant, and other separatist variations of pietism in the Republic, the orthodox Dutch Reformed Church itself comprised its own type of pietism (*gereformeerd Piëtisme*), which was characterized by the 'inward experience of Reformed doctrine' and 'sanctification of life at the personal, familial, ecclesiastical, and societal levels', rested on 'stringent exegesis and application of the Ten Commandments' (Op 't Hof, 'Willem Teellinck', 389).

[22] Huber, *Historia vitae meae*, 250; Vitringa, *Oratio funebris*, 8. Nisener, too, was of German origin (probably from Sayn, north of Koblenz) and matriculated at the University of Franeker on 11 August 1627. After Lippenhuizen (1633–) and Blija (1639–), he was called in March 1646 to serve the Reformed Church at Hallum and died there in 1654. See J. Engelsma, *Volglyst van predikanten, wie, waar, wanneer zedert de gelukkige Hervorminge onder de Classis van de Zevenwouden in dienst geweest zyn* (Leeuwarden: Pieter Koumans, 1763), 221; T. A. Romein, *Naamlijst der predikanten, sedert de Hervorming tot nu toe, in de Hervormde gemeenten van Friesland* (Leeuwarden: Meijer, 1888), 112–113, 533, 594; A. J. van der Aa, *Biographisch woordenboek der Nederlanden*, 21 vols. (Haarlem: van Brederode, 1852–1878), 13: 263–264; G. A. Wumkes, 'Johannes Nisener', in *Nieuw Nederlandsch biografisch woordenboek*, 10 vols., eds. P. C. Molhuysen, P. J. Blok, et al. (Leiden: Sijthoff, 1911–1937), 10: 671; Georg Becker, *Die Deutschen Studenten und Professoren an der Akademie zu Franeker* (Soest: Meilenstein, 1943), 43.

[23] William Bradshaw, *Bruylofts-kleed der tafel-ghenoten Christi. Dat is: twee tractaten van de voor-bereydinghe tot de weerdighe ontfanginghe des h. Avondmaels. Beide voor desen in het Engelsch beschreven.[...] Nu in de Neder-duytsche sprake overgeset, door Iohannem Nisenerum* (Leeuwarden: Dirck Alberts, 1639). C. W. Schoneveld, *Intertraffic of the Mind: Studies in Seventeenth-Century Anglo-Dutch Translation with a Checklist of Books Translated from English into Dutch, 1600–1700* (Leiden: Brill/Universitaire Pers Leiden, 1983), 181–182 (no. 119). Further bibliographical information on this volume can be found in the digital bibliography *Pietas*, http://www.pietasonline.nl/pietas. For the importance of Dutch and Latin translations of English puritan literature to Dutch Reformed Pietism, see W. J. op 't Hof, *Engelse pietistische geschriften in het Nederlands, 1598–1622* (Rotterdam: Lindenberg, 1987), esp. 415 (refers to another translation of Bradshaw); id., 'Nadere reformatie in Friesland?' *De zeventiende eeuw* 20 (2004): 53–65 (56).

[24] [Bradshaw/Ames,] *Puritanismus Anglicanus, sive praecipua dogmata eorum, qui inter vulgo dictos Puritanos in Anglia, rigidiores habentur* (Frankfurt: Aubrianus, 1610).

discussed further below.[25] Huber departed from Hallum for Franeker in November 1651 and pursued his study of Greek with a group of three other theology students, including another Nisener, using Homer as their exercise material.[26]

Although no further information about Johannes Nisener's tutorship of Huber is currently available, Vitringa suggests that Johannes Nisener's role in his education was not trivial.[27] Huber could also have had connections to the contemporary pietistic scenes through marriage: his first wife Agnes Althusius's (1641–1663[28]) uncle, Samuel Althusius (1600–1669), was a minister of the German-speaking Reformed community in Leiden (since 1645) and translated several English puritan works into Dutch.[29] Young Huber's pietistic cast of mind can most clearly be observed in an episode of spiritual 'rebirth' that occurred in 1654–1655, during his study at Utrecht. Huber recalled this event on his deathbed as something that touched his soul at its deepest part: '[i]n about the same period', namely around the death of Matthaeus II on 25 December 1654, 'I felt a big change in my heart and engaged myself in holy supper. I was reborn during the end of 1654 and the beginning of the next year. May God not turn this hope deceptive.'[30] It should be noted that Nisener also died in 1654 (the exact date is unknown). The experience of a spiritual rebirth from the death of sin was of central importance for a true believer's life as idealized in the Reformed Pietism.[31] Vitringa's *Oratio funebris* correspondingly highlights this Utrecht conversion, praising Huber as being 'invited by God to an intimate, innermost communion, from which many theologians are excluded'.[32] The centrality of this experience to

---

[25] On Ames, see W. B. S. Boeles, *Frieslands Hoogeschool en het Rijks Athenaeum te Franeker*, 2 vols (Leeuwarden: Kuipers, 1878–1889), 2.1: 116–119; Keith L. Sprunger, 'Ames, William', in *Oxford Dictionary of National Biography*, online edition (2004): https://doi.org/10.1093/ref:odnb/440; W. van't Spijker, 'Amesius, Guilielmus', *Encyclopedie Nadere Reformatie*, ed. W. J. op't Hof et al. (Utrecht: Groot Goudriaan, 2015), 1: 35–44.

[26] Huber, *Historia vitae meae*, 250; Vitringa, *Oratio funebris*, 10. These sources mention as Huber's peers Abraham de Graeu (1632–1683, son of a minister, later professor of mathematics at Franeker, and Huber's life-long friend), Daniël Nisener (?–1667, died young as minister at Hindelopen), and Johannes Isenberg (fl. 1651, died young as pastoral candidate).

[27] Vitringa, *Oratio funebris*, 8.

[28] In December 1659 Huber married Agnes Althusius, the granddaughter of the famous political thinker Johannes Althusius (1557–1638).

[29] Jan van de Kamp, 'Althusius, Samuel', in *Encyclopedie Nadere Reformatie*, 1:26–30. Van de Kamp suggests that Samuel's activities at the classis of Leiden and his translations of English devotional works show a certain distance from the rigorist, Voetian interpretation of piety especially regarding the question of Sabbath.

[30] Huber, *Historia vitae meae*, 251.

[31] Graafland, Op 't Hof, and Lieburg, 'Nadere Reformatie', 120 and *passim*.

[32] Vitringa, *Oratio funebris*, 11.

Huber's life as a Christian jurist can be seen in the personal emblem which he adapted for the title pages of his mature publications in about the 1680s. Under the motto *lex et ratio*, the emblem shows a female personification of *prudentia* (or *sapientia*) holding a sceptre and a book, and upon her breast Huber always has a star-like object shine, which represents the inner light given by the Holy Spirit.[33]

The religious features of Huber's life give rise to a question about his place in the confessional constellation within the United Provinces at that time. The fact that his religious conversion occurred at the Reformed Church of Utrecht in the middle of the 1650s requires special attention in this regard.

In particular, Utrecht was then the foremost place in the Republic where pietistic inspirations, stemming, importantly, from English Puritanism, merged with the *Nadere Reformatie*, a domestic movement for the 'further' reformation of an all-too-tepid church and an all-too-corrupt society. The *Nadere Reformatie* overlaps much with international Pietism and was a particular national expression of it within the Reformed context, but differs from Pietism in terms of its historical origin, which consisted in particluar in a critical reaction to the transformation of the Calvinist church from a gathering of saints in exile into the 'state religion' of the Dutch Republic.[34] A theocratic spirit, or an effort to purge the whole of society from existing evils in a much more intensive way than Pietism in general, characterized the *Nadere Reformatie*.[35] Communities where these ideals caught the majority of local ministers often experienced an uncompromising confrontation between the church and the civil authority, especially when regents with opposing convictions or interests held the upper hand as regards their pro-church colleagues among the magistracy.[36] Utrecht, where the magistracy and the church had been quarrelling since the 1640s about the teaching of

---

[33] Except for smaller publications, the earliest use of this emblem seems to be in 1682 for *Positiones sive lectiones juris contractae* and *Auspicia domestica* (respectively nos. 187 and 191 in *Bibliografie Franeker*). An enlarged version of the emblem adapted to a full-page illustration is found inserted in the frontmatter of the 1694 edition of *De jure civitatis* (no. 150 in *Bibliografie Franeker*, mentioned above, n. 15). This version more emphatically depicts the object shining like a sun with a face emitting dazzling rays on the goddess's breast. A digitalized image is offered online as an attachment to this 1694 edition on the *Short-Title Catalogue, Netherlands* (STCN), though in a low resolution.

[34] Graafland, Op 't Hof, and Lieburg, 'Nadere Reformatie', especially at 117, 123, and 143–145.

[35] On this difference between the *Nadere Reformatie* and pietism in general, see Graafland, Op 't Hof, and Lieburg, 'Nadere reformatie', 143–149; Op 't Hof, 'Nadere reformatie in Friesland?' 53.

[36] Graafland, Op 't Hof, and Lieburg, 'Nadere reformatie', 124, offer several examples of such conflicts between church and state including the Utrecht case, while drawing attention to the existence of sympathizers of the *Nadere reformatie* among the ruling class of the Republic. For one important example of such a regent and his ideas, see Wim Decock, 'The Law of

Cartesianism at Utrecht University, became a typical example of such divisiveness.[37] In 1653 the leading theologian of the *Nadere Reformatie*, Gisbertus Voetius (1589–1676), published the famous *Theologische advys (Theological Advice)*.[38] Voetius argued that the convention by which the political establishments of Utrecht earned private profits from former Catholic church properties was a sin that cried to heaven.[39]

Huber's stay at Utrecht coincided with the period of heated discord that followed the publication of *Theologische advys*. Jodocus van Lodenstein (1620–1677) and Justus van den Bogaert (at office 1653–1663), whom Vitringa's *Oratio funebris* names as Huber's principal mentors at the Utrecht church,[40] belonged to the ministers who sided with Voetius against the civil authority.[41] In contrast, Cyprianus Regneri ab Oosterga (1614–1687), a professor of law whose lectures Huber followed after the death of Matthaeus II[42] (and who therefore was the likely promotor of Huber's doctoral degree), was the central opponent of Voetius among the executives of Utrecht University.[43] In 1655, the year Huber left Utrecht, Ab Oosterga published two counter-pamphlets against the *Theologische advys*, although anonymously.[44]

Conscience in the Reformed Tradition: Johannes A. van der Meulen (1635–1702) and his *Tractatus theologico-juridicus*', in *Das Gewissen in den Rechtslehren der protestantischen und katholischen Reformationen / Conscience in the Legal Teachings of the Protestant and Catholic Reformations* (Leipzig: Evangelische Verlagsanstalt, 2017), vol. 31, 87–110. See also Chapter 6: Janwillem Oosterhuis, 'Hugo Grotius', and Chapter 7: Johannes van Kralingen, 'Paulus Voet', both in this volume.

[37] Theo Verbeek, *Descartes and the Dutch: Early Reactions to Cartesian Philosophy, 1637–1650* (Carbondale [etc.]: Southern Illinois University Press, 1992).

[38] [Gisbertus Voetius,] *Theologisch advys over 't Gebruyck van kerkelijcke goederen van Canonisyen, vicaryen, &c. Eerste deel* (Amsterdam: Jodocus Hondius, 1653).

[39] A. C. Duker, *Gisbertus Voetius*, 4 vols. (Leiden: Brill, 1897–1915), 2 (1910): 294–340; Rienk Vermij, *The Calvinist Copernicans: The Reception of the New Astronomy in the Dutch Republic, 1575–1750* (Amsterdam: Koninklijke Nederlandse Akademie van Wetenschappen, 2002), 225–227.

[40] Vitringa, *Oratio funebris*, 11.

[41] P. J. Proost points out a division among the ministers belonging to the Reformed Church of Utrecht in *Jodocus van Lodenstein: eene kerkhistorische studie* (Amsterdam: Brandt, 1880), 199–200.

[42] Huber, *Historia vitae meae*, 251; Vitringa, *Oratio funebris*, 10; Veen, *Oratio [III]*, 2–3.

[43] On Cyprianus Regneri ab Oosterga, see Johann Friedrich Jugler, *Beyträge zur juristischen Biographie oder genauere litterarische und critische Nachrichten von dem Leben und den Schriften verstorbener Rechtsgelehrten auch Staatsmänner, welche sich in Europa berühmt gemacht haben* (Leipzig: Kummer, 1775), 2: 331–339; van der Aa, *Biographisch woordenboek der Nederlanden*, 14: 155–158; J. van Kuyk, 'Regneri ab Oosterga (Cyprianus)', *Nieuw Nederlandsch biografisch woordenboek* 2 (1912): 1179–1180.

[44] Duker, *Gisbertus Voetius*, 2: 155–157, 305, n. 3; Margreet Ahsmann, *Bibliografie van hoogleraren in de rechten aan de Utrechtse Universiteit tot 1811* (Amsterdam: North-Holland, 1993), 123–124 (nos. 312 and 313).

Huber's short time at Utrecht thus established his religious self-awareness decisively in the form of a pietist's spiritual rebirth, while, as the evidence suggests, exposing him to political, social, and even personal divisions brought about by the intensification of pietistic engagement with social issues. A certain degree of similarity to the Voetians' programmes can also be observed regarding the later life of Huber. Commentators have pointed out an antagonism toward Herman Alexander Röell's (1653–1718) extension of the Cartesian method to questions of faith,[45] intensive efforts to combat the absolutist and rationalistic consequences of Hobbes's and Spinoza's political theories,[46] and an endorsement of Calvin's standpoint against those forerunners of the (Radical) Enlightenment.[47] Does this mean that Huber represented Voetian ideals in jurisprudence? The next sections investigate this question.

Huber Against Theocratic Ministers

Although Huber undoubtedly was a man of strong religious conviction, there is also evidence suggesting he cannot be unequivocally aligned with a particular group such as the Voetians. If anything, he was among the broad band of 'eclectics' who carefully charted their paths through radicalism, both religious and philosophical.[48] The privileges that the Frisian stadtholder's court and the States of Friesland offered Huber in order to keep the star professor at Franeker secured him a unique freedom to stay proudly far above all striving parties.

An example of Huber's public image of proud independence can be seen in a letter of dedication written by his former student and protégé, Hadriaan Beverland (1650–1716).[49] Beverland, a typical Dutch Enlightenment intellectual

---

[45] Veen, *Recht en nut*, 182–183; Jacob van Sluis, *Herman Alexander Röell* (Leeuwarden: Fryske Akademy, 1988), 59–79.

[46] Veen, *Recht en nut*, 160–214; Atsuko Fukuoka, *The Sovereign and the Prophets: Spinoza on Grotian and Hobbesian Biblical Argumentation* (Leiden: Brill, 2018), 311–343.

[47] Aza Goudriaan, 'Ulrik Huber (1636–1694) and John Calvin: The Franeker Debate on Human Reason and the Bible (1686–1687)', *Church History and Religious Culture* 91, nos. 1–2 (2011), 165–178.

[48] For assessments of Huber as a moderate Cartesian, see C. Louise Thijssen-Schoute, *Nederlands Cartesianisme*, rev. by Theo Verbeek (Utrecht: HES, 1989), 132; Kossmann, *Political Thought*, 111.

[49] Beverland belonged to the seventeen students to whom Huber dedicated the first edition of *De jure civitatis* published in 1672 (*Bibliografie Franeker*, no. 145). Not much is known about Beverland's study at Franeker; see R. De Smet, *Hardianus Beverlandus (1650–1716), Non unus e multis peccator: Studie over het leven en werk van Hadriaan Beverland* (Brussels: Koninklijke Academie voor Wetenschappen, 1988), 20; Karen E. Hollewand, *The Banishment of Beverland: Sex, Sin, and Scholarship in the Seventeenth-Century Dutch Republic* (Leiden: Brill, 2019), 24.

who extravagantly invested his talent in questions of sexuality and erotica, dedicated one of his highly controversial treatises, *De stolatae virginitatis jure* (Leiden, 1680 [1679]⁵⁰) to Huber, who was then a member of the *Hof van Friesland*. In that dedication, dated 18 July 1679, Beverland writes:

> I assume that you [Huber] won't look down from the lofty summit at these shady and infamous sparks [of anger] that disputes and sentences emit; if you regard them in their naked entirely, you would laugh at many, while censuring most.⁵¹

Beverland probably had in mind a Provincial Synod of Gouda, held between 11 and 21 July, where his freshly published writing, the second edition of *De peccato originali* (n.p., 1679), was critically discussed.⁵² It is not known whether Huber did anything for Beverland: Huber probably remained aloof, while Beverland was eventually banished from Holland.⁵³

Whatever Huber thought of Beverland's predicament, he did not fear to openly confront Calvinist ministers when it concerned his principles—especially the question of conscience. This was clearly proven in a dispute about the introduction of dancing lessons for students at the University of Franeker.⁵⁴ On 16 December 1682 the Friesian Government accepted a request from the university and ordered Jan (or Jean) Baptista de Cadillan (?–1714), the dancing master at the stadtholder's court in Leeuwarden, to appear at least three times per week in Franeker to give lessons. It was Huber himself who took the initiative for the appointment and it was Huber that ignited the controversy. He anonymously published a short pamphlet, *Dansmeester van Franequer geheekelt ende geholpen* (*Dancing Master of Franeker Heckled and Helped*, Franeker, 1683), in which he eloquently defended the appointment as a legitimate attempt to offer students an

---

⁵⁰ For the correct year of publication and other background, see De Smet, *Hardianus Beverlandus*, 39; Hollewand, *The Banishment of Beverland*, 36, 41, 267.
⁵¹ Beverland, *Justinianaei de stolatae virginitatis jure lucubratio academica* (Leiden: Johannes Lindanus, 1680), sig. A3r.
⁵² Hollewand, *The Banishment of Beverland*, 30, n. 50.
⁵³ De Smet, *Hardianus Beverlandus*, 46; Hollewand, *The Banishment of Beverland*, 34–40.
⁵⁴ Besides Boeles, *Frieslands Hoogeschool*, 1: 345–346, a series of articles by Brooks offers a neat study of related primary sources, without, however, fully situating them within the wider contemporary religious context and Huber's theory about church and state: Lynn Matluck Brooks, 'Dancing at a Dutch University, Part I: The Franeker Dancing Master, 1682', *Dance Chronicle* 9.2 (1986): 157–176; Brooks, 'Dancing at a Dutch University [Part II]', *Dance Chronicle* 9.3 (1986): 356–385; Brooks, 'Court, Church, and Province: Dancing in the Netherlands, Seventeenth and Eighteenth Centuries', *Dance Research Journal* 20.1 (1988): 19–27.

opportunity for decent recreation, while piquantly caricaturing opposing ministers.[55]

Op 't Hof was probably right in asserting that the opposition of the Friesian Reformed Church to the introduction of dancing lessons at the University of Franeker was an aspect of the *Nadere Reformatie*'s programme.[56] Johannes van Holst (?–1691), one of the ministers who disputed with Huber, invoked *De choreis* (Utrecht, 1644; Amsterdam, 1667[57]) by Voetius as the foremost authority regarding the orthodox view on this issue.[58] Dancing itself had been contested since the last decades of the sixteenth century by Dutch Calvinist ministers, including those in Friesland.[59] Along with gambling, earning usuries, sabbath desecration and similar things, dancing became the object of intensified protest in the context of the *Nadere Reformatie*.[60] Voetius denounced quite a comprehensive range of dancing, excepting only dancing as physical exercise or dancing with the same sex or with one's spouse, so long as it was done without an audience.[61] According to him, a reformed Christian should refrain not only from performing but also watching dancing;[62] the head of a family must firmly refuse to offer any opportunities for such sins in his household;[63] likewise, the magistracy should not tolerate dance schools or the activities of dancing masters.[64] Indeed, Voetius considered the profession of dancing masters illegal, along with those of actors at theatres and masked

---

[55] Huber acknowledged his authorship in the pamphlet that followed, writing that he himself mediated the requests of students to the university's authorities. Ulrik Huber, *Antwoort op een missive wegens een boekje genaemt 'De dansmeester van Franeker geheeckelt en geholpen'* (Franeker: Hans Gyselaar, 1683), 6–7.

[56] Op 't Hof, 'Nadere reformatie in Friesland?' 64.

[57] The treatise derives from a disputation held on 30 September 1643 and was long known through its Dutch translation published the next year, *Een kort tractaetjen van de danssen* (Utrecht: Willem Strick, 1644). The Latin version appeared in 1667 as a part of Gisbertus Voetius, *Selectarum disputationum theologicarum pars quarta* (Amsterdam: Johannes Janssonius à Waesberge, 1667).

[58] Johannes van Holst, *Missive aan een vriend, tegen de 'Antwoordt op een Missive'* (Leeuwarden: Hauke Egberts Heringa, 1683), sig. A2r. On van Holst, see Ph. H. Breuker, 'Holst, Johannes van', in *Encyclopedie Nadere Reformatie*, 1: 358–340.

[59] F. G. Naerebout, 'Snoode exercitien: Het zeventiende-eeuwse Nederlandse protestantisme en de dans', *Volkskundig Bulletin* 16 (1990), 125–155; Herman Roodenburg, *Onder censuur: De kerkelijke tucht in de gereformeerde gemeente van Amsterdam, 1578–1700* (Hilversum: Verloren, 1990), 321–329. For examples from the church history of Friesland, see W. Bergsma, *Tussen Gideonsbende en publieke kerk: Een studie over het gereformeerd protestantisme in Friesland, 1580–1650* (Hilversum: Verloren, 1999), 255, 298.

[60] Duker, *Gisbertus Voetius*, 2:235–246.

[61] Voetius, *Een kort tractaetjen*, 27–28.

[62] Voetius, *Een kort tractaetjen*, 58.

[63] Voetius, *Een kort tractaetjen*, 59.

[64] Voetius, *Een kort tractaetjen*, 60.

jugglers.⁶⁵ Young Huber must have witnessed corresponding church discipline cases while he actively visited the Reformed Church at Utrecht.⁶⁶

Huber, however, now 46 years old, comically presented the clerics' zeal for social reform in his *Dansmeester van Franequer* and, due to this, was sued for libel.⁶⁷ The pamphlet takes the form of a fictive conversation between a foreign student studying theology at Franeker and two local ministers of the Reformed Church, whom the student coincidentally meets at an inn. Huber describes the ministers as drinking huge glasses of beer and smoking pipes, which is, as Lynn Matluck Brooks writes, already 'a most unflattering picture' of the servants of God.⁶⁸ And yet the most decisive point of Huber's caricature entails in the fact that he mimics typical idioms and methods that those theocratically minded ministers had been employing for the social mobilization of their desired reforms.

In particular, the older minister plays the role of the typical clergy zealous for theocratic reform in the dialogue. Huber has him denounce the decision of the university as a 'sin crying to heaven [*tot de hemel roepende zonde*]', using the iconic expression that frequently accompanied the *Nadere Reformatie*'s combat against abominable sins.⁶⁹ The old minister condemns this decision of the university as 'giving so much of an ear to the devil', which is reminiscent of the frequent affiliation of dancing with Satan's manoeuvres in Voetius's text and references.⁷⁰ What is particularly 'scandalous and unheard of' for the older minister is that a dance school was not only 'connived', but is now 'founded and maintained by the public authority'. The university hereby violated a very important 'cultural fiction', to use Benjamin J. Kaplan's words,⁷¹ namely, that everyone in the Republic must at least pretend to acknowledge a fictive wall of separation between the officially recognized position on morals (i.e. the Calvinist position) and all other unofficial positions.

---

⁶⁵ Voetius, *Een kort tractaetjen*, 59–60.
⁶⁶ Duker offers several examples from the minutes of the church council at Utrecht, dating from the 1640s to 1660s, in which dancing activities by members of the church are reported and censured. See Duker, *Gisbertus Voetius*, 2: 239–246.
⁶⁷ Brooks, 'Dancing at a Dutch University, Part I', 165.
⁶⁸ Brooks, 'Dancing at a Dutch University, Part I', 161.
⁶⁹ E.g. Voetius, *Een kort tractaetjen*, 23. See also Willem J. van Asselt, 'Een roepende zonde' Gisbertus Voetius (1589–1676) en zijn strijd tegen de lombarden', in *Armzalig of armlastig? Armoede als vraagstuk en inspiratiebron voor de theologie*, eds. M. F. Farag et al. (Utrecht: Faculteit Godgeleerdheid Universiteit Utrecht, 2006), 86–103.
⁷⁰ E.g. Voetius, *Een kort tractaetjen*, 43: 'giving the soul to the devil;' 45: 'the procession of the devil;' 55: 'rogueness of the devil'.
⁷¹ Benjamin J. Kaplan, *Divided by Faith: Religious Conflict and the Practice of Toleration in Early Modern Europe* (Cambridge, MA: Harvard University Press, 2007), 176.

The university's act was all the more scandalous because it occurred in the institution that had originally been 'specially consecrated to Christ and His community'.[72] Huber's older minister deplores the university's fall into 'a school of idleness and godlessness, not fearing the wrath of God'.[73] Invoking an implicit parallel to the faithful city Jerusalem's fall into whoredom, Huber has the minister cry out: 'my hair raises up like a mountain out of the fright, when I think of God's judgement that hangs over the head of our country'.[74] The popular image of the Netherlands as the Second Israel is at work here, connected with that of the divine wrath which would afflict the country if it continued to tolerate sinners.[75]

Huber also caricatures the Dutch clerics' typical pattern of exerting pressure upon their opponents. When confuted by the student (the proxy for Huber's own view), the old minister angrily stands up and threateningly states his last words: 'we have discussed the issue already two times at the classis; now we are going to bring it to the synod. A further investigation will be executed there in order to uncover the instigators of this godlessness.'[76] Needless to say, this was the way in which the Reformed Church mobilized its internal organizations against audacious figures inside and outside the church. Provincial synods often issued the result of their discussion as requests to municipal or provincial magistracies, or sometimes to universities (as in Beverland's case[77]), asking them to exercise their power and jurisdiction in order to suppress what the church recognized as an evil. As a result, the church–state relationship in the Dutch Republic depended upon whether these civil servants rendered a willing or deaf ear to such requests from the Reformed Church.[78] In this respect, Huber shows a clear preference for moderation and dialogue over zero-toleration activism and open confrontation. In *Dansmeester van Franequer*, the younger minister remains seated with the student, while his older colleague, the representation of hardline clergy, stomps out of the room in rage. Huber narrates: '[h]is colleague stayed seated and resumed the

---

[72] [Huber,] *Dansmeester van Franequer*, sig. A2r.
[73] [Huber,] *Dansmeester van Franequer*, sig. A2r.
[74] [Huber,] *Dansmeester van Franequer*, 4.
[75] [Huber,] *Dansmeester van Franequer*, 4. On the Dutch Republic as the Second Israel, see G. Groenhuis, *De Predikanten: De sociale positie van de gereformeerde predikanten in de Republiek der Vereinigde Nederlanden voor ±1700* (Groningen: Wolters-Noordhoff, 1977); Simon Schama, *The Embarrassment of Riches: An Interpretation of Dutch Culture in the Golden Age* (New York: Knopf, 1987), 93–125; Kaplan, *Divided by Faith*, 116.
[76] [Huber,] *Dansmeester van Franequer*, 7.
[77] Hollewand, *The Banishment of Beverland*, 34.
[78] On the contemporary Church–State relationship and related literature, see Fukuoka, *The Sovereign and the Prophets*, 242–244.

discourse, and yet in a more unpretentious and patient manner, trying to understand the argument'.[79] This communicates Huber's belief that the readiness for a dialogue is prerequisite to constructing a sound relation between church and state.

Jus circa sacra *and* adiaphora

What Huber has the student and the younger minister discuss in *Dansmeester van Franequer* reflects and supplements his general theory of *jus circa sacra summarum potestatum* expounded in his main work, *De jure civitatis*. For example, Huber's orientation to the middle path is clearly expressed in this treatise where he presents the *status controversiae* regarding contemporary views on *jus circa sacra*.[80] While denouncing Erastus's and Hobbes's standpoints as 'opinions which error in their deficiency', Huber rejects the clerical struggles, observable on both Catholic and Protestant sides, for supremacy over the secular authority, denouncing them both as 'opinions which error in their excessiveness'.[81] 'Keeping ourselves away from extremism', Huber argues, 'we should follow the middle path among all.'[82] Huber's main argument in *Dansmeester van Franequer* corresponds to this 'middle path'.

Central to Huber's middle-of-the-road standpoint is a distinction between *necessaria* and other matters, that is, between 'what God demanded explicitly and without mediation' and what God did not order in this way.[83] God's explicit command and prohibition, comprising the revealed and natural laws of God, bind human conscience with necessity, allowing no deviation. In contrast, the matters about which no such will of God has been expressed can and do vary depending on time, place, and other circumstances. This distinction serves in turn as the boundary that limits the otherwise absolute power of the sovereign. While the sovereign may exercise their legislative, executive, and judicial powers over the latter, only God may rule and judge the former, which pertain to questions of conscience. In this context, Huber defends *jus internum conscientiae*, a series of entitlements that are reminiscent of liberty of conscience and free exercise of religion. Each individual may exercise this

---

[79] [Huber,] *Dansmeester van Franequer*, 7.
[80] Huber, *De jure civitatis*, 1.5.1, 149–150.
[81] Huber, *De jure civitatis*, 1.5.5, 165, and 1.5.6, 169, both chapter titles.
[82] Huber, *De jure civitatis*, 1.5.1, 150, § 20.
[83] Huber, *De jure civitatis*, 1.5.2, 152, § 4. For more on this distinction, see Fukuoka, *The Sovereign and the Prophets*, 322–325.

jus, even against the will of human authority, primarily secular, but also ecclesiastical.[84]

Applied to the issue of dancing, the pivotal question becomes whether dancing truly belongs to the things that God has explicitly forbidden. As Huber's proxy, the student repeatedly points out that God has not judged dancing either good or bad. Huber in *Dansmeester van Franequer* calls this kind of matter 'middelbare' (intermediate), which refers to the notion of so-called *adiaphora*, or 'things indifferent'.[85] When the younger minister invokes the Israelites' dancing around the Golden Calf (Exod. 32) and Salome's dance for the head of John the Baptist (Matt. 14:1–12, Mark 6:14–29), Huber's student replies that no clear condemnation about dancing can be inferred from these examples.[86] In addition, he continues, the Bible approvingly speaks of dancing with respect to Miriam (Exod. 15:20–21) and David (2 Sam. 6:14–16, 20–23). Implicitly rejecting Voetius's interpretation, the student states that 'neither aye nor nay can be explicitly inferred from the Bible; it shows that an exercise of body as such is neither good nor bad, but be in the middle [*middelbaer*]'.[87] Similar examples, such as wearing wigs, and a local Frisian banquet entertainment that included kissing someone's wife many times (called *zommertjes*, which the student, being a foreigner, refers to as an embarrassingly obscene custom), strengthen Huber's argument that many moral matters, including dancing, are actually dependent much on time and place.[88]

When viewing the student's reasoning in light of the *De jure civitatis*, his conclusion might seem to lead to an étatist argument that the sovereigns can regulate such *adiaphora* matters in whatever ways they please and that ministers cannot rightfully criticize their decision. Whereas a Hobbesian would approve of such an idea, Huber sees it as one form of extremism. What Huber understands to be the primary question with regard to the dancing lessons at the university is less about sovereigns' absolute power than it is about ministers' entitlement to censure sins. The *Dansmeester van Franequer* concretizes, as well as supplements, the theory of *De jure civitatis* in this respect.

---

[84] Huber, *De jure civitatis*, 1.5.2, 156, § 45.

[85] Sometimes also *middelmatig* (middle-range), as employed in § 76 of the Church Order of Dordrecht (1574). For the historical context that surrounded this concept, see Brian Tierney, *Liberty and Law: The Idea of Permissive Natural Law, 1100–1800* (Washington, DC: Catholic University of America Press, 2014).

[86] [Huber,] *Dansmeester van Franequer*, 9–10.

[87] [Huber,] *Dansmeester van Franequer*, 10. Compare Voetius, *Een kort tractaetjen*, 62–63, 82–83.

[88] [Huber,] *Dansmeester van Franequer*, 5–6, 13.

In *De jure civitatis*, the right for the church to censure religious misconduct derives from *jus internum conscientiae*, especially from the collective aspect of this right. While regarding the individual to be the primary agent of this *jus*, Huber also recognizes its collective dimension quite widely, because he considers the 'entitlement to organize meetings of believers in such numbers as necessary to stimulate religiosity and communion of believers' highly pertinent to that *jus* itself.[89] From this follows a series of derivative rights for exercising religion in organizational form and for keeping the unity of such religious association. One of these rights is *jus clavium*.[90] To investigate the sins of members and to subject them to corresponding disciplinary measures including excommunication is *per se* a legitimate right of the church,[91] because the entitlement to organize meetings of believers accompanies the 'jurisdiction to escape from a company with those who by their own moral misbehaviour have disclosed that their pursuit of faith was actually faked'.[92]

However, if the church's right to censure the sins of believers is thus founded upon *jus internum conscientiae*, it would also be true that the limit of the *jus* would limit the extent of the church's right as well. This implication is made explicit in the *Dansmeester van Franequer* through the debate between the student and the younger minister. The younger minister, representing more pragmatic clerics, mildly concedes to the student's argument that dancing belongs to *middelbare* things. But he points to a repercussion that would follow if the university and the magistracy, notwithstanding the dissent of the Reformed Church, officially approved what they had been suppressing by disciplinary measures since Calvin's time. Such a policy would amount to disrespect of the church's authority, or at least deserve to be seen as unwise, according to the younger minister. The student offers a counterargument based on rightfulness in response to this utilitarian reasoning:

> But don't you yourself consider if these arguments are substantial enough to impose an ill-founded fastidiousness upon the conscience of humankind? This is by no means less culpable than to condemn what God did not condemn or to declare not sinful what God condemns.[93]

In other words, the church has no legitimate claim to authority beyond the extent that it correctly represents Christ's reign over human conscience, the ultimate foundation of the *jus internum conscientiae*. An unfounded

---

[89] Huber, *De jure civitatis*, 1.5.3, 156, § 2.
[90] Huber, *De jure civitatis*, 1.5.3, 156, §§ 4–5.
[91] Huber, *De jure civitatis*, 1.5.3, 157, § 7.
[92] Huber, *De jure civitatis*, 1.5.3, 156, § 3.
[93] [Huber,] *Dansmeester van Franequer*, 17–18.

expansion of the *necessaria* by the church is no less an infringement of Christian conscience than a wilful retrenchment of the same by the sovereign.

GENERAL APPRAISAL AND INFLUENCE

As the analyses above have shown, Huber's objections to theocratic clergy and his theoretical use of conscience to neutralize their claims make it difficult to identify him, in spite of his pietistic background and mentality, with the political intervention of the *Nadere Reformatie*, which extended far beyond the spiritual reform of individual minds. Such differentiation from theocratic aspirations is also embedded in the main text of *De jure civitatis*, as elsewhere proven.[94] In this regard, W. J. op 't Hof is probably right when he points to a difference between Pietism and the *Nadere Reformatie*: Huber's life and works give a concrete example of a person who was a pietist but not precisely a *Nadere Reformist*.[95] Simultaneously, it would also be wrong to assume Huber the pietist a 'weak' conformist to the status quo, as is implied in Op 't Hof's view. According to him, the 'average pietist does not go beyond complaining about the status quo and, if necessary, make some weak attempts to bring about an improvement', while the *Nadere Reformist* 'do their utmost best in order to implement a rectification of errors and wrongdoings through a programme of reformation'.[96] In contrast, Huber's differentiation from the *Nadere Reformists* was a more principled one than is supposed in Op 't Hof's characterization above quoted. Huber's sound acceptance of the concept of sovereign power as the pivot of his *jus publicum universale*, and the principle of conscience as an integral part of *jus publicum universale*, necessitated such differentiation.

This important characteristic of Huber's intellectual position is confirmed by the other war front to which his religious conviction brought him. Huber's certainty about his religious rebirth and his firm belief in the veracity of supernatural experience simultaneously invigorated his confrontation with the doctrines of Hobbes and others, such as Röell, which relativized the role of the Holy Spirit in favour of reason, and therefore the holy inviolability of human conscience. According to Huber's assessment, Hobbes's absolutist

---

[94] Atsuko Fukuoka, 'A Path Between Scylla and Charybdis: Ulrik Huber (1636–1694) and the Theologico-Juridical Paradigm of Constantine the Great', in *De rebus divinis et humanis: Essays in Honour of Jan Hallebeek*, eds. Harry Dondorp et al. (Göttingen: V&R unipress, 2019), 151–166.
[95] Op 't Hof, 'Nadere reformatie in Friesland?' 53. See also Graafland, Op 't Hof, and Lieburg, 'Nadere reformatie', 145.
[96] Op 't Hof, 'Nadere reformatie in Friesland?' 53.

concept of the sovereign as the sole interpreter of religious truth derived ultimately from the philosopher's epistemological denial of the Holy Spirit.[97]

Toward such 'Hobbesians', who were the polar opposite of the Voetians, Huber decidedly behaved as an apologist of the Reformed creed. He wrote a detailed theological article to demonstrate that the true source of certainty about the divinity of Scripture is 'the inner revelation of the Holy Spirit', and not reason.[98] This kind of engagement, undoubtedly one pillar of Huber's intellectual activity, earned him the name of 'a dilettante theologian'.[99] Christian Thomasius (1655–1728) did not appreciate Huber's emphasis on supernatural testimony, because it could lead to religious fanaticism and because it is unable to discern true from false testimonies among mutually dissenting parties.[100] Still then, the postulation of an inviolable core in each human existence, however philosophically unfounded and practically unworkable it might have been seen, functions in Huber's state theory as the bulwark of constitutionalism—not in its modern sense, but in the sense of a principle that supports the moderate exercise of human authority in accordance with divine precepts, both natural and revealed. By defending *jus internum conscientiae* as a right executable even against the explicit will of the sovereign, Huber is exempted from the classical criticism of Early Modern natural law theories that '[t]he inborn freedom of humankind was imagined by many authors, still in the eighteenth century, as compatible with the unfreedom created by positive law' (Gerog Jellinek).[101]

Huber's works enjoyed a reputation far beyond the border of the Dutch Republic. They are available especially at libraries in German-speaking territories, Britain (importantly including Scotland), Denmark, and South Africa.[102] In particular, Thomasius repeatedly employed *De jure civitatis* as the basis of his lectures at Halle and published another edition loaded with (often critical) annotations.[103] He also recommended that his students read the *Praelectiones*, and published an enlarged edition of this treatise in Germany,

---

[97] Huber, *De jure civitatis*, 1.6.1, 173, § 2. Fukuoka, *The Sovereign and the Prophets*, 341–343.
[98] Huber, *De jure civitatis*, 1.6, 173–198 (the quotation is from 1.6.2, 176, § 4).
[99] Boeles, *Frieslands Hoogeschool* (1879), 2.1: 224.
[100] Thomasius's commentary is included in Huber, *De jure civitatis* [...] *cum novis adnotationibus et novo indice in usum auditoria Thomasiani* (Frankfurt and Leipzig: Johannes Fridericus Zeitlerus, 1708), 1.6.5, § 16, 242. *Bibliografie Franeker*, no. 156.
[101] Georg Jellinek, *Die Erklärung der Menschen- und Bürgerrechte*, 4th edn, ed. Walter Jellinek (Berlin: Dunker & Humblot, 1927), 41.
[102] *Bibliografie Franeker* offers a list of existing library copies for each edition. These lists are by no means exhaustive but give a useful overview.
[103] See supra n. 100 and Max Fleischmann, *Christian Thomasius: Leben und Lebenswerk* (Halle: Niemeyer, 1931; repr. Aalen: Scientia, 1979), 206–214.

too.[104] Upon this tradition, Otto von Gierke respectfully mentions Huber, together with Leibniz, Pufendorf, and other German theoreticians, as those who strove to 'make a breach somewhere in the armor of the sovereign's attributes, which Hobbes declared to be indestructible'.[105]

Furthermore, Huber's experience as judge also produced rich fruit: the *Heedensdaegse rechtsgeleertheyt soo elders als in Frieslandt gebruikelijk* (Leeuwarden, 1st edn 1686), one of the earliest systematic elucidations in the vernacular of Dutch law with an emphasis on Friesland. This treatise was also influential through colonial channels, so that a modern English translation appeared in 1939 at Durban in South Africa.[106] Another focus of modern attention to Huber consists in his theory of conflict of laws. Anglophone scholarship on international private law since the late nineteenth century has treated Huber's succinct explanation of this issue as one of the classical authorities next to other great jurists such as Paul Voet (1619–1667) – a son of Gisbertus. In turn, a Portuguese translation of Huber's *De conflictu legum* appeared in Rio de Janeiro (1951)[107] and a Japanese translation with extensive commentary in Tokyo (1996),[108] making the proud, independent mind known in the furthest places from Franeker.

RECOMMENDED READINGS

Bergh, Govaert C. J. J. van den. *Die holländische elegante Schule: Ein Beitrag zur Geschichte von Humanismus und Rechtswissenschaft in den Niederlanden 1500–1800.* Frankfurt am Main: Vittorio Klostermann, 2002.

Davies, D. J. Llewelyn, 'The Influence of Huber's *De conflictu legum* on English Private International Law', *British Yearbook of International Law* 18 (1937): 49–78.

Feenstra, Robert. 'Ulrik Huber'. In *Juristen: Ein biographisches Lexikon von der Antike bis zum 20. Jahrhundert*, edited by Michael Stolleis, 300–301. Munich: Beck, 1995.

Feenstra, Robert. *Bibliografie van hoogleraren in de rechten aan de Franeker universiteit tot 1811.* With the assistance of Margreet Ahsmann and Theo Veen. Amsterdam: Koninklijke Nederlandse Akademie van Wetenschappen, 2003.

---

[104] Christian Thomasius, *Kleine teutsche Schriften* (Halle: Salfeld, 1701, repr., Hildesheim: Olms, 1994), 370. On various editions of the *Praelectiones* with Thomasius's contributions, see *Bibliografie Franeker*, nos. 246–263.

[105] Otto von Gierke, *Johannes Althusius*, 178. See also Nifterik, 'Ulrik Huber on Fundamental Laws', 2–3.

[106] *Jurisprudence of My Time*, trans. Percival Gane (Durban: Butterworth, 1939). *Bibliografie Franeker*, no. 218.

[107] *Conflito de leis de Ulrich Huber*, trans. Haroldo Valladão (Rio de Janeiro: Pontificia Universidade Católica do Rio de Janeiro, 1951) *Bibliografie Franeker*, no. 272.

[108] *Ulricus Huberus 'Hou Teishoku Ron' Chukai* (Commentary on Ulrik Huber's *De conflictu legum*), trans. Jun-ichi Akiba (Tokyo: Shougaku-sha, 1996). *Bibliografie Franeker*, no. 273.

Fukuoka, Atsuko. *The Sovereign and the Prophets: Spinoza on Grotian and Hobbesian Biblical Argumentation*. Leiden: Brill, 2018.
Fukuoka, Atsuko. 'A Path between Scylla and Charybdis: Ulrik Huber (1636–1694) and the Theologico-Juridical Paradigm of Constantine the Great'. In *De rebus divinis et humanis: Essays in Honour of Jan Hallebeek*, eds. Harry Dondorp, Martin Schermaier, and Boudewijn Sirks, 151–166. Göttingen: V&R unipress, 2019.
Goudriaan, Aza. 'Ulrik Huber (1636–1694) and John Calvin: The Franeker Debate on Human Reason and the Bible (1686–1687)'. *Church History and Religious Culture* 91, nos. 1–2 (2011): 165–178.
Hewett, Margaret. *Ulric Huber (1636–1694): De ratione juris docendi et discendi diatribe per modum dialogi nonnullis aucta παραλιπομένοις, with a Translation and Commentary*. Nijmegen: Gerard Noodt Instituut, 2010.
Kossmann, E. H. *Political Thought in the Dutch Republic: Three Studies*. Amsterdam: Koninklijke Nederlandse Akademie van Wetenschappen, 2000.
Lomonaco, Fabrizio. *Lex regia: diritto, filologia e fides historica nella cultura politico-filosofica dell'Olanda di fine Seicento*. Naples: Guida, 1990. Translated as *New Studies on Lex Regia: Right, Philology and Fides Historica in Holland between the 17th and 18th Centuries*. Bern: Lang, 2011.
Mohnhaupt, Heinz. 'Von den Leges fundamentales zur modernen Verfassung in Europa. Zum begriffs- und dogmengeschichtlichen Befund (16. -18. Jahrhundert)'. In *Historische Vergleichung im Bereich von Staat und Recht: Gesammelte Aufsätze*, 35–72. Frankfurt am Main: Vittorio Klostermann, 2000.
Nifterik, Gustaaf van. 'Ulrik Huber on fundamental laws: A European perspective'. *Comparative Legal History* 4.1 (2016): 2–18.
Nifterik, Gustaaf van. 'Property Beyond Princely Authority: The Intellectual and Legal Roots of Ulrik Huber's Fundamental Law'. *Tijdschrift voor Rechtsgeschiedenis* 84 (2016): 225–244.
Raath, A. W. G. and J. J. Henning. 'Political Covenantalism, Sovereignty and the Obligatory Nature of Law: Ulrich Huber's Discourse on State Authority and Democratic Universalism'. *Journal for Juridical Science* 29.2 (2004): 15–55.
Veen, Theo J. *Recht en nut: Studiën over en naar aanleiding van Ulrik Huber (1636–1694)*. Zwolle: Tjeenk Willink, 1976.
Veen, Theo J., ed. *Ulrici Huberi: Oratio [III]*. With a translation by Fokke Akkerman, Theo J. Veen, and A. G. Westerbrink. Zwolle: Tjeenk Willink, 1978.

9

Zeger-Bernard van Espen

Jan Hallebeek

BIOGRAPHICAL INTRODUCTION

Zeger-Bernard van Espen was born in Leuven 8 July 1646 as son of the legal practitioner Joannes van Espen and his wife Elisabeth Zegers. He was the youngest of nine children. In 1656 he began attending the college of the Oratorians in Temse. In 1663 he entered *'t Varken* (Pig College) in Leuven to study Philosophy at the Faculty of Arts. In 1665 he assumed clerical status, received a scholarship at the *Heilige-Geestcollege* (Holy Spirit College) and pursued his studies at the Faculty of Law. In 1670, after five years of studying canon law, he obtained the licentiate in both laws. In 1673, he was ordained priest and one year later he was appointed to the chair of the so-called 'six weeks lectures', an extraordinary professorship, meant for teaching an annual course during the academic holiday (August and September). In 1675 van Espen took his doctoral examinations and was promoted to doctor in both laws. From 1677 until 1703 he also delivered a weekly lecture in Church History in the *Pauscollege* (Pope's College).

From the outset, van Espen took a clear stand in the various debates which dominated the intellectual climate at Leuven University.[1] He can be considered an adherent of Jansenism, in the sense that he adopted a critical attitude toward moral laxism and did not accept the Formulary of Alexander VII (1656) or the constitution *Unigenitus* (1713), not even at an advanced age, when seriously ill and put under pressure. The Formulary condemned five propositions, allegedly derived from the *Augustinus* of Cornelius Jansenius (1585–1638). *Unigenitus* condemned 101 propositions derived from the *Réflexions morales* of Pasquier Quesnel (1634–1719). In France, and later also

---

[1] Sometimes van Espen is also considered to adhere to Conciliarism, but that can be questioned.

in the Southern Netherlands, clerics were expected to sign or accept under oath these documents, for example, when making confession.

His Gallican sympathies made van Espen an advocate of the competency of the local church and its diocesan bishop against claims laid by regular clerics, appealing to their exempt status, and by the central ecclesiastical authorities in Rome. As a practical consequence of this view he supported the Catholic Church in the Northern Netherlands that is, the Church of Utrecht and its Vicars Apostolic in their efforts to maintain their position.

His regalist views made van Espen an advocate of the *ius placiti* of the sovereign and the so-called *recursus ad principem*. The former was the right of the sovereign to grant binding force to ecclesiastical legislation. The latter was an appeal to secular courts in case ecclesiastical authorities did not observe procedural rules or lacked competence. It was either aimed at possessory protection of prebends (*manutenentia*) or at cassation of ecclesiastical judgements (*appellatio ab abusu* or *appel comme d'abus*). It was up to the sovereign and his magistrates to defend the local church and her clerics against any kind of violence, including abuse of authority by bishops and ecclesiastical officers.[2] More than once, protection by secular courts played a part in van Espen's own academic or personal life. He delivered legal advice to Willem van de Nesse (†1716), parish priest of Saint Catherine's in Brussels, who, in 1706, was suspended by Humbertus Willem de Précipiano (1627–1711), Archbishop of Malines. Van de Nesse successfully contested the suspension before the Council of Brabant.[3] Moreover, Bernard Désirant (1656–1725), an opponent of van Espen's who had spread falsified letters indicating that van Espen was involved in a political conspiracy (the so-called 'Villainy of Leuven' or *Fourberie de Louvain*), was in 1718 sentenced by the Council of Brabant. Furthermore, in a civil trial before the Great Council of Malines, van Espen sued the Vicar Apostolic of 's-Hertogenbosch, Pieter Govaerts (1644–1726), because of reputational injury. In a letter Govaerts had branded van Espen 'this heretical yeast' (*hoc novum fermentum*) because of his unwillingness to sign the constitution *Unigenitus*. Van Espen demanded retraction of the insulting words and in 1722 won the case.

In his *Responsio epistolaris* of 1725, van Espen defended the validity and legitimacy of the election and consecration of Cornelis Steenoven (1661–1725) as Archbishop of Utrecht, which had been condemned by the Pope. The

---

[2] Bart Wauters, 'Zeger-Bernard Van Espen. Regalisme, conciliarisme en corporatisme. Bijdrage tot de kerkrechtsgeschiedenis in de Nederlanden', *Pro Memorie* 3 (2001): 213.

[3] Van Espen supported more clerics in their appeal against ecclesiastical sanctions, such as inter alia Jérôme Zegers, Willem van Roost (1661–1746), and Jean-Charles Leydecker.

Council of State declared this writing to be injurious toward the briefs and decrees which the Holy See had issued on the matter. In 1727, van Espen was ordered by the *rector magnificus* of Leuven University to retract his opinion within three weeks. Van Espen appealed that decision to the university tribunal but did not await the eventual outcome. He left his native city and, after a stay at Maastricht, took up residence in the seminary of the Church of Utrecht in Amersfoort, where he died on 2 October 1728. The epitaph designed for his tomb was reminiscent of the departure from Leuven: '*Patriam maluit in extrema senectute quam justitiam et veritatem deserere*'.

MAJOR THEMES AND CONTRIBUTIONS

Introduction

The major themes, characteristic of van Espen's teachings, mentioned above, were also determinative of his life story. Roughly speaking, we can bring his main scholarly writings under three headings. First, there is his principal and most influential work, which appeared in 1700, the *Jus Ecclesiasticum Universum*. Virtually all other works were written with reference to certain events or in order to defend controversial opinions. Some of these emphasize regalist premises, while others are of a more Gallican or Episcopalistic nature. A strict separation between the second and third categories cannot be made. Regalism is sometimes an instrument in the service of Gallicanism, that is, when sovereigns set themselves up as protectors of the rights of the local church.[4] Such a subdivision into three categories may create the impression that van Espen discussed only certain distinct issues but that is not the case. In his extensive oeuvre, he deals with the entire canon law of his days. The issues mentioned here are just characteristic of this oeuvre. Within the three categories we have observed the chronological order in which the various works came into being. It is also advisable to read and analyze van Espen's writings in chronological order since his views often progressed with time.

The Jus Ecclesiasticum Universum

The *Jus Ecclesiasticum Universum* deals with all possible questions related to the polity of the Catholic Church. The work is systematically structured. The

---

[4] The paragraphs below do not contain an exhaustive enumeration of the works of van Espen, but the most important ones. A complete survey can be found in the monographs of Leclerc and Nuttinck.

subject matter is discussed not according to the sequence of the titles in the *Liber Extra* but split up into three parts, that is, (i) persons (*de personis*), (ii) things (*de rebus*), and (iii) litigation, delicts, and ecclesiastical sanctions (*de judiciis, delictis, et poenis ecclesiasticis*).[5] The second part (things) is subdivided again into four sections: sacraments (*de sacramentis*), churches and feasts (*de ecclesiis et festis*), prebends (*de beneficiis*), and temporal goods (*de bonis*).

Van Espen pays considerable attention to the historical development that resulted in the rules of canon law in force in his own days. Time and again he emphasizes the fact that in the twelfth century, spurious texts, the so-called Pseudo-Isidorian decretals, had snuck into the compilations of canon law. In his treatment of many issues, these texts constitute the dividing line between the 'old law', based on the canons of the early ecumenical and regional councils, and the 'new law', primarily based on papal decretals. Due to the false decretals, the 'new law' ascribes a much stronger position to the Roman Pontiff than was possible according to 'old law'. In many cases, van Espen adopts the 'old law' as a kind of ideal and in accordance with the *ressourcement*-theology, as practised at Leuven University, he takes the original sources as a starting point to explain the 'old law', thus not just the fragments as they were, deprived from their context and sometimes reworded, adopted in the *Decretum Gratiani*.

Most of the subjects dominating van Espen's later writings can already be traced in the *Jus Ecclesiasticum Universum*. The *Jus Ecclesiasticum Universum* contains clear traces of regalist theories. The church has competence only in the spiritual realm. As regards secular affairs and temporal goods, the sovereign is competent.[6] Also the *ius placiti* and the *recursus ad principem* are dealt with already.[7] His episcopalist theory, however, is not elaborated as in later works. Van Espen mentions and describes the prerogatives which the canon law of his days attributed to the Roman Pontiff but does not say what the source of such competency is. Moreover, he does not yet maintain that all bishops, including the bishop of Rome, have equal authority, although he does say that bishops have a plenitude of power, which is not described as derived from the Pope. It finds its limits and restrictions in the church (*Ecclesia*).[8] Also, as regards the origin of jurisdiction, the *Jus Ecclesiasticum Universum* does not yet display van Espen's later, more particularized, thoughts. It states that

---

[5] Such a structure is clearly reminiscent of the outline of Justinian's Institutes.
[6] *Jus Ecclesiasticum Universum*, Pars III, Tit. II, Cap. I, n. V.
[7] *Jus Ecclesiasticum Universum*, Pars II, Sect. III, Tit. VII, Cap. VI and *Jus Ecclesiasticum Universum*, Pars III, Tit. X, Cap. IV.
[8] *Jus Ecclesiasticum Universum*, Pars I, Tit. XVI, Cap. I, n. IX.

bishops acquire their plenitude of power through their consecration, which is at odds with statements in later works, as we shall see below.

In 1704, the *Jus Ecclesiasticum Universum* was condemned by a decree of the Holy Office, reissued in 1713 and 1732, because of its regalist ideas.[9] Despite being put on the index, the work was reprinted many times and had considerable influence in major parts of continental Europe. Pope Benedict XIV (1675–1758) in his work *De synodo diocesana* (1755) referred to the work several times.[10] A supplement was published posthumously. In some later editions of van Espen's *Opera omnia* this *Supplementum* was not edited separately but incorporated into the text of the *Jus Ecclesiasticum Universum* itself.[11]

Regalist Works

In 1699, Pieter Govaerts, at the time vicar general of the archdiocese of Malines, published his *Certamen immunitatis sacerdotum Belgii in causis personalibus*, which was directed against parish priests who appealed to secular courts after being suspended from their office and/or deprived of their prebend for alleged Jansenism. Govaerts accused these priests of revolting against the ecclesiastical authorities. In response to this writing, in around 1700 van Espen wrote two treatises, in which he pronounced upon the rights of the sovereign. Both were published only in 1721. The first, *Concordia immunitatis ecclesiasticae et juris regii*, deals with the protection by secular courts of the unhampered possession of prebends. Van Espen bases the appeal to these courts on Natural Law, which allows anyone to defend himself. The second, *Dissertatio de asylo templorum*, is specifically directed toward Govaert's opinion that ecclesiastical immunity has its origin in the sacred character of the church building. It was prompted by the case of Frans van Ophoven who in March 1700 shot a Spanish officer and subsequently took refuge in a Dominican monastery.[12] Van Espen teaches that asylum in churches is

---

[9] Also, many other writings of van Espen were put on the *Index*.
[10] Especially for van Espen's accurate description of the customary law of the Southern Netherlands.
[11] The additions from the *Supplementum* are recognizable by the 'hands' at the beginning and end of each fragment. When investigating van Espen's teachings on the basis of such editions, one has to realize that the fragments derived from the *Supplementum* were not written as early as 1700, but towards the end of van Espen's academic life.
[12] Carlotta Latini, 'Le droit d'asile dans la pensée de Van Espen. Profils juridiques de la formation du ius publicum ecclesiasticum dans les Pays-Bas catholiques', in *Zeger–Bernard Van Espen at the crossroads*, eds. Guido Cooman, Maurice van Stiphout, and Bart Wauters (Leuven: Peeters, 2003), 115–132. Jan Hallebeek, 'Church asylum in late Antiquity. Concession

a concession granted by the secular authorities.[13] Although some decretals which may substantiate ecclesiastical immunity were received in the western church, van Espen maintains that the sovereign is still entitled to determine the extent of church asylum and the way it is practised.

The case of van de Nesse was already briefly mentioned above. It triggered van Espen to write a thorough legal opinion on the possessory remedy van de Nesse brought before the Council of Brabant. This reply, the *Motivum juris pro van de Nesse* (1707), describes the facts, justifies the refusal to accept the Formulary of Alexander VII, and discusses both the remedy used, that is, the possessory action against the non-regulatory and thus violent infringement of unhampered possession of a prebend (*manutenentia*), and the protective competency of the secular authorities. This includes an ideological justification for appealing to the sovereign and his magistrates.[14] In 1707, the Council of Brabant decided in favour of van de Nesse.

Regalist tendencies can also be found in the *Tractatus de censuris ecclesiasticis* (1709), a treatise on ecclesiastical sanctions primarily written in view of measures taken by the authorities in Rome against clerics in the Northern Netherlands (see below). It not only describes which procedural rules the ecclesiastical authorities must observe when sentencing someone but also deals with what can be done if these rules are violated. Apart from appealing to a superior ecclesiastical instance, there is again the possibility of bringing a possessory action before a secular court.[15]

The *Tractatus de promulgatione legum ecclesiasticarum* of 1712 is a treatise on the *ius placiti*, mentioned above. The work was largely provoked by the fact that in 1705, the bull *Vineam Domini* was promulgated in the Southern Netherlands without *placet*. This bull ruled that it was no longer permissible to accept the condemnation of the five propositions from Jansenius's *Augustinus* with a restriction (viz. that the propositions cannot be found in the book and that the author had not taught these in their heretical sense). The *Tractatus de promulgatione legum ecclesiasticarum* deals extensively with the controversial question of whether a royal *placet* is also obligatory for bulls of

---

by the Emperor or competence of the Church?' in *Secundum Ius: Opstellen aangeboden aan prof. mr. P. L. Nève*, ed. Chris Coppens (Nijmegen: Gerard Noodt Instituut, 2004), 163–182.

[13] According to the bull *Cum alias nonnulli* (1591) of Pope Gregory XIV (1535–1591) churches could offer asylum, but this bull was controversial and in many territories, like the Southern Netherlands, it had not received a *placet*.

[14] See further Bart Wauters, '"Sonder eenige ordre van 't recht te onderhouden". Een analyse van een zaak van recursus ad principem voor de Raad van Brabant in het begin van de 18de eeuw: Bezitsvordering of buitengewoon rechtsmiddel', *Tijdschrift voor rechtsgeschiedenis* 73 (2005): 111.

[15] Van Espen may have written this treatise in view of the threatening excommunication of van Erckel for not obeying the brief of 7 April 1703. See below.

a doctrinal nature, something which had not yet been discussed in the *Jus Ecclesiasticum Universum*. Here, van Espen follows the opinion of Pieter Stockmans (1608–1671), defended in the latter's *Jus Belgarum circa bullarum pontificiarum receptionem* (1645). According to van Espen, no ecclesiastical rule may be promulgated under the pretext of religion whenever this may disturb public order. A doctrinal bull has an external and an internal aspect. The sovereign will judge the former: is the content of the bull sufficiently clear? What are the sanctions for subjects who do not accept the bull? Are there other clauses which may be detrimental for the inhabitants of his realm? Etc.[16]

The *Tractatus de ecclesiastica et politica potestate* (1718) – notes resulting from a series of lectures on secular and ecclesiastical powers and published only posthumously – is composed of two parts. The first part deals with ecclesiastical competence. It emphasizes that the only purpose of the church is eternal salvation of the faithful, which can only be aimed at by spiritual means. Accordingly, in temporal affairs, the church has no power whatsoever. The second part deals with the rights of the sovereign in relation to the church. Here we again find regalist teachings: the foundations of royal jurisdiction (Pars II, Caput I), the subordination of clerics to secular authority (Caput II), ecclesiastical freedom (Caput III), restricted immunity of ecclesiastical persons (Caput IV), the sovereign supervising the temporal goods of the church (Caput V), this supervision making the sovereign an 'external bishop' (Caput VI), and the merely spiritual nature of ecclesiastical competence (Caput XI).

In the case file of the civil procedure against Pieter Govaerts, mentioned above, which was edited in 1724 under the title *Aequitas sententiae Parlamenti Mechliniensis*, van Espen replies to the accusation of having taught that doctrinal bulls are not binding in conscience before being promulgated. Van Espen answers that he did not pronounce on such a theological question. As a specialist in canon law, he maintained only that doctrinal bulls cannot be promulgated or gain force of law without *placitum* (*additionalis deductio*).

At an advanced age, van Espen wrote his most outspoken and thorough treatise on the principles of regalism, the *Tractatus de recursu ad principem*, published in 1725. The immediate cause for taking up his pen was the ruling of Emperor Charles VI (1685–1740) of 26 May 1723 that *Unigenitus* should be considered lawfully promulgated in the Southern Netherlands and that opponents should be prosecuted before ecclesiastical courts. At the same time, the Emperor encouraged the bishops to observe some restraint and his own

---

[16] *De promulgatione legum ecclesiasticarum*, Pars II, Cap. II, § I–III and Pars V, Cap. II, § I–IV.

magistrates not to thwart the bishops.[17] According to van Espen such a ruling is not in conformity with the sovereign's obligation to do justice to his subjects. Time and again, he expounds copiously the responsibility which rests on Catholic rulers. He criticizes the regular ecclesiastical remedy of appeal, which is factually not capable of putting an end to injustice but rather makes appeal to the secular courts (*recursus ad principem*) necessary.[18] In earlier works, van Espen had primarily dealt with possessory protection against abuse of power. Now he also extensively discusses the special remedy of requiring the royal magistrate to declare judgments of ecclesiastical courts null and void (*appel comme d'abus*) from lack of competence or breach of procedural prescriptions (*remedium cassationis*). In order to enforce such cassation the secular authorities are competent to confiscate ecclesiastical goods. Also, in ecclesiastical affairs the sovereign has unlimited coercive powers (*potestas coactiva*). As a restraint upon the lust for power (*libido dominandi*) of certain clerics, temporal goods of the church can also be seized. The sovereign may use the temporal sword to punish abuse by those who hold the spiritual sword. To support all this, reference is made to the legal practice in the Southern Netherlands, the German realm, France, and Spain.[19] Some scholars had argued that canon 3 of session XXV of the Council of Trent (1535–1563) would be an obstacle to royal protection of oppressed subjects, but van Espen follows the opinion of Francisco Salgado de Somoza (†1664) that the sovereign's obligation to offer protection derives from Natural and Divine law. Referring to Diego Covarruvias de Leyva (1512–1577), who had attended the Council, he maintains that it could not have been the Council's genuine intent that this canon be interpreted as such an obstacle.[20]

The concluding chapter of the *Tractatus de recursu ad principem* almost constitutes an emotional culmination of the entire treatise. Van Espen now addresses the royal magistrates and officers who, in fear of ecclesiastical sanctions, are hesitant to take cognizance of the appeal made to them by the

---

[17] Maurice van Stiphout, 'Van de paus of van de koning? Zeger-Bernard Van Espen en het appel comme d'abus', *Pro Memorie* 1 (1999): 100–114. Remco van Rhee, 'De obligatione principis protegendi subditos ... Some remarks on recursus ad principem', in *Zeger-Bernard Van Espen at the crossroads*, eds. Guido Cooman, Maurice van Stiphout, and Bart Wauters (Leuven: Peeters, 2003), 147–158. Bart Wauters, *Recht als religie. Canonieke onderbouw van de vroegmoderne staatsvorming in de zuidelijke Nederlanden* (Leuven: Universitaire Pers Leuven, 2005), 266–285. Jan Hallebeek, 'Appel comme d'abus dans l'oeuvre de Zeger-Bernard van Espen. Principes, contexte, développements', in *Justices croisées. Histoire et enjeux de l'appel comme d'abus (XIVe–XVIIIe siècle)*, eds. Anne Bonzon and Caroline Galland (Rennes: PUR, 2021), 251–269.

[18] *Tractatus de recursu ad principem*, Cap. VII, § V.

[19] *Tractatus de recursu ad principem*, Cap. VI, §§ I–VII.

[20] *Tractatus de recursu ad principem*, Cap. VI, § VIII.

oppressed. They should trust in God, even when the servants of the church would brand them as disbelievers. When excommunicated, they are as banished from the Synagogue for the sake of the name of Christ (John 16.2). If they are reluctant to confirm the truth out of fear for excommunication, they are as the chief rulers, in the Gospel according to Saint John, who did not openly confess Jesus in order not to be banished from the Synagogue (John 12.42–43). Similarly, the parents of the man, blind from his birth, had no courage to speak the truth out of fear of being expelled from the Synagogue (John 9.21–23). However, the man born blind himself spoke the truth and subsequently he was cast out. He said to Jesus 'Lord, I believe' (John 9.39). Saint Augustine stated that the Pharisees had expelled him, but the Lord had accepted him, since rather than being an outcast he had become a Christian. Accordingly, magistrates and officers who fight for justice will similarly be welcomed by the Lord, when they are by unjust sanctions banished from the worldly community of faithful. They are expelled from the Synagogue of the wicked but enter the community of saints.[21]

Writings in Defence of Gallicanism, Episcopalism, and the Rights of the Church of Utrecht

In van Espen's view, the local church, that is, the diocese, is the most important element in the constitution of the church. Its bishop, clergy, and faithful should never be subordinated to a coercive superior authority. Apart from some prerogatives of the Roman Pontiff, the jurisdiction of the diocesan bishop is restricted only by the universally received doctrines and canons of the church. The bishop's responsibility and competency should also be observed by clerics with an exempt status. In van Espen's works, more tersely in his later works, we trace various ecclesiological principles which support this view: such as the idea that the local church has her own indefeasible rights (Gallicanism); that all diocesan bishops have equal authority (Episcopalism); and that it is the local church herself which entrusts jurisdiction to her bishop.

Van Espen did not deal with these ecclesiological principles only in a doctrinal or theoretical way. They were also determinative for his stand in various controversies in legal practice, including those related to the Church of Utrecht, that is, the Church Province in the Northern Netherlands, which since the establishment of the Reformed Church as the privileged religion, was deprived of her former church buildings, monasteries, and other ecclesiastical goods. Moreover, the presence of diocesan bishops was no longer

---

[21] The statement of Saint Augustine can be found in his *Tractatus in Joannem* (Tract. 44, § 15).

permitted by the secular authorities and in 1622 the congregation *De propaganda fide* in Rome started to exercise supervision. Nevertheless, major parts of the pre-reformation structures continued to exist. The dioceses and archprebyterates were extant, while many parishes continued to function or were reorganized. The Chapter of Haarlem still functioned and the Chapters of Utrecht were in 1633 reorganized as the 'Vicariate', since all canonries were henceforth given to Protestants. A Vicar Apostolic, appointed by the Pope but usually also elected and in any case accepted by the 'Vicariate', took the place of the Archbishop. These Vicars Apostolic had to face various difficulties. Not only was the Catholic Church oppressed by the Protestant authorities, but its inalienable traditional rights were also increasingly ignored by both the Roman authorities and the regular clerics, especially the Jesuits. Van Espen, being the advocate of the local church, on many occasions hastened to assist the Church of Utrecht by producing sound scholarly support for her position toward Rome. There were already longstanding relations between the Church of Utrecht and Leuven. Since seminaries or theological colleges were not permitted in the Dutch Republic, many secular clerics from the North received their theological training in Leuven, where since 1617 the diocese of Haarlem had the college *Pulcheria*. Furthermore, between 1670 and 1680, the college *Alticollense* of the Utrecht diocese was transferred to Leuven from Cologne.

In an early work, the *Repagulum canonicum adversus nimiam exemptionum a jurisdictione episcoporum extensionem* (1688), van Espen had already dealt with the exact extent of the exempt status of regular clerics. He argues that in many matters these clerics are still subordinate to the jurisdiction of the diocesan bishop. In the *Jus Ecclesiasticum Universum* of 1700 he maintains, as stated above, that diocesan bishops have a plenitude of power of their own (*per se*), thus not derived from the Pope, but at the same time this authority would be received by virtue of their consecration (*vi suae ordinationis*).[22] It has to be noted, though, that the latter is not entirely in conformity with later thinking, as outlined below.

Van Espen also intervened in the internal debate within the Church of Utrecht concerning a number of topical questions. In 1702, after having summoned him to appear in Rome, the Pope suspended Vicar Apostolic Petrus Codde (1648–1710) and appointed Theodorus de Cock (1650–1720) as pro-vicar to replace him. Moreover, he restrained Codde from returning to the Netherlands. For the Chapter of Haarlem and the Vicariate of Utrecht, de Cock was not an acceptable successor. In this situation questions were first

---

[22] *Jus Ecclesiasticum Universum*, Pars I, Tit. XVI, Cap. I, n. IX.

raised as to whether one should invoke the help of the secular, Protestant authorities, more specifically the States of Holland, to secure Codde's return. Van Espen was quite hesitant about this.[23] Nevertheless, the States, which had already forbidden Catholics to acknowledge de Cock, issued a resolution demanding the return of Codde.[24] The second question had to do with the four pro-vicars appointed by Codde himself before going to Rome. Could these priests appeal to the Pope against the appointment of de Cock? Van Espen provided the arguments to support their position. The four pro-vicars, he argued, derived their jurisdiction not only from the now-deposed Vicar Apostolic but also from the Chapter and the Vicariate.[25] Here, we touch upon an important basic principle in the teachings of van Espen: ecclesiastical jurisdiction resides in the local church and *sede vacante* or *sede impedita* is exercised by the Chapter. He expounded this principle extensively in a letter to the dean of the Chapter of Haarlem, who was in doubt whether the Chapter was competent to appoint administrators of parishes, since there was no longer a Vicar Apostolic in office.[26] Van Espen repeated his arguments in the *Motivum juris pro capitulo Harlemensi* of 1703, arguing that the diocese of Haarlem was extant and that, since its see was vacant (from 1587), all jurisdiction was exercised by the Chapter. The Vicar Apostolic could only exercise jurisdiction in the diocese of Haarlem through delegation by the Chapter. In the archdiocese of Utrecht this was apparently different. Van Espen acknowledged that the Vicariate could exercise jurisdiction, albeit not *sede vacante* but *sede impedita*. The underlying thought was that Codde was the *Ordinarius* of the diocese and accordingly the see could not be considered vacant. A third controversial question had to do with the brief which the Pope had issued on 7 April 1703, threatening Catholics with excommunication *lata sententia* if they refused to accept the suspension of Codde.[27] According to van Espen, excommunication could not result from the mere fact of

---

[23] *Epistola* XLV of 7 February 1703.
[24] In approaching informally the civic authorities a major role was played by Joan Christian van Erckel (1654–1734), member of the Utrecht Vicariate. He had studied law in Leuven, was a kindred soul of van Espen and may even have encouraged the latter's regalist ideas.
[25] A letter from the summer of 1702. There is a reference to this letter in *Epistola* XLIII.
[26] *Epistola* XLIV of 17 January 1703.
[27] This brief may have been one of the events which prompted van Espen to write his *Tractatus de censuris ecclesiasticis* of 1709. By that time van Erckel was threatened with excommunication for not obeying this brief. On 16 January 1711 he was excommunicated by the nuncio at Cologne. Van Espen considered this excommunication null and void and advised van Erckel not to petition absolution from this excommunication, since that was entirely redundant. See *Epistola* C of 6 August 1711.

disobedience but required a proper procedure.²⁸ A fourth question, which emerged after Codde returned from Rome in June 1703, was whether he should reassume office. Van Espen answered this question in the affirmative. Codde should not resign but should take up office again.²⁹ Van Espen considered all sanctions taken against Codde as null and void for lack of proper procedure and probably also contrary to the *ius de non evocando* of secular law, which prohibited inhabitants of the Republic being summoned before a foreign court. Codde, however, definitively dismissed in 1704, refused to resume office and it appeared difficult to find a successor acceptable to all who would administer the church for a longer period. As a consequence, the Church of Utrecht was for many years administered by the Vicariate.

The *Tractatus de promulgatione legum ecclesiasticarum* of 1712, mentioned above, not only deals with the *ius placiti* of the sovereign but also lays down that without publication by the diocesan bishop, papal decrees have no binding force.³⁰ Again such an opinion is indicative of van Espen's episcopalist teachings.

From 1715 onwards, van Espen was consulted about the question whether the Utrecht Vicariate could exercise jurisdiction in the diocese of Haarlem if the Chapter of Haarlem refused to do so. In 1705, the Chapter of Haarlem had resigned itself to Rome, and no longer performed its ecclesiastical duties. Van Espen replied that the rights of the Chapter of Haarlem can devolve to the Vicariate because *sede impedita* the rights of the Metropolitan are exercised by the Metropolitan Chapter. This was confirmed by the fact that the Vicariate exercised jurisdiction in the diocese of Deventer. Moreover, extreme necessity may justify it, van Espen argued.³¹ At the same time the Vicariate started, as van Espen previously had advised,³² to issue *litterae dimissoriales* for candidates for the priesthood, so that they could obtain their ordinations from foreign bishops. In order to convince these bishops of the legitimacy of such requests, in 1717 van Espen composed a treatise under the title *Resolutio doctorum Lovaniensium*. It was signed by four other scholars from Leuven and later approved by scholars from the Sorbonne. In short, the treatise maintained that the archdiocese of Utrecht was still in existence and that the Metropolitan Chapter lived on in the Vicariate, which now had the right to issue dimissorial letters and to appoint parish priests and administrators of

---

²⁸ *Epistola* XLVIII of 4 May 1703 by Joannes Opstraet (1651–1720) also on behalf van Espen.
²⁹ *Epistola* LIV of 13 June 1704 and *Epistola* LVI of 20 July 1704.
³⁰ *Tractatus de promulgatione legum ecclesiasticarum*, Pars I, Cap. III, § VI.
³¹ *Epistola* CVIII of 27 September 1716 by Opstraet also on behalf of van Espen and others and *Epistola* CXII of 26 February 1719.
³² *Epistola* CIII of 1715 by Opstraet on behalf of van Espen.

parishes. Moreover, bishop and Chapter derive their jurisdiction from the church.[33] Again van Espen pointed out that *sede vacante* jurisdiction is retained in the local church and exercised by the Chapter, for which opinion he referred to the French theologian and Oratorian Louis Thomassin (1619–1695).

In the *Tractatus de ecclesiastica et politica potestate* of 1718, van Espen further develops his episcopalist thought. Bishops, including the Pope, basically have the same position as regards ecclesiastical jurisdiction. Everything Christ had spoken to Saint Peter concerning the guidance of the church was, in the person of Peter, addressed to all Apostles.[34] Christ gave the power of the keys directly to the church, although only the pastors use and apply it. The *Tractatus* is less clear regarding the way pastors acquire their jurisdiction: 'Immediately from God' the *Tractatus* says, 'but through the ministry of those who elect and consecrate them'.[35] It may be that van Espen is more cautious here than in the *Resolutio doctorum Lovaniensium* but that is difficult to say, since the *Tractatus* is only a posthumously edited series of lecture notes.

In 1722, van Espen, together with two other scholars from Leuven, produced an extensive legal and ecclesiological treatise to justify and substantiate the intention of the Vicariate of Utrecht to elect an Archbishop. In this writing, the *Casus resolutio sive dissertatio de misero statu Ecclesiae Ultrajectinae*, it is argued that the bishop elect could be consecrated in default of papal confirmation. In case neighbouring bishops are unwilling to cooperate, any bishop ready to rescue the Church of Utrecht would be competent to perform the consecration, if necessary without the assistance of two other bishops.[36] Accordingly, the Vicariate elected Cornelis Steenoven (1661–1725) Archbishop of Utrecht and had him consecrated in 1724 by the French missionary bishop Dominique-Marie Varlet (1678–1742), who stayed in Amsterdam. Pope Benedict XIII (1649–1730) declared the election to be void and illegal, and the consecration illicit and reprehensible. He did not deny, though, the validity of the consecration. In his *Responsio epistolaris* (1725) van Espen defended the view that in cases of emergency one consecrating bishop could suffice and that the consecration of Steenoven was permissible. As stated above, this *Responsio epistolaris* had far-reaching consequences for van Espen's position in Leuven.

---

[33] For the latter statement van Espen was criticized by Laurent Boursier (1679–1749).
[34] *Tractatus de ecclesiastica et politica potestate*, Pars I, Cap. VI, propositio I–II.
[35] *Tractatus de ecclesiastica et politica potestate*, Pars I, Cap. VI, propositio III.
[36] Jan Hallebeek, 'Questions of canon law concerning the election and consecration of a bishop for the Church of Utrecht: The casus resolutio of 1722', *Bijdragen: International Journal in Philosophy and Theology* 61 (2000): 17.

At an advanced age, he also justified the intention to again occupy the see of Haarlem. In his *Responsum juris circa institutionem Episcopi Harlemensis* he argued that if the Chapter of Haarlem neglects its duty to elect a bishop, the Archbishop is obliged to assume this task of the negligent Chapter and consecrate a bishop for the diocese of Haarlem.

At the end of his life van Espen wrote a doctrinal work, revisiting his defence of the rights of the Vicariate ten years earlier in the *Resolutio doctorum Lovaniensium*. This work, entitled *Vindiciae resolutionis doctorum Lovaniensium* (1727) is, in many respects, more outspoken than earlier works. The source of all spiritual jurisdiction is the church. As the church fathers taught, Christ had spoken to the church when he gave Saint Peter the power of the keys. Jurisdiction is derived from the church and, accordingly, the Vicars Apostolic in the Northern Netherlands were genuine Archbishops of Utrecht.[37] Here, we also trace van Espen's episcopalism in its further elaborated form: all bishops are 'vicars of Christ', 'high priests', and 'successors of Saint Peter'. Since all are successors of the Apostles, there cannot be any hierarchy between bishops.[38] Also, his doctrine on the origin of jurisdiction can be found here in its ultimate shape and in terser form than in the *Tractatus* of 1718: Saint Peter represented the church when he received the power of the keys. As a consequence, ecclesiastical jurisdiction resides fundamentally with the entire church. By electing a bishop, the local church entrusts and grants only the exercise of such jurisdiction to the bishop. *Sede vacante* jurisdiction remains with the church and is exercised by the Chapter or the clergy.[39]

The Principles and Religious Motives Underlying van Espen's Work and Life

The focus on the Early Church seems to constitute the most important motive underlying van Espen's thoughts and acts. It appeared to be determinative for his scholarly work as well as for his personal life. In his works on canon law he followed the *ressourcement* of the Leuven theology and focused, beyond the medieval law of the decretals, on the roots of the legal sources in the Early

---

[37] *Vindiciae resolutionis doctorum Lovaniensium*, Disquisitio II, § VII. It was the purpose of the entire *Disquisitio secunda* to demonstrate that the Vicars Apostolic were in fact diocesan bishops.

[38] *Vindiciae resolutionis doctorum Lovaniensium*, Disquisitio II, § VII, n. IV–XI.

[39] *Vindiciae resolutionis doctorum Lovaniensium*, Disquisitio III, § V. Many opinions as formulated in the *Vindiciae resolutionis* can also be found in the *Supplementum* to the *Jus Ecclesiasticum Universum*. See Jan Hallebeek, 'Die Autonomie der Ortskirche im Denken von Zeger-Bernard van Espen', *Internationale Kirchliche Zeitschrift* 92 (2002): 87–89.

Church. He adopted this Ancient Church, that is, Scripture. the Early Ecumenical Councils. and the authoritative writings of the church fathers, time and again as a normative ideal, albeit not in order to reject the canon law in force but to interpret and apply it. In such a way, legal history served as an interpretative principle. In his days the Pseudo-Isidorian decretals were exposed and in van Espen's opinion these spurious texts had depraved canon law, just as the probabilism of the Jesuits had depraved moral theology. Within the limits offered by canon law as in force and the decrees of the Council of Trent, van Espen aimed at purging canon law of the belief that such things would be beneficial for the church.

Moreover, van Espen's personal life was permeated with this ideal. He held to premises which he, based on his own scholarly investigations and insight, considered to be the right ones, as long as they could be legitimately defended in conformity with the Catholic theology and canon law of his days. As he grew older and encountered increasing opposition, he accentuated his points of view and phrased them more succinctly. In so doing, he by no means denied, as did Protestants, that it is the church that holds the power of the keys, but held the opinion that such competence may not be abused or employed for political aims that do not answer to the truth. As far as possible, it is compulsory to search for the truth and follow that truth in conscience. For van Espen, who abhorred any probabilism or laxism, it was not an option to make concessions to the truth. The safe course he adopted, however, appeared not to be an easy one: he suffered continuous attacks on the legitimacy of his views, there was no prospect of a full chair at Leuven University, and eventually he was obliged to make an involuntary retreat to the Northern Netherlands.

GENERAL APPRAISAL AND INFLUENCE

In the Northern Netherlands, where separation between Catholics took a definite shape, those faithful to Rome commonly described van Espen as the evil genius behind the schism whereas the followers of the Vicariate saw him as the dedicated mainstay of the church. In the Southern Netherlands it was rather van Espen's teachings concerning relations between church and state which were prominent, especially in the nineteenth-century debate as to whether, under the Belgian Constitution of 1831, there was still room for the *appel comme d'abus* of the *ancien régime*.[40] Since the middle of the twentieth century, however, a non-polemical approach, characterized by scholarly

---

[40] Leo Kenis, 'Un jurist et canoniste de cour. The prevailing image of Zeger-Bernard Van Espen in the theological faculty of Louvain during the 19th century', in *Zeger–Bernard Van Espen at*

distance, has gained the upper hand, although the traditional sentiments are not yet entirely gone.

Outside the Low Countries, the works of van Espen were considerably influential, especially during the eighteenth century. In the German lands van Espen's defence of Episcopalism was taken up and further elaborated. The famous work *De statu Ecclesiae et legitima potestate Romani Pontificis*, written by Johannes Nikolaus von Hontheim (1701–1790) under the pseudonym Justinus Febronius, claimed full autonomy for the diocesan bishop. Hontheim had studied in Leuven and became auxiliary bishop of Trier. So-called Febronianism, based on his teachings, sought to restrict the jurisdictional primacy of the Pope in a similar way to what van Espen had done.[41] It had an enormous influence in Austria, especially under the reign of Emperor Joseph II (1741–1790), where it became an organic part of the Emperor's domestic policy, so-called Josephinism.

Soon the works of van Espen were read and taught in Spain, where many of his ideas were received by politicians and scholars. In this way, his teachings were disseminated and affected the religious policy of King Charles III (1716–1788), while during the reign of Charles IV (1748–1819) attempts were made to put his regalist principles into practice.[42]

At first sight it seems striking that van Espen is only occasionally quoted by French authors. It was sometimes suggested that this was caused by the fact that van Espen published in Latin.[43] In present-day secondary literature

>   *the crossroads*, eds. Guido Cooman, Maurice van Stiphout, and Bart Wauters (Leuven: Peeters, 2003), 331–345. See also Maurice van Stiphout, 'Legal continuity and discontinuity in the Low Countries in search of a recursus ad principem in ecclesiastical cases in the 1990s', in *Zeger-Bernard Van Espen at the crossroads*, eds. Guido Cooman, Maurice van Stiphout, and Bart Wauters (Leuven: Peeters, 2003), 441–476, at 449–451. Arguments to support the idea that the Church is subordinate to the State were derived from the works of van Espen, see François Laurent, *Van Espen. Étude historique sur l'eglise et sur l'état en Belgique* (Brussels: Lacroix, 1860).
> [41] Wolfgang Seibrich, 'Aufgeklärtes Kirchenrecht als restaurative Reform: Die deutschen Episkopalisten und Johann Nikolaus von Hontheim und ihre Beziehung zu Zeger-Bernard Van Espen', in *Zeger-Bernard Van Espen at the crossroads*, eds. Guido Cooman, Maurice van Stiphout, and Bart Wauters (Leuven: Peeters, 2003), 229–265. Michael Printy, *Enlightenment and the Creation of German Catholicism* (Cambridge: Cambridge University Press, 2009), 31–36.
> [42] Antonio Mestre Sanchis, 'La influencia del pensamiento de Van Espen en la España del siglo XVIII', *Revista de historia moderna: Anales de la Universidad de Alicante* 19 (2001): 405–430. Antonio Mestre Sanchis, 'El católico y sapientísimo Van Espen. La réception de la pensée de Zeger-Bernard van Espen dans l'Espagne du XVIIIe siècle', in *Zeger-Bernard Van Espen at the crossroads*, eds. Guido Cooman, Maurice van Stiphout, and Bart Wauters (Leuven: Peeters, 2003), 267–297.
> [43] Jean-Claude Lucet (1755–1806) published in 1788 under the title *Principes du droit canonique universel, ou manuel du canoniste*, a French compendium of the *Jus Ecclesiasticum Universum*, which soon passed into oblivion.

various other explanations are put forward. For typical Gallican ideas, it is argued, the French did not need another authority to refer to. Moreover, van Espen's strong Episcopalism was not always compatible with the mainstream opinions of the French Gallican theologians. In his conception of the constitution of the church, the exercise of jurisdiction was entirely concentrated in the hands of the diocesan bishop or the Chapter, whereas in France much more authority was ascribed to the 'second order' (*second ordre*), that is, the parish priests. Moreover, van Espen taught, at least in his later works, that bishop and Chapter derive their jurisdiction immediately from the church, whereas France stuck to the older opinion of Edmond Richer (1559–1631) that the exercise of jurisdiction is directly acquired from Christ.[44]

In many Italian territories, the works of van Espen were widely known. Their dissemination was surely supported by the Neapolitan edition of van Espen's *Scripta Omnia* (1766–1769) and the five editions of the same collected writings which appeared in Venice between 1732 and 1782. In the Kingdom of Naples, a partial reception of his thoughts can be traced, especially the doctrine that jurisdiction in the proper sense is that of the state, since the state has the monopoly on violence and only the state has genuine coercive competence. Moreover, there were scholars who attempted to revive the pastoral role of the diocesan bishop. Similarly, theologians such as Pietro Tamburini (1737–1827) and Giovanni Battista Zanzi (1758–1835) argued a new kind of Synodality, based on among other things episcopalist and regalist premises: the pastoral mission of the diocesan bishop and the sovereign's competence to grant synodical decrees force of law. Such ideas could have been inspired by van Espen's works.[45]

RECOMMENDED READINGS

Bilsen, Bertrand van. *De invloed van Zeger-Bernard van Espen op het ontstaan van de kerk van Utrecht*. 's-Gravenhage: Algemeene Landsdrukkerij, 1944.

Cooman, Guido, Maurice van Stiphout, and Bart Wauters, eds. *Zeger-Bernard van Espen at the Crossroads of Canon Law, History, Theology, and Church-State Relations*. Leuven: Peeters, 2003.

---

[44] Jaques Grèzs-Gayer, 'Un "auteur à bons principes": Zeger-Bernard Van Espen en pays gallican', in *Zeger–Bernard Van Espen at the crossroads*, eds. Guido Cooman, Maurice van Stiphout, and Bart Wauters (Leuven: Peeters, 2003), 211–228.

[45] For the reception of van Espen's doctrines by the Synod of Pistoia (1786) see Pietro Stella, 'Espenius inter canonistas princeps: Débats doctrinaux et combats politiques autour de Zeger-Bernard Van Espen dans l'Italie du XVIIIe siècle', in *Zeger–Bernard Van Espen at the crossroads*, eds. Guido Cooman, Maurice van Stiphout, and Bart Wauters (Leuven: Peeters, 2003), 299–330.

[Dupac de Bellegarde, Gabriel], *Vie de M. van Espen*. Naples: Antoine Cervone, 1770.

Hallebeek, Jan. 'Die Autonomie der Ortskirche im Denken von Zeger-Bernard van Espen'. *Internationale Kirchliche Zeitschrift* 92 (2002): 76–99.

Leclerc, Gustave. *Zeger-Bernard van Espen (1646–1728) et l'autorité ecclésiastique*. Zürich: Pas Verlag, 1964.

Nuttinck, Michel. *La vie et l'œuvre de Zeger-Bernard van Espen: Un canoniste janséniste, gallican et régalien à l'Université de Louvain (1646–1728)*. Louvain: Université de Louvain, 1969.

Schulte, Johann Friedrich von. *Die Geschichte der Quellen und Literatur des canonischen Rechts* III/1. Stuttgart: Enke, 1880. Reprint Graz: Akademische Druck- u. Verlaganstalt, 1956, 704–707.

Wauters, Bart. *Recht als religie. Canonieke onderbouw van de vroegmoderne staatsvorming in de zuidelijke Nederlanden*. Leuven: Universitaire Pers Leuven, 2005.

10

Dionysius van der Keessel

Egbert Koops*

BIOGRAPHICAL INTRODUCTION

Dionysius Godefridus van der Keessel was born in Deventer on 22 September 1738 as the youngest son of the Reformed church minister Dionysius van der Keessel (1700–1755), himself the son of a physician in Dordrecht, and Johanna Wilhelmina Cabeljau (c. 1705–1775).[1] To have a minister or physician in the family background was hardly extraordinary for a Dutch law professor in the eighteenth century.[2] Van der Keessel senior had been rather combative in protecting the unity of the Reformed church. Separatists, pietists, quietists, enthusiasts, and mystics were but a few of the groups he attacked in the lengthy titles of his pamphlets.[3] He published several

---

* Egbert Koops is professor of legal history at Leiden University, The Netherlands.

[1] Biographical and bibliographical information is taken mainly from Johan de Wal, biographical notice [1855] to Dionysius G. van der Keessel, *Select Theses of the Laws of Holland and Zeeland*, trans. Charles A. Lorenz (Cape Town: Juta, 1901), xi–xx; Abraham J. van der Aa, 'Keessel (Dionysius Godefridus van der)', in *Biographisch Woordenboek der Nederlanden* (Haarlem: Van Brederode, 1862), 10:87–88; Willem B. S. Boeles, 'Levenschetsen der Groninger Hoogleeraren', in *Gedenkboek der Hoogeschool te Groningen ter Gelegenheid van Haar Vijfde Halve Eeuwfeest*, ed. Willem J. A. Jonckbloet (Groningen: Wolters, 1864), 84–85; Johannes van Kuyk, 'Keessel (Dionysius Godefridus van der)', in *Nieuw Nederlandsch Biografisch Woordenboek*, eds. Petrus J. Blok and Philipp C. Molhuysen (Leiden: Sijthoff, 1914), 3:674–675; Margreet J. A. M. Ahsmann and Robert Feenstra, *Bibliografie van Hoogleraren in de Rechten aan de Leidse Universiteit tot 1811* (Amsterdam: NHUM, 1984), 132–138; Bert Krikke and Sjoerd Faber, 'Dionysius Godefridus van der Keessel (1738–1816)', in *Zestig Juristen: Bijdragen tot een Beeld van de Geschiedenis der Nederlandse Rechtswetenschap*, eds. Theo Veen, Peter C. Kop, and Govaert C. J. J. van den Bergh (Zwolle: Tjeenk Willink, 1987), 185–189; Theodoor H. Lunsingh Scheurleer, C. Willemijn Fock, and A. J. van Dissel, *Het Rapenburg. Geschiedenis van een Leidse Gracht* (Leiden: LUP, 1992), VIb: 742–747.

[2] Jan H. A. Lokin, *De Groninger Faculteit der Rechtsgeleerdheid (1596–1970)* (The Hague: Boom, 2019), 205.

[3] Abraham J. van der Aa, 'Keessel (Dionysius van der)', in *Biographisch Woordenboek der Nederlanden* (Haarlem: Van Brederode, 1862), 10:85–87.

against the Groningen preacher Wilhelmus Schortinghuis between 1744–1755, and had Schortinghuis's book on 'Heartfelt Christianity' banned by the synod of Overijssel, embarrassing the theological faculty at Groningen, which had already given its approbation.[4] The first son was stillborn but the second son, Samuel Rudolphus van der Keessel (1737–1799), followed in his father's footsteps and became a minister of the Reformed church in Dordrecht. It seems Dionysius considered theology too, but chose law instead.[5] Van der Keessel's father and grandfather had both studied at Leiden University. Dionysius and his brother Samuel would attend there as well,[6] enrolling simultaneously in 1756 after spending two years studying liberal arts at the Athenaeum Illustre in Deventer. That both sons were able to attend university at Leiden despite the death of their father in the preceding year shows that the family was well to do, or could at least call on an extended family network to finance both a degree in theology and a degree in law. Dionysius van der Keessel obtained his degree from Leiden University in 1761 with a dissertation on the acquisitive prescription of the offspring of stolen slaves and animals.[7] It is obvious from the complexity and style of the dissertation that he was preparing himself for a university career. Indeed, after a brief stint as an advocate in The Hague,[8] he was invited to take up the post of professor at Groningen University in 1762.

Van der Keessel did not stay at Groningen for long. The faculty of law was marred at the time by the controversies surrounding professor F. A. van der Marck (1719–1800), a vocal and belligerent proponent of natural law who had been attempting to conscript local customary law into his assault on the status of Roman law, by explaining it from first principles.[9] Van der Keessel was both too practical and too historicist to be convinced. In his teaching, he preferred to remain with the tried-and-tested examples of Böckelmann's *Compendium* for the course on the Institutes and van Eck's *Principia* for the Digest course.[10]

[4] Johannes C. Kromsigt, *Wilhelmus Schortinghuis. Een Bladzijde uit de Geschiedenis van het Piëtisme in de Gereformeerde Kerk van Nederland* (Groningen: Wolters, 1904), 231–241.
[5] Boeles, 'Levenschetsen', 84.
[6] Willem N. du Rieu, ed., *Album Studiosorum Academiae Lugduno Batavae 1575–1875* (The Hague: Nijhoff, 1875), 1053. The grandfather Godefridus had enrolled in 1682 (at 655) and the father Dionysius in 1718 (at 859).
[7] Dionysius G. van der Keessel, *Dissertatio Juridica Inauguralis de Usucapione Partus et Fœtus Rei Furtivae* (Leiden: Le Mair, 1761). See De Wal, biographical notice to *Select Theses*, xii.
[8] One shouldn't make too much of van der Keessel's (limited) experience of practising law. Krikke and Faber, 'Van der Keessel', 185.
[9] Corjo J. H. Jansen, *Natuurrecht of Romeins Recht. Een Studie over Leven en Werk van F. A. van der Marck (1719–1800) in het Licht van de Opvattingen van zijn Tijd* (Leiden: Brill, 1987).
[10] Boeles, 'Levenschetsen', 85; Lokin, *Groninger Faculteit*, 183–184; Willem Otterspeer, *Groepsportret met Dame* (Amsterdam: Bert Bakker, 2005), 3: 409.

Together with the advocate J. Wolbers he produced a lengthy advice on a matter of testamentary inheritance in Overijssel in 1766.[11] In complete opposition to van der Marck, from 1767 van der Keessel began to teach an amalgam of Roman law and local customary law, the *ius hodiernum*, as a product of particular *historical* development that could be understood and systematized by applying the terms and categories of Roman law.[12] He served a term as rector of Groningen university in 1768–1769, but it seems van der Keessel had had enough. Whether for the increase in pay and status, the proximity to family, or simply to escape the controversies in Groningen, in 1769 van der Keessel informed the curators that he would be leaving for Leiden.[13] As a result, he was not involved in the head-on collision between van der Marck and the Reformed church at Groningen between 1770–1773, which resulted in the removal of van der Marck from office until 1795.

As is clear from his inaugural lecture at Leiden, van der Keessel had developed into a proponent of the *usus modernus*. The first public course he taught was an explication of difficult passages in the *Corpus Iuris*,[14] probably based on van Eck's *Theses juris controversi*, which he had first taught as a private course in Groningen. In 1771 he added some criminal law to his repertoire, followed by Roman legal history in 1772 and a disputation course on conflict of laws in 1773.[15] From a report submitted by the Senate in 1807 and again from the series of 1815, it appears that by that time van der Keessel held a regular course of lectures on the Institutes,[16] on the Digest, on criminal law,[17]

---

[11] This advice of 9 December 1766 was published in Lambertus C. H. Strubberg, *Overysselsch Advysboek, Behelzende Merkwaardige, Zo Consultatoire Als Decisoire Advysen en Sententien, van Veele Voornaame Rechtsgeleerden in Overyssel* (Kampen: De Chalmot, 1785), 2: 40. Also noted by Krikke and Faber, 'Van der Keessel', 187.

[12] Margreet J. A. M. Ahsmann, 'Teaching the *Ius Hodiernum*: Legal Education of Advocates in the Northern Netherlands (1575–1800)', *Legal History Review* 65 (1997): 426 and 447–448. Also see Corjo J. H. Jansen, 'De Ontdekking van het Vaderlandse Recht in de Achttiende Eeuw', *Documentatieblad Werkgroep Achttiende Eeuw* 24. 1 (1992): 57–71.

[13] He was appointed ordinary professor by the curators of Leiden on 10 October 1769 on a salary of fl. 1,400. Philipp C. Molhuysen, ed., *Bronnen tot de Geschiedenis der Leidsche Universiteit* (The Hague: Nijhoff, 1923), 6: 56. His salary was raised to fl. 1,600 in 1799 (7:129) and to fl. 2,000 in 1802 (7:207), which in turn was raised to fl. 2,800 for all Leiden professors (partly to compensate for the loss of other emoluments) by art. 132 of the Organiek Besluit of 2 August 1815, *Staatsblad* 14. Also see Krikke and Faber, 'Van der Keessel', 185–187.

[14] Series February 1770, in Molhuysen, *Bronnen*, 6:7*.

[15] Series September 1771 through September 1773, in Molhuysen, *Bronnen*, 6:15*–16*.

[16] The lecture notes have been published as Dionysius G. van der Keessel, *Dictata ad Justiniani Institutionum Libros Quattuor, Observato Ordine Compendii Auctore Johanne Frederico Böckelmann*, ed. and trans. Ben Beinart, B. L. Hijmans Jr., and Paul van Warmelo, 2 vols. (Cape Town: Balkema, 1965–1967).

[17] The lecture notes have been published as Dionysius G. van der Keessel, *Praelectiones in Libros 47 et 48 Digestorum, Exhibentes Jurisprudentiam Criminalem ad Usum Fori Batavi Applicatam*

and on the *Introduction to Dutch Jurisprudence* of Hugo Grotius,[18] as well as a private disputation course.[19] In the meantime he had married Catharina Adriana Bodel, in 1772, and had moved to a capacious house on Rapenburg 71 adjacent to the Academy Building.[20] The couple had no children and so the house provided enough space for three library rooms and an auditorium with a separate entrance for private lectures.[21] These private lectures were an important source of additional income for professors at Leiden and elsewhere. They also allowed professors to take a select few students under their guidance free of charge.

In his *Theses selectae*[22] on the *Introduction to Dutch Jurisprudence* of Grotius, published in 1800, van der Keessel returns to the relationship between local law and Roman law. To answer the question of when Roman law should be applied as received law, he develops a systematic approach to the question of whether local law leaves any gaps and when Roman law may provide an answer.[23] Even the (comparative) customary law of neighbouring regions may be taken into account, but natural law is the very last resort. In the preface to this work, which at 345 pages is the only major work van der Keessel published during his lifetime, he explains his choice of a commentary on Grotius by stating his intention to provide a *systematic* introduction to the *ius patrium*, which is sorely lacking for those who leave the university to work in legal practice. Far from being superseded by the already-promised codifications, a commentary bringing Grotius up to date will aid in forming and interpreting the system of new national codes.[24] Even without the thousands of pages of

---

(*Duce Cornelio van Eck*) *et in Novum Codicem Criminalem*, 1809, ed. and trans. Ben Beinart and Paul van Warmelo, 6 vols. (Cape Town: Juta, 1969–1981).

[18] The lecture notes have been published as Dionysius G. van der Keessel, *Praelectiones Iuris Hodierni ad Hugonis Grotii Introductionem ad Iurisprudentiam Hollandicam*, 6 vols., ed. and trans. Paul van Warmelo, Lucas I. Coertze, and Henri L. Gonin (Cape Town: Balkema, 1961–1975).

[19] Molhuysen, *Bronnen*, 7:86*; Otterspeer, *Groepsportret*, 3: 409.

[20] Catharina Bodel died in 1811. The house was purchased by the university following van der Keessel's death in 1816 and annexed to the Academy Building on Rapenburg 73.

[21] Voorda attacked van der Keessel for giving his lectures 'in the smoke and fumes of a stove in a room at home'. Lambertus van Poelgeest, 'Mr. Bavius Voorda (1729–1799). Een Rechtlijnig Fries Jurist aan de Leidse Academie', *Leids Jaarboekje* 79 (1987): 117.

[22] Dionysius G. van der Keessel, *Theses Selectae Iuris Hollandici et Zelandici, ad Supplendam Hugonis Grotii Introductionem ad Iurisprudentiam Hollandicam* (Leiden: Luchtmans, 1800).

[23] Theses 7–24. Also see review of *Theses Selectae [etc.]*, by Dionysius G. van der Keessel, *Algemeene Vaderlandsche Letter-Oefeningen* 1 (1803): 59–63; De Wal, biographical notice to *Select Theses*, xviii–xix; Anne S. de Blécourt, *Pro Excolendo en de Rechtsgeschiedenis* (Groningen: Wolters, 1937), 85–87. Further literature in Jansen, 'De Ontdekking', 59.

[24] Ben Beinart, 'Van der Keessel's addresses to his students', *Acta Juridica* 1 (1972): 24–25. It should be noted that Grotius's *Inleiding* had already been updated and expanded by Groenewegen van der Made (1644), Schorer (1767), and Schorer/Van Wijn (1777). See

lecture notes published since the 1960s, this book alone would have cemented van der Keessel's reputation for producing a final statement of Roman–Dutch law that was workable in practice.[25]

Living in troubled times, van der Keessel often attempted to walk the middle of the road politically. That does not detract from his belligerent temperament. Molhuysen characterizes him as such regarding discussions in the Senate and mentions the intransigent professor Bavius Voorda in the same breath.[26] With good reason, as the two became embroiled in a bitter quarrel over the right to teach the *ius hodiernum* (and the proper way to teach it) that only ended with Voorda's death in 1799.[27] Personal and political animosity aside, a major difference of opinion on the place of the *ius hodiernum* in the curriculum was at stake in this altercation between two Romanists.[28] Voorda wanted to give Roman law pride of place instead of wasting time on particularities better learnt in practice, treating statute and customary law as an afterthought best learnt by looking for parallels to and differences from Roman law. Almost as a precursor to Savigny, van der Keessel instead wanted to construct a system as complex as, and built upon, Roman law to explain the *ius hodiernum* from internal principles.[29] This meant teaching Grotius and the customs of Holland in full, in a packed two-year course that ignored other provinces, which was both more and less than Voorda had in mind.

Van der Keessel served as rector of Leiden University for three terms, 1773–1774, 1785–1786, and 1791–1792. His interest in statute and custom coupled with his faculty seniority meant he had a keen sense of the symbols of power including university privilege. Some instances may be illustrative. In 1792 and again in 1802 he was occupied with the question whether the magistrate of Leiden could impose certain taxes on professors as they were citizens of the academy and not of the city. Not without the Senate's permission, van der Keessel concluded, which was always granted when properly

---

A. J. Boudewijn Sirks, 'Hugo de Groot, Inleiding tot de Hollandsche Recht-Geleertheyd, 1631', in *Juristen die Schreven en Bleven. Nederlandstalige Rechtsgeleerde Klassiekers*, eds. Georges G. G. M. M. Martyn, Louis A. M. J. A. Berkvens, and Paul Brood (Hilversum: Verloren, 2020), 45.

[25] The book was reprinted in 1860 and went through many editions after an English translation was published in 1855. See Ahsmann and Feenstra, *Bibliografie Leiden*, 134–135; Otterspeer, *Groepsportret*, 3: 330.

[26] Molhuysen, *Bronnen*, 6: vii: 'strijdlustig'.

[27] Van Poelgeest, 'Voorda', *passim*; Ahsmann, 'Teaching the *Ius Hodiernum*', 449–450.

[28] Ahsmann, 'Teaching the *Ius Hodiernum*', 450: 'in Leiden at least there was no room yet for two courses on the *ius hodiernum*'.

[29] Van Poelgeest, 'Voorda', 113–114; Ahsmann, 'Teaching the *Ius Hodiernum*', 450.

asked but should still be requested beforehand.[30] After the regime change of 1795, he approached the curators for a new text for the doctorate bull, now that the 'ancient rights' conferred in it had disappeared.[31] When the inevitable proposal came in 1799 to abolish the academic tribunals, he fought a tenacious rearguard action together with Smallenburg and Luzac for this final academic privilege, extending its life until 1811.[32] In 1806 and again in 1807 he petitioned for a new university seal.[33] When a shipload of gunpowder exploded in Leiden that same year to terrible effect, killing both Kluit and Luzac and levelling part of the city, he went to King Louis Napoleon on behalf of the Senate to narrate what had happened, and immediately sent him a petition for relief as well, asking inter alia for the 'Hogeschool' at Leiden to be named the Royal University of Holland instead, a request which was granted.[34] Academic privilege had its drawbacks too. In 1807, senior faculty including van der Keessel complained that the citizens of Leiden had been compensated with a temporary remittance of taxes while as citizens of the academy the professors received none.[35]

From these brief biographical details, a general picture may be drawn. Van der Keessel was neither a convinced orangist nor a convinced patriot, but rather a staunch proponent of the old multilayered legal order, guarding established privilege while navigating the shoals of regime change. Preluding on the argument to be developed, he may also be characterized as a true believer in the orthodoxy of the Dutch Reformed church, a professor with an aversion to Enlightenment thought, and someone who became more and more truculent as he grew older. Yet when confronted with the new order, when Napoleon visited the soon-to-be Imperial University of Leiden in 1811, it seems the 73-year-old van der Keessel, then dean of the faculty, was left dumbfounded.[36] The restoration of the old order brought his pension too, in the form of compulsory retirement for professors over 70 as ordered by article

[30] Molhuysen, *Bronnen*, 6: 411–420 (residential tax), 7: 30 (taxes in general), 7: 195–198 (pauper tax).
[31] Molhuysen, *Bronnen*, 7: 4.
[32] Matthijs Siegenbeek, *Geschiedenis der Leidsche Hoogeschool van Hare Oprigting in den Jare 1575 tot het Jaar 1825* (Leiden: Luchtmans, 1829), 1: 385; Molhuysen, *Bronnen*, 7: 117, 7: 136–138, and 7: 149–154. The final meeting of the tribunal took place on 28 February 1811: Molhuysen, *Bronnen*, 7: 95*.
[33] Molhuysen, *Bronnen*, 7: 279 and 331.
[34] Molhuysen, *Bronnen*, 7: 297–302 and 328.
[35] Molhuysen, *Bronnen*, 7: 331.
[36] J. van Geuns, 'Napoleon te Leyden', *Vaderlandsche Letter-Oefeningen* 2 (1826): 523; Otterspeer, *Groepsportret*, 3: 219. Van Geuns is quoting from a period letter to his father and was present at Napoleon's reception. A different version, no doubt tainted with *esprit d'escalier*, is found in the diary of Willem de Clercq, an entrepreneur, poet, and Réveil friend of

140 of the Organic Decree regarding education of 1815.[37] Less than a year later, van der Keessel died in Leiden on 7 August 1816.[38]

MAJOR THEMES AND CONTRIBUTIONS

In the preface to his dissertation of 1761, van der Keessel mentions Cujas, Noodt, Bynkershoek, and Schulting with admiration, and names Scheltinga and Rücker in particular as his teachers. Both the subject and the methodology place him squarely within the 'Dutch Elegant School' of jurisprudence.[39] It is an erudite attempt to marry dogmatic interpretation with the textual reconstruction of classical Roman law, with little regard for practical relevance. A 'modern' argument from natural law or first principles is absent from the dissertation, although it surfaces in full in the accompanying theses, which breathe a spirit of natural theology perhaps surprising in the son of a Reformed church minister.[40] In light of this work, van der Keessel must have known that he was entering the proverbial hornet's nest when he accepted a position at Groningen University in 1762.

Shortly before van der Keessel's arrival, van der Marck had argued that local law should not be interpreted from Roman law but from first principles (1761) and that Roman law neither had, nor should have, subsidiary force of law (1761

Bilderdijk and Da Costa. Writing in 1822, he notes 'Desire of Napoleon always to say something nasty to everyone. He tells the prof. at Leiden that all jurisprudence except for the Code Napoleon was foolish to which the old prof. van der Keessel responded that he had always considered him a great man but now saw he was only a *breteur* [swashbuckler].' Willem de Clercq, *Diaries*, diary entry 1822, from University of Amsterdam special collections, Ms. RA F IX, 9: 47.

[37] Organiek Besluit of 2 August 1815, *Staatsblad* 14. Van der Keessel was declared emeritus along with many others by a Royal Decree of 16 October 1815; see *Algemene Konst- en Letterbode* 45 (1815): 189. Siegenbeek, *Leidsche Hoogeschool*, 1: 428 is correct but De Wal, biographical notice to *Select Theses*, xix; van der Aa, BWN, 10: 87; and Boeles, 'Levenschetsen', 85 have the wrong year (1808).

[38] Boeles, 'Levenschetsen', 85 has the wrong date. Like many other Leiden professors of that period, van der Keessel was buried in the Old Graveyard at Katwijk. The grave has been cleared but a memorial stone bearing the university seal was placed at its approximate site in 2016. Korrie J. J. Korevaart, 'Begraven in Katwijk. Frisse Lucht voor Leidse Leden van de Maatschappij', *Nieuw Letterkundig Magazijn* 35.2 (2017): 1–5.

[39] Govaert C. J. J. van den Bergh, *Die Holländische Elegante Schule: Ein Beitrag zur Geschichte von Humanismus und Rechtswissenschaft in den Niederlanden 1500–1800* (Frankfurt: Klostermann, 2002).

[40] Theses VI–IX argue that humans are bound by natural law because it has been ordered by God to perfect the happiness of rational beings (thesis VI), which leads to the precept to love that which God loves (thesis VII), which in turns leads to the precept to not only cultivate piety and true religion, but also to surrender to each what is owed and increase human happiness (thesis VIII), which is only possible by working within and through human society (thesis IX).

and 1762) in Groningen or the neighbouring provinces. Building on his dissertation, van der Keessel (who had just turned 24) entered this debate with his inaugural lecture on 1 October 1762, on the question whether those parts of Roman law supposedly not in present use should still be taught at the universities – yes, was the answer.[41] Unused parts of Roman law may still find use when the occasion arises, so the argument goes; universities should not merely educate for national service, but should keep foreign students and the colonies in mind too; and a full knowledge of Roman legal history sharpens the mind, serves as a repository for solutions, and aids the interpretation of other, received parts of Roman law. One example adduced by van der Keessel is the use of torture to extract confessions: if the Roman law of slavery had been studied more, he argues, it would have been realized that the Romans had restricted torture to the bodies of slaves, so that the institution should have disappeared in Europe together with slavery.[42]

Conflict with van der Marck eventually became unavoidable.[43] It comes as no surprise that van der Keessel refused to join the learned society van der Marck had founded in 1761 for the furtherance of 'national' law, *Pro Excolendo jure patrio*.[44] In 1764, at the instigation of the rector Chevallier, a theologian, the Senate refused to allow a pupil of van der Marck's by the name of Schukking to defend the proposition as part of his dissertation that Roman law had no force of law in the neighbouring province of Drenthe.[45] It was clear that the thesis had been drafted and approved by van der Marck, who protested

---

[41] Dionysius G. van der Keessel, *Oratio Inauguralis, qua Disquiritur an Capita Illa Juris Romani Quae in Usu Hodie Non Esse Dicuntur in Academiis Doceri Expediat* (Groningen: Spandaw, 1762). Also see: review of *Oratio [...] an Capita Illa Juris Romani Quae in Usu Hodie Non Esse Dicuntur in Academiis Doceri Expediat*, by Dionysius G. van der Keessel, *Maandelyke Uittreksels of Boekzaal der Geleerde Waerelt* 96 (1763): 432–443; De Wal, biographical notice to *Select Theses*, xiii; De Blécourt, *Pro Excolendo*, 69–70.

[42] Reviewing the oration, Luzac remarked that this particular example signalled that too much attention had been paid to history, not enough to natural law and philosophy. Elie Luzac, review of *Oratio [...] an Capita Illa Juris Romani Quae in Usu Hodie Non Esse Dicuntur in Academiis Doceri Expediat*, by Dionysius G. van der Keessel, *De Nederlandsche Letter-Courant* 99 (1762): 371–374. Beccaria's well-known treatise dates from 1764 and appeared in Dutch translation in 1768. Van der Keessel may have returned to the topic at the end of his rectorate in 1769, in an address on 'subjection or rather freedom through laws', but it seems the oration has never been printed and no manuscript copy is known today: *Oratio de Legum Servitute Vera Libertate* (4 September 1769). Mentioned in *Bibliotheca Hagana Historico-Philologico-Theologica* 5.1 (1773): 666; Boeles, 'Levenschetsen', 85.

[43] Frederik A. van der Marck, *Waaragtig Verhaal van het Geene [...] Is Voorgevallen* (Lingen: Bauer, 1775), 6–15; De Wal, biographical notice to *Select Theses*, xiv–xv; Jansen, *Natuurrecht of Romeins Recht*, 206 et seq.

[44] De Blécourt, *Pro Excolendo*, 31 and 40; Lokin, *Groninger Faculteit*, 183. Van Poelgeest, 'Voorda', 113 is mistaken.

[45] Van Kuyk, 'Keessel', 3:817; Lokin, *Groninger Faculteit*, 180–181.

the rector's decision. The candidate agreed to withdraw the proposition, then published it anyway as an appendix, with a note stating the rector had forced him to withdraw it. The Senate was not amused and started court proceedings against Schukking, which eventually came to nothing. A year later, in 1765, a comparable incident occurred when another pupil of van der Marck's by the name of Hovingh defended a dissertation under van der Marck after it had been refused by his colleague Schröder, claiming that Roman law should not be applied in the courts of Groningen. Annoyed, van der Keessel responded with a long anonymous letter in print, arguing that the discussion was moot since as a matter of fact Roman law was applied, often providing superior solutions, while most rules of statutory or customary law had no basis in the precepts of natural law at all, and running through a wealth of examples.[46] Whatever its merits, the letter opens with an *ad hominum* attack on van der Marck. He is assumed to be the real author of Hovingh's dissertation because of the mudslinging it contains, at which no one in Groningen was as adept as van der Marck, to cover his complete lack of arguments. He had been ghost-writing dissertations 'for incompetent or time-wasting candidates'[47] to enhance his own stature, as if his ideas were gaining momentum.

The tone of the letter was lamented by a reviewer, who noted that even if the allegations were true, van der Marck had not attacked anyone the way this anonymous author had tried to do.[48] Of course van der Keessel's anonymous letter invited more pamphleteers to enter the arena in defence of van der Marck,[49] but its author did not respond any further. He left for Leiden instead. But he could not resist slinging a final barb at van der Marck from the safety of his new chair.

---

[46] [Dionysius G. van der Keessel], *Brief van een Groninger Rechtsgeleerde, over Zekere Dissertatie Onlangs te Groningen Uitgegeven Aangaande de Vrage, of 't met de Goede Staatkunde Overeenkome, in de Groninger Rechtbanken Vreemde, en Byzonder de Roomsche Wetten, te Gebruiken; Waar in de Argumenten door den Heere Prof. Van der Marck Bygebragt, Onpartydig Onderzogt, en Zedig Wederlegt Worden* (Groningen: Spandaw, 1765). The attribution to van der Keessel was doubted by De Wal, biographical notice to *Select Theses*, xv, but the rumour came on the authority of Tydeman and was canonized by Jan I. van Doorninck, *Vermomde en Naamloze Schrijvers Opgespoord op het Gebied der Nederlandsche en Vlaamsche Letteren* (Leiden: Brill, 1883), 1: 524.

[47] Van der Keessel had been annoyed with this phenomenon in any case. According to an anecdote reported by Tydeman, he dismissed an ignorant candidate from an examination, only for the candidate to receive his dissertation from another university two weeks later. See Johan Huizinga, *Verzamelde Werken* (Haarlem: Tjeenk Willink, 1951), 8: 51; Lokin, *Groninger Faculteit*, 195 fnt. 185.

[48] Review of *Brief van een Groninger rechtsgeleerde [etc.]*, *Bibliothèque des Sciences et des Beaux Arts* 24.1 (1765): 280–282.

[49] Under pseudonyms such as 'Alethophilus Eleutherius' (Eilardus W. Uchtman) and 'Urbanus Hilarius'. De Blécourt, *Pro Excolendo*, 73–74.

On 12 March 1770, van der Keessel delivered his inaugural lecture at Leiden 'on the wisdom of the Dutch lawmakers in receiving Roman law'.[50] He declares that the use of Roman law as a subsidiary system of law has come under attack from adepts of natural law, and that he is coming to its defence because he fears the consequences for legal practice. At most he will admit that natural law somehow informs equity, but it is inconstant and prone to arbitrariness while a great amount of certain positive law is necessary to order society. Local custom and statute contain so many omissions that a more extensive subsidiary system of law is indispensable. Natural law is too abstract and philosophical to be applied or understood by the people, and so either new laws should be promulgated, or recourse had to a system that has already produced written law in extenso – Roman law of course. Although new civil laws can be made, the task is exceedingly difficult and often leads to imperfections, as has happened in Prussia. It is also nearly impossible to unify the separate systems of the provinces of the Netherlands. And so the Dutch lawmakers are to be congratulated on their wisdom in appreciating the equity of Roman law, which contains solutions to all possible cases or at least the materials to arrive at one through interpretation. Van der Keessel then proceeds to clear away three objections. It is moot that Roman law is not in the vernacular: Latin is the scientific language, it can safely be translated, and laws will not be understood by an untrained readership no matter the language. It is also not pertinent that the interpretation of Roman law is not secure: that does not mean it is inconsistent, any more than the existence of discussion about the Bible or natural law proves these to be inconsistent. And finally, it is irrelevant that Roman law found its origin in a different political community: a large part is *ius gentium*, and what is particularly Roman is not based on the Roman constitutional order but on unchanging relations between people.

The period between 1783 and 1795 was marked by the collapse of the Dutch Republic as a result of the struggles between orangists and patriots, both backed by foreign powers. Within this period the future King William I, then prince William Frederic, was enrolled at Leiden in 1789–1790 for a one-year course in international law, political history, and private law to finish his education. The staunch orangists Kluit and Pestel would teach the first and second part; the third part was given to van der Keessel in spite of the

---

[50] Dionysius G. van der Keessel, *Oratio Inauguralis de Legislatorum Belgarum in Recipiendo Jure Romano Prudentia* (Leiden: Le Mair, 1770). Also see: review of *Oratio Inauguralis de Legislatorum Belgarum in Recipiendo Jure Romano Prudentia*, by Dionysius G. van der Keessel, *De Regtsgeleerde in Spectatoriale Vertogen* 4.4 (1770): 81–98, De Blécourt, *Pro Excolendo*, 40.

misgivings of princess Wilhelmina, who ascribed to him a '*patriottisme voilé*'.[51] Van der Keessel had never voiced anti-orangist sentiments in public, and in fact had lauded stadtholder William V in his rectoral address of 1774 on instilling love of country, proclaiming that the office of hereditary stadtholder was the best way to unify the sovereign States and guarantee the wellbeing of all.[52] Likewise, in his rectoral address of 1786 shortly before the patriot troubles, he had argued that the best way to restore peace to the Republic was to uphold the laws but with equity in mind.[53] He swore an orangist oath of loyalty in 1788 and was accused by Voorda, who refused to take this oath, of 'swerving patriotism' in consequence.[54] If anything, van der Keessel was politically rather middle of the road.[55] But the princess must have had in mind the affair of the summer of 1789 concerning the dissertation of J. J. Th. Duval. This pupil of the orangist Kluit had argued that the stadtholder had never originally been subject to the States. Van der Keessel disapproved the dissertation and tried to persuade Duval to withdraw it and obtain a doctorate on propositions instead. With the backing of Kluit, Duval refused and had the dissertation printed without faculty approval, which led to the faculty denying him the doctorate altogether, giving as its unofficial reason that he had attempted to undermine the accepted theory of the sovereignty of the States at the time of the foundation of the Dutch Republic. In the preface to his Latin 'dissertation' Duval blamed van der Keessel for the whole affair, who responded with a public *narratio* of events, supported by Pestel as dean of

---

[51] Ben Beinart and Paul van Warmelo, 'Van der Keessel en de Studie van de Erfprins Willem Frederik, de Latere Koning Willem I, te Leiden 1789–1790', *Verslagen en Mededelingen van de Vereeniging tot Uitgaaf der Bronnen van het Oud-Vaderlandsche Recht* 14 (1974): 21–69; Otterspeer, *Groepsportret*, 3: 114.

[52] Dionysius G. van der Keessel, *Oratio de Amore Patriae in Juventute Belgica Excitando Prudenterque Dirigendo* (Leiden: Le Mair, 1774). See Cornelis van Engelen, review of *Oratio de amore patriae [etc.]*, by Dionysius G. van der Keessel, *De Denker* 12 (1775): 121–136; review of *Oratio de amore patriae [etc.]*, by Dionysius G. van der Keessel, *Nederlandsche Bibliotheek* 3.1 (1775): 103–107.

[53] Dionysius G. van der Keessel, *Oratio de Aequitate Judicantium, Optimo Turbatae Reipublicae Remedio* (Leiden: Luchtmans, 1786).

[54] Van Poelgeest, 'Voorda', 117.

[55] After the regime change, van der Keessel (and Voorda) were required to swear another oath in 1797 to uphold the Batavian Republic. Voorda bluntly refused, van der Keessel took it with incomprehensible qualifications. See van Poelgeest, 'Voorda', 118–119. The text of the oath is in Molhuysen, *Bronnen*, 7:90–91: 'I declare the Batavian people to be a free and independent people and pledge to it my loyalty. I declare to have an immutable loathing of government by the stadtholder, federalism, aristocracy and anarchy. So I declare.' Van der Keessel wanted to have it noted that he was taking the oath 'as a declaration of his intended duty toward the fatherland'.

the faculty.⁵⁶ Van der Keessel argued half-heartedly that in refusing the dissertation he had wished to save the house of Orange from false friends, but in light of the tense mood after the orangist *restoration* of 1787, it comes as no surprise that anything less than staunch orangism was considered suspect. In any case, the prince had to attend van der Keessel's lectures under supervision.

The prince was fêted at Leiden. The Senate even attempted to impress him with the academic splendour attached to a promotion *more majorum*, for the first time in 15 years and at great cost to the candidate J. C. van der Kemp.⁵⁷ Van der Keessel served as promotor, which gave him the opportunity, in front of stadtholder William V and prince William Frederic, to expound his didactic programme in an oration on the effects of the study of civil law on the formation of good morals.⁵⁸ Unsurprisingly, some part of the oration is taken up with extolling the virtues of prince William Frederic as a student of law, and the remainder with the argument that the study of law grants a better understanding of both private virtue and public virtue, not by looking at particular rules but by understanding the underlying principles and causes, which are best grasped from Roman law. The study of law instils fear of God, love of good behaviour, and love of country next to the virtues of a good magistrate and the wisdom of a lawmaker. Whatever prince William Frederic made of all this, he seems not to have held any '*patriottisme voilé*' against van der Keessel, to whom he granted an important chivalric order in 1815.⁵⁹

Van der Keessel served three terms of a year as rector of Leiden university.⁶⁰ As was customary, he ended each term with an oration delivered on the occasion of the *dies natalis* of the university. After the love of country in 1774 and the equitable judge in 1786, van der Keessel turned to the Christian advocate in 1792.⁶¹ Can such a thing exist? The advocate is occupied

---

⁵⁶ Johan J. Th. Duval, *De Vera Mente Foederis Traiectini circa Gubernatores Hollandia et Zelandiae* (Leiden: Koet, 1789); trans. *Over het Recht Verstand der Unie van Utrecht met Betrekking tot de Heeren Stadhouders van Holland en Zeeland* (Utrecht: Wild, 1790); Dionysius G. van der Keessel, *Narratio de Rebus a Se et a Facultate Juridica Gestis circa Nuper Evulgatam Dissertationem Joh. Jacob. Thom. Duval* (Leiden: Luchtmans, 1789).

⁵⁷ *Algemene Konst- en Letterbode* 96 (1790): 138–139; Siegenbeek, *Leidsche Hoogeschool*, 1: 325–326.

⁵⁸ Dionysius G. van der Keessel, *Oratio de Studio Juris Civilis ad Bonos Mores Formandos et Virtutem Colendam Aptissimo* (Leiden: Luchtmans, 1790). See De Wal, biographical notice to *Select Theses*, xviii.

⁵⁹ Van der Keessel was named knight in the Order of the Lion of the Netherlands on 18 November 1815. *Algemene Konst- en Letterbode* 49 (1815): 353.

⁶⁰ In 1805 and 1809 he refused to have his name added to the nomination, claiming bad health. Molhuysen, *Bronnen*, 7: 251 and 7: 339.

⁶¹ Dionysius G. van der Keessel, *Oratio de Advocato Christiano* (Leiden: Luchtmans, 1792).

with earthly matters, with the works of gentile jurists, with controversy in court (and not even his own), while the necessity of his office is not exactly apparent if judges dutifully adhere to the precept to hear both sides of an argument. But suits are brought daily and time-stressed judges find it difficult to be impartial, so that advocates are necessary to instruct the judge and ensure a fair hearing for their clients. Such a task is not unworthy of Christians and may be informed by Christian ethics, as van der Keessel then attempts to show. First he defines his terms. A Christian believes in God from natural reason, knows that he is fallen and cannot raise himself, but reads with gladness in revealed Scripture that he may be saved through Christ, who participated in human nature to fulfil the law; and for this reason he surrenders himself to Christ fully, to ponder his example and perform his work for the glory of God. It may be clear if unsurprising that van der Keessel is not straying an inch from the orthodoxy of the Dutch Reformed church.

From a different affair, it is equally clear that van der Keessel held no love at all for the new 'natural theology'.[62] In 1785 the German professor Johann Christoph Schwab, a follower of Wolff and Leibnitz, had been awarded first prize in the prestigious competition attached to the *legatum Stolpianum*[63] for an entry arguing that prejudice, ignorance, and blind faith in authority were the reasons Christian faith did not instil virtue in everyone. A year later, the dean of the faculty of theology, Broes, found it necessary to declare in public that none of the Leiden theologians had been involved in awarding the prize. Van der Keessel read Schwab's work in 1787 and objected greatly to it.[64] It was built on a notion of intercultural natural religion rather than Scripturally revealed Christianity and completely glossed over the fundamental religious truth of salvation through grace, turning Christ into a moral teacher and the crucifixion into a moral example. Van der Keessel wanted the entire Senate to distance itself publicly from the work, much to the chagrin of the curators of the Stolpian legacy. But it seems that apart from Broes he stood relatively alone, and nothing happened.

Returning to his oration on the Christian advocate, van der Keessel next argued that since a large amount of law is necessary to order society, trained jurists are necessary to interpret these laws. A Christian jurist, then, feels

---

[62] Otterspeer, *Groepsportret*, 3: 71–73.
[63] The alumnus Jan Stolp left a great amount of money to Leiden university in 1753 to institute a biennial prize of a gold medal worth fl. 250 for an essay in support of natural religion or moral philosophy, to be awarded by a committee of eight professors. Abraham J. van der Aa, 'Stolp (Jan)', in *Biographisch Woordenboek der Nederlanden* (Haarlem: Van Brederode, 1874), 17-2: 1021; Otterspeeer, *Groepsportret*, 3:70.
[64] Molhuysen, *Bronnen*, 6: 304–306.

bound by justice, honesty, and Christian virtue to interpret and decide cases as if he were Divine justice itself, both in giving advice and taking up a case. He will not argue from uncertainty but, conforming to his oath, will take up neither cases that go against law nor those unapproved by law. Van der Keessel seems to attempt to set Christian advocates to a higher standard than others. He should not take up a case where the law is certain but the outcome uncertain because of difficulties of proof. Neither should he take up a case on the mere grounds that the law is uncertain, but should ask himself in good conscience whether he considers the case just. When it comes to a difference between strict law and equity though, the matter is different. Applied to the case of a creditor minority holding out against a creditor majority that wants to compromise with the debtor, a Christian advocate should not extend his office merely because it seems equitable to support the majority – because what is equitable varies with the persons, facts, and qualities from case to case, and so support of the strict law should take pride of place whenever there is any doubt, just to be sure.

The orator then gets into full reactionary swing.[65] Tax evaders do not deserve advocacy because they steal from the common good, and one should render to Caesar what is owed. In criminal law, no advocate should take up the case of a criminal whom he knows to be guilty. 'I am not unaware of the voices crying that it is better to leave a wrongdoer unpunished, than to condemn the innocent. But all these things do not move me from this opinion.' If a judge has to condemn once the crime has been established, then this is all the more true for an advocate bound by law, by oath, and by conscience. An advocate defending someone he knows to be guilty is himself guilty of furthering new crimes. In consequence, he should not petition for a pardon for convicted criminals, because the common good requires them to be punished. Turning from defence advocacy to bringing suit, the Christian advocate should realize that a right that can be claimed in court does not equate to a just cause; as in his private life, he should take piety and charity to heart. In separation proceedings, for instance, he should not take any case before describing the full horrors of separation and appeal to his client's conscience and sense of morality. In matters of *iniuria*, clients should be dissuaded and court is the last resort, and in fact, the true Christian advocate will counsel against all litigation and first attempt to compromise the matter before arbiters. Should the just cause ever go to court though, then the

---

[65] De Wal, biographical notice to *Select Theses*, xvii: 'The picture of the true Christian, sketched in the first part of this work, is not wanting in vivacity; but the examples by which he, in the second, explains the duties of Christian advocates are perhaps less justly chosen'.

Christian advocate is well advised to be unafraid, steadfast and quick, diligent, and lofty in spirit, certain of himself and the support of the laws, wary of his opponent, etc. If he takes this advice to heart, then confirmed and aided by God's grace, the advocate may look back on a life well spent, knowing that as an instrument of grace he has aided the miserable, established the force of law, and been most useful to human society. It must be said: the peroration is as gratuitous as the advocate's pay (*gratuitam operam*).

Van der Keessel's final rectoral address was not received well. An anonymous reviewer[66] paid it a backhanded compliment: 'although not providing a specimen of eloquence, it presents the duties of a good and honest advocate with good intentions and meticulousness'.[67] The reviewer objected more to the title, arguing that what was presented was in fact a deontology of honest lawyers in general, 'be they Christian, Jew, or Muslim', which could not be used to distinguish Christian advocates. 'In the entire oration on the Christian advocate, one will fruitlessly search for such a [Christian] duty, that is not inseparable from any honest advocate with every people, no matter their religion, that know the office of advocates'.[68] Moreover, in as far as the professor argued that advocates should not take cases 'against the law, nor unapproved by law', he was letting his oratory run away with him, at least if that meant he would deny fellow citizens advocacy when pursued for an act not forbidden by any explicit law. Where there is no law, there is no transgression (Rom. 4:15). In van der Keessel's discussion of strict law versus equity, the reviewer was hard pressed to find any trace of Christian charity; and in prohibiting an advocate from petitioning for a reprieve, he was not only trying to think for a sovereign government that was very capable of thinking for itself, but also displaying a marked lack of Christian forgiveness. Should not van der Keessel's Dutch Reformed Christian advocate, of all people, realize that he himself was only saved from certain ruin by grace, and then recognize the same condition in an unfortunate criminal? 'The professor', so the reviewer concluded, 'seems to us somewhat too precise. Exaggerated ethics bring

---

[66] Possibly the lawyer and historian Jacobus Scheltema (1767–1835), a sympathizer of the Patriot party who often contributed to the *Algemene Konst- en Letterbode*. Following the Prussian intervention of 1787, Scheltema went into exile in Steinfurt and befriended F. A. van der Marck there.

[67] Review of *Oratio de Advocato Christiano*, by Dionysius G. van der Keessel, *Algemene Konst- en Letterbode* 199 (1792): 124–125 and 200 (1792): 133–135 (quote at 124); also see Bernard H. D. Hermesdorf, *Licht en Schaduw in de Advocatuur der Lage Landen* (Leiden: Brill, 1951), 124–126.

[68] At 124. Also see review of *Oratio de Advocato Christiano*, by Dionysius G. van der Keessel, *Vaderlandsche Bibliotheek van Wetenschap, Kunst en Smaak* 5.1 (1793): 72–73.

prejudice to true virtue by their weak grounds, and often give reason to cast aside the one with the other.'[69]

Fortunately, van der Keessel usually tempered his tone a little when addressing his students at the beginning or end of his lecture series. A collection of those addresses has survived.[70] 'Throughout they are filled with an almost feigned humility, with deep religious faith, and with respect and love for his students for which he seemed to yearn in return', as the editor of the addresses, Beinart, notes.[71] In particular in an address dated 1773, after considering that nothing is grander than the glory derived from his pupils, he offers them the advice he claims he has given many times before: namely to appreciate the burden that is entrusted to their good faith, wisdom, and integrity as judge or advocate. They are called to a path of justice, to defend only just causes and never vile acts, never to take money for service against a just cause, not to look for affection or favour, so that they may claim to have acted with justice when the time of judgement comes at the end of their life.[72] In 1807, following the gunpowder disaster at Leiden, he grieved with his students and reminded them all life and fortune is in the hands of God.[73] This far more traditional piety may have resonated more with his students than the strangely stern and unforgiving words he spoke as rector in 1792.

Van der Keessel taught public and private courses in criminal law from 1771 until at least 1809.[74] His autographed manuscript of the lectures is dated 1780 but the many copies made by pupils show that he updated his course several times, and more often toward the end of his life to keep abreast of developments in the draft, revised draft, and eventually the promulgated version of the Criminal Code for the Kingdom of Holland of 1809.[75] For the greater part, his course consisted of a vastly expanded commentary on the *Principia* of van Eck, a synoptic Digest commentary from which van der Keessel lifted the part on books 47 and 48 of the Digest, the *libri terribiles* dealing with crime and punishment. Van Eck's *Principia* were widely used in teaching, running

---

[69] At 135.
[70] Published and translated in Beinart, 'Addresses', 1–37.
[71] Beinart, 'Addresses', 8.
[72] Beinart, 'Addresses', 14–15.
[73] Beinart, 'Addresses', 36–37.
[74] Beinart and van Warmelo, preface to *Praelectiones*, xix. They refer to the series of 1772 (nt. 5) but the series of September 1771 already has van der Keessel teaching on book 48 of the Digest, see Molhuysen, *Bronnen*, 6:15*–16*.
[75] Paul van Warmelo, 'Van der Keessel en Beccaria', *Legal History Review* 35 (1967): 574; Beinart and van Warmelo, preface to *Praelectiones*, xxi–xxii.

through seven editions between 1689 and 1784.[76] It is a curious book, containing a summary of the Digest with a wealth of further references to parallel texts, writers, Scripture, and even canon law, strung together as if each carries the same authority. Van der Keessel's method is to follow the very brief text of van Eck with extensive discussion of Roman history and institutions, bringing the references up to date with some recent literature.[77] With the noticeable exceptions of torture and the death penalty, he is more interested in the historical background and systematic construction of Roman law than in the philosophy, politics, or even practice of 'modern' criminal law.[78]

Van Eck's text provides plenty of opportunity for reflecting on the relation between criminal law and divine law. Yet none of that appears in van der Keessel's lecture notes. More often than not, he completely glosses over van Eck's references to discuss Roman law instead. To give examples: punishment for acts or intentions, theft from necessity, slaying a thief in self-defence at night, *talio* and money punishments, abortion, intimate relations with housemaids, irrelevance of the moment of death for murder, witchcraft, visits to astrologers, violence against parents, kidnapping, public acquittal, and the treatment of the bodies of executed criminals are all subjects for which van Eck refers to Scripture but which van der Keessel treats solely on the basis of Roman law.[79] As is understandable in a Roman–Dutch Protestant author, canon law is hardly mentioned either. Its stance on the penalty for defloration belongs to received law, though later interpretation has shifted it from its true intent.[80] Likewise, its rule on elopement with a betrothed differs from Roman law because of a different appreciation of the betrothal in both systems.[81] Simony is treated in the context of Pertschius's 1719 dissertation on the matter: Protestants should not draw too many conclusions from canon law since it assumes the crime to be related to apostolic succession, but from a Protestant viewpoint, though still grave, simony merely means to solicit ecclesiastical office through payment.[82] The canon law stance on usury, kissing another

---

[76] Cornelis van Eck, *Principia Juris Civilis secundum Ordinem Digestorum in Usum Domesticarum Scholarum seu Collegiorum, Quae Vocant, Vulgate et in Duas Partes Divisa* (Franeker: Gijselaar, 1689). See Margreet J. A. M. Ahsmann, *Bibliografie van Hoogleraren in de Rechten aan de Utrechtse Universiteit tot 1811* (Amsterdam: North Holland, 1993), 73–74.

[77] Beinart and van Warmelo, preface to *Praelectiones*, xxv.

[78] Krikke and Faber, 'Van der Keessel', 188.

[79] Van der Keessel, *Praelectiones in Libros 47 et 48*, 1:4, 1:74, 1:116, 1:294, 1:340; 2:790; 3:1084, 3:1090, 3:1138, 3:1150, 3:1286; 4:1642, 4:1690; 6:2426–2428.

[80] Van der Keessel, *Praelectiones in Libros 47 et 48*, 2:822–828.

[81] Van der Keessel, *Praelectiones in Libros 47 et 48*, 2:890.

[82] Van der Keessel, *Praelectiones in Libros 47 et 48*, 4:1620.

man's wife, inferred adultery, and bestiality are referred to in passing.[83] That seems to be the full of it.

As a matter of fact, in 1,370 quarto pages of lecture notes, van der Keessel employs a verbatim Bible quotation only twice.[84] The first concerns Genesis 9:6, to which van der Keessel refers with supporting Scripture and modern writers for his statement that all murderers (not homicides) should be punished with death, and that not even a sovereign may grant a reprieve, as he is also bound by divine law except for pressing reasons of state. Modern writers like Thomasius are mistaken when they want to read this passage as prophecy instead of law. It is law, and although the Mosaic law has no authority in a Dutch court, it may be used to supplement the gaps in Dutch and Roman law.[85] The second Bible quotation falls in a prolonged discussion of the arguments for and against the use of torture in the criminal law of evidence.[86] It may be remembered that some of van der Keessel's interest in criminal law already appeared in his inaugural lecture in Groningen of 1762, when he stated that torture should have been abandoned when slavery fell into disuse. In his later lectures he qualifies that statement to the extent of turning it around completely. Now that torture belongs to received Roman law, it should certainly be maintained.[87] One of the many arguments against torture has been that it has no basis in Scripture, but others have argued that this silence implies tacit approval of the institution, and Leyser even draws an argument from Matthew 18:34–35 (quoted) arguing that the Greek refers to torturers instead of jailers. But van der Keessel will not weigh one quotation from Scripture against another.[88] One may wonder whether a Christian judge may give an accused over to torture, but that path leads nowhere since judges are slaves to the law (quoting Cicero) and cannot rule on its equity, but should excuse themselves from office if they feel moral compunction – *lex dura sed lex*.[89] It appears that van der Keessel turns to Scripture purely for those issues,

---

[83] Van der Keessel, *Praelectiones in Libros 47 et 48*, 1:500; 2:758 fnt. 11 (Ms. DE), 2:806, 2:862.

[84] Gen. 9:6: 'Whoever sheds human blood, by humans shall their blood be shed; for in the image of God has God made mankind', quoted in *Praelectiones in Libros 47 et 48*, 3:994. Matth. 18:34–35: 'In anger his master handed him over to the jailers to be tortured, until he should pay back all he owed. This is how my heavenly Father will treat each of you unless you forgive your brother or sister from your heart', quoted in *Praelectiones in Libros 47 et 48*, 5:1750.

[85] Van der Keessel, *Praelectiones in Libros 47 et 48*, 3:994–996 and fnt. 70a (Ms. DE, addition before 1792).

[86] Van der Keessel, *Praelectiones in Libros 47 et 48*, 5:1742–1778.

[87] Van der Keessel, *Praelectiones in Libros 47 et 48*, 5:1774–1778. See Van Warmelo, 'Van der Keessel en Beccaria', 574–580.

[88] Van der Keessel, *Praelectiones in Libros 47 et 48*, 5:1746 and 1750.

[89] Van der Keessel, *Praelectiones in Libros 47 et 48*, 5:1752.

the death penalty and the use of torture, that had been singled out for reform by Enlightenment thought, but largely left divine law out elsewhere.

The conclusion is warranted that in the thought of van der Keessel, divine law held little to no relevance to the practice of criminal law, but could be used to buttress a traditional position against the attacks of Enlightenment philosophers. Again, van der Keessel proves himself to be a lawyer and not a philosopher or a theologian. It is precisely from this standpoint that he attacks Beccaria: not only on these two issues of torture and the death penalty,[90] but more in general – '[Beccaria] not being an adequate legal expert, but one who seeks distinction in philosophy, has been able in the atmosphere of the present century to choose no more suitable road for earning glory than audaciously to criticize and to deprecate the criminal laws which have been received to date among most nations of Europe', van der Keessel notes in the 1783 preface to his lectures.[91] *Philosophia simulata* is placed against *studio legum*, those who cogitate reform against those who wisely interpret received law – that is to say the law of Rome. One must say that van der Keessel has been remarkably consistent in developing the programme he had sketched in his Leiden inaugural lecture of 1770.

GENERAL APPRAISAL AND INFLUENCE

With good reason, van der Keessel is often referred to as the last great exponent of Roman–Dutch law. His only rival for the title is the Amsterdam advocate Joannes van der Linden, who was a pupil of van der Keessel.[92] He did not publish much during his lifetime but has had an enduring influence through his students, who preserved lecture notes amounting to thousands of pages, edited and published half a century ago through the indefatigable work of the South African professors Beinart and van Warmelo. These lecture notes provide a final statement of Roman–Dutch private and criminal law on the eve of national codification. In his professorial career of over fifty years, van der Keessel lived through political upheavals that gave rise to six different regimes in twenty years. He often took

[90] See Van Warmelo, 'Van der Keessel en Beccaria', 573–583.
[91] Van der Keessel, *Praelectiones in Libros 47 et 48*, 1:lii (trans. Beinart and Van Warmelo at liii).
[92] Maarten W. van Boven, 'Linden, Joannes van der', in *Biografisch Woordenboek van Nederland 1780–1830*, Huygens Instituut, http://resources.huygens.knaw.nl/bwn1780-1830/lemmata/data/Linden [04–07-2018]; Janwillem Oosterhuis, 'Joannes van der Linden, Regtsgeleerd, Practicaal en Koopmans Handboek, 1806', in *Juristen die Schreven en Bleven. Nederlandstalige Rechtsgeleerde Klassiekers*, eds. Georges G. G. M. M. Martyn, Louis A. M. J. A. Berkvens, and Paul Brood (Hilversum: Verloren, 2020), 84–88. Van der Keessel thanks van der Linden in the preface of the *Theses Selectae* for preparing the registers.

a principled position in favour of a practical application of 'technical' Roman law and against philosophical Enlightenment thought that wished to sweep it away and replace it with natural law.

On Tuesdays, van der Keessel taught a private lecture series from his home on the Rapenburg for most of his working life. Among the prized pupils he invited to this disputation course were many of the future leaders of the Dutch Réveil movement of the early nineteenth century. He taught the polymath Willem Bilderdijk,[93] his later colleague as professor Hendrik Willem Tydeman,[94] the advocate and politician Maurits Cornelis van Hall,[95] and a generation later the poet Isaäc da Costa (who composed an epitaph for van der Keessel).[96] What connects these lawyers, writers, and poets is a common theme of orthodox Protestant, counter-revolutionary, conservative romanticism. A specific ideological influence cannot be established, but the question warrants further investigation as to how much the Dutch Réveil movement, or Bilderdijk as its central figure at least, was influenced by van der Keessel (and Pestel for that matter).[97] Bilderdijk's lecture notes from 1781, which he kept his whole life, show that the seminars concerned technical cases of private law that had to be analyzed and argued.[98] Even so, Tydeman considered van der Keessel's approach to Roman law to form a 'school' that was in conflict with the ideas about natural law promoted by the Amsterdam professor Hendrik Cras and by Seerp Gratama, van der Marck's successor to the chair in Groningen.[99] And when Bilderdijk asked Tydeman whether any real 'civilists' still existed apart from van der Keessel, Tydeman referred him to

---

[93] Heleen C. Gall, 'Bilderdijk en Van der Keessel', *Het Bilderdijk-Museum* 1 (1984): 2–6; Heleen C. Gall, *Willem Bilderdijk en het Privatissimum van Professor D. G. van der Keessel* (Leiden: Jongbloed, 1986).

[94] Johan W. Tydeman, 'Levensberigt van Mr. Hendrik Willem Tydeman', *Handelingen Maatschappij der Nederlandsche Letterkunde* 2 (1863): 407 ('his best and most advanced disciples attended the disputation course'). Van der Keessel figures prominently in the correspondence between H. W. Tydeman and Bilderdijk.

[95] Gall, 'Bilderdijk en Van der Keessel', 3.

[96] Isaäc da Costa, *Da Costa's Kompleete Dichtwerken* (Haarlem: Kruseman, 1861), 1: 343.

[97] Already desired by Allard Pierson, 'Dr. Kollewijns Bilderdijk', in *Uit de Verspreide Geschriften van A. Pierson Verschenen in 1889–1895* (The Hague: Nijhoff, 1902), 1, 2: 122–123. Samuel Iperusz. Wiselius probably was a pupil of van der Keessel too, considering his dissertation *Tractatus Academicus Inauguralis de Successionibus Hollandorum* (Leiden: Mostert, 1790).

[98] Gall, 'Bilderdijk en Van der Keessel', 3–4.

[99] Hendrik W. T. Tydeman, *Briefwisseling van Mr. W. Bilderdijk met de Hoogleraren en Mrs. M. en H. W. Tydeman Gedurende de Jaren 1807 tot 1831* (Sneek: Van Druten, 1866), 1: 233 (21 May 1810); De Wal, biographical notice to *Select Theses*, xvi–xvii. Gratama would later become one of Tydeman's and Bilderdijk's fiercest opponents: Lokin, *Groninger Faculteit*, 236–242. Also compare Isaäc da Costa, *Bezwaren tegen den Geest der Eeuw* (Leiden: Herdingh, 1823), 42–43.

Thibaut and Savigny (with whom he was in correspondence) and a select few others in the Netherlands, two of whom also were pupils of van der Keessel.[100]

Van der Keessel's professional life was marked from the first to the last by the debate about the relative merits and position of Roman law and natural law. His way out of this morass was to attempt to develop the *ius hodiernum* of Holland systematically on the largely Romanist basis of Grotius's *Introduction to Dutch Jurisprudence*.[101] Regime change brought a new order and would bring codified laws, as he foresaw in the 1800 preface to the *Theses selectae*. His students were not to worry, he told them, because Grotius and the law of Holland would remain a major influence on any codification project, and (unlike his well-prepared students) those involved would have a bitter time wedding Roman law and Dutch law to modern practice.[102] Codified laws did come, but in a different form than imagined and with a heavier influence of French law. Van der Keessel's project could still be salvaged though, considering that the Napoleonic codes were to be adapted to local Dutch customs and legal traditions following the intercession of Louis Napoleon. For the drafts of the Commercial Code and Civil Code this task fell to his pupil Joannes van der Linden. In the case of the Criminal Code, the drafting committee was led by J. E. Reuvens, another pupil, while C. F. van Maanen, yet another pupil, was largely responsible for its final draft and implementation.[103] Even if van der Keessel's direct influence is not traceable and he may have disliked the entire idea and project of codification,[104] there was good reason to think the *ius hodiernum* would enter the codes and could play a part in providing a systematic framework for interpretation. But the Kingdom of Holland was short-lived and its adapted Napoleonic codes were

---

[100] Tydeman, *Briefwisseling*, 2:52 (29 April 1815) and 2:64–65 (26 May 1815). One is Albertus Jacobus Duymaer van Twist, professor of Roman law and the new 'ius gallicum' at Groningen. Lokin, *Groninger Faculteit*, 246–247. The other is Angelus Jacobus Cuperus, van der Keessel's nephew and heir to half his estate, who was close to receiving a chair in natural law at Leiden in 1796. See Eduard van Biema, 'Cuperus (Angelus Jacobus)', in *Nieuw Nederlandsch Biografisch Woordenboek*, eds. Petrus J. Blok and Philipp C. Molhuysen (Leiden: Sijthoff, 1914), 1: 660–661; Krikke and Faber, 'Van der Keessel', 186–187; Otterspeer, *Groepsportret*, 3: 88. Maurits C. van Hall, *Ter Nagedachtenis van Mr. Angelus Jacobus Cuperus* (Amsterdam: Gartman, 1831), 8–12 notes that Thibaut had Cuperus's 1789 dissertation on the nature of possession translated and printed in 1804, and that Savigny praised it highly. See Friedrich C. von Savigny, *Das Recht des Besitzes* (Giessen: Heyer, 1803), xxviii–xxx. According to Tydeman's letter, however, some part of the dissertation had been ghost-written by van der Keessel.

[101] Beinart, 'Addresses', 32–33.

[102] Beinart, 'Addresses', 24–27.

[103] Beinart and van Warmelo, preface to *Praelectiones*, xxiii–xxiv.

[104] Beinart and van Warmelo, preface to *Praelectiones*, xxiii.

replaced by unmistakably foreign, French codifications. It would seem that once Napoleon came to Leiden in 1811, van der Keessel and the Roman–Dutch *ius hodiernum* indeed had little more to say.

One option was to doggedly pretend that nothing had happened. Following the abolition of torture in 1798, an unconvinced van der Keessel reduced his discussion of it from thirty pages of lecture notes to five, but still kept arguing its efficacy.[105] In a letter of 1809, Tydeman asks Bilderdijk whether he thinks the new Codes should influence the teaching of Roman law, or should the lectures continue, 'just as good old van der Keessel keeps teaching criminal law on the basis of van Eck's Terrible Books, in spite of all the new philosophy?'[106] Again, in 1814, having given up the full two-year course on Grotius and the *ius hodiernum*, van der Keessel taught the law of bills of exchange instead, but still on the basis of Grotius instead of the Code de Commerce.[107] This behaviour may be considered an ostrich strategy by an elderly professor who loathed change, but the ostrich is also the emblematic bird of lady Justice, believed to be able to digest even the hardest materials over time. The victory of codified law over van der Keessel's *ius hodiernum*, understood as a layered order of statute and custom infused with principles derived from Roman law, was neither as immediate nor as total as it would perhaps seem.

First, a large part of codified law followed Roman law, as was apparent from every published draft.[108] Next, article 63 of the Organic Decree of 1815 placed courses on the Institutes, the Digests, natural law, public law, contemporary private law, and contemporary criminal law on the curriculum, leading to a doctorate in Roman law and contemporary law under article 85, with a little more weight placed on the Digests in final examinations. Third, since most practising lawyers and judges had been trained in Roman law and the *ius hodiernum*, and the French codes were initially considered to be a fleeting state of affairs, Roman–Dutch law carried great weight in the courts and would continue to do so until a generation or two had passed.[109] It was not until 1838 that a Dutch Civil Code and Commercial Code gained force of law, and not until 1886 that a Dutch

---

[105] Van Warmelo, 'Van der Keessel en Beccaria', 575; van der Keessel, *Praelectiones in Libros 47 et 48*, 5:1780–1783.

[106] Tydeman, *Briefwisseling*, 1:137 (14 June 1809).

[107] Beinart, 'Addresses', 30–33.

[108] Already noted by van der Keessel in a post-1804 addition to his preface of 1783, *Praelectiones in Libros 47 et 48*, 1:lvi–lvii.

[109] Eduard M. Meijers, 'Rede van prof. mr. E. M. Meijers', in *Herdenking Honderdjarige Burgerlijke Wetgeving 1838–1938* (Zwolle: Tjeenk Willink, 1939), 18; Hendrik Kooiker, *Lex Scripta Abrogata. De Derde Renaissance van het Romeinse recht. Een Onderzoek naar de*

Criminal Code came into being to replace the patched-up Napoleonic code. It turns out that although he lost some battles, van der Keessel eventually and unwittingly won his war to found the private law and criminal law of the early nineteenth century on Roman–Dutch law instead of natural law. He did so by arguing not from theology or philosophy, but from received law. His reasons are his own, but his traditionalist, orthodox Dutch Reformed church outlook reveals itself everywhere. Much like the Dutch Réveil of the 1820s, centred around so many of his pupils, for a short while this orthodox Christian, Romanist and romantic, conservative, and even reactionary professor had history on his side.

RECOMMENDED READINGS

Ahsmann, Margreet J. A. M. 'Teaching the *Ius Hodiernum*: Legal education of advocates in the Northern Netherlands (1575–1800)'. *Legal History Review* 65 (1997): 423–457.

Ahsmann, Margreet J. A. M. and Robert Feenstra. *Bibliografie van Hoogleraren in de Rechten aan de Leidse Universiteit tot 1811*. Amsterdam: NHUM, 1984.

Beinart, Ben. 'Van der Keessel's addresses to his students'. *Acta Juridica* 1 (1972): 1–37.

Beinart, Ben and Paul van Warmelo. 'Van der Keessel en de Studie van de Erfprins Willem Frederik, de Latere Koning Willem I, te Leiden 1789–1790'. *Verslagen en Mededelingen van de Vereeniging tot Uitgaaf der Bronnen van het Oud-Vaderlandsche Recht* 14 (1974): 21–69.

Blécourt, Anne S. de. *Pro Excolendo en de Rechtsgeschiedenis*. Groningen: Wolters, 1937.

Gall, Heleen C. *Willem Bilderdijk en het Privatissimum van Professor D. G. van der Keessel*. Leiden: Jongbloed, 1986.

Keessel, Dionysius G. van der. *Oratio de Advocato Christiano*. Leiden: Luchtmans, 1792.

Keessel, Dionysius G. van der. *Theses Selectae Iuris Hollandici et Zelandici, ad Supplendam Hugonis Grotii Introductionem ad Iurisprudentiam Hollandicam*. Leiden: Luchtmans, 1800.

Keessel, Dionysius G. van der. *Praelectiones Iuris Hodierni ad Hugonis Grotii Introductionem ad Iurisprudentiam Hollandicam*. 6 vols. Edited and translated by Paul van Warmelo, Lucas I. Coertze, and Henri L. Gonin. Cape Town: Balkema, 1961–1975.

Keessel, Dionysius G. van der. *Praelectiones in Libros 47 et 48 Digestorum, Exhibentes Jurisprudentiam Criminalem ad Usum Fori Batavi Applicatam (Duce Cornelio van Eck) et in Novum Codicem Criminalem, 1809*. 6 vols. Edited and translated by Ben Beinart and Paul van Warmelo. Cape Town: Juta, 1969–1981.

Doorwerking van het Oude Recht na de Invoering van de Civielrechtelijke Codificaties in het Begin van de Negentiende Eeuw (Nijmegen: Ars Aequi Libri, 1996).

Lokin, Jan H. A. *De Groninger Faculteit der Rechtsgeleerdheid (1596–1970)*. The Hague: Boom, 2019.

Molhuysen, Philipp C., ed. *Bronnen tot de Geschiedenis der Leidsche Universiteit*. 7 vols. The Hague: Nijhoff, 1913–1924.

Poelgeest, Lambertus van. 'Mr. Bavius Voorda (1729–1799). Een Rechtlijnig Fries Jurist aan de Leidse Academie'. *Leids Jaarboekje* 79 (1987): 96–123.

Tydeman, Hendrik W. T. *Briefwisseling van Mr. W. Bilderdijk met de Hoogleraren en Mrs. M. en H. W. Tydeman Gedurende de Jaren 1807 tot 1831*. 2 vols. Sneek: Van Druten, 1866–1867.

Warmelo, Paul van. 'Van der Keessel en Beccaria'. *Legal History Review* 35 (1967): 573–583.

11

Pieter Paulus

Matthijs de Blois [1]

BIOGRAPHICAL INTRODUCTION [2]

The Republic of the Seven Provinces

Pieter Paulus was born 9 April 1753 at Axel, in the part of Zelandic Flanders which was governed by the States of the Province of Zeeland. It belonged to the Republic of the Seven Provinces, a confederation of Provinces, each of them governed by an Assembly of States, considered to be sovereign. The Provinces shared common institutions, representing the Republic as such. The most prominent was the assembly of the States-General, composed of representatives from all Provinces. A central political figure was the pensionary of the Province of Holland. Next to these, let us say, aristocratic institutions, the Republic also embodied a monarchical element in the person of the stadtholder. The incumbent was from the very beginning of the Republic a Prince of the house of Orange-Nassau. In 1747, the stadtholdership had become hereditary. The Republic had no official state church, although the Reformed Church enjoyed many privileges. Depending on local policies, Protestant dissenters (Mennonites, Lutherans, Remonstrants), Roman Catholics, and Jews, had in many but not all cases, freedom of worship.

---

[1] Dr Matthijs de Blois was until 1 August 2017 assistant professor at the Faculty of Law, Economics and Governance of Utrecht University. He is senior fellow of The Hague Initiative for International Co-operation (thinc).

[2] See E. J. Vles, *Pieter Paulus (1753–1796). Patriot en Staatsman* (Amsterdam: De Bataafsche Leeuw, 2004); Arianne Baggerman and Rudolf Dekker, 'Pieter Paulus (1753–1796) in kleine kring. 'Ach stel u die brave man tog ten voorbeelde', *Nieuw Letterkundig Magazijn* 20 (2002): 34–42.

Early Life, Studies, and First Publications

Pieter Paulus was scion of a family of local magistrates, possibly of Huguenot origin. He was baptized two days after his birth in the local Reformed Church. After preparatory schooling at 's-Hertogenbosch and Vlissingen, he entered Utrecht University in 1770. Still a student, at the age of nineteen, he published a remarkable work, displaying his broad knowledge of history and constitutional law, on the *Utility of the Stadtholder's Government*.[3] He expressed at that time his preference for a mixed system of government, including monarchical, aristocratic, and democratic elements. While supporting the Prince of Orange, he was critical of foreign advisors and the extension of the powers of the stadtholder. That was not just a general observation, but also an expression of concern about the political influence of Ludwig Ernst, Duke of Brunswick-Wolfenbüttel (1717–1788), who acted as ward of Prince Willem V of Orange (1748–1806) – the stadtholder – during the latter's minority. Also after the Prince became of age the Duke remained his advisor. In the *Utility* Paulus also defended freedom of religion. He declared himself to be a committed adherent of the reformed religion, but believed that all kinds of sects should be granted the right of free public worship. Paulus continued his studies in Leyden University, where he defended in 1775 his doctoral thesis on the question whether Zealand had ever been a Flemish fiefdom.[4] In the same year he published the first volume of a *Commentary on the Union of Utrecht*, the treaty of 1579 that functioned as a constitution of the Republic of the Seven Provinces.[5] The second volume appeared in 1776 and the last came out in 1777.

Professional Life and the Strife of Orangists and Patriots

In 1776, Pieter Paulus was admitted to the bar and became an advocate at the Court of Holland at The Hague. He was married in 1781 to Françoise Henriëtte Vockestaert (1755–1807). A year later a boy, their only child, was born, but died soon after. More and more the political sympathies of Paulus became clear. He admired the works of Enlightenment authors, such as Richard Price's (1755–1807) book *Observations on the Nature of Civil Liberty* (1776). Paulus shared Price's idea that governments are servants of the people. Paulus had contacts with John Adams (1735–1826), the ambassador of the newly created United States of America. He became more and more involved in the circles of

---

[3] Pieter Paulus, *Het Nut der Stadhouderlijke Regering* (Alkmaar, etc.: Waagh, etc., 1772/3).
[4] Pieter Paulus, *Dissertatio Inauguralis de origine, progressu & solutione nexus feudalis Flandriam inter & Zeelandiam*, Lugdunum Batavorum: apud P. Van Der Eyk et D. Vygh, 1775).
[5] Pieter Paulus, *Verklaring der Unie van Utrecht, Eerste Deel* (Utrecht: Van Schoonhoven, 1775).

the Patriots in the Republic. They shared the (political) ideals of the Enlightenment, such as the sovereignty of the people, human rights, and the separation of church and state. They had great sympathies for first the American and later the French Revolution. Their opponents, the Orangists, supported the Prince of Orange, and were in favour of the traditional political structures in the Republic. The struggle between the Patriots and the Orangists dominated the political life of the Republic during the greater part of Paulus's lifetime. He became well known in the Republic as a man with Patriotic sympathies. That may have contributed, next to his interest in naval affairs, to the decision of the States-General to appoint him in 1785 as Advocate-Fiscal of the Meuse, an important position at the Admiralty of Rotterdam. His task was to instruct those employed by the Admiralty, to supervise the finances, and to act as public prosecutor on behalf of the Admiralty in case of complaints against navy officers. Tensions within the Republic culminated in 1785 when the Prince and his family felt forced to leave The Hague and the Republic was on the verge of civil war. However, the King of Prussia, the Prince's brother-in-law, intervened with his army and the stadtholder was restored in 1787 to his position for the time being. Many Patriots were dismissed from their positions in government. Paulus also was pressed to resign. He was provisionally dismissed, pending the investigation into his support for the actions of the Patriots against the stadtholder. In vain Paulus asked for fair proceedings. He felt himself to be a victim of injustice and in his farewell letter he invoked the infallible testimony of God Omniscient. Until 1795, he lived the life of a private citizen, leaving him more time for his family. He also visited the Austrian Netherlands and France, to meet Dutch Patriots who lived there in exile and to speak to French politicians. He also had time to write.

The Treatise on Equality, the Establishment of the Batavian Republic, and an Early Death

In 1793 Paulus published his most famous work, a *Treatise on the question in what sense human beings are considered to be equal, and the rights and duties that result therefrom*.[6] It is the main source of his ideas on the relationship between Christianity and the law and it will therefore be explored more thoroughly below. This work illustrates the intellectual development of Paulus against the background of the political and ideological earthquake

---

[6] Pieter Paulus, *Verhandeling over de vrage: In welken zin kunnen de menschen gezegd worden gelyk te zyn?: en welke zyn de regten en pligten, die daaruit voordvloeien?* (Haarlem: C. Plaat, 1793).

that was brought about by the French Revolution in 1789 and subsequent events, among which were many things deplored by Paulus. He shows himself in this book fully committed to democratic values and a political system in which there was no longer room for a stadtholder. The Patriots, still without political power, had found in Paulus their most important ideologist and spokesman. The French Revolution and its aftermath also kindled again in the Dutch Republic the fire of revolution among the Patriots, both inside the country and abroad. Next to that the new French rulers had declared war on tyrants, including the stadtholder. A first attack in 1793 resulted in a defeat. When, during the bad winter of 1794/1795, French troops were successful in crossing the frozen rivers, the days of the *ancien régime* in the Seven Provinces were numbered. The stadtholder and his family escaped to England in January 1795. The Republic became the Batavian Republic, recognized by France. Government positions on the local, provincial, and national level were now taken by Patriots committed to the revolutionary ideals. Paulus played a central role in what he himself preferred to be a 'velvet' revolution, without the excesses that had accompanied the French example. He became member of the new municipal Council in Rotterdam and alderman. As First Citizen of the city, he welcomed the French troops. Representatives of the towns of Holland conferred at The Hague and called themselves the Provisional Representatives of the People of Holland. Paulus was elected as their president. On 31 January 1795, both the abolishment of the stadtholdership and sovereignty of the people were proclaimed. Next to that a Declaration on the Rights of the Man and the Citizen was promulgated, a text strongly influenced by the French Declaration of 1789, but also with some influence by Paulus. The Batavian Revolution entailed important changes to the institutional framework of the old Republic. A National Convention replaced the States-General. It was composed of representatives chosen by the people of all the Provinces. Paulus represented his city of residence, Rotterdam. He became the Convention's first President. On 1 March 1796, he opened its first session. It was a very cold day. He walked at the head of a cortege bareheaded and without a coat from the assembly hall to his lodgings. After a few days, he fell ill. Pieter Paulus did not recover and died on 17 March 1796 from pneumonia.

MAJOR THEMES AND CONTRIBUTIONS

In his valedictory address on 27 September 2012, professor of Parliament at Maastricht University, Joop van den Berg, sometime prominent senator of the Social Democratic Party, made a remarkable proposal. He suggested calling the ancient assembly hall at the Houses of Parliament at The Hague after

Pieter Paulus.⁷ For sure, many people in the Netherlands had not the slightest idea who this person was. In van den Berg's address he made clear that the lawyer Pieter Paulus (1753–1796) should be honoured as the, or at least one of the, founding fathers of real democracy and human rights in The Netherlands. The professor underlined that Pieter Paulus based his defence of equality before the law and of human rights in general primarily on the New Testament and the teaching of Jesus. That should trigger our interest in the quest for Christian jurists in the history of the Low Countries. The choice of Pieter Paulus is not self-evident. In the political struggles in the Dutch Republic at the end of the eighteenth century, we observe a sharp divide between adherents of the Enlightenment (Patriots) and those defending the status quo of the *ancien régime* (Orangists). The former, including Pieter Paulus, were defending democracy and human rights, and were opponents of the stadtholder, the Prince of Orange. Not completely without reason the Patriots were suspected of being very critical of religion in general and Christianity in particular, having regard to the writings of French authors in particular. On the other hand, the defenders of the ancient bonds with the House of Orange and the traditions of the Republic were also defenders of the prominent role of the Christian Reformed religion in the public life of the Republic. While the first group welcomed the American and French Revolutions as the dawn of a new era of equality, freedom, and democracy, the second group saw, especially in the French Revolution, an outburst of the abyss, a revolt against God, the church, and all sources of authority. A Christian jurist belonging to this group, Willem Bilderdijk (1756–1831), inspired the founders of the first Christian political party in the nineteenth century, which was called the 'Antirevolutionary party', a name which expresses their view of the French Revolution. Would it be possible to be both an advocate for revolutionary ideals on democracy and human rights and a committed Christian at the same time? We will see.

Pieter Paulus as a Christian Jurist

To qualify as a Christian jurist requires a person not only to be both a Christian and a jurist, but also necessitates evidence of a sensible relationship between these two aspects of his personality. There are indications of this in the life of Pieter Paulus. We may think of his activities as advocate-deacon in the Reformed Church at The Hague. In that capacity, he applauded the

---

⁷ J. T. J. van den Berg, *De dominee en 'de tweede apostel Paulus'* (Maastricht: Maastricht University, 2012), https://doi.org/10.26481/spe.20120927jb.

establishment of a flax mill by the church, to provide work for the poor.[8] Maybe we can next think of the way he used his powers as advocate-fiscal of the Admiralty.[9] In addition, his efforts to ensure moderation and cautiousness during the political transition that accompanied the Batavian Revolution were most likely related to his Christian convictions. In this connection it is interesting to take note of what an observer, Charles Bentinck, whose brother was imprisoned as a supporter of the Prince of Orange, wrote in 1795 on the 'leader' of the Batavian Revolution, also referring to the work we will discuss below:

> Pieter Paulus ... seems to be the leading man and has with great art and ability, endeavoured to reconcile the people to this systema by the way he modified it. By the strain of religious enthusiasm that runs throughout the work, calculated to make a strong impression on a religious people... He endeavours further to recommend this system by the apparent moderation and humanity of every syllable that comes from his mouth or his pen.[10]

First and foremost, however, we encounter Paulus as a Christian jurist in his writings.

An early example is his *Commentary on the Union of Utrecht*. Commenting upon Article XIII, on religion, Paulus is critical of the powers of the Provinces to regulate in the field of religion (apart from the individual conscience, which should be left untouched). He defends the freedom to change one's religion. The search for the truth, which is of vital importance for one's eternal salvation or perdition, should not be impeded. According to the law of nature, a person should be free to investigate the Scriptures and to serve God in the way he thinks most befitting the divine will. Imposing some form of outward conformity with forms of worship prescribed by the government is of no avail. According to Pieter Paulus Jesus Christ has taught us differently. We should not rely on outward conformity, but believe in Him.[11] This already clearly illustrates the Christian conviction of the author, but in his *Treatise on the question in what sense human beings are considered to be equal, and the rights and duties that result therefrom*,[12] published in 1793, the argumentation based on Christian beliefs is more prominent. In this work, he develops the basics of

---

[8] Vles, *Pieter Paulus*, 45–46.
[9] Vles, *Pieter Paulus*, 80–81.
[10] As quoted in the original language and spelling in Vles, *Pieter Paulus*, 104.
[11] Pieter Paulus, *Verklaring der Unie van Utrecht, Tweede Deel* (Utrecht: Van Schoonhoven, 1776), 245–247.
[12] Pieter Paulus, *Verhandeling over de vrage: In welken zin kunnen de menschen gezegd worden gelyk te zyn?: en welke zyn de regten en pligten, die daaruit voordvloeien?* (Haarlem: C. Plaat, 1793) also referred to in our text as *Treatise on Equality*.

a legal 'new order' for society. He takes the opportunity to explain his Enlightened views on the main issues of law and politics of his time. Especially interesting is the first part of this book, where he discusses the biblical foundations of equality, as it exists in the state of nature. In the second part, he argues that the principle of equality should be the basis of the rights and duties human beings have in civil society. The last part of the book is devoted to the equality of nations on the international level. It is important to see how in this part he addresses the evils of slavery and slave trade from a clear Christian perspective.

The Foundation of Equality

Paulus's *Treatise on Equality* is full of references to the Bible, both to the Old and the New Testament. Already in the Introduction, where he explains his motives for writing the work, he notes the evil of the humiliation of man, notwithstanding the fact that he is created in the image and likeness of God.[13] When he starts his defence of the equality of men, he underlines that he means equality in a moral, not in a physical sense.[14] As the equality of the sexes belongs to this latter realm, he will not address it.

The Old Testament[15]

The equality of men is, first of all, founded on the idea in the Old Testament that the earth and everything in it has been bestowed by the Universal Father and Omnipotent Creator on all men, without distinction.[16] Paulus points at the first commandment in Genesis 1:28 'Be fruitful, and multiply, and replenish the earth, and subdue it.'[17] This commandment is directed to human beings in general. It makes clear that in the state of nature, no one has more rights over his fellow human being, or over the earth, seas, rivers, etc. and their natural yields, than anyone else. Without equality, the law of the jungle would have been part of creation, which would have necessitated a commandment to destroy each other. God created man in His image; He did not create him noble or ignoble.[18] The sketch Moses has given of

---

[13] Paulus, *Verhandeling over de vrage*, 3.
[14] Paulus, *Verhandeling over de vrage*, 8.
[15] We follow the common term used to refer to the Hebrew Bible, the *Tanakh*.
[16] Paulus, *Verhandeling over de vrage*, 12–13.
[17] Paulus, *Verhandeling over de vrage*, 13. The text from the Bible quoted here is from the King James Version, as are the other quotes from the Bible elsewhere in the text.
[18] Paulus, *Verhandeling over de vrage*, 14.

patriarchal life (in the Bible) is according to Paulus a monument of the original freedom and equality of men.[19] Human beings are independent from each other, and only dependent on God.[20]

The biblical account of creation provides Paulus with another important argument for the equality of men. It is their descent from one couple, Adam and Eve. This is accepted as a historical fact by Paulus, who stresses the truth of the Books of the Old Testament.[21] That was of course to the point, having regard to the rising biblical criticism among many protagonists of the Enlightenment. Paulus explains that the text of the Old Testament has been delivered to us by God's special provision. It tells us about the special people chosen to preserve the knowledge of the One and True God (the people of Israel). The Old Testament also prepared humanity for the better and more general dispensation at the coming of Jesus Christ.[22] Paulus challenges those who do not accept the authority of the Scriptures to prove that mankind did not descend from one couple. Paulus is in any case sure that all men belong to the same family.[23] Another argument for the equality of men, mentioned by Paulus, is that we all have One God, as our Father, Protector, and Judge. We all have the same relationship with Him. God has no preference for special human beings above others, so nobody can claim to have priority over other people.[24]

The New Testament

Having discussed the Old Testament Paulus moves on to the arguments for equality in the New Testament, which relate to the coming into the world and the earthly life of the person he calls the divine founder of the Christian religion.[25]

The Life of Jesus

Paulus first points at remarkable facts in the life of Jesus. He refers to his humble birth from ordinary people, living in very poor conditions, in a small town. Jesus was raised among his fellow citizens and worked as a carpenter like

---

[19] Paulus, *Verhandeling over de vrage*, 14.
[20] Paulus, *Verhandeling over de vrage*, 15.
[21] Paulus, *Verhandeling over de vrage*, 15.
[22] Paulus, *Verhandeling over de vrage*, 16.
[23] Paulus, *Verhandeling over de vrage*, 16.
[24] Paulus, *Verhandeling over de vrage*, 18–19.
[25] Paulus, *Verhandeling over de vrage*, 20.

his father.[26] Later, after having accepted his ministry, Jesus taught universal fraternal love, without distinction of human beings or peoples. He was not often in the company of great men, or those who were in high esteem. He preferred to be among the poor and the humble, having an interest in their lives. He selected humble and ordinary people to be his disciples and special friends. He promised them the gifts of the Holy Spirit, the outpouring of which really took place. Paulus points at the benefits of Jesus's life and death, which are bestowed on all people, without distinction whatsoever of status, rank, shape, colour, or nation. He also mentions the promise of eternal salvation for all people, without distinction, who walk in accordance with Jesus's commandments and by doing so fulfil the will of His Father in heaven; that means loving God and loving their neighbour as themselves, the commandments encompassing the Law of Moses and the Prophets.[27]

His Teaching

Paulus then moves on to the teaching of Jesus in the New Testament. It is Paulus's view that if we take it seriously, we will discover that the principle of equality of all human beings is its foundation and main purpose. Without equality and equal freedom, the religion of Jesus Christ cannot have its wholesome influence on all human beings.[28] To underpin his argumentation Paulus quotes extensively from the Gospels. First, he cites five of the eight Beatitudes, which proclaim blessings for the poor in spirit, the mourners, the meek, the merciful, and the peacemakers.[29] Paulus further quotes Matthew 11:25, where Jesus thanks his Father for having hid His message from the wise and the prudent (Paulus explains: the would-be wise and the proud) and for having revealed it unto babes (meaning according to Paulus those who are humble, eager to learn, and as unbiased as children).[30] Paulus interprets the encouragement of Jesus in Matthew 11:29 to take his yoke, because he is meek and lowly in heart, as an admonishment against selfishness, haughtiness, self-conceit, ambition, and imperiousness.[31] A long quote from Matthew 12:47–50, where Jesus declares those who do the will of His heavenly Father to be his mother, brothers, and sisters, is seen by Paulus as the strongest defence of

---

[26] Paulus, *Verhandeling over de vrage*, 21.
[27] Paulus, *Verhandeling over de vrage*, 21–22.
[28] Paulus, *Verhandeling over de vrage*, 22. The expression 'religion of Jesus Christ' is used by Paulus.
[29] Paulus, *Verhandeling over de vrage*, 23. Paulus refers to Matthew 5:3, 4, 5, 7, and 9.
[30] Paulus, *Verhandeling over de vrage*, 23–24.
[31] Paulus, *Verhandeling over de vrage*, 24.

universal fraternal love and the equality of all men.[32] He develops his biblical arguments for the idea of equality further by citing the story in the Gospel of Matthew where Jesus called a child and presented it to his disciples to urge them to become humble as children, if they wanted to enter the kingdom of heaven.[33] Another event related in this Gospel is then quoted, where Jesus instructed his disciples not to exercise dominion over each other, as princes of the gentiles do, but to be a servant if they wanted to be a chief, 'as the son of man [that is, Jesus] came not to be ministered unto, but to minster, and to give his life a ransom for many'.[34] Paulus continues by including a long quote from Matthew where first the Pharisees are criticized for hypocrisy and subsequently the disciples are admonished not to call each other rabbi or father, for one is their Master, the Messiah, and only one is their Father (God), while they are just brothers and the greatest among them is their servant, 'whosoever shall exalt himself shall be abased; and he that shall humble himself shall be exalted'.[35] While most citations are from Matthew, there are also some from the other Gospels. From Mark is the story about the rebuke Jesus made to his disciples when they discussed who among them should be the greatest: 'If any man desire to be the first, the same shall be last of all, and servant of all.'[36] The teaching on humility in Luke 14, illustrated by the behaviour of a wedding guest who should not opt for the highest place, but take the lowest, and may be invited to go higher up, is also recorded, as well as the urge to invite not your friends, but the poor, the maimed, the lame, and the blind for dinner.[37] Paulus makes abundantly clear from the New Testament that a humble attitude is a prerequisite for equality. But equality is threatened not by haughtiness only. He points at another danger, as he quotes Mark 10:23–25, where Jesus warns that the entrance into the Kingdom of God may be very hard for the rich.[38] Paulus explains that for the rich it will be difficult to comply with the laws of the kingdom his heavenly Father wanted to establish on the earth.[39] He stresses on the one hand the vanity of earthly riches and greatness and on

---

[32] Paulus, *Verhandeling over de vrage*, 24–25.
[33] Paulus, *Verhandeling over de vrage*, 25. The quotation is from Matthew 18:2–4 (in the original the reference is mistakenly to Matthew 17).
[34] Paulus, *Verhandeling over de vrage*, 26. The quotation is from Matthew 20:25–28, the final part of which is cited here.
[35] Paulus, *Verhandeling over de vrage*, 26–27. The quotation is from Matthew 23:5–12, the final part of which is cited here.
[36] Paulus, *Verhandeling over de vrage*, 27. The quotation is from Mark 9:33–35, the final part of which is cited here.
[37] Paulus, *Verhandeling over de vrage*, 27–28, where Luke 14:8–11 and 13–14 are quoted.
[38] Paulus, *Verhandeling over de vrage*, 28–29.
[39] Paulus, *Verhandeling over de vrage*, 29–30. Paulus quotes Mark 12:30–31.

the other hand the value of each and every human being also by citing in full two parables told by Jesus. The first, about the rich man and the beggar Lazarus, shows that the merciless rich man will suffer forever in hell, while the poor beggar was carried by the angels into Abraham's bosom.[40] The second, on the Pharisee and the publican, shows that the latter, a repentant sinner who humbles himself, is justified, rather than the Pharisee who exalted himself and feels he is better than the publican.[41]

Fulfilment of Prophecy

Universal fraternal love, this unity of nations and men, was presented by Jesus Christ on earth as the fulfilment of prophecies. Paulus points at what the visionary Simeon had in mind when he saw the infant Jesus in the Temple, where he spoke about the salvation brought by this child, in words recorded in Luke 2:29–32.[42] Paulus also cites the words spoken by Jesus when he inaugurated his ministry in the synagogue of Nazareth, by reading a passage from the book Isaiah about preaching the Gospel to the poor, healing the brokenhearted, delivering captives, restoring sight to the blind, and setting at liberty the bruised, in short to preach the year of the Lord's favour.[43] Paulus underlines the same point about the fulfilment of prophecies by the coming of Jesus, again by quoting from another text in Luke, based on Isaiah.[44] By making this point Paulus recognizes the unity of Old and New Testament, especially in respect of the message of the equality of all human beings.

Action Speaking Stronger Than Words

Paulus finally shows that the teaching of Jesus, which he had expounded to convince his readers of the cause of equality, was underscored by the practice of Jesus's relationship to his disciples. He describes the episode where Jesus washes the feet of his disciples on the eve of the Last Supper, as recorded in John 13:3–12.[45] Paulus underlines the words of Jesus that all men will recognize the disciples of Jesus if they have love one to another[46] and stresses that action

---

[40] Paulus, *Verhandeling over de vrage*, 31–32. The text is Luke 16:19–25.
[41] Paulus, *Verhandeling over de vrage*, 32. The text is Luke 18:9–14.
[42] Paulus, *Verhandeling over de vrage*, 30.
[43] Paulus, *Verhandeling over de vrage*, 30. The text is from Luke 4:18–20, which itself is a quote from Isaiah 61:1–2.
[44] Paulus, *Verhandeling over de vrage*, 30–31, quoting from Luke 3:5–6, which itself is a text from Isaiah 40:3–5.
[45] Paulus, *Verhandeling over de vrage*, 33. Paulus quotes John 13:13–17.
[46] Paulus, *Verhandeling over de vrage*, 33, quoting John 13:35.

speaks stronger than words.[47] Paulus concludes that if he wanted to discuss all the passages in the New Testament that provide the foundation of the doctrine of the equality and universal fraternal love, he would have been obliged to discuss almost all special sermons and teachings of Jesus Christ. But what has been related suffices, according to Paulus, to convince every non-partisan and unbiased person.

Refutation of Sceptics

We have already seen that Paulus was aware of possible criticism of this biblical argumentation in respect of his inferences from the Old Testament. He is also sure that his reasoning, based on the New Testament, will not convince the sceptics who do not believe, and who consider it a fable or the history of an impostor.[48] But here again he challenges them to indicate who rather than Jesus could meet their expectations of a person, coming from God, who will enlighten humanity and bring them to the true knowledge of God. The opponents he has in mind are apparently not atheists. Paulus is convinced that only Jesus could address the blindness and superstition of the pagans and also what he qualifies, rather insultingly, as the haughtiness, bumptiousness, and ignorance of the Jews.[49] He continues by stating that Jesus's message could convince only because it was accompanied by miracles, but he adds that its content also points at its divine origin. This point is supported by a long quote from the Sermon on the Mount, about inter alia the love of one's enemy, reflecting the care of the heavenly Father for both the just and the unjust.[50] Paulus continues to defend, again with a number of biblical references, the uniqueness of Jesus's teaching by stating that no one, whether a prophet, philosopher, statesman, or priest, has stressed more the necessity of forgiveness.[51] Again, nobody urged more the love of one's neighbour without distinction than Jesus, and nobody gave a more comprehensive description of the duties we owe to our neighbours. It is for Paulus impossible to conclude that Jesus is an impostor.[52] He adds that many philosophers, who deny the truth of Jesus's history or consider him an impostor, nevertheless present his

---

[47] Paulus, *Verhandeling over de vrage*, 34.
[48] Paulus, *Verhandeling over de vrage*, 35.
[49] Paulus, *Verhandeling over de vrage*, 35–36.
[50] Paulus, *Verhandeling over de vrage*, 37–38. The quote is from Matthew 5:43–48.
[51] Paulus, *Verhandeling over de vrage*, 38–39. The references are to Matthew 6:14–15, Matthew 18:15–17, II Thessalonians 3:14, and Matthew 18:21–22 and 25.
[52] Paulus, *Verhandeling over de vrage*, 40.

teaching as something new. It appears that ethical systems developed by later philosophers familiar with Jesus's teaching are based on his principles.[53]

Equal Rights in Practice

Based on the solid foundation of equality in the Bible, Paulus addresses in the second and third parts of his book its practical inferences for the national and the international legal order. It will take too long to go into detail here. However, a few interesting points deserve to be mentioned, because they throw light on the implications of his beliefs. In one of the few passages where he enters into the debate with contemporary authors, he takes issue with one of the core ideas of Jean-Jacques Rousseau (1712–1778). This author held that on entering a civil society a human being transfers all his natural rights to the society in order to receive in return civil rights.[54] Paulus strongly disagrees. In his view there are rights a human being cannot transfer to society, for example, the right to serve God, or in respect of religious truths the right to make one's own conscience the rule of one's behaviour.[55]

Other remarkable examples can be found in the third part of his treatise, on the application of his theory to international relations. He calls the peoples to submit to the will of their Creator, the universal Father, Who has given the earth to all human beings.[56] Paulus argues in favour of free trade, but against useless exploitation of the earth,[57] and also against usurpation of other nations, which is against the laws of nature – God's law.[58] A major concern in this last part of his book is the evil of slavery and the slave trade. It is a flagrant violation of the principle of equality. It is contrary to the commandment to love one's neighbour as oneself and against the rule that we should do to all men whatever we want them to do to us (the Golden Rule).[59] Paulus observes that it is not a surprise that peoples from Africa and America have an aversion to the religion of Jesus Christ, having regard to the fact that Christians had been involved in the practice of slave trade for more than three centuries.[60] He admonishes his readers that they are responsible to the Supreme Judge of

---

[53] Paulus, *Verhandeling over de vrage*, 41.
[54] See Jean-Jacques Rousseau, *Du contrat social ou principes du droit politique* [1761] (Paris: René Hilsum, 1933), 24–25.
[55] Paulus, *Verhandeling over de vrage*, 91–93.
[56] Paulus, *Verhandeling over de vrage*, 178.
[57] Paulus, *Verhandeling over de vrage*, 178–179.
[58] Paulus, *Verhandeling over de vrage*, 184.
[59] Paulus, *Verhandeling over de vrage*, 199 (Matthew 7:12).
[60] Paulus, *Verhandeling over de vrage*, 199–200.

heaven and earth.⁶¹ True Christians should ransom slaves.⁶² That would bring people to accept the religion of Jesus Christ, rather than the practice of purchasing human beings for weapons, necklaces, or liquor, in order to bring them to eternal slavery.⁶³ Paulus invites servants of the Gospel to take an interest in the fate of the victims of slavery, underlining with a reference to Colossians 3:11 ('there is neither Greek nor Jew, circumcision nor uncircumcision, Barbarian, Scythian, bond or free: But Christ is all and in all') that the Gospel is also for them.⁶⁴ This missionary argument strongly affirms the explicit Christian nature of Paulus's approach throughout his work.

GENERAL APPRAISAL AND INFLUENCE

We now come to the appraisal of Pieter Paulus and his work, especially having regard to his identity as a Christian jurist. As has been said already in the Introduction, Pieter Paulus is almost forgotten today. In his day, the man and his ideas were very well known but also controversial. He was admired by many Patriots in and before the days of the Batavian Republic, which was partly his creation.⁶⁵ His popularity fitted the strong moderate tendencies in the Dutch provinces where liberals abhorred the excesses of the French Revolution. He was hailed as the 'philosopher Paulus', as the 'Apostle of Mankind', and as a second Hugo Grotius (1583–1645), who was likewise a child prodigy who became an oracle.⁶⁶ Paulus's popularity was definitely also related to his identity as a Christian jurist. In particular, Christian groups that had a positive attitude to the ideas of the Enlightenment were enthusiastic. He was seen as 'the second Apostle Paul (in Dutch Bible translations called 'Paulus'), that noble friend of mankind'.⁶⁷ He was seen by them as one of the three most important champions of freedom in Dutch history.⁶⁸ Paulus was applauded because he valued freedom-loving Christianity. These liberal

---

[61] Paulus, *Verhandeling over de vrage*, 202.
[62] Paulus, *Verhandeling over de vrage*, 209.
[63] Paulus, *Verhandeling over de vrage*, 210.
[64] Paulus, *Verhandeling over de vrage*, 213.
[65] Ernestine van der Wall, 'Geen natie van atheïsten. Pieter Paulus (1753–1796) over godsdienst en mensenrechten', *Jaarboek van de Maatschappij der Nederlandse Letterkunde* (1996), 45–58, https://www.dbnl.org/tekst/_jaa003199601_01/_jaa003199601_01_0005.php.
[66] W. J. Goslinga, *De Rechten van den Mensch en Burger, een overzicht der Nederlandsche geschriften en verklaringen* ('s Gravenhage: A. J. Oranje, 1936), 60.
[67] Quoted in Goslinga, *De Rechten*, 50–51, footnote 28.
[68] The two other champions were Claudius (Julius) Civilis, who led the uprising of the Batavians against the Romans in the first century, and Hendrik van Brederode (1531–1568), who was one of the leaders of the Dutch revolt against the Spanish King Philip II (1528–1598).

Christians appreciated that he presented Jesus as what was called the architect of the eternal citizen's sanctuary and that he made clear that Jesus taught equality.[69] But there were also other voices. An example is the already mentioned Willem Bilderdijk (1756–1831). This lawyer, historian, poet, and visionary was originator of the Christian revival in the Netherlands in the nineteenth century. As an Orangist he was a political opponent of Paulus. Bilderdijk even refused to take the oath of allegiance to the Batavian Republic. Paulus's work on equality did not appeal to him. He wrote that Pieter Paulus would not believe the Gospel if he had not found there the doctrine of freedom and equality.[70] Others expressed in even stronger terms their doubts as to the sincerity of Paulus's beliefs. A professor in Franeker, Johan Hendrik Swildens (1745–1809), a Patriot, qualified Paulus's work as French Jacobinism in Christian garb.[71] That suggests an opportunistic choice of arguments to ensure the success of his message in a predominantly Christian society. No doubt Paulus's approach contributed strongly to the acceptance of the political ideals of the Enlightenment in the Dutch provinces. But that does not make him insincere or opportunistic. I am sure neither the authors mentioned nor anybody else has had access to Paulus's heart, to his deepest convictions. Therefore, without further indications it is not possible to conclude that Paulus's views on the foundations of equality should not be taken seriously. More strongly, having read his passionate plea for equality, completely based on biblical arguments, it is difficult to conclude that he did not express his true feelings on the matter. Having regard to the philosophical climate of his days, especially among the adherents of the Enlightenment, the use of these arguments was not very popular. Swimming against the current requires a serious persuasion.[72]

All this does not mean that the content of Paulus's reasoning is beyond criticism. Several questions can be raised by way of example. First, as to his use of the Bible. Is the choice of his sources not one-sided? The focus is primarily on the New Testament. Important parts of the Old Testament, especially of the Pentateuch, the Torah, but also the Prophets, which are especially interesting when it comes to questions of law and the state, are not touched upon. Moreover, the author rather easily accepts that the moral admonishments to Jesus's disciples in, for example, the Sermon on the Mount are forthwith applicable to the structuring of the legal order. Furthermore, is there not

---

[69] Goslinga, *De Rechten*, 60, footnote 69.
[70] Quoted in Goslinga, *De Rechten*, 51.
[71] Goslinga, *De Rechten*, 49 and 51.
[72] See also Goslinga, *De Rechten*, 52 and J. W. Sap, *Wegbereiders der revolutie. Calvinisme en de strijd om de democratische rechtsstaat* (Groningen: Wolters-Noordhoff, 1993), 305.

also a certain one-sidedness in the message proclaimed? The equality of the worth of every human being entails automatically equal political rights. Paulus is convinced that the Bible points in the direction of democracy. He will have been aware that this was not at all a common understanding within the Christian tradition. Hugo Grotius, for example, defends in *De Republica Emendanda* the position that aristocracy, rather than democracy, represents the biblical ideal.[73] Paulus stressed further the idea of God being the Father of all mankind and the need for universal fraternal love, but should he not also have paid attention to the sharp distinctions made in Scripture? We find the chosen people of Israel as opposed to the *goyim* (peoples), as well as the dividing line between believers and non-believers. Is the universalism he proclaims not at odds with this? No doubt his universalistic approach would not appeal to more orthodox Christians, among them Calvinists, who were more inclined to an antithetical position in the world. What is true is that Paulus's universalism fits the general idea of the Enlightenment.

That brings us to a related question. Both the political activities of Paulus and his treatise on equality show that he as a Christian embraces the political ideals of the Enlightenment. At the same time it cannot be denied that this movement has aptly been characterized by Kelly as 'a shared mood or temper, or attitude to the world, in which the dominant note was one of profound scepticism toward traditional systems of orthodoxy (*especially those of religion*), and a strong faith in the power of the human reason and intelligence to make unlimited advances in the sciences and techniques conducive to human welfare'.[74] And if we see the strongly anti-clerical French Revolution for a moment as the Enlightenment in action, it cannot be a surprise that many Christian authors, among them Edmund Burke, have seen the Enlightenment and its social and political implications as a real threat to Christianity and its impact on society.[75] Paulus needs many words in his treatise on equality to refute Burke on the issue of equal political rights, but he does not enter a discussion with him on the issue addressed by Burke on the fundamentals of the Enlightenment in respect of the role of religion.[76] Maybe the polarized

---

[73] See Hugo de Groot, 'De Republica Emendanda: a juvenile tract by Hugo Grotius on the emendation of the Dutch polity (ed. by Arthur Eyffinger; in collab. with P. A. H. de Boer, J. Th. de Smidt, L. E. van Holk)', *Grotiana* 5 (1984): 3–135.

[74] J. M. Kelly, *A Short History of Western Legal Theory* (Oxford: Clarendon Press, 1993), 249–250, emphasis added.

[75] See Edmund Burke, *Reflections on the Revolution in France* [1790], ed. Frank M. Turner (New Haven, CT; London: Yale University Press, 2003). See on Burke inter alia Matthijs de Blois, 'The true spirit of toleration': Edmund Burke on establishment and tolerance', *Rechtsfilosofie en Rechtstheorie* (2008) 3: 212–229.

[76] Paulus, *Verhandeling over de vrage*, 155–168.

atmosphere in the revolutionary climate at the end of the eighteenth century did not provide the ideal context for such a debate. It is clear from what we discussed above that Paulus did not share the scepticism of many of the Enlightenment thinkers vis-à-vis religion in general and the authority of the Scriptures in particular. Paulus sticks to the traditional Christian (and Jewish) attitude to the authority of the Scriptures. In that sense he qualifies as a pre-modern thinker rather than a pure adherent of the Enlightenment. He is in that respect more congenial to Locke and Burke.[77]

Finally, it was said that Paulus is now almost forgotten. Almost, not completely. In 1936, W. J. Goslinga defended his doctoral thesis at the (Protestant) Free University of Amsterdam. His subjects were the Dutch declarations on the rights of man and citizen.[78] He paid tribute to Pieter Paulus with an extensive discussion of his life and work, focusing on his contribution to the drafting of the first Dutch declaration in 1795. Fifty-seven years later, J. W. Sap defended at the same university a doctoral thesis on Calvinism as predecessor of the revolution.[79] He also discussed Paulus's work and took seriously its intentions to develop a theory on equality on a biblical basis. In 2009, Peter C. Kop, in his treatise on the history of fundamental rights, paid ample attention to the contribution of Pieter Paulus.[80] And, as we have seen, as recently as 2012, a professor of the Parliamentary System, van den Berg, did his best to bring Pieter Paulus back from oblivion.[81] There are good reasons for that. It is not only that it is relevant to honour him as the first president of a democratic representative body in the Netherlands. There is an even more important reason to draw attention to the work of Pieter Paulus. We are living in a time where religion is sometimes presented as the antithesis of human rights. It has even been submitted that 'the fundamental tenets of monotheistic religions are at odds with the basis of the human rights doctrine'.[82] Therefore it makes sense to highlight the biblical basis of the ideas of equality, freedom, and human rights as elaborated by Pieter Paulus.

---

[77] Locke, *Political Essays*, ed. Mark Goldie (Cambridge etc.: Cambridge University Press, 1997), 204–209; Victor Nuovo, 'Locke's proof of the divine authority of Scripture', in *Philosophy & Religion in Enlightenment Britain*, ed. Ruth Savage (Oxford: Oxford University Press, 2012), 56–76; Matthijs de Blois, 'The true spirit of toleration' Edmund Burke on establishment and tolerance', *Rechtsfilosofie en Rechtstheorie* (2008) 3: 212–229.

[78] Goslinga, *De Rechten*, 48–77.

[79] Sap, *Wegbereiders*, 305. See also J. A. Hofman, J. W. Sap, and I. Sewandono, *Grondrechten in evenwicht* (Deventer: Kluwer, 1995), 57.

[80] Peter C. Kop, *Mens en Burger. Een geschiedenis van de grondrechten* (Zutphen: Walburg Pers, 2009), 116–123.

[81] Van den Berg, *Dominee*.

[82] F. Raday, 'Culture, religion and gender', *I. Con* 1 (2003): 663–715, at 668.

RECOMMENDED READINGS

Baggerman, Arianne and Rudolf Dekker. 'Pieter Paulus (1753–1796) in kleine kring. "Ach stel u die brave man tog ten voorbeelde"'. *Nieuw Letterkundig Magazijn* 20 (2002): 34–42.

Goslinga, W. J. *De Rechten van den Mensch en Burger, een overzicht der Nederlandsche geschriften en verklaringen*. 's Gravenhage: A. J. Oranje, 1936.

Israel, Jonathan. *The Dutch Republic. Its Rise, Greatness and Fall 1477–1806*. Oxford: Oxford University Press, 1998.

Kok, G. Chr. *Rotterdamse juristen uit vijf eeuwen*. Hilversum: Uitgeverij Verloren, 2009.

Kop, Peter C. *Mens en Burger. Een geschiedenis van de grondrechten*. Zutphen: Walburg Pers, 2009.

Sap, J. W. *Wegbereiders der revolutie. Calvinisme en de strijd om de democratische rechtsstaat*. Groningen: Wolters-Noordhoff, 1993.

Van den Berg, J. T. J. *De dominee en 'de tweede apostel Paulus'*. Maastricht: Maastricht University, 2012. https://doi.org/10.26481/spe.20120927jb.

Van der Wall, Ernestine. 'Geen natie van atheïsten. Pieter Paulus (1753–1796) over godsdienst en mensenrechten'. *Jaarboek van de Maatschappij der Nederlandse Letterkunde* (1996): 45–58. https://www.dbnl.org/tekst/_jaa003199601_01/_jaa003199601_01_0005.php.

Vles, E. J. *Pieter Paulus (1753–1796). Patriot en Staatsman*. Amsterdam: De Bataafsche Leeuw, 2004.

12

Guillaume Groen van Prinsterer

Jan Willem Sap [1]

BIOGRAPHICAL INTRODUCTION

The Dutch anti-revolutionary and Protestant thinker, historian, jurist, and politician Guillaume (Willem) Groen van Prinsterer (Voorburg, 21 August 1801 – The Hague, 19 May 1876) played an important role in the Netherlands after 1813, the period after the Batavian–French era. He came from an enlightened–conservative family from Holland. His father was a doctor and court physician and his mother was very wealthy. After finishing his studies at Leiden University, he graduated as a doctor of literature and law, and in 1823 became a lawyer in The Hague. He was a very gifted child who grew up to become a gentleman and mingled in high society, attending balls and parties. In 1827, he started working in Brussels and later became secretary to King William I (1829–1833). He married Betsy van der Hoop in 1828, a well-educated and pious woman. Groen van Prinsterer was a member of the Dutch Reformed Church, the same church as the royal family of the House of Orange-Nassau.

During his time in Brussels, Groen van Prinsterer was in daily contact with William I, king of a relatively large kingdom. The unification of the Northern and Southern parts of the Netherlands had been devised by the powers of Europe after the Treaty of Vienna to serve as a neutral buffer on the northern border of France between France and Germany. The Belgian Revolt in 1830 (ratified in 1839) against King William I was a tremendous shock for his secretary, the young Groen van Prinsterer. It can be argued that his writing was an ongoing reflection on the Belgian uprising, a Revolution against his king, which led to the loss of what would later become Belgium. Groen van Prinsterer had to deal with this challenge, a complicated union of Jacobinism and

---

[1] Prof. Dr J. W. Sap (1962) is professor of European Union law at the Open University in the Netherlands and associate professor of European Union law at the Vrije Universiteit Amsterdam.

Catholicism. As a conventional lawyer and monarchist working under the regime of William I (who reigned from 1813 to 1840), Groen van Prinsterer favoured restoration. However, he also understood certain arguments of orthodox Protestant dissidents who wanted to create a separate free church in 1834, although Groen van Prinsterer personally did not believe in that ideology. He pointed out that the measures of the government against the Seceders were unconstitutional, unDutch, and unChristian. Groen van Prinsterer valued their argument, the liberty to worship God according to the dictates of their conscience, without being subjected to any penalties, disqualification, or persecution. He also stressed that Holland, the Dutch Republic, and its successor the Kingdom of the Netherlands, had always been a free country.[2]

In Brussels, Groen van Prinsterer came into contact with the evangelical renewal movement 'Réveil'. This was a revival of Protestantism initiated by British and Swiss–French evangelicals and also linked to a Lutheran resurgence in Germany. The Réveil was conservative in politics yet concerned for the suffering. For young people who in an earlier generation might have chosen a more rational path, the Réveil attracted attention for a sense of being, the experience with Christ, spiritual depth, moral earnestness, and philanthropy. Especially important for Groen van Prinsterer was the Swiss Revival preacher and historian Jean-Henri Merle d'Aubigné (1794–1872), pastor of the Brussels Protestant Church. From this period, Groen van Prinsterer stepped forward as a confessional and devout Christian. Merle d'Aubigné influenced him to connect the history of Europe with the re-creating power of Christianity. In that context, Groen van Prinsterer believed that his era was apocalyptic.[3] His beliefs strengthened and he started to criticize conventional Christianity for being too lax.

Religious motive was the moving power for Groen van Prinsterer. It dictated most of his actions. Direct contact with the Bible brought man in direct contact with Christ. From 1845 Groen van Prinsterer was chair of the so-called 'Christian Friends', where one could discuss Christian interests. In addition, initiatives were organized concerning the church, philanthropy, social affairs, and publicity. Groen van Prinsterer was in contact with leading figures of the international Réveil.

In the years between 1833 and 1849, Groen van Prinsterer was primarily active as a historian, being keeper of the records of the Dutch Royal House

---

[2] G. Groen van Prinsterer, *De maatregelen tegen de Afgescheidenen aan het staatsregt getoetst* [*The Measures Against the Seceders Tested Against Constitutional Law*] (Leiden: Luchtmans, 1837), 4, 41–45, 47–58; D. Nauta, 'Groen van Prinsterer en de kerk', *Kerkblad Amsterdam*, 29 May 1976.

[3] J. Bijl, *Een Europese antirevolutionair. Het Europabeeld van Groen van Prinsterer in tekst en context* (Amsterdam: VU University Press, 2011), 553.

since 1831. He published some important works about the family of Orange, written in French. This gave him an excellent reputation among historians in Europe.[4] In 1840, he was a member of the 'Double Chamber' for Holland concerning Constitutional Reform. In 1846, he published his *Handboek der geschiedenis van het vaderland* [*Handbook of the History of the Fatherland*]. Groen van Prinsterer presented an orthodox Protestant view on the history of the Netherlands. As such, it was also a political pamphlet. In the next year, 1847, he published his most famous work, *Unbelief and Revolution*. In the years 1849 to 1857 and 1862 to 1865, Groen van Prinsterer was a member of the Second Chamber of Dutch parliament. He dedicated most of his political life to Christian education. In the years 1871 to 1876, he defended the political and religious liberties in Europe. In 1876, he died in The Hague.

MAJOR THEMES AND CONTRIBUTIONS

It was during the time when Groen van Prinsterer lived in Brussels that the Historical Law School and nationalism became stronger in Europe.[5] According to Groen van Prinsterer, the restoration of the political and societal structure was only possible if it was based on Christian-historical or anti-revolutionary principles. To him, values seemed more important than facts. Groen van Prinsterer was a committed European but very strongly rejected the liberal and atheistic principles of the French Revolution. His reading of works of the Historical Law School like the books of the great scholar Friedrich-Carl von Savigny (1779–1861) made him dislike constructionist rationalism. According to Groen van Prinsterer, ideas such as society as a social contract and the sovereignty of the people were contrary to the acknowledgement of God as the highest sovereign. The principles of the French Revolution had led to a tragic secularization of politics and society. Revolution was not just the events that had happened in Paris since 1789, it was a total upheaval in thinking and mentality. It was a disregard of the Bible as spiritual foundation and the fruitful lessons of history over the ages. Groen van Prinsterer even defended the concept of *droit divin*, although more in the sense of limited government.[6]

---

[4] R. Kuiper, 'Groen van Prinsterer', in *Christelijke Encyclopedie. Volume II*, ed. G. Harinck (Kampen: Kok, 2005), 715–717.

[5] T. Hammar, *Democracy and the Nation State. Aliens, Denizens and Citizens in a World of International Migration* (Aldershot: Avebury Ashgate Publishing, 1990), 46–51.

[6] G. Groen van Prinsterer, *Ongeloof en Revolutie. Een reeks historische voorlezingen* (1847, 1868), ed. H. Smitskamp (Franeker: Wever, 1976), 47–51.

Here we notice the deep influence of the writings of the Irish–English philosopher and politician Edmund Burke (1729–1797), who wrote his *Reflections on the Revolution in France* in the first half of 1790, but predicted many dramatic events, such as the rise of Napoleon.[7] It was Merle d'Aubigné who told Groen van Prinsterer about Burke's ideas. Readers of Burke, one of the fathers of modern conservatism, seemed to make progress in constitutional wisdom. Burke did influence Groen van Prinsterer concerning the anti-revolutionary principles.

According to Groen van Prinsterer, the seventeenth century was the golden age. The Netherlands was a blessed country because of the deep influence of the Gospel on Dutch culture and society. Groen van Prinsterer also defended a providential role for the House of Orange-Nassau, famous members of which defended the Dutch against attacks from abroad, especially France and Spain. A Dutch prince as King William III on the English throne had even defended the liberties of Europe against the French dictator Louis XIV. Groen van Prinsterer stressed the holy links between God, the Netherlands, and the house of Orange.[8]

That the reformer Jean Calvin (1509–1564) had a distaste for the pomp and extravagance characteristic of monarchs did not really seem to bother Groen van Prinsterer.[9] The fact is that these stories about the history of the Dutch people and their leaders helped readers to gain more control over the chaos of their past and in that way helped the people forward – teachers, ministers – building the Dutch nation-state, giving the Netherlands a meaningful place in Europe and the world after the very complex Batavian–French period (1795–1813). The stories about Prince William 'the Silent' of Orange, the founding father of the Dutch republic, who had been murdered in Delft in 1584, or about Prince Maurits and Oldebarnevelt, provided guidance on how to deal with complex new situations, divisions, and identities in Dutch society.

Spiritual Vacuum

Because of his fear of new revolutions in Europe, Groen van Prinsterer held lectures about the danger of the anti-religious principles and ideology that had

---

[7] E. Burke, *Reflections on the Revolution in France and on the Proceedings in Certain Societies Relative to that Event* (1790), ed. C. C. O'Brien (Harmondsworth, Middlesex, etc.: Penguin Books, 1987).

[8] Groen van Prinsterer, *Ongeloof en Revolutie*, 48–52, 313. See H. Algra, 'De overheid onder het gezag van God – het huis van Oranje', in *Anti-revolutionair bestek. Toelichting op het beginsel- en algemeen staatkundig programme van de Anti-Revolutionaire Partij* (Aalten: De Graafschap, 1964), 34–42.

[9] H. Höpfl, *The Christian Polity of John Calvin* (Cambridge: Cambridge University Press, 1982), 169.

influenced the politicos of his day. Revolution could lead to uncontrollable situations: tyranny, anarchy, masses in the streets, etc. Revolution was not just a political fact in the past, it was a present-day challenge, it was directed against the sovereignty of God, it was man in the place of God, aimed at a re-creation of the world. In fact, he saw it as the spread of atheism. These lectures were published as *Ongeloof en Revolutie* (1847) [*Unbelief and Revolution*], his most famous work, one year before the publication of *The Communist Manifesto* by Marx and Engels, a year before another year of revolutions in Europe, meaning that the timing was excellent. In his work, Groen van Prinsterer wanted to make a strong connection between the Gospel and the development of Europe. He distinguished between 1) the Christianization of Europe, 2) the Reformation, and 3) the Revolutionary Era, with the latter of course in strong contrast to the first two.[10]

Groen van Prinsterer stressed that there was a tremendous breach in European history because of the French Revolution. To the impacts of the French Revolution, he added the wars of Napoleon, permanent revolutions in politics and science, isolation of the church, and the decay of religious convictions. He saw all this as a threat to Christianity. The French Revolution was an attack on the old idea that God led history. The ideas of the French Revolution had led to the situation of spiritual vacuum. The revolt of the masses against common sense was the result of atomization and their loss of social status and communal relationships.[11] Because of the French Revolution, man became the prisoner of a violent ideology, as under Robespierre. What was left of respect for freedom, independence, the rule of law, and the government?

The only way to redemption was the Gospel. Groen van Prinsterer placed the atheist French Revolution with centralization on one side, and the Gospel with widespread reach on the other side.[12] This was not without risk, because sometimes Groen van Prinsterer saw and defended his very personal opinions as the hand of God in history. He also turned a blind eye toward the moderate optimism of some of the authors of the period of the Batavian Revolution (1795–1798), for instance concerning the equal rights of women.[13] In opposition to speculative political theory and natural law constructions of the

---

[10] Groen van Prinsterer, *Ongeloof en Revolutie*, 24.
[11] See H. Arendt, *The Origins of Totalitarianism* (1951) (San Diego: Harcourt, 1976), 352.
[12] Groen van Prinsterer, *Ongeloof en Revolutie*, 173–174.
[13] G. Paape, *De Bataafsche Republiek, zo als zij behoord te zijn, en zo als zij wezen kan: of Revolutionaire droom in 1798: wegens toekomstige gebeurtenissen tot 1998*, eds. P. Altena and M. Oostindië (Nijmegen: Vantilt, 1998), 78; J. C. Karels, 'Wakker worden na 200 jaar', *Reformatorisch Dagblad*, September 15, 1999.

state, Groen van Prinsterer always noted the adage *'It is written!* [in the Bible]. *And it has happened!* [in history]'.[14] This can be seen as a non-theoretical attitude of experience, but with Groen van Prinsterer the model of history had not yet become a problem of thought.[15] His strength was that he had a certain moral compass and could categorize ideas as right or wrong. This was connected with his upbringing and relations. This was the reason why he dared to be so judgemental, why he did not like moral relativism, why he could advise people how to live and could fight for the religious education of the new generation. It was probably for political reasons that Groen van Prinsterer made the strong contrast in his structure a bit too absolutist to be really true.[16]

During his career and lifetime, his fears of radical revolutions were linked directly to his fears of international communism and socialism, the most consistent sects of the new secular religion.[17] This was a real challenge for a monarchist. Already by the summer of 1848, some of the 'Demands of the People' formulated by the communists in Amsterdam were extremely clear: general suffrage or else revolution and republic.[18]

In the revised edition of *Unbelief and Revolution* in 1868, Groen van Prinsterer added some quotes of Tocqueville without being fully aware of the contradictions between revolutionary or liberal and anti-revolutionary or conservative political theory. However, his book did help to make the Liberals and their dominant leader Johan Rudolf Thorbecke (1798–1872), Prime Minister from 1849 to 1853, 1862 to 1866, and 1871 to 1872, aware of Groen van Prinsterer as one of their important opponents. The Liberals attacked Groen van Prinsterer's views strongly. In their eyes, the anti-revolutionary principles would serve only conservative politics, while the French Revolution had to be acknowledged as a necessary movement, in the democratic struggle of the citizens for a greater say in politics.

Unbelief and Revolution

What were Groen van Prinsterer's most important arguments? The title made very clear that he believed:

---

[14] Groen van Prinsterer, *Ongeloof en Revolutie*, 13.
[15] H. Dooyeweerd, *A New Critique of Theoretical Thought. Volume II* (Amsterdam: Paris, 1955), 192–193.
[16] J. W. Sap, *Paving the Way for Revolution. Calvinism and the Struggle for a Democratic Constitutional State* (Amsterdam: VU University Press, 2001), 289–302.
[17] A. J. van Dyke, *Groen van Prinsterer's Lectures on Unbelief and Revolution* (Jordan Station, Ontario: Wedge Pub. Foundation, 1989), 3–4.
[18] D. Bos, *Waarachtige volksvrienden. De vroege socialistische beweging in Amsterdam 1848–1894* (Amsterdam: Bert Bakker, 2001), 52.

that there is a natural and necessary relation between *unbelief* and *revolution*, that the school of thought which holds sway today in constitutional law and learning arose from a rejection of the Gospel.[19]

The self-elevation of man had led to the rise of the Revolutionary ideas, and by a natural development to the French Revolution in 1789, and more. Groen van Prinsterer states:

> By *Revolution* I do not mean one of the many events whereby a government is overthrown. Nor do I just mean by it the storm of upheaval that has raged in France. Rather, by Revolution I mean the whole inversion of the general spirit and mode of thinking that is now manifest in all Christendom.
>
> By *Revolution [Revolutionary] ideas* I mean the basic maxims of liberty and equality, popular sovereignty, social contract, the artificial reconstruction of society by common consent – notions which today are venerated as the cornerstone of constitutional law and the political order.[20]

Groen van Prinsterer's book was confrontational. He signalled errors that had become popular among academics and politicians. Not the philosophers of the Enlightenment, not Jean-Jacques Rousseau, but the Bible should be the foundation, with history as the teacher.[21] For Groen van Prinsterer the French Revolution was not caused by perversity of the former law, whether it be with regard to the *principles*, the *forms* of government, or indeed the *abuses* that prevailed at the time. Considering the old regime, he addressed the four main objections put forward by the supporters of the French Revolution: (1) too much attention was paid to questionable historic rights, to the detriment of general principles of justice; (2) too little attention was paid to the rule 'No state within the state', with the result that multiple internal clashes thwarted a strong and unified political power; (3) the divine origin of authority served as a pretext in support of despotism; (4) the forced union of church and state confused disparate things and so had many bad effects.[22]

(1) While the philosophers of the Enlightenment said that the exaggerated respect for the historical rights of the old regime and the ties to the *status quo* led to a misinterpretation of the general principles of law, Groen van Prinsterer explained that the historical rights have to be seen as a reflection of these universal principles of justice. He states:

[19] Groen van Prinsterer, *Ongeloof en Revolutie*, 8.
[20] Groen van Prinsterer, *Ongeloof en Revolutie*, 19; van Dyke, *Lectures*, par. 6 [note by Gr.v.P.: 'The Revolution is the unfolding of a wholesale skepticism in which God's Work and Law have been thrust aside'].
[21] Groen van Prinsterer, *Ongeloof en Revolutie*, 26, 29, 32.
[22] Groen van Prinsterer, *Ongeloof en Revolutie*, 44–59.

Historic rights were not simply derived from history, from the welter of all that comes to pass, beyond the control of higher powers, but on the contrary, they were respected as the slowly ripening fruits of the principles of justice whose action in time, far from bowing to the events, subjects the uninformed mass of facts and circumstances to its regulating and purifying influence. Justice, in a philosophical sense essential and historical par excellence, was placed above History. It was this dominion of Rights over fact that gave rise to a whole series of acquired rights. Now, any particular combination of these rights determined the distinctiveness of a state, forming its natural condition.[23]

(2) The assertion of the philosophers of the Enlightenment that the political authority of the state was enfeebled by the independence allowed to its divisions and subdivisions, (the principle of 'No state within the state'), was a useful warning. Nobody in a well-ordered kingdom or commonwealth possesses complete independence; every inhabitant is a subject who, either alone or in union with others, is to some degree subordinate to the authorities in everything that falls under the jurisdiction of the state. But Groen van Prinsterer also defended a historically won 'independence within one's own sphere', that is, within the sphere of their own competence, for citizens, provinces, municipalities, corporations, and societal organizations. The criticism made by these philosophers was of a tendency toward administrative centralization, and in his respect for autonomy, Groen van Prinsterer followed the warnings of Tocqueville.[24]

(3) The godly origin of authority was seen by the revolutionaries as a legitimation of tyranny. Groen van Prinsterer held on to the *droit divin*. All power is ordained by God. However, he did reject the identification of the will of the government with the will of God. A civil power is God's *lieutenant* and God's *minister*. He rejected Napoleon using God to confirm his power and to avoid limitations on his power. The government is the servant of God for the welfare of the people. If *droit divin* was used to justify tyranny, Groen van Prinsterer considered a right to resist and refusal by citizens not to be out of the question.[25] The 'crowned robber', who had banished the legitimate prince, does not have to be seen as ordained by God.[26]

---

[23] Groen van Prinsterer, *Ongeloof en Revolutie*, 44–45.
[24] Groen van Prinsterer, *Ongeloof en Revolutie*, 46.
[25] H. E. S. Woldring, *De Franse revolutie. Een aktuele uitdaging* (Kampen: Kok, 1989), 140.
[26] Groen van Prinsterer, *Ongeloof en Revolutie*, 48–49; van Dyke, *Lectures*, par. 51. This was an important element for Dutch Calvinists fighting the Nazis during the German occupation (1940–1945).

(4) Concerning the relation between church and state, Groen van Prinsterer states:

> If a sovereign is God's lieutenant, he is obliged publicly to confess and worship Him, to aid others in the exercise of worship, and as far as his legitimate authority extends to apply the standards of God's law to all his deeds and ordinances ... As for the church, she is called to be the light, the salt, and the heaven of the world. The church ought not to seek martyrdom or humiliation. She should not withdraw if the state requests her co-operation. The church must endeavour to secure authority and influence for the Gospel, in order that the divine commandments be observed. These are the grounds for the union of Church and State. Note that it is not an option but an obligation.[27]

Groen van Prinsterer was against regulation by the government that would place the church in custody and limit her legal rights. A church should defend its autonomy. Nowadays the principle of autonomy is of fundamental importance to the freedom of religious organizations; it is indispensable for pluralism in a democratic society.[28]

Groen van Prinsterer did not deny that abuses were among the secondary causes of the French Revolution. He admitted the influence of every wrongdoing that had become intertwined with the political arrangements. Yet he was convinced that their negative effect, when compared with the effect of the revolutionary ideas, was very subordinate. Following Burke, Groen van Prinsterer stressed that the *ancien régime* in France had not been as wicked as the despotism of Turkey.

From today's perspective, it is disappointing that Groen van Prinsterer was quite negative about the *Declaration of the Rights of Man and the Citizen* (1789). He noted that every freedom depended on the government. Groen van Prinsterer states:

> Such is the fate of the 'imprescriptible, inviolable, sacred Rights'. Supposedly beyond the reach of government, they are the toy of every regime that is in power. What the one hand gives, the other takes away. The liberties are exhibited, not conferred. Everything is allowed, with one fatal proviso: everything *insofar* as the state, the collective despot, is pleased to grant. I would not be understood. That the rights are restricted does not offend me, this is inherent in every right. The cause of my complaint is that whereas rights used to be circumscribed and confirmed by the unchangeable laws and ordinances of God, they are now made to depend on the good pleasure of the

---

[27] Groen van Prinsterer, *Ongeloof en Revolutie*, 52.
[28] Norman Doe, *Law and Religion in Europe* (Oxford: Oxford University Press, 2011), 114.

State, that is to say, on the will of changeable men, and for that reason must, by definition, perish. The revolutionary state affords liberty, insofar as it is possible, useful, desirable; insofar as the interest of the state allows; insofar as it is considered compatible with the circumstances; insofar as it is in keeping with the interests and demands and desires and whims and fancies of those placed over you. Liberty, complete liberty, unrestricted liberty is the promise, and in the end not liberty but the restrictions are unrestricted. Perfect liberty there is, with one restriction – one only, but one which revokes everything just granted: perfect liberty, subject to perfect slavery.[29]

If we think about the Protestant revolution in Germany, Martin Luther attacking the system of indulgences (in Wittenberg in 1517), teaching the 'priesthood of all believers' against the corrupt hierarchy, we can be sure that Groen van Prinsterer was aware of the most fundamental element in the genesis of the Reformation. This was 'the emerging spirit of rebellious, self-determining individualism, and particularly the growing impulse for intellectual and spiritual independence'.[30] The Reformation had a conservative side, the revival of a Bible-based Judaic Christianity, a religious reaction to corruption. But it was also a radical libertarian revolution.[31] In this cultural transformation in Europe the individualism of Luther (in Worms, 1521) was protected by German rulers and other northern countries. One of the consequences was that the individual could be alone outside the institutions of the Roman Catholic Church, and also alone directly before God. In that sense the Reformation was the assertion of Christian liberty. Groen van Prinsterer managed to escape this paradox by warning of the powers of the state. Groen van Prinsterer states:

> Later authors, like Benjamin Constant and Guizot, have looked for a safeguard in the 'doctrine of individualism', arguing that there are rights so weighty, so sacred, so intimately intertwined with the nature and destiny of man, that they ought to be withdrawn from the supreme power of the state. Altogether true; unfortunately, they have not shown as well how these rights can possibly be wrested from the state once it has taken over.[32]

Why was Groen van Prinsterer so conservative in his *Unbelief and Revolution*? We mentioned the influence of Burke earlier, but it also had to do with Carl Ludwig von Haller (1768–1854). Von Haller's reactionary patrimonial theory

---

[29] Groen van Prinsterer, *Ongeloof en Revolutie*, 182–183; van Dyke, *Lectures*, 249.
[30] R. Tarnas, *The Passion of the Western Mind. Understanding the Ideas that Have Shaped Our World View* (1991) (New York: Ballantine Books, 1993), 234.
[31] Tarnas, *Passion*, 237.
[32] Groen van Prinsterer, *Ongeloof en Revolutie*, 182–183; van Dyke, *Lectures*, 249.

of the state, defending monarchy founded on largescale land ownership, had a big influence on the first edition of *Unbelief and Revolution*. Groen van Prinsterer even thought he had found the real historical fundamentals of the 'Christian-Germanic State idea', this in opposition to the republican idea of the body politic defended by natural law like in the French Revolution. Later Groen van Prinsterer regretted following this too reactionary approach. Since 1850, Groen van Prinsterer had become increasingly influenced by the Historical Law School, the meaning of public justice, and the work of the Lutheran legal philosopher Friedrich Julius Stahl (1802–1861), famous for his saying 'Authority, not majority.'

While Marx and Engels had expected a battle between the classes, Groen van Prinsterer expected a battle between philosophies of life. His 'ghost' was not communism, but the spirit of the French Revolution. In a way, one can even assert that in Groen van Prinsterer's view on revolution there is a prophetic element. Members of the Dutch resistance movement were inspired by *Unbelief and Revolution* in the fight against the German occupation (1940–1945).[33]

Democracy, Secularization, and Religious Education

King William I was not enthusiastic about the modernizing of the Dutch Constitution. In the old Constitution (1814, 1815), the House of Orange had a fixed position; there were no specific articles on sensitive issues like the sovereignty of the people or the separation of church and state. There was no catalogue of human rights yet (only since 1983). But King William II, probably out of fear, accepted a group that would work on constitutional reforms. The final result was Thorbecke's Constitution of 1848. It confirmed a constitutional monarchy, dividing sovereignty between the monarch and the States-General. The Second Chamber was directly elected by (a limited group) of citizens. The agent of government was a Cabinet formally commissioned by the monarch. After a long struggle of twenty years, the Cabinet became responsible to the Second Chamber in 1868.

Although the Constitution of 1848 was a smart compromise – it kept the House of Orange on the throne and brought more democracy – most orthodox Protestants had a serious problem with the neglect of a religious foundation

---

[33] H. Smitskamp, 'Voorbericht van den bewerker', in G. Groen van Prinsterer, *Ongeloof en Revolutie. Een reeks historische voorlezingen* (1847, 1868) (Franeker: Wever, 1976), 5. See also R. Kuiper, 'Ter inleiding', in G. Groen van Prinsterer, *Ongeloof en Revolutie* (1847) (Barneveld: Nederlands Dagblad, 2008), 16.

and transcendent authority. It also appeared that the franchise was very restricted because of property qualifications. When Thorbecke accepted allowing Roman Catholics to reintroduce the hierarchy in their church, the Calvinist populace was afraid their old position would be threatened by the influence of the Roman Catholic network of bishops, with at its head in the Netherlands the archbishop of Utrecht. The reinstatement of the dioceses in April 1853 led to huge protests among Protestants and by King William III as well, although he was supposed to be politically silent.

After the introduction of greater democracy in the new Netherlands Constitution of 1848, Groen van Prinsterer became a member of the Second Chamber (Lower House) of the States-General (Dutch Parliament). He did not present himself as contra-revolutionary. He was not against the positive results of the French Revolution. He worked very hard. Was he aware of the fact that the French people hated aristocrats because to them wealth without function was intolerable?[34] Just as Tocqueville had done, he too warned against the dangers of oppression.[35] As the most important spokesman of the anti-revolutionary movement he presented himself not as a statesman, but as a confessor. It was quite a lonely job, but he contributed to the culture of having real debates between the government and the opposition in parliament, more or less following the English example, so striving for a parliament with more powers and debates with the government than for instance in France. Groen van Prinsterer had fierce but respectful debates with Thorbecke, who had managed to find a working balance between the king and revolutionary principles.[36] A complicating factor between them may have been that Thorbecke being a Lutheran belonged to a Protestant minority that used to be discriminated against in the Netherlands before 1795, whereas the elite, including Groen van Prinsterer, adhered to the Reformed tradition as developed by Jean Calvin.[37]

Although Groen van Prinsterer was very suspicious of the French *Declaration of the Rights of Man and the Citizen* (Paris, 1789) and considered it too abstract, it is possible to list some principles and human rights he fought for during his life as a researcher and politician, always conscious of the

---

[34] Arendt, *Origins*, 4.

[35] J. W. Sap, 'De angst voor revolutie bij de democratisering van de rechtsstaat. Groen van Prinsterer en Tocqueville', in *Groen van Prinsterer in Europese context*, eds. J. de Bruijn and G. Harinck (Hilversum: Verloren, 2004), 25–35; I. Broekhuijse and J. W. Sap, eds., *De Amerikaanse droom van Tocqueville* (Nijmegen: Vantilt, 2016), 145–147.

[36] J. W. Sap, *The Netherlands Constitution 1848–1998. Historical Reflections* (Utrecht: Lemma, 2000), 47–56.

[37] V. Hoel, *Faith, Fatherland and the Norwegian Seaman. The work of Norwegian's Seamen's mission in Antwerp and the Dutch ports (1864–1920)* (Hilversum: Verloren, 2016), 262.

spiritual and moral heritage of Europe, including the Netherlands. Because he, just like Tocqueville, was sensitive about the dangers of equality, he favoured liberty, but most important to him was the religious origin of the human being, man created by God. So, that could be placed under *human dignity*, which nowadays is valued higher than *liberty* and *equality*. Also important for Groen van Prinsterer was that no one should be held in slavery. It is striking that Groen van Prinsterer was the chair of a committee to abolish slavery in the Dutch colonies (1853), but that slavery in the colonies would last until 1863. His endeavours for the implementation of classical freedoms should also be mentioned: freedom of thought, conscience, and religion; freedom of expression and communication; and freedom of assembly and association. But above all his life was committed to the right to religious education. Groen van Prinsterer was also aware of the importance of principles. He fought for the emancipation of and respect for minorities. To him, just like Tocqueville, democracy should always be controlled by rule of law. Uncontrolled democracy was dangerous because of the danger of the tyranny of the majority. Going back in time, the early protests of Groen van Prinsterer had not reached many supporters. In the beginning, adversaries even named Groen van Prinsterer 'a general without an army'. But that would slowly change because he was a strong political writer and debater. Between the periods 1849–1857 and 1862–1965, he grew very active in parliament defending Christian education in the Netherlands. This should have been organized by the Dutch government, as an expression of the character of the Dutch nation and as a means for restoration. In that light, he defended religious liberties against the old papism, the struggle of the Dutch against Spain, but also against state liberalism. However, his dream of Christian education in state schools failed, because the majority in parliament decided that state education should be neutral. The Liberals feared that religious education would damage national unity. Groen van Prinsterer had to accept this as a political fact and therefore decided to focus his efforts on organizing special Christian education through civil society. The members of these non-governmental organizations would become his new 'army'.

Parliament did not have the power to fulfil the wishes of neglected groups in society. This meant that these groups had to organize activities outside of parliament. After 1870, these groups no longer accepted the dominance of the wealthy Liberal citizens who had been in control for many years. The new groups felt that they were being discriminated against in economic, political, ideological, and cultural ways. So religious protesters and socialist protesters started to organize themselves against the dominant Liberal order in church, state, and society. It was the struggle of groups who did not yet have the right to vote, being discriminated against by the (wealthy) citizens with their vested interests. For orthodox Protestants the fact that the strong relationship between the king and the Protestants had weakened was a problem. The sympathy of King William III (who had reigned since 1849) was not with somebody like the orthodox Protestant Groen van Prinsterer and the *'kleine luyden'* [little men, lower middle class]. For constitutional and personal reasons King William III was not prepared to let the orthodox Protestants use his position in the fight for religious education; he would sign the liberal School Act of 1878. The King was not happy with orthodox Protestants who wanted to break the unity in church, state, and society.[38]

King William III was even more worried about the socialist movement because their frustration was directed against the monarchy. The *'Sociaal Democratische Bond'* [Social Democratic Union] of Ferdinand Domela Niewenhuis (1846–1916) fought for general suffrage to bring about the revolution. They wanted social renewal and rejected authorities that stood in the way. The constitutional reform of 1887 made important changes possible, leading to the typical Dutch pillarization of society. The organizations of these pillars protected minorities against other groups and the state. The aim of the pillars was to stick to an orthodox Protestant, Catholic, Socialist, or even Liberal identity in a secularizing state. That is why Groen van Prinsterer had at first not liked neutral education by the state, because that would lead to secularization. According to confessional Christians, it was a fact that society needed Christian education. They wanted to emancipate their group, the *kleine luyden*, in a period when most of them did not have the right to vote. The fascinating thing is that the first orthodox Protestant political party in the Netherlands was built on a popular initiative concerning religious education. This initiative, organized by Abraham Kuyper (1837–1920) in 1878, involved a revolutionary form of citizen participation. In 1879, three years after the death of Groen van Prinsterer, the first political party in the Netherlands was founded by Kuyper, named the Anti-Revolutionary Party. It was an example for socialists and Catholics and the start of, roughly speaking, the four pillars that confirmed a pluralistic society: Liberal, orthodox Protestant, Roman Catholic, and Socialist.[39]

---

[38] C. A. Tamse, 'Koning Willem III en Sophie', in *Nassau en Oranje in de Nederlandse geschiedenis*, ed. C. A. Tamse (Alpen aan den Rijn: A.W. Sijthoff, 1979), 309–356, especially 318–320.

[39] Tamse, 'Willem III', 320. It is possible to use the concept of 'subculture'; no implications of inferiority are intended. See Peter Burke, *History and Social Theory* (Cambridge: Polity Press, 2005), 123.

In the period after 1848, Groen van Prinsterer commented strongly on all the political developments. Notwithstanding his conservative philosophical ideas about the French Revolution, he favoured reforms in the area of constitutional law and accepted greater participation in government by citizens. He warned of Bonapartism, the search for world monarchy and attempt to destroy historical international law. As a historian and a jurist, he kept on defending the religious and political liberties of Europe. In his search for peace, he held Napoleon III and Bismarck responsible for the outbreak of the Franco–Russian War, blaming them for breaching the Christian family tie. Although Groen van Prinsterer formally stayed with his anti-revolutionary principles, directed against the atheistic principles of the French Revolution, he decided to stop wandering the endless aristocratic, monarchist, absolutistic, and theocratic paths. After 1856, he chose a more democratic path. Around 1870 he was disappointed in his passive aristocratic and anti-revolutionary friends. During the elections of 1871, he supported three orthodox Protestant candidates of the middle class, A. Kuyper, M. D. van Otterloo, and L. W. C. Keuchenius. At the end of his political life, in February 1874, Groen van Prinsterer embraced the 'Christian liberalism' of Abraham Kuyper.[40]

GENERAL APPRAISAL AND INFLUENCE

One of the reasons Groen van Prinsterer became more 'modern' at the end of his career had to do with the consequences of Calvinism. There is a big difference between the principalities in Germany on one side and the cities ruled by an elite of citizens in Switzerland on the other side, especially concerning trust in government. Calvinists had discovered early the need to control government and valued the role of local governments and the right to resist. Roughly put, Lutheranism risked promoting absolutism. According to Dooyeweerd, history stood closer to democratic theory than Groen van Prinsterer had been aware of. The so-called democratic form of government of a medieval town 'was not typically founded in economical forms of power... all the citizens of a town had to join one of the guilds ...' So they became *political members*.[41]

---

[40] Groen aan Kuyper, February 7, 1874, in *Briefwisseling van Mr. G. Groen van Prinsterer met dr. A. Kuyper 1864–1876*, ed. A. Goslinga (Kampen: Kok, 1937), 283; A. Kuyper, *Het Calvinisme. Oorsprong en waarborg van onze constitutionele vrijheden. Een Nederlandse gedachte* (1874) (Kampen: Kok, 2004); A. Kuyper, 'Calvinism: source and stronghold of our constitutional liberties', in *Abraham Kuyper, A. Centennial Reader*, ed. James D. Bratt (Grand Rapids, MI: Eerdmans, 1998), 279–322.

[41] H. Dooyeweerd, *A New Critique of Theoretical Thought. Volume III* (Amsterdam: Paris, 1957), 477–478.

Although his book *Unbelief and Revolution* was influential in starting the anti-revolutionary movement, the work is not easy to read. It is a mix of constitutional law and a long debate about the psychology of revolution. It appears academic, but is in fact a political pamphlet, although a slightly too long one.[42] The book, however, is relevant because it had such great influence on aristocratic and orthodox Protestant circles, and could be read as a serious warning about populism and totalitarian systems such as communism and national socialism, just like the work of Tocqueville. Groen van Prinsterer warns of the radical revolutionary party of the French Revolution—terrorists who are said to have been striving for universal brotherhood.[43] The approach of Groen van Prinsterer would become an important guide for many orthodox Christians, because they were afraid that the modernity of the Enlightenment was deliberately trying to free Western culture from its Christian historical roots.[44] At the same time *Unbelief and Revolution* is full of errors regarding modern perspectives of political and legal philosophy.

It took Groen van Prinsterer many years to understand that the idea of the restoration of church and culture of the Netherlands, the search for order alone, could not be the dominant purpose of his life. For many years the gentleman Groen van Prinsterer, the Leader of his Majesty's most loyal opposition but not the leader-in-waiting, hesitated about the need for a Christian political party. After his death in 1876, it was his successor, and later prime minister, Abraham Kuyper who knew that the best way to go forward was to support the concept of an active Christian political party in the liberal system of political parties, stimulating the concept of a political party based on Christian democratic principles. To make this move Kuyper was not so much focused on the principles of the French Revolution as Groen van Prinsterer was, although Kuyper did write to Groen van Prinsterer in 1873 stating how he loved reading the entire work of Edmund Burke. Kuyper, in contrast to Groen van Prinsterer, drew his inspiration more from the United States of America, with its 'sovereignty of the people' not as a general principle but as given by God. In his view, separation of church and state was not always the result of the struggle against the church.

But without the impressive struggle of Groen van Prinsterer, without his influential lectures and his book *Unbelief and Revolution* (even if the work was not convincing in a theoretical sense), Kuyper could never have implemented this dream. Groen van Prinsterer was one of the architects and builders during

---

[42] R. Kuiper, 'Ter inleiding', 9.
[43] Groen van Prinsterer, *Ongeloof en Revolutie*, 11.
[44] Kuiper, 'Ter inleiding', 7.

the work in progress after the Batavian–French era, building a house of many mansions with room for all, a house that allowed people to make religious arguments in the public sphere. He made room for the opposition in and outside parliament. It was Groen van Prinsterer's brave political life as a Christian that made the dream come true, although he would never enter the promised land of the Anti-Revolutionary Party. For more than a century, since 1917, countless numbers of children and students in the Netherlands have benefited from religious school education subsidized by the state. Even today, three Christian political parties in the Netherlands still consider Groen van Prinsterer one of their most important heroes, although none agrees with him completely. But that is typically Dutch.

RECOMMENDED READINGS

Bijl, J. *Een Europese antirevolutionair. Het Europabeeld van Groen van Prinsterer in tekst en context*. Amsterdam: VU University Press, 2011.
De Bruijn, J. and G. Harinck, eds. *Groen van Prinsterer in Europese contect*. Hilversum: Verloren, 2004.
Groen van Prinsterer, G. *Ongeloof en Revolutie. Een reeks historische voorlezingen* (1847, 1868). Edited by H. Smitskamp. Franeker: Wever, 1976.
Groen van Prinsterer, G. *Handboek der geschiedenis van het vaderland*. Amsterdam: Höveker & Zoon, 1895.
Kuiper, R. *Tot een voorbeeld zult gij blijven. Mr. G. Groen van Prinsterer* (1801–1876). Amsterdam: Schipper & Buitenheijn, 2001.
Sap, J. W. *Wegbereiders der revolutie. Calvinisme en de strijd om de democratische rechtsstaat*. Groningen: Wolters-Noordhoff, 1993.
Sap, J. W. *Paving the Way for Revolution. Calvinism and the Struggle for a Democratic Constitutional State*. Amsterdam: VU Uitgeverij, 2001.
Van Dyke, A. J. *Groen van Prinsterer's Lectures on Unbelief and Revolution*. Jordan Station, Ontario: Wedge Pub. Foundation, 1989.

13

Edouard Ducpétiaux

Frank Judo

BIOGRAPHICAL INTRODUCTION[1]

If the name of Edouard Ducpétiaux (1804–1868) still rings a bell for some people today, it is without any doubt for his role as a reformer of the Belgian prison system, having influenced reflection on this theme all over Europe. But although there is surely a link between the law and the existence of prisons, his role was more what we today would call that of political activist, journalist, and senior civil servant, rather than that of a jurist in the more classical sense of the word.

Nevertheless, Ducpétiaux, born in Brussels into a family of wealthy merchants who dealt in lace, received his legal education at the universities of Ghent, Liège, and Leiden, where he was influenced by Kantian and Spinozist thinking in the tradition of Johannes Kinker (1764–1845). After his graduation, he established himself as an attorney in Brussels, but focused his activity, like many of his colleagues, on the press, where he gained fame as a staunch opponent of the government of King William I of the Netherlands. His most important achievement was the publication of a book on capital punishment in 1827, which provoked the anger of the legal elites of those days. One year later, he was thrown into prison after publishing an article in the liberal newspaper *Courrier des Pays-Bas* in favour of two expelled colleagues, making him a martyr for freedom of the press. During these years, he was also a member of the reformist and anti-clerical *Société belge pour la propagation de l'instruction et de la morale*.

When the 1830 revolution broke out, Ducpétiaux proved to be a keen supporter of the alliance between progressive Catholics and moderate liberals which formed the backbone of the revolutionary forces. Despite his reputation as a victim of the defeated regime, he was not elected as a member of the

---

[1] This biographical introduction is mostly based on the only full-scale biography of Ducpétiaux, written by Edmond Rubbens, *Edouard Ducpétiaux 1804–1868*. I/II (Louvain-Brussels: Dewit, 1922/Paris: Société d'études morales sociales et juridiques, 1934).

provisional parliament, the National Congress. In turn, he was appointed inspector-general of the prisons and welfare institutions of the country, a position he kept until 1861, making him the moral conscience of the country in this field. One of the reasons for his authority in this regard was his constant presence in the public debate, fuelled by the articles, brochures, and books he wrote, using the possibilities of the new science of statistics to support his calls for social reform. It was therefore not a coincidence that, when the government instituted a Central Commission for Statistics in 1841, Ducpétiaux was one of its founding members. His reputation soon passed the national borders, which gave him the opportunity to augment his argumentation with data and experiences from abroad.

Although he had been one of the more radical voices in the early days of the 1830 revolution, and even until the 1840s, Ducpétiaux soon considered himself a middle-of-the-road man very attached to the collaboration of liberal and Catholic moderates in the so-called unionist governments of the young kingdom of Belgium. Once the new state had acquired internal stability and international acceptance, the old fault lines again became more important. The replacement of the last unionist government by a cabinet that relied exclusively on liberal opinion profoundly shocked Ducpétiaux, who had learnt to appreciate the contribution of Catholic laymen and religious to the development of welfare initiatives and thus did not share the anti-clerical approach of his friends in government. *Nolens volens*, the old radical found himself on the other side of the trenches, although he was convinced that his worldview was still the same as in the days of King William.

During the last years of his life, Ducpétiaux proved his ability as an organizer, this time in the interests of the Catholic aspect of Belgian public opinion. In 1863, influenced by the example of the German *Katholikentag*, he was the driving force behind the organization of the Catholic Congress of Malines, an experience that was repeated in 1864 and 1867, each time with Ducpétiaux as its secretary general and chief organizer. Also in 1864, he founded the *Revue générale*, established to be the intellectual voice of Belgian Catholicism. Only his death in 1868 prevented him from undertaking further initiatives in the organization of Catholic opinion in Belgium and all over Europe.

MAJOR THEMES AND CONTRIBUTIONS

Pragmatism and the Use of Modern Sciences

While it may seem easy to define Ducpétiaux's major themes, it is not easy to sum up his most important contributions to Christian legal thinking, for various reasons. In the first place, Ducpétiaux was more a man of action than a theorist: he was influential by choosing his battles and insisting for many years on the reforms he thought necessary. And although he had been trained as a lawyer and had been a member of the Brussels bar for some years, his scientific method was more influenced by such 'modern' sciences as statistics and the rising science of sociology than by more traditional legal thinking.

Regarding Ducpétiaux as a 'Christian jurist', another problem arises. Both from a religious and from an intellectual and political perspective, there seems to be a bit of a paradox between the liberal and anti-clerical Ducpétiaux of his early years and the Catholic intellectual of his last years. However, Ducpétiaux himself denied the existence of any rupture between these two periods in his life. On the face of it, there is indeed an important continuity in his thinking. But how to explain the change of allegiance if not by the commonplace that not he but instead those who used to be his allies had changed?

For this reason, we will try to do the reverse exercise. Starting with Ducpétiaux's role in the Malines Congresses, we will try to understand to what extent there was a form of continuity in Ducpétiaux's thinking before and after his political and religious conversion of the 1850s.

Of course, this approach also presents some disadvantages. First, it tends to reduce the intellectual life of Ducpétiaux to a simple antithesis between liberalism and Catholicism. As rightly stated by Hans Moors,[2] Ducpétiaux's legacy is far more complex, including also pre-socialist influences. Nevertheless, the way the continuity question is presented here is also the way the older Ducpétiaux himself felt it should be presented.

Once a Liberal, Always a Liberal?

On the other hand, the question of the intellectual evolution of an author cannot be reduced to his evolution in a world that would remain stable otherwise. This is especially relevant for the relationship between Catholicism and liberalism in Belgium in the second third of the nineteenth century. As we mentioned before, the 1830 revolution in Belgium was supported by an alliance between moderate liberals and progressive Catholics – implying that on both sides there were groups that did not join the revolutionary movement or at least were less prominent in the new order of things. This is especially true for the older generation of liberals, whose anticlericalism prevented them from joining

---

[2] Hans Moors, 'Edouard Ducpétiaux (1804–1868): scènes uit een steeds weer vergeten leven', in *Universalis. Liber amicorum Cyrille Fijnaut*, eds. Toine Spapens, Marc Groenhuijsen, and Tijs Kooijmans (Antwerp; Cambridge: Intersentia, 2011), 529–544.

forces with Catholics in order to put an end to the enlightened, but authoritarian, reign of William I of the Netherlands. These people and their political heirs abstained from Belgian mainstream politics in the first years after the revolution and formed the backbone of the counter-revolutionary Orangist party. The same goes also for a smaller but socially influential section of reactionary Catholics.

When after some twenty years it became clear that the 1830 revolution and its product, the Kingdom of Belgium, would not be a nine-day wonder, more and more former counter-revolutionaries decided to integrate with the new structures and to collaborate loyally, if not enthusiastically, with the new regime. While they abandoned their rejection of the new state, they did not, however, leave behind all of their former convictions. This is especially true for the bulk of the former Orangists, who joined the mainstream liberal party, bringing along their tradition of radical anticlericalism.

The formal reunification of the liberal forces during the founding congress of the official liberal party in 1846 was also the beginning of the end for the tradition of governing the country by 'unionist' governments, in which liberals and Catholics worked together. From 1847 onward, Belgium started experimenting with party government. Already by 1848, Ducpétiaux was very critical of the organization of the public service under the new government, which he criticized for its attempts to limit civil servants' independence.[3] However, at this time, Ducpétiaux did not consider this question to be linked to more fundamental or ideological questions. The rift between him and his former liberal friends would only increase during the following years.

Ducpétiaux was not completely wrong in considering himself to belong with a different type of liberal to those in charge of the party in the 1860s. If anybody could appropriately state that it was not he, but his party, that had changed, it was Ducpétiaux – even if this was to mean that his brand of liberalism had become a relic of a bygone age by 1865. In his 1857 book *La question de la charité et des associations religieuses en Belgique* he explicitly compared the liberal attack on religious welfare institutions to the politics that had caused the end of the Kingdom of the Netherlands in 1830.[4] In his eyes, he had always attacked those politics, and if this attitude brought him first into

---

[3] R. Depré, *De topambtenaren van de ministeries in België* (Leuven: Faculty of Social Sciences, 1973), 87.
[4] During the second Malines congress, the president of the congress, de Gerlache, went even further during a toast in honour of Ducpétiaux, calling the liberal demonstrations against a legislative initiative in order to give legal standing to (mostly Catholic) welfare initiatives 'a kind of counterrevolution', *Assemblée générale des catholiques en Belgique. Deuxième session à Malines*, II (Brussels: Devaux, 1865), 675.

the ranks of the liberal party, and later that of their adversaries, he was ready to accept this.

In other words, Ducpétiaux suggested that his principles were unchanged, even if the way he chose to realize them was completely different. Even if during the first Malines Congress, Ducpétiaux stayed mostly behind the scenes, stressing his role as the director of the Congress, he abandoned his restraint on some occasions to defend one of his favourite ideas – the idea of a 'statistics' of Catholicism, to which we will revert later, but also to remind his fellow believers of the importance of such liberal values as liberty and transparency. Even when the discussion concerned the organization of Catholics in Belgium and Europe, Ducpétiaux defended the principle of liberty as a starting point, rather than a strictly hierarchical blueprint.[5]

When defending his darling idea of a statistics of Catholicism, Ducpétiaux seized the opportunity to stress the fundamental importance of this instrument, even at the level of principle:

> Catholicism has nothing to fear from publicity, it has nothing to hide, it is even interested in bringing out into the open all the facts that concern it, in order to make the light it carries shine as far as possible. Its constitution, its institutions, its works, its progress, its situation at all times and in all places, must inspire it with legitimate confidence [...] It is by truth and truth alone that it will overcome [...]. It has been said that statistics is a two-edged sword that often hurts the helpless or unfaithful hands that handle it. We want it to become a sincere instrument, a wide-open book where everyone can read without fear of error.[6]

Even if this belief was mainly aimed at a specific point regarding the publishing of facts and figures about Catholic initiatives and organizations, it also reflected a more fundamental part of Ducpétiaux's thinking, namely that truth, and not force, would be the source of victory for Catholic principles – a belated echo of the battle cry of the revolutionaries of 1830, that is, 'a free church in a free state'.

---

[5] *Assemblée générale des catholiques en Belgique. Première session à Malines*, I (Bruxelles: H. Goemaere, 1864), 166.

[6] *Assemblée générale des catholiques en Belgique. Première session à Malines*, I (Bruxelles: H. Goemaere, 1864), 224: '*Le catholicisme n'a rien à redouter de la publicité, il n'a rien à cacher, il est intéressé même à produire au grand jour tous les faits qui le concernent, afin de faire rayonner au plus loin la lumière qu'il porte en lui. Sa constitution, ses institutions, ses œuvres, ses progrès, sa situations dans tous les temps et dans tous les lieux, doivent lui inspirer une légitime confiance [...] C'est par la vérité et par la vérité seule qu'il vaincra les uns et qu'il fortifiera les autres. On a dit que la statistique était une arme à deux tranchants qui blessait souvent les mains inhabiles ou infidèles qui la maniaient. Nous voulons, nous, qu'elle devienne un instrument sincère, un livre largement ouvert où chacun puisse lire sans crainte d'erreur*'.

During the second session in 1865, Ducpétiaux not only elaborated his plan regarding a statistics of Catholicism, but added another theme to his repertoire. Indeed Ducpétiaux intervened in the working group on 'the organisation of modern industry', this being the code word for the social responsibility of Catholic entrepreneurs.[7] Soon, he came to understand that his more interventionist approach did not appeal to the majority of the participants, and steered away from the subject.

Indeed, although Ducpétiaux acquired most of his reputation as the reformer of prisons, his vision of welfare was undoubtedly larger. Over the years, he wrote on the funding of the working class,[8] the importance of workers' associations as a means to the solution of the social question[9] and on primary education.[10] Being the opposite of a materialist, he had always stressed the importance of the ethical, spiritual, and religious element in social reform, for instance in the rehabilitation of former convicts:

> But the success of this organization depends above all on the introduction of the moral and religious element in the discipline of prisons; the most perfect constructions, the best regulations, will be powerless unless the voice of the pious man strikes the culprit in his loneliness and gives him the strength and courage to bear his punishment with resignation and to work for his amendment.[11]

This emphasis on the moral element was in fact not limited to the context of prison reform but was an important element of Ducpétiaux's social thinking. In some way his approach can be qualified as holist, as he deemed it inevitable to establish cross-connections between the different fields of social action: prison reform; education, including compulsory education; reform of the asylums for the insane; minimum wages; the limitation of child labour; an improved food regime for the poor ... These were for him

---

[7] *Assemblée générale des catholiques en Belgique. Deuxième session à Malines*, I (Brussels: Devaux, 1865), 244.
[8] *Budgets économiques des classes ouvrières en Belgique* (Brussels: Hayez, 1855).
[9] *De l'association dans ses rapports avec l'amélioration du sort de la classe ouvrière* (Brussels: Hayez, 1860).
[10] *Quelques mots sur l'état actuel de l'instruction primaire en Belgique* (Brussels: Weissenbruch, 1839).
[11] Quoted in Rubbens, *Ducpétiaux*. I, 169: '*Mais le succès de cette organisation dépend avant tout de l'introduction de l'élément moral et religieux dans la discipline des prisons; les constructions les plus parfaites, les règlements les mieux combinés, seront impuissants, si la voix de l'homme pieux ne va frapper le coupable dans sa solitude et ne lui donne la force et le courage de supporter sa peine avec résignation et de travailler à l'œuvre de son amendement*'.

aspects of the general question of social progress, rather than separate issues.[12]

On the other hand, he did not believe that the voluntary effort of the rich, inspired by Christian virtues, would be sufficient to solve the social question. Already by 1843, he had proclaimed that the rich lacked in charity, and he advocated a 'ministry of progress'.[13] However, the intervention of the state in the field of welfare should not free the rich from their moral and charitable duties: both had their own task in the organization of welfare, and only their collaboration could bring about a stable solution to the social question. It was the state's responsibility to create a framework, including a legislative framework, that would allow private initiative to flourish and to fill the gaps left by the temporary or structural absence of these private initiatives – but nothing more[14] – as virtue was for Ducpétiaux eminently a personal characteristic, while vice was a collective phenomenon.[15] It is interesting that he favoured a parallel approach to the organization of education: rather than a model of total liberty, as defended by most Catholic authors in Belgium in those days, or a model of state-organized education, Ducpétiaux preferred a model in which the state would establish the framework, which should be filled in by private, including religious, initiative.[16]

The most striking example of Ducpétiaux's approach in this sense was, however, his influence on the legislation regarding the reintegration of former offenders into society. In this field, the state appealed in an almost systematic way to the help of well-meaning citizens, but this did not imply that the relationship between the public authorities and private benefactors was seamless.[17] For Ducpétiaux the reason for these problems was fundamentally a question of organization: the volunteers and religious worked under the authority of the management of the prisons, which underestimated the moral element of reintegration and mistook the penitentiary system for a mere repressive system.[18] According to Ducpétiaux, this

---

[12] M.-S. Dupont-Bouchat, *De la prison à l'école. Les pénitenciers pour enfants en Belgique au XIXe siècle* (Heule: UGA, 1996), 28.
[13] Th. Juste, *Notice sur Edouard Ducpétiaux* (Brussels: Devaux, 1871), 32 ; R. Riche, *Ducpétiaux* (Brescia: La Scuola, 1950), 84–85.
[14] Edouard Ducpétiaux, *La question de la charité et des associations religieuses en Belgique* (Brussels: Goemaere, 1858), 37 and Riche, *Ducpétiaux*, 126.
[15] Rubbens, *Ducpétiaux. I*, 198.
[16] Riche, *Ducpétiaux*, 136.
[17] M.-S. Dupont Bouchat, 'La Belgique capitale internationale du patronage au XIXe siècle', in *La Belgique criminelle. Droit, justice, société (XIVe-Xe siècles). Marie-Sylvie Dupont-Bouchat*, eds. X. Rousseaux and G. Le Clercq (Louvain-la-Neuve: Bruylant, 2006), 385–431.
[18] Rubbens, *Ducpétiaux. I*, 128, 215.

approach was in complete contradiction to the roots of a modern approach to prisons: it was precisely in the history of ecclesiastical penal law, in which improving the offender's moral standards was more important than punishing him, that the idea of imprisonment as a form of punishment had originated.[19] In order to make this approach work, the prisons needed staff members who were better qualified than the average ushers. The least expensive way to involve such people in the management of the prisons was to employ religious, most notably the Brothers of Scheppers, in the Belgian prisons.[20]

It was therefore no coincidence that Ducpétiaux's breach with the liberal movement did not take place immediately after the breakdown of unionist government, but at the precise moment when the liberal government unfolded its plans to take more or less the whole field of welfare into the government's hands. His 1857 book *La question de la charité et des associations religieuses en Belgique* was his personal crossing of the Rubicon. It is therefore not amazing that his first biographer, Théodore Juste, considers this book to be his most important work.[21]

In this book, he also clearly stated his ambition to stay a liberal – although in a specific understanding of the term:

> If we take this word [liberalism] in its most vulgar and at the same time most true acceptance, liberalism is the application of law, justice, truth, tolerance in the political sphere and in social relations. [...] Have I changed since then, and like so many others have I abdicated my independence to court the powerful of the day and beg the applause of the crowd? No. What I was before 1830, I still am today.[22]

His vigorous denial of being a renegade was not only a firm declaration, but also demonstrated his views, for instance, his ongoing belief in the theories of Thomas Malthus, not exactly an author who enjoyed particular sympathy in

---

[19] M.-S. Dupont-Bouchat, 'Ducpétiaux ou le rêve cellulaire', *Déviance et Société* 12.1 (1986): 1, 3–4 and B. Vanhulle, 'Dreaming about the prison: Edouard Ducpétiaux and Prison Reform in Belgium (1830–1848)', *Crime, History & Societies* 14.2 (2010): 14.

[20] Vanhulle, 'Dreaming', 39.

[21] Juste, *Ducpétiaux*, 36.

[22] Ducpétiaux, *Charité*, xiv: '*Si l'on prend ce mot [libéralisme] dans son acceptation la plus vulgaire et en même temps la plus vraie, le libéralisme est l'application du droit, de la justice, de la vérité, de la tolérance dans la sphère politique et dans les relations sociales. [...] Ai-je varié depuis, et comme tant d'autres ai-je abdiqué mon indépendance pour courtiser les puissants du jour et mendier les applaudissements de la foule ? Non. Ce que j'étais avant 1830, je le suis encore aujourd'hui*'.

Catholic circles.[23] In this context it is worth noting that Ducpétiaux's political conversion predated his religious conversion for some years, the former being the logical consequence of his own thinking, the latter also being influenced by the personal evolution of his second wife.[24] This might be seen as representative of his worldviews, which gave priority to political and practical questions above philosophical, theological – and even legal – debates.

A Catholic and a Child of His Time

That Ducpétiaux did not deny his liberal antecedents is also clear when we analyze his readings and friendships. His library, which can be found today in the Royal Academy of Belgium in Brussels,[25] contained above all plenty of technical studies and pamphlets on the topics about which he was passionate, such as prison reform and welfare policies. When we look at his choice of contemporary authors on questions of philosophy, politics, and social science, we find plenty of early socialist authors, with a prominent place for the Spanish anarchist author Ramon de la Sagra (1798–1871), which may corroborate the views of Hans Moors.[26] These authors are only outnumbered by kindred spirits of Ducpétiaux, who belong to the category of more progressive and socially active Christians. Notorious examples of those writers, and very present in his library, are people like Augustin Cochin (1823–1872), who was a lifelong adversary of slavery and a promotor of the synthesis of Christianity and liberty. Another name that pops up regularly is that of Charles Dupin (1784–1873), the French mathematician and middle-of-the-road politician, who wrote a lot on social reform but remarkably was in favour of slavery. A third name that should be mentioned is that of Willem Hendrik Suringar (1790–1872) who played in the Netherlands more or less the same role as Ducpétiaux in the context of prison reform, although from a Protestant background.

On the other hand, his stand on social and ideological matters would indicate that he would not join the new and growing group of politically

---

[23] Riche, *Ducpétiaux*, 101. For an example, see Edouard Ducpétiaux, *Les ordres monastiques et religieux* (Brussels: Devaux, 1865), 76, where he invokes Malthus to defend the requirement of celibacy for Catholic priests.
[24] Riche, *Ducpétiaux*, 27.
[25] An inventory can be found at https://tresorsdelacademie.be/fr/bibliotheque/fonds-speciaux#Ducpetiaux.
[26] See note 2. Ducpétiaux had also been visiting Saint-Simonist meetings in the early 1830s, according to Dupont-Bouchat, 'Rêve cellulaire', 7.

active Catholics called ultramontanes.[27] If there had been any doubt on this, an incident during the third Malines Congress finally made clear that there was a watershed between this type of Catholicism and Ducpétiaux's. Indeed, although he had always resisted the view that welfare policy had to be a monopoly of the state, his pragmatic approach had brought him to recognize the necessity of legislative measures to protect basic rights for workers, and especially for the women and children among them. Joseph de Hemptinne (1822–1909), an industrialist from Ghent and spokesman for the more conservative group in the Congress, opposed the discussion in the context of a Catholic congress of relations between labour and capital – and even more so if this discussion was about putting legislative measures in place.[28] Later on, the two clashed again, this time on the question whether lay people could make proposals to the clergy in order to improve their work for the good of the church. What seemed evident to Ducpétiaux was experienced by other lay people as a lack of respect.

This altercation can be seen as illustrative of Ducpétiaux's brand of Christianity. His Catholicism was all but clericalism, and rather than stressing the specific position of priests and the clergy in society, he tended to remind his adversaries and his allies that they were, in the first place, citizens of their country, and thus holders of all the fundamental rights that the Belgian constitution of 1831 guaranteed. His defence of the rights of the church was therefore not based on arguments inspired by theological or natural law thinking, but by post-revolutionary positive law and the new sciences of sociology and statistics. Ducpétiaux warned both his adversaries and some of his allies that a strong bond between the church and the state had been the root of different forms of abuse.[29] Those who tended to glorify the pre-revolutionary times, known for the alliance of the church and the state, in Ducpétiaux's eyes opened the door for a new form of submission of the religious order to the political order. On the other hand, some heralds of freedom seemed to forget that it was logically impossible to state that freedom of religion and association were fundamental rights in a modern state, while simultaneously denying these freedoms to religious associations, as if their nature could be a ground for stringent limitations to their freedom. The principle of the free church in a free state, which had been one of the more popular slogans of the Belgian

---

[27] On the growth of ultramontanism in Belgium in the second half of the nineteenth century, see E. Lamberts, ed., *De kruistocht tegen het liberalisme. Aspecten van het ultramontanisme in België in de negentiende eeuw* (Louvain: Peeters, 1984).

[28] *Assemblée générale des catholiques en Belgique. Troisième session à Malines.* II (Brussels: Devaux, 1868), 70 and 114.

[29] Ducpétiaux, *Les ordres*, vii.

revolution of 1830, stayed at the heart of Ducpétiaux's thinking about the relationship between church and state.

In fact, Ducpétiaux argued, there was a confusion between the question whether liberties could be subject to limits and conditions and the question whether these limits and conditions should be justified and proportioned.[30] For him, liberal radicals jumped to conclusions when they assumed that every measure against religious orders could be justified by the possibility of restricting fundamental freedoms. The real question was whether these restrictions were justified by urgent needs of society and were commensurate with the goal they pursued, the burden of proof resting with those who wanted to impose a restriction on the principle of freedom,[31] for liberty had to be the basic principle of modern society:

> Freedom! This must be the motto of all men of good faith, whatever opinion they profess. It is on this ground alone that the great problems that trouble the world can be discussed widely and fairly. Solutions by coercion, by force, are no longer of our age; those who resort to them lack confidence in their principle; they offend the truth by implying that it is not powerful enough to triumph on its own, through the legitimate action of reasoning and persuasion.[32]

But Ducpétiaux would not have been Ducpétiaux if he had limited his argument to the level of the general principles. Above all, he stressed the utility of many initiatives that had been taken from religious inspiration at grassroots level. To restrict these bottom-up initiatives would leave needy people without help, and especially those categories of needy people who saw themselves confronted with new forms of misery. To set up a state-sponsored, top-down answer to these new challenges would take lots of time, money[33] and energy, at the expense of the poor.

---

[30] This approach can be read as an echo of the programme of the Catholic government, led by Pieter De Decker in 1855: 'Liberté de la charité, mais aussi garanties sociales contre les abus éventuels de cette liberté', see Juste, Ducpétiaux, 36.
[31] Ducpétiaux, Charité, xi.
[32] Ducpétiaux, Charité, xix: 'Liberté! Telle doit être la devise de tous les hommes de bonne foi, quelle que soit l'opinion qu'ils professent. C'est sur ce terrain seul que peuvent se débattre largement, loyalement les grands problèmes qui agitent le monde. Les solutions par la contrainte, par la force ne sont plus de notre âge; ceux qui y ont recours manquent de confiance dans leur principe; ils outragent la vérité en faisant supposer qu'elle n'a pas assez de puissance pour triompher par elle-même, par l'action légitime du raisonnement et de la persuasion'.
[33] Typical for Ducpétiaux was the use of detailed figures about the financial impact of the Christian welfare initiatives in order to make his point – see for instance Ducpétiaux, Les ordres, 204.

This kind of pragmatism can already be found in Ducpétiaux's debut, his 1827 essay *De la peine de mort*, where he explicitly stated that not legal science nor metaphysics but personal experience and facts would be decisive for his reasoning.[34] And indeed, arguments that are deduced from belief or philosophy are strikingly absent in this controversial work. Although the author did not hesitate to call himself a Christian, the only references to religion in the book seem to concern the condemnation of religious fanaticism that were a usual topos in the post-Enlightenment literature of those days. Nevertheless, Ducpétiaux had not the slightest problem in repeating his more than thirty-year-old views on the question in an article of the *Revue générale* in 1865,[35] although his position in the public debate had dramatically shifted in the meantime. His consistent refusal to mix his views on society in general and on the law in particular with his philosophical and ideological standpoints was the precondition for his ability to evolve in the political and religious debate without losing his credibility.

GENERAL APPRAISAL AND INFLUENCE

For today's readers it is difficult to understand Ducpétiaux's influence, especially if we want to define this influence as that of a 'Christian jurist'. When we define 'Christian' as being persistently and in every field influenced by the Gospel and Christian tradition, Ducpétiaux does not answer to this definition. When we define 'jurist' as someone whose professional or scientific contribution consists in the production of legal documents or doctrine, Ducpétiaux does not fit this definition either.

Nevertheless, for at least a century after his passing, he has been promoted as a key figure of social Catholicism in Belgium and abroad, as the man who made it possible to find predecessors for the more progressive strand of Christianism that was dominant in Belgian intellectual and political circles in the second half of the twentieth century.

In part, this view of Ducpétiaux can be qualified correctly as the 'myth Ducpétiaux', a romanticized story, based on Ducpétiaux's own view of his life, consecrated by an uncritical biographer and freed from criticism thanks to the absence of a personal archive of Ducpétiaux.[36] Yet, the fact that Ducpétiaux himself supported the birth of this approach to his thinking makes it difficult to

---

[34] Edouard Ducpétiaux, *De la peine de mort* (Brussels: Tarlier, 1827), xii and xxiii.
[35] Printed separately as Edouard Ducpétiaux, *La question de la peine de mort envisagée dans son actualité* (Brussels: Comptoir universel d'imprimerie, 1865).
[36] Vanhulle, 'Dreaming', 16.

set it aside as a complete myth without any connection with his actual ideas. However, the 'reduction' of Ducpétiaux to the historical predecessor of a specific brand of Christian social thinking does not take into account the complexity and the evolution of his ideas.

It is clear that this multiple interpretation finds its source at least in part in a kind of vagueness regarding Ducpétiaux's thinking – or stated more positively – in the independence of any philosophical, ideological, or religious presupposition of the most fundamental elements of his views. It may be the most objective way to qualify this fact to say that his thinking as such was not precisely a form of Christian thinking, but that it was nevertheless very influential among Christian thinkers of the following generations. Two of these were Jules Le Jeune, minister of justice between 1887 and 1894 and an influential reformer of criminal law in Belgium, and Ducpétiaux's biographer Edmond Rubbens, who was inter alia minister of social affairs and a well-known polemic against the influence of more reactionary forms of Catholic social thinking, as represented by the French author Charles Maurras.

That leaves the question whether Ducpétiaux can reasonably qualify as a jurist – at least when a law degree is not deemed sufficient to so qualify. Even if none of the dozens of books, brochures, and articles Ducpétiaux wrote can be considered part of legal literature in the strict sense of the term, one cannot deny that the overwhelming majority deals with problems of a legal nature. These are predominantly the two fields in which Ducpétiaux established the core of his reputation, namely capital punishment and prison reform. But his other writings mostly discuss improvements to the legal framework of his time, which makes it difficult to deny him qualification as a jurist. As in the House of the Father, there are many dwelling places in the law.

RECOMMENDED READINGS

Dupont-Bouchat, Marie-Sylvie. 'Ducpétiaux ou le rêve cellulaire'. *Déviance et Société* 12.1 (1986): 1–27.
Dupont-Bouchat, Marie-Sylvie. *De la prison à l'école. Les pénitenciers pour enfants en Belgique au XIXe siècle*. Heule: UGA, 1996.
Juste, Théodore. *Notice sur Edouard Ducpétiaux, membre de l'Académie*. Brussels: Devaux, 1871.
Rubbens, Edmond. *Edouard Ducpétiaux 1804–1868*. I/II. Louvain-Brussels: Dewit, 1922/Paris: Société d'études morales sociales et juridiques, 1934.
Vanhulle, Bert. 'Dreaming about the prison: Edouard Ducpétiaux and Prison Reform in Belgium (1830–1848)'. *Crime, History & Societies* 14.2 (2010): 107–130.

14

Charles Périn

Fred Stevens

BIOGRAPHICAL INTRODUCTION

Henri Xavier Charles Périn was born in Mons on 25 August 1815. He was the son of Paul François Charles, Imperial Receiver-General in Mons, and Mary F. J. F. Gigault, who emigrated to Germany at the arrival of the French revolutionary armies. This resulted in a counter-revolutionary family tradition. After his secondary education in his hometown, he continued his studies at the Faculty of Law of the Catholic University of Louvain. He was strongly influenced by Charles de Coux, the first holder of the Chair of Political Economy, appointed as professor in 1834 at the newly created Catholic University. On 2 November 1842 Périn enrolled as a lawyer–trainee at the Brussels Bar under the supervision of the liberal advocate Dolez, also a native of Mons.

On 15 September 1844, Périn was appointed professor at the University of Louvain for courses in internal and external public law and administrative law. The following year, when de Coux returned to Paris to take charge of *L'Univers*, the bishops decided to appoint Périn to the course in political economy and statistics. Later he would be also responsible for the course in the law of nations. After his move to Louvain, he enrolled in 1851 at the bar of this city. He remained a lawyer until his resignation from the university in 1881. From 1882 until his death in 1905, he was registered as a lawyer at the bar in Mons. On 28 November 1848, he married Elise-Sabine Dubois.[1]

The relationship of conflict between the Liberals, who had formed into a party in 1846, and their Catholic opponents, would worsen as a result of growing internal conflicts (the law of the convents, liberal school policy ...)

---

[1] Victor Brants, 'Charles Périn: notice sur sa vie et ses travaux', *Annuaire de l'Université catholique de Louvain* 70 (1906): XIV–LIV; Armand Louant, 'Périn', *Biographie nationale* 30 (1958): 665–671.

and external sources (the unification of Italy ...).² The rejection of modern freedom and liberalism and socialism by Pius IX in the encyclical *Quanta Cura* and the *Syllabus Errorum* in 1864 radicalized Belgian ultramontanism. From supporter of liberal Catholicism, Périn evolved toward secular leader of the ultramontanes, opponents of constitutional freedoms. In 1868, the Pope received Périn in audience. Assertive in his ideas, he thought himself invested in the mission to defend the 'real principles'.³ Under his presidency the *ultras* would form the *Confrérie de Saint-Michel* in 1875.

When the bishops of northern France decided in 1875 to create the Catholic University of Lille, they offered him the post of professor of the law of nations and political economy courses. However, as he was not French, the French minister, Waddington, refused him the necessary authorization.

After the war of 1870, social action was organized in France. In January 1876, Périn contributed to the first issue of *La revue de l'Association catholique*. Soon differences would break out. At the Congress of Chartres, in September 1878, Périn opposed Count de Mun on the question of mandatory corporatism. *Catholic economists*, along with Périn, constituted a group which was soon called the School of Angers. They declared themselves opponents of a return to the mandatory corporate system and advocated freedom of labour and freedom of association between boss and worker.

In Louvain, in mid-1878, Woeste and Beernaert denounced remarks to cardinal Deschamps vis-à-vis the teaching of Périn.⁴ Within the Faculty of Law Périn was not uncontroversial. Progressives such as Thonissen opposed him personally, and opposed ultramontanism. The split became clear in the case of canon Ferdinand Moulart. If, within the episcopate, Cardinal Deschamps was a defender of constitutional liberalism, the bishops of Mons, Namur, and Tournai argued for the ultramontanes. Monseigneur Dumont, bishop of Tournai, strove to condemn Moulart's book *L'Église et l'État* [Church and State] to Rome. The response of Périn to this work was completely negative. The death of Pius IX, on 7 February 1878, was a real game changer. The advent of Leo XIII allowed the book's publication. Many times,

---

² Emiel Lamberts, 'Het ultramontanisme in België 1830–1914', in *De Kruistocht tegen het Liberalisme*, ed. Emiel Lamberts (Louvain: Universitaire Pers Leuven, 1984), 38–63; Karel van Isacker, *Werkelijke en wettelijk land. De katholieke opinie tegenover de rechterzijde 1862–1884* (Antwerp: Standaard Boekhandel, 1955), 62–85.
³ Armand Louant, 'Charles Périn et Pie IX', *Bulletin de l'Institut historique belge de Rome* 27 (1952): 181–220.
⁴ Emiel Lamberts, 'De Leuvense universiteit op een belangrijk keerpunt tijdens het rectoraat van A. J. Namèche en C. Pieraerts (1872–1887)', in *L'Église et l'État à l'époque contemporaine. Mélanges dédiés à la mémoire de mgr Aloïs Simon'*, eds. Gaston Braive and Jacques Lory (Brussels: Presses de l'Université Saint-Louis, 1975), 337–369.

Périn had severely judged Cardinal Deschamps, the University, liberal Catholics, and the parliamentary right in letters to Bishop Dumont. Affected by madness, Dumont was removed on 22 October 1880 by Leo XIII. Furious at having to resign, Dumont published these documents in liberal newspapers. The Belgian bishops requested a letter of reparation from Périn addressed to the cardinal and to the university. Supported by the bishop of Namur, he refused. A further publication of letters by Dumont precipitated the conflict. At the request of Monseigneur Goossens, Périn was summoned to Rome. Périn was blamed implicitly in the encyclical *Licet Multa* of 3 August 1881, addressed to the Belgian bishops, who advocated the unity of Catholics and disavowed ultramontane activities. He left the University of Louvain and retired to Ghlin.[5]

From that moment, Périn no longer involved himself in Belgian affairs, and returned to France. In 1896, he published his last work, the second edition of the *Premiers principes de l'économie politique*. He died on 4 April 1905.

MAJOR THEMES AND CONTRIBUTIONS

Unshakeable Faith

On the occasion of the publication of the book of Émile Keller *L'encyclique du 8 décembre 1863 et les principes de 1789* (Paris: Poussielgue, 1865/1866) [The encyclical of December 8, 1862 and the principles of 1789], Périn published in the newspaper *Le Catholique* on 22 September 1866 his article *L'encyclique de 8 décembre et le progrès social* [The encyclical of December 8, 1826 and social progress]. He defended the principle that the rule of conduct of Catholics 'is still, for civilian life as for the spiritual life, in the decisions of the Roman Pontiff, who received the mission to define, in the name of God himself and of his authority, the grand principles of the dogmatic and moral order'. A first condition of progress in social life was the acceptance of the teachings and the discipline of the church. The church professed the principle of submission to God, which was followed as a practical consequence by the duty of sacrifice and charity. The Revolution however professed man as master of himself. The idea of obedience was the guiding principle for the ideas of Périn. It was found explicitly in his article *La proclamation du dogme et de l'infaillibilité pontificale* [The proclamation of the dogma and the papal infallibility], published in *Le contemporain* of 1 August 1870: 'Catholics are fully obedient Christians.'

---

[5] M. Becqué and Armand Louant, 'Le dossier "Rome et Louvain" de Charles Périn', *Revue d'Histoire Écclésiastique* 50 (1955): 36–124.

Périn and Political Economy

By June 1839, Périn had published *Du progrès des idées religieuses en économie politique* [Progress of religious ideas in political economy], a conference he had held in the *Société Littéraire* of the Catholic University of Louvain under the leadership of Professor Arendt, in the *Revue de Bruxelles* (pp. 101–129). Before showing the progress of Catholic ideas in political economy, he wanted to demonstrate in this paper how and why the science of political economy had departed from these Catholic ideas. With exceptional rhetorical talent, he had already advanced the principle of the necessity of sacrifice, a principle which dominated the entire moral world. Catholicism was only the development, the practical implementation, of this idea.

The following year, at the end of 1840, he published his article *Les intérêts matériels dans la société moderne* [Material interests in modern society], which constituted a continuation of the first article, in the *Société Littéraire*.[6] He argued that some sophists had made modern nations, whose great concern was material interests, believe that there was a fundamental incompatibility between material interests and the moral interests of which Catholicism was the natural defender. The result was the prejudice that Catholicism was an enemy of prosperity, and thus there was an obligation to demonstrate that Catholics do not intend to destroy material development, but, in the interest of social equilibrium, they seek to direct it, to bring it into harmony with the moral development of nations. For Périn, in contrast to individualism, source of many evils, the church proposed charity. Referring to history, he objected to Protestantism, '[which] had declared that reason was sufficient to itself for the explanation of the Holy Books', while the *Philosophes* went so far as to give reason 'a sovereign and absolute authority'.

The following year, as a result of the events of 1848, he published *Les économistes, le socialisme et les chrétiens* [Economists, socialism and Christians]. In this book, he argued that the English economy, with its principle of the indefinite development of needs, 'by constituting social science on sensualist data, prepared the way for the socialist destroyers'. The principle of indefinite development of the needs of the political economy cannot be reconciled with Christian doctrine, in which the ideas of good and virtue are inseparable from charity. For Périn, there is no real progress for society or for the individual without the principle of moral development. Against the seductions of sensualism, he proposed the severities of Christian

---

[6] Charles Périn, 'Des intérêts matériels dans la société moderne', *Société littéraire de l'Université catholique de Louvain. Choix de mémoires*, I (Louvain: Vanlinthout et Vandenzande, 1841), 84–130.

renunciation. Renunciation, sacrifice, was the source of all progress. In all his work on political economy, the principle of 'Christian renunciation' constituted his guideline. He developed this idea in *Du socialisme dans les écrits des économistes* [Socialism in the writings of economists], published in *Le Correspondant* (Paris) on 25 September 1850 and in *Du progres matériel et du renoncement chrétien* [Material progress and Christian renunciation], published in the same review on August 25 and October 25, 1854.

The idea of 'Christian renunciation' is also the guideline of his book *Les richesses dans les sociétés chrétiennes* [Wealth in Christian societies], whose first edition dates to 1861, the second to 1868, and the third, revised and completed, to 1882. Its purpose was to reconcile material progress and Christian renunciation.[7] The first book, *De la richesse et du progres matériel en general* [Wealth and material progress in general], sets out its fundamental thesis. Renunciation was the law of any free creature. This renunciation, which reconciled itself with self-interest, also reconciled individual interest with social interest. Individual interest was even one of the indispensable forces of social order. From the fact that God created mankind improvable followed the legitimacy of moral and material progress. For Périn, the law of renunciation offered various aspects. It was through the spirit of renunciation that wealth was able to grow. These were the products of work and savings. Work was pain, sacrifice, so renunciation was necessary for the creation of wealth. The concept of the association, which required the participation of everyone in the requirements of the common action, demanded personal self-sacrifice. But this sponsorship had to be voluntary, freely granted, and freely accepted. He fully accepted the principle of free competition, while expressing the wish that the spirit of justice and charity would soften the harshness of its application. The production of wealth required exchange, while the spirit of renunciation brought men together in a Christian spirit of moderation. Renunciation ensured equitable distribution of wealth and stopped oppression and exploitation. On the question of population, Périn considered that doctrines which encouraged population growth to meet the needs of production were the consequences of an indefinite will to enjoyment. He argued that the growth of the population was not a scourge that led to decadence and misery, but on the contrary, was 'a blessing, a sign, at the same time as a source of progress and strength', regulated by Providence. He opposed the doctrine of

---

[7] L. de Lavergne, 'De l'accord de l'économie politique et de la religion', *Revue des Deux Mondes* 42 (1862): 421–448; Paul-Lambert Michotte, *Études sur les théories économiques qui dominèrent en Belgique de 1830 à 1886* (Louvain: Charles Peeters, 1904), 377–378; Maarten van Dijck, *De wetenschap van de wetgever: de klassieke politieke economie en het Belgisch landbouwbeleid 1830–1884* (Louvain: Universitaire Pers Leuven, 2008), 4–77.

Thomas Malthus and argued that the church, by fortifying the man against himself, gave the means to wait in celibacy before starting a family. He even invoked the example of religious celibacy. With regard to salaries, for Périn, the spirit of charity and Christian equity was of great importance to soften the application of free competition. The sixth book dealt with ease and misery, the seventh with charity. Subtly, he distinguished poverty from misery. If poverty consisted in a state of embarrassment, it did not deprive man of freedom or dignity. Misery on the other hand led to moral and material decline. According to him, poverty extended in proportion to the influence exerted by the principles and customs of industrialism, with the example of England to support his argument. He traced a frightening picture of the state of the working classes of this country. As one of the main causes of this situation, he considered 'the absence of any serious action by the Anglican clergy and other heretical clergy on these classes'. It was on the other hand by the principle of charity that the principle of solidarity between the rich and the poor in the Catholic countries was fulfilled. The great merit of wealth remained the attempt to reconcile political economy and religion. For Périn, 'the Christian harmonies of the economic order' would ensure the equitable distribution of wealth, stop oppression and exploitation by the mighty, and enforce the laws of justice and the benefits of charity. The work was the result of long meditation. Périn fought materialism at the basis of economic liberalism and proposed as ideal 'the free and Christian corporation, uniting patrons and workers by achieving peace and progress through the generous effort of charity and renunciation under the legal guarantee of justice'. He opposed any intervention in economic and social matters.

At the General Assembly of Catholics meeting in Mechelen on 10 August 1863, Périn held the conference *De la mission sociale de la charité* [From the social mission of charity].[8] He supported the thesis that the workers' association, with a view to mutual assistance, was charity from 'the little ones to the little ones'. The upper classes had to return to patronage, 'the charity of the great towards the little ones'. By making acceptable to workers' associations the purely free and charitable patronage of the upper classes, the charity of the great and the little ones, responding to the same inspiration, merge into the same work: 'This is the plan that seems to respond to the situation that Providence has made us.' In his speech, Périn argued that he did not want to provoke a return to the old corporations: 'Free competition is the only law

---

[8] Paul Gérin, 'Les Écoles sociales belges et la lecture de rerum novarum', in *'Rerum novarum'. Écriture, contenu et réception d'une encyclique* (Rome: École française de Rome, 1997), 270–276.

that our societies can accept.' The purpose of the workers' associations was mutual assistance, mutual charity. However, according to Périn, associations too had to be charitable, they had to be essentially religious, since there was no charity without sacrifice and there was no sacrifice without religion. In the association reconstituted by Catholic charity, the working classes would find welfare, freedom, and dignity. Patronage, which he considered charitable, was the proper mission, the true dignity, and at the same time the greatest strength of the superior classes. In the providential order, the mission of these classes was to serve the societies. It was to charity in patronage that the upper classes appeared to the working classes as 'agents of Providence'. Clergy and religious orders should best exercise charitable patronage in all its forms.

In France, in 1862, a major investigation was opened on freedom of interest rates. A majority agreed the repeal of 1807 usury legislation. On 19 March 1862, the Senate considered the question of a petition signalling the inequality resulting from the legislation in force in the banking sector and that vis-à-vis foreign trade. The question was referred to the minister of Commerce. An investigation was opened by the State Council on the interest rate of the money. At the meeting of the Council Committee of 31 October 1864, Périn was heard. The following year he published the book *L'usure et la loi de 1807* [Usury and the law of 1807]. In this book, he regarded usury, in a traditional approach, as an exploitation of labour by capital, and established that society had the right to intervene against it, and that the interest of the weak incited its repression. Considering that usury was a circumstance of guilt, he argued that society had the right to intervene. Against the principle of letting go, let it pass, Périn argued that natural freedom was not an absolute freedom. It had to conform to the principles of morality, which had to regulate all acts: 'The principle of freedom taken absolutely is destructive of the social order.' Usury was for him a real injustice, an exploitation of the weak and poor by the strong and rich, against which society had the right to intervene. He was therefore seeking the means by which usury could be punished. The productive power of capital, and the sacrifice imposed by refraining from enjoying it, on the other hand, legitimated normal interest. Périn opted for the maintenance of the law of 1807, while proposing mitigation through precedents established by the courts to enable traders and bankers who provided credit to follow the fluctuations that occur in the price of money in the commercial market in their discounts. In 1867, he would send a written statement to the Higher Council of Agriculture, Commerce and Industry of France.

In 1871, two years after the parliamentary elections in France, which gave rise to street fights, and one year after the defeat of Napoleon III, he published *Les libertés populaires* [Popular freedoms]. He wanted to demonstrate what true freedoms were, those that were truly 'popular', by going back to the principles and origins of freedom. For Périn, the French Revolution scrambled ideas and confused notions. Eighteen centuries of Christianity had prepared and matured social liberties, which the Revolution had corrupted. Considering social relations, there were, according to him, in the man of the people, two qualities which prevailed over all the others: he was father of the family and he was a worker. Man had the freedom of the person and the freedom of property. He had the freedom of duty because, for Périn, it was his duty to God that decreed his obligation to work for his personal preservation and improvement, and it was to God that he was accountable for the exercise of his paternal authority. The freedom of the worker required that work be done in honour. One of the greatest misdeeds of contemporary democracy was to have materialized and degraded work, while pretending to liberate and divinize it. In honour of work, freedom of association, both of patrons and of workers, was still necessary. Society cannot do without the organization of groups for activities and interests. In order to discern what was legitimate and salutary in the practice of the association, and what was reprehensible and dangerous, it was not necessary to appeal to the state, which was an appeal to coercion, but to charity, which is based on freedom. If free association could be an instrument of progress, it could also, according to Périn, be an instrument of perversion, referring to the actions of *L'International*. Nor could the state be the body that traced the rule of duty, since in this case there would be no more freedom. It would be exposing itself to tyranny. The Divine commandments must regulate limited and sanctioned freedom of association. In a writ of 16 October 1871, Pope Pius IX praised this book.

In 1880, Périn published *Les doctrines économiques depuis un siècle* [Economic doctrines for a century].[9] In 1878, the Liberals regained power. In this work, Périn wanted to demonstrate that in the economic order as elsewhere, 'the reign of Christian freedom, which stands at equal distance from the licence and absolutism, *laissez-faire, laissez-passer*, vaunted by liberalism, and the takeover of the state over individual strengths and properties, of which socialism, whatever its colour, proclaims justice and necessity'. He distinguished the doctrine of sacrifice, advocated by Christianity, and that of the deification of man. The economists of the utilitarian school, by substituting the principle of the indefinite development of needs for the law of

---

[9] M. Damoiseaux, 'Un économiste catholique belge', *Revue sociale catholique* 2 (1897–1898): 181–186; Arnaud Pellissier Tallier, 'The labour theory of value and social justice. The teaching of social Catholic criticism of Bastiat's Doctrine', *Journal des Économistes et des Études Humaines* 11 (2001): 295–309.

sacrifice, had broken with the ideas on which the Christian civilization was based. From this principle, Périn challenged economists. In this examination he wanted to separate the truth of facts to which observation had led economists, and the errors of doctrine that a false philosophy had involved. Economic sensualism led to socialism 'by the consequences that naturally come out of the laws of the production and distribution of wealth, when one makes it a mechanism driven by sensual appetites'.

Influenced by the currents of German, Austrian, and French ideas, social Catholicism developed in the years 1880 with corporatism as an ideological basis. In a tension of social conflict, this ideology was expressed at a congress in Liège in 1886, in which Périn refused to participate. At the Congress of Catholic Jurists, however, held in Lille in the same year, Périn examined systems that held that the intervention of the state had the means to put an end to the difficulties of the current crisis. For him, the solution was a return, in doctrine and in practice, to the rules of the Christian constitution of states: 'As long as the poisoned principles of 1789 prevail, nothing will be done.'[10] Reforms such as protection of women and children or measures against abuse of alcoholic drinks were necessary. The intervention of the state was therefore indispensable. In his view, a break from the absolute doctrine of *laissez-passer, laisser aller* of the liberal school was necessary. If these laws were claimed in the name of justice to the worker, they had a socialist and unacceptable character. But they could be justified as regulatory and industrial police measures, factories being dangerous establishments. New law, in the name of justice due to the worker, such as compulsory insurance, pretended to bring into the obligations of justice that which was only obligated by charity. What the boss owed to the worker only by virtue of charity, one wanted to impose on him by virtue of justice. The state would by constraint do what charity, in Christian societies, did by freedom.

Périn's appointment as a member of the Board of Development at the founding of an industrial school, annexed to the Catholic University of Lille, was the origin, in 1886, of the book *Le patron, sa fonction, ses devoirs, ses responsabilités* [The boss, his function, his duties, his responsibilities]. He described the duties of the good Christian boss. It should be noted that it was the employer's duty to avoid the use in factories of mothers of families as this would remove them from the domestic hearth. For Périn, according to the divine plan, reciprocal assistance was a law of social life. This mutual assistance had to be realized in patronage, a work of selflessness, inspired by

---

[10] Charles Périn, 'Le nouveau droit en matière économique', *Revue catholique des institutions et du droit* 14 (1886): 321–328.

the spirit of sacrifice. To be effective, patronage, under the direction of the boss, must unite the boss and the worker in professional association, or free corporation.

Périn and Public Law[11]

Périn argued in his *Lettre sur la liberté d'enseignement en Belgique* [Letter on the freedom of education in Belgium], published in the *Correspondant* in April 1844, that 'the Belgian clergy has accepted and applied the most liberal principles of our public law' and still recommended to its students in 1851 the work of Thonissen, *La Constitution belge annotée* [The Belgian Constitution annotated]. However, he would evolve more and more against the liberal spirit of the Constitution. Like the liberal Catholics, the ultramontanes had changed their target. They no longer focused on King William I and his policy of state charity and teaching, but were against liberal authoritarian government. The latter did not want the independence of the civil power or the authority of the church, but secularization of the whole of society.

In 1871, in *Les libertés populaires* [Popular freedoms], Périn distinguished 'the legitimate freedoms of the people' from the 'false freedoms of democracy'. He opposed 'the greedy and violent freedom of democracy' and advocated 'the regulated, patient and fruitful freedom that carries with constancy and honour the burden of work, which considers the public peace as its first good, and who uses political law only to make respect his civil law, with all the interests he protects'. Man is free to do well. For Périn, the ability to do wrong was an abuse of freedom. The first of the popular freedoms was to carry out his duties, according to the law that God imposed. In the freedom of the family father and the worker his popular liberties converged. 'Freedom of duty', which Périn considered to be the freedom of the good, was opposed to liberal freedom. The latter recognized no spiritual order and accepted no other law than that of the state, an organ of rational sovereignty. But according to Périn, when the state had the right to determine what was lawful and what was legal, there was no longer freedom: 'To whom would we call arbitrary decisions, if not to Caesar, which is the living expression of the sovereign reason of the people, against which no one can be right? ... Caesar is infallible.' Périn would come back several times to the danger of *caesarism*, which he considered along with socialism to be enemies of all Christian civilization and all the social improvements suggested by the Gospel.

---

[11] Vincent Viaene, *Belgium and the Holy See from Gregory XVI to Pius (1831–1859. Society and Politics in 19th-Century Europe* (Louvain: Leuven University Press, 2001), 83–112.

During his audience with Pius IX on 1 May 1868, four years after the publication of the *Syllabus*, Périn pointed out to the Pope that he had a very difficult and very delicate task to fulfil in Louvain: to teach the principles of modern constitutional law. He insisted that in fulfilling this task his greatest concern was to remain rigorously faithful to the Pope and the principles of the encyclical. The Pope stressed the need to remain true to the principles. At this audience, the Pope approved a first sketch of a book, which would become in 1875 *Les lois de la société chrétienne* [The laws of Christian society].[12] This work, of which a second edition was published in 1876, would be translated into German, Italian, Spanish, and Hungarian. Périn himself considered this book to be a 'fighting book'. He defended the doctrine that in the supernatural strength of Christian societies lay the reason for their pre-eminence over societies that lived by the principles of natural order. After his publication, a brief pontifical of 1 February 1875 praised the defence of the 'true principles' and implicitly criticized the liberal Catholics: 'Pray to God that these truths were understood by those who boast of being Catholics, while adhering obstinately to the freedom of the press and other freedoms of the same species decreed at the end of the last century by the revolutionaries . . .'

For Périn, humanity was divided into two great parties in all ways opposite and irreconcilable: 'the society of Christ, and the society of the Revolution, the divine society and the satanic society'. Catholic society had the supreme law of God-dependent morality; liberal democratic society took as sovereign rule the 'essentially mobile and capricious will of the people', which led to 'blind and indomitable passions'. It did not offer guarantees for freedom, since according to the rules of democracy, the majority always prevailed as regards reason and power. Catholic society, on the other hand, could offer public liberties without risk. By his obedience to God, man had made himself master of himself: 'He has made himself free in his moral life by his fidelity to duty.' The religious norms he recognized create a certain order of duty, to which an order of inviolable rights and freedoms responded. In 'societies where the revolution reigns', such freedom was impossible. One believed oneself to be free, to apply to the general will, by participation in suffrage, which actually consisted in enslavement. The authority of the majority, derived from universal suffrage, was absolute. No one could challenge its decrees in the name of freedom. In order to maintain the general will and order, absolute

---

[12] Alfred Jourdan, *Épargne et Capital ou du meilleur emploi de la richesse. Exposé des principes fondamentaux de l'économie politique* (Aix: A. Makaire/Paris: Librairie Guillaumin et Cie, 1879), 262–266.

centralization of the state was necessary, 'in which the lively forces of society are irritated and perished'.

In Christian societies, everyone had the right to participate, but no one could exert any influence, 'except to the degree of the social hierarchy in which he is placed and according to the measure of strength and capacity which he has been given'. National representation had to reflect this hierarchy of spiritual and moral interests. Since society was ordered hierarchically, not all citizens could qualify equally to represent their social interests in parliament. For Périn, 'in any society, the spiritual interest . . . dominates all others'. The men who were in charge of this spiritual interest had therefore to have the floor in national representation. Below the interests of moral order, which were subordinate to spiritual order, there were the interests of material order. It follows that property must be taken into consideration in the allocation of electoral law. Périn even went so far as to ask the question if it would not be fair and useful to give each owner a number of votes in proportion to the importance of his property. Egalitarian democracy on the other hand ignored any form of Christian hierarchy.

He strongly criticized the utilitarianism and liberalism of John Stuart Mill, who, according to Périn, considered society a juxtaposition of individuals who saw as the ultimate goal, under the law of strict justice, the satisfaction of their personal interest . The general interest was in this case only the addition of all special interests. The doctrine of Christianity was quite different, since 'God has constituted the human kind according to a law of solidarity and unity.'

Périn maintained that in every society there were two powers: the spiritual order, which governed human things in view of an order superior to this world, and the temporal order, which has as its object the interests of present life. Although the two powers were closely linked, they nevertheless had to remain distinct. The spiritual power that exerted its action on consciousness and eternity was always superior to the power that exerted its action on the external and temporal life. For Périn, the superiority of the church to the state was set for Catholics, beyond all contestation, by the bull *Unam Sanctam* of 1302 of Pope Boniface VIII. He considered Christian royalty the best of governments, since it could guarantee unity, stability, and freedom.

Périn and the Law of Nations

In 1888, Périn published his treaty *L'ordre international. Principes fondamentaux du droit des gens* [The international order. Fundamental principles of the law of nations]. In *Les lois de la société chrétienne* [The laws of Christian society] he had already dedicated a chapter to the 'League of Nations among themselves' and published, in 1881, in the *Revue trimestrielle* of Lille a study on *La guerre d'après le droit nouveau* [War according to the new law]. He had held a conference at the Congress of Jurists in Reims in 1882 on *L'État et l'Église dans la société internationale contemporaine* [The state and the church in contemporary international society]. In this text he developed the idea that the present events demonstrated 'that a society without God is a society without rest and without future'. As there is a political and social question, there is also an international question. On the question of the law of nations he put in opposition to liberalism and humanitarian radicalism 'the full and frank assertion of the Catholic faith and the prerogative of the Church'.

The End of an Era

In February 1878, Pius IX died and was succeeded by Leo XIII.[13] Between 1878 and 1881 the new pope urged the Belgian episcopate to admit Belgian constitutional freedoms in order to oppose the policy of liberal secularization. In 1881, Périn published his article *Le modernisme dans l'Église d'après les lettres inédites de la Mennais* [Modernism in the Church according to the unpublished letters of la Mennais] in *La Revue trimestrielle*. In this contribution he not only criticized liberal modernism, which he considered to be a known enemy, but also Catholic liberalism, 'dupe and unconscious accomplice of modernism'. He used the term 'modernism' to indicate the errors which, in his opinion, entered the church with Lamenais in an attempt to reconcile Catholic faith with a secular vision of the world. At the *Congres des oeuvres ouvrières* in Caen, in 1886, Périn presented a report on *La cooperation chrétienne* [Christian cooperation]. He supported the thesis that cooperative works brought the habit of concerted relationships, fixity of relationships, and mutual trust into all ranks.

In 1882, he published the contribution *La réaction* [The reaction] in the *Revue trimestrielle*, in which he examined the different models of reaction against the model of the Revolution, which he considered an evil that affected the whole of social society. He concluded that there were two groups within Christian society: the supporters of social reform of Le Play, which misses its goals, and the Catholic circles of workers.

---

[13] Emiel Lamberts, 'De ontwikkeling van de sociaal-katholieke ideologie in België', in *Een kantelend tijdperk. 1890–1910*, ed. Emiel Lamberts (Louvain: Leuven University Press, 1992), 49–63.

But from 1881, following disapproval of him by Leo XIII and his resignation from the university, Périn's influence weakened. When the encyclical *Rerum Novarum* appeared in 1891, Périn wrote *L'économie politique d'après l'Encyclique sur les conditions de l'ouvrier* [Political economy according to the encyclical on the conditions of the worker]. He argued that 'the Pontiff gives to the world, by an act of solemn teaching, the Catholic truth for the economic order'. He did not find any changes in his own doctrinal convictions in the encyclical. The doctrine of charity, close to the justification of property, excluded socialism and liberalism. He saw confirmation of the roles of patronage and association, which he regarded as the two forms of charity present in the economic order. He agreed with the role of the state described in the Pontifical document. He insisted on the right salary (*juste salaire*), the payment of which was one of the boss's main duties. Périn considered that Catholics now had a political economy that derived from the social teaching of the church: no more disagreement, no more doctrinal particularism.

In 1895, the first edition of the *Premiers principes d'économie politique* [First principles of political economy] appeared. The following year he published a second edition of this book, reviewed and completed, followed by a study on fair salary based on the encyclical *Rerum Novarum*. This book was in a way the scientific testament of Périn: 'It is a farewell that I address today to the public.' On several occasions he invoked his older works, as if to prove that his ideas had been constant. He noted that the encyclical that should have united Catholics on social issues had only marked divisions more clearly and aggravated dissent, although the encyclical contained all the constituent elements of economic science following the principles of Christian life. In this book he taught that freedom had to preside over the work of creation, distribution, and consumption of wealth. This freedom was not unlimited. To the ideas of the rationalist and utilitarian school, he responded with the doctrine of Christian renunciation, which he considered to be uttermost in the whole order of social sciences. Indissolubly linked to freedom was authority. This gave society the necessary unity principle. The question of weighting between freedom and regulation therefore became crucial, as Périn had demonstrated in 1879 in his book *Le socialisme chrétien* [Christian socialism]. If freedom was the general rule, regulation was only the exception. But to ask for freedom was dangerous, due to the weakness of man. To ask everything for justice was 'falling into socialism'. The real solution was for him the alliance of charity and justice. They were necessary for the evolution of the world. But in order to achieve the rapprochement of the classes, this social evolution had to be done, according to Périn, under the direction of the church. Salvation could be found only in 'the fraternal understanding between different men by the social condition, but equal, under the eye of God, by the character of the Christian and the similarity of destinies'. He finished his book by repeating to employers and workers the words of Christ: 'peace to the men of good will'. The second edition of the first principles was followed by an appendix on fair salary based on the encyclical *Rerum Novarum*. Périn brought together and completed the texts on this subject which he had published since the publication of the encyclical.

GENERAL APPRAISAL AND INFLUENCE

The ideas of Périn fitted into the tradition of those of his master Charles de Coux. By advancing the superiority of faith in God and the superiority of the church, Périn often used history to demonstrate the greatness of the religious world of the *ancien régime* and emphasized the detrimental effects of Protestantism, rationalism, and the French Revolution. In return, he proposed the Christian ethic of renunciation as a panacea for the problems of modern industry. He rejected all government intervention and recommended charity. Périn was strongly opposed to the state. In his view, the state's role was limited to guaranteeing a legal framework for private charity.

Périn must be placed in the movement of the Counter-Enlightenment, an intellectual response against the emergence of rationalism and its culmination in the French Revolution. Therefore, the laws of God and of the church opposed the temples of Reason. Périn took up and broadened the thesis of de Villeneuve-Bargemont on the Christian political economy, as indicated by the French liberal economist Frédéric Passy. In 1881, Victor Brants succeeded Périn in Louvain in teaching the course on political economy. Brants was enthusiastic about Périn's teaching and stressed that he had a large part in the religious restoration in social science.

During the second half of the nineteenth century, the influence of Périn was strong, both in Belgium and abroad. In the first place, as a teacher from 1845 until 1881, he taught his ideas to a great number of students. His radical position divided both professors and students. In addition, as noted by Victor Brants, 'the blows that they (Périn and Thonissen) gave were not all scientific'. His work was translated into various languages, but not into English. But Périn did not live in an ivory tower: he was also present in public life. He actively attended several Congresses in Belgium and France. In France, he participated in the newspaper *Anjou*, widespread in the diocese of Monseigneur Freppel. He was active with the members of *l'Association des patrons catholiques du Nord de la France*, an association of Catholic patrons. He was considered the figurehead of the ultramontanes, who opposed Catholic liberalism. He was an active correspondent. He was present in the press, even in the daily press. Until 1881, he was a member of the board of directors of the Société Saint-Pierre, owner of the *Courrier de Bruxelles*, a daily newspaper for the defence of ultramontane ideas. In 1875, he became the first president of the Confrérie de Saint-Michel, a function he exercised until 1881. This very select Confrérie stood as the ultramontane organ par excellence in Belgium.

It is obvious that Périn, as leader of the ultramontanes, was challenged by liberal Catholics. After *Les lois sur la société civile* [Laws on civil society] was published, liberal Catholics even went to refer him to the Congregation of the Holy Office and accused him of political *balinisme*, although in vain. Following the implicit papal condemnation of ultramontanism and the publication by the former bishop of Tournai of Périn's letters criticizing the Archbishop of Mechelen in liberal newspapers, Périn resigned, in 1881, as professor of the University of Louvain. Later on he concentrated his activities on Catholic action in France and at the Catholic University of Lille.

The agreement between the Catholic parliamentary right and the ultramontanes, as desired by the Pope, was crowned by Catholic success in the elections of 1884. Until the First World War, the Catholic party remained in power. The creation of a socialist party in 1885, the social revolts in 1886, and the adoption of male suffrage and the plural vote in 1893 meant the end of the democracy of the elites. The ultramontane ideas of Périn had now to give place to ideas more in line with the political reality of the late nineteenth century.

In November 1884, in the House of Representatives, the Chief of the cabinet, replying to insinuations of the left concerning contempt for the institutions, replied: 'There (at the Catholic University of Louvain) was once a publicist (Périn) who spoke without respect: he has been sent away.' Périn himself remained convinced of his ideas and the evils of the Revolution when he commented in the brochure *La Révolution française, à propos du centenaire de 1789* [The French Revolution, about the centenary of 1789]: 'It is the definitive stop on the Revolution, it is an event, and one resumes to hope when one sees this book welcomed as it is, even by people who have burned so much incense to the idol.'

RECOMMENDED READINGS

An exhaustive, but not complete, bibliography was published in: Université catholique de Louvain [Catholic University of Louvain], *Bibliography. 1834–1900*. Louvain, Charles Peeters, 1900. A large part of the works of Périn are available on www.gallica.fr and www.liberius.net/auteur.php?id_auth=46. The state archives in

Mons preserve Périn's papers: Dumont, C. and Armand Louant. *Inventaire des papiers Charles Périn*. Brussels, AGR, 1986. Louvain university archives keep several student course notes.

Fèvre, Justin. *Charles Périn. Créateur de l'économie politique chrétienne*. Paris: Arthur Savaète, 1903.

Kempeneers, J. *Charles Périn (1815–1903) de l'école libérale d'inspiration chrétienne*. Liège: La Pensée Catholique, 1930.

Michotte, Paul-Lambert. *Études sur les théories économiques qui dominèrent en Belgique de 1830 à 1886*. Louvain: Charles Peeters, 1904.

Naudet, Jean-Yves. 'Les économistes catholique français au XIXe siècle'. *Liberté. Politique. La nouvelle revue d'idées chrétienne* 14 (2000): 83–99.

Solari, Stefano. 'Catholic perspectives on poverty and misery: From nineteenth-century French Catholic social economists to the contribution of Jesuits'. *Cahiers d'économie Politique/Papers in Political Economy* 59 (2010): 185–203.

15

Léon de Lantsheere

Peter Heyrman

BIOGRAPHICAL INTRODUCTION

Léon de Lantsheere was born in Brussels on 23 September 1862 into a renowned Catholic family rooted in the region of Dendermonde.[1] His grandfather was a physician, while his father Théophile-Charles-André de Lantsheere (1833–1918) studied law in Leuven, worked as a lawyer in Brussels, and became increasingly involved in several business companies. Théophile de Lantsheere had a remarkable public career as a member (1872–1900) and chair (1884–1905) of the Belgian Chamber of Deputies, Minister of Justice (1871–1878), chair (*stafhouder*) of the Brussels Bar (1887), vice-governor (1899–1905) and governor (1905–1918) of the Belgian National Bank, and as a senator (1900–1905). In 1890 he was granted the title of Minister of State, and in 1913 he was raised to the nobility with the hereditary title of viscount.[2] Léon de Lantsheere was his oldest son. Léon's older sister Nathalie (1861–1931) would enter the so-called 'English Convent' in Bruges as a regular canoness of Saint Augustine. The second sister, Alice (1864–1944), married the Brussels notary Louis Vergote (1861–1907), and his younger brother Auguste (1870–1932) came to be governor of the *Société Générale* and lord mayor of Meldert. Due to a childhood accident, Léon de Lantsheere had lost the use of

---

[1] De Lantsheere has not yet been the subject of an academic biography, except for succinct accounts by Alain Stenmans, Paul van Molle, Jo Deferme, and Kristien Meerts. Details about his life can be found in several commemorative statements by, for instance, Paulin Ladeuze, Edouard Descamps, Maurice Defourny, Léon Dupriéz, Maurice De Wulf, Léon Noël, and Alexandre Braun (see recommended readings).

[2] Marcel de Schaetzen, 'Généalogie de la Famille de Lantsheere', in *La Noblesse Belge* (1933): 209–242, partly based on: Jan Lindemans, 'Het geslacht de Lantsheere', *Eigen Schoon* 4 (1914): 1–8. On Théophile de Lantsheere as a Minister of Justice, see Jos Monballyu, *Six centuries of criminal law: history of criminal law in the Southern Netherlands and Belgium (1400–2000)* (Leiden: Brill Nijhoff, 2014), 186–191.

one of his eyes and became extremely short-sighted. He did his secondary studies at the Jesuit Collège de Saint-Michel in Brussels and in 1880 enrolled at the Catholic University of Leuven where in 1885 he obtained a doctoral degree in law, *magna cum laude*.[3] He also followed the course *La haute philosophie selon Saint Thomas* at the Leuven Faculty of Theology, obtained the degree of *Licencié en Philosophie* in May 1885, and subsequently wrote a doctoral dissertation in scholastic philosophy,[4] which he successfully defended on 3 December 1886.[5]

In 1888 de Lantsheere was admitted to the bar of the Brussels Court of Appeal. His political career was launched at around the same time. On 2 July 1889 he was installed as a member of the Provincial Council of Brabant as a representative of the canton of Asse. That same year de Lantsheere became a member (*auditeur* and *conseiller* in 1903) of the High Council of the Congo (*Conseil Supérieur de l'Etat Indépendant du Congo*), a network of jurists set up by King Leopold II to act as the highest legal committee of the Congo Free State.[6] Meanwhile he continued his academic activities and scientific research. In 1895, the year in which he married Marguerite Kerckx (1865–1951) with whom he raised five children,[7] de Lantsheere was appointed *professor extraordinarious* of criminal law at the Leuven Law Faculty. He was the successor of Albert Nyssens (1855–1901) who in that year became the first Belgian Minister of Industry and Labour. Part of his assignment was to teach a course on comparative private law at the School of Political and Social Sciences (1892), founded by Jules van den Heuvel (1854–1926).[8] These lectures, under the title *Les institutions civiles comparées*, focused on a broad range of subjects such as 'family', 'property', 'the theory of fault', the legal position of married women and the German Imperial Civil Code. From 1893, de Lantsheere also offered weekly lectures at the Leuven

---

[3] 'Avec grande distinction', *Annuaire de l'Université Catholique de Louvain* (1886): 228.
[4] 'Doctorat en philosophie selon Saint Thomas'. Léon de Lantsheere, *Du Bien au point de vue ontologique et moral. Dissertation pour le doctorat en philosophie selon St. Thomas* (Leuven: Charles Peeters, 1886).
[5] *Annuaire de l'Université Catholique de Louvain* (1887): 287.
[6] Pierre-Luc Plasman, *Leopold II, potentat congolais. L'action royale face à la violence coloniale* (Brussels: Racine, 2017), 37–68.
[7] Théophile (1897–1958), who would become a diplomat and head of the ministerial cabinet of Foreign Affairs; Madeleine (1899–1964); Alice (1900–1956), who married Raoul Hayoit de Termicourt; Jean (1902–1974), who would become a lawyer and secretary of the royal private estate; and Emmanuel (1908–1910).
[8] Emmanuel Gerard, *Sociale wetenschappen aan de Katholieke Universiteit te Leuven, 1892–1992* (Leuven: Politica-Cahier, 1992), 32–36. It is worth mentioning that de Lantsheere's father was chairman of the Belgian *Commission Permanente pour l'Examen des Questions de Droit International Privé*, set up by Royal Decree of 3 August 1898.

Higher Institute of Philosophy, mainly on the classification of the modern sciences, the philosophy of history, and the works of modern philosophers such as Descartes, Spinoza, Kant, and Hegel.[9] In 1899 he was appointed full professor at the Leuven Law Faculty.[10]

Besides developing a remarkable academic career during the 1890s, de Lantsheere also became increasingly involved in the social and political arenas. Together with his college friend Jules Renkin (1862–1934) and Henry Carton de Wiart (1869–1951), he was one of the main protagonists of the emerging Christian Democracy and Christian labour movement in Brussels.[11] Carton and Renkin were elected to Parliament in July 1896, de Lantsheere on 27 May 1900. His expertise in legal, social, and colonial matters was noted, and his political influence grew steadily, maybe also because he often fulfilled a mediating role between the different factions of the Catholic party. However, the rising political impact of the Brussels Christian Democrats was also linked to the sympathy that they enjoyed in both the royal entourage and the church hierarchy.

When in May 1907 a new government was formed under the lead of Jules de Trooz (1857–1907), two Christian Democrats were offered ministerial responsibilities: Joris Helleputte (Railroads) and Jules Renkin (Justice). Both would remain in place after the death of de Trooz and the formation of the Schollaert cabinet on 9 January 1908. However, Renkin moved to the Department of the Colonies in October of that year, after the official takeover of Congo. De Lantsheere succeeded Renkin as Minister of Justice,[12] a role he retained until the cabinet fell on 17 June 1911. De Lantsheere renounced a mandate in the new government of Charles de Broqueville (1860–1940). He returned to his academic assignments in Leuven, again teaching criminal law at the Law Faculty and comparative private law in the School of Political and Social Sciences, and offering a weekly lecture at the Higher Institute of Philosophy.[13]

---

[9] See for instance: Léon de Lantsheere, 'Les caractères de la Philosophie moderne', Revue néo-scolastique 1.2 (1894): 101–111; Léon de Lantsheere, 'Introduction à la philosophie moderne suivie d'un fragment de leçon sur Descartes', Annales de l'Institut Supérieur de Philosophie 2 (1913): 330–393.

[10] Together with Deploige. See Revue Catholique de Droit 2 (1899–1900): 224.

[11] Henk de Smaele, 'Henry Carton de Wiart (1869–1905). Christen-democratisch politicus en literator', Trajecta 4.1 (1995): 22–41; Henry Carton de Wiart, Souvenirs politiques. 1878–1918 (Bruges: Desclée De Brouwer, 1948), 35–62; Giovanni Hoyois, Henry Carton de Wiart et le Groupe de 'La Justice Sociale' (Paris-Kortrijk-Brussels: Jos. Vermaut, 1931).

[12] Royal Decree of 30 October 1908, Belgisch Staatsblad/Moniteur Belge 31 October 1908. The nomination had already been announced on 10 October.

[13] In 1909 de Lantsheere had explicitly asked his rector to retain his professorial status and expressed his desire to come back to the university after the end of this ministerial mandate.

In late 1911 he was elected dean of the Leuven Law Faculty and also became chair of the *Association des Anciens Étudiants de la Faculté de droit de l'Université de Louvain* (1908).[14] On 15 June 1912 de Lantsheere was granted the title of Grand Officer in the Order of Leopold. After being re-elected to parliament that same month, he was named as a prime candidate for succeeding Gerard Cooreman (1852–1926) as chair of the Belgian Chamber of Deputies. However, he died unexpectedly at Putberg, his father's estate in Asse near Brussels, on the morning of Monday 26 August 1912 as a result of an acute kidney crisis.

MAJOR THEMES AND CONTRIBUTIONS

Given the different paths of Léon de Lantsheere's career, one cannot simply label him a jurist. His life's work indeed encompassed many different areas. Looking back on his life's work we can attribute to him the roles of (1) academic involved in teaching and wide-ranging scholarly research, (2) social activist, and (3) politician and policy-maker.

Scholar

As an academic de Lantsheere displayed a remarkable tendency toward multi-disciplinarity. After his death he was often portrayed as an 'encyclopaedic mind'.[15] This attribute however does not do justice to the erudite and extremely literate scholar that de Lantsheere was. Friends portrayed him as an *uomo universalis*, a 'living library' who devoured books and articles and was remembered for having said that 'a day without learning something new

---

Paulin Ladeuze, 'Discours prononcé par Monseigneur P. Ladeuze, recteur magnifique de l'Université catholique de Louvain, le jeudi 29 août 1912, aux funérailles de M. le professeur L. de Lantsheere', *Annuaire de l'Université catholique de Louvain 1913* (1913): XXXII. During his absence he was replaced by Prosper Poullet (1868–1937) and Léon Dupriez (1863–1942).

[14] De Lantsheere was one of the initiators of this new association. On 3 October 1907 he was elected as the provisional chairman. At the formal foundation meeting of 6 December 1908, however, he was already a minister and thus needed to leave the chairmanship to Prosper Poullet. In December 1911, when Poullet in his turn had become a minister, de Lantsheere succeeded him as chairman. *Revue Catholique de Droit* 12 (1909): 28–29 and 43; *Revue Catholique de Droit* 15 (1912): 17.

[15] *Annales parlementaires de la Belgique. Chambre de Représentants. Session ordinaire de 1911–1912. Séance d'ouverture du mardi 12 Novembre 1912*, 5. See also the description of de Lantsheere as 'a walking encyclopedia' or 'véritable Pic de Mirandole' in Michel Dumoulin, et al., *Nieuwe Geschiedenis van België II (1905–1950)/Nouvelle Histoire de Belgique II (1905–1950)* (Tielt: Lannoo/Brussels: Editions complexes, 2006), 758/57.

was a day lost'.[16] Nonetheless, his research resulted in a limited number of publications. In 1912–1913 the Leuven Law Faculty made great efforts to compile his more-or-less complete bibliography, but the final list contained only 49 items, more than half of them speeches and policy documents.[17] In any case, when browsing through the titles of his academic publications, it is not at all clear one can exclusively label de Lantsheere a jurist. His scientific interests ranged across many different fields. As a young student at the Jesuit Collège Saint-Michel in Brussels Léon de Lantsheere was known as a quiet but inquisitive boy who played violin and piano and had a clear talent for mathematics.[18] He was also involved in a social study circle under the inspiring guidance of his Jesuit teacher, François van Innis (1839–1889).[19] One can suppose that his decision to study law in Leuven was motivated by family tradition and the career plans that his father had set out. During his student years de Lantsheere developed a growing interest in philosophy and became the second[20] doctoral student of Désiré-Joseph Mercier (1851–1926).[21] Over the next years the young doctor ventured into many different fields, such as the origins of Christianity, modern and medieval Arabic philosophy, Babylonian

[16] Ladeuze, 'Discours', XXXIII.
[17] A bibliography of his works (still incomplete and with some errors) in 'Principaux travaux de Léon Joseph-Marie-Antoine de Lantsheere', *Annuaire de l'Université catholique de Louvain* 1913 (1913): LII–LIV.
[18] De Lantsheere would even compose a few pieces of music, for instance a wedding march and the song *Vous avez allumé les lampes* (1892), based on a text of Maeterlynck. Flavie Roquet, et al., eds., *Lexicon Vlaamse componisten geboren na 1800* (Roeselare: Roularta, 2007), 208–209.
[19] Hoyois, *Henry Carton*, 11–13; Carton de Wiart, *Souvenirs politiques*, 35. Apart from Jules Renkin and Henry Carton de Wiart, other members of this circle that continued meeting in the room of van Innis after his death were the future Cardinal Rafaël Merry del Val (1865–1930), the Liège jurist Edouard Vander Smissen (1865–1926), and the future Belgian minister, Pierre de Liedekerke (1869–1943). On van Innis: KADOC-KU Leuven: Archives of the Society of Jesus in Flanders, 6545.
[20] Mercier's first doctoral student was Théodore Fontaine (1858–1898) with his study *De la sensation et la pensée* (Leuven: Peeters, 1885). Soon afterwards Fontaine taught the course *Droit social dans ses rapports avec la question ouvrière* at the Leuven Special Schools for Engineering. He was appointed professor in the Faculty of Law (1886) and the Faculty of Philosophy and Arts (1890) but had to resign those activities in 1893 due to illness and died five years later.
[21] Roger Aubert, 'Désiré Mercier et les débuts de l'Institut de Philosophie', *Revue philosophique de Louvain* 88 (1990): 147–1967; Aloïs Simon, *Le cardinal Mercier* (Brussels: La Renaissance du Livre, 1960); Jan de Volder, *Cardinal Mercier in the First World War: Belgium, Germany and the Catholic Church*. KADOC-Studies (Leuven: UPL, 2018); Françoise Mirguet and Françoise Hiraux, *L'Institut supérieur de philosophie de Louvain (1889–1968)*. Publications des archives de l'Université catholique de Louvain, 21 (Louvain-la-Neuve: Bruylant, 2008), 520.

law, the history and language of the Hittites and Amorites, and even the metrics of Assyrian poetry.[22]

Mercier, who would become archbishop in 1906 and cardinal in 1907, played a decisive role in shaping de Lantsheere's career and mindset. The launch of Mercier's course *La haute philosophie selon Saint Thomas* in 1882, which was open to all university students and even to the general public, was a clear response to the plea of Pope Leo XIII in his brief *Aeterni Patris* (4 August 1879) that the study of the writings of St Thomas Aquinas (1225–1274) be encouraged at all Catholic schools and universities. De Lantsheere clearly supported Mercier's Thomist project and subscribed to its scholarly, educational, and apologetic objectives. Neo-Scholastic philosophy would offer future Belgian Catholic intellectual elites (not only the priests but also the laity) a new metaphysical framework, enabling them to confront the paradigms of positivist, agnostic philosophy, and to enter into a synergistic dialogue with the many emerging modern sciences, all this with respect for church doctrine and tradition.[23] In particular, Mercier's collaborator and successor Simon Deploige (1868–1927)[24] would develop Thomism into a moral philosophy that could incorporate the results of modern scientific research. In 1889 and with the explicit support of the Pope, Mercier founded the Leuven Higher Institute of Philosophy.[25] Courses in Thomist philosophy were introduced in different faculties, and students were encouraged to obtain a baccalaureate at

---

[22] Léon de Lantsheere, 'De la race et de la langue des Hittites', in *Compte Rendu du Congrès Scientifique International des Catholiques tenu à Paris du 1 au 6 Avril 1891. Sixième Section: Philologie* (Paris: Alphonse Picard, 1891), 154–179; Léon de Lantsheere, *Le Droit à Babylone et l'évolution juridique* (Brussels: Larcier, 1894); Léon de Lantsheere, 'Note sur la métrique Assyrienne', in *Compte rendu du troisième Congrès Scientifique International des Catholiques, tenu à Bruxelles du 3 au 8 septembre 1894. Sixième section: Philologie* (Brussels: Société belge de Librairie, 1895), 195–201. He also contributed to a volume in honour of the Leuven orientalist Charles de Harlez (1832–1899): Léon de Lantsheere, 'Le pied et la chaussure comme symboles juridiques', in *Mélanges Charles de Harlez. Recueil de travaux d'érudition offert à Charles de Harlez à l'occasion du vingt-cinquième anniversaire de son professorat à l'Université de Louvain, 1871–1896*, ed. Charles de Harlez (Leiden: E. J. Brill, 1896), 149–161.

[23] Carlos Steel, 'Thomas en de vernieuwing van de filosofie. Beschouwingen bij het thomisme van Mercier', *Tijdschrift voor filosofie* 53 (1991): 44–89; Kaat Wils, *De omweg van de wetenschap. Het positivisme en de Belgische en Nederlandse intellectuele cultuur 1845–1914* (Amsterdam: Amsterdam University Press, 2005), 326–341.

[24] Obtained a doctoral degree in Arts (1888) and Law (1889) and was *Licencié en Philosophie* (1890). Main works: *Le conflit de la morale et de la sociologie* (1911) and *Saint Thomas et la question juive* (1902).

[25] Georges van Riet, 'Originalité et fécondité de la notion de philosophie élaborée par le Cardinal Mercier', *Revue Philosophique de Louvain* 4, 79, 44 (1981): 532–565; Louis De Raeymaeker, *Le cardinal Mercier et l'Institut supérieur de philosophie de Louvain* (Louvain: Publications universitaires de Louvain, 1952); Louis De Raeymaeker, 'Les origines de l'Institut supérieur de Philosophie de Louvain', *Revue Philosophique de Louvain* 3, 49, 24 (1951):

the Institute. Mercier's pupils were strategically appointed to different Leuven faculties, but also at the state universities of Ghent and Liège. The Leuven Higher Institute became a central node of the growing network of Neo-Scholastic study centres throughout Europe and even beyond.[26]

As one of Mercier's earliest acolytes, de Lantsheere was strongly involved in the multifaceted network of the later archbishop. We already mentioned that from 1893/1894 onwards he offered weekly lectures at the Higher Institute. He interacted with such key figures as Deploige, Maurice de Wulf (1867–1947),[27] the editor of the *Revue Néo-Scholastique* (1894–), the cosmologist Désiré Nys (1859–1927), Maurice Defourny (1878–1953),[28] and the epistemologist Léon Noël (1878–1953).[29] De Lantsheere contributed to the *Annales de Sociologie* (1900–) of Camille Jacquart,[30] Fernand Deschamps (1868–1957)[31] and Cyrille van Overbergh (1866–1959),[32] and to the *Revue Catholique de Droit* (1898–1914) of Edouard Crahay (1872–1945).[33] He also published in the influential *Revue Sociale Catholique* (1897–1920) and was a member of the *Société Belge (des Etudes Pratiques) d'Economie Sociale* founded in 1881 by Victor Brants (1856–1917), a pupil of Frédéric Le Play (1806–1882) and the successor of Charles Périn (1815–1905) in the Leuven chair of Political Economy.[34]

The intensity of de Lantsheere's commitment to the Leuven Thomist revival movement was already apparent in his doctoral thesis.[35] In this study on the idea of the good, he highlighted the antagonisms of moral, ontological,

505–633; Emiel Lamberts and Jan Roegiers, *De Universiteit te Leuven 1425–1985* (Leuven: UPL, 1986), 220 and 261–262.

[26] Joseph-Louis Perrier, *The Revival of Scholastic Philosophy in the Nineteenth Century* (New York: Columbia University Press, 1909).

[27] Professor at the Higher Institute (1893) and at the Arts Faculty (1898). He published on the history of (medieval) philosophy.

[28] Professor at the Higher Institute, did a PhD on the 'positivist sociology of Comte' (1902), offered courses on the history of social theories and was editorial secretary of the *Revue Sociale Catholique*.

[29] Assistant editor of the *Revue Neoscholastique*, took over Mercier's courses on psychology and criteriology, and published on the question of determinism and free will. Georges van Reet, 'Noël, Léon', *Biographie Nationale* XL, 12, 2 (Brussels: Académie Royale de Belgique, 1978): 661–669.

[30] Later director of the Belgian Bureau of Statistics.

[31] Professor at the Antwerp Higher Institute for Commercial Studies.

[32] Founder and chairman of the Société Belge de Sociologie. Among many other things he studied socialism and the reform of public assistance.

[33] Professor at the Liège Law Faculty. Main work: *La Politique de Saint Thomas d'Aquin* (Leuven: Institut Supérieur de Philosophie, 1896).

[34] On Périn, see the contribution of Fred Stevens, 'Charles Périn', in this volume.

[35] Léon de Lantsheere, *Du Bien au point de vue ontologique et moral. Dissertation pour le doctorat en philosophie selon St. Thomas* (Leuven: Charles Peeters, 1886).

and logical finality in scholastic and Kantian philosophy, clearly rejecting the latter. De Lantsheere's dissertation was tributary to the works of Aloïs van Weddingen (1841–1890), a professor of theology in Leuven and one of the pioneers of the Belgian Thomist revival.[36] Following Mercier and van Weddingen, de Lantsheere defended an essentially teleological view of human existence as a continuing, destined movement toward God. On an epistemological level he rejected the existence of a priori knowledge. No knowledge, even regarding the existence of God, was possible without experiencing the natural world. The divide between the modern sciences and religion needed to be bridged.[37]

His neo-Scholastic training would also determine de Lantsheere's legal work. Maurice Defourny asserted that 'above all he was a philosopher' adding that 'his rare legal writings relate neither to the technique of the codes, nor to the text of the law, they deal with the nature, the evolution and the philosophy of law'.[38] De Lantsheere displayed a great interest in folk law symbolism. This was already apparent in his book on the Babylonian law system, but especially in his article on the foot and the shoe as legal symbols.[39] In his essay *L'évolution moderne du droit naturel* (1897–1898)[40] he joined numerous Leuven colleagues in their fight against positivism and especially against what they called 'the relativism of modern sociology'.[41] 'There is no doubt', de Lantsheere wrote, 'that Positivism can arrive at formulating a theory of legality, but it will never be able to formulate a theory of law without contradicting its own principle [...]. Every legislation of course contains rules that are its own and will vary according to the diversity of time and circumstances; but besides, or better, above this changing section, we ascertain a certain order that has to exist, goods that need to be respected, actions that need to be defended or commanded, in every era and in all circumstances.'[42] Human liberty and thus the will to break this consensus was of course also a natural

---

[36] See his popularizing summary of van Weddingen's book *Les bases de l'objectivité de la connaissance dans le domaine de la spontanéité et de la réflexion, essai d'introduction à la philosophie critique* (1889): Léon de Lantsheere, 'L'objectivité de la connaissance', *Revue Générale* 51.26 (Feb. 1890): 153–170 and (May 1890): 638–676.

[37] Léon de Lantsheere, 'L'Avenir Scientifique', *L'Avenir Social* 2. 11 (13 March 1892).

[38] Maurice Defourny, 'Léon de Lantsheere', *Revue Sociale Catholique* 16 (1911–1912): 246.

[39] Léon de Lantsheere, *Le Droit à Babylone et l'évolution juridique* (Brussels: Larcier, 1894); de Lantsheere, 'Le pied', 149–161.

[40] Léon de Lantsheere, 'L'Evolution moderne du droit naturel', *Revue néo-scolastique* 4.15 (1897): 298–306 and 4.17 (1898): 45–59.

[41] Wils, *De omweg*, 326–341; Kaat Wils, 'Les intellectuels catholiques et la sociologie en Belgique, 1880–1914', *Archives de sciences sociales des religions* 179.3 (2017): 71–88.

[42] De Lantsheere, 'L'Evolution moderne II', 54.

phenomenon. For de Lantsheere only 'the idea of the final cause' could transform the spontaneous and de facto social idea of order into a rule of law. Nonetheless, de Lantsheere warned the general public against those scholars – in particular the Ghent jurist François Laurent (1810–1887) – who had pleaded for a complete revision of the Napoleonic Belgian Civil Code. It was better, he claimed, to cautiously amend and ameliorate this collection of 'high intrinsic value', than to completely reconstruct it.[43]

De Lantsheere labelled himself a member of what he called the 'neo-classical school of criminal law'. He was willing to incorporate the findings of sociology, criminology and other modern sciences but also expressed his gladness to see 'that amidst the ongoing contemporary scientific debates, the idea of the absolute always and persistently reappears after being washed away and swallowed up by the passing and fleeting waters of relativity'. He was also confident that the ongoing 'shock of ideas' facilitated the 'rejuvenation and revitalization' of older concepts and ideas.[44] Two studies of de Lantsheere illustrate his mindset. In his essay *Le Pain volé*, he used the much debated verdict of acquittal by the *bon juge* Paul Magnaud (1848–1926) in Château-Thierry on a case of bread theft in March 1898, to elaborate on the concept of 'extreme necessity' and the relativity of property rights.[45] His thorough and elegantly written analysis culminates in a reference to the legal maxim *necessitas legem non habet*, its affirmation in canon law,[46] and the famous passage on the issue in the *Summa* of Saint Thomas.[47] De Lantsheere concluded that in the case of extreme necessity, the indigent had indeed the right to take what was necessary for the preservation of their lives.

Another important article by de Lantsheere highlighting his ideas on criminal law deals with the origin of punishment.[48] After evaluating the existing literature on the subject (Letourneau, Tarde, and of course Durkheim), de Lantsheere discarded the idea of legal punishment being rooted in (private or collective) vengeance. Instead, both punishment and vengeance originated from the desire to restore a troubled order. While the

---

[43] Léon de Lantsheere, 'Le centenaire du Code civil. Les opportunités de sa révision en Belgique', *Revue Catholique de Droit* 7.1 (1904–1905): 10–15.

[44] 'Discours de M. de Lantsheere, Ministre de la Justice', *Bulletin de l'Union internationale de droit pénal*, XVII, fasc. 2 (1910): 409–419.

[45] Léon, de Lantsheere, 'Le pain volé', *Revue Sociale Catholique* 2 (1897–1898), May and July, 193–201 and 257–266. This judgment on 4 March 1898 was confirmed by an appeal court.

[46] De Lantsheere, 'Le pain', 260–264, with special reference to several passages in the *Decretum Gratiani* and the *Liber Extra*.

[47] *Summa Theologiae*, 2, 2 quaestio 66 articulus 7.

[48] Léon de Lantsheere, 'L'origine de la peine au point de vue sociologique', *Annales de Sociologie et Mouvement sociologique* 1 (1900–1901) (1903): 311–336.

latter only mends the existing order between independent beings who are not part of the same whole, punishment aims to restore the social order, which is by definition teleological or moral in nature and based on the reciprocal relations of man and his fellow beings.[49]

Social Activist

It remains unclear whether de Lantsheere was already involved in Catholic social initiatives during his studies in Leuven, but it is more than likely that in the late 1880s he indeed followed in the footsteps of his college friend Jules Renkin (1862–1934). The latter was president of the Brussels *Jeune Garde Catholique*, the party's youth organization, and committed himself to different initiatives supporting the Catholic press and schools. After 1886, a year marked by great social unrest in Wallonia and the first Catholic Social Congress in Liège, the Catholic social infrastructure in the capital expanded in a remarkable way. The main structures were the so-called labourers' houses (*maisons des ouvriers/werkmanshuizen*), with telling names such as *Concordia, Union et Travail* or *La Paix*. Under the motto 'Family, Property and Fatherland' these houses accommodated a variety of paternalistic social organizations and services that sought to 'morally and materially improve' the industrial workers. Lavishly sponsored by the Catholic nobility and bourgeoisie, they expressed a message of class harmony and reconciliation, a clear alternative to the growing success of the socialist *Maison du Travail* in the capital. In the early 1890s and clearly inspired by the papal encyclical *Rerum Novarum* (1891), a group of young Catholic intellectuals decided to take control of this embryonic Catholic social infrastructure in the capital and steer it in a more democratic and progressive direction. Henry Carton de Wiart, another alumnus of the Brussels Jesuit Collège de Saint-Michel, has always been portrayed as the leader of this group, but de Lantsheere and Renkin, who both were seven years older, must be counted among the main protagonists of the emerging Brussels Christian Democratic movement as well.

In their periodical *L'Avenir Social* (1891–1895) Carton, Renkin, de Lantsheere, and their friends propagated and supported more emancipatory social initiatives such as social housing associations, mutual social insurance, consumer cooperatives, and even independent labour unions. Nonetheless, the goal of these Brussels Christian Democrats was above all political. They were among the early members of the *Belgische Volksbond/Ligue Démocratique*

---

[49] De Lantsheere, 'L'origine', 335–336.

Belge, founded in 1891 by Joris Helleputte (1852–1925). *L'Avenir Social* challenged the political monopoly of the conservative electoral associations; appealed for universal male suffrage and for social legislation regulating minimum wages, working hours and conditions; demanded a stricter policy on alcoholism and gambling; and pleaded for compulsory school attendance and equal subsidies for public and Catholic schools. In 1895, after the introduction of the general plural voting system for men, they founded the *Fédération Démocratique Chrétienne de l'Arrondissement de Bruxelles* and its periodical *La Justice sociale* (1895–1902), which is generally considered the cradle of the Christian workers' movement in the capital.[50]

De Lantsheere was among the founding members of both *L'Avenir Social* and *La Justice Sociale*, but cut back on his editorial activities from 1894 on, according as his academic duties increased. He was somewhat the *'philosophe tranquille'* of the group, the intellectual in the background who pleaded for more nuanced political discourses[51] and contributed elegantly written articles on more difficult subjects, such as the reform of the Belgian Senate, evolutionary theories, or social art and aesthetics.[52] He also appears to have been the author of the then often quoted witty paradox stating that 'the Catholic party would be seriously and truly conservative only if it were to become honestly and thoroughly democratic'.[53]

However, this role as an intellectual in the background did not prevent de Lantsheere from writing several more argumentative articles, again in line with the Neo-Scholastic agenda that he had embraced in Leuven. He made clear how the fight of Christian Democracy for better working conditions concurred with Christianity's deep-seated respect for human dignity.[54] De Lantsheere openly pleaded for more state intervention in the social domain[55] and as a member of the provincial council devoted himself clearly to the fight for minimum wages.[56] Referring to the 'Neo-Scholastic theories' of Wilhelm Emmanuel von Ketteler (1811–1877) on property rights, he strongly contested

---

[50] De Smaele, 'Henry Carton de Wiart', 22–41; Hoyois, *Henry Carton*.
[51] Léon de Lantsheere, 'La mort des nuances (parabole)', *L'Avenir Social* 1.13 (27 March 1892).
[52] See his contributions to *L'Avenir Social*: 'News from nowhere' (20 December 1891), 'La révision et les lois de l'évolution' (24 January 1892), 'La réorganisation du Senat' (14 February 1892), 'Le capital, la spéculation et la finance' (22 May 1892), 'Le luxe et la démocratie' (18 September 1892), 'L'art au point de vue social' (8 episodes between February 1893 and April 1894) and 'H. Taine' (12 March 1893).
[53] Hoyois, *Henry Carton*, 63.
[54] Léon de Lantsheere, 'Le travail et l'art d'après W. Morris', *L'Avenir Social* 2.27 (3 July 1892).
[55] Léon de Lantsheere, 'Les interviews de M. Huret', *L'Avenir Social* 2.35 (28 August 1892).
[56] Léon de Lantsheere, 'Le minimum de salaire au conseil provincial du Brabant', *L'Avenir Social* 2. 15 (10 April 1892).

the assertion that the church's social action had emerged only in the previous decades.[57] He also rejected the socialist plea for a clear separation of church and state.[58]

Parliamentarian and Minister

De Lantsheere was elected a member of the Belgian Chamber of Deputies on 27 May 1900. Over the next years the Brussels and other members of the Christian Democrat faction of the Catholic Party would play a remarkable role in the Belgian political scene. The *Jeune Droite*, as they were called, openly questioned aspects of Catholic government policy, actively entered into dialogue with the liberal and socialist opposition, and often disrespected the discipline of the Catholic Party, thereby challenging the leadership of its longstanding chair, Charles Woeste (1837–1922). Not surprisingly, the divide between conservative and democratic Catholic parliamentarians explicitly came to the fore when social legislation was discussed, such as the laws on professional unions (1898), the labour contract (1900), industrial accidents (1903), or obligatory Sunday rest (1905). In January 1905 de Lantsheere signed a letter to Franz Schollaert (1851–1917), then chair of the Chamber of Deputies, defending the place of Christian Democracy within the Catholic party. In April 1907 he and his Christian Democrat colleagues teamed up with members of the socialist and progressive liberal parliamentary opposition in voting through a law regulating miners' working conditions, which led to the fall of the cabinet of De Smet de Naeyer.

The *Jeune Droite* was of course far from homogeneous. De Lantsheere and his Brussels friends Renkin and Carton de Wiart were clearly well connected to the political inner circles of the capital, including the Belgian Royal Court. They were considered to be more 'governmental' than other Christian Democrats with a more rural background and an ingrained distrust of state power, such as Joris Helleputte and Arthur Verhaegen (1847–1917). Their will to compromise with Belgium's establishment became apparent during the lengthy discussions on compulsory military service and on the government's plans for the expansion of the port and military fortifications in Antwerp. When in the winter of 1905/1906 this last dossier threatened to critically divide the Christian Democratic ranks, de Lantsheere tried to reconcile the factions. Another heavily contested dossier in those years was the future of the Congo Free State. Although de Lantsheere and his friends

---

[57] Léon de Lantsheere, 'Etudes sociales catholiques', *L'Avenir Social* 2.31 (31 July 1892).
[58] Léon de Lantsheere, 'Les nouveaux doctrinaires', *L'Avenir Social* 3.18 (30 April 1893).

often expressed their admiration and gratitude for the role played by King Leopold II in Africa, they were also shocked by the growing rumours and evidence of the atrocities committed in the territory. In May 1901 de Lantsheere co-signed a proposal of August Beernaert (1829–1912) countering government policy and pleading for the immediate takeover of the Congo as a colony of the Belgian State. It was a stance that he and his friends would obstinately defend over the following years.[59] Nonetheless, they enjoyed growing royal sympathy. De Lantsheere would write the report of the parliamentary *Commission des XVII* preparing for the administrative and legal takeover of the Congo in 1907/1908, culminating in the signing of the 'Colonial Charter' on 18 October 1908.[60] In this very delicate case, de Lantsheere displayed a remarkable pragmatism, rejecting the idea of a separate Crown Domain in the colony but on the other hand pleading for a proportionate financial compensation of 50 million francs to a Royal Fund. He defended the colonial vocation of Belgium, it being the fifth economic power in the world, but of course also applauded the 'evangelising proselytism' of the country in central Africa.[61] 'The development of Africa', he declared, 'is neither a commercial affair nor a philanthropic enterprise, but a fair midpoint between both.'[62]

That de Lantsheere in October 1908 was chosen to succeed his friend Renkin as Minister of Justice in the Schollaert cabinet can be considered a reward for his successful completion of the much-disputed Congo dossier. Moreover, his expertise in this policy domain was generally acknowledged, given his academic background and having written the parliamentary reports on the Justice budget in 1901–1907. The political influence of the Brussels Christian Democrats grew steadily, mainly thanks to their clear royal and ecclesiastical backing. In 1910, for instance, Mercier intervened in Rome to have a knighthood in the order of Saint Gregory the Great granted to Renkin and de Lantsheere.[63]

---

[59] Ruben Mantels, *Geleerd in de tropen. Congo & de wetenschap, 1885–1960* (Leuven: UPL, 2007), 41–42; Jean Stengers, 'L'Etat Indépendant du Congo et le Congo belge', in *Congo. Mythes et Réalités. 100 ans d'histoire*, ed. Jean Stengers (Gembloux: Duculot, 1989), 91–119.

[60] Parliamentary Documents Belgian Chamber of Representatives, 1907–1908, nr. 146: Léon de Lantsheere, *Projet de loi réalisant le transfert à la Belgique de l'Etat Indépendant du Congo / Project de loi approuvent l'article additionnel au traité de session de l'Etat Indépendant du Congo à la Belgique. Rapport* (Brussels, 1 April 1908), 306; Alain Stenmans, 'Leon de Lantsheere, ministre de la Justice (1862–1912)', *Biographie coloniale belge* 3 (1952): 495–501; Alain Stenmans, *La Reprise du Congo par la Belgique. Essai d'histoire parlementaire et diplomatique* (Brussels: Editions Techniques et Scientifiques, 1949).

[61] De Lantsheere, *Projet de loi*, 12–13.

[62] Stenmans, 'Léon de Lantsheere', 499; see his interventions in *Parlementaire Handelingen. Kamer van Volksvertegenwoordigers*, 12 December 1906 (183–187) and 6 May 1908 (1875–1883).

[63] Henk de Smaele, *Rechts Vlaanderen. Religie en stemgedrag in negentiende-eeuws België*. KADOC-Studies 33 (Leuven: UPL, 2009), 243.

During his two-and-a-half years as Minister of Justice (30 October 1908–17 June 1911), de Lantsheere had to deal with many different political dossiers. We must certainly mention Belgium's nationality law of 1909[64] and his efforts to foster better coordination between the many bodies involved in the Belgian system for children who had been made wards of court.[65] Striving to improve policing methods in Belgium, de Lantsheere in January 1910 launched an official bulletin centralizing all relevant information on the country's most wanted felons and convicted criminals. His department also did a lot of work in preparing for the international harmonization of legislation on bills of exchange and cheques. The involvement of de Lantsheere in the legal regulation of the rapidly developing use of the automobile, for instance in the issue of the civil liability of drivers, is far less known.[66] During his last year as a minister, he also had to devote a lot of energy to settling the inheritance of King Leopold II and delicately fighting the claims of his daughter Louise (1858–1924) against the Belgian State.

Although one hesitates to concur with Léon Noël's statement that the entire political work of de Lantsheere was based on Thomist doctrine, some of his policy measures clearly bore a Catholic mark. His instructions to the public prosecutors regarding gambling and public decency in music halls, theatres, and cinemas can for instance be seen as a clear expression of Catholic government policy. In August 1909 de Lantsheere strengthened the legal framework protecting the job security of local civil servants when confronted with an alternative (liberal/socialist) political

---

[64] Frank Caestecker, 'In het kielzog van de Natie-Staat. De politiek van nationaliteitsverwerving, -toekenning en- verlies in België, 1830–1909', Belgisch Tijdschrift voor Nieuwste Geschiedenis/ Revue Belge d'Histoire contemporaine 3–4 (1997): 323–349; Frank Caestecker et al., Belg worden. De geschiedenis van de Belgische nationaliteitsverwerving sinds 1830 (Mechelen: Wolters Kluwer, 2016).

[65] These measures must be linked to the sustained efforts of his administration, since the first blueprint on the matter of Minister Jules Lejeune (1828–1911) in 1889, to create a more comprehensive legal framework on juvenile care, clearly in line with the 'social defense doctrine' of for instance Adolphe Prins (1845–1919). De Lantsheere's successor Carton de Wiart would introduce the Belgian Children's Protection Act of 15 May 1912. Marie-Sylvie Dupont-Bouchat, Les pénitenciers pour les enfants en Belgique au XIXe siècle (1840–1914) (Louvain-la-Neuve: Commission internationale pour l'histoire des Assemblées d'États, 1996); Jenneke Christiaens, 'A history of Belgium's Child Protection Act of 1912: the redefinition of the juvenile offender and his punishment', European Journal of Crime, Criminal Law and Criminal Justice 7.1 (1999): 5–21.

[66] Donald Weber, Automobilisering en de overheid in België voor 1940. Besluitvormingsprocessen bij de ontwikkeling van een conflictbeheersingssysteem (PhD diss., University of Ghent, 2009), here 291–299; Parlementaire Handelingen. Senaat, 4, 8 (10–11 June 1909).

majority.⁶⁷ Another of his religiously coloured measures concerned the repeal of the legal sanctioning of priests administering a marriage *in extremis* and thus not complying with the legal primacy of the civic marriage.⁶⁸ As his major accomplishment de Lantsheere himself mostly cited the law of 12 August 1911, granting legal personality to the two private universities of Belgium, the Catholic one in Leuven and the Free University of Brussels.⁶⁹ Although the main parliamentary discussions on the bill he had prepared took place after his resignation, his successor Carton de Wiart invited de Lantsheere to introduce the text to parliament. It was clear that both saw the law as a prelude to a more general framework that would solve the old and much-disputed absence in Belgian law of a flexible legal personality to accommodate the many social institutions (schools, hospitals, ...) that had been founded by religious institutes or other church-related actors.⁷⁰

De Lantsheere was indeed an ardent supporter of freedom of education. He applauded the fast-growing network of Catholic schools in Belgium, with a particular sympathy for the Saint-Luc art and craft schools of the Brothers of the Christian Schools.⁷¹ When the Schollaert cabinet fell in June 1911, he was clearly disappointed that due to its inner divisions, the Catholic Party had missed a unique chance to once and for all settle the long-lasting conflict on the financing of primary education. 'Equal subsidies are the alpha and omega of the school issue, we won't solve it without them', he stated to an assembly of Catholic young guards and students at the end of August 1911. In February 1912 he again demonstrated his dedication to the cause of free school choice at a celebration in Brussels on the occasion of the 100th birthday of Charles de Montalembert (1810–1870).⁷² After the Catholic electoral victory of 2 June 1912

---

67 Parliamentary Documents Belgian Chamber of Representatives, 1908–1909, nr. 157: *Project de loi relatif à la stabilité des emplois dépendant des établissements publics de bienfaisance et des mont-de-piété*, 26 May 1909.

68 Law of 3 August 1909, *Belgisch Staatsblad/Moniteur Belge*, 12 August 1909, 4441; see his interventions in the parliamentary discussions on this bill proposed by Woeste: *Parlementaire Handelingen. Kamer van Volksvertegenwoordigers*, 27 November 1908, 138–142.

69 *Belgisch Staatsblad/Moniteur Belge*, 21 August 1911; Lamberts and Roegiers, *De Universiteit te Leuven*, 212–213.

70 Léon de Lantsheere, 'Les controverses relatives à la personnification civile', *Revue Sociale Catholique* 16 (1911–1912): 178–181. On the often-shady legal constructions used by religious congregations in the 19th century to manage their assets, see Fred Stevens, 'Les associations religieuses en Belgique pendant le 19ᵉ siècle', in *Religious Institutes in Western Europe in the 19th and 20th Centuries: Historiography, Research and Legal Position*, eds. Jan De Maeyer, Sofie Leplae, and Joachim Schmiedl (Leuven: Leuven University Press, 2004), 185–202.

71 Ecole Saint-Luc Bruxelles, *Discours de M. Léon de Lantsheere, député de Bruxelles. Rapport annuel 1904. Distribution des prix 1904* (Brussels: F. van Gompel, 1904).

72 Léon de Lantsheere, 'Montalembert et les temps nouveaux', *Revue Générale* 95.48 (March 1912): 335–347.

he made clear that now the school issue had to be a top priority of the new cabinet.[73]

GENERAL APPRAISAL AND INFLUENCE

On de Lantsheere's death many different, but uniformly laudatory words were written and spoken to honour the professor and politician who had died so young and unexpectedly.[74] These texts have clearly coloured his image in historiography, although there are few studies that examine his role and contributions in any depth. De Lantsheere was the first of his political generation to disappear, while most of his friends, colleagues, and political adversaries continued their careers in the interwar period, some of them even writing memoirs. The new democratic socio-political order that arose after the Armistice somewhat obscured the memory of the political protagonists of Belgium's *belle époque*. De Lantsheere's role was quickly forgotten. Meanwhile, Catholic intellectual culture ventured into new paths. After the devastation of the First World War, neo-Scholasticism 'exploded' in many different directions, ranging from aesthetics to royalist nationalism.[75] De Lantsheere was, of course, remembered as a prominent member of the first generation that had carried Leuven's Thomist revival. However, in the new context of the 1920s his ideas and writings no longer looked relevant and were only rarely quoted.

Was de Lantsheere really 'one of the most cultivated minds of his time', as Maurice Defourny claimed in his obituary? His literacy in many different domains indeed impressed both his colleagues and students. However, this quality did not really find a lasting result in ground-breaking studies. In his main field of teaching, that of criminal law, he had hardly any publications. The comparative and subject-based way in which he and van den Heuvel approached the teaching of private law at the School for Political and Social Sciences was indeed an innovation in Leuven. But de Lantsheere did not publish any handbooks in this field either. Being a philosopher first, he showed great interest in the history/philosophy of law, but his agenda in that

---

[73] Léon de Lantsheere, 'Les élections du 2 juin 1912 en Belgique', *Revue Sociale Catholique* 16 (1911–1912): 350–364.

[74] See the references in fn. 1 and the parliamentary commemoration of the deceased members, de Lantsheere and Beernaert, in *Annales parlementaires de la Belgique. Chambre de Représentants. Session ordinaire de 1911–1912. Séance d'ouverture du mardi 12 Novembre 1912*, 4–6. In the church of Asse, a commemorative plate was unveiled on 26 July 1914. In 1913 a street in Etterbeek was named after him.

[75] Philippe Chenaux, *Entre Mourras et Maritain. Une génération intellectuelle catholique (1920–1930)* (Paris: Le Cerf, 1999).

field was far more apologetic and political than it was academic. De Lantsheere fully embraced Mercier's ambition to sculpt an integrated or mitigated modernity by encouraging the church and the Catholic elite to turn toward the popular classes and enter into a dialogue with modern society and science, incorporating their innovations, but all this moderately and circumspectly, in order to secure a harmonious synthesis with Catholic teachings and tradition.[76]

De Lantsheere was not a self-made man. His family was part of the Brussels Catholic bourgeois establishment, his father a member of the country's highest political and financial circles. This background of course brought responsibilities but on the other hand helped him to secure his future. It also enabled him to walk alternative, even deviant, paths, both intellectually and politically. Together with his Brussels Christian Democrat friends, de Lantsheere caused a new wind to blow in the somewhat stuffy Catholic Party and thus in Belgian politics. Their plea for a social and democratic turn in policy of course led to much turbulence and conflict, but was finally acknowledged. De Lantsheere was certainly not the most radical member of the *Jeune Droite*. Not forgetting his family background, his academic expertise, and both the royal and ecclesiastical protection he enjoyed, it was maybe above all this moderateness that brought him into government. As a Minister of Justice, de Lantsheere was able to implement several important legal measures, but he also experienced the harshness and disappointments of party politics.[77] It was with relief that he returned to the habitat that he cherished above all, the intellectual shelter of academia.

RECOMMENDED READINGS

Braun, Alexandre. 'Léon de Lantsheere, ministre de la Justice'. *Almanach des étudiants catholiques* (1913): 256–273.
De Wulf, Maurice. 'Nécrologie. Léon de Lantsheere'. *Revue néo-scolastique de philosophie* 19 (1912): 563–565.
Deferme, Jo. 'De Lantsheere, Léon, Marie, Joseph, Antoine'. *La Nouvelle Biographie Nationale* 10 (2009): 120–122.
Defourny, Maurice. 'Léon de Lantsheere'. *Revue Sociale Catholique* 16 (1911–1912): 343–350.

---

[76] Jan De Maeyer, 'De wending van de kerk naar het volk (1884–1926)', in *Het aartsbisdom Mechelen-Brussel: 450 jaar geschiedenis* 2 (Antwerp/Leuven: Halewijn/KADOC, 2009), 101–171.

[77] Charles Woeste remembered de Lantsheere as 'a very cultivated mind' but also claimed that 'he did not have the qualities of a politician; he acted in jest'. Woeste, *Mémoires pour servir à l'histoire contemporaine de la Belgique* 2 (Brussels: Edition Universelle, 1933), 405.

Descamps, Édouard. 'Léon de Lantsheere. Discours prononcé le 14 novembre 1912, en la Salle des Promotions de l'Université, par le baron Descamps, doyen de la Faculté de Droit'. *Annuaire de l'Université catholique de Louvain* 1913 (1913): XXXVII-XL.

Dupriéz, Léon. 'Léon de Lantsheere'. *Revue Générale* 96.48 (1912): 481–482.

Ladeuze, Paulin. 'Discours prononcé par Monseigneur P. Ladeuze, recteur magnifique de l'Université catholique de Louvain, le jeudi 29 août 1912, aux funérailles de M. le professeur L. de Lantsheere'. *Annuaire de l'Université catholique de Louvain* 1913 (1913): XXXII–XXXVI.

Ladeuze, Paulin. 'Inauguration dans l'église d'Assche, le 26 juillet 1914, d'une plaque commémorative en l'honneur de Léon de Lantsheere, professeur de droit pénal à l'Université Catholique décédé le 26 aout 1912. Discours de Mgr Ladeuze, rector magnifique de l'Université'. *Annuaire de l'Université catholique de Louvain* 1915–1919 (1924): 77–83.

Meerts, Kristien. 'Leo de Lantsheere'. In *Lovanium docet. Geschiedenis van de Leuvense Rechtsfaculteit*, edited by Guido van Dievoet, 186–188. Leuven: Faculteit Rechten KU Leuven, 1988.

Noël, Léon. 'In memoriam Leon-Marie-Joseph-Antoine de Lantsheere, professeur à la Faculté de droit de l'Universite de Louvain, maître de conférences à l'Institut Supérieur de Philosophie, député de Bruxelles, ancien ministre de la Justice du Royaume de Belgique, 23 septembre 1862–26 août 1912'. *Annales de l'Institut Supérieur de Philosophie* II (1913): 311–328.

Stenmans, Alain. 'Lantsheere (de) *(Léon-Joseph-Marie-Antoine)*'. In *Biographie coloniale belge* 3 (1952): 495–501.

Van Molle, Paul. 'De Lantsheere, Léon, Marie Joseph Antoine'. In *Het Belgisch parlement. 1894–1972*, 84–85. Antwerp/Utrecht: Standaard, 1972.

16

Paul Scholten

Timo Slootweg

BIOGRAPHICAL INTRODUCTION[1]

Born in Amsterdam in 1875, Paulus Scholten, jurist, died aboard a ship in 1946 on his way to the United States and Canada. In 1893, he enrolled at the Faculty of Law at the Universiteit van Amsterdam. In 1895, he passed the candidate's exam, and in 1898 his (final) doctoral exam. In 1899, Scholten obtained his doctorate with distinction (*cum laude*) with a thesis on 'damages other than contract and tort'. In 1903, he married Grietje Fockema. Of this marriage two sons and one daughter were born.

Scholten settled in his native town as a practising lawyer and solicitor (1899–1907) and in 1903 was appointed deputy judge, a position he held until 1915, in which year he became deputy justice at the Amsterdam Court of Justice until 1935. In 1906, he gained a temporary post, lecturing on civil law and civil procedure at the University of Amsterdam. From 1907 to 1914 he was professor of Roman law in Amsterdam, and in addition, in 1910, he was again entrusted with civil law and civil procedure. From 1914 onward, his teaching commitment also included ancient Dutch law and the encyclopedia of law. From 1927 to 1946 he taught philosophy of law as well. His full schedule as lecturer did not prevent him from acting as editor for the journal on private law, *Notarial Profession and Registration* (WPNR), and as annotator to the journal on Dutch case law (NJ). In 1922, he was appointed member of the Royal Dutch Academy of Sciences. In 1924, he took on the task of the establishment of a school for higher education in law in former Batavia (currently Indonesia). Before and during this sojourn of several months in the Dutch East Indies he became involved in many aspects of Indonesian society. For almost twenty years Scholten was chair of the Amsterdam

---

[1] The biographical information given below draws from: W. M. Peletier, 'Scholten, Paulus (1875–1946)', in *Biografisch Woordenboek van Nederland. Vol. II* (The Hague, 1979), 536.

University Society and rector from 1932 to 1933. He was editor and active participant of many journals and chair of the Reorganization Committee of the Dutch Reformed Church.

Scholten had converted to Christianity and joined the Dutch Reformed Church in 1913. He was then 38. His faith and Christian convictions increasingly guided his thoughts and activities in the field of law. Whenever, according to Scholten, fairness or custom were at stake, the final say was not left to legal doctrine, but a solution needed to be sought that was acceptable both practically and theoretically. The law itself is not of decisive importance, as there will always be a need for interpretation of laws and facts. This problem is extensively treated in the first, General Part of Mr C. Asser's *Manual for the Practice of Dutch Civil Law* (1931), which dealt with the nature and method of private law. In time Scholten became intensively occupied with fundamental questions concerning the essence of law, which in his view was situated 'behind the law', in the personal responsibility of the judge. Scholten worked in a non-rationalistic way, proceeding from the human person and his conscience, from love, forgiveness, and compassion; principles that referred to an elusive form of justice, beyond the law.

In respect to his beliefs and convictions, it is not surprising that for Scholten, the Second World War and German occupation of his home country were an abomination. With his chivalrous personality he devoted himself to maintaining the fighting spirit of the Dutch people. It was on his initiative that an informal board for concerted action was established among the different universities and schools for higher education. Scholten publicly protested against the use of discriminating measures against Jewish public servants.

In addition to this, he performed a leading role in Dutch ecumenicity. In 1940 the General Synod of the Dutch Reformed Church convened a committee for ecclesiastical consultations. The main study group of this committee, chaired by Scholten, was focused on church and government, which determined the attitude of the Dutch Reformed Church toward measures taken by the German authorities: the persecution of Jews, the violation of justice, and the imposition of a National Socialist philosophy of life.

In 1942 Scholten was arrested because of these activities. He was banished to South Limburg (Valkenburg). Later in 1942 Scholten was placed under house arrest, but he managed to work for his fatherland and the Dutch Reformed Church. Through his chairmanship of the Reorganizing Committee of the Dutch Reformed Church, he had a large influence on the replacement of the standing rules of 1816, with a new church order drawn up and accepted by the Dutch Reformed Church itself.

Throughout the war Scholten protested and resisted when freedom of conscience and the principles of Dutch society were at issue. Later he was in charge of the so-called 'Scholten group', which addressed problems relating to the occupation and developed plans for the 'postwar Netherlands'. This group consisted of persons of different political and religious persuasion. Out of this group and a number of other illegal groups, the National Advisory Committee arose when the occupation ended. Paul Scholten accepted the chairmanship on 20 July 1945. The committee had among its tasks to make proposals for the appointment of members to the National Emergency Parliament.

Scholten, who until then had been a member of the Christian Historical Union (CHU), was appointed member of the first chamber of the Dutch parliament. After some time, he ended his membership of the CHU. His Christian inspirations made his political preference shift to the Labor Party (PVDA), which was newly constituted in February 1946. His sudden demise while on a journey to the United States ended this versatile life. The great comprehensive work he had begun to write in 1943, *The right of law*, would always remain unfinished.

MAJOR THEMES AND CONTRIBUTIONS

Scholten believed the principles of law to be embedded in the personal relationship of (and the 'encounter' between) man and God ('I and Thou'). All his theoretical publications bear witness to this. He was in this respect influenced by quite a few and sometimes fairly diverse sources. Originally he was under the influence of the so-called 'Ethical Theology', a strand of Dutch origin that taught the importance of existence and personal life over doctrine and dogma. An early source of this 'ethical' inspiration came especially from P. D. Chantepie de la Saussaye (1848–1920), who himself expressed strong affinity with two writers, Alexandre Vinet (1797–1847) and Søren Kierkegaard (1813–1855). Very important was the spiritual and intellectual influence of Scholten's lifelong friend and famous pedagogue Phillip Kohnstamm (1875–1951), whose personalist philosophy (according to himself) was akin to existentialist thought. In 1924 Scholten explicitly confessed to the personalistic philosophy developed by Kohnstamm. (DG 286–287/VG I 268–269)

All through his work Scholten also refers to and draws from famous foreign thinkers, such as Friedrich Gogarten (1887–1967), Ferdinand Ebner (1882–1931), Karl Heim (1874–1958), Karl Jaspers (1910–1969), and Martin Buber (1878–1965); likewise writers from the personalist, dialogical, and existentialist spectrum.

In time Scholten became more and more captivated by the latest theological developments of his time: by the 'Theology of Crisis' and by the 'Dialectical Theology', both of which originated in Switzerland. Since 1930, he increasingly focused on Karl Barth (1886–1986) and Emil Brunner (1889–1966). Eventually he, together with Dr Oepke Noordmans and others, explicitly distanced himself from the former, 'ethical' theologians and from neo-Calvinism.

With Karl Barth and others, the heteronomous 'Word of God' and the dynamics of dialogue became of even more importance to Scholten, influencing his perspectives on politics and law and his research programme. In 1939 Scholten became editor-in-chief of the ambitious new theological journal *Word and World* (*Woord en Wereld*). In his editorial preface to the first edition, Scholten committed himself explicitly to the new Protestant movement of dialectical theology. In his mission statement he dedicated this journal to the theological movement, of which Karl Barth had been the pioneer and main figure.

Scholten fought against the rationality and scientism in law with the weapons of the paradox, the person, and the personal decision. The infinite, qualitative differences, paradoxes, or antitheses between time and eternity and between world and word, between the realm of God and the realm of Caesar, implicate a (similar) unbridgeable distance between law and justice, is and ought, will and knowledge. Justice and fairness (equity) are decisive for law. As such they can never be fully codified and found in written human law. Without the law (in itself) being able to tell us what to do, adjudication is the semi-ethical practice of personal decision-making through which justice is found. It is not by means of some abstract principle, but only through the mediation of the individual person that the many contradictions in life can be surmounted. (AD/DG 128–135)

The many-sided 'brokenness' that characterizes the world is decisive for how Scholten judges law. This brokenness or paradoxicality cannot be dealt with by means of a rational (e.g. Hegelian) dialectic of some sort, or in reference to some higher principle of reason. Instead it implicates and appeals to an 'existential dialectic' that involves the responsibility of the human person. It was faith that directed Scholten to these valuable insights. To exist (as he did) in the transcendent light of infinity involves never having lasting possession of it in this world: infinity cannot be limited and 'imprisoned' in anything conceptual, intelligible, determinate, and unchangeable. Instead of courageously accepting this existential fate of always having to decide, man searches for support and certainty and 'naturally' closes himself off from the irrational. This 'natural' tendency to rationality also manifests itself in law, more specifically in its legalistic conception. In 1924, in *Law and equity* (DG

289/VG I 271), Scholten – in reference to Jaspers – argues that rationalists always cling to the determinate and general and turn it into something of absolute validity. The decision then becomes an illusory shadow play against the background of what has already been decided. However, the decision cannot be thought of as the choice between an objective good and an evil that exists prior to freedom. (DG 285/VG I 267) The distinction between good and evil has no existence outside of and beyond the sphere of freedom: outside the non-rational decision of conscience.

Law certainly responds to the appeal to justice. But it forcefully tries to secure and embody it in determinate laws, procedures, and institutions. Thus, it never succeeds in coinciding with justice. Justice requires that justice be done in the individual case, while the law always ranks the individual case under a general rule. Justice cannot be captured in a fixed legal form and neither can it be deduced from a pre-established natural order.

Law, both positive and natural law, is governed by fear. Law markedly rationalizes the moral judgements it involves. But although its method certainly has its rational and scientific moments or phases, law in essence is not a science but a form of art. Justice is served through the decision. Only decisions, not rules and norms, can be just or righteous. Just as man is not perfect and is subject to continual growth, so is the legal order (of laws, procedures, and jurisdiction) always imperfect and continually changing. Law changes in relation to an ever-changing and always concrete reality. Finding law involves having to do with concrete men of flesh and bone: our brothers and neighbours are the actual subject behind the very necessary but always far too abstract concepts of law. Therefore, in the end human conscience must have the final say. For Scholten this implies that if someone, in all conscience, is convinced that the government exceeds the limits set by law in exerting its authority, he may, if worst comes to worst, make a stand against that government. As he argues in *Law and Philosophy of Life* (1915), his would be the only justification for a civil revolution against the state. (DG 177–178/ VG I 160–161)

The General Part

Scholten is famous in particular for his 'General Part' of the Asser-series, a manual on Dutch civil law. For many contemporary Dutch reading students, scholars, and jurists, Scholten's famous *General Method of Private Law* is still a relevant source for which they find no equivalent in the international body of knowledge. The General Part (particularly its first chapter), written in 1931, describes and analyzes general issues of Legal Theory from the perspective of the judge, in the process of making legal decisions. Scholten argues that the judge's responsibility is substantially more profound than is usually acknowledged. He typically polemicizes against rationalist ideologies of all kinds (idealism, naturalism, stoicism, positivism) that tend to disguise the decision as such behind a veil of illusions: the illusory positivity of laws, facts, 'objective' natural laws, principles, and ideas.

Under the influence of so many forms of rationalism, law has often passed over the responsibility for the decision under the impression (a prejudice) that it can and should logically follow from laws, all kinds of sources of law and rational procedures. The decision has been thought of and approached in practice as being the logical 'conclusion' of a scientific syllogism. The negative consequence hereof is that personal responsibility for the decision is being evaded, to the detriment of justice. To 'thirst after justice' as every sincere judge should do, involves taking existential responsibility for one's interpretations and decisions. Without being willing to do so (on grounds often of some misconceived bureaucratic and scientific modesty), one's power of judgement is bound to fail. A decision of some sort will be always made, but without the wisdom and critical scrutiny of a personal conscience behind it. Although the difficult concept of conscience must always evade definition, description, and analysis (DG 286/VG 268), Scholten clearly argues that it is not autonomous, but relational and heteronomous: intrinsically related (or subjected) to the other, to God (the Wholly Other), to Christ and to our neighbour (the other), who is not necessarily an alter ego. The wise judge, not the smart, the judicious, or the learned judge, represents the ideal for Scholten. In view of the other, 'a wise judge subordinates his knowledge and science to the task of personal and conscientious decision-making'. (AD 134/VG I 134)

Although the General Part on the method of private law has brought him fame, it is questionable whether the recognition should not be extended to other, more profound, writings. The book does not adequately represent the full width and depth of his ideas, which are only implicated in a very indirect way. The General Part is relatively down to earth and practical, which explains some of its popularity. And although the last paragraph of the first chapter (§28) (AD/DG 129–135), which deals with the nature of the decision, opens the perspective on many fundamental theoretical and existential themes, they are not (as such) subject to much philosophical discussion. Scholten himself refers here to other writings for explanation; to his philosophy of life in particular.

This implies that the General Part can be fully appreciated only in the context of the many loose and dispersed articles that he wrote and that deal especially with the relation between law and Christian faith and theology. To name just a couple of these articles, which are all included in his collected work: 'Law and Philosophy of Life' (1915); 'Law and Love' (1917); 'Law and Justice' (1938); 'Gospel and Law' (1939); 'Principles of Society' (1934); 'What Can Man Know about God?' (1937).

Both in the General Part and elsewhere Scholten most famously focusses on the theme of decision-making. It is important to appreciate the existentialist and personalist import, influenced especially by ethical and dialectical theology. To concentrate solely on his methodology, as most of his interpreters have done, leads one to philosophically underappreciate his understanding of law as an existential phenomenon of life. Whoever separates law and philosophy of life, Scholten says, makes himself guilty of harming both. He forges and corrupts his jurisprudence by abstracting from the highest values of life and personal existence, as he argues in 'Law and Philosophy of Life'. (DG 178/VG I 161)

Law cannot be principally defined by judicial rules and the procedures. No pre-existing set of rules can be laid down to make explicit how one should decide on this or that particular case, in this or that particular situation, in relation to this or that individual person. We need to appreciate the authority and (relative) sovereignty of the judge, which is that he or she is the one who has the responsibility for having to make a genuine decision.

The philosophical implication of this insight is that we should distance ourselves from a scientific theory of law in the sense of Hans Kelsen's 'Reine Rechtslehre': a theory from which all subjective or existential elements have been eliminated.[2] Such a theory is neither feasible nor wanted. It would be unfeasible because the law in particular, as well as the meaning of laws, are neither predefined nor positive. They must be 'found' through a non-systematic process of interpretation, which is determined by all kinds of hermeneutical decisions, including the decision on how to determine the relative weight of the different products of interpretation. Without taking responsibility for interpreting the law and finding its meaning in relation to the case at hand, there is no law in the proper sense of the word. And the same applies to the so-called 'facts' of the case at hand. They also are not given without the control of the interpreter, who takes on responsibility for

---

[2] Hans Kelsen (1878–1970), *Reine Rechtslehre* (Leipzig/Vienna: Deuticke, 1934). With its pure doctrine, Kelsen aims at a strictly scientific analysis of law, in which non-legal terms are entirely omitted. According to Kelsen, scientific doctrine does not prescribe how law *should* be, but how it really is. The legal doctrine must be: a value-free (non-morally judgemental) descriptive science of the formally binding force of legal norms. Other well-known, 'later' representatives of legal scientism are: Alf Ross, *On Law and Justice* (Berkeley: University of California Press, 1959), and Herbert Hart, *The Concept of Law* (Oxford: Oxford University Press, 1961).

hermeneutically determining what the facts are. The judge is in the precarious position that he is to decide 'without the law'.

At every moment in law, the dynamic and paradoxicality of life breaks through the solidified surface of the concepts, rules, and principles of the system with which we try to do justice. This causes the judge to (have to) interpret the rules and to bend and adjust their meaning, bringing them to 'communicate' with the case at hand. At every moment in the process of judging, life interferes with what always threatens to become an estranged system of laws, and a dead mechanism of merely logical argumentation. Scholten demonstrates that the decision is not a logical 'conclusion', but an ethical decision and an artistic invention. 'Adjudication is always creative work'. (DG 292/VG 274) The wise judge is sensitive to the ultimately ambiguous, unruly, and unruled quality of human life, which does not fit our conceptual apparatus: a paradoxical reality which can never be adequately understood and measured by any set of rules, no matter how rich and complex.

The rule of men as persons must always existentially underlie the rule of law and the law of rules. To pretend otherwise, to think of the possibility of a perfect rule of law, is to invite a dangerous vulnerability. It invites judicial impotence and injustice when unforeseen and unpredictable cases and situations present themselves. The naïve, formalistic, and rationalistic paradigm of legal positivism sets us up to be overtaken by events of life that do not fit our categories of good and evil. Justice seen as such tempts us to distance ourselves from the actual human element, which is always personal and singular.

There is no provable truth here [in law]. But it is better to accept this deficiency and subjectivity than to gaze at an appearance of objectivity and certainty which is nothing more than an illusion and which does not stand up to criticism. (DG 135/AD 135)

Law in a purely scientific and positivist sense is both impossible and unwanted. Scholten stresses the human and personal quality of law and adjudication. He wants to reinstate the personal element in law, which – left to itself – has a dangerous dehumanizing tendency. It is because life is life that proper decisions will always be necessary: that judgments will always demand something more profound, more responsive and creative than the simple application of laws and the logical acumen to accomplish the underlying argumentation.

The legal judgment is more than a scientific judgement of observation and logical argument. It is not a scientific judgement, but a declaration of will: this is how it should be. Finally, it is a leap, like every deed, every moral judgement is. (DG 130/AD 130)

The knowledge of positive law serves no purpose other than that it prepares the judge for the decision that he will have to make. This scientific dimension does not take this responsibility from his shoulders, as Scholten says in Law and Morality. (DG 307/VG I 288) Scholten goes so far as to underline that adjudication involves a power of judgement that invents and 'creates law', instead of merely applying pregiven laws. Law is not a science, although it has its scientific and rational dimensions. Law in fact is a form of art: an art of invention or creation. Law is the creation of form: a 'giving form' to what is only vaguely 'there', in our imagination. Law is a human creation that as such does not automatically control us:

> It [law] is undoubtedly mental [intellectual] work that must be done here, it cannot be done without knowledge, knowledge of rules and social relations, but is it science? Perhaps the work that led to the decision was a whole or half scientific, but this handling, this judging, this process of finding law in itself might best be called 'ars'. If at least one then does not understand it as a skill or technique, but as a giving form to vague imaginations, to crystallize them into law, in short – a creation of form, which can be called art. (VG I 455)

The judge truly decides – not only observes – in favour of whom the scale of Themis tilts. The grounding of law and rules on human action and art is part of what Scholten sees as the need to defend human life. As a Christian, he wants to defend human life against the dehumanizing mechanisms of a science and bureaucracy that (as such) do not deal with persons, men of flesh and blood, but with 'conceptual mummies': rules, numbers, cases, types, instances of general principles, et cetera.

In the specialized bureaucracy of the modern state, law is transformed to the rational rule of law in which professional responsibility is reduced to the mechanical discharge of well-defined, objective, transparent, and predictable procedures, without regard for the reality of 'real' people. However, life is not intelligible without the personal concern of and for 'living' persons. In wanting to control and out of desire for calculability, transparency, and equality, man has given in to the neutralization and mechanization of law: to the 'domestication' of the personal decision, by interpreting it as a formal, mechanical, and logical application; a process devoid of (the involvement of) the sovereignty of people and the spiritual responsibility of persons.

Scholten certainly accepts that legitimacy is democratic: founded on the will of the people. And he also accepts the democratic code of the separation of powers (the notion that power must always be checked by power), in which the judicial power is limited and bounded by the laws that are given by the people.

Scholten also acknowledges that the judge is obliged to explain, motivate, and legitimize his decision in terms of the law and the facts *in casu*; that he is not free to do and decide whatever he wants. In his view, however, the separation of powers should not be interpreted in an absolute sense. Given the under- and over-determined meaning of the law, we may not assimilate legitimacy to legality, nor may we substitute procedure for personal responsibility.

Rationalism in law absolutizes what should merely have relative weight and meaning. Accordingly, law has no need of individual persons. To the reigning ideology of positivism especially, judges should act like '*êtres inanimé*' and like '*bouches de la loi*' (Montesquieu): 'lifeless beings', rule-abiding 'mouthpieces of the law', without real blood running through their veins, without any consideration for the other, and without love for our neighbour. Under the influence of rationalism and positivism, the personalistic and aesthetic elements of law have tended to disappear from the ethics of jurisprudence: they withdrew from our attention and recognition. But no matter what we do to disguise our decisions as conclusions, they (in effect) remain our personal responsibility.

Judges are bound, yet free. Although bound by the law, they are free to decide. Lawgivers on the other hand are free, yet bound. They are free to decide, yet bound to their neighbours, to the life of the persons whom they should respect and protect. According to the Principles of Society (1934), political authority depends not on power alone, but on the reverence of leaders for the unalienable right of the human person: on the subject's recognition of their (the leaders') respect for him. (DG 369–376/VG I 362–379)

Judicial decision-making certainly implies an aesthetic moment. Law is art, according to Scholten, as we have already seen. To judge is to 'creatively respond' to whatever happens: to whoever presents himself as our brother and neighbour. Adjudication can be understood on the model of God's creation. Christian faith implies that man is created 'in the image of God'. (Gen. 1; 26) He is bound to be free and creative as God (the Creator) Himself is: as such he is not subject to laid-down laws. Man is called upon to be an artist and a creator. And when he is 'on duty' as a jurist or as a judge, this remains his calling. He should not restrict himself to obeying and administering moral or judicial laws. If he does so, he is simply disobedient to God: to the law of love which demands that we transcend the law, to enter into the personal relation:

> One cannot do more violence to the deepest wisdom given to moral life, Jesus' teaching, than by moralizing it, transforming it into a series of precepts. Whoever tries to do this turns the gospel into law. (DG 287 /VG I 269)

In relation to the living God of the Bible we are equipped with a new, heteronomous or relational conscience. We no longer decide on the grounds of a pregiven truth, a law without or within, or on the grounds of an internal (subjective) quality or virtue. It is only through the living word of God that one remains bound to His free will and to the concrete neighbour. Love does not know 'the good' in advance of the relation and decision. It is precisely in this sense that she is bound to the other and not subjectively 'imprisoned in itself'. Every alienation, every legal generalization, every rationalization of human relations is relativized or held in suspense through the demand of love. Love focusses on the singular and the concrete: it is precisely in our relation to this one concrete person in which infinity lies hidden.

Law and love stand in an antithetical relationship. The distance between them can only be bridged by means of an existential dialectic: through the conscience and momentary decision of a responsible person. Man should be prepared to obey God and to suspend and transcend the law, if He, love (God is love) and the situation demand this from him. Also, the decision is not given by the law in such a way that the judge is merely its instrument. One is always under the moral obligation of having to give meaning to laws and 'facts': to respond to the divine 'demand of the moment' (Barth: 'das Gebot der Stunde'). It is only by means of the decision, made possible through the 'indecisiveness of the law', that the uniqueness or singularity of justice can be met with.

In complex and ambiguous situations, when two or more laws at the same time claim to be uniquely relevant and applicable for the case at hand, it is you and I – not the law – who must decide. We must decide, not through the workings of an isolated (solipsistic) power of judgement, but in relation and connection to 'the guiding star' of either some general 'idea' or some concrete 'person'. This important alternative, which to Scholten represents an existential choice, refers to the well-known opposition to idealism and personalism, on which we will elaborate in the next paragraph. We quote the famous but notedly difficult last sentence of §28 of the General Part in full:

> In my opinion, there are only two possibilities: either it will be an idea, the idea of the right, in one of the forms in which the spirit of the world is realized, who can be the leader here, or the conscience is subjected to a higher power, who as a Person revealed in Creation and History, confronts

individual and community with its unconditional demands. The first is the idea of idealism, especially in its Hegelian pantheistic forms; the second is the requirement of the Christian faith.   (DG 135/AD 135)

According to the Principles of Society, a passive, independent, and objective attitude (that of the distanced spectator and scientist) is both impossible and 'unlawful' in law. If this is not the case, we will turn what is serious, and what demands our participation, into a game and a joke. (DG 364/VG I 357)

Judgement and Conscience

There is a realm of wisdom from which the logician is excluded. In view of this realm, art is an essential correlative and supplement to the discipline of law. We have, according to Scholten, to be so courageous and wise as to acknowledge the aesthetic conditions of judging and deciding. Under these circumstances, we will have to limit the dangers of errancy and aberrance. If all or much comes down to our personal power of judgement, then how must our conscience be formed and constituted to ever be able to bear (in the service of law) this heavy responsibility of judging? Let us first recapitulate what we have already found: the naive faith in science, technology, and reason, the conviction that the decision (justice) results from the law itself, is 'a fruit from the tree of knowledge' and the wide and certain road to errancy. This means that we stand guilty of having to act and decide. We have no choice but to bring to bear on the process of adjudication our own personal sense of judgement. The judge stands trial before the council of his conscience: this is the first transcendental precondition of any justifiable decision. But this concept of conscience should not be understood in the sense of natural law theory: the naturalism that traditionally has been of enormous influence on Christianity. Scholten thinks that there is no inborn ('positive') set of eternal and unchangeable ethical principles to fall back on whenever we must decide on what to do or how to judge. On the basis of the naturalistic reflection on man, as he in essence is, we never arrive at what one ought to do. 'There is a breach in man, what Christianity calls sin'. According to the Principles of Society, this is why one has to reject naturalism. (DG 367–368/ VG 361–362)

During his life and all through his work Scholten consistently attacked natural law theory (immanent idealism) and categorically rejected its rigid and impotent laws and principles. (DG 158/VG I 141, 332/VG I 313) Natural conscience (as well as conscience in idealism) is bound to fail, because it is unrelated and estranged, not only from the living God, but also from Jesus Christ, who lived and still lives among us in the lives of others. We ought (for the sake of justice) to live and act 'out of grace'. Our main objective should be not to believe unconditionally in the idols of the state and its political interests in the common good, in laws, or in pregiven ethical principles. Everything in law is changed when God as a sovereign person is placed above the law (both ethical as well as judicial). Christianity means freedom of conscience: the freedom of our personal responsibility to choose and decide, with nothing to guide us but God, Christ, and the face of the other. God is community: He is the living relation with Himself, with Christ, and with His creation. Through Christ we are asked to encounter our concrete neighbour: to read the right that speaks from his countenance. We are the image of God in so far that we find ourselves in relation to the other, 'subjected' to his appeal for justice.[3] One can summarize Scholten's anthropology in contradistinction to Descartes's famous cogito: 'I respond, therefore I am'. People appear as persons and realize their being through the encounter with others. Humanity exists in the anthropological definition of existence as being together with the other. Abstracted from its relations to the other, seen and approached as either individuals or 'political animals', man is a stranger to himself and others.

A society certainly involves the constitution of a state, of political institutions and general laws that demand to be followed and upheld 'without the regard for persons', for the sake of universality and equality. But amid the organization of a legal order we still ought to be able to encounter the other who appeals to my responsibility. If not, we stand guilty of judging and convicting him as if 'in absentia'. Religion keeps me from hiding myself (like Adam) in the thicket of legal abstractions. Through love, the grip of rigid rules, norms, and procedures is loosened, so that, notwithstanding all judicial restrictions, justice remains possible, even within the sphere of law. Scholten's God is a personal God: He is the God of Abraham, Isaac, and Jacob, not the God of the philosophers (Pascal). (VG I 469–470) To have a conscience implies that one is in a free relation to God. God as a Person places us before our brothers and neighbours as persons: through Christ we

---

[3] The humanity of man exists in the determinateness of being together with the other. As indicated above, there are several different sources for Scholten's personalism, which returns on almost every page of his work. One of these is Karl Barth. For the many personalist passages in the work of Barth, see his *Kirchliche Dogmatik*, II, 2 (Zürich: Theologischer Verlag Zürich, 1942), 43 f.; 143, 337 f. as well as *Kirchliche Dogmatik*, III, 2 (Zürich: Theologischer Verlag Zürich, 1948), 288, 290–299, 315.

become related to one another as *Ich und Du* (I and Thou). The encounter with God transforms our natural, erotic, and impersonal relation to the other: thus, law becomes the law of the neighbour. Justice becomes *Gemeinschaft*, not in the sense of an aggregate of strangers, but as the community of neighbours. (DG 347–353/VG I 340–346) In this respect also, Scholten refers to dialogical and dialectical theology. He shares with these a theological personalism that to him is also of fundamental value in respect to the philosophy of law. 'The primacy of the political (*Primat des Politischen*), for which Carl Schmitt fights, does not exist.' (DG 351/VG I 344) The Person of God and the person of the neighbour ought to inform and found our political and judicial intuitions and decisions. The divine and human person is the truth behind the law. Although 'the community of law' is not (yet) the authentic community of me and you, it must always remain animated by its true destiny. We should creatively respond to the appeal of the other. Without being related (as a person) to the person involved, my decision will be abstract and idle. Working together with God (as co-creator in God's continuing work of creation), judging from grace, we should try to better and fulfil creation: we should 'thirst after justice', also within the – in many respects restricted and hostile – sphere of law. (DG 299/VG I 281)

The rule of law always threatens to install a legal abstraction in the place of the living person: a fully interchangeable subject, without content, without bonds, without environment. Religious inspiration is the perfect antidote to this – in many ways all too necessary – abstraction. Scholten stresses that the New Testament is not an ethical or juridical manual, but that the songs, stories, and parables of the Bible never fail to inspire us to transcend the simple rule of law. They do so, as he says in 'Law and Love' (1917), in a way that leads us to the essence of law, to the law 'behind' the law: a right that was and is continually forgotten, in theory as well as in practice.

Whoever has experienced the Gospel, who has come to God in a personal relationship through Jesus, will relate differently than before to the questions that world and work offer him. This applies to every work, in every sphere of life, but to law in particular. Everything in law enforcement that would be revenge or wounded pride lies behind him, but also law because of law, the '*fiat iustitia*' ('let justice prevail, even if the world perishes') can no longer be his life motto. His conviction has become another. When love has come to us, her mild mouth smiles at us, we feel fulfilled by her and then we are different, and in our actions, this will shine through and radiate. (DG 203/VG I 186)

GENERAL APPRAISAL AND INFLUENCE

Recently there has been a renewed interest in Scholten's philosophy of law and the underlying theological principles of his work. One has begun to appreciate that an adequate understanding of the theological context of Scholten's work is of enormous importance, not only for Christians and out of religious interest, but also for secular jurists and for the theory and practice of law. The reception of and the effect or follow-up on his philosophy of law has been greatly inhibited by the unwillingness or incapacity of his readers (both secular and Christian positivists) to appreciate the Christian existentialist and personalist principles of his thoughts.[4] They misrepresented his philosophy in particular by interpreting his ideas through the inappropriate prism of natural law theory and of (especially) 'Aristotle': by means of concepts (f.i. phronesis) and principles (f.i. virtue-ethics) that do not at all coincide with his (Scholten's) worldview, his personalist anthropology and morality.

The reception of 'Scholten' is for the most part founded upon a reduced, methodological interpretation of his work, of which the deeper philosophical and theological layers are largely (although not entirely) neglected and misunderstood. Most interpreters have wanted to abstract from this theological dimension in the belief that in secular times all 'irrational religiousness' should be eradicated from his teachings, on the certain grounds that for contemporary thought, religion can no longer be relevant.[5] They have argued that the relevance of his work can only be preserved if and in so far as we can detract from the theological dimension of his work. This typically 'modernist' interpretative strategy has turned out to be fatal for the veracity of his fame and for what his work could (potentially) mean for both the theory and practice of law. It has sterilized and amputated the heritage of Scholten. More so, considering the well-known 'religious turn' in contemporary (postmodern) philosophy, an appreciation of the theological content of his work is not only appropriate from a historical point of view (for the preservation of this part of

---

[4] Although J. J. H. Bruggink at least acknowledged Scholten's Christian existentialist orientation in *Wat zegt Scholten over recht?* (Utrecht; Zwolle: W. E. J. Tjeenk Willink, 1983), 90–92.
[5] See, for example, *De actualiteit van Paul Scholten* (The actuality of Paul Scholten), eds. E. Lissenberg, P. W. Brouwer, F. Jacobs, and E. Poortinga (Nijmegen: Ars Aequi Libri, 1996), published by the Paul Scholten Institute of the UVA (Scholten's alma mater). The back cover of this collection states the collective confession to which all of the authors are said to agree: 'Scholten's ideas should be stripped of their all too Christian aspects. In this disassembled form Scholten becomes topical again'.

our cultural heritage), but also of vital importance for the future effect it deserves to generate.[6]

Scholten himself wanted the reader to search further and beyond his words. He consistently expressed this in his lectures and he emphasized this again in his Farewell Speech (1945). He did not teach *iurare in verba magistri* (to 'swear by the words of the master') or *autos epha* ('he has said it himself'). (DG 414/VG I 500) For those who are examining his work, an important task is included in this word of farewell (1945). Whoever seeks no further, and honours him by taking his word as the final and decisive word, does not do him proper justice: he frustrates the further research that Scholten himself requested.

Scholten's texts, including the many telling references therein, are partly rooted in the tradition of Christian dialogical thought and existentialism. As such (in some way) they point toward contemporary philosophy. They show a point of focus that still requires much further research, but that unmistakably directs the reader toward current modern and postmodern thought for which the phenomenology of encounter, dialogue, and response in particular are quintessential.

Further research should provide insight into the affinity of Scholten with earlier famous existentialists (Kierkegaard[7] and Nietzsche) as well as with other later personalistic thinkers, in particular Nicolai Berdyaev (1874–1948) and Lev Shestov (1866–1938), as well as Emmanuel Levinas (1906–1995) and Jacques Derrida (1930–2004). This should make it even clearer that the religious dimension of Scholten's work is also of great significance outside the confines of faith, within the (agnostic) context of current philosophical ethics and the philosophy of science.

---

[6] In respect of the continuation and furtherance of what he began to think, religious readers have been reluctant to keep alive his theological heritage. They have mostly ignored or downplayed the profound existentialist and dialectical dimensions of his philosophy.

[7] Scholten does not directly refer to Kierkegaard. But many if not all of the authors to which he does refer have in common their profound indebtedness to the great Dane. This counts as much for the representatives of the aforementioned strand of Ethical Theology as it does for (to name only a few) Ferdinand Ebner, Karl Jaspers, Martin Buber, Emil Brunner, and Karl Barth. For further reference to the underlying influence and importance of Kierkegaard, see my monograph *Uit de schaduw van de wet. Inleiding tot de esthetica van het recht* ('Out of the Shadow of the Law. Introduction to the Aesthetics of Law') (Antwerp: Garant Uitgeverij, 2016), 262 ff. In this book I try to further develop the dialogical, existentialist, and postmodern contours of an Aesthetic Philosophy of Law, ideas that follow in some of the footsteps of Scholten.

RECOMMENDED READINGS[8]

Bruggink, J. J. H. *Wat zegt Scholten over recht?* Utrecht/Zwolle: W. E. J. Tjeenk Willink, 1983.
'Herdenkingsnummer – 100st geboortedag Paul Scholten'. *Weekblad voor Privaatrecht, Notariaat en Registratie* (WPNR) 106 (1975).
Peletier, W. M. 'Scholten, Paulus (1875–1946)'. In *Biografisch Woordenboek van Nederland. Vol. II.* The Hague: 1979, 536.
Scholten, Paul. *Mr. C. Asser's Handleiding tot beoefening van het Nederlandse Burgerlijk Recht, Algemeen Deel* [AD] [1931]. Zwolle: W. E. J. Tjeenk Willink, 1974.
Scholten, Paul. *Verzamelde Geschriften* [VG]. IV Volumes. Edited by G. J. Scholten, Y. Scholten, and M. H. Bregstein. Zwolle: W. E. J. Tjeenk Willink, 1949.
Scholten, Paul. *Dorsten naar gerechtigheid* [DG] [Thirsting after justice]. Edited by T. J. M. Slootweg. Deventer: Kluwer, 2010. Contains a reprint of the first chapter of the General Part, and a selection of Paul Scholten's Collected Philosophical Papers. Below is a selection from VG of some the most important essays and articles. This selection was also reprinted in DG:
Scholten, Paul. 'Recht en levensbeschouwing'. [1915] [Law and philosophy of life] In VG I, 120–161.
Scholten, Paul. 'Recht en liefde'. [1917] [Law and Love] In VG I, 162–187.
Scholten, Paul. 'Gedachten over macht en recht'. [1917] [Thoughts on power and law] In VG I, 188–215.
Scholten, Paul. 'Recht en billijkheid'. [1917] [Law and equity] In VG I, 225–281.
Scholten, Paul. 'Recht en moraal'. [1927] [Law and morality] In VG I, 282–295.
Scholten, Paul. 'Recht en gerechtigheid'. [1932] [Law and justice] In VG I, 296–317.
Scholten, Paul. 'Beginselen van samenleving'. [1934] [Principles of society] In VG I, 330–379.
Scholten, Paul. 'Gerechtigheid en recht'. [1938] [Justice and law] In VG I, 216–224.
Scholten, Paul. 'Evangelie en recht'. [1939] [Gospel and law] In VG I, 413–431.
Scholten, Paul. 'Afscheidsrede'. [1945] [Farewell speech] In VG I, 493–505.
Slootweg, Timo and Bas Hengstmengel, eds., *Recht en Persoon. Verkenningen in de rechtstheologie van Paul Scholten* [Law and Person. Explorations into Paul Scholten's Theology of Law]. Deventer: Akkermans & Hunnink, 2013.
Slootweg T. J. M. 'Persoon en geweten bij Paul Scholten'. In *Rechtvaardigheid, persoon en creativiteit. Personalisme in recht en politiek*, edited by C. Bouteligier and T. J. M. Slootweg, 25–56. Oud-Turnhout; 's-Hertogenbosch: Gompel & Svacina, 2020.

---

[8] As we indicated above, there is no equal to 'Scholten', which is why it is of vital importance that his valuable insights remain in the spotlights of contemporary (international) scholarship. We noticed however that the secondary literature on Scholten bypassed his work's crucial religious and existential dimensions. In addition to this, we must acknowledge that up to now no English translations of his work exist, and scholarship on Scholten is in the Dutch language exclusively. See however this open access preprint: Paul Scholten, General Method of Private Law. Chapter 1 of Volume I (General Part) of *Mr C. Asser's Manual for the Practice of Dutch Civil Law*. Preprint, first edition. Amsterdam: Digital Paul Scholten Project, May 2014. http://www.paulscholten.eu/dutch-english. In addition to this first English translation of the General Part, this website, hosted by the University of Amsterdam, offers a full bibliography and allows one to download most of Scholten's work in Dutch.

17

Willem Duynstee

Corjo Jansen [1]

BIOGRAPHICAL INTRODUCTION

'Fathoming someone's innermost motives is no easy matter.' It is with these apposite words that Cornelis Struyker Boudier (1937–2015), professor of philosophical anthropology at Nijmegen University in the Netherlands, began his reflections on the ideas and vision of William Duynstee. He believed that every life has its blind spots, which, for lack of evidence to remedy them, stay there for good. As he saw it, Duynstee's life was also subject to these blind spots.[2] My sketch of Willem Duynstee's life and work is therefore doomed to fall hopelessly short.

Willem Jacob Jozef Anton Duynstee was born on 6 September 1886 in Sittard. Following in his father's footsteps, he studied law at what was then known as the Municipal University of Amsterdam from 1905 to 1908. He completed his studies with the defence of a thesis.[3] Against his father's wishes, he entered the Order of the Redemptorist Fathers (C.ss.R) at the age of 21. It is not known what motivated him to make this choice. Perhaps it was a book about Saint Alphonsus Liguori (1696–1787), the founder of the Redemptorist fathers and a brilliant jurist, that tipped the scales. During his studies, Willem had been gifted the work by the Redemptorist priest Father Christianus Baker (1863–1931). At the Seminary of the Redemptorist Fathers in Wittem, Willem received a thorough education in philosophy and moral theology.

---

[1] Professor of Legal History and Civil Law, Radboud University, Nijmegen.
[2] Cornelis Struyker Boudier, 'Gerechtigheid en liefde', in *De 'oude Duyn' herdacht*, eds. Cornelis Struyker Boudier et al. (Nijmegen: Katholieke Universiteit, 1987), 64.
[3] His thesis supervisor's name is not known. Professor Willem Treub (1858–1931) is sometimes mentioned. He was a professor of political economy and statistics. But he had already resigned on 1 November 1905. It is more likely that Antonius Struycken (1873–1923), a devout Catholic who in 1906 was appointed Professor of Constitutional Law at the Municipal University of Amsterdam, was Willem's thesis supervisor.

His theological education steeped him in the work of Thomas Aquinas (1225–1274), and this was the starting point for many of his later studies, including those on the law. He was ordained a priest in 1913.

At the intercession of the Dutch bishops, in 1928 Duynstee was appointed professor of criminal law and criminal procedure at what was then the Catholic University of Nijmegen, which had been founded a few years before in 1923. He had never published an article on criminal law. That changed rather quickly.[4] He gave a lecture in 1928 entitled: *De leer der straf van den H. Thomas van Aquino* [Thomas Aquinas's Doctrine of Punishment] (1928). In his scholarly work on law, he linked criminology, constitutional law, legal philosophy, moral theology, and psychology. He wrote a great deal about the nature of punishment and the foundations of criminal law. He developed a theory of retribution inspired by Thomas Aquinas. He viewed punishment primarily as retribution for a crime that violated the God-ordained order.[5] In 1929, he became a member of the editorial board of the monthly theological journal *Nederlandsche Katholieke Stemmen* [Dutch Catholic Voices].[6] In 1933, he co-founded the *Vereeniging voor Thomistische Wijsbegeerte* [Dutch Association for Thomistic Philosophy].

In 1939, Duynstee's teaching assignment changed: he continued teaching criminal law, stopped teaching criminal procedure, and started teaching jurisprudence. Duynstee was the university's Rector Magnificus during the first year of the German occupation (from 1940 to 1 May 1941). He was forced to resign his position by order of the occupiers. After the war, in 1948, he started teaching philosophy of law instead of criminal law. To distinguish him from his nephew, Frans Duynstee (1914–1981), who was appointed professor of constitutional and administrative law at the Catholic University of Nijmegen, everyone affectionately called him 'Duyn the Elder'. His legal oeuvre included studies on civil law, including matrimonial and juvenile law, philosophy of law, commercial law, constitutional law, criminal law, and criminology. The study of positive law was often done from the perspective of the philosophy of law. In the words of Josephus van der Ven (1907–1988), professor of labour law at the University of Utrecht, 'we shall continue to see how, when it comes to specific legal topics, he drills

---

[4] For instance, between 1936 and 1943, he contributed five articles to the criminal law journal *Tijdschrift voor Strafrecht*.

[5] See also his rectoral lecture: 'Het wezen der vergelding', in *Verspreide Opstellen [van] prof. mr. W.J.A.J. Duynstee C.ss.R.* (Roermond: J. J. Romen & Zonen, 1963), 102 *et seq.*

[6] Up until 1940. He was also the editor of *Studia Catholica* and of *Monatschrift für Kriminalpsychologie und Strafrechtsreform*.

down to deeper questions, or tackles them directly from a legal-philosophical plane'.[7]

Duynstee had an interest early on in the mental health of people, particularly the clergy. He was one of the first Catholic academics to apply results from modern psychoanalysis and psychology to pastoral care. He also focused on people's physical health. He thus founded the Sint Maartenskliniek in 1936, a hospital in Nijmegen that specialized in treating nervous disorders affecting posture and mobility. He chaired the clinic's board until 1956. Finally, from 1936 to 1951, he was a member of the Board of Regents of Saint Canisius Hospital in Nijmegen, and served as chair of the board from 1951 to 1956.

In 1956, Duynstee retired from Radboud University with a lecture typical for him: *Wet en wetsverplichting bij Sint Thomas* [The Law and Legal Duty with St. Thomas], which was published in *Studia Catholica* 31 (1956). Around the time he retired from the University of Nijmegen, Duynstee was already in conflict with the Congregation of the Holy Office, which had its seat in Vatican City. The issue became known as the Duynstee-Terruwe affair. Anna Terruwe (1911–2004) was the first female psychiatrist in the Netherlands. Together with Duynstee, she had developed a psychotherapeutic treatment for people – in particular, for parish priests and other clergy – with neurotic disorders, including in the sphere of sexuality. This treatment would stand contrary to the church's moral teaching of the time. After the Holy Office handed down a 'sentence', Duynstee, who was by no means a modern moral theologian, was transferred to Rome, which he was not permitted to leave from 1957 to 1960. Only through the mediation of Cardinal Bernard Alfrink (1900–1987) was he allowed to return to Amsterdam in 1960. He was rehabilitated only in 1965. He went to live in his beloved Nijmegen monastery, the Nebo. He was travelling with Anna Terruwe on 8 November 1968 when he died quite unexpectedly in Menton, France.[8]

---

[7] Josephus van der Ven, 'Willem Duynstee, de juridisch-wijsgerige denker', in *De 'oude Duyn' herdacht*, eds. Cornelis Struyker Boudier et al. (Nijmegen: Katholieke Universiteit, 1987), 32.

[8] Jan Brabers, *De Faculteit der Rechtsgeleerdheid van de Katholieke Universiteit Nijmegen, 1923–1982* (Nijmegen: GNI, 1994), 64 *et seq.*, 274 *et seq.*; J. Elgershuizen, 'Pater Prof. Mr. Willem Duynstee', in *Een kroniek van vijfenzeventig jaar Nebo* (Nijmegen: Paters Redemptoristen, 2003), 50–53; Ad Stadhouders, 'Willem Duynstee', in *Jaarboek Numaga* (2004), 43–44; Corjo Jansen, 'W. J. A. J. Duynstee', in *Meesterlijk Nijmegen*, eds. Claartje Bulten, Louk Hermans-Brand, and Corjo Jansen (Den Haag: Boom Juridische uitgevers, 2008), 71–72; Cornelis Struyker Boudier et al., eds., *De 'oude Duyn' herdacht* (Nijmegen: Katholieke Universiteit Nijmegen, 1987); Johannes de Valk, 'Duynstee, Willem Jacobus Antonius Joseph (1886–1968)', in *Biografisch Woordenboek van Nederland* http://resources.huygens.knaw.nl./bwn1880-2000/lemmata/bwn2/duynstee.

MAJOR THEMES AND CONTRIBUTIONS

Main Writings and Inspiration

Duynstee's first major publication was at the crossroads of law and pastoral work: *Burgerlijk recht en Zielzorg* [Civil Law and Pastoral Care] (first edition 1919).[9] In the preface, he made his intentions for this book clear:

> On the one hand, we have sought to introduce the seminarians to Dutch [civil] law, by systematically setting out the basics and the overall system of various legal provisions ...; on the other hand, we have sought to summarize everything that may be of importance to practical pastoral care, so that the priest can immediately look up one and another item *in cura* and provide the information required.[10]

The first explanation of his views on natural law came in 1929. It was a lecture for the Dutch Association for the Philosophy of Law, and was titled simply: *Natuurrecht* [Natural Law]. In 1939, the Dutch Association for Thomistic Philosophy put out a more fully developed version of these views: *Het Natuurrecht* [Natural Law]. In 1940, Duynstee published an overview of the historical development of natural law in the Netherlands: *Geschiedenis van het natuurrecht en de wijsbegeerte in het recht in Nederland* [The History of Natural Law and Philosophy of Law in the Netherlands] (1940). The book begins with a review of the earliest Dutch practitioners of the philosophy of law, who worked in the Middle Ages and were few and far between, and ends with the work of the Dutch legal philosophers from the period 1880 to 1890. It focuses primarily on the work of Hugo de Groot (1583–1645) and the influence of Samuel von Pufendorf (1632–1694), Christian Wolff (1679–1745), and Immanuel Kant (1724–1804). In 1956, *Over recht en rechtvaardigheid* [On Law and Justice], finally appeared. This book contained Duynstee's most detailed views on natural law.

Duynstee's greatest inspiration is Thomas Aquinas, *Doctor Angelicus*. Duynstee's writings are steeped in Aquinas's thought. Van der Ven observed that, 'in his writing [Duynstee] was guided almost exclusively by [Aquinas's] pronouncements'.[11] Duynstee himself wrote in his study *Over recht en rechtvaardigheid*: 'Our starting point has been St. Thomas Aquinas, not

---

[9] His second book, which was not really about the law, was *De Leer der Kuischheid* [The Doctrine of Chastity] (Roermond: J.J. Romen, 1927).

[10] Willem Duynstee, *Burgerlijk recht en Zielzorg*, fourth edition ('s-Hertogenbosch: Malmberg, 1937): preface.

[11] Van der Ven, 'Willem Duynstee', 55.

because of who he was, but because we saw the truth in what he wrote.'[12] In his farewell address to the Catholic University of Nijmegen in 1956, Duynstee said he had only one wish for the Catholic University: 'that the spirit of Thomas always remain the basis for what is taught here'.[13] Another inspiration for Duynstee was the Neothomistic priest Josephus Beysens (1864–1945), who was professor of ethics, metaphysics, and psychology at Utrecht University. Among his works, the most frequently cited in legal circles is *Ethiek of natuurlijke zedenleer* [Ethics, or Natural Moral Philosophy] (I, 1913). Beysens was partly responsible for the revival of Aristotelian–Thomistic thought between the First World War and Second World War (the so-called interwar period) in the Netherlands. Nothing is known about any contact between Duynstee and Beysens. And from the few times Duynstee cites Beysens's work, we cannot conclude to what extent he was influenced by him. A third – especially theological–philosophical source of inspiration – was the *Theologia Moralis secundam doctrinam S. Alfonsi de Liguorio Doctoris ecclesiae*, in two parts and numerous editions, the first of which was written by the Redemptorist priest Joseph Aertnijs (1828–1915), and revised by his fellow Redemptorist, Cornelius Alphonsus Damen (1881–1953). They were both professors at the seminary in Wittem. Duynstee was Damen's assistant from 1914 to 1921, when he succeeded him. He revised that part of the *Theologia Moralis* that treated of the virtues. The moral theologian Father Ludovicus Wouters (1864–1933), who was also at the seminary in Wittem, had considerable influence on Duynstee's theological views.[14]

Natural Law and Positive Law

The distinction between natural law and positive law is as old as the hills. The Roman jurist Ulpian recounted in his *Institutes* that private law was made up of three parts: rules derived from nature (*ex naturalibus praeceptis, ius naturale*), from the law which all nations use (*gentium, ius gentium*), and from the law peculiar to the community of citizens itself (*civilibus, ius civile*, positive law). The difference between *ius naturale* and *ius gentium* was, he believed, easy to see: natural law was common to all living beings, while *ius gentium* was common to all human beings. Natural law was not only proper to

---

[12] Willem Duynstee, *Over recht en rechtvaardigheid* ('s-Hertogenbosch: Malmberg, 1956), preface.
[13] Willen Duynstee, 'Wet en wetsverplichting bij Sint Thomas', in *Verspreide Opstellen [van] prof. mr. W.J.A.J. Duynstee C.ss.R.* (Roermond: J. J. Romen & Zonen, 1963), 135–136.
[14] Struyker Boudier, 'Gerechtigheid', 68.

the human race, but was common to all living beings on the earth or in the sea: even the birds were part of it. The bond between a male and a female, known as marriage, emerged from it. And it also led to the procreation and raising of children.[15]

The fact that the Romans made the distinction between natural law and positive law meant that this pair of concepts belonged to the legal culture of the Continent, based on the reception of Roman law and its principles. Almost every European jurist from the *ancien régime* devoted some attention to it. The Dutch history of natural law was one of ups and downs, and reached an apex in the eighteenth century.[16] The monopoly that Grotius and Pufendorf had had in this area at Dutch universities disappeared in the middle of this century. Wolff's pupils got the upper hand and taught courses on 'natural law' at many of these universities.[17] This apex lasted only a short time. Natural law, and in its wake the philosophy of law, were in decline in the nineteenth century, and reached rock-bottom in the Netherlands – following Germany's lead – at the end of the nineteenth century. The renowned Dutch lawyer Gerard Langemeijer (1903–1990) was quite clear about what he saw as the death of the philosophy of law: 'One can safely say that in Netherlands at that time [about 1880] the philosophy of law ceased to be practiced.'[18] The same applied to natural law. The famous Utrecht professor of commercial law Willem Molengraaff (1858–1931) argued in his inaugural lecture that the law had no absolute, supernatural character. 'There can be no question of immutable, eternal true foundations of the law that are valid everywhere, independent of time and place.' The law was a product of human experience that had, by nature, a purely relative character.[19] The Utrecht jurist–philosopher Cornelis Opzoomer (1821–1892) held the German jurists responsible for the demise of philosophy and natural law:

---

[15] See D. 1,1,1,2 and D. 1,1,1,4.
[16] See Willem Duynstee, *Geschiedenis van het natuurrecht en de wijsbegeerte in het recht in Nederland*, Geschiedenis der Nederlandsche Rechtswetenschap, II-I (Amsterdam: Noord-Hollandsche Uitgevers Mij, 1940), 31 *et seq.*, 59 *et seq.*
[17] See Corjo Jansen, 'Over de 18ᵉ-eeuwse docenten natuurrecht aan Nederlandse universiteiten en de door hen gebruikte leerboeken', *Legal History Review* LV (1987): 103 *et seq.*
[18] Gerard Langemeijer, *De wijsbegeerte des rechts en de encyclopaedie der rechtswetenschap sedert 1880*, Geschiedenis der Nederlandsche Rechtswetenschap, VI (Amsterdam: Noord-Hollandsche Uitgevers Mij, 1963), 6.
[19] Willem Molengraaff, *Het verkeersrecht in wetgeving en wetenschap* (Haarlem: De Erven F. Bohn, 1885), 12. See also the harsh words K. Bergbohm used in *Jurisprudenz und Rechtsphilosophie. Kritische Abhandlungen*, I (Leipzig: Duncker & Humblot, 1892), 118: '... das Unkraut Naturrecht auszurotten'.

Through exaggeration, German legal scholars, who are more used than those in other countries to the philosophical analysis of concepts, easily turn virtues into faults, and turn philosophy into an infertile, impractical scholasticism.[20]

However, the founder of the Dutch Association for the Philosophy of Law, Professor Willem van der Vlugt (1853–1928), a professor at Leiden University, for his part held Opzoomer responsible, as a representative of empirical positivism, for 'the unphilosophical age that is behind us'. For him the hallmark of Dutch philosophy had been the concentration on facts, the facts alone or 'knowledge and understanding of facts alone', while he dismissed the content of philosophy as stargazing, cabbala, and theology. Van der Vlugt was convinced that empirical positivism was to answer for the death not only of natural law but also of the philosophy of law.[21]

The tide turned for Dutch legal philosophy and natural law in the first decades of the twentieth century. By the time Duynstee wrote his book *Burgerlijk recht en Zielzorg*, interest in natural law was on the rise again in Germany, largely thanks to the work of Josef Kohler (1849–1919) and Rudolf Stammler (1856–1938) on legal philosophy. Although they represent a completely different natural law tradition to that of Duynstee, their work stimulated interest in natural law in the Netherlands. In addition, the work of francophone Neothomistic Catholic authors, such as Georges Renard (1876–1943) and Jean Dabin (1889–1971)[22] inspired Roman Catholic lawyers in the Netherlands, such as Egidius van der Heijden (1885–1941), who was professor of civil and commercial law at Nijmegen University from 1923 until his death.[23] In 1929 and 1939, Duynstee published his reflections on natural law. As we have noted, his later book, *Over recht en rechtvaardigheid* (1956), contained a complete statement of his views on natural law.

The Distinction Between Natural Law and Natural–Rational Law

Duynstee distinguished three types of legal norms: strictly natural (or 'natural law proper'), natural–rational, and positive. He also referred to strictly natural

---

[20] Cornelis Opzoomer, *Het Burgerlijk Wetboek, verklaard*, Part 3, second edition (Amsterdam: J. H. Gebhard & Comp., 1876), 463, note 1.

[21] Willem van der Vlugt, 'Openingswoord', *Handelingen van de Vereeniging voor de Wijsbegeerte des Rechts (HVWR)* (1919): 2 *et seq.*, 6. See also R. Kranenburg, 'De rechtsphilosophie en de juridische vakwetenschappen', *HVWR* (1921): 6 *et seq.*

[22] *Compare* Georges Renard, *Le droit, l'ordre et la raison* (Paris: Recueil Sirey, 1927) and *La valeur de la loi* (Paris: Recueil Sirey, 1928); Jean Dabin, *La philosophie de l'ordre juridique positif* (Paris: Recueil Sirey, 1929).

[23] He reviewed Dabin's book, *La philosophie de l'ordre juridique positif* in *The Legal History Review* (1931): 450–457.

legal norms as primarily natural law prescriptions that concerned the essential objects of people's aspirations. He saw the natural–rational norms as secondary natural law regulations that concerned additional objects of people's aspirations.[24] By strictly natural law, he understood 'the norms that have been put forward as part of nature itself, that is, those that meet people's naturally imperative aspirations, the norms that express in words ... what they, as reasonable beings, must strive for.'[25] The first and most basic norm when it comes to human aspirations is that people must pursue good and avoid evil. In the depths of every person's nature there is the quest for universal good that has no limitation: God. God is every person's ultimate goal. Thus, God is the primary source of all law, and any legal order must derive from Him.[26]

The starting point of natural law proper was what, by virtue of people's nature, was necessarily of benefit to them. For example, as a matter of natural necessity, people are ordained by God to life. Duynstee referred for support to the definition offered by Ulpian in D. 1,1,1,3: natural law is the law that nature has taught to all creatures – humans and animals. When it came to most other goods, people had to create an ordination with the help of their reason. The result was natural–rational law. This law contained norms that were associated so closely with nature that reason had to establish them practically always and everywhere. The contents of natural–rational law thus emerged from reason, not nature. It was the law that Ulpianus and Gaius were referring to, in the first book of their *Institutes*, when they wrote about the law that natural reason had brought into being among all people and that all peoples respect in the same way: the *ius gentium*.[27] This meant that, despite certain points of agreement, natural law proper was, as Duynstee saw it, fundamentally different from natural–rational law. While natural–rational law applied almost everywhere and while people spontaneously recognized it as correct, it was not – as natural law proper was – dictated directly by nature. Human judgement was always necessary to establish natural–rational law. Natural law proper was, moreover, immutable, while it was the circumstances in a given case that determined whether natural–rational law applied. As Duynstee saw it, the natural–rational thus concerned the norms 'that are so closely bound up with human nature

---

[24] Willem Duynstee, 'Het Natuurrecht' [1939], in *Verspreide Opstellen [van] prof. mr. W.J.A.J. Duynstee C.ss.R.* (Roermond: J. J. Romen & Zonen, 1963), 84–88; Duynstee, *Over recht en rechtvaardigheid*, 41–42. As he noted himself, he borrowed this triad from St. Thomas.

[25] Duynstee, *Over recht en rechtvaardigheid*, 23. In 1929, Duynstee defined natural law as 'all the moral powers and obligations, whereby the natural order laid down by God, between men is accomplished'. Duynstee, 'Natuurrecht', *HVWR* (1929): 171.

[26] Duynstee, *Over recht en rechtvaardigheid*, 23–25; Duynstee, 'Natuurrecht' [1929], 169.

[27] Gai. Inst. I, 1. '(...) vero quod omnes homines constituit inter naturalis ratio (...)'. See also D. 1,1,9.

that, regardless of which circumstances of time or place human nature is located in, one particular way of treating people's welfare will necessarily have to be considered'.[28]

The question arises as to which norms Duynstee thought fell under natural law proper, and which ones under natural–rational law. I will give a few examples, first, of natural law proper. Duynstee distinguished six naturally imperative ordinations that were naturally of benefit to people and belonged to natural law proper: (1) the ordination to life; (2) the ordination to reproduction; (3) the ordination by virtue of which people could make concretely sensuous goods subservient to them; (4) the ordination to contacts with other people; (5) the ordination to knowledge of the truth, and (6) the ordination to act reasonably. Life occupied the first place, and people had to emulate that first and foremost. Suicide was thus always against natural law. People also had a natural duty to take care of their health. The preservation of the species was by nature of benefit to people. In view of it, people had a natural right to reproduce. The act the church father Origen committed in castrating himself (185–253/254), was thus not objectively justifiable. Another natural benefit to people was fundamental disposition to their fellow human beings. Truth in social exchanges was thus a postulate of natural law, and deceit was an offence under it. Finally, it was in people's nature for their actions to be guided by reason, and this was, as we have seen, the basis for positive law in a general sense. From this overview, it follows that the legal norms under natural law proper were only of a very elementary nature.[29] By their very nature, the six ordinations not only were focused on the wellbeing of the one person, but were also of benefit for the other. In relation to the other person, this meant that one person was not permitted to intervene in another's life or in their capacity to reproduce, and that one person was not permitted to deprive another of the ability to engage in interpersonal contact.[30] In short, everyone had to give to everyone what was theirs by decree of the natural order, that is to say, the practice of justice. Here, Duynstee followed Ulpian's words: justice is the unshakeable and abiding will to give everyone his due.[31]

The ordination to life, reproduction, and reasonable behaviour were important especially to jurists. They could be translated into legal norms in accordance with which people had to act. These norms could take the form of a subjective right. Natural law proper delivered only the bare-bones framework

---

[28] Duynstee, *Over recht en rechtvaardigheid*, 46–50 (quote on 50).
[29] Duynstee, 'Het Natuurrecht' [1939], 89–91; Duynstee, *Over recht en rechtvaardigheid*, 25–29.
[30] Duynstee, *Over recht en rechtvaardigheid*, 29–31.
[31] Duynstee, 'Natuurrecht' [1929], 171. See D. 1,1,10: *Iustitia est constans et perpetua voluntas ius suum cuique tribuere*.

for all human actions. Natural–rational law saw to it that this was fleshed out. It was the law that was established by natural reason. Natural reason arranged the secondary objects of human endeavours, which, as we have seen, were so closely associated with human nature that reason practically always and everywhere had to establish them as a norm. Natural–rational law was thus closely related to the *ius gentium* in Roman law – the law which all nations on earth use (see D. 1,1,1,4). Respect for human personality and private property belonged to this natural–rational law. Another important natural–rational norm was that parties to a sale had to keep their word about the agreed moment of the delivery of the goods and the payment of the agreed price at the moment of purchase (*pacta sunt servanda*), and that, if one person has given something for safe keeping, the person keeping it was obliged to return it.[32]

The Eternal and Immutable Character of Natural Law Proper

As Duynstee saw it, the validity of natural law proper was general and complete. It applied to anyone endowed with human nature because it was endowed by nature itself. Natural law proper had been applicable always and everywhere, and that would remain the case in the future. '[People] remain, of course, entitled, always and everywhere, to subject external goods to their own ends; and by nature they retain, always and everywhere, the right to life.' Natural law proper was, in this regard, independent of people and their knowledge. It was also 'entirely immutable'. It could not be changed by any circumstances of any kind. After all, nature remained the same, however much circumstances changed. Neither people nor any worldly authority such as the state could alter natural law proper. 'No state can ever, in its systems, go against the law of nature; rather, it must always take it as a foundation.' In fact, as Duynstee saw it, 'a state that could not exist without damaging these laws has already lost all its *raison d'être* as a state: for the first goal of the state is precisely to safeguard people's natural rights'.[33]

The fact that natural law proper was both generally valid and immutable did not mean that it was an obstacle to the development of the law. 'No, natural law is not an obstacle to progress in the law; rather, it is the basis and the condition for it, because it provides a guiding light and clear orientation.'[34] Natural–rational law, which had a basis in natural law proper, was not valid

---

[32] Duynstee, 'Het Natuurrecht' [1939], 91, 92, and 94; Duynstee, *Over recht en rechtvaardigheid*, 41–43 and 50 and 51.
[33] Duynstee, 'Natuurrecht' [1929], 162, 163, and 174 (first quote); Duynstee, 'Het Natuurrecht' [1939], 85; Duynstee, *Over recht en rechtvaardigheid*, 32–34 (quotes on 33 and 34).
[34] Duynstee, 'Natuurrecht' [1929], 175.

always and everywhere. The state could make rules and apply restrictions regarding national–rational law, depending on the social circumstances and in view of the interests of the community. Moreover, natural–rational law was often drafted so generally that positive law was needed to make it concrete. This granted any positive law the complete freedom to adapt to circumstances that changed with country, people, and time. This law contained only a precise system of certain concrete circumstances and was thus by its nature changeable, temporary, and variable.[35]

Elaboration of Duynstee's View of Natural Law

As Duynstee saw it, one of the merits of natural law proper was the dismantling of the idea that all law was to be found in statutes. In his view, natural law supported a free role for the judiciary in relation to the statutes and distanced itself from the primacy of the legislature in the development of new law. 'People are becoming increasingly aware that legislation (...) can be unjust; people have managed to give courts authority, and this has drawn a shudder from the orthodox legal positivists.'[36] Duynstee's view on the role of the judiciary with regard to legislation also held true for criminal law. One of the most basic principles of criminal law was to be found in the maxim, *nulla poena sine lege* (no penalty without a previous penal provision), which had made its way into Article 1 of the Dutch Penal Code. In Duynstee's view, there were two possible interpretations of this adage. On the one hand, one could read it as *nulla poena sine praevia lege poenali* (no punishment without a previous *statutory* penal provision). On the other hand, one could read it as *nulla poena sine lege normativa* (no penalty without the existence of a normative prescription that has been violated). On the first reading, the maxim did not belong, in his view, to natural law proper. The existence of a penalty in a *statute* was for natural law proper not relevant to the state's right to mete out punishment. The fact that there was a culpable breach of the legal order was enough for that. In the second reading of the maxim, it did belong to natural law proper, in Duynstee's view. A penalty could never be imposed without a breach of a normative prescription that was somehow part of the legal order. The question arises as to how the word *lex* is to be understood. According to Duynstee, it is not only as statute. The most fundamental norms – those of natural law – were valid without being put into force by

---

[35] Duynstee, 'Natuurrecht' [1929], 174; Duynstee, 'Het Natuurrecht' [1939], 94–95; Duynstee, *Over recht en rechtvaardigheid*, 52.
[36] Duynstee, 'Natuurrecht' [1929], 164. In other words, Duynstee rejected legalism.

the state. Examples of these (natural) fundamental norms include the rule that one should not kill another and that one must respect the property of another. The recognition of norms of natural law that are not included in legislation made it possible to punish an immoral act that by its nature was criminal, even if there was no statute with a penal provision. 'Because in that case an act has been committed against the legal order – not, perhaps, against that which has been codified in a statute, but against the legal order that naturally prevails.' The approach that Duynstee followed can be characterized as reasoning by analogy.[37] He granted the courts in the area of criminal law as much freedom as in the area of civil law. He was not the only one to do so during the interwar period. Also, the later Catholic Supreme Court judge, Bernardus Taverne (1874–1944), and Duynstee's predecessor as professor of criminal law at Nijmegen University, the professor of criminal law Willem Pompe (1893–1968), were proponents of reasoning by analogy in criminal law. However, they belonged to a minority among Dutch criminal lawyers.[38]

According to Duynstee, natural law was of the utmost importance to the practical application of the law. It offered a firm foundation on which the courts and the legislature could further build. Without natural law there was no criterion against which to test the justice and the fairness of positive law. Abandoning natural law led to a hopeless opportunism in legislation. Moreover, the court was no longer one to apply the law mechanically and blindly, but was a *iudex boni et aequi*. 'The good and the fair' had a strong foundation, according to Duynstee's firm conviction, in natural reason and in natural justice. Reason and justice had prevented arbitrariness from entering into the administration of justice. 'When in certain circumstances positive law would be too harsh or unfair, that will be corrected in accordance with the requirements of natural law...'[39]

Finally, natural law was a tool for interpreting positive law. I will give two examples. The first example has to do with the following question: was restriction of ownership possible? According to the doctrine of natural law, according to Duynstee, property was, by virtue of being a subjective power,

---

[37] Duynstee, 'Nulla poena sine lege' [1936], in *Verspreide Opstellen [van] prof. mr. W.J.A.J. Duynstee C.ss.R.* (Roermond: J. J. Romen & Zonen, 1963), 68 *et seq.*, 74 *et seq.*, 78–79 (quotes).
[38] See the article by D. van Eck, a pupil of Duynstee and his successor at Nijmegen as Professor of Criminal Law: 'Some Reflections on the *Nulla Poena Principle*', in *Opstellen over recht, wet en samenleving op 1 oktober 1948 door vrienden en leerlingen aangeboden aan Prof. mr. W. P. J. Pompe* (Nijmegen/Utrecht: Dekker & Van de Vegt, 1948), 55 *et seq*. For the *nulla poena* principle in the interwar period, see Corjo Jansen, 'Enige beschouwingen over het "nieuwe" strafrechtsdenken in de jaren dertig van de 20ᵉ eeuw aan de hand van het legaliteitsbeginsel', *Delikt en Delinkwent* (2006): 415 *et seq*.
[39] Duynstee, 'Natuurrecht' [1929], 176–178 (quote on 178).

susceptible to restriction, and the legal limits were not 'unnatural' curtailments, but 'detailed provisions' regarding property that were entirely in accordance with the nature of property.[40] A second example concerned the following question: through an agreement in a bankruptcy, in which creditors get only a certain percentage of their claim, is the debtor released in his conscience for the whole amount? Duynstee answered this question in the affirmative: he rejected the creation of a natural obligation after the conclusion of an agreement, a position held by some of the writers. By the agreement, the existing commitments came to nothing.[41] Duynstee's conclusion was that, generally, the provisions of Dutch civil law were in accordance with natural law, so that they generally entailed an obligation in one's conscience. For example, the right to marry constituted an exception. The law did not distinguish a marriage between people who were baptized and one between those who were not. However, Christ had exalted the natural marriage contract between two people who were baptized to the level of a sacrament, and that should be put beyond the jurisdiction of the state in all its aspects: 'it is not for the state to judge, only to accept'.[42]

The power of Duynstee's conception of natural law did not lie in its concrete implementation. He also wrote relatively little about positive law. According to Struyker Boudier, for Duynstee, the appeal of the Redemptorist fathers was concentrated in two spheres: study, penetrating to the essence of things in absolute obedience to the natural order created by God; and spiritual welfare, especially as expressed in the sacrament of confession. His great love was therefore not law or philosophy, but had to do with theology.[43] A consideration of Duynstee's philosophical–anthropological, psychological, psychotherapeutic, and psychiatric beliefs is beyond the scope of this contribution. They have indeed determined in large measure his disposition as

---

[40] Duynstee, *Burgerlijk recht en Zielzorg*, no. 132, 107. On Thomas Aquinas and the right of ownership, see the thesis of Jan Hallebeek, *Quia natura nichil privatum. Aspecten van de eigendomsvraag in het werk van Thomas van Aquino* (Nijmegen: Gerard Noodt Institute, 1986).

[41] Duynstee, *Burgerlijk recht en Zielzorg*, no. 235, 186. On the necessity of mutual consensus as a 'natural law' requirement for the validity of a contract: no. 203, 158.

[42] Duynstee, *Burgerlijk recht en Zielzorg*, no. 4, 6. On marriage as a contract under natural law, see no. 42, 31–32. Impotence, the natural law impediment to marriage, was, for instance, kept out of the Dutch Civil Code (no. 50, 42). According to Articles 549–551 of the Dutch Civil Code, a first marriage was dissolved by a new marriage if one of the spouses had been absent for 10 years or more. According to Duynstee, these provisions did not apply 'in foro conscientiae'. 'Coram Deo', the first marriage remained in force until the actual death of the absent spouse (no. 70, 58–59).

[43] Struyker Boudier, 'Gerechtigheid en liefde', 65, 69, 74.

a spiritual leader of others, in particular of priests and other clergymen dealing with psychological problems.

GENERAL APPRAISAL AND INFLUENCE

Reception: 'Natural Law Restored to Honour'

According to Pieter Kamphuisen (1897–1961), who was professor of constitutional and administrative law at the Catholic University of Nijmegen from 1933 to 1945, with his 1956 book *Over recht en rechtvaardigheid*, Duynstee did ground-breaking work and 'developed a doctrine that in my view trumps all objections to natural law'.[44] The reception that natural law met with in the Netherlands had, however, already begun before the Second World War. Duynstee was not the only Dutch protagonist of natural law in the interwar period, and maybe not even the most important one. That honour goes to another professor from the Catholic University of Nijmegen, Egidius van der Heijden. Little to nothing is known about the relationship between the three Nijmegen 'heavyweights': van der Heijden, Kamphuisen, and Duynstee. They no doubt worked together within the faculty, but van der Heijden and Kamphuisen were averse to the influence of the bishops on their scholarly work and on day-to-day business in the Nijmegen Faculty of Law. The 1928 appointment of Duynstee through the intervention of the bishops will likely have made the other two men reticent about intensively interacting with him, someone who in general stuck to the teachings of the Church in Rome. Duynstee and van der Heijden had a pupil in common, Willem van der Grinten (1913–1994), professor of civil law at Nijmegen University from 1957 to 1984. His work reflected the rise and fall of natural law in the Catholic legal circles in the Netherlands. After completing his doctorate in criminal law under Duynstee, he continued working in the natural law tradition of van der Heijden. For example, in the 1940s van der Grinten formulated a general norm grounded in natural–rational law as a basis for positive civil law.[45] Later, his work was purely within the framework of positive law.

---

[44] Pieter Kamphuisen, 'Contractsvrijheid' [1957], in *Verzameld werk van Prof. Mr. P. W. Kamphuisen* (Zwolle: W. E. J. Tjeenk Willink, 1963), 120.

[45] The title of van der Grinten's thesis was *Rechtmatigheid van de doodstraf* (Nijmegen: De Gelderlander, 1937). See Corjo Jansen, Sebastian Kortmann, and Gerard van Solinge, 'Willem Christiaan Leonard van der Grinten (1913–1994)', in *Verspreide Geschriften van W. C. L. van der Grinten*, eds. Jansen, Kortmann, and van Solinge (Deventer: Kluwer, 2004), xxiii–xxx.

The best-known work by van der Heijden on natural law can be found in his lecture as Rector, *Natuurlijke normen in het positieve recht* [Natural Norms in Positive Law] (1933). In it, he discussed the meaning of legal concepts such as reasonableness, fairness, good faith, and *iusta causa*. Van der Heijden noticed in his day the growing influence of these natural norms in positive law. 'A return to natural norms is essentially a recognition that the law is more than what the people determine, and that there is a higher reality in the nature of things.' Was the fairness in van der Heijden's day a living factor that shaped the law, alongside and sometimes even over and above legislation? To this question, he gave a resolutely affirmative answer. Catholic doctrine had never left room for the delusion that legislation and the law were synonymous.[46] The recognition of natural law entailed the rejection of the idea that in mind the sum total of the law was to be found in statutes. It also led to a rejection of legal certainty as a core legal value. '[I]t shows people's eternal longing for justice that they prefer legal uncertainty over the certainty of injustice, which is inseparable from all forms of rigid legality.'[47] According to van der Heijden, the law was more than what a legislature composed of people had set down. 'See what people achieve when they practice the law as science: positive law became thus the ultimate rule (...).' The grounds for the binding character of positive law derived, however, not from the will of a legislature made up of people, but from the will of Him who established the law, which everyone had to obey.[48]

Not only van der Heijden but also his close colleague Kamphuisen was a proponent of natural law as the foundation of positive law. In 1939, together with Duynstee, he gave an introduction to natural law for the Dutch Association for Thomistic Philosophy. Kamphuisen struggled with the concretization of the content of the norms of natural law. Everyone agreed on the fundamental standard – give each person their due – but the standards of natural law were necessarily so general that they were to be found hardly at all in legislation and case law. Maybe it was better, then, for scholars to focus on identifying institutions that had the characteristics of natural law, such as

---

[46] See Egidius van der Heijden, 'Recht en billijkheid', *De Nieuwe Eeuw* (1924): no. 381 (in response to Paul Scholten, *Beschouwingen over recht* (Haarlem: De Erven F. Bohn, 1924)).

[47] Egidius van der Heijden, *Natuurlijke normen in het positieve recht* (Nijmegen/Utrecht: Dekker & Van de Vegt, 1933), 27–28. See also van der Heijden, 'De Advocaat in dezen tijd', *De Nieuwe Eeuw* (1924): nr. 335.

[48] Egidius van der Heijden, 'Recht en vrijheid', in *Verslagboek Cultureele Week van het Nijmeegsche Studentencorps Carolus Magnus* (1934): 51, 54 (Katholiek Documentatie Centrum Nijmegen, Archive E. J. J. van der Heijden (817), no. 31). Also Egidius van der Heijden, foreword to *Handboek voor de naamlooze vennootschap naar Nederlandsch recht*, second edition (Zwolle: W. E. J. Tjeenk Willink, 1931), v.

private property, the doctrine of *justum pretium* (just price), and the principle of *pacta sunt servanda*. Kamphuisen believed that a degree of contractual freedom was a requirement of natural–rational law. Reflection on human society showed that it could not function well without freedom of contract. This meant that the state had considerable authority to impose controls and limitations.[49] He also believed that relinquishing legislation did not mean that legal certainty was lost: 'And I ... respect the fact that our case law can maintain good faith and fairness, which is of far greater importance than the existence of a nevertheless problematic legal certainty.'[50] His conclusion was clear: 'Thus the doctrine of natural law provides a philosophical foundation for the law and the state, sets the boundaries for state power, and suggests guidelines; but by no means does it bind the government in a straitjacket.'[51] Regarding the actuality of the natural law standpoint, the Roman Catholic lawyer Carel van Nispen tot Sevenaer (1895–1995) pointed to the Germany and Russia of his time: 'Not on religious grounds, but solely on the grounds of natural law, the exclusion of Jews from the state community in which they were born and raised, is to be rejected, as is the sentencing to death of the guilty, not to mention of the innocent, without due process.'[52]

The publication of van der Heijden's rectoral address, *Natuurlijke normen in het positieve recht*, was greeted enthusiastically by Jules van Oven (1881–1963), professor of Roman Law at Leiden University, who was also Editor-in-Chief of the *Nederlands Juristenblad*. Van Oven named his study: *Het natuurrecht in eere hersteld* [*Natural Law Restored to Honour*]. 'It seems to me that natural law exists, but that our human imperfection is getting in the way of its realisation.' And still he warned against giving legal certainty too little ground: 'A lawyer must be careful lest the moralist in them runs away with them.'[53] There were other reactions besides praise. Van Oven called on

---

[49] Kamphuisen, 'Contractsvrijheid', 122.
[50] Pieter Kamphuisen, 'Depreciatie van vreemde valuta' [1931], in *Verzameld werk van Prof. Mr. P. W. Kamphuisen* (Zwolle: W. E. J. Tjeenk Willink, 1963), 213.
[51] Pieter Kamphuisen, 'Het natuurrecht' [1939], in *Verzameld werk van Prof. Mr. P. W. Kamphuisen* (Zwolle: W. E. J. Tjeenk Willink, 1963), 78 et seq., 84–85, 87 (quotation); Pieter Kamphuisen, 'De leer van het justum pretium herleefd' [1933], in *Verzameld werk van Prof. Mr. P. W. Kamphuisen* (Zwolle: W. E. J. Tjeenk Willink, 1963), 222, 231. In his essay on freedom of contract, Kamphuisen gave a comprehensive overview of Duynstee's views on natural law. Kamphuisen, 'Contractsvrijheid', 119–123.
[52] Carel van Nispen tot Sevenaer, 'De strijd om de grenzen van het natuurrecht', *NJB* (1934): 673 et seq., 685 et seq. (quote on 692–693). Also Carel van Nispen tot Sevenaer, 'Natuurlijke normen als ondergeschoven kinderen', *Weekblad van het Recht* 12692 (1934): 3–4.
[53] Jules van Oven, 'Het natuurrecht in eere hersteld', *NJB* (1933): 593 et seq. (quote on 598) and 605 et seq. (quote on 610). Also Paul Scholten, '[Bookreview of] E. J. J. van der Heijden, Natuurlijke normen in het positieve recht', *Rechtsgeleerd Magazijn* (1934): 427–428.

van der Heijden to justify his position further and to explain why the natural standards of good faith and decency should be called natural law, preferably on the basis of concrete examples drawn from private law. In addition, there were also lawyers who simply denied the existence of a natural law of divine origin.[54]

Duynstee, van der Heijden, and Kamphuisen all rejected emphatically the 'new', non-neothomistic views of their day on natural law. These views emerged from natural law that had varying contents – the so-called '*richtige Recht*'. Positive law had to conform to this '*richtige Recht*', the social ideal such as could be found in a community of free people. The content of this law changed with time and place, but could remain unchanged for a longer period of time in a given culture. The interpreter par excellence of this 'relative' natural law in the first half of the 20th century was Stammler, whom we have mentioned above. Paul Scholten (1876–1946), professor of civil law and legal philosophy at the University of Amsterdam, was most impressed with Stammler's take on natural law. In expounding his view, Scholten avoided, as he said himself, the use of the concept of natural law, 'even though I am aware that what I want to propose is close to many views on what they call natural law'.[55] Duynstee found this modern natural law concept a 'mistake': it did not take an essential immutability as its starting point. In addition, this natural law emerged, not from the nature of people, but from the nature of culture. Duynstee did not see the system of natural or cultural law as having any great value. On the 'minus' side, however, it was significant that the system 'proclaimed the utter untenability of legal positivism'.[56]

Appreciation

Duynstee was a priest and a lawyer. He felt at home on philosophical, anthropological, legal, psychological, and theological terrain – he could not be defined by just one or two interests. In his view, however, there was a hierarchy at work between these disciplines. He had no ambition to be a professor of law. He sought out the legal world hardly at all, and he wrote relatively few legal articles. Once he became a professor, he performed his work conscientiously. Above all else, however, he felt himself to be the

---

[54] See Cornelis Westrate, 'Natuurrecht contra positivisme', *NJB* (1934): 227 *et seq.* and L. Polak, *HVWR* (1929): 178 *et seq.*

[55] See Corjo Jansen and Eke Poortinga, 'Het onderwijs in de rechtsfilosofie van Paul Scholten', *Recht en kritiek* 19.2 (1993): 191 *et seq.* (quote on 201).

[56] Willem Duynstee, 'Verdelende rechtvaardigheid', in *Verspreide Opstellen [van] prof. mr. W.J. A.J. Duynstee C.ss.R.* (Roermond: J. J. Romen & Zonen, 1963), 118 *et seq.*

theologian he was, and he was at home with his order, the Redemptorist Fathers, also known as the Congregation of the Most Holy Redeemer. It was theology that defined his views on law and natural law.

Duynstee's legal principles lay firmly in the nature of people, whom God had created, and in the natural order He had also created. They were subject to the *lex aeterna* (eternal law). This eternal law was absolute – that is, immutable and valid as a general matter. Its content was natural law proper. Natural law proper formed the basis of natural–rational law. Natural reason had derived natural–rational law from the natural law proper. As we have seen, Duynstee's view was closely bound up with his Catholic faith. During the interwar period in the Netherlands, he blossomed into a Catholic figurehead, albeit on the sidelines of the law. Together with van der Heijden and Kamphuisen, in the 1930s he put the Faculty of Law of the Catholic University of Nijmegen (an institution that had been founded only in 1923) on the Dutch scholarly map. He did not have many law students, however.[57] Just like van der Heijden and Kamphuisen, Duynstee did not like the adherents of the 'new' natural law, such as Stammler, who had severed the link with God.[58] In the 1960s and 1970s, natural law would slowly but surely disappear from the Nijmegen Faculty of Law and from the legal domain altogether.

Duynstee saw 'give each person their due' as the cardinal rule of natural law.[59] Through a cynical twist of fate, this rule appeared above the gate to the Buchenwald Nazi concentration camp: '*Jedem das Seine*'). Duynstee spent his entire life in the service of others, relying on the fact that this was what God intended for him. He was a sincere and honourable scholar. His work had the power of Dogmatics: as methodologically pure as possible, he built a system of concepts, rules, and principles, from the general to the particular. However, he never forgot that the law was there for the people. He was known as a good, avuncular, and cheerful professor. The letter of the law was sometimes hard, but the practice of the law should be merciful.

---

[57] See Dick van Eck, *Causaliteit en aansprakelijkheid voor gevolgen in het strafrecht* (Nijmegen: Dekker & Van de Vegt, 1947). In 1948, van Eck succeeded Duynstee as Professor of Criminal Law. He also took over legal philosophy when Duynstee left the University. Duynstee was also a source of inspiration for the 'Thomistic' psychologists and psychiatrists, such as Petrus Calon (1905–1973) and Joseph Prick (1909–1978).

[58] Duynstee's work contained almost no references at all to such work as H. Welzel, *Naturrecht und Materiale Gerechtigkeit* (Göttingen: Vandenhoeck und Ruprecht, 1955) and the oeuvre of E. Wolf (1902–1997). He did refer to the Jesuit Johannes Hoogveld, *Overzicht van beginselen der algemeene rechtsfilosofie naar peripateties-thomistische beginselen* (Nijmegen/Utrecht: Dekker & Van de Vegt, 1935).

[59] See Duynstee, 'Verdelende rechtvaardigheid', 118 *et seq.*

RECOMMENDED READINGS

De Valk, Johannes. 'Duynstee, Willem Jacobus Antonius Joseph (1886–1968)'. In *Biografisch Woordenboek van Nederland* http://resources.huygens.knaw.nl./bwn1880-2000/lemmata/bwn2/duynstee.

Duynstee, Willem. 'Natuurrecht' [Natural Law], *Handelingen van de Vereeniging voor de Wijsbegeerte des Rechts* (1929): 161ff.

Duynstee, Willem. *Geschiedenis van het natuurrecht en de wijsbegeerte in het recht in Nederland* [The History of Natural Law and Philosophy of Law in the Netherlands], Geschiedenis der Nederlandsche Rechtswetenschap, II-I. Amsterdam: Noord-Hollandsche Uitgevers Mij, 1940.

Duynstee, Willem. *Over recht en rechtvaardigheid* [On Law and Justice]. 's-Hertogenbosch: Malmberg, 1956.

Duynstee, Willem. 'Het Natuurrecht'. [Natural Law] [1939]. In *Verspreide Opstellen [van] Prof. mr. W. J. A. J. Duynstee C.ss.R.*, 82ff. Roermond: J. J. Romen & Zonen, 1963.

Duynstee, Willem. *Verspreide Opstellen [van] prof. mr. W. J. A. J. Duynstee C.ss.R.* [Collected Writings of Willem Duynstee C.ss.R.] Collected and published by Petrus Calon. Roermond: J. J. Romen & Zonen, 1963.

Struyker Boudier, Cornelis, et al., eds. *De 'oude Duyn' herdacht* [Commemorating 'Duyn the Elder']. Nijmegen: Katholieke Universiteit Nijmegen, 1987.

18

Jules Storme

Dirk Heirbaut

BIOGRAPHICAL INTRODUCTION

Jules Storme[1] was born in 1887 in Gentbrugge, near the city of Ghent, the son of Marcel Storme, an intellectual who had not been able to receive a higher education and had compensated by becoming very active as founder, president, and board member of many local and regional Catholic organizations.[2] Jules went to grammar school in Ghent and studied at the university there. He started at the Arts faculty, where he obtained a doctorate with a thesis on the dictionary in Dutch of the sixteenth-century humanist Cornelis Kiliaan, for which the Royal Flemish Academy of Dutch language and literature awarded him a prize. Although he could easily have become a philologist, Jules Storme studied law in Ghent and also went abroad in order to develop himself. In 1915 he obtained his doctorate in law, but although he was only an apprentice lawyer during the war, he had already made an impression, as some people wanted to recommend him for a chair at the 'von Bissing University'.

---

[1] Unless mentioned differently the biographical details mainly come from: Veerle van Conkelberghe, *Jules Jacob Storme* (Unpublished thesis, Ghent University, 1994) (accessible at lib.ugent.be). Other biographies of Jules Storme are: Petra Gunst, 'Storme, Jules (1887–1955)', in *UGentMemorie* (2015; www.ugentmemorie.be/personen/storme-jules-1887-1955); Peter Heyrman, *Jules Storme* (2005; http://www.odis.be/lnk/PS_51303); Marcel van Meerhaeghe, 'Jules Storme 1887–1955', in *Rijksuniversiteit te Gent. Liber memorialis 1913–1960*, ed. Theo Luyx (Ghent: UGent rectoraat, 1960), 119–120. See also the personal memories of his son: Marcel Storme, *Storme(n) over recht en gerecht. 60 jaar leven met justitie* (Ghent: Story-Scientia, 2010); Marcel Storme, 'Mijn leven op de Coupure', in *De Coupure in Gent: scheiding en verbinding* (Ghent: Academia press, 2009), 237–248; Lieke Coenraad and Remco van Rhee, 'Jurist zonder grenzen: interview met M. L. L. V. Storme', *Pro Memorie* 6 (2004): 144–167 and the history of the Storme-Leroy-van Parijs law firm (*SLVP 1915–2015. Een advocatenkantoor 'de longue durée'* (Ghent: private edition SLVP, 2016)).

[2] On Marcel Storme, not to be confused with his grandson Marcel, the son of Jules, see 'In memoriam Marcel Storme', *Maandbericht christelijke arbeidersbeweging*, April 1930.

However, Jules Storme himself did not want to be associated with this institution established by the German occupiers in Ghent.[3]

After the war Jules Storme's career really took off. From 1918 he acted as a legal advisor to social organizations of the Catholic workers, in which his father had played an important role, and to the middle class. In 1919 he enrolled as a lawyer at the Ghent Bar and in 1920 he became a lecturer at an agricultural college, where he taught law and also economics. All this enabled him to marry Maria Bosteels, a marriage blessed with four children. In 1924 Jules Storme also started to teach economics at the Special School of Commerce, a subsidiary of Ghent University's Law Faculty. This enabled him to teach economics and social law at the Law Faculty and finally led to a position as extraordinary professor at the Law Faculty in 1935 and ordinary professor in 1938. His teaching in the law school, however, mainly concerned economics. During the interwar years Storme also came to the fore as a prominent leader of the Ghent middle class, a subject which this text explores below, as it is hard to understand Jules Storme's ideas on the Christian middle class outside the context of his own involvement. Although he could only be active part-time at the Bar, Storme served before the Second World War as a board member of the Flemish Conference of the Ghent Bar, an organization which fought for the use of Dutch in the courts of Dutch-speaking Belgium. After the war his colleagues at the Bar elected him several times as a member of the Council of the Ghent Bar.

His many activities in Ghent society also gave wings to Jules Storme's political career. Elected to the Ghent city council in 1921, he was the first representative of the middle class to become alderman of Ghent for the Catholic party in 1934 and he remained alderman until the start of the German occupation. Although he was at the time only the fourth alderman of Ghent, he accepted the position of acting mayor, the mayor and others having fled or being less qualified than Storme, who spoke fluent German. He seems, like many others to have been torn between continuing in office and trying to alleviate the occupation on the one hand and his dislike of the occupiers.[4] It seems that the personal request of the bishop of Ghent, who wanted to assure the defence of Catholic schools in the local administration, played a crucial role in his decision to remain in office.[5] Storme's tenure as acting mayor did not last long, as already after a few months the Germans

---

[3] On this institution, see Kristof Loockx, '1916 Vlaamse Hogeschool', in *UGentMemorie* (2016; www.ugentmemorie.be/gebeurtenissen/1916-vlaamse-hogeschool).
[4] See Peter Taghon, *Gent, mei 1940* (Ghent: Historica, 1986).
[5] Interview with Marcel Storme by the author, 19 December 2016.

nominated a new mayor-commissioner, who belonged to a collaborationist group that had previously accused him of incompetence. No data seems to justify that and it seems that discrediting Jules Storme was just part of a larger plot of collaborationist Flemish nationalists to displace local administrators with the help of the Germans.[6] Storme continued as alderman, but finally resigned in 1943. When he refused to address a group of local volunteers who would leave to fight for Germany on the eastern front, the Germans invaded his house, destroyed furniture, and terrorized his family. Nevertheless, after the war Storme did not hesitate to defend persons accused of collaboration, but he did not return to local politics.[7]

The Storme household was very religious. Parents and children did not celebrate anniversaries, but only Catholic holidays. When the family moved in 1937, the location of the house was determined by two factors, the vicinity of a church and the vicinity of a good Catholic school. Jules Storme even walked the distance to both to ensure that they were near enough. Apart from the regular church services, he went to confession every Saturday. When he wanted to read the *Essais of Montaigne*, a book put on the index by the Pope, he asked the bishop of Ghent's permission first. Even in his work as a lawyer, Jules Storme strictly followed the Catholic authorities and never took on divorce cases.[8] Given all this, it does not come as a surprise, that in 1954, one year before his death, the Pope awarded him the *Pro Ecclesia et Pontifice* decoration for his service to the church.

MAJOR THEMES AND CONTRIBUTIONS

Unlike today's academics, Jules Storme was not that eager to publish.[9] He published one book and at least twenty smaller publications.[10] Of the latter, even in the library of his own university, only two can still be found. Thanks to Matthias Storme, his grandson, and Peter Heyrman, researcher at KADOC, I could find eight others. Their length points to their origins. Generally the smaller publications contain around thirteen pages of text, indicating that they all started as lectures. Newspaper reports on Jules Storme leave no doubt as to

---

[6] On the Belgian war mayors, see Nico Wouters, *Oorlogsburgemeesters 40/44. Lokaal bestuur en collaboratie in België* (Tielt: Lannoo, 2004) and specifically on Storme, 120, 128–129.

[7] He was one of many Catholic candidates in Ghent for the senate in 1949 (*De Standaard*, 21 May, 6).

[8] Interview with Marcel Storme by the author 19 December 2016.

[9] Even the prize-winning thesis led to only one small publication: Jules Storme, 'Een van de bronnen van Kiliaans etymologieën', *Tijdschrift voor Nederlandsche taal- en letterkunde* 33 (1914): 116–122.

[10] For a survey, see van Conkelberghe, *Jules Storme*, 26.

his talent in bringing complicated issues to ordinary people.[11] It seems that in many cases publication was due only to the wish of the audience to have Storme's words in writing. In one case, the text we have consists mainly of notes taken by an enthusiastic member of the audience.[12] In short, Storme's texts only give a limited impression of the impact he had in contemporary society.

The popular acclaim of Jules Storme's speeches should be seen in the context of Belgium's interwar history. In 1918 the breakthrough of universal equal suffrage led to political earthquakes. Nobles and upper bourgeoisie, who had previously dominated Belgian politics and society, would have to give way to the lower and middle class. For the Catholics this implied the replacement of the old Federation of Catholic Circles of the high bourgeoisie by a Christian democratic party. However, the Federation proved hard to dislodge. Within the 1921 established Catholic Union of Belgium, the 'estates' of the workers, farmers, and middle class had to fight for adequate political representation. It took them until 1936 and the establishment of a new political structure to eliminate the Federation and only in 1945 did the newly named Christian Social Party have a name that indicated the triumph of the Christian democrats.[13]

The conservative element of the Catholic party was able to resist its democratic opponents for such a long time because the democrats lacked the qualified leaders the conservatives had. If no leaders of their own could be found or created, the democratic movements had to turn to outsiders. Among those two groups stand out: clerics,[14] but also lawyers. Turning to the former was self-evident for Catholics, but it also made sense to look toward lawyers for leadership, as they already served as advisors on legal issues.[15] Jules Storme's career was unique in that he contributed to the development of not just one but two of the three estates of the Catholic party, namely the workers and the 'middle estate'. Although he lectured at an agricultural college, he never reached out to the third estate of the Belgian Catholic party, the farmers. His one text for this audience deals with the prices and rents of farmland in

---

[11] See e.g. 'Oud-leerlingenbond van 't St.-Gregoriuscollege te Ledeberg', *De Gentenaar*, 19 September 1934, 4.

[12] Jules Storme, *Jacob van Artevelde* (Gent: Het Volk, s.d.).

[13] On the evolution of the Catholic party in Belgium, see Emmanuel Gerard, *De katholieke partij in crisis. Partijpolitiek leven in België 1918–1940* (Leuven: Kritak, 1985).

[14] See e.g. on the monk who united the Catholic workers in Belgium, Emmanuel Gerard, 'Rutten, Georges A.', in *Nieuwe encyclopedie van de Vlaamse Beweging*, III, eds. Reginald De Schryver et al. (Tielt: Lannoo, 1998), 2676–2677.

[15] See for Jules Storme, *Het Volk*, 14 December 1919, 2.

a more technical way than usual for him.[16] The explanation may be twofold: the farmers already had a very strong organization from the end of the nineteenth century, the Farmers Union,[17] and in the city of Ghent farmers were absent anyway.

At first Jules Storme mainly worked on the challenges facing the Catholic workers. In 1904 the Christian Unions in Belgium established a common organization, which in 1912 became the General Confederation of Christian and Free Unions of Belgium, but there was no national organization to channel the political aspirations of Catholic workers. The latter arose only in 1921, the Christian Workers Movement. It followed the example of Belgium's socialist party, although the Movement was not a party in itself, as it remained active within the broader Catholic party, of which it was only one of four estates, although it could boast of the most extensive network of organizations. In the years 1918–1921 however, that future success was still far from certain, as the organizations of Catholic workers had to cope with internal divisions and conservative resistance.[18] In those circumstances they eagerly looked for outsiders who could both show the righteousness of their claims and a common way forward.

Jules Storme came to the attention of the Catholic workers in Ghent[19] in 1916 when he gave a lecture on James of Artevelde, the fourteenth-century leader of the first Ghent republic, for the local Christian Workers Union (Werkliedenbond). He had not been researching Artevelde himself but offered a simplified overview which made a great impression on his audience, according to the enthusiastic press.[20] The newspaper *Het Volk* published his text in a small cheap edition which was clearly meant to be widely read.[21] This interest of factory workers from Ghent and elsewhere in a medieval leader seems strange, but readers may have felt that Storme used James of Artevelde as an excuse to comment on his own time. Thus, when he described the plight of working men before Artevelde and their lack of political representation, his contemporaries did not fail to compare this with their own situation. Jules Storme praises Artevelde as a statesman, the creator of a constitutional,

---

[16] Jules Storme, *Over pachtwaarde (grondrente) en bodemprijs* (Gent: s.e., 1926).
[17] Leen van Molle, *Ieder voor allen. De Belgische Boerenbond 1890–1990* (Leuven: Boerenbond, 1990).
[18] On the organizations of the Catholic workers in Belgium, see Emmanuel Gerard, ed., *De christelijke arbeidersbeweging in België* (Leuven: Universitaire pers Leuven, 1991).
[19] On the Christian workers in Ghent, see Jan De Maeyer, 'De Poel. Huis de Nockere. De christelijke arbeidersbeweging aan het feest', in *Geloven in Gent. Plaatsen van het religieuze verleden*, eds. Ruben Mantels et al. (Ghent: Academia press, 2015), 86–92.
[20] *Het Volk*, 21 October 1916, 2; *Het Vlaamsche Nieuws*, 22 October 1916, 2.
[21] Jules Storme, *van Artevelde*.

parliamentary state long before the nineteenth century. In fact, implicitly Storme indicates that Artevelde's state was even superior to nineteenth-century Belgium, as Artevelde took into account social differences and ensured that all the classes of Ghent's population were represented in its administration. Jules Storme's view of Artevelde is somewhat exaggerated. Artevelde at times behaved like a dictator, but he did indeed try to come to social and political harmony in Ghent by also involving the working and middle class in Ghent politics.[22] Storme's view, however, turns Artevelde into a Christian democrat *avant la lettre*. As such, the lecture on Artevelde reveals more about Jules Storme than about Artevelde.

Given Jules Storme's open sympathy for the Christian workers in Ghent, they hired him as their advisor.[23] The newspaper of a Ghent Catholic worker's union, *Het Volk* (*The People*),[24] wanted to offer him a broader platform in 1918 by organizing a competition for the best publication on the reconstruction of post-war Belgium, which should take into account the reasonable aspirations of the workers but in terms of a good understanding with the employers and the government.[25] The 'competition' looks like a set up from the start. Storme, who professed to have had many talks with union leaders,[26] seems to have suggested the question, as it allowed him fully to expose his ideas on the future of his country. The book *Maatschappelijke vrede en economische wederopbloei* (Social peace and economic reconstruction) published by *Het Volk* in 1919 must have been based on earlier work by Storme and on discussions with union leaders during the war,[27] else it is hard to explain how he could have written it in such a short time.

Storme splits his book into three parts, covering the situation before the war, the war years, and his proposals. The author makes a few elements clear from the start. He wants to achieve social peace. In order to achieve it, the ethical dimension has to be taken into account and employers and labourers need to cooperate.[28] As Storme himself admits the first two parts of his book want to make the readers aware of the workers' situation.[29] His description of

---

[22] On Artevelde, see Patricia Carson, *James van Artevelde. The man from Ghent* (Ghent: Story-Scientia, 1980).
[23] *Het Volk*, 19 December 1919, 2.
[24] On this paper, see Bart De Wilde, 'De Forelstraat. Het Volk. Katholiek dagblad voor Vlaanderen', in *Geloven in Gent*, 146–153.
[25] Jules Storme, *Maatschappelijke vrede en economische wederopbloei* (Ghent: Het Volk, 1919), v.
[26] Storme, *Maatschappelijke vrede*, 44.
[27] Compare Storme, *Maatschappelijke vrede*, 120.
[28] Storme, *Maatschappelijke vrede*, vi.
[29] Storme, *Maatschappelijke vrede*, 123.

the situation before 1914 reads even today as a good account of the actual events.[30]

Storme keenly analyzes the differences between socialist and Catholic unions and also between union activity in Flanders and Wallonia. Whereas the socialists wanted class struggle, Catholics preferred to avoid it. In this context Storme expressly mentions *Rerum Novarum* by Pope Leo XIII, 'the great Pope'.[31] However, Storme also indicates that socialist fervour was weakening and that socialism in Belgium had recently turned to more peaceful means of action. He especially mentions the socialist cooperatives, which formed the distinctive element of socialism in Flanders and which have left their mark in Ghent even today.[32] He pays less attention to the influence the socialists had on Catholic workers, although he mentions in passing that Catholic cooperatives also started to appear.[33] Moreover, Storme did not completely rule out strikes. He preferred amicable settlements, but could accept strikes as an ultimate remedy.[34]

Although Storme in the historical part tries to present a neutral view, he cannot completely escape his own origins and preferences. He describes the squalid living conditions of the working class, but also blames the workers for sometimes having loose morals[35] and not making enough effort to keep their homes clean, failing, however, to see that their long working days did not leave them much time for hygiene. In this Storme shared a common perception of the working class held by middle- and upper-class Belgians. However, Storme pulled no punches in his description of wage policies in Belgium and he does not at all hesitate to deem the workers' demands for higher wages justified.[36]

The second part of the book, on the war years, has less appeal to later readers than the rest of the book. Yet, for his intended readership it may have been essential. Surprisingly, Storme praised the Germans for offering high wages and an eight-hour workday to those who volunteered to work for them. To Storme, this and the example of England proved that it was not impossible to ameliorate the conditions of the workers after the war.[37]

---

[30] For an overview of Belgian social and economic history and legislation, see Dirk Heirbaut, *Een beknopte geschiedenis van het sociaal, het economisch en het fiscaal recht in België* (Tielt: Lannoo, 2019).
[31] Storme, *Maatschappelijke vrede*, 72.
[32] Storme, *Maatschappelijke vrede*, 65–83.
[33] Storme, *Maatschappelijke vrede*, 75.
[34] Storme, *Maatschappelijke vrede*, 81–82, 262.
[35] Storme, *Maatschappelijke vrede*, 148.
[36] Storme, *Maatschappelijke vrede*, 46–50.
[37] Storme, *Maatschappelijke vrede*, 121–122.

His proposals for post-war Belgium reflect Storme's general views on law and religion. Although he was a jurist, in his opinion, law was not the best means for ordering society. In a text on the 'sociological' foundations of law, he states that *boni mores* trump *bonae leges*. In this context, he refers not only to morals, but also to religion, which he deemed more important than law.[38] For ordering society, Storme's fundamental axiom was: 'Love your neighbour as yourself' (Mark 12:31).[39] To him this ruled out both socialism and unfettered capitalism. He pleads for a middle road, which he finds in the works of Christian economists and sociologists, although also in the publications of a few others,[40] like the French lawyer and politician Léon Bourgeois, who was a freemason and thus anti-religious.[41] Storme's main inspiration is Heinrich Pesch,[42] of whom he quotes in particular the first volume of the *Lehrbuch der Nationalökonomie*.[43] Like Pesch, Storme had studied in Berlin under Gustav Schmoller and Adolph Wagner.[44] Pesch, and in his wake Storme,[45] proposed 'solidarism' for the organization of society. Pesch was not alone in advocating solidarism, which tried to balance the interests of the individual and society. For this purpose, Pesch attributed a crucial role to autonomous social groups, which served as links between the individual and the state and which should work together to achieve social harmony. Christian authors like Pesch firmly based solidarism on religion. In practice, this meant the recognition of the activities of organically grown groups in society, in particular the Catholic organizations which had sprung up after *Rerum Novarum*. Christian solidarism provided a framework for their activities.

The fundamental difference between Marxism and solidarism was the attitude toward class struggle. Although writing for the workers and defending their cause, Storme emphasized that they also should keep in mind the interests of other social groups.[46] Unlike in his 1916 lecture on Artevelde, he

---

[38] Jules Storme, *De sociologische ondergrond van het recht* (Ghent: Erasmus, 1924). Storme did not mean sociology in the current sense, but rather sociology as a part of ethics, which determined the rights and duties of man as a social being.

[39] Storme, *Maatschappelijke vrede*, 124.

[40] Storme, *Maatschappelijke vrede*, 131–136.

[41] See on him, Marc Sorlot, *Léon Bourgeois: un moraliste en politique* (Paris: Bruno Leprince, 2005).

[42] On Pesch, see Hermann-Josef Große Kracht, Tobias Karcher, and Christian Spieß, eds., *Das System des Solidarismus – Zur Auseinandersetzung mit dem Werk von Heinrich Pesch SJ* (Berlin: Lit Verlag, 2006).

[43] Heinrich Pesch, *Lehrbuch der Nationalökonomie* I (Freiburg im Breisgau: Herder, 1905).

[44] On both professors and their ideas, see J. Backhaus et al., eds., *Gustav von Schmoller and Adolph Wagner. Legacy and lessons for civil society and the state* (Springer: New York, 2018).

[45] Storme, *Maatschappelijke vrede*, 131–136.

[46] Storme, *Maatschappelijke vrede*, 146.

avoids the concept of class when later describing social groups. Associations of the concept of class with struggle had made it preferable for German Christians to use another word, '*Stand*' (estate). Thus, Pesch, building upon the work of Schmoller, spoke of a division of society in '*Stände*' (estates),[47] based on the economic sector in which persons were active: agriculture, industry, or trade. Dutch, which also had the word '*stand*', easily caught up with this German terminology. Hence, Jules Storme stated that Belgium was a society of estates in the making.[48] However, the idea of 'estates' only held for the Catholic party, and the quadripartite division of the 1921 Catholic Union into farmers, workers, the middle estate, and the conservatives of the Federation corresponded more to political reality than to a theory.

As already indicated, the challenge facing Christian democracy in Belgium was in meeting the demands of those estates which had previously been deprived of power. In *Maatschappelijke vrede* Storme focuses only on the workers and the cooperation he wants between them and the employers. Storme judged that psychologically the time was right for the employers to respect their employees' rights, including the right to unionize, but also for the latter to be aware of their duties. Both sides had to make concessions, but Storme indicated that the employers had a larger margin than they assumed. He suggests several efficiency-enhancing measures that should create possibilities for better pay, shorter working hours, and better working conditions.[49]

The cooperation of employers and workers does not eliminate the need for state intervention.[50] For Storme 'the protection of the weakest is the most important objective of democratic legislation'.[51] Storme shrewdly explained that this general legislation on workers' rights is also in employers' interest. State legislation ensured a level playing field, so that less charitable employers would not enjoy a competitive advantage.[52] Storme pleaded for accession to most of the workers' demands – higher wages, shorter working days, better working conditions – although not completely.[53] For example, the eight-hour workday (a very popular demand of the socialists who regularly named the seat of their activities the 'eight-hours house') did not yet seem feasible to him.[54] Nevertheless, Storme went quite far, advocating adequate institutions for

---

[47] Heinrich Pesch, *Lehrbuch der Nationalökonomie* II (Freiburg im Breisgau: Herder, 1926), 320–324.
[48] Storme, *Maatschappelijke vrede*, 129.
[49] Storme, *Maatschappelijke vrede*, 146–181.
[50] Storme, *Maatschappelijke vrede*, 184.
[51] Storme, *Maatschappelijke vrede*, 60.
[52] Storme, *Maatschappelijke vrede*, 184.
[53] Storme, *Maatschappelijke vrede*, 184–253.
[54] Storme, *Maatschappelijke vrede*, 241.

enforcing social legislation, maximum rewards for necessary goods, and all kinds of social insurance mechanisms. He even promoted the Ghent system, which supported the unions' allowance to unemployed members through paying them a supplement.[55]

For Jules Storme the law had to accommodate his objectives. The labour contract to him could no longer be a contract of lease of work because a labourer's work was linked to his person. How the jurists defined a labour contract was less important and could be solved later. Moreover, the contract was a collective labour agreement, because only in this way could workers act together in solidarity.[56] Storme's enthusiasm for the collective labour agreement fits with the general attitude of the Catholic church in Belgium. After all, the first Belgian publication to study collective labour agreements extensively was written by Valerius Claes, a Capuchin friar.[57] Storme also devoted a lot of attention to the institutions which could bring together employers and workers, thus contributing to social peace. He criticized the existing labour and industry commissions and proposed reform.[58]

Needless to say, Storme disliked the ban on trade unions which had existed in Belgium until 1867. In an article on the right to unionize, he even wrote: 'Nothing should be allowed to stand in the way of the success of the unions.'[59] However, in 1867 the legislature had accompanied the abolition of the ban with new measures against strikers who hindered colleagues who wanted to work and had even strengthened this anti-picketing measure in 1892, just before the arrival of universal but unequal suffrage. After the First World War, this legislation had to go, but Storme, following the Catholic unions, had some reservations. The existing law helped the Catholic union, which could mobilize less than one-sixth of the number of members of the socialist union. Under those circumstances, legislation which forbade the socialists to put pressure on Catholic workers had its advantages and Storme therefore also defended the freedom not to become a member of a union,[60] which was exactly the solution the Belgian

---

[55] Storme, *Maatschappelijke vrede*, 253.
[56] Storme, *Maatschappelijke vrede*, 220–221, 255.
[57] Valerius Claes, *L'organisation professionnelle et le contrat collectif de travail des imprimeurs allemands* (Leuven: A. Uystpruyst, 1908).
[58] Storme, *Maatschappelijke vrede*, 64, 276–288 and in more detail Jules Storme, 'De hervorming onzer arbeids- en nijverheidsraden', *Gids op maatschappelijk gebied* (1920), 1–4 and Jules Storme, *Het voorkomen en regelen der arbeidsgeschillen*, *Gids op maatschappelijk gebied* (1922), 3–16.
[59] Jules Storme, *Het coalitierecht der arbeiders. Syndicalisme en coöperatie. Doel en middelen* (Antwerp, 1921).
[60] Storme, *Maatschappelijke vrede*, 258–259, 271; Storme, *Coalitierecht*, 4–7.

legislature came to in 1921. Workers had the unrestricted right to unionize, but also the right to remain out of any union.

As this shows, Storme's proposals always had the Catholic worker in mind, but Storme cared not so much for the individual worker as for his family, the cornerstone of society.[61] The protection of family life implied a ban on child labour, but also, as much as possible, on women in the workplace. Storme wanted to forbid women to work in factories or in jobs for which they were physically less apt. If women remained at home, this would lessen immorality at work and lead to higher wages for the male workers, but also to cleaner houses.[62] The workman's family had to be Christian foremost. After all: 'The most valuable treasure a worker possesses is his religious conviction.'[63] A large Christian family would also ensure the country had a great group of productive workers.[64] Hence, Storme foresaw additional measures for helping families with more than the three children a normal wage should support.[65]

The needs of a Catholic family also necessitated Catholic unions. Socialists only looked at the material element, but the moral element was equally important, as 'the foundation of all social theories has to be a solidly grounded religion'.[66] Following in the footsteps of medieval thinkers, Storme declared that 'Labour is also religion',[67] or 'Labour is a prayer',[68] but he contrasts this with the working conditions in his own time. Labourers have turned into cogs in a machine and can no longer find pleasure in their work. Instead of bringing them closer to God, it turns them away from Him. Workers have to rediscover the joy of life, by looking at both their material and moral needs. Therefore, unions need to look at both and this can only happen when they are religious.[69]

Jules Storme's book found acclaim among its target public. The academic world received it less favourably. Storme wrote in Dutch at a time when any serious book in Belgium had to be in French and the last part of his work reads as the programme of the Christian democratic movement.[70] This may help to explain why academics forgot this book, even though many elements of the programme it envisioned became reality during the next decades. Storme

---

[61] Storme, Maatschappelijke vrede, 185.
[62] Storme, Maatschappelijke vrede, 197–203.
[63] Storme, Maatschappelijke vrede, 191.
[64] Storme, Maatschappelijke vrede, 192.
[65] Storme, Maatschappelijke vrede, 234.
[66] Storme, Maatschappelijke vrede, 290.
[67] Storme, Maatschappelijke vrede, 293.
[68] Storme, Maatschappelijke vrede, 294.
[69] Storme, Maatschappelijke vrede, 294–298.
[70] 'Prix Adelson Castiau', Annuaire de l'Académie royale de Belgique 87 (1921): 128–134.

himself is also to blame. He saw his involvement with the workers movement as only provisional. The unions needed their own leaders, workers exempt from their normal job and trained by the union.[71] Last but not least, Storme felt that another group needed him more, the 'middle estate'.

Jules Storme and the Catholic 'Middle Estate'

In 1919 Jules Storme became legal advisor to and a board member of the General Committee of 'The Middle Estate' (*Algemeen Comiteit 'De Middelstand'*).[72] Until his death in 1955 Storme would be the great man behind this *Comiteit*, and its splinter organization and later successor.[73] The word '*Middelstand*' in the name of the *Comiteit* refers to the group it represented: the 'middle estate'. This terminology needs some explanation. As indicated, Christian authors in Germany, followed by Dutch-speaking Belgians and Dutch, tried to avoid the Marxist terminology of class warfare by using 'estate' instead of 'class'. But neither French nor English ever copied it. For Christian theory the concept of a middle estate took on importance when Gustav Schmoller, later Storme's teacher in Berlin, lectured on it for the eighth Evangelical social congress in 1897 and Pesch also wrote on the subject.[74]

Storme's involvement with the middle estate at first sight clashes with his original activity on behalf of the workers movement. In his *Maatschappelijke vrede* he encouraged the establishment of cooperatives.[75] These enjoyed great popularity in Ghent, with an extremely strong socialist cooperative movement[76] and a smaller Catholic one in its wake. The small shopkeepers and independent craftsmen who made up the core of the middle estate may not have liked Storme's original attitude toward the cooperatives which

---

[71] Storme, *Maatschappelijke vrede*, 260–264.
[72] Its full name was: Algemeen Comiteit ter verdediging van de belangen der kleine burgerij 'De Middelstand'. On this organization in particular and the Catholic middle estate in Belgium in general, see Peter Heyrman, *Voor eigen winkel. Honderd jaar middenstand en middenstandsbeweging in Oost-Vlaanderen* (Ghent: Provinciebestuur Oost-Vlaanderen, 1991); Peter Heyrman, *Middenstandsbeweging en beleid in België 1918–1940* (Leuven: Universitaire pers, 1998); Peter Heyrman, 'De Lange Kruisstraat. Het Middenstandshuis. Zelfstandigen in het geloof', *Geloven in Gent*, 78–85.
[73] Van Conkelberghe, 'Jules Storme', 14–16.
[74] Klaus-Jürgen Gantzel, *Wesen und Begriff der mittelständischen Unternehmung* (Wiesbaden: Springer, 1962), esp. 7–8. See also Klaus-Peter Sick, 'Le concept de classes moyennes. Notion sociologique ou slogan politique?', *Vingtième siècle* 37 (1993): 13–34.
[75] Storme, *Maatschappelijke vrede*, 268–269. See also Storme, *Coalitierecht*, 15–16.
[76] See on this, Hendrik Defoort, *Werklieden bemint uw profijt! De Belgische sociaaldemocratie in Europa* (Ghent: Amsab, 2006).

wanted to eliminate them. Storme was also an internationalist who pleaded for free trade, even during the crisis of the 1930s,[77] and supported the establishment of the International Labour Organization and the international protection of workers.[78] Among the middle estate there was also a strong dislike of lawyers.[79] Yet, given the lack of qualified leaders of their own the middle estate had to turn to others. Thus, the driving forces behind the establishment of the *Comiteit* were a notary and a lawyer[80] and they called on Jules Storme.

Whereas Storme's short activity for the Christian workers resulted in the majority of his published work, his lifelong work for the middle estate produced only two publications on the middle estate and only one has been preserved.[81] Nevertheless, his written material on this topic must have been greater, as newspapers report several lectures by Storme covering problems of the middle estate.[82] Unfortunately, only in one case does a newspaper extensively cover a lecture, in 1935.[83] Apart from this report, the main source on Storme's thoughts on the middle estate can be found in the text of his solemn address in 1929 to an audience of vocational trainers and professionals. To Storme this sympathetic audience would welcome his views on the problem of the middle estate (*middenstandsprobleem*).[84]

Many elements justified seeing the situation of the middle estate as problematic, as even the concept itself was unclear. Schmollers's 1897 lecture had already struggled with its main problem.[85] The 'middle estate' denominated the group in-between the upper and the lower classes, but it turned out to be hard to define exactly who belonged to it. For Pesch, for example, the primary division of social groups was into agriculture, industry, and trade. The middle groups of each of these together formed the 'middle estate'.[86] The landscape of Catholic movements in Belgium did not conform to Pesch's theories. In French-speaking Belgium the low number of Catholics made it necessary to

---

[77] Jules Storme, *Vrijhandel of protectie* (Ghent: Erasmus, 1932).
[78] Jules Storme, *Het verdrag van Versailles en de internationale arbeidersbescherming* (Ghent: Erasmus, 1932).
[79] Compare Heyrman, *Middenstandsbeweging*, 125–126.
[80] Heyrman, *Winkel*, 87.
[81] Jules Storme, *De economische en sociale betekenis van den middenstand* (Ghent: Erasmus, 1929). I could not find Jules Storme, *De taak der gemeente tot bevordering van handel en ambachtswezen* (1937).
[82] E.g. 'Gents nieuws. Algemene middenstandsbond Gent', *De Gentenaar*, 19 February 1948, 2.
[83] Jules Storme, 'Slotrede Christen Middenstandsdag te Gent', *Het Nieuwsblad*, 30 December 1935, 3 (summary).
[84] Storme, *Betekenis*, 3.
[85] Gustav Schmoller, *Was verstehen wir unter dem Mittelstande?* (Göttingen: Vandenhoeck, 1897).
[86] Pesch, *Lehrbuch*, II, 320–324.

band together, whereas in Dutch-speaking Belgium the different estates were more prominent. Farmers, workers, and the conservatives had their own organizations, so that the middle estate could only take the terrain they had not yet covered. Storme first of all thought of independent craftsmen and shopkeepers, but in a broader view also included white collar workers, liberal professionals, and famers.[87] However, his discourse mainly reflects the views of the independent craftsmen and shopkeepers. After all, the additional groups belonged to other estates of the Catholic party.

Storme in 1929 and 1935 lamented the neglect of the middle estate by the politicians. He railed against taxes. The 'middle estate' had to bear the burden of them, but the authorities used its revenue to finance social legislation, which did not profit the middle estate. Thus, he demanded just taxes.[88] He seems to ignore that the reform of the Belgian tax system between 1919 and 1921 took as its basic principle the 'ability to pay' thanks to Jules Ingenbleek's 1918 *La justice dans l'impôt*, which defended this principle.[89] Storme does not offer any alternative. In his 1929 lecture Storme clamours for the support of the authorities, but remains rather vague about what he wants. One part of the problem, in his opinion, is the lack of general appreciation of the public at large for the middle estate. Therefore, he wants the government to inform the citizens better on the middle estate. He also pleads for more statistical data on the middle estate.[90] The 1935 lecture contains more details, but remains vague. The state has to defend the middle estate, just as it defends the other estates, by an effective 'Middle estate policy' (*Middenstandsbeleid*). This means that the state must ensure just taxes and equal rights for members of the middle estate, and must act against supermarkets, but also against monopolies and state enterprises, in so far as these are unnecessary.[91] In this, Storme's discourse does not differ from that of other defenders of the middle estate, who felt that politicians ignored their problems.[92]

Storme's 1935 lecture and other documents show that he wanted to organize the middle estate in the Catholic party at the level of the organizations of the workers and the farmers. Therefore, he entreated the middle estate to be united under 'the banner of Christ'.[93] He and others completely failed in this endeavour. Only a small minority of professionals wanted to rally to an

---

[87] Storme, *Betekenis*, 2–3.
[88] Storme, *Betekenis*, 4.
[89] Jules Ingenbleek, *La justice dans l'impôt* (Paris: Berger-Levrault, 1918).
[90] Storme, *Betekenis*, 3–13.
[91] Storme, 'Slotrede', 3.
[92] See e.g. Heyrman, *Middenstandsbeweging*, 161.
[93] Storme, 'Slotrede', 3.

organization.⁹⁴ Those who wanted to do so had to confront organizational chaos. In Ghent alone two 'Catholic' organizations competed for representation of the middle estate with a group headed by Fernand van Ackere facing off against Storme's *Comiteit*.⁹⁵ The *Comiteit* could draw the rank and file, but van Ackere had the luck that he had 'inherited' the funds and organizations that Karel van der Cruyssen had built up in Ghent before he took orders and became abbot of Orval.⁹⁶ Van der Cruyssen's work meant that both in Ghent and at the national level van Ackere could go his own way. The national organization, the Christian National Union of the Belgian Middle Estate (*Christelijke Landsbond van de Belgische Middenstand*), could not impose itself against van Ackere and local organizations, so that it remained the weakest link of the Catholic party.

Many professionals preferred their organizations to be neutral.⁹⁷ For the *Comiteit*, which, to a greater extent than van Ackere, had to take its members into account, this proved to be a serious obstacle. The lawyers on its board, like Storme, tried to steer the organization as far as possible in a Catholic direction, whereas the professional organizations behind the *Comiteit* liked neutrality. In practice the *Comiteit* acted like a Catholic organization. This changed in the 1930s. New order movements found it easy to seduce the middle estate by sharing and enhancing its complaints against corrupt politicians. In spite of Storme's efforts, the *Comiteit* moved toward the extreme right, which led him to secede and establish the General Catholic Middle Estate Union of Ghent (*Algemeen Katholiek Middenstandsverbond*) in 1936. When the war ended the *Comiteit* disappeared and its remaining members re-joined their brethren in Storme's organization. In the meantime, the middle estate had found its unity and in 1949 Storme's General Catholic Middle Estate Union of Ghent became the Ghent chapter of the National Christian Middle Estate Union (*Nationaal Christelijk Middenstandsverbond*).

The organizational chaos of the middle estate and its reluctant Catholicism have many causes, such as personality clashes. A crucial element, however, was the lack of a Christian theory of the middle estate. The 1891 *Rerum Novarum* mentioned labourers and farmers, but not the middle estate. Intellectuals also largely ignored it. In this context Storme got not much further than a vague neo-thomistic view of society. The middle estate was a social necessity. 'If it would not exist, one should have to create it.'⁹⁸ As the

---

[94] Heyrman, *Middenstandsbeweging*, 171.
[95] On van Ackere, see Heyrman, *Winkel*, 174–175.
[96] On van der Cruyssen, see Heyrman, *Winkel*, 90–91.
[97] Heyrman, *Middenstandsbeweging*, 118, 173–176.
[98] Storme, *Betekenis*, 13.

estate in the middle, it served as a buffer between the upper and the lower estates, so that struggle between them could be avoided. As binding link between the upper and lower estates, the middle class ensured solidarity and social mobility. For the lowest in society it was impossible to climb in one generation to the highest level, but the children of a worker could ascend to the middle estate and thanks to that his grandchildren could reach the highest levels in society. The engine of this upward mobility were the virtues of the middle estate: hard work, thrift, order, and self-discipline, and of course, Christian family life.[99] In this, Storme did not particularly distinguish himself from other leaders of the middle estate who pronounced the same ideas.[100]

However, Storme's Christian democratic ideas had first formed when he wrote on the working class. In his *Maatschappelijke vrede* he had already presented the Christian family values of the middle estate as the ideal that Christian workers should aspire to.[101] Storme pleaded for a strong middle estate, but he wanted all estates harmoniously working together to the benefit of society. Solidarity with the other estates had to be paramount.[102] It therefore sorely disappointed him that the other estates of the Catholic party did not support the justified claims of the middle estate, even though the latter had helped them.[103] Storme's own *Maatschappelijke vrede* had benefited the Catholic workers movement, but it galled him that the workers did not return the favour.

In 1935 Storme based his theories on *Rerum Novarum* and *Quadragesimo anno*, in which the Pope, forty years after *Rerum Novarum*, once again considered the challenges of an industrialized society. In *Quadragesimo anno* Pope Pius XI gave his blessing to the Christian organizations established in the wake of *Rerum Novarum*, advocating a corporatist organization of society. What the Pope exactly meant by the latter remains disputed, because Catholics interpreted his message according to their own preferences. In Belgium the conservatives of the Federation of Catholic Circles found in *Quadragesimo anno* ammunition in the fight against their democratic opponents, as to them it meant the establishment of a corporative state, and the abolition of separate workers organizations and their replacement by new organizations under their control. The Christian Workers Movement in Belgium, however, saw things differently. It found a justification for its

---

[99] Storme, *Betekenis*, 13–14.
[100] See e.g. Heyrman, *Middenstandsbeweging*, 161.
[101] Storme, *Maatschappelijke vrede*, 189–192.
[102] Storme, 'Slotrede', 3.
[103] Peter Heyrman, 'De middenstand in de jaren 1930. Verslagboek Middenstandsverbond Oost-Vlaanderen', *Kadoc nieuwsbrief* 9/10 (2005): 5.

autonomous organizations in *Quadragesimo anno* and limited the corporatist element to the establishment of joint organizations in the economic sphere.[104] Jules Storme wanted a corporatist reorganization of society in 1935,[105] but his view turned out to be far removed from what the conservatives wanted. In his *Maatschappelijke vrede* and other publications he had already defended unions and rejected associations dominated by employers. He had also promoted the idea that some aspects of the economy could be better left to the actors involved.[106] In 1935, he had not changed his mind. He continued to defend autonomous organizations of workers, but wanted next to them autonomous organizations of the 'middle estate' which would be just as strong and would be able to themselves take care of some aspects of economic regulation.[107] In short, whatever message the Pope had wanted to convey, like other Belgian Catholics, Jules Storme used *Quadragesimo anno* only to support his own agenda.

GENERAL APPRAISAL AND INFLUENCE

Looking at Jules Storme's work, he seems to have offered a prophecy of Christian democracy in Belgium during the second half of the twentieth century, when the Christian People's Party channelled the aspirations of strong organizations of farmers, workers, and the middle estate. Storme's main contribution consisted of promoting these ideas during the interwar years through his publications and most of all his speeches. Exceptionally, he defended the interests of not one but two estates, which shows his commitment to the idea of social harmony and cooperation among the estates of the Catholic party in Belgium.

Last but not least, Jules Storme does not stand on his own. There is a remarkable continuity in his family: from his father Marcel to Jules himself, his son Marcel, grandson Matthias, and the latter's children. In spite of the secularization Belgium underwent, the Storme family has remained as Catholic at the dawn of the twenty-first century as it was on the eve of the nineteenth. The three successive law professors – Jules, Marcel, and Matthias – nevertheless show that the political face of Catholicism in Belgium and its relationship with society changed radically. Whereas Jules

---

[104] Compare Dirk Luyten, 'Politiek corporatisme en de crisis van de liberale ideologie (1920–1944)', *Belgische tijdschrift voor nieuwste geschiedenis* 23 (1992): 493–546; 24 (1993): 107–139.
[105] Storme, 'Slotrede', 3.
[106] See note 58.
[107] Compare Storme, 'Slotrede', 3.

Storme stands for the growing pains of Christian democracy, Marcel Storme incarnates its triumph[108] and Matthias Storme, *éminence grise* of a Flemish-nationalist party which more belligerently adheres to a cultural Catholicism, can stand for a new era in which traditional Christian democracy has to give way to newcomers. Thus, a comparison of three generations of Storme law professors will be an interesting topic of study for future historians.

RECOMMENDED READING

Gerard, Emmanuel. *De katholieke partij in crisis. Partijpolitiek leven in België 1918–1940*. Leuven: Kritak, 1985.

Gerard, Emmanuel, ed. *De christelijke arbeidersbeweging in België*. Leuven: Universitaire pers Leuven, 1991.

Gunst, Petra. 'Storme, Jules (1887–1955)'. UGentMemorie (2015; http://www.ugentmemorie.be/personen/storme-jules-1887-1955).

Heyrman, Peter. *Voor eigen winkel. Honderd jaar middenstand en middenstandsbeweginginOost-Vlaanderen*. Ghent: Provinciebestuur Oost-Vlaanderen, 1991.

Heyrman, Peter. *Middenstandsbeweging en beleid in België 1918–1940*. Leuven: Universitaire pers, 1998.

Heyrman, Peter. *Jules Storme* (2005; http://www.odis.be/lnk/PS_51303).

Mantels, Ruben, et al., eds. *Geloven in Gent. Plaatsen van het religieuze verleden*. Ghent: Academia press, 2015.

Van Conkelberghe, Veerle. *Jules Jacob Storme*. Unpublished thesis, Ghent university, 1994 (accessible at lib.ugent.be).

Van Meerhaeghe, Marcel. 'Jules Storme 1887–1955'. In *Rijksuniversiteit te Gent. Liber memorialis 1913–1960*, edited by Theo Luyx, 119–120. Ghent: UGent rectoraat, 1960.

---

[108] On Marcel Storme, son of Jules and not be confused with his eponymous grandfather, see Dirk Heirbaut, 'Storme, Marcel (1930–2018)', *UGentmemorie* (2018; https://www.ugentmemorie.be/personen/storme-marcel-1930-2018).

19

Herman Dooyeweerd

Bas Hengstmengel

BIOGRAPHICAL INTRODUCTION

Herman Dooyeweerd was born in Amsterdam on 7 October 1894.[1] His family strongly sympathized with the ideas of the Dutch neo-Calvinist theologian, statesman, and prolific author Abraham Kuyper (1837–1920). As a commentator rightly notes, 'Kuyper's influence permeated Dooyeweerd's life in every way'.[2] Dooyeweerd attended the Reformed gymnasium in Amsterdam. In 1912, he enrolled at the Free University (Vrije Universiteit) in Amsterdam at the Faculty of Law. Legal study was more or less a pragmatic choice for Dooyeweerd, who was very interested in literature and wrote poetry. The Free University, founded in 1880 by Kuyper and others, was still very small in those years, with only a few professors of law. In 1917, Dooyeweerd completed a dissertation on the role of the cabinet in Dutch Constitutional law.[3] Afterwards he worked as a civil servant for a few years. In 1922 Dooyeweerd was appointed first deputy director of the Dr Abraham Kuyper Stichting, the newly founded think tank of the Anti-Revolutionary Party (ARP), the first political party in the Netherlands. Until 1926, he worked at the party's Kuyper Institute, located in the former residence of Abraham Kuyper in The Hague. In 1924, Dooyeweerd founded the monthly journal *Antirevolutionaire Staatkunde* (Anti-Revolutionary Politics) and served as its first editor-in-chief. This was a period of intense and fundamental study in which Dooyeweerd read and wrote about the nature and sources of law, the foundations of the state,

---

[1] For a good general introduction to Dooyeweerd's life and work see: Marcel E. Verburg, *Herman Dooyeweerd: The Life and Work of a Christian Philosopher* (Grand Rapids: Paideia Press, 2009).
[2] Albert Wolters, 'The intellectual milieu of Herman Dooyeweerd', in *The Legacy of Herman Dooyeweerd*, ed. C. T. McIntire (Lanham: University Press of America, 1985), 2.
[3] Herman Dooyeweerd, *De ministerraad in het Nederlandsche staatsrecht* (Amsterdam: Wed. G. van Soest, 1917).

philosophy, and the history of Christian thought. He studied a lot with his brother-in-law, the philosopher and theologian D. H. Th. Vollenhoven (1892–1978). Besides the general introduction to philosophy that was offered to every student at the Free University, Dooyeweerd was never educated as a philosopher. His philosophical knowledge was mainly gained through self-study. He also learnt a lot by discussing philosophy with his brother-in-law Vollenhoven.[4]

In 1926, Dooyeweerd was appointed professor of law at the Vrije Universiteit. He remained at this position until his retirement in 1964. He taught in the areas of the encyclopaedia of the science of law, jurisprudence, and legal history. Although he was first and foremost a legal scholar, he rapidly developed as a general philosopher. Initially he was very impressed by neo-Kantianism and later by Edmund Husserl's phenomenology, but eventually he opposed both currents. However, the dominant school of neo-Kantianism remained his main interlocutor, especially the so-called Marburg school of neo-Kantianism of which Herman Cohen (1842–1918), Paul Natorp (1854–1924), and Ernst Cassirer (1874–1945) were the main representatives. Neo-Kantianism was highly influential in the Netherlands in the first half of the twentieth century and dominated philosophy of law. The most important neo-Kantian legal philosophers Dooyeweerd argued with were Rudolf Stammler (1856–1938), Gustav Radbruch (1878–1949), and Hans Kelsen (1881–1973).

Dooyeweerd became the systematic philosopher of neo-Calvinism and was one of the founders of what is known as *reformational philosophy*. The voluminous work in which his thoughts were systematically worked out in their full breadth for the first time was *De Wijsbegeerte der Wetsidee* (three volumes, 1935–1936). Through this work, Dooyeweerd's philosophy has become known as the Philosophy of the Cosmonomic Idea (or 'law idea'). His brother-in-law Vollenhoven was his fellow thinker and one of the organizers of the Calvinistic philosophy movement in the Netherlands. They were the founders of the journal *Philosophia Reformata* (1935), still published today. Dooyeweerd was its editor-in-chief from 1936 to 1976. The journal was originally published in Dutch, regularly also containing articles in English, German, and French. Since 2010, it has been published as an English-language journal. Three other collaborators are worth mentioning who were influenced by Dooyeweerd's thought (and vice versa). First, the South African philosopher Hendrik Gerhardus Stoker (1899–1993) at

---

[4] See e.g. Anthony Tol, *Philosophy in the Making: D. H.Th. Vollenhoven and the Emergence of Reformed Philosophy* (Sioux Center: Dordt College Press, 2010), 263–380.

Potchefstroom University, who was a pupil of Max Scheler (1874–1928); second, the Dutch–American theologian and philosopher Cornelius van Til (1895–1987) at Westminster Theological Seminary; and third, the Czech–Austrian philosopher and theologian Josef Bohatec (1876–1954), who was a prominent Calvin scholar.

From 1953 on, an English translation and expansion of *De Wijsbegeerte der Wetsidee* was published under the title *A New Critique of Theoretical Thought* (four volumes, 1953–1958).[5] The *New Critique of Theoretical Thought* can be regarded as the ultimate *magnum opus*. As a consequence of this translation and his many lectures abroad (both in English, French, and German) Dooyeweerd was internationally known. He held talks and lectures in South Africa, France – where he was introduced by philosophers like Paul Ricoeur and Gabriel Marcel – and many times in the United States (at Harvard and Princeton, among others) and in Canada. Dooyeweerd also maintained contact with the eminent Italian legal philosopher Giorgio del Vecchio. Outside the Netherlands, Dooyeweerd's philosophy was especially influential in Canada, the United States, and South Africa, but he also had students in France, Scandinavia, Australia, New Zealand, Japan, and Korea.

Dooyeweerd was a fellow of the Royal Dutch Academy of Sciences. Besides his scholarly work Dooyeweerd also had editorial and administrative functions in society (e.g. in prisoner rehabilitation). After a highly productive life, Dooyeweerd died on 12 February 1977 in Amsterdam.

MAJOR THEMES AND CONTRIBUTIONS

Dooyeweerd can be regarded as a (legal) philosopher *sui generis*. He does not have a clear place in one of the existing traditions and schools of legal philosophy. This may be a reason for – but also a consequence of – his typical 'Dooyeweerdian' technical vocabulary, which is an eclectic mixture of philosophical and theological origins. Dooyeweerd's thought is characterized by one commentator as 'both unconventional and highly complicated' and as a 'labyrinthian system' by a second.[6] A third commentator calls him 'not only

---

[5] Herman Dooyeweerd, A *New Critique of Theoretical Thought*, 4 Volumes (Amsterdam/Philadelphia: Paris/Presbyterian and Reformed Publishing Company, 1953–1958; second print 1969); published again: Grand Rapids: Paideia Press, 1983–1984; New York: Edwin Mellen Press, 1997; and Grand Rapids: Paideia Press/Reformational Publishing Project, 2016 (Collected Works of Herman Dooyeweerd, Series A, volumes 1–4).

[6] R. D. Henderson, *Illuminating Law: The Construction of Herman Dooyeweerd's Philosophy. 1918–1928* (Amsterdam: Vrije Universiteit, 1994), 182; Jeremy Begbie, 'Creation, Christ, and Culture in Dutch Neo-Calvinism', in *Christ in our Place: The Humanity of God in Christ for*

a very complex thinker but also a difficult and often obscure writer'.[7] Dooyeweerd uses 'numerous novel terms bearing distinctive and sometimes quite idiosyncratic meanings'. The terminology that Dooyeweerd used is partly taken from neo-Kantian philosophy, partly from phenomenology, and partly from the heritage of Augustine, Calvin, and Kuyper.

Dooyeweerd can be regarded as the systematic philosopher of neo-Calvinism. In order to understand his position and as a necessary introduction to central motives and themes in his thought I will first introduce neo-Calvinism in general and Kuyper's thought in particular.

Neo-Calvinism

Neo-Calvinism was a Dutch religious and social reform movement in the second half of the nineteenth and first half of the twentieth century. It was opposed to the influence of liberal thought, in the first place in theology. The anti-revolutionaries opposed the principles of 'modernity' which culminated in the French Revolution (1789). Under the influence of Kuyper a revival of the comprehensive Calvinist worldview took place. This revival applied not only to theology, but also areas such as science, politics, and art. An important ally of Kuyper was the theologian and pedagogue Herman Bavinck (1854–1921).

Kuyper established Christian organization in all areas of society: the Anti-Revolutionary Party (1878) in politics, Christian schools and the Free University (1880) in Amsterdam, newspapers (*De Heraut* and *De Standaard*), trade unions, and social care. Kuyper was mainly a theologian, politician, and organizer, not a philosopher. He did however deliver philosophical building blocks that were taken up and elaborated by Dooyeweerd and others. Kuyper was a student of Augustine and Calvin, but he was also of romantic mind, influenced by German romantic idealism. Kuyper had some international influence, mainly in the United States and South Africa. In the United States, he lectured at the famous Stone Lectures (*Lectures on Calvinism*, 1898) and had much influence at Princeton Theological Seminary, especially on the theologian B. B. Warfield (1851–1921), and on the philosopher W. H. Jellema (1893–1982). In South Africa, he influenced the philosopher H. G. Stoker (1899–1993), who became an ally of Herman Dooyeweerd.

---

the Reconciliation of the world, eds. Trevor Hart and Daniel Thimell (Allison Park: Pickwick, 1989), 120–121.

[7] Jonathan Chaplin, *Herman Dooyeweerd: Christian Philosopher of State and Civil Society* (Notre Dame: University of Notre Dame Press, 2011), 2.

Worldview and Perspective: Augustinianism

The term 'neo-Calvinism' 'refers not so much to a theological system, but to an all-embracing worldview (*levens- en wereldbeschouwing*) or *Weltanschauung* which has a bearing on the whole of human life'.[8] Therefore, when Kuyper speaks of 'Calvinism' (meaning neo-Calvinism) he does not mean an ecclesiastical or denominational position, but a general worldview, a 'life principle':

> Calvinism is rooted in a form of religion which was peculiarly its own, and from this specific religious consciousness there was developed first a peculiar theology, then a special church order, and then a given form for political and social life, for the interpretation of the moral world order, for the relation between nature and grace, between Christianity and the world, between church and state, and finally for art and science; and *amid* all these life-utterances it remained always the self-same Calvinism, in so far as simultaneously and spontaneously all these developments sprang from its deepest life-principle.[9]

When all of life is guided by a religious principle, there is no 'neutral' domain that is not influenced by the worldview a person has. Likewise, there can be a Calvinist philosophy, because when philosophy is not Calvinist it will be influenced ('directed') by another worldview. A 'neutral' philosophy does not exist. Pre-theoretical worldview and theoretical philosophy are 'like the two foci of an ellipse comprising all the giants of the philosophical tradition'.[10] This has an interesting implication. Unlike large parts of the natural sciences, theology, philosophy, and the human sciences are unavoidably 'perspectival', according to Kuyper.

The different worldviews are in a position of *antithesis*. The neo-Calvinist concept of antithesis can be traced back to the Augustinian doctrine of the two cities (as developed in *De Civitate Dei*) supplemented by the biblical idea of 'enmity' between the offspring of the snake and the offspring of the woman (Genesis 3:15). There is a radical contradiction between the power of sin and of Christ. There is no such thing as a profane and a sacred atmosphere in the world, everything belongs to God. Kuyper's typical statement is: 'There is not a square inch in the whole domain of our human existence over which Christ, who is Sovereign over all, does not cry, Mine!'[11] There are different 'world

---

[8] Albert Wolters, 'Dutch Neo-Calvinism: Worldview, Philosophy and Rationality', in *Rationality in the Calvinian Tradition*, eds. H. Hart, J. van der Hoeven, and N. Wolterstorff (Toronto: UPA, 1983), 117.
[9] Abraham Kuyper, *Lectures on Calvinism* (Grand Rapids: Eerdmans, 1999), 14, 15, 17.
[10] Wolters, 'Dutch Neo-Calvinism', 115.
[11] Abraham Kuyper, 'Sphere Sovereignty', in *Abraham Kuyper: A Centennial Reader*, ed. James D. Bratt (Grand Rapids, MI: Eerdmans, 1998), 488.

views' or life-systems, which are fundamentally *religious* perspectives. The different worldviews are not alternatives, but opposites, or in Kuyper's terminology 'principle against principle'.[12]

The Augustinian motive of antithesis is very important in Dooyeweerd's thought, although Dooyeweerd hardly uses the Kuyperian term.[13] He does however frequently use another Augustinian term, namely 'the heart'. One of the core Augustinian notions in neo-Calvinism is the heart as a religious point in man. In the heart is the 'unity of life', so the whole of life is religious. The heart is the contact point between God and man. Kuyper writes about 'that point in our consciousness in which our life is still undivided and lies comprehended in its unity, not in the spreading vines but in the root from which the vines spring. This point, of course, lies in the antithesis between all that is finite in our human life and the infinite that lies beyond it.'[14]

Transcendental Critique

The concept of the heart as religious core is closely connected to the religious perspective of man. The perspective is rooted in the heart of man. In Dooyeweerd's philosophy the thinking 'I' is a religious mind. Therefore, the philosopher himself cannot stay out of the picture. The act of thinking presupposes an act of faith.[15] Dooyeweerd opposes the autonomous self-complacency of human reason, as he finds it among many modern philosophers. By means of a 'transcendental critique of theoretical thought' he shows the non-self-sufficiency of every philosophy. A transcendental critique examines the conditions of theoretical thought as such. In Dooyeweerd's early formulation: every philosophy (and science as such) presupposes a conception of the coherence and unity of reality, the totality of meaning (*zintotaliteit*). It needs a firm ground, an Archimedian point. This conception is fundamentally religious in nature.[16] In his mature formulation (called the 'second way'), Dooyeweerd focused on the act of theoretical thought as such.[17]

---

[12] Kuyper, *Lectures on Calvinism*, 11–12.
[13] Herman Dooyeweerd, *Roots of Western Culture: Pagan, Secular and Christian Options* (Grand Rapids: Paideia Press, 2012).
[14] Kuyper, *Lectures on Calvinism*, 20.
[15] Herman Dooyeweerd, *Encyclopedia of the Science of Law: Introduction (The Collected Works of Herman Dooyeweerd, Series A, Volume 8/1)* (Grand Rapids: Paideia Press, 2012), 37–48.
[16] Herman Dooyeweerd, *A New Critique of Theoretical Thought. Volume I: The Necessary Presuppositions of Philosophy* (Amsterdam/Philadelphia: Paris/Presbyterian and Reformed Publishing Company, 1953), 3–21.
[17] Dooyeweerd, *A New Critique of Theoretical Thought*, 1:34–68; Herman Dooyeweerd, *In the Twilight of Western Thought: Studies in the Pretended Autonomy of Philosophical Thought*

A transcendental critique is 'a critical inquiry (respecting no single so-called theoretical axiom) into the universally valid conditions which alone make theoretical thought possible, and which are required by the immanent structure of this thought itself'.[18] Immanuel Kant's critique did not reach far enough and finally ended in dogmatism. A *new* critique of theoretical thought is needed (hence the title of Dooyeweerd's *magnum opus*). In the first volume of *A New Critique of Theoretical Thought* Dooyeweerd develops his theory about the necessary presuppositions of philosophy.

Under neo-Kantian influence, epistemology became the 'gateway' to Dooyeweerd's philosophy. Dooyeweerd's epistemology is a critical reflection upon the possibility and foundation of theoretical thought. It is both highly critical of neo-Kantianism and heavily influenced by it. Dooyeweerd himself states:

> Originally I was strongly under the influence first of the neo-Kantian philosophy, later on of Husserl's phenomenology. The great turning point in my thought was marked by the discovery of the religious root of thought itself, whereby a new light was shed on the failure of all attempts, including my own, to bring about an inner synthesis between the Christian faith and a philosophy which is rooted in faith in the self-sufficiency of human reason.'[19]

Creation Order

Neo-Calvinism can to a certain extent be regarded as a philosophical translation of Calvin's thought. The neo-Calvinists did not simply want to copy Calvin's sixteenth-century thoughts; rather, they wanted to actualize them and make them in accordance with the actual time.[20] New elements were added. Some thoughts of Calvin are emphasized, like the biblical words creation, sin, and salvation. Creation means that God, in his creation of the world, has established a creational order and has given laws, both to nature and to humans (laws of nature and laws of culture). God's law is not only a moral law, but also a law through which God creates and sustains the cosmos. This leads to a philosophical interest in the law-like structures of reality.

(Grand Rapids: Paideia Press, 2012); Herman Dooyeweerd, *Transcendental Problems of Philosophical Thought: An Inquiry into the Transcendental Conditions of Philosophy* (Grand Rapids: Wm. B. Eerdmans Publishing Company, 1948); Dooyeweerd, *Encyclopedia of the Science of Law. Vol. I*, 26–37.

[18] Dooyeweerd, *A New Critique of Theoretical Thought. Vol. I*, 37.
[19] Dooyeweerd, *A New Critique of Theoretical Thought. Vol. I*, v.
[20] Arie L. Molendijk, 'Neo-Calvinist Culture Protestantism: Abraham Kuyper's Stone Lectures', *Church History and Religious Culture* 88.2 (2008): 235–250.

Neo-Calvinists, more so than other Reformed groups, emphasize the intellectual elaboration of God's sovereignty. Every *thought* should be brought into captivity to God.[21]

There is a distinction between God and creation.[22] 'Creation' is what is not God. God and creation cannot be reduced to each other. Closely connected to this is the distinction between 'heaven' and 'earth'. The earth, broadly understood as 'the horizon of normal human experience', is the domain, but also the limit, of human knowledge, scientific investigation, and analysis. There is also a distinction between God's creational ordinances and what is subject to these ordinances. Creation is defined in terms of law. The relationship between God and creation is one of law and subject, both in the natural and cultural realm. In the natural realm natural laws simply exist, while in the cultural and societal realm the law needs implementation. Kuyper speaks of 'ordinances' of creation. Within the earthly cosmos, there is a developmental potential. Man has a 'cultural mandate' to 'subdue' the earth and develop the cultural potential that is in it.[23] This 'opening process' is to God's glory. An important aspect of this is that a philosophical investigation of creation is possible. Kuyper, like Calvin, regards science as a gift of God that should be accepted in gratitude.[24]

Sin and Salvation

Sin (the Fall) is a distortion of God's order and is essentially opposition to God. Sin works through the heart of man, the religious centre of human existence, into all of life. Neo-Calvinists have a negative assessment of the human mind and the noetic effects of sin in man's unredeemed state. They do however have a rather optimistic conception of the redeemed mind. Salvation is restoration of the disturbed relationship with God, but also a re-direction of all things onto Him. Important also is God's sovereignty over all areas of life and God's revelation, both in the Bible and in nature.[25]

An important distinction in neo-Calvinism is between 'structure' and 'direction'. 'Structure' is the world as it is with all its potential, while 'direction' is how the world can be developed, for example, the world's creational

---

[21] Richard J. Mouw, 'Dutch Calvinist philosophical influences in North America', *Calvin Theological Journal* 24.1 (1989): 98–99.
[22] Wolters, 'The intellectual milieu of Herman Dooyeweerd', 5–8.
[23] Wolters, 'Dutch Neo-Calvinism', 121.
[24] John Calvin, *Institutes of the Christian Religion*, II.2.15–16.
[25] Mouw, 'Dutch Calvinist Philosophical Influences in North America', 98–99.

possibilities. Man can be misdirected by sin or redirected by Christ. Sin and redemption have a cosmic scope (not only an individual one), including nature, culture, and society. Salvation is re-creation; therefore grace does not destroy or supplement nature, but restores it.[26] Regarding 'direction' there is the Augustinian battle between two opposing forces: the City of God and the Earthly City, or the antithesis between belief and unbelief. This is also an antithesis between regenerate and unregenerate science.[27]

The Cosmic Order of the Modal Aspects

The words with which Dooyeweerd opens his *magnum opus* immediately give a first introduction to several basic ideas in his philosophy. He writes:

> If I consider reality as it is given in the naïve pre-theoretical experience, and then confront it with a theoretical analysis, through which reality appears to split up into various modal aspects then the first thing that strikes me, is the original *indissoluble interrelation* among these aspects which are for the first time explicitly distinguished in the theoretical attitude of mind.[28]

The key ideas that are introduced are: (1) the distinction between 'naïve', pre-scientific and everyday experience of reality versus a theoretical attitude of analysis and abstraction, (2) the different aspects (modalities, functions) that can be distinguished in reality, and (3) the relationship that exists between all aspects of reality – Dooyeweerd speaks of a 'cosmos' (an ordered and coherent whole). He continues: 'The coherence of all the modal aspects of our cosmos *finds its expression in each* of them, and also *points beyond* its own limits toward a central totality, which in its turn is expressed in this coherence.' Our cosmos is a created cosmos. It is an expression of God's sovereignty in all aspects of life. This also has anthropological implications. 'Our ego expresses itself as a totality in the coherence of all its functions within all the modal aspects of cosmic reality. And man, whose ego expresses itself in the coherence of all its temporal modal functions, was himself created by God as the *expression* of His image.'

Dooyeweerd's doctrine of the so-called 'modalities' or 'modal aspects' has been called the 'jewel' ('show piece') of his philosophy.[29] This can be regarded as an original working-out of Kuyper's doctrine of sphere sovereignty.

---

[26] Wolters, 'Dutch Neo-Calvinism', 122.
[27] Wolters, 'Dutch Neo-Calvinism', 122–123.
[28] Dooyeweerd, *A New Critique of Theoretical Thought. Vol. I*, 3.
[29] Th. de Boer, 'De filosofie van Dooyeweerd', *Algemeen Nederlands Tijdschrift voor Wijsbegeerte* 76.4 (1984): 258.

Sphere Sovereignty

One of the intellectual fathers of neo-Calvinism is the Dutch politician, jurist, and historian Guillaume Groen van Prinsterer (1801–1876). According to Groen van Prinsterer the French Revolution was an expression of a religion of 'unbelief'.[30] In his book *Ongeloof en revolutie* (1847, *Unbelief and Revolution*) he regarded the rationalism of the Enlightenment as a system of belief rejecting Christianity. It destroys the Christian spiritual foundation of Europe. Two themes in Groen van Prinsterer's thought are especially relevant. The first is the religious motive behind every thought, whether it is Enlightenment rationality and revolutionary unbelief or Christianity.[31] This is also an important motive in Dooyeweerd's philosophy. The second thought is what came to be known as *soevereiniteit in eigen kring* ('sphere sovereignty' or 'sovereignty in its own sphere'). This concept, originating from the Calvinist legal philosopher Johannes Althusius (1557–1638), was further developed by Groen van Prinsterer regarding the separation of church and state.[32] It was however given its full societal expression in the thought of Groen's political successor, Abraham Kuyper.[33]

In 1880, Kuyper opened the Free University with the speech *Soevereiniteit in eigen kring* (Sphere sovereignty).[34] Kuyper distinguished, among other things, between marriage, family, company, state, church, school, and university. Each of these social spheres has its own role, nature, and internal authority structure. They are both interwoven and relatively independent (sovereign). These spheres have their own intrinsic normative principles and their own nature and structure, based on God's creational order. The spheres have no control over each other and are responsible only to God about the way they exercise their internal authority. The Free University Kuyper established was called free because of its independence from both church and state. Each sphere has its own standard, its own 'law of life' (*levenswet*). For the state it is justice, for a company the economic standard, for the family it is love.

Dooyeweerd adopted the idea of sphere sovereignty, developing a non-hierarchical view of society. However, he worked it out not only in a social but also in a philosophical direction as an ontological principle. Just like Kuyper distinguished different social spheres and their own sovereign laws,

---

[30] Guillaume Groen van Prinsterer, *Unbelief and Revolution*, ed. Harry van Dyke (Amsterdam: The Groen van Prinsterer Fund, 1973), Lecture I.
[31] See e.g. Groen van Prinsterer, *Unbelief and Revolution*, Lecture VIII.
[32] See e.g. Groen van Prinsterer, *Unbelief and Revolution*, Lecture III.
[33] Johan van der Vuyver, 'The jurisprudential legacy of Abraham Kuyper and Leo XIII', *Journal of Markets & Morality* 1 (Spring 2002): 211–249.
[34] Abraham Kuyper, *Soevereiniteit in eigen kring* (Amsterdam: J. H. Kruyt, 1880).

Dooyeweerd distinguishes various modal aspects of reality that cannot be reduced to each other. These aspects are ways of experiencing reality, ways of being, ways of functioning, also called 'modalities' or 'modal aspects' (Latin: *modus*) or 'law-spheres'. In philosophical terms, Dooyeweerd cosmology can be called an ontology and the aspects ontic modes. They are about the *how* of reality, not the *what*. Dooyeweerd calls his philosophy a *transcendental* philosophy because the modal aspects are necessary presuppositions for the existence, functioning, and knowledge of reality, both epistemic and ontic.[35]

Dooyeweerd distinguishes fifteen of these aspects:

> An indissoluble inner coherence binds the numerical to the spatial aspect, the latter to the aspect of mathematical movement, the aspect of movement to that of physical energy, which itself is the necessary basis of the aspect of organic life. The aspect of organic life has an inner connection with that of physical feeling; the latter refers in its logical anticipation (the feeling of logical correctness or incorrectness) to the analytical–logical aspect. This in turn is connected with the historical, the linguistic, the aspect of social intercourse, the economic, the aesthetic, the jural, the moral aspect and that of faith. In this inter-modal cosmic coherence no single aspect stands by itself; everyone refers within and beyond itself to all the others.[36]

Reality is not a chaos, but an ordered and coherent whole, a cosmic order in which the different modal aspects of reality refer to each other in an indissoluble interrelation.

Ontology

In the second volume of *A New Critique of Theoretical Thought* Dooyeweerd develops his theory of modal aspects. This ontology outlines the characterization and definition of the aspects, their order, and references. Each aspect has a so-called 'meaning-kernel' or 'meaning-nucleus' (*zinkern*) that characterizes the specific nature of the aspect. It is the kernel or core of a modal aspect.[37]

This specific nature of a modal aspect has as a consequence that the meaning-kernel cannot be defined in terms of another aspect. A meaning-kernel can only

---

[35] Gerrit Glas and Jeroen de Ridder, 'Introduction to the philosophy of creation order, with special emphasis on the philosophy of Herman Dooyeweerd', in *The Future of Creation Order. Vol. 1, Philosophical, Scientific, and Religious Perspectives on Order and Emergence*, eds. Gerrit Glas and Jeroen de Ridder (Cham: Springer, 2018), 1–30.

[36] Dooyeweerd, *A New Critique of Theoretical Thought. Vol. I*, 3.

[37] Herman Dooyeweerd, *A New Critique of Theoretical Thought. Volume II: The General Theory of the Modal Spheres* (Amsterdam/Philadelphia: Paris/Presbyterian and Reformed Publishing Company, 1955), 74–79.

be approached intuitively. It must be 'grasped' in a phenomenological way. For example, the legal aspect of reality cannot be reduced to the linguistic, social, economic, or moral aspect. Simply put, in reality there is something we call 'law' or 'right' or 'justice', which has something to do with language, social order, and the like, but does not coincide with these aspects and cannot be reduced to them. The legal aspect is a unique aspect with its own meaning-kernel that we do not exactly understand but intuitively know about. So it is with the other aspects.[38]

The modal aspects (and meaning kernels) are: the quantitative aspect (amount), the spatial aspect (space or extent), the kinematic aspect (movement), the physical aspect (cause and effect), the biotic/organic aspect (life processes), the sensitive/psychical aspect (feeling, the sensitive), the logical–analytical aspect (analytical distinction), the cultural–historical/formative aspect (history, development, culture), the lingual aspect (symbolic meaning), the social aspect (social interaction), the economic aspect (scarcity, savings), the aesthetic aspect (harmony, form), the jural aspect (justice, rights, retribution), the ethical/moral aspect (moral love) and faith/pistic aspect (belief).[39] As has been said, man functions in all the aspects, unlike a stone, a flower, or an animal.

The modal aspects have their own modal laws (spheres of law). The aspects up to the logical–analytical aspect are called the *natural side* and are independent of human design. The laws of nature simply work. Think about the laws of physics and chemical processes. The aspects from the logical–analytical aspect onward however are norms, standards, an 'ought'. Thus, there are rules of logic, language standards, aesthetic laws, but also moral standards. These laws are not a matter of taste and personal preference but are created normative structures in the world. These laws require actualization, which means they must be recognized and realized by man. They can be violated, but their effect is not eliminated by that. This second category of laws is called the *cultural* or *normative side*. Modal aspects of both 'sides' are called 'law-spheres'. There are ontic laws and norms in reality.[40]

The modal aspects are in a certain order, meaning that every aspect presupposes the preceding aspect, while it is presupposed by the subsequent aspects. There is no feeling without life, but there is life without feeling and no economy without social interaction, but there is social interaction without economy. Dooyeweerd speaks of *earlier* and *later* aspects. The sequence in

---

[38] Dooyeweerd, *Encyclopedia of the Science of Law. Vol. 1*, 94–112.
[39] Dooyeweerd, *A New Critique of Theoretical Thought. Vol. II*, 55–180; Dooyeweerd, *Encyclopedia of the Science of Law. Vol. 1*, 26–34.
[40] Dooyeweerd, *Encyclopedia of the Science of Law. Vol. 1*, 26–34.

modal aspects is not a hierarchy with 'higher' and 'lower' modal aspects. The sequence only indicates that later modal aspects presuppose earlier ones.[41]

The modal aspects thus refer to each other. Dooyeweerd distinguishes between *anticipations* (reference to subsequent aspects) and *retrocipations* (references to previous aspects). Thus, the term 'legal scope' retrocipates from the legal to the (previous) spatial aspect. 'Legal guilt' is an anticipation to the (subsequent) moral aspect. The latter doctrine is only found in developed legal systems, in which the legal aspect has 'opened up' to the moral aspect. The *opening process* (disclosure, unlocking) is the developing of a modal aspect into a normative direction.[42] This element in Dooyeweerd's philosophy must be connected to Kuyper's doctrine of common grace (*gemene gratie, algemene genade*), a Calvinian legacy. In his three-volume work *De gemeene gratie* (1902–1904) Kuyper sketches both the 'negative' and 'positive' goals of common grace. The negative goal is restraining from sin and maintaining creation, although affected by sin. The positive goal, which plays an important role in Dooyeweerd's philosophy, is the 'opening process' or 'disclosure' of the creational potential.[43] It is the dynamic factor in Dooyeweerd's theory of modal aspects. Previous aspects 'found' later ones, while later aspects 'disclose' earlier ones. For example, there is no love (the moral aspect) without law (the legal aspect), but love brings law to a higher level, without abolishing it. Together, the anticipations and retrocipations are called the 'analogies' or 'analogical structure moments' or 'references'.[44]

After this introduction, we can understand that the neo-Calvinist doctrine of sphere sovereignty becomes a 'cosmological principle' in Dooyeweerd's philosophy, that is, the structuring principle for the order in reality. The different 'law-spheres' or modal aspects have their own normativity. They are both interconnected and independent, both irreducible and referring to each other, just like the different spheres in society.

Anti-Reductionism

An important distinction Dooyeweerd makes is between, on the one side, the 'naïve' pre-theoretical thought and experience, and, on the other side,

---

[41] Dooyeweerd, *A New Critique of Theoretical Thought*. Vol. II, 49–54. See also Johan van der Hoeven, 'In *memory of Herman Dooyeweerd*: Meaning, Time and Law', *Philosophia Reformata* 43 (1978): 130–144.

[42] Dooyeweerd, *A New Critique of Theoretical Thought*. Vol. II, 181–192.

[43] Abraham Kuyper, *De gemeene gratie, deel II. Het leerstellig gedeelte* (Kampen: J. H. Kok, 1903), 616–623.

[44] Dooyeweerd, *A New Critique of Theoretical Thought*. Vol. II, 74–79.

scientific or theoretical thought. Theoretical (scientific) thought is, according to Dooyeweerd, placing the logical–analytical function against a different aspect of reality (a *Gegenstand*). This aspect is analyzed (cut into pieces, laid apart) and abstracted. Biologists analyze the biotic aspect, psychologists the sensitive aspect, and economists the economic aspect. The logical–analytical aspect however is itself an aspect of reality. People can argue (logical–analytical function), but also feel (sensitive function), have an aesthetic experience (aesthetic function), have a legal opinion (legal function), have a moral consideration (moral function), and have a religious experience (belief function). Being human therefore takes place in all these aspects. In other words: human beings have different functions. The logical–analytical function is not the highest one.[45]

Dooyeweerd disputes the idea that one science would be the most fundamental. This would be making one aspect of reality absolute, at the expense of other aspects. Such absolutism leads to an 'ism' as psychologism, physicalism, historicism, or economism. For example, there are more aspects of reality than the aspects that are 'measurable' in a (quasi-)scientific method. Dooyeweerd's philosophy is anti-reductionist.[46]

Being and Meaning

Reality is not sufficient to itself, that is, it does not exist in isolation. The whole of reality, in all its modal aspects, refers to and is an expression of its origin. Dooyeweerd writes: 'This universal character of *referring* and *expressing*, which is proper to our entire created cosmos, stamps created reality as *meaning*, in accordance with its dependent non-self-sufficient nature. *Meaning* is the *being* of all that has been *created* and the nature even of our selfhood. It has a *religious root* and a *divine origin*.'[47] In this sense we can say that reality does not *have* a meaning (*zin*), but *is* meaning (i.e. referring). Reality is referral and expression. It is a meaningful whole. It is noteworthy that according to Dooyeweerd creation actually does not have *being* itself, but only *meaning*, that is, non-self-sufficient referring and expressing.

Anyone familiar with *Sein und Zeit* (1927) of Martin Heidegger (1889–1976) will have noticed an echo of Heidegger's discussion of *Sinn* (meaning) and

---

[45] Dooyeweerd, *Encyclopedia of the Science of Law. Vol. I*, 21–26, 37–48.
[46] Dooyeweerd, *A New Critique of Theoretical Thought, Vol. I*, 46–47; Dooyeweerd, *A New Critique of Theoretical Thought. Vol. II*, 187–188; Dooyeweerd, *Encyclopedia of the Science of Law. Vol. II*, 34–37.
[47] Dooyeweerd, *A New Critique of Theoretical Thought. Vol. I*, 4.

Sein (being). Dooyeweerd studied the book intensely. He reportedly read it thirteen times.[48]

The Jural Aspect

Although Dooyeweerd gradually developed more and more as a general philosopher, his first calling was to be a professor of law. Consequently, it is not surprising that his philosophy has been elaborated most extensively in this field.[49] Therefore we will take a closer look at the jural aspect. The meaning-kernel of the jural aspect is – somewhat confusing – indicated as 'retribution' by Dooyeweerd. The term is used 'in the pregnant sense of an irreducible mode of balancing and harmonizing individual and social interests. This mode implies a standard of proportionality regulating the legal interpretation of social facts and their factual social consequences in order to maintain the juridical balance by a just reaction (...)'[50] Retribution clearly refers to the economic, the aesthetic, and the social. The term *retribution* 'designates the irreducible meaning-kernel of what is signified by the words δικη, jus, justice, recht, diritto, droit, etc'.[51]

As has been said the modal aspects refer to each other. In every modal aspect all the other aspects are present, although in a modified and unique way. Legal causality refers to physical causation but has a unique legal qualification. It cannot be reduced to, for example, laws of nature. Legal will cannot be reduced to psychological will. Likewise, legal guilt refers to moral or religious guilt, but has a limited and unique legal qualification. The blurring of these legal and non-legal meanings causes significant confusion in legal theory.[52]

The jural or legal aspect of reality is a universal aspect. There are legal phenomena in every social structure. They are not limited to state-law or to law that is based on state-law because law is a modal aspect of reality as such. There is also law in the family, the church, the company, and the association. Even stronger, every social structure *has* a juridical aspect and

---

[48] Wolters, 'The intellectual milieu of Herman Dooyeweerd', 15.
[49] See especially Dooyeweerd, *Encyclopedia of the Science of Law*. Vol 1 and Herman Dooyeweerd, 'Die Philosophie der Gesetzidee und ihre Bedeutung für die Rechts- und Sozialphilosophie', *ARSP: Archiv für Rechts- und Sozialphilosophie* 53.4 (1967): 1–22, 465–499.
[50] Dooyeweerd, *A New Critique of Theoretical Thought*. Vol. II, 129.
[51] Dooyeweerd, *A New Critique of Theoretical Thought*. Vol. II, 132.
[52] Dooyeweerd, *Encyclopedia of the Science of Law*. Vol. I, 185–188.

functions in the juridical or legal aspect of reality. Dooyeweerd is a legal pluralist.[53]

The modal character of the jural aspect of reality explains Dooyeweerd's classical conception of the encyclopaedia of law. The encyclopaedia of law is not only a general introduction for students in the discipline of law but also a study of the place of the jural aspect in the coherence of all the modal aspects. Dooyeweerd's ontology establishes the place of the science of law in the entire context of the special sciences ('*vakwetenschappen*'). The encyclopaedia of the science of law also studies the basic concepts of law. These concepts do not belong to a particular division of the science of law because they have a foundational character. They concern the foundational legal character of the jural aspect.[54]

Elementary basic concepts of law (*elementaire grondbegrippen*) are necessary and constitutive elements of every legal order: legal norm, legal subject, legal object, legal fact, subjective right, legal duty, area of validity, locus of a legal fact, lawfulness and unlawfulness, jural attribution and accountability, jural will and jural causality, jural positivizing, legal organ and jural competence (legal power), jural interpretation and legal significance, jural fault or guilt, good morals, good faith, etc.[55] Together these basic concepts constitute the central Concept of Law (*rechtsbegrip, Rechtsbegriff*).[56] If the most fundamental principles (constitutive principles) are violated there is no law. These fundamental principles can even be found in the most primitive legal systems in history. However, law must be disclosed on the basis of regulative principles, like equity, good faith, and guilt. They can be found only in developed legal systems. Together these regulative principles constitute the Idea of Law (*rechtsidee, Rechtsidee*).[57] The distinction between *Rechtsbegriff* and *Rechtsidee* is a legacy of neo-Kantianism in general and the German philosopher of law Rudolph Stammler (1856–1938) in particular.

---

[53] Dooyeweerd, *Encyclopedia of the Science of Law. Vol. I*, 185–204.
[54] Dooyeweerd, *Encyclopedia of the Science of Law. Vol. 1*, 197–198.
[55] Dooyeweerd, *Encyclopedia of the Science of Law. Vol. 1*, 197–198.
[56] Herman Dooyeweerd, *Encyclopaedie der rechtswetenschap: Deel II* (Amsterdam: Studentenraad V. U. [c. 1960]), chapter III. A translation will be published in *The Collected Works of Herman Dooyeweerd, Series A*, Volumes A9 and A10 as *Encylopedia of the Science of Law: A History of the Concept of Encyclopedia and the Concept of Law. Volume 2* and *Encylopedia of the Science of Law: The Elementary and Complex Basic Concepts of Law. Volume 3* (Grand Rapids: Paideia Press, in press).
[57] Herman Dooyeweerd, 'The structure of jural principles and the method of the science of law in light of the Cosmonomic Idea', in *Time, Law, and History: Selected Essays (The Collected Essays of Herman Dooyeweerd, Series B, Volume 14)* (Grand Rapids: Paideia Press, 2017), 111–154.

Law and Morality

A noteworthy element in Dooyeweerd's philosophy of law is the relationship between law and morality. Principles of law are no moral principles. They belong to the jural aspect of reality, not the moral.[58] Just like legal positivists Dooyeweerd sharply distinguishes law and morality. Morality is not the foundation of law. Does that mean that Dooyeweerd can be regarded a legal positivist? Not at all. One has to remember that law is understood by Dooyeweerd as a modal aspect. The jural aspect has its own normativity. Law cannot violate fundamental legal principles otherwise it cannot be law. The principles however are not understood as moral principles. The concept of law is what makes a phenomenon a jural phenomenon. There is however a moral analogy within the jural aspect. Law has a normative direction. It must be 'opened up'. Legal–moral principles however are regulating principles, not constitutive ones.[59]

Law is bound to normative principles (*rechtsbeginselen*) that are non-random. They do however require human positivation. That is: we have to *form* law, but cannot *create* it. Through the functioning of the jural modal aspect law is bound to creation order. Law is a normative phenomenon, not only because it proclaims a norm, but because it is rooted in the jural modal aspect which is governed by normative legal principles.[60] As one commentator rightly observes, Dooyeweerd developed 'a normative theory of law that is both part of the natural law tradition and highly critical of many natural law conceptions'.[61] Another commentator called it 'a sophisticated natural law approach'.[62]

A Theory of Things

As has been sketched, the modal aspects concern the ways of being, the 'how' of things. This theory is concentrated in the second volume of *A New Critique of Theoretical Thought*. Besides that, Dooyeweerd has developed a theory of 'structures of individuality' or 'typical structures' (entities), that is, things,

---

[58] Dooyeweerd, *A New Critique of Theoretical Thought. Vol. II*, 140–149.
[59] Dooyeweerd, *A New Critique of Theoretical Thought. Vol. II*, 140–149.
[60] Dooyeweerd, 'The Structure of Jural Principles and the Method of the Science of Law in Light of the Cosmonomic Idea', 111–154.
[61] David S. Caudill, 'On realism's own "hangover" of natural law philosophy: Llewellyn *Avec* Dooyeweerd', in *On Philosophy in American Law*, ed. Francis J. Mootz (New York: Cambridge University Press, 2009), 23.
[62] David VanDrunen, *Natural Law and the Two Kingdoms: A Study in the Development of Reformed Social Thought* (Grand Rapids: Eerdmans, 2010), 359.

processes, events and social relations, the 'what' of things. This theory is founded on his ontology of the modal aspects and functions of reality. It is concentrated in the third volume of Dooyeweerd's *magnum opus*. It is the basis for his social and political philosophy.[63] I will briefly sketch its main elements.

All things (or entities or artefacts) have both a 'foundational function' and a 'leading function'. The foundational function is the aspect qualifying the formation of a thing, while the leading function (or 'qualifying function') is the aspect qualifying the intrinsic destination of a thing. For example: a family is founded biologically but is qualified morally (love). It functions as a moral subject, but it can also function as an object, for example, in the economic or jural aspect. It is not qualified as a legal institute, although it also has a legal expression. A family has sovereignty in its own sphere and can never become a part of, for example, the church or state.[64]

I will work out (still briefly) Dooyeweerd's conception of the state.[65] The state is characterized by a tension between power and law. This tension led to many one-sided conceptions of the state (e.g. sociological). The state has its foundational function in the cultural–historical aspect. It has the monopoly of power (sword power) in a certain territory. There is no state without power. However, it is more than a robber gang. The power of the state has to be 'opened up' toward the jural aspect. The state has to develop in a normative direction toward its qualifying destination: legality (rule of law). The state is a public–legal community of government and citizens. It must promote public social justice and harmonize interests. However, within the public law sphere the state must respect the internal law spheres of the other spheres in society (churches, families, businesses, associations, etc.).[66]

Just like his ontology of modal aspects and functions, Dooyeweerd's theory of things is a rich frame of thought and a very fruitful instrument for analysis. Both theories have only been briefly summarized in the above. They ask for a thorough but rewarding study by the reader himself or herself.

---

[63] See for example Herman Dooyeweerd, *A Christian Theory of Social Institutions* (La Jolla: The Herman Dooyeweerd Foundation, 1986).
[64] Herman Dooyeweerd, *A New Critique of Theoretical Thought. Volume III: The Structures of Individuality of Temporal Reality* (Amsterdam/Philadelphia: Paris/Presbyterian and Reformed Publishing Company, 1957), 265–304.
[65] Dooyeweerd, *A New Critique of Theoretical Thought*. Vol. III, 379–508.
[66] For an extensive discussion, see Chaplin, *Herman Dooyeweerd: Christian Philosopher of State and Civil Society*. See also David T. Koyzis, 'Political theory in the Calvinist tradition', in Herman Dooyeweerd, *Political Philosophy: Selected Essays (The Collected Works of Herman Dooyeweerd, Series B, Volume 19)* (Grand Rapids: Paideia Press, 2012), 1–16.

GENERAL APPRAISAL AND INFLUENCE

When Dooyeweerd took leave of his position as a professor (in 1965), he was offered a collection of essays titled *Philosophy and Christianity* to which well-known legal philosophers like Hans Kelsen and Jacques Ellul (1912–1994) contributed. This can be regarded a confirmation of the international recognition Dooyeweerd had acquired in philosophy in general and philosophy of law in particular. Notwithstanding this recognition, Dooyeweerd's work never got a prominent position in the handbooks and curricula of general or legal philosophy. One can wonder why. Part of the explanation may be the specific neo-Calvinist theological context in which Dooyeweerd developed his thought and which has been closely associated with it since.[67] Another part of an explanation may be the typical 'Dooyeweerdian' technical vocabulary of his work.

Although Dooyeweerd has been lauded – slightly exaggeratedly – as 'the most original philosopher Holland has ever produced, not even Spinoza excepted' and has been regarded – more realistically – as 'undoubtedly the most formidable Dutch philosopher of the 20th century', his work is perhaps better known outside of the Netherlands than it is inside.[68]

There is a strong living legacy in the work of Dooyeweerd scholars around the world. The journal *Philosophia Reformata* is an important platform for them. The journal has focused on the legacy of Dooyeweerd, Vollenhoven, and their students for a long time. At present, the scope has broadened, including Reformed Epistemology (Alvin Plantinga (1932), Nicholas Wolterstorff (1932), and others). Students of Dooyeweerd apply his thought in diverse disciplines, ranging from aesthetics and philosophy of mind to physics and international relations. Some stay close to Dooyeweerd's original thought, others are critical and propose adjustments. Most of them use elements of his thought and try to develop them in a specific discipline. They all value his legacy.

The Association for Reformational Philosophy in the Netherlands (founded in 1935) has special chairs within the major universities in the Netherlands since 1947. Introductions to Dooyeweerd's thought are offered on a regular basis, introducing his philosophy to new generations of students. The Association is

---

[67] Dooyeweerd's successor at the Free University, Hendrik van Eikema Hommes (1930–1984), elaborated Dooyeweerd's thought in a strictly 'dogmatic' way.
[68] Appraisals by G. E. Langemeijer, chairman of the Royal Dutch Academy of Sciences, in the newspaper *Trouw*, 6 October 1964, and P. B. Cliteur, legal philosopher and chairman of the Dutch humanist league, in *Trouw*, 8 October 1994.

actually the largest philosophical association in the Netherlands. Apart from the Association, the Free University of Amsterdam has its own Dooyeweerd chair.

The Dooyeweerd Centre for Christian Philosophy at Redeemer College in Ancaster, Ontario (Canada) publishes *The Collected Works of Herman Dooyeweerd*, in English translation. More than twenty volumes are planned. Some volumes have already been published.[69] This project shows the continued interest in Dooyeweerd's work.

Together with his brother-in-law Vollenhoven, Dooyeweerd will be remembered as the founder of a unique orthodox Christian school of thought. His work is no easy reading but it is highly rewarding in the end. The reader of this chapter is invited to discover that for himself or herself.[70]

RECOMMENDED READINGS

Cameron, Alan. 'Dooyeweerd on Law and Morality: Legal Ethics – A Test Case'. *Victoria University of Wellington Law Review* 28 (1998): 263–281.

Cameron, Alan C. 'Implications of Dooyeweerd's Encyclopedia of Legal Science. Legal theory and practice in common law countries: Legal causality as a case study'. In *Contemporary Reflections on the Philosophy of Herman Dooyeweerd*, edited by D. M. F. Strauss and Michelle Botting, 191–238. Lewinston, Queenston, Lampeter: The Edwin Mellen Press, 2000.

Caudill, David S. 'Christian legal theory: The example of Dooyeweerd's critique of Romanist Individualism and Germanic Communitarianism in property law'. *Georgetown Journal of Law & Public Policy* 5 (2007): 531–560.

Caudill, David S. 'On Realism's Own "Hangover" of Natural Law Philosophy: Llewellyn *Avec* Dooyeweerd'. In *On Philosophy in American Law*, edited by Francis J. Mootz, 19–26. New York: Cambridge University Press, 2009.

Chaplin, Jonathan. *Herman Dooyeweerd: Christian Philosopher of State and Civil Society*. Notre Dame: University of Notre Dame Press, 2011.

Henderson, Roger. *Illuminating Law: The Construction of Herman Dooyeweerd's Philosophy 1918–1928*. Amsterdam: Vrije Universiteit, 1994.

Kalsbeek, L. *Contours of a Christian Philosophy: An Introduction to Herman Dooyeweerd's Thought*. Lewinston, Queenston, Lampeter: The Edwin Mellen Press, 2002.

---

[69] The Collected Works consist of four series. Series A contains multi-volume works by Dooyeweerd: *A New Critique of Theoretical Thought* (A1–A4), *Reformation and Scholasticism in Philosophy* (A5–A7), and *Encyclopedia of the Science of Law* (A8–A12). Series B contains smaller works and collections of essays. Series C contains reflections on Dooyeweerd's philosophy and legacy. Series D contains systematic selections from series A and B.

[70] A good work to start with is Dooyeweerd, *Roots of Western Culture: Pagan, Secular and Christian Options* (Grand Rapids: Paideia Press, 2012).

Marshall, Paul. 'Dooyeweerd's Empirical Theory of Rights'. In *The Legacy of Herman Dooyeweerd*, edited by C. T. McIntire, 119–142. Lanham: University Press of America, 1985.

Skillen, James W. 'Philosophy of the Cosmonomic Idea: Herman Dooyeweerd's political and legal thought'. *Political Science Reviewer* 32 (2003): 318–380.

Strauss, D. F. M. 'Dooyeweerd's Legal and Political Philosophy: A Response to the Challenge of Historicism'. *Journal for Juridical Science* 39.1 (2014): 75–96.

VanDrunen, David. *Natural Law and the Two Kingdoms: A Study in the Development of Reformed Social Thought*. Grand Rapids: Eerdmans, 2010.

Verburg, Marcel E. *Herman Dooyeweerd: The Life and Work of a Christian Philosopher*. Grand Rapids: Paideia Press, 2009.

Witte, John. 'The Development of Herman Dooyeweerd's Concept of Rights'. *South African Law Journal* 110 (1993): 543–562.

20

Josse Mertens de Wilmars

Laurent Waelkens

BIOGRAPHICAL INTRODUCTION

Joseph (Josse) Marie Honoré Charles Mertens de Wilmars was a Belgian lawyer, a barrister in Antwerp, cofounder of the Christian democratic party CVP/PSC, one of the first assessors of the Conseil d'État in Brussels, for six years a representative in the Belgian Chamber, and a professor and curator at the Catholic University of Louvain. He was also one of the first justices of the European Court in Luxemburg, over which he presided from 1980 to 1984. The main sources for this article have been an excellent study made by Vera Fritz about the first members of the European Court of Justice,[1] the memoirs of Josse Mertens de Wilmars,[2] a long interview with him conducted by researchers of the University of Leuven,[3] the political archives he left to the same institution,[4] his

---

[1] Vera Fritz, *Juges et avocats généraux de la Cour de Justice de l'Union européenne (1952–1972), Une approche biographique de l'histoire d'une révolution juridique*. Rechtshistorische Studien 312 (Frankfurt/Main: Vittorio Klostermann, 2018). In this excellent study based on an extensive bibliography and on archival research, V. F. analyzes the biographies and the ideological positions of the first members of the Court of Justice of Luxemburg (1952–1972).

[2] Josse Mertens de Wilmars, *Liber memorialis Mertens de Wilmars* (Lier: Van In & C°, 1994). The book has not been distributed commercially, but some libraries have a copy of it, as for instance the library of the *Office généalogique et héraldique de Belgique*, which is housed in the town hall of Woluwe-Saint-Pierre. The author wrote the book when he was in his eighties. It breathes out a memory that is still incredibly fresh. It contains very few inaccuracies (as we found e.g. p. 160: as a student the author probably did not go dancing in the house of the old Nobels family in Mechlin, but in Sint-Niklaas) and seems more than once to have been based on documents rather than memory.

[3] Josse Mertens de Wilmars, 'Interview', interview by Jozef Smits, KADOC [= Katholiek Documentatiecentrum], *Verzameling interviews CVP-prominenten*, BE/942855/901, 15 April 1986, audio. The recording was transcribed and indexed by KADOC. Further quoted as *Interview*.

[4] KADOC Leuven, Arch. Josse Mertens de Wilmars (thirty archive boxes). When quoting them below we refer to the numbers of the folders collected in the boxes.

publications,[5] and some of my own recollections.[6] He was a keen jurist and lawyer and a devout Christian in daily life. Was his influence dictated by his faith? There is no precise method to measure the action of the Holy Spirit in the development of law and institutions. We will let the reader judge.

Born in Flemish Catholic Bourgeoisie

Josse Mertens de Wilmars was born in Sint-Niklaas, a city situated twenty-five kilometres south of Antwerp in the former County of Flanders. The county was one of the cradles of Calvinism in the Early Modern Period and of anti-Catholic liberalism in the nineteenth century, but a Catholic belt which includes Sint-Niklaas cuts across it from the south-west to the north-east. Throughout his life Josse Mertens de Wilmars was marked by his birth in and descent from Flemish French-speaking Catholic bourgeoisie, a milieu with child-rich families, and with social and political commitment. His family was acquainted with many representatives of the Catholic Party in the Belgian Parliament.

Josse Mertens de Wilmars's grandfather Henri Mertens[7] (1851–1920) was a brewer in Kruibeke.[8] He was mayor of the township (1893–1920) and sat in the Belgian Senate as a Catholic Party senator for the constituency of Sint-Niklaas (1900–1920). Henri Mertens's spouse Marie-Josèphe Erix (1851–1926) was the daughter of a public notary from Puurs. Josse's father Albert Mertens (1879–1942) was the fourth of their fourteen children. He was educated at the Jesuit colleges of Alost and Antwerp and studied at the Catholic University of Louvain.[9] In 1902 he graduated as a building engineer and in 1903 as an electrical engineer at the special schools of the Faculty of Sciences of the

---

[5] The bibliography of the works of Josse Mertens de Wilmars has been compiled by Marc Boes, 'Bibliografie', in *Liber amicorum Josse Mertens de Wilmars* (Antwerpen-Zwolle: Kluwer-Tjeenk Willink, 1982), IX–XIV.

[6] In 1948 Mrs Albert Mertens, mother of Josse Mertens de Wilmars, travelled to Rome with two goddaughters and invited the author's mother to join the party. She was the sister of Paul and Frantz van Dorpe mentioned in footnote 28. Together with Prof. Fernand De Visscher, professor of Roman law in Louvain and director of the Belgian Academy of Rome at the time, they were received privately by Pope Pius XII. It created a sense of attachment.

[7] The affix 'de Wilmars' was added to the family name in 1950: *L'intermédiaire des généalogistes* (1978): 452.

[8] The Mertens brewery in Kruibeke existed until 1961.

[9] We write 'Catholic University of Louvain' for the unitarian university which existed until 1970 and 'KU Leuven' or 'University of Leuven' for the Flemish university which stayed in Louvain after the scission of the unitarian university and the relocating of the French-speaking Université Catholique de Louvain to Louvain-la-Neuve.

University of Louvain. In that same institution he was then appointed as an assistant to professor Gustave Gillon (1874–1966), a specialist in electrical engineering. In 1903, Albert's oldest brother, brewer Adolphe Mertens, fell ill. He died in 1911. Albert took over the management of the family brewery in Kruibeke for a few years. In Louvain he befriended brewery specialist and professor canon Frans A. Janssens (1863–1924).[10] Under his influence Albert Mertens switched from electrical engineering to agronomy. From agronomy he evolved to industrial chemistry. In 1908 he married Jeanne Meert in Sint-Niklaas. She originated from the same milieu. Her father Emile Meert (1848–1922) was justice of the peace in Sint-Niklaas. Her mother was Céline Fiévé (1854–1896), the daughter of Ghent industrialist Désiré Fiévé (1825–1908), who served in the Belgian Parliament for the Catholic Party from 1886 until his death.[11] Jeanne was the first of their eight children. The young couple established themselves in the city centre of Sint-Niklaas.[12] They would have five sons. The first three were born in Sint-Niklaas. Josse was the second. Albert Mertens was appointed lecturer in the Catholic University of Louvain in 1908, and part-time professor in 1910, and, after his brother Antoine took over the management of the brewery, full professor in 1914.[13] He wished to move his family to Louvain, but they were confronted with the burning down of the city by the *furor teutonicus* in late August/early September 1914. The family fled to Southern France and from there travelled to Oxford, where they stayed until 1918 and where their fourth son was born.[14] In 1921 the family built a new house in

[10] Frans Alphonse Janssens was also born in Sint-Niklaas, as the seventh child of Theodore Janssens (1825–1889), who represented Sint-Niklaas for the Catholic party in the Belgian Parliament from 1852 until 1889.
[11] Désiré Fiévé began his career as a wood merchant. In 1857, he drew the Désiré-Fiévé-Street, two hundred fifty meters long, through the former estate of his parents in the city of Ghent. He started up the production of printed and compressed cement tiles which competed with the French and Italian ceramics. He sold his merchandise as far as Argentina. He offered cheap shipments by promoting his tiles as ballast for ships who brought agricultural products to Antwerp and had to return empty. At the end of the nineteenth century he merged his company Fiévé and Crul with local competitor Dutry and Massy. Sources: documents from Ghent about real estate heritage. The other daughter of Désiré Fiévé, Augusta (1859–1887), was the mother of the law professors Charles (1884–1973) and Fernand De Visscher (1885–1964). Charles married his cousin Hélène Meert, daughter of Céline Fiévé.
[12] In the Hofstraat, the elegant street of Sint-Niklaas. In the archives of the Catholic University of Louvain this 'Court Street' is translated in a funny way as 'Rue du Jardin'.
[13] *Annuaire de l'Université catholique de Louvain*, 1910, 54; 1911, 25; 1942–43, part 3 v–vii.
[14] At that moment their brother-in-law Charles De Visscher was already in Oxford with his family. Fernand De Visscher would join them coming from Switzerland. On Charles De Visscher see e.g. François Rigaux, 'Charles De Visscher, An exemplary lawyer's life (1884–1973)', *European Journal of International Law* 11 (2000): 877–886; on Fernand De Visscher e.g. Jean-François Gerkens, 'Fernand De Visscher als Archäologe', in *Aus der Werkstatt römischer Juristen, Vorträge der Europäisch-Ostasiatischer Tagung 2013 in*

Louvain, where the youngest son was born.[15] Albert Mertens was director of the Agronomy Department of the Faculty of Sciences from 1928 to 1932. His brother Eugène joined the faculty in 1923 and received the chair of industrial chemistry in 1930.[16] Albert Mertens invested in a company of industrial chemistry in Antwerp and moved his family home from Louvain to Antwerp. In 1928 he had a marvellous house built in the posh Jan van Rijswijcklaan, which would later become the family home of Josse Mertens de Wilmars.[17] The family moved there in in 1929. Albert Mertens died in 1942, exhausted by business problems and worries about the war.[18]

The Catholic Party in whose orbit the family lived was controlled by the Belgian bishops until the First World War.

Growing Up in Roaring Times

Josse Mertens de Wilmars was born in Sint-Niklaas in 1912. From 1921 he lived in Louvain and from 1924 he attended secondary school in the Holy Trinity College of the Josefites. In 1928 he moved to the French-speaking boarding school of the Benedictines in Loppem near Bruges. He came back to Louvain to study law (1929–1934) and political sciences (1934–1936) at the Catholic University. While acting as a barrister in Antwerp, he would obtain a PhD in political sciences in Louvain in 1945.

During the roaring thirties in Louvain Josse Mertens de Wilmars passed for a Catholic student but was uncommitted to clubs or circles. He was interested in the personalism of Emmanuel Mounier and Jacques Maritain and attended lectures about this new Christian philosophy. He later considered Mounier his *'maître de pensée'*.[19] Jean Dabin (1899–1971) was the enthusiastic advocate of personalism in the law faculty. He lectured in family law, but impressed Josse Mertens de Wilmars with his underlying legal theory and his continuous

---

Fukuoka. Freiburger Rechtsgeschichtliche Abhandlungen, Neue Reihe 75, eds. Ulrich Manthe et al. (Berlin: Dunckler & Humblot, 2016), 111–130.

[15] The Mertens houses were built at Maria-Theresiastraat 98-100-102, on a plot of houses burnt down in 1914. From 1921 to 1929, Josse lived in number 100, built by architect Alphonse Stevens and nowadays a Grade 1 listed town house.

[16] And became his brother's neighbour at Maria Theresiastraat 102. He died in 2019.

[17] Jan van Rijswijcklaan 192; the move was for business purposes, if we can trust the author of the obituary of his son Charles: J. J. Hoet, 'Charles Mertens de Wilmars, Éloge à l'Académie de Médecine', *Bulletin de l'Académie de Médecine de Belgique* 150 (1995): 305; compare the obituary of Albert Mertens in *Annuaire de l'Université Catholique de Louvain*, part III (1942–43).

[18] Mertens de Wilmars, *Liber memorialis*, 170.

[19] KADOC, *Verzameling interviews CVP-prominenten*, BE/942855/901, 3; compare Mertens de Wilmars, *Liber memorialis*, 154–156.

balancing of juridical norms and human liberty. Mertens was still a student when the young 'personalist' priest Albert Dondeyne was appointed professor of philosophy in 1933. He did not yet know him as a student – Dondeyne was appointed in the Dutch-speaking section – but followed his lectures and publications afterwards.

In 1931, during the great depression, Pius XI issued the social encyclical *Quadragesimo anno*, in which he renewed the idea of a political collaboration of the classes and in which, through his sympathy for Italian corporatism, he seemed to accept the authoritarian regime of Mussolini. In 1921, the Belgian Catholic Party had been replaced by the Catholic Union, which had adapted to the corporatism of *Rerum Novarum*. It was a union of the Christian Democratic League of Belgium, the Farmers Union, the Federation of Middle Classes, and the Federation of Catholic Associations and Circles. It was mainly financed by the Farmers Union, which was established in Louvain and of which the presidents were Louvain professors. In 1933, the Catholic Union was again in crisis and appointed a commission to revise its structure. In 1937, it would be replaced by the Catholic Bloc, which for the first time was divided into a Dutch-speaking *Katholieke Vlaamse Volkspartij* and a French-speaking *Parti catholique social*. Many discussions about the political presence of Catholics in the Belgian Parliament were held in the small university city of Louvain, which is situated twenty kilometres from Brussels. As mentioned, as a student Josse Mertens de Wilmars was not committed to Catholic party politics. However, he was aware of what was happening in the surroundings of the law faculty and read the national newspapers. He recognized a certain sympathy in Belgium for authoritarian regimes like the *Action française* of Charles Maurras. He assessed the success of Léon Degrelle, who in 1932 edited the student edition of *Le vingtième siècle* in the Louvain publishing office *Christus Rex* and eventually founded the authoritarian Catholic Rex party, which took one-third of the voices of the Catholic union in the elections of 1936. From 1931 onwards he watched the actions of the *Vereniging der Dietse Nationaal Solidaristen* (Verdinaso), a Catholic movement which dreamt of restoring the Low Countries of 1585 and which converted to an authoritarian political party. It stood for a strong government led by a political and cultural elite with a tradition of honesty and sobriety. In 1936, aiming to restore an orderly Catholic political life, the Belgian bishops gathered a conference in Mechlin to discuss the events and to consider the position of the Catholic Church in party politics. Young Josse Mertens de Wilmars participated in the conference as an independent intellectual. He never knew who had invited him.

MAJOR THEMES AND CONTRIBUTIONS

A Strong Law Practice in Antwerp

In 1936, Josse Mertens de Wilmars established himself as a barrister in Antwerp. He joined the Wynen law firm, which had a clientele of Antwerp industrial companies. In 1943, at the demise of Marcel Wynen, he continued alone. He took over a large part of the clientele and built up a profitable law practice. In 1945, when he was involved in the start-up of the Christian social party, he became the regular barrister of the city of Antwerp and of the Belgian Department of Finance. Due to his later specialization in administrative law and subsequently his PhD, he was appointed lecturer at the Antwerp Provincial Institute for Administrative Sciences (1945–1967). He was gifted at explaining changing state structures to students.[20] Most of his early publications dealt with administrative law.[21] He became a strong proponent of administrative courts being installed in Belgium and was appointed assessor in the *Conseil d'État* from 1950–1952, where he had to review bills for new legislation. Thanks to his law practice he never had financial worries.

In 1939, Josse Mertens de Wilmars married Elisabeth van Ormelingen, whose father was a member of the Belgian Parliament from 1914 to 1929. They lived in spacious houses in Antwerp city centre.[22] Their eight children were educated in the Catholic tradition. It is, however, impossible to evaluate whether his law practice would have been different if he had not been a Christian. We did not see any files from his law practice which would have allowed us to explore this idea. In his political archives we find files indicating that he counselled religious orders in Brussels and Boom,[23] which probably contacted him because of his personal convictions. The advices are not especially Roman Catholic but provide a way for investment in Christian social works according to Belgian law. An anti-clerical barrister would probably have recommended the same measures but would not have had the opportunity to do so. Let us repeat like Saint Josemaría Escrivá, who was

---

[20] One can discover this talent in for instance: Josse Mertens de Wilmars, 'De evolutie van de overheidsstructuren', in *Facetten van onze evoluerende wereld, 1946–1966, Huldebetoon gouverneur R. Deklerck* (Antwerp: Inrichtend Comité Huldebetoon Goevemeur R. Declerck, 1966), 29–47; compare his contribution 'De parlementaire democratie, Evolutie en toekomstperspectieven', in *Het politieke beleid, Vijfde Vlaamse studiedagen, Houthalen 7-8-9 September 1964*, eds. R. Houben et al. (Brussels: CEPESS, 1965), 47–62.

[21] See Boes, 'Bibliografie', IX–XIV.

[22] First in Britselei 52; in 1948 Lange Leemstraat 274; in 1957 Jan van Rijswijcklaan 192.

[23] KADOC, Arch. Josse Mertens de Wilmars, 40 and 80/3; these files were probably mistakenly classified with his political archives.

a jurist and priest, that a barrister ought to be a good lawyer *and* a good Christian.

Architect of the Christian Social Party

In 1940, Josse Mertens de Wilmars was mobilized as an officer of the Belgian army and was marched away to Nuremberg as a prisoner of war. As a bilingual Belgian citizen who never gave preference to either the Dutch or to the French language,[24] he was shocked by the different treatment given to Dutch- and French-speaking prisoners of war by Belgian aids of the German army. After six months, Flemish officers could re-join their homes while French-speakers had to remain in the prison camp. He returned home but opted to remain a Belgian citizen with a bilingual culture. Later he realized that the division in his country which he had discovered as a prisoner of war was irreversible. His preference for a country with a bilingual administration proved impossible to realize.[25] As an inhabitant of Antwerp, he would for the rest of his life be on the Flemish side, at least in politics.

Back in Antwerp during the war, Josse Mertens de Wilmars met the industrialist Antoine Herbert through an army doctor.[26] Herbert was the son of Louis Herbert (1872–1929), who had been a French-speaking representative for Sint-Niklaas in the Belgian Parliament.[27] Josse Mertens de Wilmars joined his Brussels think tank, which gathered in order to prepare the future of Belgium after the war. The core of the group consisted of members of the pre-war Catholic Action and the Verdinaso.[28] They tried to discourage

---

[24] In his archives personal annotations are written in both languages. In 1955, he writes letters in French and in Dutch for the parents' association of the Dutch-speaking school of his children: KADOC, Arch. Josse Mertens de Wilmars, 93. Even his *Liber memorialis* is bilingual, French on the left pages and Dutch on the right side.
[25] KADOC, Arch. Josse Mertens de Wilmars, 19/3 and 100.
[26] In the *Liber memorialis*, 166, he is called Hubert Vandermeiren, in the *Interview*, 3, Vandermeersch.
[27] Louis Herbert (1872–1929), born a Frenchman, had been naturalized Belgian in 1883; his son Antoine (1902–1959) was a Flemish nationalist. In 1924, he was dismissed from the university of Louvain because of his claims for it to be Dutchified. He became a textile entrepreneur in Kortrijk. Tony Herbert was one of the founders of the Flemish VNV party in 1933 but left the party soon after. He was also an inspiration for the Verdinaso but by that time no longer engaged in party politics. At the beginning of the war the VNV and the Verdinaso were seized by the German occupiers, but by then the group of Dutch-speaking Belgian nationalists joined by Josse Mertens de Wilmars no longer had any ties with VNV or Verdinaso.
[28] As explained by Mertens de Wilmars, *Interview*, 5; they met in the Brussels apartment of Jef van Bilsen, who had already been a member of the board of Verdinaso as a law student in 1932 and remained as such until 1939; Josse Mertens de Wilmars had not known him as a student, as van Bilsen was in the Flemish section. Frantz van Dorpe was also a former leader of the

cooperation with Germany and especially to keep the Catholic youth from signing up for the anti-communist war in Russia. A central theme in their reflection was determining the role of public authority in society. A clear example of what they discussed was William Beveridge's *Full employment in a free society*, London 1944. Josse Mertens de Wilmars was tasked with propagating their ideas in Antwerp, and to that end he had many conversations with the Catholic trade unionist Paul-Willem Segers and with Joseph Deschuyffeleer, who from 1931 until 1947 led the movement of Young Catholic Workers founded by Joseph Cardijn (1882–1967, cardinal in 1965).[29] The encounters with Herbert's think tank sparked in Josse Mertens de Wilmars an interest in becoming active in party politics. In the meantime, he studied political sciences for his PhD in Louvain. His doctoral thesis dealt with the legal force of the special Belgian legislation issued at the end of the First World War.

At the end of the war, he was one of the only members of Tony Herbert's Christian-inspired think tank to continue intellectual reflection about the role of the state in the post-war years. Most members settled in business. Josse Mertens de Wilmars grew to become the ideologue and one of the architects of Christian democracy in Belgium. His fellows would serve the party as full politicians, but he continued for the sake of Christian democracy. In 1944, he was asked to write the bylaws of a new Flemish Christian party.[30] From 1945 he would be focused on the national Christian social party *Christelijke Volkspartij/Parti social chrétien*, to whose founding meeting he was invited. In the party he met future prime ministers and political celebrities, but also his former professor Jean Dabin. In 1945–1946 he was co-author of the bylaws of the party. In 1948, the party would start up a Flemish section and a French-speaking section.[31] He would be co-opted by the Flemish section, which was to become the Flemish CVP in 1969. In the party he was always concerned with documentation and research. He strongly influenced the scientific analysis of social and economic problems.[32]

From 1945 until 1967, he was at the helm of a new political party, which immediately became the main Belgian party in the elections of 1946 and

---

Verdinaso, and left it in 1938 and founded the more realistic Benelux-movement; in the PoW-camp Josse Mertens de Wilmars had met his brother Paul van Dorpe, who was a close friend of Antoine Herbert as well. The van Dorpes conformed to his old criteria: their mother originated from Sint-Niklaas and they had ancestry in Belgian Congress and Parliament.

[29] Mertens de Wilmars, *Interview*, 7–8.
[30] KADOC, Arch. Josse Mertens de Wilmars, 1.1.
[31] KADOC, Arch. Josse Mertens de Wilmars, 12.
[32] See for instance: KADOC, Arch. Josse Mertens de Wilmars, 71; 154; 158/1; 161/2–3; 162.

which obtained an absolute majority in 1950 and 1958. It was in power until his retirement.[33] He created the Antwerp section and was its vice-president for two decades. He inspired, gave advice, and wrote bills and legal texts on the most diverse issues.[34] He regularly met with ministers and resolved their juridical problems. In 1961 he advised the government on special laws issued after the war in 1919. Prime Minister Lefèvre answered that the government had never received advice of that quality and relevance and suggested sending him an honorarium bill. It was, however, free of charge.[35] His political archives attest to his active presence behind major political issues after the war, like ending repression, the language to be used in administrative affairs,[36] the equal treatment of Catholic schools, the expansion of the universities, the cultural autonomy of Dutch-speakers and French-speakers (which necessitated modifications to the constitution), decolonization, etc. And nevertheless, Josse Mertens de Wilmars dreamt of active participation in the process of legislation as a member of parliament, but never succeeded in being registered in an eligible place on the election lists which he himself drew up.[37] He never rose higher on the ballots than as a substitute. He explained that he was perhaps too independent and did not represent any political movement in the party.[38] Three times, however, he received a mandate in parliament as a substitute, and he sat in the Chamber for six years.[39] Within the Chamber he was

[33] The history of the foundation and the first year of the party is explained well by Mark van Den Wijngaert, *Ontstaan en stichting van de C. V. P.-P. S. C., De lange weg naar het kerstprogramma* (Brussels: Instituut voor politieke vorming, 1976), or in French: Wilfried Dewachter et al., *Un parti dans l'histoire, 1945–1995, Cinquante ans d'action du parti social-chrétien* (Louvain-la-Neuve: Duculot, 1995).

[34] For instance, on the statute of municipalities, provinces and agglomerations: KADOC, Arch. Josse Mertens de Wilmars, 27–29; 32; 64; bylaws for the National Office for Reintegration of People with a handicap: KADOC, Arch. Josse Mertens de Wilmars, 43; the new status of accountants: KADOC, Arch. Josse Mertens de Wilmars, 41/3; of company auditors: KADOC, Arch. Josse Mertens de Wilmars, 17/4; the new law about advocacy: KADOC, Arch. Josse Mertens de Wilmars, 99; arbitration in the new judicial code: KADOC, Arch. Josse Mertens de Wilmars, 99/2.

[35] KADOC, Arch. Josse Mertens de Wilmars, 167.

[36] KADOC, Arch. Josse Mertens de Wilmars, 140 (1952) and 154 (1958).

[37] Fritz, *Juges et avocats*, 119 writes that he was disappointed that he never became a member of the Belgian government. We found, however, no evidence that he wanted to become a minister. As long as he was a barrister, he did not have time for it: see KADOC, Arch. Josse Mertens de Wilmars, 57. He nevertheless continued to long for a seat as a representative in parliament.

[38] In the fifties, the party was mainly paid for by the Christian trade union, the Farmers Union, and the Christian employers: KADOC, Arch. Josse Mertens de Wilmars, 17/12.

[39] From 1952 to the elections of 1954, when François-Xavier van der Straten-Waillet, with whom he was associated in his law firm, became ambassador in Buenos Aires; again, for some months

indefatigable as a member of the commission of justice,[40] the commission of constitutional reform,[41] the commission for colonial affairs,[42] the cultural commission,[43] the commission for home affairs,[44] the commission for foreign affairs[45] and foreign trade.[46] In 1957, he presided over a special commission which was unique in Belgian public law: it dealt with a decision of the *Cour des Comptes* which had been overturned by the *Cour de Cassation* and had to be revised.[47] Nevertheless, when he finished his last term in 1962, he knew he would still not obtain a place on the electoral list and returned to his former seat in the party cenacle.[48]

Pacemaker of the European Court of Justice

Josse Mertens de Wilmars's European career has been described by Vera Fritz.[49] In 1947, his party delegated him to the *Nouvelles équipes internationales* of the international Christian democrat movement, in whose congresses he participated until 1959, and in 1949 to the European Movement of the Christian democrats. In this capacity, he travelled through Western Europe and met many foreign politicians. He also once represented the Belgian government in the UN in New York.[50] From the early years of the CVP/PSC onwards he followed the emergence of the European institutions.[51] He pleaded more than once as a barrister in the Court of Justice of the CECA and the European Court in Luxemburg.[52] In 1967, he applied for the vacant position of Belgian justice in the European Court of Justice and was selected by the Belgian government. He sat as justice until 1980 and presided over the European Court from 1980 until 1984. He was a keen European jurist, as is

---

in 1957–58 when the Antwerp representative Hendrik Marck died and from 1958 to 1962, after the demise of Antwerp representative Bert Verlackt.

[40] See e.g. KADOC, Arch. Josse Mertens de Wilmars, 35–36: e.g. in 1960 he wrote the report about the new insurance bill.
[41] KADOC, Arch. Josse Mertens de Wilmars, 48/1 and 2.
[42] KADOC, Arch. Josse Mertens de Wilmars, 117–133; 142/1–153.
[43] KADOC, Arch. Josse Mertens de Wilmars, 135/1.
[44] KADOC, Arch. Josse Mertens de Wilmars, 47.
[45] KADOC, Arch. Josse Mertens de Wilmars, 111 and 113–116.
[46] KADOC, Arch. Josse Mertens de Wilmars, 112.
[47] KADOC, Arch. Josse Mertens de Wilmars, 166.
[48] Fritz, *Juges et avocats*, 255–256.
[49] Fritz, *Juges et avocats*, 74; 119–120; 253–257.
[50] KADOC, Arch. Mertens de Wilmars, 169.
[51] See e.g. KADOC, Arch. Josse Mertens de Wilmars, 111 and 114.
[52] Mertens de Wilmars, *Liber memorialis*, 190.

evident from his many publications on European law.[53] In her study Ms Fritz has also analyzed the political influences on the Court of Justice and how it fitted into the contemporary legal structures. A special role for the first generations of justices (1952–1972) was to discuss the relationship between the Court and the member states. In this process Christian democracy had an important role. In the decisions of the Court the hierarchy of legal norms was still to be established – as well as what president Koen Lenaerts called the hierarchy of 'desires' formulated in the treaties in the 1990s. Josse Mertens de Wilmars actively promoted the court. Was it as a lawyer and jurist who sensed the juridical reality of his environment or as an agent of the Holy Spirit? The answer is as written on so many war graves in the surroundings of Ypres: known unto God.

In 1971, Josse Mertens de Wilmars became a member of the Organising Authority of the Flemish University of Leuven and he could still be found there in 1991.[54] This committee was composed of five bishops and four laymen. As such, for the first time he sat on a committee together with bishops and presided over by the Archbishop of Brussels. The four laymen were always selected from among influential Christian democrats, until Walter van Gerven was appointed there as a lawyer and jurist.[55] From 1971 to 1982, Josse Mertens de Wilmars was a part-time professor at the KU Leuven Law Faculty.

GENERAL APPRAISAL AND INFLUENCE

Throughout his legal and political career Josse Mertens de Wilmars remained a devout Catholic, member of his parish council and of the fraternity of the Venerable Chapel of the Antwerp Cathedral. The first time he sat in parliament, in 1952, he announced his intention to defend the Christian social ideas there.[56] He liked Jef Deschuyffeleer 'who must have been a saint on earth'.[57] In his political archives we find a rare unequivocal expression of Christian convictions applied to a professional career. In 1955 and 1956, he held lectures

---

[53] Boes, 'Bibliografie', IX-XIV; from 1962 on nearly all publications concern European law.
[54] After 1991, the university preferred privacy and no longer published the composition of this committee. The five Flemish bishops were members of it until 2012.
[55] Walter van Gerven (1935–2015) was a barrister and afterwards full professor of law at KU Leuven. He was advocate-general in the European Court of Luxemburg (1988–1994) and had the advantage vis-à-vis Josse Mertens de Wilmars of originating from Sint-Niklaas.
[56] KADOC, Arch. Mertens de Wilmars, 17/5.
[57] Mertens de Wilmars, *Interview*, 4. J. Deschuyffeleer was the president of the Catholic Workers Youth movement (KAJ) from 1935 until 1944. In 1944, he became secretary of the Brussels Christian trade union. From 1951 until 1958, he was national secretary of the Belgian Christian trade union.

in The Hague and Haarlem about freedom of education. In Haarlem he stated: 'As Catholics we have a duty to contribute to the church's task of apostolate and Christianization, but we do not ask for privileges. We have sufficient faith in the radiance of the truth, of the devotion, of the sacrifices, of the example that we do not want any other weapon than that of freedom.'[58] Indeed, his own political career was defined by conviction, detachment, and incredible patience, and it remained without privileges.

In party politics he was, however, strictly opposed to confessional influence. This already shone through in discussions of the drafts of the bylaws of the CVP/PSC[59] and in the 'Christmas programme' of the party, which he drew up with Jean Dabin in 1945.[60] Both texts had to defend the basic foundations of a Christian society and the social and economic stance based on the major social encyclicals,[61] but as they were read in the workplace – not as dictated by the clergy. Instead of confessional influence he listened to the policy wishes of Christian citizens. The party had to be un-confessional. It had to return to Christians the freedom either to support it or to contest it.[62] The church can have a public policy or a special need to intervene in political matters, but let it do this in favour of all Catholics and in the open, not by means of one specific political party.[63] Josse Mertens de Wilmars had a special interest in economic policy and nurtured an economy with Christian solidarity and mutual respect between employers and employees which emphasized freedom of enterprise.[64] He feared the socialists, who wanted to control the administration,[65] and the 'amoral' communists.[66] He opposed giving trade unions too large a role in his party, as it weakened the French-speaking section of the party.[67] In 1948, he revised the law reorganizing the *société anonyme* (large company with limited liability),[68] but did not in any way mention the ideas of participation defended by Christian social thinkers in those years. He was eager to listen to the social and economic doctrine of the church, but as it

---

[58] KADOC, Arch. Mertens de Wilmars, 92; from a lecture held in Haarlem, 13 January 1956; the translation is ours.
[59] KADOC, Arch. Mertens de Wilmars, 2.2.
[60] Mertens de Wilmars, *Interview*, 15.
[61] KADOC, Arch. Mertens de Wilmars, 2.2.
[62] Mertens de Wilmars, *Interview*, 14–15.
[63] Mertens de Wilmars, *Interview*, 14.
[64] His first benchmark was the creation of wealth, his second the fair distribution of it: see e.g. KADOC, Arch. Mertens de Wilmars, 103–106.
[65] KADOC, Arch. Mertens de Wilmars, 17/5; 17/7; 17/12; 85.
[66] KADOC, Arch. Mertens de Wilmars, 17/7 and 116 (1956).
[67] KADOC, Arch. Mertens de Wilmars, 44; 53/1.
[68] KADOC, Arch. Mertens de Wilmars, 17/4.

appeared in the newspapers and the public debate of his time. No episcopal letters are to be found in his political records. The same conclusion can be drawn regarding his views about Catholic schools. In his political archives one finds the text of the encyclical *Divini Illius Magistri* (Pius XI, 1930) about Christian education but as it was published by *La Libre Belgique* in 1955.[69] He kept a papal message from 1951, but as it was published in *De Vlaamse Linie*.[70] In the files from 1950 about the role of women in society and party, we find the guidelines of Pius XII about the social role of women (1945), but in the form of an extract from a magazine.[71] When in parliament in 1957, he received a long report from the Association of Christian Lawyers about the reform of matrimonial property law, but he did not integrate these comments into the parliamentary bill he wrote.[72] He followed the Second Vatican Council, but through the reports that Mgr van Cauwelaert sent to the priests of his Congolese diocese.[73] He condemned the political role the bishops played when they tried to keep a French-speaking university in the Dutch-speaking part of Belgium, because it would accelerate the scission of the country.[74] As president of the Commission for University Expansion in Antwerp, he defended a pluralistic university and preferred the viewpoints of the new council of rectors to those of the bishops.[75]

Two issues could reveal strongminded Christian convictions: the launch of a Christian newspaper and an attitude of forgiveness toward collaborators during the Second World War.

In 1944, Tony Herbert's think tank and the Christian employers tried to start up a Christian press group. They founded *De Gids* and hired the titles of *De Standaard* and *Het Nieuwsblad*, which were considered Christian-minded and were not issued during the war, from the Sap family.[76] Josse Mertens de Wilmars was a small stakeholder in *De Gids* but became a commissioner of the group and was associated with the editorial office. The undertaking worked well from 1945 to 1947, but then ran into conflict with the owners of the titles because of the forgiving attitude toward collaborators. The reporting about the conviction and execution of August Borms shocked the Sap family, which was

---

[69] KADOC, Arch. Mertens de Wilmars, 92.
[70] KADOC, Arch. Mertens de Wilmars, 111.
[71] KADOC, Arch. Mertens de Wilmars, 17/3.
[72] KADOC, Arch. Mertens de Wilmars, 35.
[73] KADOC, Arch. Mertens de Wilmars, 134.
[74] KADOC, Arch. Mertens de Wilmars, 164; KADOC, Arch. Mertens de Wilmars, 17/12 (1965): 'Neither the bishops nor the Catholic university will resolve the question, but the consequences will affect Brussels'.
[75] KADOC, Arch. Mertens de Wilmars, 164 (1968).
[76] KADOC, Arch. Mertens de Wilmars, 168/1–5.

less indulgent toward Borms.⁷⁷ The family reclaimed their titles and resumed their own publication of *De Standaard* and *Het Nieuwsblad*. *De Gids* launched a new title, *De Nieuwe Gids*, but there was no market for two independent Christian newspapers and in 1950 *De Nieuwe Gids* had to merge with the newsgroup of the Christian trade union. It is not impossible that the strong opinions of Josse Mertens de Wilmars about repression and forgiveness affected the case. Against his personal convictions that the classical restrictions of penal law had to be taken into account for war crimes, the party took a step back in its policy concerning repression and epuration. This, however, led to the creation of the competing *Christelijke Vlaamse Volksunie* in 1953, which adopted the views of the ideologist of the Christian social party on amnesty. In the elections of 1954, it took one-third of the votes given to the CVP/PSC in 1952 and it remains the main contender of the Flemish Christian social party until this day.

Indeed, one could argue that the view of Josse Mertens de Wilmars on repression and amnesty was linked with the Catholic attitude of resetting and forgiving sinful behaviour. In his private practice he defended civil servants who were indicted for war crimes and was the advocate of the Ministry of Finances for cases of economic collaboration.⁷⁸ But his basic stance was that of a lawyer: the tradition of criminal law had to be restored as quickly as possible. He emphasized the necessity of full rehabilitation once prison sanctions had been served, with restoration of social rights. He opposed death sentences and proposed to convert them to imprisonment. The government followed him in this.⁷⁹ He promoted individual measures of mercy and collective amnesty. He condemned senseless seizures. He proposed to adapt disciplinary regulations for administrations and state-owned companies.⁸⁰ As a member of parliament he tried to change the famous art. 123/6 of the Criminal Code, which foresaw perpetual loss of civil rights.⁸¹ He proposed a bill to remove the notion of civil disloyalty. In 1959 this brought him a series of swastikas on the façade of his house.⁸² But while screening these archive

---

[77] This is a hot topic in contemporary Belgian history. See e.g. Luc Vandeweyer, 'August Borms', in *Nieuwe Encyclopedie van de Vlaamse beweging* (Tielt: Lannoo, 1998), 559–563. For Josse Mertens de Wilmars, August Borms could have been a typical protégé: a devout Catholic originating from Sint-Niklaas, who had eight children. For many commentators it was a 'Christian' testcase, because a first death sentence for Borms in 1919 had given rise to a request for leniency by Pope Benedict XV.

[78] KADOC, Arch. Josse Mertens de Wilmars, 87/1.

[79] KADOC, Arch. Josse Mertens de Wilmars, 4.2.2; Fritz, *Juges et avocats*, 253.

[80] KADOC, Arch. Josse Mertens de Wilmars, 87/2; 88–90.

[81] KADOC, Arch. Josse Mertens de Wilmars, 91.

[82] KADOC, Arch. Josse Mertens de Wilmars, 87/2.

files, one might again consider that he was a keen lawyer who appreciated the strength of traditional criminal law. Is it necessary to see it as an attitude of Christian forgiveness?

The same kind of conclusion can be reached about the files in the political archives concerning the defence of Catholic schools.[83] Privately Josse Mertens de Wilmars sent his children to the Antwerp Jesuit College and the Dames of Christian Education. He was convinced that freedom of education led to better schools, Catholic or not, and by public spending in free schools the government would get more value for its money. But when guiding the party's reflection on the financing of private schools, he organized a public opinion poll in 1955,[84] which resulted in the signatures of 3,404,742 inhabitants, presented to the king of the small country in 1957.[85] Is this still Christian conviction or should we consider it smart politics?

In his memoirs he explained that in his quiet old age, he was pleased to meet family members and people of his parish – yes, but no longer as a lawyer. Nevertheless, in the notes we made while reading through his political archives, we wrote several times – mainly when reading the repression cases, the defence of free schools, the texts about the cultural autonomy of Dutch- and French-speaking Belgians, and reform of the constitution – that he must have been extraordinarily patient and tolerant. Saint Ambrose quoted *prudentia, iustitia, fortitudo,* and *temperantia* as the cardinal virtues. But Ambrose was a lawyer. Did he separate those virtues from *fides, spes,* and *charitas*?

RECOMMENDED READING

Since its foundation in 1974, the KADOC study centre, which is to be found at www.kadoc.kuleuven.be, focuses on the interactions between Christianity and democracy. The origins of the Christian democracy in Belgium and the foundation of the Christian popular party CVP have been thoroughly covered by KADOC. For the last couple of years, the research field has been expanded to the history of Christian democracy in the European Union. An easy way to discover this history is through the publications of Peter Heyrman, who is research director of KADOC,[86] and the publications of Steven Van Hecke[87] and Emmanuel Gerard[88] of

---

[83] KADOC, Arch. Josse Mertens de Wilmars, 17/6; 92–98.
[84] KADOC, Arch. Josse Mertens de Wilmars, 17/6.
[85] KADOC, Arch. Josse Mertens de Wilmars, 94; the petition was organized by the association 'Freedom and Democracy' of which Josse Mertens de Wilmars was a founding member and the secretary was Rik Vermeire, who was also party secretary at the time.
[86] Publications on http://lirias.kuleuven.be/cv?Username=U0002027.
[87] Publications on http://lirias.kuleuven.be/cv?Username=U0026593.
[88] Publications on http://lirias.kuleuven.be/cv?Username=U0004364.

the KU Leuven Center of Political Sciences. They give an overview of the matter and the state of the research, and point toward further references.

The integration of the European Court of Justice in the political context of the 1950s and 1960s has been thoroughly studied by Vera Fritz. *Juges et avocats généraux de la Cour de Justice de l'Union européenne (1952–1972), Une approche biographique de l'histoire d'une révolution juridique*. Rechtshistorische Studien, 312. Frankfurt am Main: Vittorio Klostermann, 2018. On the life and career of Josse Mertens de Wilmars it is pleasant to read his *Liber memorialis Mertens de Wilmars*. Lier: Van In & Co, 1994, but the book is difficult to find.

Index

Abbé Pottier, 15
Adam and Eve, 47, 101, 208
Adams, John, 202
adiaphora, 153
administrative law, 249, 364
Alexander VII, 159, 164
Alger of Liège, 1, 5, 19–37
Althusius, Johannes, 8, 103, 116, 347
Ambrose, 31, 373
Ames, William, 143, 144
amnesty, 100, 372
anticlericalism, 238, 239
anti-revolutionary movement, 230, 234, 239, 249
Anti-Revolutionary Party, 205, 232, 235, 338, 341
anti-revolutionary principles, 221, 222, 224, 233
Aquinas, Thomas, 45, 48, 64, 68, 69, 105, 134, 271, 302, 304, 313
Archdukes Albert and Isabella, 64, 65, 72, 75, 90
Aristotle, 69, 117, 298
Arminians, 106, 108, 111, 124, 130
Arminius, Jacobus, 98, 102, 106, 108
atheism, 4, 223
Augustine, 9, 23, 30, 31, 32, 39, 45, 48, 125, 167, 266, 341

Baldus de Ubaldis, 41, 125
Barth, Karl, 287, 294, 296, 299
Batavian Republic, 187, 204, 214
Batavian Revolution, 223
Bavinck, Herman, 341
Beccaria, Cesare, 184, 195
Bekker, Balthasar, 9, 10
Belgian Revolution, 11, 12, 219, 236, 237, 238, 239
Benedict XIII, 171

Berman, Harold, 2, 3, 4, 18
Beverland, Hadriaan, 147, 148, 151
Beysens, Josephus, 305
Beza, Theodore, 8, 103, 116
Bible, 3, 8, 31, 62, 66, 83, 100, 103, 111, 116, 119, 125, 129, 153, 156, 173, 186, 189, 192–194, 207, 208, 213–217, 220, 224, 225, 228, 294, 297, 345
Bilderdijk, Willem, 183, 196, 198, 205, 215
Bont, Johannes, 41, 47
Bradshaw, William, 143
Brants, Victor, 13, 78, 263, 272
Burke, Edmund, 216, 222, 227, 228, 234

Calderini, Gaspar, 38
Calderini, Giovanni, 40, 42
Calvin, John, 2, 3, 55, 57, 58, 99, 103, 116, 130, 147, 154, 222, 230, 340–341, 344, 345
Calvinism, 8, 97, 119, 217, 233, 341, 360
Calvinist orthodoxy, 100, 103, 121
Calvinists, 57, 102, 106–109, 117, 119, 120, 129, 216, 226, 233
canon law, 4, 5–7, 20, 21, 26, 33–36, 38–49, 52–55, 56, 57, 60, 61, 66–67, 81, 84, 85, 88, 89, 124, 126–130, 132, 135, 136, 159, 161–165, 172, 173, 193, 274
canon lawyer, 1, 5, 38–43, 44, 48, 67, 81, 83, 84, 87–95
capital punishment, 12, 116, 119, 193, 195, 236, 248
Castelein, Auguste, 15
Catholic Church, 4, 6, 17, 29, 42, 58, 69, 80, 89, 111, 146, 160, 161, 168, 228, 329, 363
Catholic Party, 277, 280, 282, 360, 362, 363
Catholic schools, 271, 276, 280, 321, 367, 371, 373

Index

Catholicism, 9, 13, 52, 58, 59, 101, 220, 237–241, 245, 247, 250, 252, 257, 334, 336
Catholics, 4, 12, 14, 107, 169, 173, 201, 230, 232, 236–240, 245, 251, 254, 257–260, 262, 264, 323, 326, 332, 335, 363, 370
charity, 3, 13, 28, 190, 191, 242, 251–255, 256–258, 262–263
Charles III, 174
Charles IV, 174
Charles V, 53, 89, 91–93, 94
Christian advocate, 188, 189, 190, 191
Christian belief, 2, 11, 12, 13, 18
Christian democracy, 17, 268, 276, 277, 328, 336, 337, 366, 369
Christian democratic party, 323, 359
Christian Democrats, 268, 275, 277, 278
Christian education, 221, 231, 232, 371
Christian faith, 1–4, 6, 9, 10, 13, 18, 57, 107, 129, 189, 289, 293, 295, 344
Christian People's Party, 18, 336
Christian Social Party, 323, 364, 366, 372
Christian thinking, 2, 248
Christian Workers, 324, 335
Christianity, 1, 4, 5, 10, 18, 119, 120, 178, 189, 203, 205, 214, 216, 220, 223, 228, 244, 245, 256, 260, 270, 276, 285, 295, 296, 342, 347, 356
church and state, 2, 4, 9, 99, 111, 145, 148, 151, 152, 173, 203, 225, 227, 229, 234, 246, 250, 277, 342, 347
Church of Utrecht, 9, 145, 160, 161, 167, 168, 171
Cicero, 41, 105, 125, 194
civil authorities, 2–4, 13, 90, 99, 108, 145, 146
Civil Code, 197, 198, 267, 274, 313
clergy, 3, 19, 80, 84, 150, 151, 155, 167, 172, 245, 254, 258, 303, 370
Codde, Petrus, 168
colonies, 105, 157, 184, 231, 268, 278, 368
comitas, 133, 134, 135, 137
Commercial Code, 197, 198
Common Life, Brethren of the, 39, 53
contract law, 66–68, 77, 114
corporatism, 250, 257, 363
Counter-Reformation, 52, 55
Criminal Code, 192, 197, 199, 372
criminal law, 3, 5, 15, 179, 190, 192–196, 198, 248, 267, 268, 274, 281, 302, 311, 314, 372
customary law, 6, 88, 89, 135, 163, 178, 180, 181, 185

da Costa, Isaäc, 183, 196
Dabin, Jean, 307, 362, 366, 370
de Cock, Theodorus, 168
de Coux, Charles, 13, 249, 263
de Groot, Willem, 94
de Lantsheere, Léon, 14, 266–283
death penalty. *See* capital punishment
Decalogue, 3, 44, 57, 111, 116–119, 120, 129, 143
decision-making, 287, 289, 290, 293
Declaration of the Rights of Man, 204, 230
Decretum Gratiani, 5, 52, 61, 62, 162, 274
deontology, 10, 81, 191
Descartes, René, 7, 9, 124, 268, 296
dialectical theology, 287, 290, 297
divine law, 102, 103, 112, 115, 116, 118, 119, 127, 131, 166, 193–195
divine will, 110, 116, 119, 206
Dooyeweerd, Herman, 17, 233, 338–357
Ducpétiaux, Edouard, 12, 236–248
Durand, Guillaume, 40, 41
Dutch Elegant School, 8, 183
Dutch Reformed Church, 15, 98, 108, 123, 124, 143, 182, 189, 199, 219, 285
Dutch Republic, 3, 6, 7, 10, 11, 89, 90, 94, 97, 99, 105, 106, 123, 125–128, 130, 132, 135, 145, 151, 156, 168, 186, 204, 205, 220, 222
Dutch Revolt, 6, 97, 99, 139
Duynstee, Willem, 16, 301–319

ecclesiastical authorities, 7, 16, 93, 160, 163, 164
ecclesiastical courts, 4, 83, 89, 92–94, 165
ecclesiastical jurisdiction, 92, 94, 169, 171, 172
Enlightenment, 9, 10, 12, 13, 78, 120, 147, 182, 195, 196, 202, 205, 208, 214, 216, 225, 226, 234, 247, 263, 347
Episcopalism, 167, 174, 175
Epo, Boëtius, 6, 52–63
equality, 11, 12, 69, 70, 73, 75, 105, 113, 205–217, 225, 231, 292, 296
Erasmus, Desiderius, 14, 100, 102
European Court of Justice, 18, 359, 368
European Union, 18
Everaerts, Nicolaes, 41, 49

Fontaine, Théodore, 15, 270
forgiveness, 191, 212, 285, 371–373
Frederick, Henry, 100
free will, 58, 78, 102, 104, 107, 115, 116, 119, 272, 294
freedom of association, 231, 250, 256
freedom of education, 258, 280, 370, 373
freedom of religion, 202, 245

French Revolution, 1, 11, 203, 205, 214, 216, 221, 222–234, 256, 263, 341, 347
Further Reformation, 7, 8, 124, 142, 145, 149, 150, 155

Gallicanism, 161, 167
Gallicanists, 87
Gheyloven, Arnoldus, 5, 10, 38–51
Gomarus, Franciscus, 99, 106, 108, 130
Gospel, 11, 117, 167, 210, 214, 222–225, 227, 247, 258, 290, 297
Govaerts, Pieter, 160, 163, 165
grace, 9, 27, 28, 32, 34, 58, 78, 189–192, 296, 297, 342, 346, 350
Gratian, 25, 33–35, 61, 62
Gregorian Reform, 5, 27
Gregory XIII, 57, 62, 86
Gregory the Great, 23, 29, 31, 80, 278
Groen van Prinsterer, Guillaume, 11, 13, 219–235, 347
Groenendaal, monastery of, 5, 39, 43
Groote, Geert, 5, 39
Grotius, Hugo, 7, 10, 77, 88, 97–122, 130, 179–181, 197, 198, 214, 216, 304, 306

Habsburg Low Countries, 6, 85, 89, 93
Hegel, Georg Wilhelm Friedrich, 268
Hobbes, Thomas, 8, 103, 125, 136, 147, 152, 155, 157
Holy Scriptures. *See* Bible
Holy Spirit, 85, 145, 155, 156, 159, 209, 360, 369
Hoppers, Joachim, 54
Huber, Ulrik, 8, 132, 134, 137, 139–158
human conscience, 8, 152, 154, 155, 288
human nature, 114, 115, 119, 189, 308, 310
human rights, 203, 205, 217, 229, 230
humanism, 5, 7, 13, 14, 50, 83, 101, 103, 107, 114, 119, 121, 140, 141, 320, 356

idealism, 289, 294, 295, 341
image of God, 102, 104, 119, 194, 293, 296
individualism, 13, 228, 252
indulgence, 28
international private law, 7, 132, 135, 137, 157
Investiture Controversy, 19, 22, 23, 26, 27, 31–34, 36, 62
irenicism, 98, 103
Israel, 3, 109, 151, 208, 216
ius commune, 1, 6, 67
ius hodiernum, 179, 181, 197, 198

ius placiti, 9, 160, 162, 164, 170
Ivo of Chartres, 22, 25, 29, 31, 35, 61–62

James I, 108
Jansenism, 9, 91, 159, 163
Jansenists, 95, 124
Jansenius, Cornelius, 9, 89, 159, 164
Jaspers, Karl, 286, 288, 299
Jesuit college, 6, 54, 64, 66, 67, 94, 267, 270, 275, 360, 373
Jesuits, 9, 15, 64–67, 69, 73, 76–77, 83, 86, 124, 168, 173
Jesus, 11, 64, 66, 114, 167, 205–215, 293, 296, 297
Jews, 116, 201, 212, 285, 316
Joseph II, 174
judgement, 69, 274, 289, 292, 294, 295, 308
July Revolution, 11
Junius, Franciscus, 98, 107
jus circa sacra, 152
jus publicum universale, 155
justice, 3, 16, 21, 22, 27–31, 34, 67–70, 74, 103–107, 111–114, 117–119, 166, 167, 190, 192, 225, 226, 229, 243, 253, 256, 257, 260, 262, 285, 287–289, 291, 294–297, 309, 312, 315, 347–349, 352, 355
Justinian, 8, 88, 125, 135, 162

Kamphuisen, Pieter, 314, 315, 317, 318
Kant, Immanuel, 268, 304, 344
Kelsen, Hans, 290, 339, 356
Kierkegaard, Søren, 286, 299
Kingdom of Belgium, 11, 12, 239
Kingdom of the Netherlands, 11, 220, 239
Kuyper, Abraham, 12, 17, 232–234, 338, 341–343, 345, 347, 350

Langemeijer, Gerard, 306, 356
Laurent, François, 4, 274
law of nations, 104, 261
laxism, 159, 173
legal philosophy, 234, 302, 307, 318, 340, 356
legal theory, 352, 362
Leo XIII, 14, 250, 261, 262, 271, 326
Leopold II, 267, 278, 279
Lessius, Leonardus, 6, 7, 10, 15, 16, 64–79, 83, 105, 124, 134
liberalism, 231, 233, 238–239, 243, 250, 254, 256, 260–262, 264, 360
liberty, 5, 8, 12, 91, 104, 139, 152, 211, 220, 225, 228, 231, 240, 242, 244, 246, 273, 363
Lipsius, Justus, 7, 14, 98, 101

Louis XIII, 114
Louis XIV, 222
Louis Napoleon, 182, 197
love, 17, 28–31, 102, 104, 107, 119, 183, 209–212, 213, 216, 285, 293, 294, 296, 297, 347, 349, 350, 355
Lubbertus, Sibrandus, 108
Luther, Martin, 2, 3, 129, 228

magistracy, 110, 145, 149, 154
magistrates, 3, 7, 92, 110–112, 118, 130, 160, 164–167, 181, 188, 202
Marx, Karl, 223, 229
Matthaeus, Anthonius, 136
Matthaeus II, Anthonius, 3, 140, 144, 146
Matthaeus III, Anthonius, 128
Maurice of Nassau, 98, 222
Mercier, Désiré-Joseph, 270–273, 278, 282
mercy, 21, 22, 27–31, 34, 44, 372
Merle d'Aubigné, Jean-Henri, 220, 222
Mertens de Wilmars, Josse, 18, 359–374
middle class, 232, 233, 321, 323, 325, 335
ministers, 8, 84, 89, 90, 109, 110, 130, 145, 146, 148–150, 153, 222, 366, 367
Modern Devotion, 5, 50
modernity, 14, 17, 234, 282, 341
Molengraaff, Willem, 306
Molina, Ludovicus, 67, 68
Montes Pietatis, 72–77
moral theologians, 6, 43, 45, 66, 68, 71, 72, 76, 86, 119, 303, 305
moral theology, 4, 40, 43, 47, 50, 67, 73, 77, 78, 83, 173, 301, 302
morality, 5, 9, 10, 11, 17, 50, 190, 255, 259, 298, 354
Mosaic law, 116, 120, 194
Moses, 3, 116, 207, 209
Mounier, Emmanuel, 362

Nadere Reformatie. See Further Reformation
Napoleon, 11, 182, 222, 223, 226
Napoleon III, 233, 255
natural law, 6, 10, 14, 17, 69–71, 73, 103, 104, 107, 113–117, 119, 121, 131, 136, 156, 166, 178, 180, 183–186, 196–198, 206, 223, 229, 245, 288, 295, 298, 304, 305–318, 354
natural law proper, 16, 307–311, 318
natural order, 16, 259, 288, 308, 309, 313, 318
natural religion, 7, 118, 119, 189
natural theology, 126, 183, 189
natural–rational law, 16, 307–311, 314, 316, 318

necessaria, 8, 152, 155
neo-Calvinism, 340–343, 344
neo-Calvinists, 344, 345
neo-Kantianism, 17, 339, 344, 353
neo-Scholasticism, 281
New Testament, 105, 117, 143, 205, 207–209, 211, 212, 215, 297
Nicholas of Liège, 19, 21, 22
Nisener, Johannes, 142, 144

Old Testament, 3, 116, 135, 207–208, 212, 215
ontology, 348, 353, 355
Opzoomer, Cornelis, 306, 307
Orange, Prince of, 202, 203, 205, 206
Orange-Nassau, House of, 188, 201, 219, 221, 222, 229
Orangists, 182, 186, 203, 205, 239
Otbert, 5, 20, 22, 32, 33

Patriots, 11, 182, 186, 187, 203, 204, 205, 214
Paul V, 65
Paulus, Pieter, 11, 12, 201–218
Périn, Charles, 12, 249–265, 272
personalism, 294, 296, 297, 362
Pesch, Heinrich, 327, 328, 331, 332
Petrus, Suffridus, 53, 54
Philip II, 7, 54, 55, 60, 85, 92, 214
philosophy of law, 17, 273, 281, 284, 297, 298, 302, 304, 306, 307, 339, 354, 356
Pietism, 7, 142–147, 155
Pius IX, 250, 256, 259, 261
Plantinga, Alvin, 17, 356
political economy, 12, 78, 249, 250, 252–254, 262, 263, 301
Pompe, Willem, 312
positive law, 10, 14, 113, 114, 118, 156, 186, 245, 292, 302, 305, 306, 309, 311–315
positivism, 14, 15, 273, 289, 291, 293, 307, 317
poverty, 11, 12, 38, 49, 86, 254
prison reform, 241, 244, 248
prison system, 12, 236
prisons, 236, 237, 241–243
private law, 137, 186, 196, 198, 267, 268, 281, 285, 289, 305, 317
probabilism, 71, 72, 173
Protestantism, 143, 220, 252, 263
Protestants, 3, 12, 14, 57, 58, 89, 93, 168, 173, 229, 232
pseudo-Isidorian decretals, 162, 173
public law, 7, 12, 84, 142, 198, 249, 258, 355, 368
Pufendorf, Samuel von, 78, 120, 157, 304, 306

Index

punishment, 28, 91, 104, 105, 111–112, 114, 118, 192, 193, 241, 243, 274, 302, 311
Puritanism, 7, 143, 145

Quadragesimo anno, 335, 363

rationalism, 221, 263, 289, 293, 347
rationality, 9, 15, 102, 104, 107, 113, 115, 287, 347
recursus ad principem, 9, 92, 160, 162, 164, 166
Reformation, 2, 6, 52, 55, 57, 58, 61, 101, 130, 223, 228
Reformed Church, 98, 99, 143, 145, 146, 149, 150, 151, 154, 167, 177, 179, 183, 201, 205
Reformed religion, 2, 5, 6, 7, 97, 98, 106, 202, 205
Regalism, 161
Regneri ab Oosterga, Cyprianus, 127, 146
renunciation, 13, 253, 262, 263
repression, 367, 372, 373
ressourcement, 52, 162, 172
Réveil, 11, 182, 196, 199, 220
Röell, Herman Alexander, 147, 155
Roman law, 5, 6, 55–56, 60, 61, 67, 70, 75, 88, 105, 113, 124, 126, 130, 132, 135, 178–186, 188, 192–198, 284, 306, 310
Roman pontifical authorities, 96, 168
Roman–Dutch law, 10, 123, 135, 137, 181, 195, 198
Rousseau, Jean-Jacques, 213, 225

salvation, 10, 14, 20, 28, 31, 32, 58, 165, 189, 206, 209, 211, 262, 344, 345, 346
Savigny, Friedrich-Carl von, 181, 197, 221
scholasticism, 7, 64, 66, 78, 120, 137, 307
Scholastics, 102, 114, 119
Scholten, Paul, 15, 18, 284–300, 317
School of Salamanca, 6, 67, 83
Schortinghuis, Wilhelmus, 178
Scripture. *See* Bible
secular authorities, 4, 6, 8, 18, 88, 91, 92, 94, 110, 112, 131, 152, 163–166, 168
secular courts, 160, 163, 166
secularization, 1–4, 18, 258, 261
simony, 5, 32, 193
Sixtus V, 55, 62, 86
slavery, 184, 194, 207, 213, 228, 231, 244
socialism, 13, 224, 250, 252, 256, 258, 262, 272, 326, 327
Socinians, 108, 124
sovereignty of the people, 203, 204, 221, 229, 234
sphere sovereignty, 346–348, 350
Spinoza, Baruch de, 17, 147, 268, 356

Stammler, Rudolf, 307, 317, 318, 339, 353
statistics, 237, 238, 240–241, 245, 249, 301
Steenoven, Cornelis, 160, 171
Stockmans, Petrus, 9, 95, 165
Storme, Jules, 16, 320–337
Suárez, Francisco, 66, 76, 105, 113
subjective right, 70, 113, 114, 309, 353
Suringar, Willem Hendrik, 244

Taylor, Charles, 2, 3, 13, 14
Ten Commandments. *See* Decalogue
Thomasius, Christian, 156, 194
Thomism, 15, 271
Thomist revival, 272, 281
Thorbecke, Johan, 11, 224, 229–230
Tocqueville, Alexis de, 224, 226, 230, 231, 234
torture, 184, 193, 194, 195, 198
trade unions, 329, 341, 370
Trent, Council of, 73, 81, 83, 85, 166, 173
Tydeman, Hendrik Willem, 185, 196, 198

Ulpian, 305, 308, 309
ultramontanism, 95, 245, 250, 264
ultramontanists, 13, 90, 95, 245, 250, 258, 263, 264
universities
  Free University of Amsterdam, 12, 17, 217, 338, 341, 347, 356, 357
  Free University of Brussels, 280
  University of Amsterdam, 284, 301, 317
  University of Douai, 6, 7, 54–56, 58, 64, 66, 98
  University of Franeker, 8, 9, 142, 148, 149
  University of Ghent, 16, 321
  University of Groningen, 178, 183
  University of Leiden, 7, 98, 140, 178, 181, 182, 202, 219, 307, 316
  University of Lille, 250, 257, 264
  University of Louvain, 5, 6, 9, 12, 18, 249, 251, 252, 264, 267, 359–361, 369
  University of Nijmegen, 16, 302, 303, 305, 314, 318
  University of Orléans, 98
  University of Utrecht, 7, 123–126, 136, 146, 202, 302, 305
usurious contracts, 42, 43, 84, 92
usury, 43, 68, 73–77, 84, 130, 193, 255
usus modernus, 179

van der Grinten, Willem, 314
van der Heijden, Egidius, 307, 314, 316

van der Keessel, Dionysius Godefridus, 10, 177–200
van der Linden, Joannes, 10, 127, 195, 197
van der Marck, Frederik Adolf, 178, 183, 184, 185, 191, 196
van der Meulen, Johannes Andreas, 8
van Espen, Zeger-Bernard, 9, 91, 95, 159–176
van Oldenbarnevelt, Johan, 98, 119, 222
van Ruusbroec, Jan, 39
van Vollenhoven, Cornelis, 120
Viglius of Aytta, 54, 55
Voet, Gijsbert, 7, 123, 124, 125, 126, 129, 146, 149–150, 153
Voet, Johannes, 8, 123, 132, 134, 135, 137
Voet, Paulus, 7, 107, 123–138, 157
Vollenhoven, Dirk Hendrik Theodoor, 339, 356, 357
Voorda, Bavius, 180, 181, 187
Vorstius, Conrad, 108

William Frederic, 186, 188
William I, 11, 186, 219, 229, 236, 239, 258
William III, 222, 230, 232
William V, 187, 188, 202
William of Orange, 7, 222
welfare, 104, 216, 226, 237, 239–245, 246, 255, 309, 313
Windesheim, Congregation of, 39, 43, 50
Wissenbach, Johannes Jacobus, 140
Woeste, Charles, 250, 277, 280, 282
Wolff, Christian, 120, 189, 304, 306
Wtenbogaert, Johannes, 98, 101, 109, 110

Zabarella, Francesco, 38, 45, 48
Zypaeus, Franciscus, 6, 10, 80–96

For EU product safety concerns, contact us at Calle de José Abascal, 56–1°,
28003 Madrid, Spain or eugpsr@cambridge.org.

www.ingramcontent.com/pod-product-compliance
Ingram Content Group UK Ltd.
Pitfield, Milton Keynes, MK11 3LW, UK
UKHW020925110825
461507UK00030B/442